TOUCHSTONE

I
Asia Minor, Greece and Italy: The Classical World and Its Background

II
India, China and Elsewhere

III
Britain and Europe

IV
America

THE
WORLD
OF THE
PAST

VOLUME II

EDITED, WITH AN INTRODUCTION

AND INTRODUCTORY NOTES, BY

JACQUETTA HAWKES

A TOUCHSTONE BOOK
PUBLISHED BY SIMON AND SCHUSTER

Contents

II : INDIA, CHINA AND ELSEWHERE

III : BRITAIN AND EUROPE

IV : AMERICA

List of Plates

PLATE

XV   LIST OF PLATES

PLATE

Maps

ACKNOWLEDGMENTS

The drawings on pp. 107, 112, 114, 116 are reproduced from *The Palace of Minos* by Arthur Evans, Macmillan & Co. Ltd., London, 1921, by kind permission of Agathon Press, Inc., which is reprinting *The Palace of Minos.* The drawings on pp. 350, 422, 470, 475, 492 are reproduced from *The Testimony of the Spade,* © 1956 by Geoffrey Bibby, Alfred A. Knopf, Inc., New York. The drawing on p. 382 is reproduced from *Stonehenge* by Richard Atkinson, Hamish Hamilton Ltd., London, 1956, by kind permission of the publishers. The drawings on pp. 458, 459, 460 are reproduced from *The Scythians* by Tamara Talbot Rice, Thames and Hudson Ltd., London, 1957, by kind permission of the publishers. The drawings on pp. 542, 612, 640, 645, 653, 656 are reproduced from *Indian Art of Mexico and Central America* by Miguel Covarrubias, © 1957 Alfred A. Knopf, Inc.

I

Asia Minor, Greece and Italy

The Classical World and Its Background

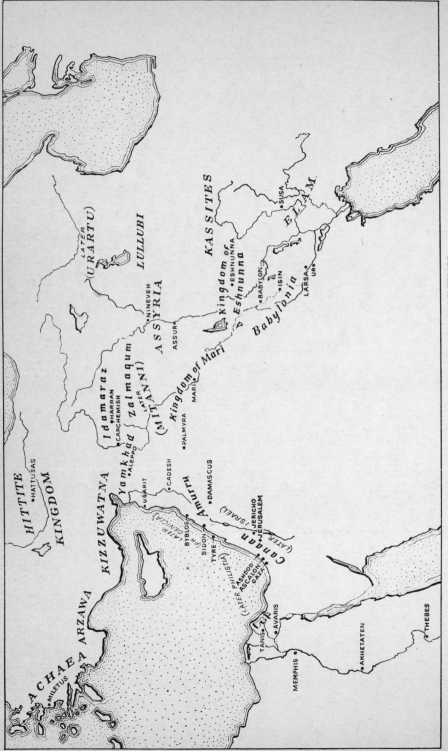

THE NEAR EAST IN THE TIME OF HAMMURABI

INTRODUCTORY

THROUGHOUT history the huge peninsula of Asia Minor (or Ana-
tolia) has served as a passageway linking the continents of Asia and
Europe. Its western coast was inevitably a part of the Aegean world,
bound by ties of migration, commerce and war with Greece and
Crete. At its other extremity, the Cilician plain was wide open to
Syria and Palestine, while the fact that the Tigris and Euphrates
rise in the east Anatolian mountains led to frequent involvement
with the great powers of Mesopotamia. In addition, north-eastern
Asia Minor was easily accessible from Armenia and the other Cau-
casian lands. A territory with so great a range of external contacts
could have little unity, and in fact the peninsula shows a bewildering and always shifting pattern of different cultures, peoples and
languages.

The close association between western Anatolia and Greece,
familiar in Homeric and classical Greek times, extends back to the
beginning of settled life in the Mediterranean. The early Neolithic
farmers of southern Anatolia had much in common with those of
Greece and Thessaly, and may indeed have provided settlers for the
European lands. It is more certain that a little later (about 5000
B.C.) the earliest peopling of Crete was due to Anatolian immigrants. Contacts of various kinds continued throughout the Bronze
Age, emerging into history in the Late Bronze Age Mycenaean world
of Homer. Although the development of Italy was always made to
differ from that of her eastern neighbours by incursions of western
and northern peoples over the Alps, Sicily and southern Italy were
very much involved with Greece and Asia Minor in the Neolithic
and Bronze Ages, as they were in historical times. Most authorities
now accept the classical tradition that the Etruscans came from
Asia Minor, while the Greek colonies in Italy were early established
and, of course, profoundly influential.

NOTE

THE editor's notes that precede many se-
lections are identified by the use of Italic
capitals for the first word or words. The
typographic ornament shown here separates it from the selection.

THE text of the selection invariably starts
with the first word or words in capital and
small capitals.

I. *Asia Minor*

HEINRICH SCHLIEMANN

Schliemann
Introduces Himself

IF I begin this book with my autobiography, it is not from any feeling of vanity, but from a desire to show how the work of my later life has been the natural consequence of the impressions I received in my earliest childhood; and that, so to say, the pickaxe and spade for the excavation of Troy and the royal tombs of Mycenae were both forged and sharpened in the little German village in which I passed eight years of my earliest childhood. I also find it necessary to relate how I obtained the means which enabled me, in the autumn of my life, to realize the great projects I formed when I was a poor little boy. But I flatter myself that the manner in which I have employed my time, as well as the use I have made of my wealth, will meet with general approbation, and that my autobiography may aid in diffusing among the intelligent public of all countries a taste for those high and noble studies, which have sustained my courage during the hard trials of my life, and which will sweeten the days yet left me to live.

I was born on the 6th of January, 1822, in the little town of Neu Buckow, in Mecklenburg-Schwerin, where my father, Ernest Schliemann, was a Protestant clergyman, and whence, in 1823, he was elected in that capacity to the parish of the village of Ankershagen between Waren and Penzlin, in the same duchy. In that village I spent the eight following years of my life; and my natural disposition for the mysterious and the marvellous was stimulated to a passion by the wonders of the locality in which I lived. Our garden-house was said to be haunted by the ghost of my father's predecessor, Pastor von Russdorf; and just behind our garden was a pond

From Autobiographical Introduction to *Ilios*. London: John Murray; 1880, pp. 1-18, 65-6.

called "das Silberschälchen," out of which a maiden was believed to rise each midnight, holding a silver bowl. There was also in the village a small hill surrounded by a ditch, probably a prehistoric burial-place (or so-called *Hünengrab*); in which, as the legend ran, a robber knight in times of old had buried his beloved child in a golden cradle. Vast treasures were also said to be buried close to the ruins of a round tower in the garden of the proprietor of the village. My faith in the existence of these treasures was so great that, whenever I heard my father complain of his poverty, I always expressed my astonishment that he did not dig up the silver bowl or the golden cradle, and so become rich. There was likewise in Ankershagen a medieval castle, with secret passages in its walls, which were six feet thick, and an underground road, which was supposed to be five miles long, and to pass beneath the deep lake of Speck; it was said to be haunted by fearful spectres, and no villager spoke of it without terror. There was a legend, that the castle had once been inhabited by a robber knight of the name of Henning von Holstein, popularly called "Henning Bradenkirl," who was dreaded over the whole country, for he plundered and sacked wherever he could. But, to his vexation, the Duke of Mecklenburg gave safe-conducts to many of the merchants who had to pass by his castle. Wishing to wreak vengeance upon the duke, Henning begged him to do him the honour of a visit. The duke accepted the invitation, and came on the appointed day with a large retinue. But a cowherd, who was cognizant of Henning's design to murder his guest, hid himself in the underwood on the roadside, behind a hill a mile distant from our house, and lay in wait for the duke, to whom he disclosed his master's murderous intention, and the duke accordingly returned instantly. The hill was said to have derived its present name, "Wartensberg" or "Watch-mount," from the event. Henning, having found out that his design had been frustrated by the cowherd, in revenge fried the man alive in a large iron pan, and gave him, when he was dying, a last kick with his left foot. Soon after this the duke came with a regiment of soldiers, laid siege to the castle, and captured it. When Henning saw that there was no escape for him, he packed all his treasures in a box and buried it close to the round tower in his garden, the ruins of which are still standing, and he then committed suicide. A long line of flat stones in our churchyard was said to mark the malefactor's grave, from which for centuries his left leg used to grow out, covered with a black silk stocking. Nay, both the sexton Prange and the sacristan Wöllert swore that, when boys, they had themselves cut off the leg and used its bone to knock down pears from the trees, but that, in the beginning of the present century, the leg had suddenly stopped growing out. In my childish simplicity I of course believed all this; nay, I often begged my father to excavate the tomb or to allow me to excavate it, in order to see why the foot no longer grew out.

A very deep impression was also made upon my mind by the terracotta relief of a man on the back wall of the castle, which was said to be the portrait of Henning Bradenkirl himself. As no paint would stick to it, popular belief averred that it was covered with the blood of the cowherd, which could not be effaced. A walled-up fire-place in the saloon was indicated as the place where the cowherd had been fried on the iron pan. Though all pains were said to have been taken to obliterate the joints of that terrible chimney, never-theless they always remained visible; and this too was regarded as a sign from heaven, that the diabolic deed should never be for-gotten.

I also believed in a story that Mr. von Gundlach, the proprietor of the neighbouring village, Rumshagen, had excavated a mound near the church, and had discovered in it large wooden barrels con-taining Roman beer.

Though my father was neither a scholar nor an archaeologist, he had a passion for ancient history. He often told me with warm enthusiasm of the tragic fate of Herculaneum and Pompeii, and seemed to consider him the luckiest of men who had the means and the time to visit the excavations which were going on there. He also related to me with admiration the great deeds of the Homeric heroes and the events of the Trojan war, always finding in me a warm defender of the Trojan cause. With great grief I heard from him that Troy had been so completely destroyed, that it had dis-appeared without leaving any traces of its existence. My joy may be imagined, therefore, when, being nearly eight years old, I re-ceived from him, in 1829, as a Christmas gift, Dr. Georg Ludwig Jerrer's *Universal History*, with an engraving representing Troy in flames, with its huge walls and the Scaean gate, from which Aeneas is escaping, carrying his father Anchises on his back and holding his son Ascanius by the hand; and I cried out, "Father, you were mistaken: Jerrer must have seen Troy, otherwise he could not have represented it here." "My son," he replied, "that is merely a fanciful picture." But to my question, whether ancient Troy had such huge walls as those depicted in the book, he answered in the affirmative. "Father," retorted I, "if such walls once existed, they cannot possibly have been completely destroyed: vast ruins of them must still re-main, but they are hidden away beneath the dust of ages." He main-tained the contrary, whilst I remained firm in my opinion, and at last we both agreed that I should one day excavate Troy.

What weighs on our heart, be it joy or sorrow, always finds utter-ance from our lips, especially in childhood; and so it happened that

I talked of nothing else to my playfellows, but of Troy and of the mysterious and wonderful things in which our village abounded. I was continually laughed at by every one except two young girls, Louise and Minna Meincke, the daughters of a farmer in Zahren, a village only a mile distant from Ankershagen; the former of whom was my senior by six years, the latter of my own age. Not only did they not laugh at me, but, on the contrary, they always listened to me with profound attention, especially Minna, who showed me the greatest sympathy and entered into all my vast plans for the future. Thus a warm attachment sprang up between us, and in our childish simplicity we exchanged vows of eternal love. In the winter of 1829-30 we took lessons in dancing together, alternately at my little bride's house, at ours, and in the old haunted castle, then occupied by the farmer Mr. Heldt, where, with the same profound interest, we contemplated Henning's bloody bust, the ominous joints of the awful fireplace, the secret passages in the walls, and the entrance to the underground road. Whenever the dancing-lesson was at our house, we would either go to the cemetery before our door, to see whether Henning's foot did not grow out again, or sit down in admiration before the church-registers, written by the hand of Johann Chr. von Schröder and Gottfriederich Heinrich von Schröder, father and son, who had occupied my father's place from 1709 to 1799; the oldest records of births, marriages, and deaths inscribed in those registers having a particular charm for us. Or we would visit together the younger Pastor von Schröder's daughter, then eighty-four years of age, who was living close to us, to question her about the past history of the village, or to look at the portraits of her ancestors, of which that of her mother, Olgartha Christine von Schröder, deceased in 1795, was our special delight, partly because we thought it a masterpiece of workmanship, partly because it resembled Minna.

We also often visited the village tailor Wöllert, who was one-eyed, had only one foot, and was for this reason called "Peter Hüppert," or Hopping Peter. He was illiterate, but had such a prodigious memory that he could repeat my father's sermon word by word after having heard it in church. This man, who might possibly have become one of the greatest scholars of the world, had he had a university education, was full of wit, and excited our curiosity to the utmost by his inexhaustible stock of anecdotes, which he told with a wonderful oratorical skill. Thus, to give but one of them: he told us how, being desirous to know whither the storks migrated for the winter, he had, in the time of my father's predecessor, Pastor von Russdorf, caught one of the storks which used to build their nests on our barn, and had fastened round its foot a piece of parchment, on which, at his request, the sexton Prange had written that he himself, the sexton, and Wöllert the tailor, at the village of Ankershagen in Mecklenburg-Schwerin, humbly begged the proprietor of the barn, on which the stork had its nest in the winter, to inform them of the name of his country. When the stork was again caught by him in the spring, another parchment was found attached to its foot, with the following answer in bad German verse:—

> Schwerin Mecklenburg ist uns nicht bekannt,
> Das Land wo sich der Storch befand
> Nennt sich Sankt Johannes-Land.

"We do not know Schwerin Mecklenburg: the country where the stork was is called Saint John's Land."

Of course we believed all this, and would have given years of our life to know where that mysterious Saint John's Land was to be found. If this and similar anecdotes did not improve our knowledge of geography, at least they stimulated our desire to learn it, and increased our passion for the mysterious.

From our dancing-lessons neither Minna nor I derived any profit at all, whether it was that we had no natural talent for the art, or that our minds were too much absorbed by our important archaeological investigations and our plans for the future.

It was agreed beween us that as soon as we were grown up we would marry, and then at once set to work to explore all the mysteries of Ankershagen; excavating the golden cradle, the silver basin, the vast treasures hidden by Henning, then Henning's sepulchre, and lastly Troy; nay, we could imagine nothing pleasanter than to spend all our lives in digging for the relics of the past.

Thanks to God, my firm belief in the existence of that Troy has never forsaken me amid all the vicissitudes of my eventful career; but it was not destined for me to realize till in the autumn of my life, and then without Minna—nay, far from her—our sweet dreams of fifty years ago.

My father did not know Greek, but he knew Latin, and availed himself of every spare moment to teach it me. When I was hardly nine years old, my dear mother died: this was an irreparable misfortune, perhaps the greatest which could have befallen me and my six brothers and sisters. But my mother's death coincided with another misfortune, which resulted in all our acquaintances suddenly turning their backs upon us and refusing to have further intercourse with us. I did not care much about the others; but to see the family of Meincke no more, to separate altogether from Minna—never to behold her again—this was a thousand times more painful to me than my mother's death, which I soon forgot under

my overwhelming grief for Minna's loss. In later life I have undergone many great troubles in different parts of the world, but none
of them ever caused me a thousandth part of the grief I felt at the
tender age of nine years for my separation from my little bride.
Bathed in tears and alone, I used to stand for hours each day before Olgartha von Schröder's portrait, remembering in my misery the
happy days I had passed in Minna's company. The future appeared
dark to me; all the mysterious wonders of Ankershagen, and even
Troy itself, lost their interest for a time. Seeing my despondency,
my father sent me for two years to his brother, the Reverend Friede-
rich Schliemann, who was the pastor of the village of Kalkhorst in
Mecklenburg, where for one year I had the good fortune of having
the candidate Carl Andres from Neu Strelitz as a teacher; and the
progress I made under this excellent philologist was so great that,
at Christmas 1832, I was able to present my father with a badly-
written Latin essay upon the principal events of the Trojan war
and the adventures of Ulysses and Agamemnon. At the age of
eleven I went to the Gymnasium at Neu Strelitz, where I was placed
in the third class. But just at that time a great disaster befell our
family, and, being afraid that my father would no longer have
the means of supporting me for a number of years, I left the Gymnasium after being in it only three months, and entered the *Real-
schule* of the same city, where I was placed in the second class.
In the spring of 1835 I advanced to the first class, which I left in
April 1836, at the age of fourteen, to become apprentice in the
little grocer's shop of Ernest Ludwig Holtz, in the small town of
Fürstenberg in Mecklenburg-Strelitz.

A few days before my departure from Neu Strelitz, on Good Friday 1836, I accidentally met Minna Meincke, whom I had not seen
for more than five years, at the house of Mr. C. E. Laué. I shall
never forget that interview, the last I ever had with her. She had
grown much, and was now fourteen years old. Being dressed in
plain black, the simplicity of her attire seemed to enhance her fascinating beauty. When we looked at each other, we both burst into a
flood of tears and fell speechless into each other's arms. Several
times we attempted to speak, but our emotion was too great; neither
of us could articulate a word. But soon Minna's parents entered
the room, and we had to separate. It took me a long time to recover
from my emotion. I was now sure that Minna still loved me, and
this thought stimulated my ambition. Nay, from that moment I
felt within me a boundless energy, and was sure that with unremitting zeal I could raise myself in the world and show that I was
worthy of her. I only implored God to grant that she might not
marry before I had attained an independent position.

I was employed in the little grocer's shop at Fürstenberg for five

years and a half; for the first year by Mr. Holtz and afterwards by
his successor, the excellent Mr. Theodor Hückstaedt. My occupation
consisted in retailing herrings, butter, potato-whiskey, milk, salt,
coffee, sugar, oil, and candles; in grinding potatoes for the still,
sweeping the shop, and the like employments. Our transactions
were on such a small scale, that our aggregate sales hardly a-
mounted to 3000 thalers, or £450 annually; nay, we thought we had
extraordinary luck when we sold two pounds' worth of groceries in
a day. There I of course came in contact only with the lowest classes
of society. I was engaged from five in the morning till eleven at
night, and had not a moment's leisure for study. Moreover I rapidly
forgot the little that I had learnt in childhood; but I did not lose
the love of learning; indeed I never lost it, and, as long as I live,
I shall never forget the evening when a drunken miller came into
the shop. His name was Hermann Niederhöffer. He was the son
of a Protestant clergyman in Roebel (Mecklenburg), and had almost completed his studies at the Gymnasium of Neu Ruppin, when
he was expelled on account of his bad conduct. Not knowing what
to do with him, his father apprenticed him to the farmer Langer-
mann in the village of Dambeck; and, as even there his conduct
was not exemplary, he again apprenticed him for two years to the
miller Dettmann at Güstrow. Dissatisfied with his lot, the young
man gave himself up to drink, which, however, had not made him
forget his Homer; for on the evening that he entered the shop he
recited to us about a hundred lines of the poet, observing the
rhythmic cadence of the verses. Although I did not understand a
syllable, the melodious sound of the words made a deep impression
upon me, and I wept bitter tears over my unhappy fate. Three times
over did I get him to repeat to me those divine verses, rewarding his
trouble with three glasses of whiskey, which I bought with the few
pence that made up my whole fortune. From that moment I never
ceased to pray God that by His grace I might yet have the happiness of learning Greek.

There seemed, however, no hope of my escaping from the hapless
and humble position in which I found myself. And yet I was relieved
from it, as if by a miracle. In lifting a cask too heavy for me, I hurt
my chest; I spat blood and was no longer able to work. In despair I
went to Hamburg, where I succeeded in obtaining a situation with
an annual salary of 180 marks, or £9 sterling: first in the grocer's
shop of Lindemann junior, on the Fishmarket in Altona; and
afterwards in that of E. L. Deycke junior, at the corner of the
Mühren and Matten-Twiete in Hamburg. But as I could not do the
heavy work, owing to my weakness in the chest, I was found useless by my employers, and was turned away from each place, after
having occupied it for only eight days. Seeing the impossibility of

filling a situation as grocer's shopman, and prompted by want to engage in any work, however humble, merely to earn my food, I endeavoured to obtain employment on board a ship, and at the recommendation of a very kind-hearted shipbroker, Mr. J. F. Wendt, a native of Sternberg in Mecklenburg, who when a child had been brought up with my late mother, I succeeded in obtaining a situation as cabin-boy on board the little brig *Dorothea*, commanded by Captain Simonsen, owned by the merchants Wachsmuth and Kroogmann of Hamburg, and bound for La Guayra in Venezuela.

I had always been poor, but never yet so utterly destitute as at that time; I had even to sell my only coat in order to buy a blanket. On the 28th of November, 1841, we left Hamburg with a fair wind; but in a few hours it turned contrary, and we were accordingly detained for three days in the river Elbe, near Blankenese, until on the 1st of December the wind again became fair. On that day we passed Cuxhaven and entered the open sea, but we had no sooner reached Heligoland than the wind returned to the west, and remained there up to the 12th of December. We were continually tacking, but made little or no progress, until in the night of the 11th-12th December we were shipwrecked in a fearful storm off the island of Texel, on the bank called "de Eilandsche Grond." After escaping innumerable dangers, and having been tossed about by the fury of the elements for nine hours in a very small open boat, the crew, consisting of nine men, were all saved. I shall always remember with gratitude to Heaven the joyful moment when our boat was thrown by the surf on a bank close to the shore of the Texel, and all danger was over. I did not know the name of the land we had been cast upon, but I perceived that it was a foreign country. I felt as if on that bank a voice whispered to me that the tide in my earthly affairs had come, and that I had to take it at its flood. My belief was confirmed when, on the very day of our arrival, my little box, containing a few shirts and stockings, as well as my pocketbook with the letters of recommendation for La Guayra procured for me by Mr. Wendt, was found floating on the sea and was picked up, while all my comrades and the captain himself lost everything. In consequence of this strange event, they gave me the nickname of "Jonah," by which I was called as long as we remained at the Texel. We were kindly received there by the consuls Sonderdorp and Ram, who proposed to send me, together with the rest of the crew, by way of Harlingen, back to Hamburg. But I declined to return to Germany, where I had been so overwhelmingly unfortunate, telling them that I regarded it as my destiny to remain in Holland, that I intended to proceed to Amsterdam to enlist as a soldier, for I was utterly destitute, and saw, for the moment, no other means of obtaining a living. At my urgent request, therefore,

Messrs. Sonderdorp and Ram paid 2 guilders (3s. 4d.) for my passage to Amsterdam.

The wind having now changed to the south, the little vessel by which I was forwarded had to stay a day at the town of Enkhuyzen, and it took us no less than three days to reach the capital of Holland. For want of clothes I suffered fearfully on this passage. Fortune did not smile on me at first at Amsterdam: winter had set in; I had no coat, and was suffering cruelly from the cold. My intention to enlist as a soldier could not be realized so soon as I had imagined; and the few florins which I had collected as alms on the island of Texel and in Enkhuyzen, as well as the two florins which I obtained from Mr. Quack, the consul for Mecklenburg at Amsterdam, were soon spent in the tavern of Mrs. Graalman in the Ramskoy at Amsterdam, where I had taken my lodgings. As my means of living were entirely exhausted, I feigned illness and was taken into the hospital. From this terrible situation I was released by the kind shipbroker already mentioned, Mr. Wendt of Hamburg, to whom I had written from the Texel, informing him of my shipwreck and my intention to try my fortune at Amsterdam. By a lucky chance my letter reached him when he was sitting at a dinner party with numerous friends. The account of the disaster which had befallen me excited universal compassion, and a subscription which he at once raised for me produced the sum of 240 florins (£20), which he sent me through Consul Quack. At the same time, he recommended me to the excellent Consul-General of Prussia at Amsterdam, Mr. W. Hepner, who procured me a situation in the office of Mr. F. C. Quien.

In my new situation my work consisted in stamping bills of exchange and getting them cashed in the town, and in carrying letters to and from the post-office. This mechanical occupation suited me, for it left me time to think of my neglected education.

First of all I took pains to learn to write legibly, and this I succeeded in doing after twenty lessons from the famous calligraphist Magnée, of Brussels. Afterwards, in order to improve my position, I applied myself to the study of modern languages. My annual salary amounted only to 800 francs (£32), half of which I spent upon my studies; on the other half I lived—miserably enough, to be sure. My lodging, which cost 8 francs a month, was a wretched garret without a fire, where I shivered with cold in winter and was scorched with the heat in summer. My breakfast consisted of rye-meal porridge, and my dinner never cost more than two-pence. But nothing spurs one on to study more than misery and the certain prospect of being able to release oneself from it by unremitting work. Besides, the desire of showing myself worthy of Minna created and developed in me a boundless courage. I applied myself with extraordinary diligence to the study of English. Necessity taught me a method which greatly facilitates the study of a language. This method consists in reading a great deal aloud, without making a translation, taking a lesson every day, constantly writing essays upon subjects of interest, correcting these under the supervision of a teacher, learning them by heart, and repeating in the next lesson what was corrected on the previous day. My memory was bad, since from my childhood it had not been exercised upon any object; but I made use of every moment, and even stole time for study. In order to acquire a good pronunciation quickly, I went twice every Sunday to the English church, and repeated to myself in a low voice every word of the clergyman's sermon. I never went on my errands, even in the rain, without having my book in my hand and learning something by heart; and I never waited at the post-office without reading. By such methods I gradually strengthened my memory, and in three months' time found no difficulty in reciting from memory to my teacher, Mr. Taylor, in each day's lesson, word by word, twenty printed pages, after having read them over three times attentively. In this way I committed to memory the whole of Goldsmith's *Vicar of Wakefield* and Sir Walter Scott's *Ivanhoe*. From over-excitement I slept but little, and employed my sleepless hours at night in going over in my mind what I had read on the preceding evening. The memory being always much more concentrated at night than in the day-time, *I found these repetitions at night of paramount use*. Thus I succeeded in acquiring in half a year a thorough knowledge of the English language.

I then applied the same method to the study of French, the difficulties of which I overcame likewise in another six months. Of French authors I learned by heart the whole of Fénelon's *Aventures de Télémaque* and Bernardin de Saint Pierre's *Paul et Virginie*. This unremitting study had in the course of a single year strengthened my memory to such a degree, that the study of Dutch, Spanish, Italian, and Portuguese appeared very easy, and it did not take me more than six weeks to write and speak each of these languages fluently.

Whether from my continual readings in a loud voice, or from the effect of the moist air of Holland, my complaint in the chest gradually disappeared during my first year's residence in Amsterdam, and it has never returned. But my passion for study caused me to neglect my mechanical occupation in the office of Mr. F. C. Quien, especially as I began to consider it beneath me. My principals would give me no promotion; they probably thought that a person who shows his incapacity for the business of a servant in an office proves thereby his unfitness for any higher duties. At last, however, through the intercession of my worthy friends, Louis Stoll of Mannheim and

J. H. Ballauf of Bremen, I had on the 1st of March, 1844, the good fortune to obtain a situation as correspondent and book-keeper in the office of Messrs. B. H. Schröder & Co. of Amsterdam, who engaged me at a salary of 1200 francs (£48); but when they saw my zeal, they added 800 francs a year more by way of encouragement. This generosity, for which I shall ever be grateful to them, was in fact the foundation of my prosperity; for, as I thought that I could make myself still more useful by a knowledge of Russian, I set to work to learn that language also. But the only Russian books I could procure were an old grammar, a lexicon, and a bad translation of *Les Aventures de Télémaque*. In spite of all my enquiries, I could not find a teacher of Russian, since, with the exception of the Russian Vice-Consul, Mr. Tannenberg, who would not consent to give me lessons, there was no one in Amsterdam who understood a word of the language. So I betook myself to the study of it without a master, and, with the help of the grammar, I learned the Russian letters and their pronunciation in a few days. Then, following my old method, I began to write short stories of my own composition, and to learn them by heart. As I had no one to correct my work, it was, no doubt, extremely bad; but I tried at the same time to correct my mistakes by the practical exercise of learning the Russian *Aventures de Télémaque* by heart. It occurred to me that I should make more progress if I had some one to whom I could relate the adventures of Telemachus; so I hired a poor Jew for four francs a week, who had to come every evening for two hours to listen to my Russian recitations, of which he did not understand a syllable.

As the ceilings of the rooms of the common houses in Holland consist of single boards, people on the ground-floor can hear what is said in the third storey. My recitations therefore, delivered in a loud voice, annoyed the other tenants, who complained to the landlord, and twice while studying the Russian language I was forced to change my lodgings. But these inconveniences did not diminish my zeal, and in the course of six weeks I wrote my first Russian letter to Mr. Vasili Plotnikoff, the London agent for the great indigo-dealers, Messrs. M. P. N. Malutin Brothers, at Moscow, and I found myself able to converse fluently with him and the Russian merchants Matweieff and Froloff, when they came to Amsterdam for the indigo auctions. After I had completed my study of the Russian language, I began to occupy myself seriously with the literatures of the languages I had learned.

In January, 1846, my worthy principals sent me as their agent to St. Petersburg. Here, as well as in Moscow, my exertions were in the very first two months crowned with the fullest success, which far exceeded the most sanguine expectations of my employers and myself. No sooner had I rendered myself indispensable to Messrs.

B. H. Schröder & Co. in my new career, and thus obtained a practically independent position, than I hastened to write to the friend of
the Meincke family, Mr. C. E. Laué of Neu Strelitz, describing to
him all my adventures, and begging him to ask Minna at once for
me in marriage. But, to my horror, I received a month later the
heartrending answer, that she was just married. I considered this
disappointment at the time as the greatest disaster which could
have befallen me, and I was for some time utterly unfit for any
occupation and sick in bed. I constantly recalled to mind all that
had passed between Minna and myself in early childhood, all our
sweet dreams and vast plans, for the ultimate realization of which
I now saw such a brilliant chance before me; but how could I think
of realizing them without her participation? Then again I bitterly
accused myself for not having demanded her in marriage before
proceeding to St. Petersburg; but again I recollected that I could
not have done so without exposing myself to ridicule, because while
in Amsterdam I was only a clerk, and my position was a dependent
one, subject to the caprice of my employers; besides, I was not sure
of succeeding at St. Petersburg, where instead of success I might
have made a complete failure. I fancied that neither could she be
happy with anyone else besides me, nor that I could possibly ever
live with another wife but her. Why then should fate be so cruel as
to tear her from me when, after having for sixteen long years striven
to reach her, I seemed at last to have succeeded in attaining her? It
had indeed happened to Minna and me as it often happens to us
in our sleep, when we dream that we are pursuing somebody and
can never catch him, because as often as we reach him he escapes
us again. I thought I could never get over the misfortune of losing
Minna as the partner of my life; but time, which heals all wounds,
at last healed mine, so that, although I remained for years mourning
for her, I could at least continue my mercantile pursuits without
further interruption.

In my very first year at St. Petersburg my operations had already
been so successful, that in the beginning of 1847 I was inscribed
in the Guild as a wholesale merchant. But, in spite of my new
functions, I remained in connection with Messrs. B. H. Schröder
and Co. of Amsterdam, whose agency I kept for nearly eleven years.
As I had acquired in Amsterdam a thorough knowledge of indigo,
my transactions were almost exclusively limited to that article; and,
as long as my fortune was below 200,000 frs. (£8000), I never
gave credit except to merchants of the very first standing. Thus I
had to content myself at first with very small profits, but my business
was a perfectly safe one.

Not having heard of my brother, Louis Schliemann, who in the
beginning of 1849 had emigrated to California, I went thither in

the spring of 1850, and found that he was dead. Happening, therefore, to be in California when, on the 4th of July, 1850, it was made a State, and all those then resident in the country became by that very fact naturalized Americans, I joyfully embraced the opportunity of becoming a citizen of the United States.

At the end of 1852 I established a branch-house at Moscow for wholesale dealing in indigo, first under the direction of my excellent agent, Mr. Alexei Matweieff, and after his death under the direction of his servant Jutchenko, whom I raised to the dignity of a merchant of the Second Guild, considering that an able servant may easily become a good director, whilst a director can never become a good servant.

As I was always overwhelmed with work at St. Petersburg, I could not continue my linguistic studies there, and it was not until the year 1854 that I found it possible to acquire the Swedish and Polish languages.

Divine Providence protected me marvellously, and on more than one occasion I was saved from apparently certain destruction by a mere accident. All my life long I shall remember the morning of the 4th of October, 1854. It was at the time of the Crimean war. The Russian ports being blockaded, all the merchandise intended for St. Petersburg had to be shipped to the Prussian ports of Memel or Königsberg, thence to be forwarded overland. Some hundreds of chests of indigo, as well as large quantities of other goods, had been thus shipped by Messrs. J. Henry Schröder & Co. of London and Messrs. B. H. Schröder & Co. of Amsterdam, on my account, by two steamers to my agents, Messrs. Meyer & Co. of Memel, to be sent on by the latter overland to St. Petersburg. I had just returned from the indigo auctions at Amsterdam in order to see after my goods at Memel, and had arrived late in the evening of the 3rd of October at the Hôtel de Prusse in Königsberg, when, happening to look out of the window of my bedroom on the following morning, I saw the following ominous inscription, written in large gilt letters on the tower of the gate close by, called "das Grüne Thor:"

> Vultus fortunae variatur imagine lunae,
> Crescit decrescit, constans persistere nescit.

Though I am not superstitious, the inscription made a profound impression upon me, and I was seized with a kind of panic, as though an unknown disaster were hanging over me. In continuing my journey by the mail-coach, I was horror-stricken to learn, at the first station beyond Tilsit, that the whole city of Memel had been consumed on the previous day by a fearful conflagration; and I saw this but too well confirmed on my arrival before the city, which resembled an immense graveyard on which blackened walls and chimneys stood out like tombstones, mournful monuments of the fragility of human things. Almost in despair, I ran among the smouldering ruins in search of Mr. Meyer. At last I found him, and asked him whether my goods were safe: by way of answer, he pointed to his smouldering warehouses and said, "There they are buried." The blow was tremendous: by eight and a half years' hard labour in St. Petersburg I had only saved 150,000 thalers, or £22,500, and this was now all lost. But no sooner had I acquired the certainty that I was ruined, than I recovered my presence of mind. It gave me great comfort to think that I had no debts to pay, for it was only at the beginning of the Crimean war, and business being then very unsafe, I had bought only for cash. So I thought Messrs. Schröder of London and Amsterdam would give me credit, and I felt confident that I should make up the loss in course of time. In the evening, when on the point of leaving by the mail for St. Petersburg, I was telling my misfortune to the other passengers, when a bystander suddenly asked me my name, and, having heard it, exclaimed: "Schliemann is the only man who has not lost anything! I am Meyer & Co.'s first clerk. Our warehouse being crammed full of goods when the steamers arrived with his merchandise, we were obliged to build close to it a wooden barrack, in which all his property lies perfectly safe."

The sudden transition from profound grief to great joy is difficult to bear without tears: I was for some minutes speechless; it seemed to me like a dream and incredible that I alone should have escaped unhurt from the universal ruin. But so it was. The strangest thing was that the fire had originated in Meyer & Co.'s stone warehouse, at the northern extremity of the town, whence, owing to a furious gale which was blowing from the north at the time, the flames rapidly spread over the whole city; whereas, under the protection of the same storm, the wooden barrack remained unhurt, though it was not more than a couple of yards north of the warehouse. My goods having thus been preserved, I speedily sold them to great advantage; turned the money over and over again; did a large business in indigo, dyewoods, and war material (saltpetre, brimstone, and lead); and, as capitalists were afraid to do much business during the Crimean war, I was able to realize large profits, and more than doubled my capital in a single year. I was greatly assisted in my transactions during the Crimean war by the great tact and ability of my agent, my dear friend Mr. Isidor Lichtenstein, senior, partner in the house of Messrs. Marcus Cohn & Son at Königsberg, and his junior partner, Mr. Ludwig Leo, who forwarded all my transit goods to me with a promptitude really wonderful.

My wish to learn Greek had always been great, but before the Crimean war I did not venture upon its study, for I was afraid

that this language would exercise too great a fascination over me
and estrange me from my commercial business; and during the
war I was so overwhelmed with work, that I could not even read
the newspapers, far less a book. When, however, in January 1856,
the first tidings of peace reached St. Petersburg, I was no longer
able to restrain my desire to learn Greek, and at once set vigorously
to work, taking first as my teacher Mr. Nicolaos Pappadakes and
then Mr. Theokletos Vimpos, both from Athens, where the latter is
now archbishop. I again faithfully followed my old method; but
in order to acquire quickly the Greek vocabulary, which seemed to
me far more difficult even than the Russian, I procured a modern
Greek translation of *Paul et Virginie*, and read it through, comparing every word with its equivalent in the French original. When
I had finished this task, I knew at least one-half the Greek words the
book contained, and after repeating the operation I knew them all,
or nearly so, without having lost a single minute by being obliged
to use a dictionary. In this manner it did not take me more than
six weeks to master the difficulties of modern Greek, and I next
applied myself to the ancient language, of which in three months
I learned sufficient to understand some of the ancient authors, and
especially Homer, whom I read and re-read with the most lively
enthusiasm.

I then occupied myself for two years exclusively with the literature of ancient Greece; and during this time I read almost all the
classical authors cursorily, and the *Iliad* and *Odyssey* several times.
Of the Greek grammar, I learned only the declensions and the verbs,
and never lost my precious time in studying its rules; for as I saw
that boys, after being troubled and tormented for eight years and
more in schools with the tedious rules of grammar, can nevertheless none of them write a letter in ancient Greek without making
hundreds of atrocious blunders, I thought the method pursued by the
schoolmasters must be altogether wrong, and that a thorough knowledge of the Greek grammar could only be obtained by practice,—
that is to say, by the attentive reading of the prose classics, and by
committing choice pieces of them to memory. Following this very
simple method, I learnt ancient Greek as I would have learnt a
living language. I can write in it with the greatest fluency on any
subject I am acquainted with, and can never forget it. I am perfectly
acquainted with all the grammatical rules without even knowing
whether or not they are contained in the grammars; and whenever
a man finds errors in my Greek, I can immediately prove that I am
right, by merely reciting passages from the classics where the
sentences employed by me occur.

Meanwhile my mercantile affairs in St. Petersburg and Moscow
went on steadily and favourably. I was very cautious in my business;

and although I received severe blows during the fearful commercial crisis of 1857, they did not hurt me much, and even in that disastrous year I made, after all, some profits.

In the summer of 1858 I renewed with my friend, Professor Ludwig von Muralt, in St. Petersburg, my study of the Latin language, which had been interrupted for nearly twenty-five years. Now that I knew both modern and ancient Greek, I found the Latin language easy enough, and soon mastered its difficulties.

I therefore strongly recommend all directors of colleges and schools to introduce the method I have followed; to do away with the abominable English pronunciation of Greek, which has never been in use outside of England; to let children first be taught modern Greek by native Greek professors, and only afterwards begin ancient Greek when they can speak and write the modern language with fluency, which it can hardly take them more than six months to do. The same professors can teach the ancient language, and by following my method they will enable intelligent boys to master all its difficulties in a year, so that they will not only learn it as a living language, but will also understand the ancient classics, and be able to write fluently on any subject they are acquainted with.

This is no idle theory, but a stubborn fact, which therefore ought to be listened to. It is a cruel injustice to inflict for years upon an unhappy pupil a language of which, when he leaves college, as a general rule he knows hardly more than when he first began to learn it. The causes of this miserable result are, in the first place, the arbitrary and atrocious pronunciation of Greek usual in England; and in the second place the erroneous method employed, according to which the pupils learn to disregard the accents entirely, and to consider them as mere impediments, whereas the accents constitute a most important auxiliary in learning the language. What a happy effect would be produced on general education, and what an enormous stimulus would be given to scientific pursuits, if intelligent youths could obtain in eighteen months a thorough knowledge of modern Greek, and of that most beautiful, most divine, and most sonorous language, which was spoken by Homer and Plato, and could learn the latter as a living tongue, so as never to forget it! And how easily, at how small an expense, could the change be made! Greece abounds with highly-educated men, who have a thorough knowledge of the language of their ancestors, who are perfectly acquainted with all the classics, and who would gladly and at moderate salaries accept places in England or America. How greatly the knowledge of modern Greek assists the student in mastering ancient Greek I could not illustrate better than by the fact, that I have seen here in Athens office-clerks who, feeling no inclination for commerce, have left the counting-house, settled

down to study, and been able in four months' time to understand
Homer, and even Thucydides.

Latin should, in my opinion, be taught not before, but after,
Greek.

In the year 1858 I thought I had money enough, and wished to
retire from commercial pursuits. I travelled in Sweden, Denmark,
Germany, Italy, and Egypt, where I sailed up the Nile as far as the
Second Cataracts. I availed myself of this opportunity to learn
Arabic, and I afterwards travelled across the desert from Cairo to
Jerusalem. I visited Petra, and traversed the whole of Syria; and in
this manner had abundant opportunity of acquiring a practical
knowledge of Arabic, the deeper study of which I continued afterwards in St. Petersburg. After leaving Syria I visited Smyrna, the
Cyclades, and Athens, in the summer of 1859, and I was on the
point of starting for the island of Ithaca when I was seized with
fever. At the same time I received information from St. Petersburg
that a merchant, Mr. Stepan Solovieff, who had failed, owing me a
large sum of money, and with whom I had agreed that he should
repay it in the course of four years by annual instalments, not
only had not made his first payment, but had brought a suit against
me in the Commercial Court. I therefore hurried back to St.
Petersburg, was cured of fever by the change of air, and promptly
gained my cause. But my antagonist appealed to the Senate, where
no lawsuit can be terminated in less than three and a half or four
years; and my presence on the spot being necessary, I went into
business once more, much against my will, and on a much larger
scale than before. My imports from May to October 1860 reached
as high a sum as £500,000. Besides indigo and olive oil, I also in
1860 and 1861 embarked largely in cotton, which gave great profits,
owing to the Civil War in the United States of America, and the
blockade of the Southern ports. But when cotton became too dear,
I abandoned it, and in its stead went into tea, the importation of
which by sea was permitted from May 1862 and onwards. My first
tea order to Messrs. J. Henry Schröder and Co. of London was for
30 chests; and when these were advantageously disposed of, I
imported 1000, and afterwards 4000 and 6000 chests. I also bought
of Mr. J. E. Günzburg of St. Petersburg, who was withdrawing from
the trade in goods, his whole stock of tea, at a cheap rate, and
gained in the first six months £7000 on my transactions in that
commodity. But when in the winter of 1862-3 the insurrection
broke out in Poland, and the Jews, profiting by the disorder then
prevailing there, smuggled immense quantities of tea into Russia,
I could not stand this competition, being obliged to pay the high
import duty. I therefore retired again from the tea trade, but it took
me a long time to sell at a small profit the 6000 chests which had

remained on my hands. But my staple commodity always remained indigo; for, as I knew the article well, and was always favoured by Messrs. John Henry Schröder and Co. of London with choice and cheap purchases, and as I also imported large quantities direct from Calcutta, and never confided the sale of indigo to clerks or servants, as others did, but always stood myself in my warehouse, and showed and sold it personally and wholesale to the indigo dealers, I had no competition to fear, and my net profit on this article was on an average £10,000 annually, with 6 per cent interest on the capital employed.

Heaven continued to bless all my mercantile undertakings in a wonderful manner, so that at the end of 1863 I found myself in possession of a fortune such as my ambition had never ventured to aspire to. But in the midst of the bustle of business I never forgot Troy, or the agreement I had made with my father and Minna in 1830 to excavate it. I loved money indeed, but solely as the means of realizing this great idea of my life. Besides, I had recommenced business much against my will, and merely in order to have some occupation and distraction while the tedious lawsuit with the merchant who had attacked me was going on. When therefore his appeal had been rejected by the Senate, and I had received from him the last payment, in December 1863, I began to liquidate my business. But before devoting myself entirely to archaeology, and to the realization of the dream of my life, I wished to see a little more of the world. So I started in April, 1864, for Tunis, to investigate the ruins of Carthage, and went thence, by way of Egypt, to India. I visited in succession the island of Ceylon, Madras, Calcutta, Benares, Agra, Lucknow, Delhi, the Himalaya Mountains, Singapore, and the island of Java, and stayed for two months in China, where I visited Hong Kong, Canton, Amoy, Foochoo, Shanghai, Tin-Sin, Peking, and the Great Wall. I then went to Yokohama and Jeddo in Japan, and thence crossed the Pacific Ocean in a small English vessel to San Francisco in California. Our passage lasted fifty days, which I employed in writing my first work, La Chine et le Japon. From San Francisco I went, by way of Nicaragua, to the Eastern United States, travelled through most of them, visited Havana and the city of Mexico, and in the spring of 1866 settled down in Paris to study archaeology, henceforth with no other interruption than short trips to America. . . .

As on my last journey to England and Germany I have heard it repeatedly stated that, carried away by ambition, I am ruining myself in my archaeological explorations, to the prejudice of my children, who will be penniless after my death, I find it necessary to assure the reader that, although on account of my present scientific pursuits I am bound to keep aloof from all sorts of speculation and am compelled to content myself with a small interest on my capital, I still have a yearly income of £4000 as the net proceeds of the rents of my four houses in Paris, and £6000 interest on my funded property, making in all £10,000; whilst, inclusive of the large cost of my excavations, I do not spend more than £5000 a year, and am thus able to add £5000 annually to my capital. I trust, therefore, that on my death I shall leave to each of my children a fortune large enough to enable them to continue their father's scientific explorations without ever touching their capital. I avail myself of this opportunity to assure the reader that, as I love and worship science for its own sake, I shall never make a traffic of it. My large collections of Trojan antiquities have a value which cannot be calculated, but they shall never be sold. If I do not present them in my lifetime, they shall at all events pass, in virtue of my last will, to the Museum of the nation I love and esteem most.

HEINRICH SCHLIEMANN

Schliemann Finds "Priam's Treasure" at Troy

HISSARLIK, the site of Troy, lies on a fold of rock in the north-west corner of Asia Minor, near the entrance to the Dardanelles. Troy was founded in the Early Bronze Age of the third millennium B.C. Soon it was a flourishing little fortress city with walls of mudbrick and timber on stone foundations, and massive, towered gateways. It had a large assembly hall of the *megaron* plan (with an entrance porch), and nearby a modest palace for the ruling family. This Early Bronze Age Troy (at a stage of its development known to modern archaeologists as IIg) was burnt down after about 2300 B.C., and it was the vitrification of the walls and other marks of conflagra-

From *Ilios*, pp. 40-3.

tion that led Schliemann to identify it with the city of the Homeric story, and to attribute the "treasure" he found in it to King Priam. Homer's city is now identified usually with Troy VIIa—dating from over a millennium later.

WHILE following up this circuit-wall, and bringing more and more of it to light, close to the ancient building and north-west of the Gate, I struck upon a large copper article of the most remarkable form, which attracted my attention all the more, as I thought I saw gold behind it. On the top of it was a layer of red and calcined ruins, from 4¾ to 5¼ ft. thick, as hard as stone, and above this again the above-mentioned wall of fortification (5 ft. broad and 20 ft. high), built of large stones and earth, which must have been erected shortly after the destruction of Troy. In order to secure the treasure from my workmen and save it for archaeology, it was necessary to lose no time; so, although it was not yet the hour for breakfast, I immediately had *païdos* [time for rest] called. While the men were eating and resting, I cut out the treasure with a large knife. This required great exertion and involved great risk, since the wall of fortification, beneath which I had to dig, threatened every moment to fall down upon me. But the sight of so many objects, every one of which is of inestimable value to archaeology, made me reckless, and I never thought of any danger. It would, however, have been impossible for me to have removed the treasure without the help of my dear wife, who stood at my side, ready to pack the things I cut out in her shawl, and to carry them away. All the different articles of which this treasure was composed will be described at the proper place in the precise order in which they were taken out of the ruins.

As I found all these articles together, in the form of a rectangular mass, or packed into one another, it seems certain that they were placed on the city wall in a wooden chest. This supposition seems to be corroborated by the fact that close by the side of these articles I found a copper key. It is therefore possible that some one packed the treasure in the chest, and carried it off, without having had time to pull out the key; when he reached the wall, however, the hand of an enemy, or the fire, overtook him, and he was obliged to abandon the chest, which was immediately covered, to a height of 5 ft., with ashes and stones of the adjoining house. But as in 1878 and 1879 I found, at a distance of but a few yards from the spot where this treasure was discovered, four more treasures, which must evidently have fallen from an upper storey of the town-chief's house, I now rather think that the same may have been the case with the large treasure.

Perhaps the articles found a few days previously in a room of the chief's house, close to the place where the treasure was discovered, belonged to this unfortunate person. These articles consisted of a helmet and a silver vase, with a cup of electrum, which will be described in the chapter on this Third City.

On the thick layer of *débris* which covered the treasure, the builders of the new city erected a fortification-wall already mentioned, composed of large hewn and unhewn stones and earth. This wall extended to within 3¼ ft. of the surface of the hill.

That the treasure was packed together at a moment of supreme peril appears to be proved, among other things, by the contents of the largest silver vase, consisting of nearly 9000 objects of gold, which will be described in the subsequent pages. The person who endeavoured to save the treasure had, fortunately, the presence of mind to place the silver vase, with the valuable articles inside it, upright in the chest, so that nothing could fall out, and everything has been preserved uninjured.

Hoping to find more treasures here, I pulled down the upper wall, and I also broke away the enormous block of *débris* which separated my western and north-western trenches from the great massive walls which I used to call the "Tower." But to do this I had to pull down the larger of my wooden houses, and to bridge over the Gates, so as to facilitate the removal of the *débris*. I found there many interesting antiquities; more especially three silver dishes 1 ft. 9 in. below the place where the treasure was discovered: two of them were broken in pieces by the labourer's pickaxe; the third is entire. That the treasure itself escaped injury from the pickaxes, was due to the large copper vessel, which projected in such a way that I could cut everything out of the hard *débris* with a knife.

RUDOLF VIRCHOW

Schliemann's
Scholarly Supporter

RUDOLF VIRCHOW was a German of many abilities, who had won fame as a pathologist and anthropologist, and interested himself in liberal politics. He took some part in the study of lake dwellings, and went with Schliemann to Troy in 1879. Although he had no great archaeological knowledge, his support must have been valuable to Schliemann in his controversies with the scholarly world (p. 57, I).

❧

WHO could fail to feel the thrilling interest of such a view? From the oldest times the Hellespont has been not merely the boundary, but, in a much higher degree, the connection between Asia and Europe. Here the armies of the two continents met in conflict. What the Persians failed to do, the Turks have done. The enterprise in which Alexander succeeded was attempted over again by the Crusaders. The shores of the Dardanelles provide the easiest passage from Europe to Asia, or from Asia to Europe. History has taught us that the Asiatic stream has, on the whole, been the stronger one. It is probable even that our own ancestors, the Aryan immigrants, came by this passage on their victorious career into Europe, long before the *Iliad* was composed, and still longer before the history of mankind began to be written.

Such thoughts as these were constantly present to my mind as I turned my eyes to the little bit of Europe which was visible from our wooden hut on Hissarlik. A very little bit it was, and I cannot say that I wished it larger. All we saw of it was the southern point of the Thracian Chersonese, a low rising ground beyond the Hel-

From an appendix to *Ilios*, pp. 679-85.

lespont, at the south end of which the ancients placed the grave
of Protesilaus. In the evening, when I had put out my lamp and
looked out once more, the only visible sign which remained to
connect me with Europe was the beacon-light at the end of this
promontory, which shone straight into my little window. But what
a crowd of memories did its beam awaken!

As I looked out in the morning from the same window, I saw
stretching far away the deep-blue sea with its islands. In the distance, separated from the Chersonese by a wide stretch of sea,
lay rocky Imbros, with its long jagged ridge; and just behind it rose
the towering peak of Samothrace. How majestic this island looks
from Ujek Tepeh! What Ida is in the far southeast, Samothrace is in
the far northwest: the former the seat of Zeus, the mightiest of
all the gods; the latter that of the next mightiest, Poseidon.

The Northerner, especially if he lives where the sky is often
clouded, finds it hard to understand how the religious ideas of
Southern nations attached themselves so prevailingly to the
phenomena of the atmosphere, or, to speak more mythologically,
of "Heaven." It is necessary to see the wide horizon and the pure
blue of the Trojan sky, in order to appreciate the effect produced
here by the formation of clouds. When, on a sudden, while sea and
land are lying apparently at rest, a dark mass of cloud gathers
round the peak of Samothrace, and, sinking deeper every moment,
enshrouds one sharp line of rock after another, till the storm at last
descends, and, after lashing the sea with its gusts, wraps even it in
darkness, we find it easier to see how it was that a childlike spirit
looked for the presence of the sea-god himself in the secret recesses
of the clouds. And if far away in the southwestern sky, in the
direction of Greece, a single cloud appears over the Aegean, and
gradually rises and spreads, draws nearer and nearer, and at last
touches the summit of Ida, there to thicken and cling for hours and
even days together, and if then lightning breaks from this cloud-
mass whole nights through, while all the face of Nature seems to
lie beneath it in fright, who can help thinking of the poet's descriptions of the journey and sojourn of the Thunderer?

From the height of Ujek Tepeh may be seen several other islands
of the Aegean, rising high, with clear rock outlines. Close at hand,
just opposite to Besika Bay, lies the vine-clad Tenedos, behind which
the Achaean fleet hid by way of preparing for their attack on Ilium.
Far to the south, though only when the air is very clear, we may see
the angular lines of Lesbos, or, as it is called in modern times,
Mitylene. Sometimes a cloud rises far out at sea, which makes for
Lesbos and Cape Baba, the Lectum of the ancients, and which
passes from mountain to mountain till it reaches Ida. It takes
exactly the path which Hera took when she sought out her angry

spouse on Gargarus, and accomplished the loving reconciliation portrayed in one of the most charming passages in the *Iliad*.

Who would not feel the captivating charm of such scenes as these? and who can fail to see that the great poet has created out of them the magnificent picture he gives us of the ways and workings of the Olympian gods? I will not here describe these natural phenomena in detail. I will even forbear to portray the grand spectacle presented by the lifting and sinking of the clouds at the foot of Mount Ida. But I cannot conceal my amazement that it should have been thought possible to darken the wondrous beauty of the Trojan scenery by the light of the student's lamp, and to call in question the background of reality which gave shape to the visions of the immortal poet.

This attempt would probably never have been made if the site of ancient Ilium had been known. But even in the days of Demetrius of Scepsis, a native of the Troad, who lived about two hundred years before the beginning of the Christian era, not a trace was to be seen of the old city anywhere in the plain. This country was left isolated at an early time by the ruin of many kingdoms; and thousands of years elapsed before the search actually began for the real site of the city. Since the commencement of that search, scarcely a part of the country has been safe from the conjectures of the learned. Beginning with the Gulf of Adramyttium and Cape Lectum, they have sought the city, now here, now there. The points which occupied for the longest time the attention of scholars were Alexandria-Troas, the site of the extensive ruins of a metropolis founded on the Aegean by Antigonus, and so post-Homeric, and Bounarbashi, a wretched Turkish hamlet at the southern extremity of the Trojan plain. It was only fifty years ago that Maclaren first ventured to fix on the hill and fortress of Hissarlik as the spot where Troy once stood. Others, among whom was Von Eckenbrecher, adopted his view. The first actual excavations were conducted by Mr. Frank Calvert. These excavations, however, were confined to the surface. It has been reserved for Dr. Schliemann, by the application of resources such as can hardly ever have been devoted by a private individual to such an object before, to lay bare, by digging down to an amazing depth, the ruins of settlements of immense antiquity, and thereby to make Hissarlik an object of the highest interest to all educated men.

Does this settle the question about the site of the ancient Ilium? Opponents say, No. And why? While they condemn Schliemann for taking the *Iliad* literally, they think it a sufficient refutation of his views if they prove that the ruins of Hissarlik do not correspond to Homer's descriptions. Correspond they certainly do not. Homer's

idea of his sacred Ilios is very different from any conception we can
form from the testimony of the ruins.

No one doubts that Ilium was destroyed centuries before the
Iliad was composed. How many centuries, is a question which
divides even those who take Homer's side. Even if the interval were
not more than two or three hundred years, still Ilium itself could
never have been seen by the poet. *The Ilium of fiction must, under
any circumstances, be a fiction itself.* It is possible that legend
may have preserved many topographical particulars about the
ancient city, but it is not to be imagined there should have been
preserved a detailed and authentic description of the city or the
fortress as it existed before its destruction. "Grass" had no doubt
"grown" meanwhile over the ruins. New settlers had built on the old
spot dwellings which had perhaps lain long in ruins themselves
when the poet began his work. It is very questionable whether he
ever saw with his eyes even the ruins of the fallen city. The place
where it stood he saw no doubt, *but the city itself he saw only in a
vision.* Just as Zeus and Hera, Poseidon and Athene, Ares and
Aphrodite, were creatures of his fancy, so the city of Ilium was itself
"a dream." No one can expect the actual ruins to correspond to every
imagination of the poet; and when it is established that Homer had
in his mind much that never existed, at all events on this spot, it
simply comes to this, that the *Iliad* is not an historical work, but
a poetical one.

And yet the correspondence of the poetical representation with
the local conditions is far from being so imperfect as it is represented. The situation of Hissarlik satisfies in the main all the demands of the Homeric topography. From this spot, as from Ujek
Tepeh, we get a view over the whole of the anterior Troad. The
plain with its rivers and brooks, the side-valleys, the encompassing
hills, the circlet of volcanic mountains, the Hellespont and the
Aegean, lie spread out before our eyes as we stand on the height
of Hissarlik. The only difference is that we are ever so much nearer
to the plain, and especially to that part of it which is best suited
for a battle-field, and which, if we overlook the present altered
courses of the rivers, completely answers to the topography of the
Homeric field of battle. The separate objects on this plain are
clearly distinguishable, and it is not quite impossible that Helen
should have been able to point out the individual chieftains of the
Achaeans to her royal father-in-law. The distance, too, is quite
visible enough for the purposes of the Homeric landscapes. We see
the Thracian Chersonese, and we have Imbros and Samothrace
before us. Further to the left lies Tenedos, and right behind in the
south-east the snowy top of Ida rises above the nearer range of

hills. At sunset even the pyramid of Athos may sometimes be seen for a few minutes in the far west.

It is true that the old city did not stand as high as the top of the hill of Hissarlik did before the excavations were begun. Dr. Schliemann had to go deep down—from 25 to 30 feet or more—before he came on the walls and houses of Ilium under the *débris* of later settlements. But even if we sink the level of Ilium to such a depth, it is still high enough to preserve to the city its commanding position. Its houses and towers, even though they were of a very moderate height, must have risen far enough above the surface to reach the level of the later hill. This would still make it a lofty, "windy" fastness. Our wooden huts, which had been put up at the foot of the hill, well below the level of the old city, looked straight down upon the plain from a height of at least 60 feet, and the winds blew about us with such force that we often felt as if our whole settlement might be hurled down the precipice.

The fortress-hill of Hissarlik, as it appeared to travellers before Dr. Schliemann started his huge excavations, was then, properly speaking, an artificial hill, most nearly comparable perhaps with the earth hills of the Assyrian plain which covered the ruins of the royal castles; only it had not been set up on the plain itself, but on the west end of the second ridge of tertiary rock above described. Consequently it lay right over the plain, and must have looked high from the first. Its subsequent increase in height must have been very gradual indeed. In digging down from the surface fresh ruins are constantly encountered, belonging to various epochs. One people has lived here after another, and each fresh one which settled on the ruins of its predecessor levelled the surface anew by clearing away some of the ruins and throwing them over the precipice. In this way the surface of the hill grew gradually in extent, and it is conceivable that, now that last year's excavations have almost completely laid bare the boundaries of the old city, the vast pit should present the aspect of a funnel, at the bottom of which the ruins of Ilium lie within a pretty small compass. We must admit the justness of the objection that this Ilium was no great city, capable of finding room for a great army of foreign warriors in addition to a large population of its own. Such an Ilium as that existed only in the poet's vision. Our Ilium hardly deserves to be called a city at all. In our part of the world we should call such a place a fortress or a stronghold. For this reason I prefer to call the place a *fortress-hill (Burgberg)*; a term which, strictly speaking, is merely a translation of the Turkish word Hissarlik.

But why take these very ruins at the bottom of the funnel to be Ilium? To this I answer that it is a question again whether there ever was a place called Ilium. Is it not questionable whether

there ever was any Heracles or any Argonauts? Perhaps Ilium,
Priam, and Andromache, are just as much poetical fictions as
Zeus, Poseidon, and Aphrodite. But this does not amount to saying
that we ought not to look for the Ilium of the poet at the bottom
of our funnel. There lies a close array of houses surrounded by a
mighty wall of rough-hewn stone. The walls of houses and rooms
have been preserved to such an extent, that it is possible to give a
ground-plan of the place. A pretty steep street, paved with large
flags, leads through a single gate on the western side into the
fortress. Only a narrow passage is left between the houses. The
whole place is full of the rubbish left by a conflagration. Great clay
bricks, half a yard square, have been melted by a fierce heat and
turned to a glassy paste. Heaps of corn, especially wheat, pease,
and beans, have been turned to charcoal. The remains of animal
food, oyster-shells and mussels of all kinds, bones of sheep and
goats, of oxen and swine, have likewise been partially burnt away.
Of charcoal proper there is but little to be seen, and what
there is is mostly oak. The conflagration must have lasted long
enough to destroy entirely almost all the woodwork. Even the
metal, and especially the bronze, is for the most part molten and
reduced by fire to an undistinguishable mass.

It is evident that this fortress was destroyed by a conflagration
of great extent, which lasted long enough to destroy utterly all
inflammable materials. Such a fire as corresponds to Homer's description has only taken place once in the settlements on Hissarlik.
In the numerous strata of ruins which lie one above the other there
are several other traces of fire, but none on the scale on which
they occur in the "burnt city." Even below it there are still strata,
going down at some points to a depth of 20 or 25 feet or more,—
for the "burnt city" was not the oldest settlement on Hissarlik,—but
even in these oldest strata there is nowhere the trace of such an
extensive conflagration.

It is the "burnt city," however, where, among numerous objects
of art-work—of pottery especially—some of which are of rare
excellence, gold has repeatedly been brought to light, sometimes
in connection with objects of silver, bronze, and ivory. All these
discoveries have been eclipsed in splendour by the "Treasure of
Priam," upon which Dr. Schliemann lighted in the third year of his
successful excavations. And not a year has passed since, without
the discovery of at least some articles of gold. I was myself an
eye-witness of two such discoveries, and helped to gather the articles together. The slanderers have long since been silenced, who
were not ashamed to charge the discoverer with an imposture.
Especially since the Turkish government, on the occasion of the fur-
tive appropriation of a portion of the discoveries by two of the

workmen, has laid an embargo on all objects of the kind,—as is the case with such collections elsewhere,—such envious spite has retreated to the privacy of the family hearth. Since that time, objects of gold of the same type as those from Hissarlik have been found not only in Mycenae, but also in other Greek graves. One of the gold treasures which were excavated in my presence contained stamped plates of gold, the ornamentation of which is in the minutest details the counterpart of that found at Mycenae.

The "burnt city" was then also the "city of gold." It is only in it that we find this wealth of marvellous and at the same time distinctly foreign treasures. For it is clear that we have here no product of native industry, but articles brought from abroad either by trade or plunder. Their character is Oriental, and more particularly Assyrian. Consequently the burnt fortress must have been the seat of a great and prosperous hero—or of the son of such a man—who had amassed treasures of the rarest value in his small but secure home.

The chief treasure was found all together at one spot, in a kind of cupboard. It appeared to have been originally stowed away in a wooden chest. It was near the wall of a very strongly built stone house, in other parts of which were found numerous other treasures, in vases of terracotta, in a good state of preservation, and which was evidently the residence of the prince. For in no other place were any such treasures discovered; and, as the area of the burnt city has now been completely brought to light, we may assert definitely that *on this spot was the palace. The old city wall runs close by it, and the street which comes up through the single gate of the fortress leads up to it.*

Was this gate the Seaean gate, and this house the house of Priam? Dr. Schliemann, overawed by his learned adversaries, now talks only of the house of the "chief of the city" (*Stadthaupt*). But can the "chief of the city," who was master of so much gold at a time when gold was so scarce, have been anything but a prince? And why not call him Priam? Whether Priam ever existed or not, the prince of the golden treasure who lived on this spot comes near enough to the Priam of the *Iliad* to make us refuse to forego the delight of giving the place his name. And what harm can there be in assigning to the western gateway, *the only one which exists in the city wall at all,* to which a steep road led up from the plain, the famous name of the Seaean gate?

Do not let us cut ourselves off from all poetry without the slightest need. Children that we are of a hard and too prosaic age, we would maintain our right to conjure up again before our old age the pictures which filled our youthful fancy. It saddens but it also elevates the soul when we stand on a place like Hissarlik, and

read the course of history from the series of successive strata as
from a geological disclosure. This history is not written for us, but
set bodily before our eyes in the relics of bygone times, in the
actual objects used by men who lived in them. Huge masses of
ruins are piled in layers above the burnt stronghold, between it
and the first layer containing hewn stones and a wall of square
blocks. This was perhaps the wall which Lysimachus, one of
Alexander's generals, is recorded to have built on Ilium. Anyhow
this wall resembles the walls of the Macedonian period, and the
corresponding layer conceals Greek walls and pottery. Here then
we have a definite limit of time. From this point we have got to
reckon the time backwards, and it is easy to see that this reckoning
is not unfavourable to our interpretation of the Trojan legend.

Perhaps then Homer's song is not pure fiction, after all. Perhaps
it is true that in a very remote prehistoric time a rich prince really
dwelt here in a towering fortress, and that Greek kings waged a
fierce war against him, and that the war ended in his own fall
and the destruction of his city by a mighty conflagration. Perhaps
this was the first time that Europe and Asia tried each other's
strength on this coast, the first time that the young but more and
more independent civilization of the West put to the rough test
of force its superiority over the already effeminate civilization of
the East. To me this seems a probability, but it is one which I will
not press any one else to accept.

Of this we may be sure, that even the oldest and earliest settlement on Hissarlik was made by a people which had already felt
the influence of civilization. True, it still used stone weapons, but
these weapons were finely polished and bore witness by the delicacy
of their outline to a knowledge of metals. In fact, traces of metals
are not wanting even in the oldest strata. It is impossible therefore
to assign these strata to the Stone age. They are indications of
what we may undoubtedly assert to be *the oldest known settlement
in Asia Minor of a people of prehistoric times, of some advance
in civilization*. Hence the hill-fortress of Hissarlik is certain to hold
an enduring place as a trustworthy witness in the history of civilization. It will be to our descendants an important geographical position, and a fixed starting-point for the flights of their fancy. For
it is to be hoped that, however the strife may end about the existence of Ilium or of Priam, the young will never lose the *Iliad*.

CARL BLEGEN

Troy Revisited

CARL BLEGEN renewed excavation at Troy in 1932 (p. 59, I).

❧

SOME explanation might seem to be required for the action of the sponsors of the University of Cincinnati Expedition in deciding to devote another large-scale effort and a considerable sum of money to supplementary research on the Trojan hill which had already been so thoroughly churned over. It might well be asked—not only by the layman—if more novel and sensational discoveries could not have been anticipated from the excavation of some hitherto untouched site in the same general region. Not much is needed in the way of justification. In the Bronze Age the fortress of Troy, now represented by the ruins at Hissarlik, was obviously the key stronghold of northwestern Anatolia; there is no other like it. Moreover, whatever contrary theories and speculations may be brought forward by those who oppose the identification, it was also surely the actual citadel—if there ever was one—that came to be immortalized, magnified, and gilded with poetic glamor, in the *Iliad*. Both from the side of general human interest and from the strictly archaeological point of view it was, and is, consequently a place of unique appeal; and the chance of finding new evidence to settle some of the major unsolved Trojan problems, in history, culture, and relations with other centers, was judged to be preferable to the possibility, or even probability, of unearthing novel material from some less significant site.

Archaeology had been steadily marching forward. The three or four decades following the conclusion of Schliemann's and Dörpfeld's excavations at Troy had seen a remarkable advance in our

From *Troy*, Vol. I, pp. 5-7. Reprinted from *Troy* by Carl Blegen, by permission of Princeton University Press, Princeton. © 1950 by Princeton University Press.

knowledge of preclassical civilization in the Aegean. New and illuminating discoveries in Crete, in the Cyclades, on the mainland of Greece, in Macedonia, along the western littoral of Asia Minor and in Cyprus, had yielded a huge increment of detailed information, unveiling an ever-broadening vista that led back into the unrecorded past of the Eastern Mediterranean world. The brilliant researches of Sir Arthur Evans at Knossos, supplemented by those of colleagues at many other island and mainland sites, had provided a substantial basis for the reconstruction, by Evans, in an orderly general outline, of a historical development that ran its course through a Bronze Age of more than two millennia.

In the meantime Troy had remained more or less neglected, just beyond the periphery of these new discoveries. It was not possible to determine exactly how the series of Trojan settlements—the Nine Cities of Schliemann and Dörpfeld—corresponded with the newly ascertained periods and subperiods of the Aegean Bronze Age. Dörpfeld had indeed shown that deposits laid down in Troy VI and VIIa produced Mycenaean pottery of types commonly found at Mycenae and Tiryns, and a general contemporaneity of the two cultures had thus been established; but precise points of contact had not been fixed. For the earlier settlements at Troy, moreover, no specific synchronisms with the Aegean system of chronology had been satisfactorily demonstrated, nor had the cultural relations of the Troad with the West been clarified. The problem of dating the older strata at Troy had meanwhile been steadily growing more important as archaeologists began to make increasing use of Trojan comparisons and analogies in their attempts to build up an absolute chronology for some of the periods in European prehistory.

For these and other reasons it seemed desirable, timely, and worth while to return to Troy to undertake an exhaustive, painstaking re-examination of the entire site. There was ground for believing that a considerable amount of "certified" material could still be recovered from each one of the principal layers represented in the stratified deposit covering the mound, and that a careful study of this material might clear up not a few of the vexing uncertainties of the site itself, permitting a sharper and more exact differentiation of the earlier periods than had been possible in previous excavations. And there was also reason to hope that such a study, taking into consideration all the Aegean comparisons now available, might shed fresh light on the external relations of Troy in all phases of its occupation.

From the start the excavations at Troy were planned as a work of sober, serious research, and there was no compulsion to recover objects of startling or sensational character with high publicity value. The principal objectives of the expedition, laid down at the inception of the project, were kept steadily in mind throughout the entire undertaking. There were three such main lines of investigation.

The first and paramount task envisaged was to re-examine the whole problem of the Trojan stratification in the light of present-day knowledge of Aegean archaeology. This meant finding and "isolating" undisturbed deposits belonging to each one of the chief layers; and it was believed that careful digging would then permit the recovery of a substantial collection of material and evidence of all kinds that could in each instance be certainly and authoritatively attributed to its proper stratum; and that it would thus ultimately be possible to build up an unbroken series of objects representing all the successive periods during which the site was occupied. Such a collection, without gaps, was particularly needed for a better understanding of Settlements II, III, IV, and V, which had not been clearly differentiated in the excavations of our predecessors, as well as for a clarification of the relationship between Settlements I and II, V and VI, and VIIa and VIIb. It was further proposed to seek out by a patient and thorough scrutiny whatever evidence might shed new light on the external relations of Troy in all directions and might make possible a more specific dating—especially of the early settlements—in terms of the chronology now established, at least tentatively, for the Aegean Bronze Age.

The second aim was to renew and to intensify the search for pre-classical tombs in the immediate neighbourhood of Troy. Schliemann and Dörpfeld had devoted no little time and effort to this quest, but all their explorations had unfortunately proved fruitless. The nonexistence of early cemeteries in the vicinity of the site—if really a fact—was a curious phenomenon, constituting one of the most striking differences that could be noted between Troy and the Aegean world. The whole problem definitely called for further patient investigation; and this the Cincinnati Expedition was prepared to undertake, although it could not boast of possessing methods of tomb-divination not available to the previous excavators. Nevertheless, the chance of a fortunate discovery that might contribute some enlightenment on Trojan burial customs was naturally a strong incentive to work in this field.

As a third line of investigation the expedition proposed to conduct a systematic exploration of the entire Troad—or at least the northwestern part of it—in an attempt to discover and map all ancient sites; and it was planned to make trial soundings at the more important-looking places of this kind, especially those which had at one time or another been brought into the controversial discussion over the identification of Troy, or which might have been

suggested as alternative sites in preference to the mound of Hissarlik.

In retrospect it may be said that the first and main objective was
attained in a measure somewhat beyond expectation: a nearly full
series of "certified" material was secured, yielding new evidence
for an understanding and differentiation of the successive Trojan
settlements, and providing a broader foundation for dating than
was heretofore available. Some slight success may likewise fairly
be claimed in the search for tombs which ultimately brought to
light scanty remains of what might be called a cremation cemetery
of the Sixth Settlement. Also in our third field of endeavor, exploration in the Troad, some accomplishment may be entered on the
credit side of the expedition's ledger: several previously unknown
preclassical sites were discovered, one of which, Kumtepe, was
tested in a small trial excavation, while exploratory trenches were
dug at three other already recorded places: Balli Dag, Eski Hissarlik, and Karatepe.

A. H. SAYCE

The Hittites: an Inspiration

ARCHIBALD HENRY SAYCE was to become professor of Assyriol-
ogy at Oxford in 1891. His brilliant recognition of the unity underlying various sculptures and inscriptions scattered through Asia
Minor quickly led to a coherent understanding of the Hittite empire (p. 62, I).

IT was a warm and sunny September morning (of 1879) when I
left the little town of Nymphi near Smyrna with a strong escort

From *The Hittites*. London: Religious Tract Society; 1925, pp. 75-88.

of Turkish soldiers, and made my way to the Pass of Karabel. The
Pass of Karabel is a narrow defile, shut in on either side by lofty
cliffs, through which ran the ancient road from Ephesos in the
south to Sardes and Smyrna in the north. The Greek historian
Herodotus tells us that the Egyptian conqueror Sesostris had left
memorials of himself in this place. "Two images cut by him in
the rock" were to be seen beside the roads which led "from Ephesos
to Phokæa and from Sardes to Smyrna. On either side a man is
carved, a little over three feet in height, who holds a spear in the
right hand and a bow in the left. The rest of his accoutrement is
similar, for it is Egyptian and Ethiopian, and from one shoulder
to the other, right across the breast, Egyptian hieroglyphics have
been cut which declare: 'I have won this land with my shoulders.'"

These two images were the object of my journey. One of them
had been discovered by Renouard in 1839, and shortly afterwards
sketched by Texier; the other had been found by Dr. Beddoe in
1856. But visitors to the Pass in which they were engraved were
few and far between; the cliffs on either side were the favourite
haunt of brigands, and thirty soldiers were not deemed too many
to ensure my safety. My work of exploration had to be carried on
under the shelter of their guns, for more than twenty bandits were
lurking under the brushwood above.

The sculpture sketched by Texier had subsequently been photographed by Mr. Svoboda. It represents a warrior whose height is
rather more than life-size, and who stands in profile with the right
foot planted in front of him, in the attitude of one who is marching. In his right hand he holds a spear, behind his left shoulder
is slung a bow, and the head is crowned with a high peaked cap.
He is clad in a tunic which reaches to the knees, and his feet are
shod with boots with turned-up ends. The whole figure is cut in
deep relief in an artificial niche, and between the spear and the
face are three lines of hieroglyphic characters. The figure faces
south, and is carved on the face of the eastern cliff of Karabel.

It had long been recognized that the hieroglyphics were not those
of Egypt, and Professor Perrot had also drawn attention to the
striking resemblance between the style of art represented by this
sculpture and that represented by certain rock-sculptures in Cappadocia, as well as by the sculptured image of a warrior discovered
by himself at a place called Ghiaur-kalessi, "the castle of the in-
fidel," in Phrygia, which is practically identical in form and character with the sculptured warrior of Karabel.

What was the origin of this art, or who were the people it commemorated, was a matter of uncertainty. A few weeks, however,
before my visit to the Pass of Karabel, I announced that I had
come to the conclusion that the art was Hittite, and that the hiero-

glyphics accompanying the figure at Karabel would turn out, when carefully examined, to be Hittite also. The primary purpose of my visit to the pass was to verify this conclusion.

Let us now see how I had arrived at it. The story is a long one, and in order to understand it, it is necessary to transport ourselves from the Pass of Karabel in Western Asia Minor to Hama, the site of the ancient Hamath, in the Far East. It was here that the first discovery was made which has led by slow degrees to the reconstruction of the Hittite empire, and a recognition of the important part once played by the Hittites in the history of the civilized world.

As far back as the beginning of the present century (in 1812) the great Oriental traveller Burckhardt had noticed a block of black basalt covered with strange-looking hieroglyphics built into the corner of a house in one of the bazaars of Hama. But the discovery was forgotten, and the European residents in Hama, like the travellers who visited the city, were convinced that "no antiquities" were to be found there. Nearly sixty years later, however, when the American Palestine Exploration Society was first beginning its work, the American consul, Mr. Johnson, and an American missionary, Dr. Jessup, accidentally lighted again upon this stone, and further learned that three other stones of similar character, and inscribed with similar hieroglyphics, existed elsewhere in Hama. One of them, of very great length, was believed to be endowed with healing properties. Rheumatic patients, Mohammedans and Christians alike, were in the habit of stretching themselves upon it, in the firm belief that their pains would be absorbed into the stone. The other inscribed stones were also regarded with veneration, which naturally increased when it was known that they were being sought after by the Franks; and the two Americans found it impossible to see them all, much less to take copies of the inscriptions they bore. They had to be content with the miserable attempts at reproducing them made by a native painter, one of which was afterwards published in America. The publication served to awaken the interest of scholars in the newly discovered inscriptions, and efforts were made by Sir Richard Burton and others to obtain correct impressions of them. All was in vain, however, and it is probable that the fanaticism or greed of the people of Hama would have successfully resisted all attempts to procure trustworthy copies of the texts, had not a lucky accident brought Dr. William Wright to the spot. It is to his energy and devotion that the preservation of these precious relics of Hittite literature may be said to be due. "On the 10th of November, 1872," he tells us, he "set out from Damascus, intent on securing the Hama inscriptions. The Sublime Porte, seized by a periodic fit of reforming zeal, had appointed an honest man, Subhi Pasha, to be governor of Syria. Subhi Pasha brought a conscience to his work, and, not content with redressing wrongs that succeeded in forcing their way into his presence, resolved to visit every district of his province, in order that he might check the spoiler and discover the wants of the people. He invited me to accompany him on a tour to Hama, and I gladly accepted the invitation." Along with Mr. Green, the English Consul, accordingly, Dr. Wright joined the party of the Pasha; and, fearing that the same fate might befall the Hamath stones as had befallen the Moabite Stone, which had been broken into pieces to save it from the Europeans, persuaded him to buy them, and send them as a present to the Museum at Constantinople. When the news became known in Hama, there were murmurings long and deep against the Pasha, and it became necessary, not only to appeal to the cupidity and fear of the owners of the stones, but also to place them under the protection of a guard of soldiers the night before the work of removing them was to commence.

The night was an anxious one to Dr. Wright; but when day dawned the stones were still safe, and the labour of their removal was at once begun. It "was effected by an army of shouting men, who kept the city in an uproar during the whole day. Two of them had to be taken out of the walls of inhabited houses, and one of them was so large that it took fifty men and four oxen a whole day to drag it a mile. The other stones were split in two, and the inscribed parts were carried on the backs of camels to the" court of the governor's palace. Here they could be cleaned and copied at leisure and in safety.

But the work of cleaning them from the accumulated dirt of ages occupied the greater part of two days. Then came the task of making casts of the inscriptions, with the help of gypsum which some natives had been bribed to bring from the neighbourhood. At length, however, the work was completed, and Dr. Wright had the satisfaction of sending home to England two sets of casts of these ancient and mysterious texts, one for the British Museum, the other for the Palestine Exploration Fund, while the originals themselves were safely deposited in the Museum of Constantinople. It was now time to inquire what the inscriptions meant, and who could have been the authors of them.

Dr. Wright at once suggested that they were the work of the Hittites, and that they were memorials of Hittite writing. But his suggestion was buried in the pages of a periodical better known to theologians than to Orientalists, and the world agreed to call the writing by the name of Hamathite. It specially attracted the notice of Dr. Hayes Ward of New York, who discovered that the inscriptions were written in *boustrophedon* fashion, that is to say,

that the lines turned alternately from right to left and from left
to right, like oxen when plowing a field, the first line beginning on
the right and the line following on the left. The lines read, in fact,
from the direction towards which the characters look.

Dr. Hayes Ward also made another discovery. In the ruins of
the great palace of Nineveh Sir A. H. Layard had discovered numerous clay impressions of seals once attached to documents of
papyrus or parchment. The papyrus and parchment have long since
perished, but the seals remain, with the holes through which the
strings passed that attached them to the original deeds. Some of
the seals are Assyrian, some Phoenician, others again are Egyptian,
but there are a few which have upon them strange characters such
as had never been met with before. It was these characters which
Dr. Hayes Ward perceived to be the same as those found upon the
stones of Hama, and it was accordingly supposed that the seals
were of Hamathite origin.

In 1876, two years after the publication of Dr. Wright's article,
of which I had never heard at the time, I read a Paper on the
Hamathite inscriptions before the Society of Biblical Archaeology.
In this I put forward a number of conjectures, one of them being
that the Hamathite hieroglyphs were the source of the curious
syllabary used for several centuries in the island of Cyprus, and
another that the hieroglyphs were not an invention of the early
inhabitants of Hamath, but represented the system of writing employed by the Hittites. We know from the Egyptian records that
the Hittites could write, and that a class of scribes existed among
them, and, since Hamath lay close to the borders of the Hittite
kingdoms, it seemed reasonable to suppose that the unknown form
of script discovered on its site was Hittite rather than Hamathite.
The conjecture was confirmed almost immediately afterwards by
the discovery of the site of Carchemish, the great Hittite capital,
and of inscriptions there in the same system of writing as that
found on the stones of Hama.

It was not long, therefore, before the learned world began to
recognize that the newly discovered script was the peculiar possession of the Hittite race. Dr. Hayes Ward was one of the first to
do so, and the Trustees of the British Museum determined to institute excavations among the ruins of Carchemish. Meanwhile notice
was drawn to a fact which showed that the Hittite characters, as
we shall now call them, were employed, not only at Hamath and
Carchemish, but in Asia Minor as well.

More than a century ago a German traveller had observed two
figures carved on a wall of rock near Ibreez, or Ivris, in the territory
of the ancient Lykaonia. One of them was a god, who carried in
his hand a stalk of corn and a bunch of grapes, the other was a

man, who stood before the god in an attitude of adoration. Both figures were shod with boots with upturned ends, and the deity wore a tunic that reached to his knees, while on his head was a peaked cap ornamented with hornlike ribbons. A century elapsed before the sculpture was again visited by a European traveller, and it was again a German who found his way to the spot. On this occasion a drawing was made of the figures, which was published by Ritter in his great work on the geography of the world. But the drawing was poor and imperfect, and the first attempt to do adequate justice to the original was made by the Rev. E. J. Davis in 1875. He published his copy, and an account of the monument, in the *Transactions of the Society of Biblical Archaeology* the following year. He had noticed that the figures were accompanied by what were known at the time as Hamathite characters. Three lines of these were inserted between the face of the god and his uplifted left arm, four lines more were engraved behind his worshipper, while below, on a level with an aqueduct which fed a mill, were yet other lines of half-obliterated hieroglyphs. It was plain that in Lykaonia also, where the old language of the country still lingered in the days of St. Paul, the Hittite system of writing had once been used.

Another stone inscribed with Hittite characters had come to light at Aleppo. Like those of Hamath, it was of black basalt, and had been built into a modern wall. The characters upon it were worn by frequent attrition, the people of Aleppo believing that whoever rubbed his eyes upon it would be immediately cured of ophthalmia. More than one copy of the inscription was taken, but the difficulty of distinguishing the half-obliterated characters rendered the copies of little service, and a cast of the stone was about to be made when news arrived that the fanatics of Aleppo had destroyed it. Rather than allow its virtue to go out of it—to be stolen, as they fancied, by the Europeans—they preferred to break it in pieces. It is one of the many monuments that have perished at the very moment when their importance first became known.

This, then, was the state of our knowledge in the summer of 1879. We knew that the Hittites, with whom Hebrews and Egyptians and Assyrians had once been in contact, possessed a hieroglyphic system of writing, and that this system of writing was found on monuments in Hamath, Aleppo, Carchemish, and Lykaonia. We knew, too, that in Lykaonia it accompanied figures carved out of the rock in a peculiar style of art, and represented as wearing a peculiar kind of dress.

Suddenly the truth flashed upon me. This peculiar style of art, this peculiar kind of dress, was the same as that which distinguished the sculptures of Karabel, of Ghiaur-kalessi, and of

Cappadocia. In all alike we had the same characteristic features, the same head-dresses and shoes, the same tunics, the same clumsy massiveness of design and characteristic attitude. The figures carved upon the rocks of Karabel and Cappadocia must be memorials of Hittite art. The clue to their origin and history was at last discovered; the birthplace of the strange art which had produced them was made manifest. A little further research made the fact doubly sure. The photographs Professor Perrot had taken of the monuments of Boghazköy in Cappadocia included one of an inscription in ten or eleven lines. The characters of this inscription were worn and almost illegible, but not only were they in relief, like the characters of all other Hittite inscriptions known at the time, among them two or three hieroglyphs stood out clearly, which were identical with those on the stones of Hamath and Carchemish. All that was needed to complete the verification of my discovery was to visit the Pass of Karabel, and see whether the hieroglyphs Texier and others had found there likewise belonged to the Hittite script.

More than three hours did I spend in the niche wherein the figure is carved which Herodotus believed was a likeness of the Egyptian Sesostris. It was necessary to take "squeezes" as well as copies, if I would recover the characters of the inscription and ascertain their exact forms. My joy was great at finding that they were Hittite, and that the conclusion I had arrived at in my study at home was confirmed by the monument itself. The Sesostris of Herodotus turned out to be, not the great Pharaoh who contended with the Hittites of Kadesh, but a symbol of the far-reaching power and influence of his mighty opponents. Hittite art and Hittite writing, if not the Hittite name, were proved to have been known from the banks of the Euphrates to the shores of the Aegean Sea.

C. W. CERAM

Winckler and the
Hittite Hieroglyphs

HUGO WINCKLER first went to Boghazköy, site of the great Hittite capital of Hattusas in 1906 (p. 64, I). The Kültepe to which he refers was the site of Kanesh, a Cappadocian city. Early Assyrian traders had settled there, and vast numbers of tablets recording their commercial dealings with the Hittites, written in cuneiform in the Akkadian language, have been found on the site. Arzawa was a state in south-west Asia Minor which the Hittites repeatedly fought against, but never lastingly subjected. Excavations at Beycesultan on the Maeander have discovered what was probably the capital city.

❧

THE PROBLEMS summed up by the very word "Hittites" were coming to a head. Now it is easy to apply hindsight and pick out the one coherent theme concealed amid the confusion of interpretations and misinterpretations advanced by the early investigators. But it was far from easy then. Let us see what the archaeologist destined to make the next important discoveries had to say. In December 1907 Hugo Winckler wrote in the *Communications of the German Orient Society*:

"Along with the monuments of pure Asia Minor or Hittite civilization, occasional evidence had been turned up showing strong Babylonian influence upon these countries also. As chance would have it, at about the same time that the Tell el Amarna documents

From *The Secret of the Hittites*. New York: Alfred A. Knopf; 1956, pp. 46-59. Reprinted by permission of Alfred A. Knopf, Inc., © 1955 by Alfred A. Knopf, Inc.; and by permission of Victor Gollancz Ltd., who published it in London as *Narrow Pass, Black Mountain*.

were discovered, clay tablets in cuneiform script came to light in
Asia Minor. The site at which they were found proved to be a
mound of ruins called Kültepe, near the village of Kara Hüyük
about three hours' journey to the east of Kayseri. Difficult to interpret and yielding little information, these tablets nevertheless
proved the influence of the cuneiform script countries in Asia
Minor, and so they added welcome evidence to the few letters
from Asia Minor to the Egyptian Pharaoh which had been found
at Tell el Amarna. Of these there were only a few items, meagre in
content, from Suppiluliumas, King of the Hatti, and two others
which offered more enigmas than enlightenment. These were:
(1) A letter to King Tarchundaraus of Arzawa from Amenophis
III. That the land of Arzawa must have been situated somewhere
in Asia Minor could be deduced; the precise location could not be
determined. (2) A letter naming a certain Prince Lapawa who is
elsewhere mentioned as a northern neighbour of the Kingdom of
Jerusalem and whose seat must therefore have been somewhere in
the vicinity of Carmel. How these isolated facts could be put
together was a total puzzle. Nor could it be explained how a language which appeared to be that of the country of Arzawa came to
be used in Palestine, in the area later occupied by Israel (Samaria).

One possible solution had not as yet occurred to Winckler or the
other archaeologists of his day. Could the Arzawa letters have been
written in the *Hittite* language?

Would that question be answered by the excavators' spades?

But first let us briefly sum up once more what the young science
of Hittitology had accomplished up to the point where Winckler
entered the picture. What, in other words, was the status of Hittite
research at the beginning of the twentieth century?

First: Several travellers, Texier in particular, had reported monuments, reliefs, and inscriptions of a completely unfamiliar type in
Central Anatolia and Northern Syria.

Second: A. H. Sayce had recognized that these monuments, scattered all the way from Smyrna to Northern Syria, must be relics of
a single folk which he correctly identified with the Hittites mentioned in the Bible.

Third: From Egyptian and Assyrian sources, from certain clay
tablets found in the area between Boghazköy and Kayseri, and
above all from the Egyptian-Hittite correspondence in the Amarna
archives, it had been amply demonstrated that Sayce's and Wright's
hypothesis was right: the Hittites had indeed been a Great Power.
Moreover, the names of a few Hittite kings were now known.

Fourth: Scholars had determined that three principal languages
and scripts had been in use among the Hittites: the Akkadian
language in cuneiform script (readable and intelligible); the Hittite

language in cuneiform script (readable but not intelligible); and hieroglyphic Hittite, as found on the Hamath Stones (neither readable nor intelligible). In the next chapter we will deal with these perplexing matters.

Fifth: On the basis of the Arzawa letters, a single scholar, the Norwegian Knudtzon, had come to the conclusion that cuneiform Hittite was an Indo-European language. He had, however, retracted this assertion.

Sixth: Sayce and several others had deciphered the first few symbols of hieroglyphic Hittite, in particular the ideograms for "city," "country," and "king"; but they could not prove that their readings were correct and were nowhere near being able to read the language.

Seventh: On the basis of all other documens which at that time could be read, it had been assumed that the centre of Hittite power had lain in Central or Northern Anatolia, not, as the Biblical texts suggested, in Northern Syria. The finds at Zinjirli, where the first sizable excavations in a Hittite cultural area were undertaken, had been recognized as Late Hittite, thus neither proving nor disproving this important theory. Still, the reliefs and the outlines of the city uncovered there permitted some conclusions about the religion, architecture, and general cultural influences in the life of the Late Hittites.

Such was the body of knowledge at Winckler's disposal when he started out on his expedition. Actually, what was known consisted largely of questions. But in science it is the framing of the right questions that leads to new discoveries.

Winckler's first expedition was rather amateurish even though there were great models which could have provided him with guidance. A few years before, Arthur Evans had begun his excavations at the palace of Knossos on the island of Crete. Robert Koldewey had only recently started digging at Babylon. Both these expeditions were splendidly conducted.

It may be that the cloud which overhung the expedition from the start had something to do with Winckler's personality. Born in Graefenhainichen, a small town in Saxony, in 1863, Winckler became a prominent Assyriologist. He had already done some excavating at Sidon in 1903-4 before he went to Anatolia. Nevertheless, he affected everyone as he did Ludwig Curtius, who became his assistant the following year. Curtius, who had distinguished himself as an archaeological annalist, wrote: "I had looked forward with great eagerness to working with an Orientalist whom I could not help imagining as a much-travelled man-of-the-world. I was consequently not a little surprised, upon meeting Winckler in Constantinople, to find an unimpressive looking fellow with a brown, unkempt beard, wearing a sports shirt with red silk trim, and conducting himself in a petty-bourgeois manner little suited to the real Orient. There was nothing at all of the man-of-the-world about him."

Moreover, Winckler was one of those unfortunates who always make enemies and seldom find friends, and he was "full of resentment against everyone who was more successful than himself." In addition he was utterly intolerant of scientific opponents. He was fanatically convinced that everything worthwhile in the world had originated in Babylon; any other view he took as a personal affront and forthwith despised any humanist who dared to speak up for the umbilical tie between Western and Greek culture.

To top it all off, he was an anti-Semite—very odd indeed for a passionate Orientalist. It may be that the protracted, ultimately fatal, illness that struck him in 1913 was to blame for his irascibility and for his numerous inconsistencies. In spite of his anti-Semitism he was content to have his first archaeological explorations subsidized by Jewish financiers. And far from transposing his profound dislike for Jews into racial theories, Winckler was the man who wrote a sentence that the jack-booted anti-Semites and race theorists ought to have learned by heart: "Civilized peoples are never racially pure; rather they are always the product of a large number of strata formed by more or less different races."

Funds for the exploratory probe were provided by Baron Wilhelm von Landau, a disciple of Winckler's, who had already financed the Sidon expedition. Companion, collaborator, government official, and executive head of the expedition all rolled into one was Theodore Macridy-Bey, who had worked with Winckler at Sidon. A functionary of the Ottoman Museum in Constantinople, Macridy-Bey was the Oriental counterpart to Winckler. Curtius, who in all the five hundred-odd pages of his memoirs has hardly an unkind word to say for any person he describes, speaks of Macridy-Bey as a man "with impenetrable black eyes in a smooth-shaven face yellowed by malaria . . . Macridy-Bey," he continues, "was the most curious mixture of half-taught dilettante and passionate enthusiast; of secret dickerer and loyal official faithfully obeying the orders of his superior, Halil Bey. . . . He would without warning drop all interest in archaeology and devote himself solely to his own pleasure. He might be full of noblesse and charm today, might be a cynical intriguer tomorrow . . . Sometimes he seemed to me like Iago in *Othello!*"

Although Winckler and his associates were by no means inexperienced, they set out on their first exploration like the rankest amateurs. They travelled by railroad as far as Angora; there they expected to stock up in short order on the things they most urgently needed. Aside from the fact that in the Orient you cannot buy anything at all if you attempt to do it in a hurry, Angora at that time was an insignificant group of mud huts surrounding the old castle hill. (Today, under the new name of Ankara it is the capital of Turkey, has 287,000 inhabitants, broad boulevards, modern bank buildings, and a man-made lake—all the creation of the dictator Kemal Atatürk.) The party took three days to make its purchases. Winckler, who could ill adapt to new situations, was driven to the point of madness by all the haggling. They could not even find good horses; nothing but worn-out mares were available. "For saddles we had those painful Oriental devices which in Europe would undoubtedly find a place of honour in the torture chambers."

They set off at last on October 14, very late in the year for Turkey. Winckler, the Orientalist, felt the Orient as a hostile place. By day he suffered from the heat, by night from the cold. He was upset by the most trivial incidents and argued about everything and nothing.

The ride lasted five days. Nights the company camped around a fire or put up at a *musafir-oda*, the shelter which even tiny villages provide for wayfarers (the custom is for each villager in turn to provide hospitality for a day). Winckler preferred these to the *khans*, the old caravanseries where he found too many *tacht-biti*—vermin. On the other hand, in the *musafir-odas* he often had to share his bed with cattle. "However," he remarked, "these beasts are decidedly good-tempered and far less repugnant to human nature than the rest of the inhabitants, whose importunate servility toward outsiders is equalled only by the Christian Syrians."

Conditions were different in Boghazköy, however. Outwardly nothing had changed here since Texier's visit seventy-one years before. But in the past two decades a good many outlandish foreigners had come by and almost immediately upon their arrival had asked with unseemly haste whether any old walls were to be seen. And all these foreigners had found the same cordial host, the landowner Zia Bey. Endless tracts of land belonged to him, but he was not allowed to cross the borders of his province—for he was a member of the ancient Seljuk nobility still feared by Sultan Abdul-Hamid, a hypochondriac perpetually terrified of plots. Zia Bey had become a mixture of farmer and aristocrat; he rode the noblest horses, always accompanied by his magnificently uniformed body-servant Ismail, but he himself preferred to dress in the collarless peasant blouse, with slippers on his feet instead of riding boots. It was he who had sent a clay tablet, brought him by one of his peasants, to Constantinople where Macridy-Bey had seen it and called Winckler's attention to it.

Zia Bey, then, gave them a warm welcome. As prominent strangers they were entitled to silk mattresses. As Winckler tells the story,

Macridy was the first to jump up and begin scratching himself. Winckler demanded a new bed. The servants were delighted; what an inexhaustible topic of conversation this would be; men who made a fuss about a few little bugs. With much to-do they brought new beds—which were no less alive.

On October 19 the work began. Winckler and Macridy examined the ruins and retraced the footsteps of Texier and all the other travellers after him. They themselves, however, were looking for something particular now; where was the spot where the tablets with the curious symbols had been found? When the natives of Boghazköy finally grasped what the strangers were after, they amiably brought fragments of tablets—as far as they were concerned there was nothing precious about these things. When they herded their sheep along the great old walls and one of the animals started off in the wrong direction, they thought nothing of throwing such fragments of clay at it—there were plenty of the broken tablets lying around. Winckler and Macridy were up and about from dawn till dusk; they narrowed a circle around the main source of the tablets and then discovered that at the spot where, according to the natives, especially large pieces of inscribed tablets were to be found, an excavator had already been at work. "This discovery, however, did not at all arouse any resentment in us," Winckler noted—most unusually for him. The reason was that the digging revealed itself as planless and casual in the extreme. Winckler was gratified to see that his predecessor had lost courage and given up far too soon. He already sensed that he was about to make a big find. For although after three days of incessant activity they had to stop their preliminary exploration—the rainy season had caught them by surprise and turned the plain into a sea of mud—they already had with them, carefully wrapped up, no less than thirty-four fragments of Hittite clay tablets. Since in the normal experience of excavators a *single* tablet may well constitute an important find, this was a tremendous, a sensational result of their efforts. But Winckler correctly guessed that still more and different treasures could be extracted from this soil. Describing the road back and the inn in Nefesköy, he, who usually grumbled and paid not the slightest attention to the wild beauty of the Anatolian landscape, records that he could not sleep and went to the door late at night to consider the future—and to look at the stars.

In less than a year Winckler had made a find such as no one had dared to hope for.

The expedition of 1906 was financed by the German Near Eastern Society and the Berlin Orient Committee, several private patrons providing funds for these groups. On July 17, 1906, Winckler and Macridy returned to Zia Bey's *konak,* as the "palace" was called. By now they were old friends. "We had kept up the best of relations with the Bey. He had made many requests—from a bottle of good cognac to helping him out of a 'temporary embarrassment.' By way of return he had repaid us after his fashion. A strike had been settled without any further fuss by an order from him. Little friendly services are worth their while in the Orient!"

At the fortress mound (*buyukkale*) they set up their headquarters tent. Winckler, feeble and ill, suffered from the heat and the bad food prepared by the Bulgarian cook whom they had hired because he spoke a little German. The archaeologist huddled in a rude wattle hut, hat on his head, swathed in shawls, gloves on both hands. Often moaning with pain, he made copies of the clay tablets that were brought to him in a steady stream.

That Winckler, the excavator at the site, was able to draw immediate conclusions from his work was altogether unusual. It seldom happens that archaeologists are also philologists, capable of using linguistic knowledge to exploit the results of their excavations. Moreover, here at Boghazköy the political correspondence of a nation virtually unknown until recently was readable the moment it was uncovered. The reason was that the Hittites of Boghazköy had composed their important documents and letters in Akkadian which was, as we have mentioned earlier, at one time the language of international communications in the Orient. Philologists had no trouble understanding Akkadian, especially when it was written, as it was here, in a script that had also long since been deciphered: Babylonian-Assyrian cuneiform writing.

It was a tablet of this sort that Winckler, sitting in his wattle hut, received into his gloved hands one day. As he deciphered it, this sick, embittered man became wild with excitement.

He recalled the Egyptian hieroglyphic inscriptions that had given archaeologists their first hints of the existence of a nation known as the "Hatti" (or "Chatti"). Among these was an inscription on a temple wall at Karnak mentioning a treaty between Ramses the Great and Hattusilis III, King of the Hatti. (Those idiotic Egyptologists read the name as Chatasar, but he, Winckler, already knew it should be Chattusil, the "ch" representing the rough German aspirate!) Of course treaties in the ancient world were usually drawn up in several texts, just as they are today, and almost always in the languages of all the countries concerned. But was it not wildly fantastic for him to hope that after more than 3,100 years a full report on this treaty could be found, not chiselled into stone as it was in Egypt, but inscribed on a fragile clay tablet in the land of the other partner to the treaty, more than 1,200 miles from the temple wall at Karnak? Winckler had had such a dream and had put it out of his mind. Such a find would border on the miraculous;

it would be comparable to such archaeological wonders as Schliemann's discovery of Troy on the basis of the Homeric descriptions,
or Layard's finding Nimrûd. Comparable most of all, in fact, to
George Smith's amazing triumph—in the eighteen-seventies Smith
had travelled from London to Nineveh to find a few clay tablets
that were needed to complete the Gilgamesh epic, and had found
them!

And now a similar miracle had taken place. Winckler, the dry
scientist and chronic invalid, kept shaking his head in awe as he
wrote with feverish enthusiasm:

"On August 20, after some twenty days of digging, the breach
into the gravel of the hillside had advanced as far as a first sectional
wall. Below this wall a beautifully preserved tablet was found,
which even in outward appearance looked promising. I glanced at
it—and all my previous experiences vanished into nothingness.
Here it was, the very thing I might perhaps jestingly have longed
for as a pious wish: a letter from Ramses to Chattusil on their mutual treaty. True, in the past several days more and more small
fragments had been found in which there was mention of the
treaty between the two states, but here it was now confirmed; the
famous treaty, known from the hieroglyphic inscription on the
temple wall at Karnak, was now to have fresh light cast upon it by
the other treaty-making side. Ramses, with his titles and descent
given exactly as in the text of the treaty, was writing to Chattusil,
who was also quoted, and the content of the letter was in places
verbally identical with paragraphs of the treaty."

Then he went on to speak of his emotions:

"With what strange feelings I of all persons regarded this docu-
ment. Eighteen years had passed since I encountered the Arzawa
letter of el Amarna in what was then the museum of Bulaq, and
since in Berlin I learned the Mitanni language. At that time, in the
course of following up the facts disclosed by the find at el Amarna,
I had expressed the supposition that the Ramses treaty might
originally have been composed in cuneiform script—and now I
was holding in my hands one of the letters exchanged in the course
of discussion of the treaty—in the finest cuneiform script and in
good Babylonian!"

It was time to be thinking of a more thorough and carefully prepared expedition for the following year, 1907. For already Winckler
had become convinced that the object of his excavations was not
just any Hittite city, but that he was actually standing on soil covering the *capital* of the Hittite Empire. There were, after all, so
many important government documents lying around here. Would
not the state archives normally be located at the king's residence?
And was not the king's residence as a rule identical with the capital

of the country? But if that were so, what was the name of this city? In the Ancient East the name of the country and the name of the capital were frequently one and the same. Winckler therefore deduced that the "Land of Chatti" must have had as its capital the "City of Chatti." And as it turned out, his guess was right. Today we write the name of this city "Hattusas," but the principle stands; the name is only a more modern reading based upon greater philological knowledge.

It was really an incredible piece of good fortune. With his first efforts Winckler had laid bare the heart and brain of the Hittite Empire, the city which had briefly enjoyed the glory of being ranked equal to Babylon and Thebes. Recognizing the magnitude of his find, Winckler wrote in 1907: "These newly-revealed archives will keep more than one man busy far into the future." He himself went on working, and his second year proved more successful than the first—although some of the incidental circumstances were distinctly unpleasant. But Winckler was quite right—today, nearly fifty years later, profitable excavation is still going on at Boghazköy.

2. Greece and Crete

HESIOD

The Bronze Age of Hesiod

THE Greek poet Hesiod wrote his *Works and Days* in the eighth century B.C. In it he divides human history into five Ages. His pre-archaeological idea of a Bronze Age preceding an Iron Age probably owes something to genuine folk memory.

THEN Zeus the Father again made humankind,
A breed of bronze, far differently designed,
A breed from the Ash-tree sprung, huge-limbed and dread,
Lovers of battle and horror, no eaters of bread
Their hearts were hard, their adamant hearts: none stood
To meet their power of limbs and their hardihood
And the swing of the terrible arms their shoulders bore.
Bronze were their arms, bronze the armour they wore,
And their tools; for no dark iron supplied their needs . . .

From *Works and Days*. 8th century B.C.

W. E. GLADSTONE

A Prime Minister
as Archaeologist

WILLIAM EWART GLADSTONE, the great English Liberal Prime Minister, wrote his very substantial preface to Schliemann's *Mycenae* in 1877. This year falls within his period of semi-retirement, between his first and second ministries. His elaborate reconstruction of the order of events in the burial of Agamemnon and his companions in the Shaft Graves can be no more than a curiosity in the light of our knowledge that the bodies were those of Bronze Age rulers and their consorts and companions of about 1550 B.C.

❦

IT has been with much reluctance that, at the persevering request of Dr. Schliemann, I have undertaken to write a Preface to his Mycenaean volume. I have managed perhaps, though with long intermissions of the pleasant labour, to maintain a tolerable acquaintance with the text of Homer; and the due establishment of the points of contact between that text and the remains from Mycenae is without question one of the essential aims, to which comment on this work requires to be addressed. But I have a horror of all specialism which travels beyond its proper province; and in this matter I am at best no more than a specialist, probably, too, not one of very high pretensions. I have not that practised skill, that comprehensive outlook over the whole field of Hellenic, and other than Hellenic archaeology, which has conferred upon Mr. Newton his well-earned fame. The just conclusion from these premises appears to be, that I ought to have declined a charge *quod ferre recusent humeri.* But there was, in ancient poetry, a Destiny stronger than

From the Introduction to *Mycenae*. London: John Murray; 1878, pp. v-vii, xxiii-xl.

the will of gods. To me, on this occasion, Dr. Schliemann is the vice-gerent and organ of that Destiny. In view of the splendid services which he has conferred upon classical science, a power that thrusts argument out of court brings me to perceive that I cannot but accede to his desire. I have however given the reader fair warning where and why he should be on his guard; and I shall make all the use I can of the landmarks laid down in the report which Mr. Newton, after an ocular inspection of these remains, published in the *Times* of April 20, 1877; and of the valuable papers of Mr. Gardner in the *Academy* (April 21 and 28). I believe that the interest, excited by Dr. Schliemann's discoveries, has been by no means confined to classical scholars. I shall therefore endeavour to be as little technical as possible, and to write, so far as may be, for a circle wider than that of the persons among us who are acquainted with the Greek tongue.

When the disclosures at Tiryns and Mycenae were announced in England, my own first impression was that of a strangely bewildered admiration, combined with a preponderance of sceptical against believing tendencies, in regard to the capital and dominating subject of the Tombs in the Agora. I am bound to say, that reflection and a fuller knowledge have nearly turned the scales the other way. There are indeed, not only gaps to be supplied, but difficulties to be confronted, and to be explained; or to be left over for future explanation. Yet the balance, I will not say of evidence, but of rational presumption, seems as though it might ultimately lean towards the belief that this eminent explorer has exposed to the light of day, after 3,000 years, the memorials and remains of Agamemnon and his companions in the Return from Troy. But let us endeavour to feel our way by degrees up to this question, gradually and with care, as a good general makes his approaches to a formidable fortress.

[*MR. GLADSTONE* next seeks to establish parallels between descriptions in the Homeric texts and the art, architecture, ornaments, pottery, bronzes and other objects from Mycenae and Hissarlik (Troy)].

By the foregoing detail I have sought to show, that there is no preliminary bar to our entertaining the capital question whether the tombs now unearthed, and the remains exposed to view, under masks for the faces, and plates of gold covering one or more of the trunks, are the tombs and remains of the great Agamemnon and his compeers, who have enjoyed, through the agency of Homer, such a protracted longevity of renown. For the general character of the Mycenaean treasures, I take my stand provisionally on the declaration of Mr. Newton (supported by Mr. Gardner), that, in his judgment, they belong to the prehistoric or heroic age, the age antecedent to his Greco-Phoenician period; and in important out-lines of detail I have endeavoured to show that they have many points of contact with the Homeric poems, and with the discoveries at Hissarlik. But this preface makes no pretension whatever to exhibit a complete catalogue of the objects, or to supply for each of them its interpretation. We encounter, indeed, a certain number of puzzling phenomena, such as the appearance of something like visors, for which I could desire some other explanation, but which Schliemann cites as auxiliaries to the masks of the tombs, and even thinks to prove that such articles were used by the living, as well as for the dead.

Undoubtedly, in my view, these masks offer to us a great enigma, when we come to handle the question who were the occupants of the now opened sepulchres? It may be, that as Mr. Newton says, we must in the main rest content with the "reasonable presumption" that the four tombs contained royal personages, and must leave in abeyance the further question, whether they are the tombs indicated to Pausanias by the local tradition; at any rate, until the ruins of Mycenae shall have been further explored, according to the inten-tion which the Government of Greece is said to have conceived.

At the same time this is a case where the question before us, if hazardous to prosecute, is not easy to let alone.

It is obviously difficult to find any simple, clear, consistent inter-pretation of the extraordinary inhumation disclosed to us by these researches. Such an interpretation may be found hereafter: it does not seem to be forthcoming at the present moment. But the way towards it can only be opened up by a painstaking exhibition of the facts, and by instituting a cautious comparison between them and any indications, drawn from other times or places, which may ap-pear to throw light upon them. For my own part, having approached the question with no predisposition to believe, I need not scruple to say I am brought or driven by the evidence to certain conclusions; and also led on to certain conjectures suggested by those con-clusions. The first conclusion is that we cannot refer the five entomb-ments in the Agora at Mycenae to any period within the historic age. The second is that they are entombments of great, and almost certainly in part of royal, personages. The third, that they bear in-disputable marks of having been effected, not normally throughout, but in connection with circumstances, which impressed upon them an irregular and unusual character. The conjecture is, that these may very well be the tombs of Agamemnon and his company. It is supported in part by a number of presumptions, but in great part also by the difficulty, not to say the impossibility, of offering any other suggestion which could be deemed so much as colourable.

The principal facts which we have to notice appear to be as follows: —

1. The situation chosen for the interments.
2. The numbers of persons simultaneously interred.
3. The dimensions and character of the graves.
4. The partial application of fire to the remains.
5. The use of masks, and likewise of metallic plates, to adorn or shelter them, or both.
6. The copious deposit both of characteristic and of valuable objects in conjunction with the bodies.

1. Upon the situation chosen for the interments, Dr. Schliemann opines that they were not originally within the Agora, but that it was subsequently constructed around the tombs. His reasons are that the supporting wall, on which rest, in double line, the upright slabs, formerly, and in six cases still, covered by horizontal slabs as seats for the elders, is careless in execution, and inferior to the circuit wall of the Acropolis. But, if it was built as a mere stay, was there any reason for spending labour to raise it to the point of strength necessary for a work of military defence? Further, he finds between the lines of slabs, where they are uncovered, broken pottery of the prehistoric period, more recent than that of the tombs. But such pottery would never have been placed there at the time of the construction; with other rubbish, it would only have weakened and not strengthened the fabric of the inclosure. Nor can we readily see how it could have come there, until the work was dilapidated by the disappearance of the upper slabs. If so, it would of course be later in date than the slabs were.

It appears to me that the argument of improbability tells powerfully against the supposition that the Agora was constructed round the tombs, having previously been elsewhere. The space within the Acropolis appears to be very limited: close round the inclosures are "Cyclopean" houses and cisterns. When works of this kind are once constructed, their removal would be a work of great difficulty: and this is a case, where the earliest builders were followed by men who aimed not at greater, but at less, solidity. Besides which, the Agora was connected with the religion of the place, and was, as will be shown, in the immediate neighbourhood of the palace. In addition to these material attractions, every kind of moral association would grow up around it.

It can be clearly shown that the ancient Agora was bound down to its site by manifold ties, other than those of mere solidity in its construction. It stands in Mycenae, says our author, on the most imposing and most beautiful spot of the city, from whence the whole was overlooked. It was on these high places that the men of the prehistoric ages erected the simple structures, in many cases perhaps uncovered, that, with the altars, served for the worship of the gods. In Scherie, it was built round the temple, so to call it, of Poseidon (*Odyssey* vi. 266). In the Greek camp before Troy the Agora was in the centre of the line of ships (*Iliad* xi. 5-9, 806-8). There justice was administered, and there "had been constructed the altars of the gods." Further, it is clear, from a number of passages in Homer, that the place of Assembly was always close to the royal palace. In the case of Troy we are told expressly that it was held by the doors of Priam (*Il.* ii. 788, vii. 345, 6). In Scherie, the palace of Alkinoös was close to the grove of Athene (*Od.* vi. 291-3); and we can hardly doubt that this grove was in the immediate vicinity of the Posideïon, which was itself within the Agora. In Ithaca (*Od.* xxiv. 415 *seqq.*), the people gathered before the Palace of Odysseus, and then went in a mass into the Agora. While it was thus materially associated with those points of the city which most possessed the character of fixtures, it is not too much to say, considering the politics of early Greece, that it must, in the natural course, have become a centre around which would cling the fondest moral and historical associations of the people. Into the minor question, whether the encircling slabs are the remains of an original portion of the work or not, I do not think it needful for me to enter.

But, while I believe that the Agora is where it was, the honour paid to the dead by the presence of their tombs within it is not affected by either alternative; but only the time of paying it. If this be the old Agora, they were honoured by being laid in it; if it is of later date, they were honoured by its being removed in order to be built around them; if at least this was done knowingly, and how could it be otherwise, when we observe that the five tombs occupy more than a moiety of the whole available space? We know, from the evidence of the historic period, that to be buried in the Agora was a note of public honour; we cannot reasonably doubt, with the five graves before us, that it was such likewise in the prehistoric age.

It was a note of public honour, then, if these bodies were originally buried in the Agora. If we adopt the less probable supposition that the Agora was afterwards constructed around them by reason of their being there, the honour may seem even greater still.

2. Next, the number of persons simultaneously interred, when taken in conjunction with the other features of the transaction, offers a new problem for consideration. An argument to show that the burials were simultaneous, seems quite conclusive. They embraced sixteen or seventeen persons. Among the bodies one appears to be marked out by probable evidence as that of the leading personage. Lying in the tomb, it has two companions. Now Aga-

memnon had two marshals or heralds (*Il.* I. 320), whose office
partook of a sacred character. There might, therefore, be nothing
strange in their being laid, if so it were, by their lord. The most
marked of the bodies lay to the north of the two others, all three
having the feet to the westward. It was distinguished by better
preservation, which may, at least not improbably, have been due
to some preservative process at the time of interment. It carried,
besides a golden mask, a large golden breastplate (15⅗ by 9½ in.),
and other leaves of gold at various points; also a golden belt across
the loins, 4 ft. long and 1¾ in. broad. By the side of the figure
lay two swords, stated by Dr. Schliemann to be of bronze; the
ornamentation of one of them particularly in striking accordance
with the description in the *Iliad* of the sword of Agamemnon (*Il.*
XI. 29-31). Within a foot of the body, to the right, lay eleven other
swords, but this is not a distinctive mark, as the body on the south
side has fifteen, ten lying at the feet, and a great heap of swords
were found at the west end, between this and the middle body.

The entire number of bodies in the five tombs, which is stated
at sixteen or seventeen, seems to have included three women and
two or three children. The local tradition recorded by Pausanias
takes notice of a company of men with Agamemnon, and of Cassandra, with two children whom she was reported to have borne.
This is only significant as testifying to the ancient belief that children were buried in the tombs: for Cassandra could only be taken
captive at the time when the city of Troy was sacked, and the
assassination immediately followed the arrival in Greece. But it is
likely enough that these children may have been the offspring of
another concubine, who may have taken the place Briseis was
meant to fill. This is of course mere speculation; but the meaning
is that there is nothing in these indications to impair the force of
any presumptions, which the discoveries may in other respects
legitimately raise.

3. Like the site in the Agora, so the character of the tombstones,
which is in strict correspondence with the style of many of the
ornaments, and the depth of the tombs, appear with one voice to
signify honour to the dead. As I understand the plans, they show a
maximum depth of 25 to 33 feet below the surface, hollowed for
the most part out of the solid rock. But then we are met with the
somewhat staggering fact that the bodies of full-grown, and apparently tall, men have been forced into a space of only five feet
six inches in length, so as to require that sort of compression which
amounts almost to mutilation.

We seem thus to stand in the face of circumstances, that contradict one another. The place, the depth, the coverings of the
tombs, appear to lead us in one direction; the forcing and squeez-

ing of the bodies in another. But further, and stranger still, there seems to have been no necessity for placing the bodies under this unbecoming, nay revolting, pressure. The original dimensions of the tomb were 21 ft. 6 in. by 11 ft. 6 in. These are reduced all round, first by an inner wall two feet thick, and secondly by a slanting projection one foot thick (at the bottom) to 5 ft. 6 in. and 15 ft. 6 in. Why, then, were the bodies not laid along, instead of across, it? Was not the act needless as well as barbarous? And to what motive is a piece of needless barbarism, apparently so un-equivocal, to be referred? I hardly dare to mention, much less, so scanty is the evidence, to dwell upon, the fact that their bodies lie towards the west, and that the Egyptian receptacle for the dead lay in that quarter. The conflict of appearances, at which we have now arrived, appears to point to a double motive in the original entombment; or to an incomplete and incoherent proceeding, which some attempt was subsequently made to correct; or to both. But let us pay a brief attention to the remaining particulars of the disclosures.

4. We have next to observe (a) that fire was applied to these remains; (b) that the application of it was only partial; (c) that the metallic deposits are said to show marks of the action of it; so do the pebbles. We see, therefore, that the deposition of the precious objects took place either at the same moment with the fire, or, and more probably I suppose, before it had entirely burned out.

The partial nature of the burning requires a more detailed con-sideration. In the Homeric burials, burning is universal. It must be regarded, according to the Poems, as the established Achaian custom of the day, wherever inhumation was normally conducted. And for burial there was a distinct reason, namely, that without it the Shade of the departed was not allowed to join the company of the other Shades, so that the unburied Elpenor is the first to meet Odysseus (Od. XI. 51) on his entrance into the Underworld; and the shade of Patroclos entreats Achilles to bury him as rapidly as may be, that he may pass the gates of Aïdes (Il. XXIII. 71). I think the proof of the universal use of fire in regular burials at this period is conclusive. Not only do we find it in the great burials of the Seventh Book (429-32), and in the funerals of Patroclos (XXIII. 177) and Hector (XXIV. 785-800), but we have it in the case of Elpenor (Od. XII. 11-13), whom at first his companions had left uninterred, and for whom therefore we must suppose they only did what was needful under established custom. Perhaps a yet clearer proof is to be found in a simile. Achilles, we are told, wept while the funeral pile he had erected was burning, all night long, the bones of Patroclos, "as a father weeps when he burns the bones of his youthful son" (*Od.* XXIII. 222-5). This testifies to a general practice.

In the case of notable persons, the combustion was not complete. For not the ashes only, but the bones, were carefully gathered. In the case of Patroclos, they are wrapped in fat, and put in an open cup or bowl (*phiale*) for temporary custody (*Od.* XXIII. 239-44) until the funeral of Achilles, when with those of Achilles himself, similarly wrapped, and soaked in wine, they are deposited in a golden urn (*Od.* XXIV. 73-7). In the case of Hector, the bones are in like manner gathered and lodged in a golden box, which is then placed in a trench and built over with a mass of stones (*Il.* XXIV. 793-8). Incomplete combustion, then, is common to the Homeric and the Mycenaean instances. But in the case of the first tomb at Mycenae, not only was there no collection of the bones for deposit in an urn, but they had not been touched; except in the instance of the middle body, where they had simply been disturbed, and the valuables perhaps removed, as hardly anything of the kind was found with it. In the case of the body on the north side, the flesh of the face remained unconsumed.

But though the use of fire was universal in honourable burial, burial itself was not allowed to all. Enemies, as a rule, were not buried. Hence the opening passage of the *Iliad* tells us that many heroes became a prey to dogs and birds (*Il.* I. 4). Such, says Priam, before the conflict with Hector, he would make Achilles if he could (XXII. 42); and he anticipates a like distressing fate (66 *seqq.*) for himself. In the *Odyssey*, the bodies of the Suitors are left to be removed by their friends (XXII. 448; XXIV. 417). Achilles, indeed, buried Eëtion, king of Asiatic Thebes, with his arms, in the regular manner. "He did not simply spoil him, for he had a scruple in his mind" (*Il.* VI. 417); and no wonder; for Eëtion, king of the Kilikes, was not an enemy: that people does not appear among the allies of Troy in the Catalogue. Thus there was some variance of use; and there may have been cases of irregular intermediate treatment between the two extremes of honourable burial and casting out to the dogs.

5. With regard to the use of masks of gold for the dead, I hope that the Mycenaean discoveries will lead to a full collection of the evidence upon this rare and curious practice. For the present, I limit myself to the following observations:

(1.) If not less than seven of these golden masks have been discovered at Mycenae by Dr. Schliemann, then the use of them, on the occasion of these entombments, was not limited to royal persons, of whom it is impossible to make out so large a number.

(2.) I am not aware of any proof at present before us that the use of such masks for the dead of any rank or class was a custom prevalent, or even known, in Greece. There is much information, from Homer downwards, supplied to us by the literature of that country concerning burials; and yet, in a course of more than 1200 years, there is not a single allusion to the custom of using masks for the dead. It seems to be agreed that the passage on masks in the works of Lucian, who is reckoned to have flourished in the second half of the second century, does not refer to the use of such masks. This might lead us to the conjecture that, where the practice has appeared, it was a remainder of foreign usage, a survival from immigration.

(3.) Masks have been found in tombs, not in Greece, but in the Crimea, Campania, and Mesopotamia. Our latest information on the subject is, I believe, the account mentioned in Dr. Schliemann's last report from Athens (pp. xlvii, xlviii), of a gold mask found on the Phoenician coast over against Aradus, which is of the size suited for an infant only. It is to be remembered that heroic Greece is full of the marks of what I may term Phoenicianism, most of which passed into the usages of the country, and contributed to form the base of Hellenic life. Nor does it seem improbable, that this use of the metallic mask may have been a Phoenician adaptation from the Egyptian custom of printing the likeness of the dead on the mummy case. And, again, we are to bear in mind that Mycenae had been the seat of repeated foreign immigrations.

(4.) We have not to deal in this case *only* with masks, but with the case of a breastplate in gold, which, however, could not have been intended for use in war; together with other leaves or plates of gold, found on, or apparently intended for, other portions of the person.

6. Lastly, with regard to the deposit of objects which, besides being characteristic, have exchangeable value, the only point on which I have here to remark is, their extraordinary amount. It is such, I conceive, as to give to these objects, and particularly to those of the First Tomb, an exceptional place among the sepulchral deposits of antiquity. I understand that their weight is about one hundred pounds troy, or nearly that of five thousand British sovereigns. It is difficult to suppose that so large a deposit could have been usual, even with the remains of a King; and it is at this point that I, for one, am compelled to break finally and altogether with the supposition, that this great entombment, in the condition in which Dr. Schliemann found it, was simply an entombment of Agamemnon and his suite effected by Aegisthus and Clytemnestra, their murderers.

So far, with little argument, I have endeavoured fairly to set out the facts. Let me now endeavour to draw to a point the several

threads of the subject, in order to deal with the main question,
namely, whether these half-wasted, half-burned remains are the
ashes of Agamemnon and his company? And truly this is a case,
where it may be said to the inquirer, in figure as well as in fact,

· incedis per ignes
Suppositos cineri doloso.

Let us place clearly before our eyes the account given by the
Shade of Agamemnon, in the Eleventh Odyssey (405-434), of the
manner of his death. No darker picture could be drawn. It combined every circumstance of cruelty with every circumstance of
fraud. At the hospitable board, amid the flowing wine-cups, he
was slain like an ox at the stall, and his comrades like so many
hogs for a rich man's banquet; with deaths more piteous than he
had ever known in single combats, or in the rush of armies. Most
piteous of all was the death of Cassandra, whom the cruel Clytemnestra despatched with her own hand while clinging to Agamemnon; nor did she vouchsafe to her husband the last office of
mercy and compassion, by closing his mouth and eyes in death.
Singularly enough, Dr. Schliemann assures me that the right eye,
which alone could be seen with tolerable clearness, was not entirely
shut; while the teeth of the upper jawbone (see the same engraving) did not quite join those of the lower. This condition, he thinks,
may be due to the superincumbent weight. But if the weight had
opened the jaw, would not the opening, in all likelihood, have
been much wider?

Now, as we are told that Aegisthus reigned until Orestes reached
his manhood, we must assume that the massacre was in all respects
triumphant. Yet there could hardly fail to be a party among the
people favourable to the returning King, who had covered his
country with unequalled glory. There might thus be found in the
circumstances a certain dualism, a ground for compromise, such
as may go far to account for the discrepancies of intention, which
we seem to find in the entombments. There was this division of
sentiment among the people, in the only case where we know the
return of the prince from Troy to have been accompanied with a
crisis or conflict, I mean the case of Ithaca.

The assassins proceeded in such a way, that the only consistent
accomplishment of their design would have been found in casting
forth the bodies of the slain like the bodies of enemies. But this
may have been forbidden by policy. In the Julius Caesar of Shakespeare, Brutus says (III. I.)—

We are contented Caesar shall
Have all due rites and lawful ceremonies.
It shall advantage more than do us wrong.

Aegisthus was not Brutus. Even fury was apparent in the incidents of the slaughter. Yet there might be a desire to keep up
appearances afterwards, and to allow some semblance of an honourable burial. There is one special circumstance that favours the
idea of a double process, namely, that we readily find the agents
for both parts of it; the murderers for the first, with necessity and
policy controlling hatred; Orestes, on his return, for the second,
with the double motive of piety and revenge.

We are now on the road not of history, but of reasonable conjecture. I try to account for a burial, which according to all reasonable
presumption is of the heroic age, and of royal and famous personages, but which presents conflicting features of honour and of
shame. That there is no competing hypothesis, is not a good reason
for precipitate assent to the hypothesis which we may term Aga-
memnonian. Conjecture, to be admissible, ought to be consistent
with itself, to meet the main demands of the known facts, and to
present no trait at actual variance with any of them. In this view,
I present the hypothesis of a double procedure, and a double
agency: and I submit, that there is nothing irrational in the following chain of suppositions for the First Tomb, while the others are
probably included in the same argument. That the usurping
assassins, from policy, granted the honour of burial in the Agora;
hewed the sepulchre deep and large in the rock; and built the
encircling wall within it. That honour stopped with the preparation
of the tomb, and the rest, less visible to the public eye, was left to
spite or haste. That the bodies were consequently placed in the
seemingly strange and indecent fashion, which the tomb has disclosed. That, from their being protected by the rock, and by the
depth from the surface, or from physical causes, their decomposition was slow. That Orestes, on his return, could not but be aware
of the circumstances, and, in the fulfillment of his divinely ordered
mission, determined upon reparation to the dead. That he opened
the tombs, and arranged the means of cremation. That, owing to
the depth, it was imperfect from want of ventilation; we may remember that in the case of Patroclos the impersonated Winds were
specially summoned to expedite the process (*Il.* XXIII. 192-218).
In calling it imperfect, I mean that it stopped short of the point
at which the bones could be gathered; and they remained *in situ.*
That the masks, breastplate, and other leaves of gold were used,
perhaps, in part with reference to custom; in part, especially as
regards all beside the masks, to replace in the wasted bodies the
seemliness and majesty of nature, and to shelter its dilapidation.
That the profuse deposits of arms and valuables were due to filial
piety. That the same sentiment carried the work through, even to
the careful sculpturing of the four tomb-stones (others have been

found, but without sculpture); and sought, by their means, to indicate for renown and reverence, and to secure from greedy violation, the resting-place of the dead.

A complex solution, perhaps; but one applicable to very complex facts, and one of which the ground at least is laid in those facts; one also, which I offer as a contribution to a most interesting scrutiny, but with no claim or pretension to uphold it against any other, that may seem better entitled to fill the vacant place.

W. E. G.

HAWARDEN, *November*, 1877.

————

HEINRICH SCHLIEMANN

The Lion Gate at Mycenae

THE Lion Gate of Mycenae was probably built in the 14th century B.C. (The much older Shaft Graves are inside the wall to the right on entering the gate.) The lions have their paws on altars surmounted by pillars—each pillar symbolizing the divinity on whom the lion attends. The lions can also be seen as guardian attendants of the semidivine kings of Mycenae—like the griffins in the throne room at Knossos (p. 89, II). These ideas and symbols came, ultimately, from the East.

NOTWITHSTANDING the remote antiquity of Mycenae, its ruins are in a far better state of preservation than those of any of the Greek cities which Pausanias saw in a flourishing condition, and whose sumptuous monuments he describes (about 170 A.D.); and, owing to its distant and secluded position, and to the rudeness, magnitude,

From *Mycenae*, pp. 32-5.

and solidity of the ruins, it is hardly possible to think that any
change can have taken place in the general aspect of Mycenae since
it was seen by Pausanias.

In the north-western corner of the circuit-wall is the great "Lions'
Gate," of beautiful hard breccia. The opening, which widens from
the top downwards, is 10 ft. 8 in. high, and its width is 9 ft. 6 in.
at the top, and 10 ft. 3 in. below. In the lintel (15 feet long and
8 feet broad) are round holes, 6 inches deep, for the hinges, and
in the two uprights, which it roofs over, are four guadrangular
holes for the bolts. Over the lintel of the gate is a triangular gap
in the masonry of the wall, formed by an oblique approximation
of the side courses of stone. The object of this was to keep off the
pressure of the superincumbent wall from the flat lintel.

This niche is filled up by a triangular slab of the same beautiful
breccia of which the gateway and the walls consist: it is 10 feet
high, 12 feet long at the base, and 2 feet thick. On the face of the
slab are represented in relief two lions, standing opposite to each
other on their long outstretched hind-legs, and resting with their
fore-paws on either side of the top of an altar, on the midst of
which stands a column with a capital formed of four circles enclosed between two horizontal fillets. The general belief that the
heads of the lions are *broken off* is wrong, for on close examination I find that they were *not* cut out of the same stone together
with the animals, but that they were made separately and fastened
on the bodies with bolts. The straight cuts and the borings in the
necks of the animals can leave no doubt as to this fact. Owing to
the narrowness of the space, the heads could only have been very
small, and they must have been protruding and facing the spectator. I feel inclined to believe that they were of bronze and gilded.
The tails of the lions are not broad and bushy, but narrow, like
those which are seen in the most ancient sculptures of Egypt.

It is universally believed that this sculpture represents some
symbol, but many different conjectures have been made as to its
meaning. One thinks that the column alludes to the solar worship
of the Persians; another believes that it is the symbol of the holy
fire, and a *pyratheion* or fine altar, of which the lions are the
guardians; a third conjectures that it represents Apollo Agyieus,
that is, the "guardian of the gateway." I am of this last opinion,
and firmly believe that it is this very same symbol of that god
which Sophocles makes Orestes and Electra invoke when they enter
their father's house. As to the two lions, the explanation is still
more simple. Pelops, son of the Phrygian king Tantalus, migrated
hither from Phrygia, where the mother of the gods, Rhea, whose
sacred animal is the lion, had a celebrated worship. Most probably,
thcrcforc, Pelops brought with him the cultus of the patron deity

of his mother-country, and made her sacred animal the symbol of
the Pelopids. Aeschylus compares Agamemnon himself to a lion;
he also compares Agamemnon with Aegisthus as a lion with a
wolf. Thus here above the gate the two lions, either as the sacred
animals of Rhea or as the symbol of the powerful dynasty of the
Pelopids, have been united to the symbol of Apollo Agyieus, the
guardian of the gateway. To the left of the sculpture of the lions
is a large quadrangular window in the wall.

HEINRICH SCHLIEMANN

A Peaceful Garrison

Mycenae, 6th December, 1876.

FOR the first time since its capture by the Argives in 468 B.C., and
so for the first time during 2,344 years, the Acropolis of Mycenae
has a garrison, whose watchfires seen by night throughout the
whole Plain of Argos carry back the mind to the watch kept for
Agamemnon's return from Troy, and the signal which warned
Clytemnestra and her paramour of his approach. But this time the
object of the occupation by soldiery is of a more peaceful character,
for it is merely intended to inspire awe among the country-people,
and to prevent them from making clandestine excavations in the
tombs, or approaching them while we are working in them.

Ibid., p. 290.

HEINRICH SCHLIEMANN

Men in Gold Masks: the Discovery of the Shaft Graves

SCHLIEMANN excavated (p. 58, I) five of the six Shaft Graves enclosed in the circular wall inside the Lion Gate at Mycenae. The shafts were cut in the soft rock and lined with stone to make a burial chamber at the bottom. This was then roofed with wood and the shaft filled with earth. At the top a grave stone or *stela* was set, sometimes carved with spiral designs, sometimes with a relief of the dead man driving his war chariot. Very many of the gold, silver and bronze vessels and the richly-ornamented weapons buried with the dead were either imports from Minoan Crete or made by Minoan craftsmen living at Mycenae; others were local imitations of Minoan work. Some objects, however, were of purely local design, or were imports from Anatolia. This great wealth of grave goods makes it easy to date the burials to the very beginning of the Late Bronze Age, about 1550 B.C.

✻

THE mud in the *First Sepulchre,* whose site had been marked by the three *stelae* with low reliefs, having dried up in the fine weather, I continued the excavation there, and struck at last the bottom of the tomb, which is cut out in the rock, 17½ ft. deep on the north side, and 17 ft. deep on the south-east side. But from these points the slope is so abrupt that, although the upper breadth of the sepulchre does not exceed 10 ft. 10 in., yet the greater part of its west side needed only to be cut 11 ft. deep into the rock to make a

Ibid., pp. 293-312.

level bottom. This west side is close to the Cyclopean wall, with the parallel double row of large calcareous slabs, which forms the enclosure and benches of the Agora, and rises vertically over the sepulchre. For all these reasons it appeared to me, on first excavating this tomb, that the wall passed through its north-west angle. But, by propping up with planks and beams the earth and stones which cling to the wall and overhang the north-west corner of the tomb, I have now cleared the latter in its entire length, and visitors will perceive that the wall does not pass through the tomb but merely touches its brink in the north-west corner.

The length of the tomb is 21 ft. 6 in., its breadth at the bottom is 11 ft. 6 in., and thus 8 in. more than at the top. The four inner sides were lined with a Cyclopean wall, 3 ft. high and 2 ft. broad; and this had superposed on it a slanting wall of schist plates joined with clay, which reached to a height of 6½ ft., and projected on all sides a foot more than the Cyclopean wall, and thus in all 3 feet on the bottom of the tomb. The latter was covered with the usual layer of pebbles, which were, however, more irregularly strewn than in the other tombs, there being places without any pebbles; which circumstance made me at first believe that there was no layer of pebbles at all in this tomb. But on careful examination, I found such a layer, and below the bodies I found it just as regular as in any other tomb, which circumstance appears to give an additional proof that those layers of pebbles were merely intended to procure ventilation for the pyres.

The three bodies which the sepulchre contained lay at a distance of about 3 ft. from each other, and had been burnt in the very same place where I found them. This was evident from the marks of the fire on the pebbles and on the rock below and also around the bodies, and to the right and left of them on the walls, as well as from the undisturbed state of the ashes. Only with the body which lay in the midst the case was different. The ashes had evidently been disturbed; the clay with which the two other bodies and their ornaments were covered, and the layer of pebbles which covered the clay, had been removed from this body. As, besides, it was found almost without any gold ornaments, it is evident that it had been rifled. This opinion is also confirmed by the twelve golden buttons, the small golden plates, and the numerous small objects of bone, which had been found together with small quantities of black ashes at different depths below the three sculptured tombstones which adorned this sepulchre. It is further confirmed by the fragments of the usual Mycenaean pottery of later times, which in this tomb were mixed up with the very ancient hand-made or wheel-made vases. Most likely some one sank a shaft to examine the tomb, struck the body in question, plundered it recklessly, and for fear of being detected, carried off his booty in such a hurry that he only thought of saving the large massive gold ornaments, such as the mask, the large breast-cover, the diadems and the bronze swords, and, in re-mounting to the surface, dropped many of the smaller objects, such as the twelve golden buttons, etc., which I found at intervals in digging down. There can be no doubt that this larceny occurred *before* the capture of Mycenae by the Argives (468 B.C.); for, if it had been committed while the later Greek city stood on the top of the prehistoric ruins, I should also have found fragments of Greek pottery in the tomb; but of these I saw no vestige.

The three bodies of this tomb lay with their heads to the east and their feet to the west; all three were of large proportions, and appeared to have been forcibly squeezed into the small space of only 5 ft. 6 in. which was left for them between the inner walls. The bones of the legs, which are almost uninjured, are unusually large. Although the head of the first man, from the south side, was covered with a massive golden mask, his skull crumbled away on being exposed to the air, and only a few bones could be saved be-sides those of the legs. The same was the case with the second body, which had been plundered in antiquity.

But of the third body, which lay at the north end of the tomb, the round face, with all its flesh, had been wonderfully preserved under its ponderous golden mask; there was no vestige of hair, but both eyes were perfectly visible, also the mouth, which, owing to the enormous weight that had pressed upon it, was wide open, and showed thirty-two beautiful teeth. From these, all the physicians who came to see the body were led to believe that the man must have died at the early age of thirty-five. The nose was entirely gone. The body having been too long for the space between the two inner walls of the tomb, the head had been pressed in such a way on the breast, that the upper part of the shoulders was nearly in a horizontal line with the vertex of the head. Notwithstanding the large golden breast-plate, so little had been preserved of the breast, that the inner side of the spine was visible in many places. In its squeezed and mutilated state, the body measured only 2 ft. 4½ in. from the top of the head to the beginning of the loins; the breadth of the shoulders did not exceed 1 ft. 1¼ in., and the breadth of the chest 1 ft. 3 in.; but the large thighbones could leave no doubt regarding the real proportions of the body. Such had been the pressure of the *débris* and stones, that the body had been reduced to a thickness of 1 in. to 1½ in. The colour of the body resembled very much that of an Egyptian mummy. The forehead was orna-mented with a plain round leaf of gold, and a still larger one was lying on the right eye; I further observed a large and a small gold leaf on the breast below the large golden breast-cover, and a large one just above the right thigh.

The news that the tolerably well preserved body of a man of the mythic heroic age had been found, covered with golden ornaments, spread like wildfire through the Argolid, and people came by thousands from Argos, Nauplia, and the villages to see the wonder. But, nobody being able to give advice how to preserve the body, I sent for a painter to get at least an oil-painting made, for I was afraid that the body would crumble to pieces. Thus I am enabled to give a faithful likeness of the body, as it looked after all the golden ornaments had been removed. But to my great joy, it held out for two days, when a druggist from Argos, Spiridon Nicolaou by name, rendered it hard and solid by pouring on it alcohol, in which he had dissolved gum-sandarac. As there appeared to be no pebbles below it it was thought that it would be possible to lift it on an iron plate; but this was a mistake, because it was soon discovered that there was the usual layer of pebbles below the body, and all of these having been more or less pressed into the soft rock by the enormous weight which had been lying for ages upon them, all attempts made to squeeze in the iron plate below the pebble-stones, so as to be able to lift them together with the body, utterly failed. There remained, therefore, no other alternative than to cut a small trench into the rock all round the body, and make thence a horizontal incision, so as to cut out a slab, two inches thick, to lift it with the pebble-stones and the body, to put it upon a strong plank, to make around the latter a strong box, and to send this to the village of Charvati, whence it will be forwarded to Athens as soon as the Archaeological Society shall have got a suitable locality for the Mycenaean antiquities. With the miserable instruments alone available here it was no easy task to detach the large slab horizontally from the rock, but it was still much more difficult to bring it in the wooden box from the deep sepulchre to the surface, and to transport it on men's shoulders for more than a mile to Charvati. But the capital interest which this body of the remote heroic age has for science, and the buoyant hope of preserving it, made all the labour appear light.

The now nearly mummified body was decorated with a golden shoulder-belt, 4 ft. long and 1¾ in. broad, which, for some cause or other, was not in its place, for it now lay across the loins of the body, and extended in a straight line far to the right of it. In its midst is suspended, and firmly attached, the fragment of a double-edged bronze sword and to this latter was accidentally attached a beautifully-polished perforated object of rock crystal, in form of a jar, with two silver handles. It is pierced in its entire length by a silver pin. This little object has unfortunately been detached in removing the treasure from Charvati to Athens, and thus I represent it separately. Together with the shoulder-belt and the little crystal jar was found the small object of rock-crystal which has the shape of a funnel. In the extremity of the shoulder-belt, to the left of the spectator, are two perforations; at the other end there has probably been a clasp, because there are no perforations; on the fragment of the sword we see one of those small shield-like or button-like golden disks, with an ornamentation of *repoussé* work, which have decorated the sheaths of the swords in uninterrupted rows, their size being always determined by the breadth of the sheaths. The disk before us is divided by three concentric circles into three circular compartments, of which the outer and the central one represent a number of ornaments resembling horse-shoes. A glance at this shoulder-belt will convince every one that it is by far too thin and fragile to have been worn by living men. Besides, I feel certain that no living warrior has ever gone to battle with swords in sheaths of wood ornamented on either side with rows of gold plates, which are merely glued on the wood. Thus, we may consider it beyond all doubt that a great part of all the golden ornaments have been expressly prepared for funeral use. There was also found an alabaster stand for a vase.

The massive golden breast-plate of this same body is perfectly plain, and it is therefore unnecessary to engrave it. It is 15⅗ in. long and 9½ in. broad; it has no ornamentation, but two protruding breasts can be distinctly seen; they are not, however, in the middle, as they ought to be, but more to the right of the spectator. While speaking of breast-covers, I may as well give here the breast-cover of the body at the southern end of this first tomb. It is 1 ft. 9 in. long and 1 ft. 2⅗ in. broad. Here the two breasts are well represented by two protruding shield-like bosses, and the whole remaining space is richly ornamented with beautiful spirals in *repoussé* work.

The best preserved parts of the same body, at the southern end of the tomb, are two large bones and a small bone. On the latter, which is probably an arm-bone, is still attached a broad golden ribbon, with a splendid ornamentation of *repoussé* work.

I return to the body at the northern extremity. To its right lay the two bronze swords and close to them all the other objects. The handle of the upper sword is of bronze, but thickly plated with gold, which is all over covered with a magnificent intaglio work of the most varied description. On the upper part of the handle, where the blade issues from it, is fastened a broad curved gold plate with splendid intaglio work, similar to that represented below, of which we only here recognise the exact use. No doubt this sword has had a wooden sheath, which must have been ornamented with the long gold plate, with a ring and much resembling the shape of a man, which we see to the right of it. The sheath must have been further adorned with the golden button, with engraved concentric circles, which we see close to the blade. Much richer still has evidently been the ornamentation of the other bronze sword, for its wooden sheath must evidently have been adorned, in its entire length, on both sides, with a series of those large golden buttons with a magnificent intaglio work of spirals which we see below and on the right side of the sword. The sheath has evidently been also adorned with the tubular golden plate, ornamented with spirals in intaglio work, which we still see around the sword.

The handle of this sword must have been of wood, because it has entirely disappeared, and it must necessarily have been adorned with the two quadrangular golden plates which we see lying, still closely joined together, in the very place where the knob of the handle ought to have been; only on the small side, which is turned towards the spectator, the two plates are slightly disjoined. Both have ornamentation in *repoussé* work of interwoven spirals; and we see in their long sides the marks of a number of small pins, which must have served to attach both plates to a piece of wood which stuck between them, and of which some traces remain. This piece of wood must have been very thin, for otherwise the two plates could not after its disappearance have fallen together so exactly as to appear still joined. Certainly they must have served as ornaments of the sword-handle, but how this was done is altogether inexplicable to me. I find it impossible to suppose that the sword-handle terminated in a thin piece of wood, so as to be fastened between the two plates; besides, this is contradicted by their raised borders. With the two plates was found a bead of amber, the presence of which here must be only accidental, for of course it can have nothing in common with the swords. To one of these swords was doubtless attached the golden tassel which I found near them. Probably all these weapons had been suspended on a belt of embroidered work which has disappeared.

At a distance of hardly more than one foot to the right of the body I found eleven bronze swords, of which nine had suffered more or less from moisture; but the other two were pretty well preserved. One of them has the enormous length of 3 ft. 2 in., the other of 2 ft. 10 in. With the swords I found two golden plates, both of which have belonged to sword-handles; that to the left having been on the upper part of the handle, to which it was attached with no less than twelve gold pins, of which five with large globular heads are still visible. This object is so thickly covered with ashes of the funeral fire that but little of its spiral ornamentation in intaglio can be discerned. The other golden plate has been used as the cover of the wooden sword-handle, and it is perfectly similar to those which we passed in review in describing the discoveries in the fourth tomb.

I further found with the swords three tubes of gold plate, one 12½ in. long, another 10½ in. long, both containing remnants of wood, and the third 5⅗ in. long There were also 124 large round gold buttons, plain or with splendid intaglio work, two of which are two inches in diameter, and four of the size of five-franc pieces; the other 118 are smaller. Further, six large splendidly-ornamented golden buttons in the form of crosses, three of which are 3 in. long and 2¼ in. broad. All these buttons consist either of flat pieces of wood covered with gold plates, and in this case they have invariably been pasted or soldered as embellishments on sword-sheaths or other objects, or they are real wood buttons resembling our present shirtstuds and covered with gold plates, and in this case they must have been used on clothes. The magnificently engraved ornamentation of both these kinds of buttons can leave no doubt as to the importance attached to them. I may add that in this tomb not only all the cruciform gold buttons, but also all the very large round gold buttons, have on their lower side a flat piece of wood.

With the body which lay in the middle of the tomb were found some round leaves of gold with an impressed ornamentation, and the remnants of a wooden comb. With the body at the south end of the sepulchre I found fifteen bronze swords, ten of which lay at his feet. Eight of them are of very large size, and tolerably well preserved,

A large heap of more or less broken bronze swords, which may have represented more than sixty entire ones, was found on the west side, between the last-mentioned body and the middle one; also a few bronze knives and lances. Very remarkable is the battle-axe for I have never yet found this shape here, but I very frequently found it in Troy, and fourteen of them were contained in the Trojan treasure. Compared with our present axes, this Mycenean and the Trojan battle-axes have no hole in which the wooden handle could be fixed, and thus they had evidently been fastened in or on the handle instead of the handle being fastened in them. Some of the swords show traces of having been gilded; several of them have golden pins at the handle.

I also found, with the body at the south end of the tomb, the large handle with a fragment of a bronze sword. This handle is covered with thick gold plate richly ornamented with intaglio work, which can be well distinguished, though the handle is very dirty from the smoke and ashes of the funeral pyre. The ornamentation is exactly the same on both sides. In the hollow of the handle is still preserved part of the wood with which it was once filled.

I also found with the body at the southern end a large quantity of amber beads and five small plain cylinders of gold plate (in one of which still sticks a piece of wood), which have evidently covered a stick, perhaps a sceptre; further seven large sword-handle knobs of alabaster and one of wood, all ornamented with gold nails; a small piece of gold in the form of a bar of a watch-chain, which cannot but have served as a sort of clasp to a shoulder-belt; thirty-seven round gold leaves of various sizes, twenty-one fragments of gold leaves, two fragmentary silver vases, a pair of silver tongs or tweezers, and a large vase of alabaster, with a mouthpiece of bronze, plated with gold. The perforations on three sides in the upper part of the body can leave no doubt that this vase has had three handles, and the large round hole with four small perforations in front show that it has had a pipe. In this vase I found thirty-two small and three large round gold buttons with rich intaglio patterns, as well as two gold buttons in the shape of crosses, each with two very small golden handles; further a large gold button of conical shape, and a wedge-shaped golden tube.

The following engravings represent three more of those wonderful gold plates, two of which we have already passed in review. There were found twelve of them in all, to the right and left of the body at the northern extremity of the tomb. One represents a lion chasing a stag; the four feet of the former are in a horizontal line to show the great speed with which he is running; he has just overtaken the stag, which sinks down before him, and his jaws are wide open to devour it. The head of the lion, as well as the mane, are pretty well represented. On the other hand, the representation of the stag, which has no horns, is clumsy and indistinct; beyond it we see an animal with spines and a long fishtail, probably a sea monster. Above the lion are represented two long palm-fronds, and below it the crowns of two palm-trees and a palm-frond.

Another represents nearly the same subject: we see again a lion running at full speed and catching a stag, which is represented with the body turned towards his pursuer and with his head in the opposite direction; he stands on his hind-legs, into which the lion, with open jaws, is just biting. The fore-feet of the stag are uplifted, and his lower feet protrude at a right angle from the knee. Just before the uplifted loins of the stag we see the wide-open jaws of a large cow-head with two long horns of the crescent form and two enormous eyes, to which I call particular attention. Between the two large horns we see two smaller ones, the space between which is filled with small objects in the form of figs; similar objects are seen between the small and the large horns. Though the artist has given us a front view of the cow-head, yet he represents its jaws in profile. To the right of the cow-head we see five long palm-fronds, below which, in the corner to the right of the spectator, is an object which I cannot recognise; it resembles a bird's foot.

The whole scene certainly appears to be symbolic.

I think there can be no reasonable doubt that the cow-head represents Hera Boöthis, the patron deity of Mycenae, and that when, in later times, this goddess received a female head, her enormous cow's eyes alone survived of her former cow-shape; because her sole characteristic epithet βοῶπις, consecrated as it was by the use of ages, was thenceforward indiscriminately used for both goddesses and mortal women to designate large eyes. Thus, for example, Clymene, one of Helen's female servants, is called by Homer ox-eyed. Hera's representation here, with a double pair of horns and the fruits between the four horns, can, I think, have no other purpose than to glorify her. I further believe that the lion represents the house of the Pelopids, and perhaps Agamemnon himself, and that the stag represents a sacrifice offered by the lion (the house of the Pelopids or Agamemnon himself) to the patron deity of the town, and the open jaws of the cow-head may have the meaning that she benignantly receives the sacrifice.

The remaining plate represents the same spiral ornamentation which we have so frequently passed in review.

To the reverse side of these wonderful golden plates there sticks a good deal of a blackish matter, perhaps a sort of cement, which must have served to attach them to flat pieces of wood, on each side of which must have been one plate. This opinion seems also to be confirmed by the marks of nails which we see in the rims of the plates, for the nails can, of course, only have been used to fasten them to a softer substance.

As to the massive golden mask of the same body at the north end of the first tomb, unfortunately the lower part of the forehead has been so much pressed upon the eyes and the nose, that the face is disfigured, and the features cannot be well distinguished. Highly characteristic is the large round head, the enormous forehead, and the small mouth with the thin lips.

In a perfect state of preservation, on the other hand, is the massive golden mask of the body at the south end of the tomb. Its features are altogether Hellenic and I call particular attention to the long thin nose, running in a direct line with the forehead, which is but small. The eyes, which are shut, are large, and well represented by the eyelids; very characteristic is also the large mouth with its well-proportioned lips. The beard also is well represented, and particularly the moustaches, whose extremities are turned upwards to a point, in the form of crescents. This circumstance

seems to leave no doubt that the ancient Mycenaeans used oil or a
sort of pomatum in dressing their hair. Both masks are of *repoussé*
work, and certainly nobody will for a moment doubt that they
were intended to represent the portraits of the deceased, whose
faces they have covered for ages.

The question now naturally arises:—have they been made in
the lifetime, or after the death, of the persons? Probably after their
death: but then we wonder again how the masks can have been
made so quickly; because here, as in all hot climates, the dead
are buried within twenty-four hours after their decease; and this
must have been the custom here at all times. If Homer leaves the
bodies of Patroclus and Hector for ten or twelve days unburied, it
was owing to peculiar circumstances; and if they remained well
preserved, it was that Thetis dropped ambrosia into the veins of
the former, and Apollo into those of the latter. However that may
have been with the bodies before us, we are amazed at the skill of the
ancient Mycenaean goldsmiths, who could model the portraits of
men in massive gold plate, and consequently could do as much as
any modern goldsmith would be able to perform.

———————

HEINRICH SCHLIEMANN

Agamemnon's Tomb?

HAVING in the preceding pages described the five great sepulchres
and the treasures contained in them, I now proceed to discuss the
question, whether it is possible to identify these sepulchres with
the tombs which Pausanias, following the tradition, attributes to
Agamemnon, to Cassandra, to Eurymedon, and to their companions.

The Trojan war has for a long time past been regarded by many
eminent scholars as a myth, of which, however, they vainly endeavoured to find the origin in the Rig-Vedas. But in all antiquity the

Ibid., pp. 334-7.

siege and conquest of Ilium by the Greek army under Agamemnon was considered as an undoubted historical fact, and as such it is accepted by the great authority of Thucydides. The tradition has even retained the memory of many details of that war which had been omitted by Homer. For my part, I have always firmly believed in the Trojan war; my full faith in Homer and in the tradition has never been shaken by modern criticism, and to this faith of mine I am indebted for the discovery of Troy and its Treasure.

However, the want of ornamentation on the Trojan jewels, the hand-made uncoloured pottery with impressed or engraved ornamentation, and, finally, the want of iron and glass, convinced me that the ruins of Troy belong to such a remote antiquity, as to precede by ages the ruins of Mycenae, the date of which I thought I could fix by the result of the 34 shafts which I sank in the Acropolis in February 1874. I therefore believed that Homer had only known the siege and destruction of Troy from an ancient tradition commemorated by preceding poets, and that, for favours received, he introduced his contemporaries as actors in his great tragedy. But I never doubted that a king of Mycenae, by name Agamemnon, his charioteer Eurymedon, a Princess Cassandra, and their followers had been treacherously murdered either by Aegisthus at a banquet, "like an ox at the manger," as Homer says, or in the bath by Clytemnestra, as the later tragic poets represent; and I firmly believed in the statement of Pausanias, that the murdered persons had been interred in the Acropolis, differing in this respect, as I have said before, from Leake, Dodwell, O. Müller, E. Curtius, Prokesch, and other travellers in the Peloponnesus, who had all misunderstood the statement of Pausanias, and thought that he meant the murdered persons to have been buried in the lower town.

My firm faith in the traditions made me undertake my late excavations in the Acropolis, and led to the discovery of the five tombs, with their immense treasures. Although I found in these tombs a very high civilisation, from a technical point of view, yet, as in Ilium, I found there only hand-made or most ancient wheel-made pottery, and no iron. Further, writing was known in Troy, for I found there a number of short inscriptions, in very ancient Cypriote characters; and, so far as we can judge, in a language which is essentially the same as Greek; whereas we have the certainty now that the alphabet was unknown in Mycenae. Had it been known, the Mycenaean goldsmiths, who were always endeavouring to invent some new ornamentation, would have joyfully availed themselves of the novelty to introduce the strange characters in their decoration. Besides, in the remote antiquity to which the Homeric rhapsodies and the tradition of the Mycenaean tombs refer, there was as yet no commercial intercourse. Nobody travelled, except on

warlike or piratical expeditions. Thus there may have been a very
high civilisation at Mycenae, while at the very same time the arts
were only in their first dawn in Troy, and writing with Cypriote
characters may have been in use in Troy more than 1000 years
before any alphabet was known in Greece.

I have not the slightest objection to admit that the tradition
which assigns the tombs in the Acropolis to Agamemnon and his
companions, who on their return from Ilium were treacherously
murdered by Clytemnestra or her paramour Aegisthus, may be
perfectly correct and faithful. I am bound to admit this so much
the more, as we have the certainty that, to say the least, all the
bodies in each tomb had been buried simultaneously. The calcined
pebbles below each of them, the marks of the fire to the right and
left on the internal walls of the tombs, the undisturbed state of the
ashes and the charred wood on and around the bodies, give us the
most unmistakable proofs of this fact. Owing to the enormous
depths of these sepulchres, and the close proximity of the bodies
to each other, it is quite impossible that three or even five funeral
piles could have been dressed at different intervals of time in the
same tomb.

The identity of the mode of burial, the perfect similarity of all
the tombs, their very close proximity, the impossibility of admitting
that three or even five royal personages of immeasurable wealth,
who had died a natural death at long intervals of time, should have
been huddled together in the same tomb, and, finally, the great
resemblance of all the ornaments, which show exactly the same
style of art and the same epoch—all these facts are so many proofs
that all the twelve men, three women, and perhaps two or three
children, had been murdered simultaneously and burned at the
same time.

The veracity of the tradition seems further to be confirmed by
the deep veneration which the Mycenaeans and in fact the inhabitants of the whole Argolid, have always shown for these five sepulchres. The funeral pyres were not yet extinguished when they were
covered with a layer of clay, and then with a layer of pebbles, on
which the earth was thrown at once. To this circumstance chiefly
are we indebted for the preservation of so large a quantity of wood
and the comparatively good preservation of the bodies; for in no
instance were the bones consumed by the fire, and on several bodies,
which were covered with golden masks and thick breast-plates, even
much of the flesh had remained. The site of each tomb was marked
by tombstones, and when these had been covered by the dust of
ages and had disappeared, fresh tombstones were erected on the
new level, but precisely over the spot where the ancient memorials
lay buried. Only on the large fourth sepulchre with the five bodies,

instead of new tombstones, a sacrificial altar of almost circular form was built.

As before explained, the first tomb had, according to all appearance, been originally decorated with a large monument, from which came the three tombstones with the bas-reliefs, and these sculptured tombstones must have been taken out and erected on the new level.

HEINRICH SCHLIEMANN

Schliemann as Excavator

TIRYNS was another great Mycenaean citadel, standing in the plain of Argos at no great distance to the south of Mycenae itself. It was fortified with walls of huge stone blocks during the 14th century B.C.

IN the beginning of August 1876, I had worked at Tiryns for a week with 51 men, had sunk on the high plateau of the citadel 13 pits and several long trenches down to the rock, and had also examined by 7 pits the lower plateau of the citadel and its immediate neighbourhood. In a trench dug at the west side of the higher plateau I had rediscovered the rectangular plinth, together with the 3 pillar-bases, which had been found by Fr. Thiersch and Al. R. Rangabé who had dug here for one day in September 1831. In seven or eight of the pits on the higher plateau I had found walls built of large stones without mortar, which I considered to be the Cyclopean housewalls of the prehistoric inhabitants of Tiryns. But afterwards I began to doubt this, and my doubts were strengthened by the results of my excavations at Mycenae and Troy. I was therefore very desirous for years back to explore Tiryns thoroughly, but was

From *Tiryns*. London: John Murray; 1886, pp. 1-7.

prevented by other pressing work. . . . It was not till March 1884
that I was able to realise my long-deferred hope of exploring Tiryns.
The necessary permission was readily granted me by M. Boulpiotes,
the learned Minister of Education, who was constant in helping
me to overcome the many obstacles arising during the operations.
It is with great pleasure that I here repeat my thanks to this
worthy man for the inestimable services he has rendered to science,
for without his ready help, it would have been impossible to carry
out effectually the exploration of Tiryns.

In order to ensure that none of the information likely to be
obtained from architectural fragments should be lost, I again obtained the assistance of the eminent architect of the German
Archaeological Institute at Athens, Dr. Wilhelm Dörpfeld, who had
conducted for four years the architectural department of the German excavations at Olympia, and who had helped me for five
months at Troy in 1882. I also re-engaged, as overseer (at 180 frs.
per month), G. Basilopoulos from Maguliana in Gortynia, who had
served me in the same capacity under the name of *Ilos* at Troy, and
now entered on the new campaign under this title; I also engaged
Niketas Simigdalas of Thera, for 150 frs. per month. My third overseer was my excellent servant Oedipus Pyromalles, who had also
been with me in Troy, and had now much leisure.

The necessary apparatus I brought from Athens, viz. 40 English
wheelbarrows with iron wheels; 20 large iron crowbars; one large
and two small windlasses; 50 large iron shovels; 50 pickaxes; 25
large hoes, known all through the East by the name of *tschapa*, and
used in vineyards; these were again of the greatest use in filling
the baskets with *débris*. The baskets necessary, known even in
Greece by the Turkish name *senbil*, I bought in Nauplia. For the
storage of these tools, for the stabling of my horse, and for the
lodging of my overseers, I hired rooms (at 50 frs. per month) in
the buildings of the model farm started by Capo d'Istria, close to
the south wall of Tiryns. It has now decayed into a tumbledown
farmhouse.

Dr. Dörpfeld and I found this house too dirty; and as there was
near Tiryns only one suitable residence, for which they asked 2000
frs. for three months, we preferred to live in the Hôtel des
Etrangers, in Nauplia, where we got for 6 frs. per day a couple of
clean rooms, as well as a room for Oedipus, and where the worthy
host, Georgios Moschas, did all he could to make us comfortable.

My habit was to rise at 3.45 A.M., swallow 4 grains of quinine as
a preservative against fever, and then take a sea bath; a boatman,
for 1 fr. daily, awaited me punctually at 4 o'clock, and took me from
the quay to the open sea, where I swam for 5 or 10 minutes. I was
obliged to climb into the boat again by the oar, but long practice

had made this somewhat difficult operation easy and safe. After bathing, I drank in the coffee-house *Agamemnon,* which was always open at that hour, a cup of black coffee without sugar, still to be had for the old sum of 10 Lepta (a penny) though everything had risen enormously in price. A good cog (at 6 frs. daily) stood ready, and took me easily in twenty-five minutes to Tiryns, where I always arrived before sunrise, and at once sent back the horse for Dr. Dörpfeld. Our breakfast was taken regularly at 8 A.M., during the first rest of the workmen, on the floor of the old palace at Tiryns. It consisted of Chicago corned beef, of which a plentiful supply was sent me by my honoured friends Messrs. J. H. Schröder & Co., from London, bread, fresh sheep-cheese, oranges, and white resined wine (*rezinato*), which, on account of its bitter, agrees with quinine, and is more wholesome during heat and hard work than the stronger red wines. During the workmen's second rest, beginning at 12 and lasting at first an hour, in greater heat one hour ad three-quarters, we also rested, and two stones of the threshing-floor at the south end of the Acropolis, where we afterwards found the Byzantine Church, served us for pillows. One never rests so well as when thoroughly tired with hard work, and I can assure the reader, that we never enjoyed more refreshing sleep than during this midday hour in the Acropolis of Tiryns, in spite of the hard bed, and the scorching sun, against which we had no other protection than our Indian hats laid flat upon our faces.

Our third and last meal was at our return home in the evening, in the restaurant of the hotel. As my London friends had also supplied me with Liebig's Extract of Meat, we had always excellent soup; this, with fish or mutton, fried in olive-oil, cheese, oranges, and resined wine, completed our menu. Fish and many kinds of vegetables, as potatoes, broad beans, French beans, peas and artichokes, are excellent here, but are so ill-cooked with quantities of olive-oil, that to our taste they are almost useless.

Although wine mixed with resin is not mentioned by any ancient Greek author except Dioscorides, and even Athenaios makes no allusion to it, yet we may assume with high probability that it was in common use in the ancient Greek world, for the fir-cone was sacred to Dionysos, and the thyrsos, a light staff wound with ivy and vine branches, which was carried in processions by the priests of Bacchus, was ornamented at the upper end with a fir-cone. Pliny also, among the various fruits useful for making wine, enumerates the fir-cone, and says that it is dipped and pressed in the must.

The passage in Dioscorides, which is very characteristic and instructive, runs thus: "Concerning resined wine. Resined wine is prepared by various peoples, but it is most abundant in Galatia, for there, on account of the cold, the grapes do not ripen, and therefore the wine turns sour if it be not tempered with pine resin. The resin is taken off along with the bark, and half a Kotyle (a piece of two ounces) is mixed in an Amphora. Some filter the wine after fermentation, and thus separate the resin; others leave it in. When the wine is long kept it becomes sweet. But all wines so prepared produce headache and dizziness, yet promote digestion, are diuretic, and to be recommended for coughs and colds; also to those suffering from gastric complaints, dysentery or dropsy, &c., and for internal ulcers. Also the dark rezinato constipates more than the white."

I commenced the excavation on the 17th of March, with sixty workmen, who were shortly increased to seventy, and this remained the average number of my labourers during the two and a half months' campaign at Tiryns in 1884.

The daily wages of my workmen were at first 3 francs; this, however, increased as the season advanced, and before Easter rose to 3½ francs. I also employed women, finding them quite as handy at filling baskets as men; their wages at first were 1½ francs, and later were increased to 2 francs. At sunrise all the workers came with the tools and wheelbarrows from the depot to the citadel, where as soon as I had called over the roll, work began, and lasted till sundown, when all tools and wheelbarrows were again returned to the depot. In spite of these precautions, many tools and a wheelbarrow were stolen from me.

For work with the pickaxe I chose the strongest men, as it is the heaviest; the others suited for the wheelbarrows, for filling the rubbish into the baskets, and for clearing them again. As I desired to provide my people with good drinking-water, I set aside a labourer for the purpose, that he might fetch it in barrels upon a wheelbarrow from the nearest spring.

Another workman, with some knowledge of carpentry, I set aside for the repairs of wheelbarrows and tools; a third served me as groom. Unfortunately, I was debarred the pleasure of employing my old servant Nikolaos Zaphyros Giannakis, who since the beginning of 1870 had served me in all my archaeological campaigns as comptroller of the household and cashier, for, unhappily, he was drowned in August 1883, in the Skamander, on the east of Yeni Shehr, so I had to manage without him.

The labourers were mostly Albanians from the neighbouring villages of Kophinion, Kutsion, Laluka, and Aria. I had only about fifteen Greeks from the village of Charvati, who had worked with me eight years ago in Mycenae, and who distinguished themselves by their industry above the Albanians.

The winter, 1883-4, had been very mild, and on our arrival on the 15th of March the trees were already clothed in the richest green and the fields decked with flowers. We saw flocks of cranes only on the 16th of March. These birds do not nest here, but stay only a few hours, and then continue their northward flight. Storks are never seen in Argolis, though often in the marshy plains of the Phthiotis, where they build.

ARTHUR EVANS

Minoan Civilization

THE Island of Crete is so situated that, once the Bronze Age civilizations of the ancient world had been created and were developing their commerce, the Cretans had every chance of prospering as sea traders. They took the chance, and in the relative safety of their island were able to build a fine and artistically sensitive culture of their own. They were influenced by the Egyptians and the peoples of south-west Asia, and had the closest bonds with Asia Minor and the whole Aegean, yet the "form" of their civilization was always distinctive.

Soon after he began to discover this forgotten Bronze Age civilization of Crete, Sir Arthur Evans decided to call it Minoan (p. 87, II). He was naturally so enthralled by the fine palace and exquisite objects which he was finding at Knossos, and so impressed by the fact that this Minoan civilization began long before the Mycenaean which Schliemann had first revealed on the Greek mainland, that he was inclined to exaggerate the relative importance of Crete. He believed that the dominance of the Minoans over the mainland was complete, and that the Mycenaean culture was little more than a creation of Minoan overlords and colonists. As for the destruction of the palace of Knossos in 1400 B.C. which his excavations had proved, he attributed it (p. 121, II) to an earth-

From *The Palace of Minos*, Vol. I. London: Macmillan & Company Ltd.; 1921, pp. 1-4, 15-19, 25-30. Reprinted by permission of Agathon Press, Inc., which is reprinting *The Palace of Minos*.

quake, followed by social upheaval. Thereafter, Evans was convinced, the Minoans never fully recovered, but lived on at an
altogether lower standard—the palace of Knossos itself occupied
by impoverished "squatters."

As the Mycenaean civilization came to be more fully appreciated, Evans's view of Minoan dominance was disputed. Champions
of the mainland declared that during the last brilliant period of its
occupation Knossos was ruled by Mycenaean conquerors—and the
destruction was due (p. 129, II) to an insurrection by the subject
native Minoans. The argument continues—although no one questions that the Minoan civilization flowered before that of the mainland, and that its cultural influence upon the Mycenaeans was very
powerful indeed.

The argument is much involved with the question as to when
the first Greek-speaking people appeared in Greece and Crete. It
has been generally agreed that the Mycenaeans were Achaean
Greeks, and it was partly because Evans could not agree that there
had been Greeks in Crete during "Minoan" times that he refused to
believe there had been any Mycenaean control of the island. When
Michael Ventris proved (p. 153, II) to most people's satisfaction that
the inscribed tablets which Evans had assigned to the period before
the destruction were in the Greek language, the case for mainland
dominance seemed to be won. It was thought that an Achaean
dynasty must have taken over the palace and its authority some time
in the fifteenth century B.C. Now the debate has been given another
twist. In what has come to be one of the most publicized scholarly
battles of the twentieth century, Leonard Palmer has argued very
convincingly that Evans misinterpreted the stratigraphical evidence
when he said that the inscribed tablets dated from before the destruction. According to Professor Palmer all the evidence points to
these tablets being very much later than the destruction—possibly
dating not much before 1200 B.C. If so, then there is no need to
bring in any Greek rulers before 1400 B.C., and the Minoans can be
left in undisputed possession of their island until that time. It is
a curious irony that if Palmer has proved Evans to be wrong in his
dating of the tablets, he may thereby have proved him partly right
in his main historical thesis.

The iconoclastic Palmer went on to claim that the sack of
Knossos was not followed by a period of undisturbed Minoan decadence, but on the contrary that the conquering Mycenaeans set
up a ruling dynasty and enjoyed commercial prosperity and influence until the coming of the Dorians in about 1200 B.C. Indeed, he
thinks that the famous throne room, and at least the "Taureador
Frescoes" (p. 109, II) were the work of this late Mycenaean phase.
Whether or not this very different ending to the story of Knossos

is accepted, the evidence in favour of the late dating of the tablets seems hard to refute (it is discussed a little more fully in the introduction to the scripts, p. 132, II).

Apart from this disagreement concerning the later stages of Cretan history, most of what Sir Arthur Evans had to say about the enchanting island civilization he revealed to the world has stood the test of time. Probably in assessing the foreign influences on Minoan culture (pp. 89, II, 92, II) more emphasis would now be placed on the Anatolian and Asiatic sources and less on the Egyptian. Again, while Evans's general classification into the three main periods and their subdivisions (pp. 94, II, 97, II) still stands, there have been some drastic changes in the absolute dates assigned to the earlier periods. Thus the beginning of the Early Minoan (when in fact eastern Crete was more important than the central, Knossian, region) has been brought down to about 2500 B.C., and of the Middle Minoan to about 1950 B.C. On the other hand the first establishment of a great palace at Knossos remains at about 1900 B.C., and subsequent dates are little changed. The Late Minoan period after 1550 B.C. corresponds to the Mycenaean of the mainland, and both can be more broadly classified as representing the Late Bronze Age of their region.

The "Palace of Minos" at Knossos was built on the hill of Kaphala a few miles to the south of modern Heraklion (Candia). Although distinguished in architectural style and charmingly decorated, this home of the semi-divine rulers of Crete was not large by Oriental standards. It measured approximately 150 metres square, and its maze of royal and religious apartments, halls, shrines, offices, storerooms and the like were built round a rectangular open courtyard about 50 metres in length. The area has always been subject to earthquakes (p. 124, II), and several damaged the buildings. The worst was probably in 1570 B.C., but Knossos was then at the height of its prosperity and the palace was quickly restored.

THE progressive revelations, from 1900 onwards, of a high early civilization on Cretan soil entailed the urgent necessity for devising a new system and terminology for the Later Prehistoric Age in the Aegean area. The term "Mycenaean" no longer sufficed. The great palaces at Knossos and Phaestos, the smaller but exquisitely appointed building of the same class at Hagia Triada, the town sites of Gournia and Palaikastro, island settlements like Pseira, the archaic mansions of Vasilikì, the cave sanctuaries of Psychro and Kamares, primitive "tholos" ossuaries like those of Messara, the early tombs of Mochlos and a further series of discoveries, to which each season adds, have brought forth a mass of materials not only showing us a contemporary culture, parallel with that of Mycenae, in its own home, but carrying the origins of that culture stage beyond stage to an incomparably more remote period. For the first time there has come into view a primitive European civilization, the earliest phase of which goes back even beyond the days of the First Dynasty of Egypt.

To this early civilization of Crete as a whole I have proposed—and the suggestion has been generally adopted by the archaeologists of this and other countries—to apply the name "Minoan." By the Greeks themselves the memory of the great Age that had preceded their own diffusion throughout the Aegean lands was summed up in the name of Minos.

It is true that very different traditions were connected with that name. On the one side we gain a vision of a beneficent ruler, patron of the arts, founder of palaces, stablisher of civilized dominion. On the other is depicted a tyrant and a destroyer. The grim aspect of the great justiciary as impressed on the minds of a later generation is already reflected in the Homeric epithet ὀλοόφρων. It was, however, reserved for Athenian chauvinism so to exaggerate the tyrannical side of that early sea-dominion as to convert the palace of a long series of great rulers into an ogre's den. But the fabulous accounts of the Minotaur and his victims are themselves expressive of a childish wonder at the mighty creations of a civilization beyond the ken of the new-comers. The spade of the excavator has indeed done much to explain and confute them. The ogre's den turns out to be a peaceful abode of priest-kings, in some respects more modern in its equipments than anything produced by classical Greece. The monumental reliefs within its sea-gate—visible, it would appear, to a much later date—representing bull-catching scenes and, still more, the fresco panels with feats of the bull-ring in which girls as well as youths took part, go far to explain the myth. It may even be that captive children of both sexes were trained to take part in the dangerous circus sports portrayed on the palace walls.

Minos "the destroyer" may certainly have existed. That the yoke of the more civilized ruler should at times have weighed heavily on subject peoples is probable enough. But, in the main, the result of recent discovery has been to confirm the more favourable side of Greek tradition.

Until a full interpretation of the inscribed tablets is forthcoming it must remain impossible to obtain any actual excerpts from the "Laws of Minos," or to ascertain how much of the later legislation of Greece may go back to a far more ancient source. But the minute bureaucratic precision revealed by these clay documents, the official sealings and docketings, their signing and countersigning, are symptoms that speak for themselves of a highly elaborated system of legislation. In view of such evidence the legendary account of Minos, like another Moses or Hammurabi, receiving the law from the hands of the divinity himself on the Sacred Mountain, may well be taken to cover the actual existence of a code associated with the name of one of the old priest-kings of Crete.

Of ordered government we have the proof, and, in a not less striking degree, the evidence of extraordinary achievements in peaceful arts. The Palace traditionally built for Minos by his great craftsman Daedalos has proved to be no baseless fabric of the imagination. The marvellous works brought to light at Knossos and on other sites show moreover that the artistic skill associated with his name fell, if anything, short of the reality. At the same time the multiplicity of technical processes already mastered, the surprising advance in hydraulic and sanitary engineering—leaving Egypt for behind—bear witness to a considerable measure of attainment in the domain of science. Almost, we are tempted to believe in Talos "the mechanical man," or that a Cretan headland was the scene of the first experiment in aviation—the fatal flight of Ikaros!

That the word "Minoan" was used by the Greeks themselves in an ethnic or dynastic as well as a personal sense is shown by the constantly recurring term *Minoa* applied to traditional settlements from prehistoric Crete. In the neighbourhood of Gaza, the cult of the Cretan "Zeus" lived on into late classical times. The name attaches itself to towns, islands, and promontories not only in Crete itself but throughout the Aegean world. In Delos we find the "Minoid Nymphs." On the mainland of Greece itself the islet that guards the port of Megara, and a headland of Laconia, bear this appellation. It recurs in Corcyra. In Sicily, where of recent years a series of finds have come to light illustrative of a late offshoot of the Minoan civilization, the "Minoan" Herakleia bears witness to its abiding tradition. For it was said that Daedalos sought refuge on Sicilian shores, and that Minos himself, following with an ill-fated expedition, found a grave and sepulchral shrine near this westernmost Minoa.

The dynastic use of the word "Minos" may perhaps be compared with that of Pharaoh, originally signifying him of the "great house" (Per-o), and "Minoan" may thus be fairly paralleled with "Pharaonic" as a term for the dynastic civilization of Egypt. It seems certain that we must recognize in Minos the bearer of a divine title. He is of divine parentage and himself the progenitor of divine beings. Son of Zeus by Europa, herself, perhaps, an Earth-Goddess, wedded to Pasiphae, "the all-illuminating," father of Ariadne "the Most Holy"—Minos, in the last two relationships at least, was coupled with alternative forms of the Mother Goddess of pre-Hellenic Crete.

But this divine element in Minos has a special significance in view of a series of analogies supplied by the great religious centres of the geographically connected Anatolian regions. In these sanctuaries the priest not only represented the God, wore his dress, and wielded his authority, but often also bore his name. A most conspicuous instance of this is found in the case of Attis or Atys, whose chief-priest, the Archigallus, regularly took the same name. At Pessinus he was a priest-king. The divine nature of primitive kingship is of course almost universal. It is well illustrated indeed in the case of Egypt, whose Pharaohs took the titles of the "Great God," "the golden Horus," Son of the Sun-god (Ra), at times, Son of the Moon (Aah), or "engendered of Thoth," and so forth.

In Egypt, indeed, the royal and the priestly authority were kept somewhat apart, and the Temple overshadowed the Palace. In the Anatolian centres the royal and the sacerdotal abode was one and the same, and the palace was also a sanctuary. It is these last conditions that seem to have most nearly corresponded with those of Minoan Crete. The cumulative results of the exploration of the great building at Knossos have served more and more to bring out the fact that it was interpenetrated with religious elements. The constant appearance of the sacred double axe or "labrys" as a sign on its blocks, outnumbering all the other marks on the palace walls put together, and recurring on stucco and painted pottery, on seals, and in concrete shape on the altar of a shrine, is itself of special significance in connexion with the surviving traditions of the Labyrinth on this spot and the closely related Carian cult. The wall-paintings themselves have, in almost all cases, a religious connexion direct or indirect. It is now clear that a large part of the west wing of the palace was little more than a conglomeration of small shrines, of pillared crypts designed for ritual use, and corresponding halls above. The best preserved existing chamber, moreover, of this quarter, the "Room of the Throne," teems with religious suggestion. With its elaborately carved cathedral seat in the centre and stone benches round, the sacred griffins guarding on one side the entrance to an inner shrine, on the other the throne itself, and, opposite, approached by steps, its mysterious basin, it might well evoke the idea of a kind of consistory or chapter-house. A singularly dramatic touch, from the moment of final catastrophe, was here, indeed, supplied by the alabastra standing on the floor, beside the overturned oil-jar for their filling, with a view, we may infer, to some ceremony of anointing. It is impossible to withhold the conclusion that the "Room of the Throne" at Knossos was designed for religious functions.

That throughout its course Minoan civilization continued to absorb elements from the Asiatic side is, on the face of it, probable enough. This process was, in fact, the continuation of an early drift and infiltration, going back to the most primitive times, and to which probably the first acquaintance with metals was due. The cult of the Double Axe was, as we have seen, common to both areas, and there is a strong presumption that its original home is to be sought in that direction. Votive axes of terra-cotta, both double and single, were brought to light moreover during M. de Sarzec's excavations at the early Chaldaean site of Tello. The stone mace has the same wide easterly range. We have even a hint that the favourite bull-grappling sports of Minoan Crete, with their acrobatic features, had their counterparts in Cappadocia as early as 2400 B.C. The Early Minoan ivory seals in the shape of animals and the conoid types have also a wide Oriental distribution, and the "signet" form that survives into Middle Minoan times show a parallelism with certain Hittite seals. A few Cretan hieroglyphs also suggest Hittite comparisons.

Taking the data at our disposal as a whole there is little evidence of direct relations with the Easternmost Mediterranean shores before the close of the Middle Minoan Age. The Early Babylonian cylinder may indeed be regarded as an incipient symptom of such relations, and the fashion of flounced costumes may have owed its first suggestion to models from that side. Early in Late Minoan times a regular commercial intercourse was established with Cyprus and the neighbouring coastlands of North Syria and Cilicia, which was the prelude to actual colonization, eventually resulting in a distinct Cypro-Minoan School of Art. From the First Late Minoan Period onwards we trace the reflex of all this in many signs of Syrian influences. The clay tablets that form the vehicle of script continuously reflect Oriental models. That religious influences from Semitic sources were also beginning to operate is by no means improbable. Who shall say how early the old Chaldaean tradition of the legislator receiving the law from the God of the Mountain was implanted in Crete, as it had been in Israel? Of great significance, moreover, is the appearance in Cretan signets belonging to the closing part of the First Late Minoan Period of priestly figures, wearing long robes of oriental fashion, and bearing ceremonial axes of a typically Syrian form. It is clear, too, that chariots and thoroughbred horses together with their accoutrements reached the Minoan and Mycenaean princes from the same side. In the last Late Minoan Period, moreover, there occur bronze figurines of a male divinity with a peaked

headpiece which stand in a close relation to similar types from
North Syria and the Hittite regions. In all this, account must be
taken of the intermediary activities of the Keftiu people of the Egyptian Monuments.

But it must be clearly realized that the waves of higher civilizing
influences that ultimately reached Crete through Syria and Cyprus
from a more distant Mesopotamian source only affected Minoan
culture at a time when it had already reached a comparatively advanced stage. Neither were they able to penetrate as yet with effective results through the mountain ranges of the interior of Asia
Minor.

It cannot be gainsaid, indeed, that, as far as can be gathered from
the evidence before us, the civilization of the Eastern Aegean shores
at the close of the Neolithic Age stood on no higher level than that
of Crete. It could not give more than it possessed, and we must seek
on another side for the quickening spirit which about this time begins to permeate and transform the rude island culture.

In what direction then are we to look for this very early influence,
thanks to which, in the course of a few generations, the Cretans had
outstripped all their neighbours of the Aegean basin and evolved
the high early civilization to which the term "Minoan" is properly
applied?

That the main impulse came from the Egyptian side can no
longer now be doubted. Cumulative evidence, drawn from various
sides, to which attention will be called in the succeeding Sections,
shows that this influence was already making itself felt in Crete
in the Age that preceded the First Dynasty. Not only does it appear,
for instance, that stone vases of Pre-dynastic fabric were actually
reaching the island, but a whole series of Early Minoan forms can
be traced to prototypes in use by the "Old Race" of Egypt. In both
cases again we find the same aesthetic selection of materials distinguished by their polychromy, so that the beautifully coloured
vases of Mochlos find their best analogy in those of the prehistoric
tombs of Naqada rather than in those of the Early Dynastic Age.
Certain types of small images, the subjects and forms of seals, and
the game of draughts, go back to the same early Nilotic source.

That a maritime connexion between Crete and the Nile Valley
began already in very early times will surprise no one who recalls the
important part played by both rowing-galleys and sailing vessels in
the figured representations of the late Pre-dynastic Period in Egypt,
and the "Old Race" had already a Mediterranean outlet at the
Canopic mouth of the Nile. Models of boats, found in both Early
Minoan and Cycladic graves, show that the islanders themselves
were already filled with the sea-faring spirit. How comparatively
easy, indeed, under favourable circumstances, is the passage of the

Libyan Sea is shown by the fact that the sponge-fishing craft that touch on the east coast of Crete, manned at times with a crew of less than a dozen men, ply their industry as far as Benghazi. The Etesian winds of summer and accompanying current greatly aid this transit.

The proto-Egyptian element in Early Minoan Crete is, in fact, so clearly defined and is so intensive in its nature as almost to suggest something more than such a connexion as might have been brought about by primitive commerce. It may well, indeed, be asked whether, in the time of stress and change that marked the triumph of the dynastic element in the Nile Valley, some part of the older population then driven out may not have made an actual settlement on the soil of Crete.

Further waves of influence from the same side succeeded, in part due, it would seem, to some continued relations with members of the older indigenous stock of the Delta coasts, but now, in a progressive degree, to contact with the dynastic element in Egypt. Exquisite "carinated" bowls of diorite and other hard materials such as were executed for the Pharaohs of the Fourth and immediately succeeding dynasties found their way to the site of Knossos where they were imitated by the indigenous lapidaries and potters. In the darker period of Egyptian history that intervenes between the Sixth and Eleventh Dynasty this transmarine influence, as illustrated by the "button-seals" and leg amulets, takes again a character perhaps best described as "Egypto-Libyan." In the great days of the "Middle Kingdom" the purer Egyptian element once more asserts itself, and countless Nilotic models, among which the lotus and papyrus are very distiguishable, are henceforward assimilated by Minoan art. The most striking record of this connexion is the diorite monument of User, found in the Central Court of the Knossian Palace in a stratum belonging to the Second Middle Minoan Period. On the other hand, the counterpart of the evidence from Cretan soil is seen in the beautiful polychrome pottery of Middle Minoan fabric found at Kahum, Abydos, and elsewhere, in association with remains of the Twelfth and the early part of the Thirteenth Dynasty.

An astonishing series of discoveries recently made beneath the present sea-level off the former island of Pharos, at Alexandria, may place the relations of Ancient Egypt with the Minoan world in a wholly new light. The moles and wharves and capacious basins have now been traced out of a vast pre-Hellenic harbour, which rivals the Pyramids in its colossal construction.

That the intercourse with the Nile Valley was not broken off during the period of the Hyksos dominion is shown by the occurrence— again on the Palace site of Knossos, in a deposit belonging to the

earlier part of the Third Middle Minoan Period—of the alabastron
lid of King Khyan.

It was, however, during the early part of the Late Minoan Age in
Crete and of the New Empire in Egypt that these inter-relations
were most manifold in their complexion. The correspondence of
Egyptian and Minoan technique in metal-work is often such that it
is difficult to say on which side was the borrowing. Types, too, are
fused. The Egyptian griffin takes Minoan wings. The reproduction
of Nile scenes by Minoan artists is at times so accurate and detailed
as to convey the impression that guilds of Cretan craftsmen were
actually working at this time on Egyptian soil. The abundance there
of imported Late Minoan I vessels fits in, too, with a personal contact of another kind between the Minoan world and the Nile Valley
evidenced by the Egyptian representations of the People of the Isles
of the Sea and their offerings. In the latest Minoan epoch, when
Crete itself had become largely isolated through the decay of its sea-
power, the commercial relations with the Nile Valley for the most
part passed into the hands of the Cypriote and Mycenaean branch,
but this does not affect the main phenomenon with which we have
to do. This is the highly important historic fact, brought more clearly
into relief with every fresh discovery, that for some two thousand
years the Minoan civilization of Crete was in practically uninterrupted relations with that of Egypt.

The material evidence of interpenetration with Egyptian elements
cannot of course always give a clue to the more intangible influences
that may have been brought to bear in the domain of ideas—in
Cretan religion for instance, in law and government, or even in
literary tradition. That the elaborate systems of Minoan writing
were of independent evolution is certain, but there are good reasons,
for instance, to suspect the stimulus of Egyptian suggestion in the
rise of the Cretan hieroglyphic signary, and a few individual signs
seem to have been actually borrowed. The wearing of amulets of
Egyptian form, such as the leg-shaped pendants, shows a certain
community in popular superstition. The use of the Egyptian sistrum
for the ritual dance of the Hagia Triada vase is a very suggestive
symptom, and the adoption of a type of double-spouted libation
vessel associated, as it appears, with a primitive cult of Set and
Horus, may point to a very ancient religious connexion. In Late
Minoan times the evidences of a real religious syncretism accumulate—witness the constant recurrence of sphinxes and griffins and
the adoption of the Egyptian *waz* and *ankh* symbols, or of Hathoric
emblems like the cow suckling her calf. Ta-urt, the Hippopotamus
Goddess, becomes the prototype of Minoan Genii.

When it is realized how many elements drawn from the Minoan

world lived on in that of Hellas the full import of this very ancient
indebtedness to Egypt at once becomes apparent. Egyptian influences, hitherto reckoned as rather a secondary incident among late
classical experiences, are now seen to lie about the very cradle of
our civilization.

But the essential character of this influence must not be misunderstood. As regards Egypt, Minoan Crete did not find itself in the
position in which Palestine and Phoenicia, having only land frontiers, stood towards the great border powers of the Nile and of
the Euphrates. With the sea between, it could always keep the foreign civilization at arm's length. Its enterprising inhabitants continually absorbed and assimilated Egyptian forms and ideas,
developing them on independent lines. They took what they wanted,
nothing more, and were neither artistically nor politically en-
slaved.

The Egyptian relations, as above indicated, supply a certain measure, for the duration of the Minoan civilization. It has been already
suggested that the very pronounced Pre-dynastic element in Early
Minoan culture may connect itself with some actual exodus of part
of the older race of Nile-dwellers, due to the pressure of Menes'
conquest. Taking the accession of the First Dynasty as a rough
chronological guide to the beginning of the Minoan Age, and accepting provisionally Meyer's upper dating, we arrive at 3400 B.C. by a
century or more. The lowest term of anything that can be called pure
Minoan culture can hardly be brought down much below 1200 B.C.

For this considerable space of time, extending over some two
thousand two hundred years, the division here adopted into three
main Sections, the "Early," "Middle," and "Late" Minoan, each in
turn with three Periods of its own, will not be thought too minute.
It allows, in fact, for each Period an average duration of nearly two
centuries and a half, the earlier Periods being naturally the longer.
This triple division, indeed, whether we regard the course of the
Minoan civilization as a whole or its threefold stages, is in its very
essence logical and scientific. In every characteristic phase of culture we note in fact the period of rise, maturity, and decay. Even
within the limits of many of these Periods, moreover, the process
of evolution visible has established such distinct ceramic phases
that it has been found convenient to divide them into two sections
—a and b.

The three main phases of Minoan history roughly correspond
with those of the Early, the Middle, and the earlier part of the New
Kingdom in Egypt.

The Early Minoan Age, the beginning of which indeed seems to
overlap to a certain extent the close of the Pre-dynastic Age in Egypt,
supplies, in its middle Period (E. M. II), evidence of inter-relations

with the Egypt of the Fourth, Fifth, and Sixth Dynasties. Certain features that characterize its concluding Period (E. M. III), on the other hand, betray a contact with the quasi-Libyan elements that came to the fore in the Nile Valley during the troubled times that follow on to the Sixth Dynasty.

This Early Minoan Age, the beginnings of which are taken to include a phase of somewhat gradual transition, to which the name "Sub-Neolithic" may be given, must have extended over a relatively considerable space of time. The date of the accession of Menes, approximately fixed at 3400 B.C., has been taken above as supplying a rough *terminus a quo* for the beginning of this Age, while its lower limits would be about 2100 B.C.

This is an Age of gradual up-growth and of vigorous youth. The primitive culture of Crete now assumes its distinctive features. It works out its independence of the surrounding elements of wider geographical range from which it grew, and takes up a commanding position in the Aegean world. The great "hypogaea" at Knossos already foreshadow palatial arrangements.

Among its most characteristic products are the elegant stone vessels of choice and brilliantly variegated materials. The fabric of painted pottery with geometrical designs, first dark on light then light on dark, also makes considerable progress. Goldsmith's work attains a high degree of delicacy and perfection and, in this branch, as well as in the reliefs and engravings on soft stone and ivory, natural forms are at times successfully imitated. The seals show a gradual advance in pictographic expression.

The Middle Minoan Age covers the Period of the Middle Kingdom in Egypt including that of the Hyksos domination. Its first Period seems largely to coincide with that of the Eleventh Dynasty, overlapping, however, the first part of the Twelfth. Its acme, the Second Middle Minoan Period, is marked by a growing intimacy of relations with the Egypt of the Twelfth and Thirteenth Dynasty, while, in a stratum belonging to the concluding Middle Minoan III Period, occurred the alabastron lid of the Hyksos king Khyan. The chronological limits of this Age lie roughly between 2100 and 1580 B.C.

This is pre-eminently the Age of Palaces. The foundation of the great buildings at Knossos and Phaestos goes back to the close of Middle Minoan I *a*, or to shortly after 2100 B.C. The hierarchical position of the priest-kings was now consolidated. A true "Early Palace Style" had evolved itself by the end of Middle Minoan II— an epoch marked on both sites by a great catastrophe. It was followed in Middle Minoan III, however, by a monumental rebuilding and a spendid revival, leading up to the first era of expansion in mainland Greece, richly illustrated by the earliest elements in the Shaft Graves of Mycenae.

This is the Age of brilliant polychromy in ceramic decoration, and of the earliest wall-paintings. In its latest phase it is marked by an extraordinary development of naturalism in design. But what especially distinguishes this middle stage of Minoan culture is the final evolution of the art of writing from the mere pictography of the earlier periods. By Middle Minoan I we already see the full evolution of a hieroglyphic style. In Middle Minoan III, Class A of the Linear series has already taken its rise. To the same period belongs the "Phaistos Disk," but the characters differ from the Cretan and may best be ascribed to some related element in South-west Asia Minor.

The Late Minoan Age corresponds with the Eighteenth and Nineteenth Dynasties in Egypt, at most including the early part of the Twentieth. Its first and second periods would cover the reigns from Aahmes to Amenhotep III. The beginning of the mainland Late Minoan III stage is already illustrated by the earlier sherds of the "rubbish heaps" of Tell el Amarna of the time of Akhenaten and his immediate successors (c. 1370–1350 B.C.). By the thirteenth century Minoan and Mycenaean art was in full decadence, and it is difficult to believe that anything that can be described as pure Minoan culture is to be found in Crete later than the early part of Ramses III's reign.

Thus the time limits with which we have to deal for the Late Minoan Age lie approximately between 1580 and 1200 B.C.

The early part of this epoch, including the transitional phase which preserved the fine naturalistic style of Middle Minoan III, is the Golden Age of Crete, followed, after a level interval, by a gradual decline. The settlement already begun in Middle Minoan III of large tracts of mainland Greece is now continued, and the new Mycenaean culture is thus firmly planted on those shores. But the generation that witnessed this consummation saw also the final overthrow of the palace at Phaistos, and the brilliant sole dominion of remodelled Knossos that followed on this event was itself, after no long interval, cut short. The overthrow of the great palace took place at the close of the succeeding Late Minoan II Period, the result, according to the interpretation suggested below, of an internal uprising, apparently of "submerged" elements. It looks as if the mainland enterprise had been too exhausting. The centre of gravity of Minoan culture shifted now to the Mycenaean side. Finally, some hostile intrusion from the north, which is naturally to be connected with the first Greek invasions, drove away the indigenous settlers who had partially reoccupied or rebuilt the ruined sites at Knossos and elsewhere, and put an end to the last recuperative efforts of Minoan Crete. The culture of the succeeding Age when iron was coming into general use, though still largely permeated with indigenous elements, is

best described as "sub-Minoan," and lies beyond the immediate
scope of the present work.

The brilliant naturalism of the grand transitional epoch that
links the Middle with the Late Minoan Age reaches its acme in the
high reliefs of painted stucco at Knossos, in the frescoes of Hagia
Triada and such works as the "harvester" vase. The Court atmosphere at Knossos developed a greater formalism in art, well
illustrated by the ceramic designs in the later "Palace Style." Such
remains, however, as the "Room of the Throne" which dates from
the latter epoch, show the refinement in civilized surroundings then
attained. So too Class B of the linear script, now in vogue, and confined as far as is known to Knossos, represents the highest development of the Minoan system of writing. But the rococo spirit now
visible, and which, already in Late Minoan I, manifests itself in
the artificial groups of the Court ladies of the "Miniature" frescoes,
was a harbinger of the gradual decline that marks the course of the
last Minoan period.

The classification of the Minoan culture into nine successive
periods does not rest on merely theoretical deductions as to the
evolution and succession of types. In the case of the excavations
at Knossos a constant endeavour has been made to apply geological
methods, so that the sequence here adopted rests on a mass of
stratigraphical evidence. In such evidence, as indeed in that afforded
by geological strata, the succession of deposits in individual cases
presents lacunae which have to be filled up from data supplied
by other sections. Only, moreover, by considerable experience has
it been possible to guard against certain subtle causes of error, such
as, for instance, the total removal of a floor belonging to one construction and its substitution by another on the same level. In order
to revise the evidence, largely with a view to the present study, three
months of the year 1913 were devoted by me, as already mentioned,
to supplementary excavations on the palace site, in the course of
which about ninety explorations were made beneath the floors at
various spots. The result has been, while correcting some individual
errors in previous reports, to corroborate the results already obtained as to the general classification of the successive periods.

A good section resulting from the excavation of a part of the
west court of the Knossian palace shows how great a relative depth
is occupied by the Neolithic deposit, though in a neighbouring pit
it was even greater. The three Early Minoan periods were represented by distinct layers. Above these was a definite flooring, and
at this point occurred one of the lacunae in the evidence referred
to above. The First Middle Minoan period was not represented, the
floor having probably been in continuous use. In a contiguous area,
however, this gap is fully supplied. Otherwise the succession of the

Minoan periods is here complete up to the pavement of the court, laid down in Late Minoan I. Above this point the deposit was of a more unstratified nature, containing remains of the Late Minoan II and Late Minoan III periods.

The evidence supplied by the stratification of the successive cultural deposits at Knossos is more complete than that on any other Cretan site. Its general results, however, have been corroborated by the careful researches of fellow explorers on other Cretan sites, though special allowances have in these cases to be made for local conditions. Thus in great residential centres like Knossos or Phaistos changes in fashion had a tendency to set in somewhat earlier than in more remote provincial localities and to attain a more characteristic development. In the East of Crete the First Middle Minoan style shows a tendency to persist, while, on the other hand, the mature class of polychrome ware in what may be called the earlier "Palace Style" becomes decidedly sparser away from the great centres. At Palaikastro, for instance, there was a tendency, as Mr. Dawkins has observed, for the older Middle Minoan I traditions to survive to the borders of Middle Minoan III. So, too, the later "Palace Style" of Late Minoan II is the special product of Knossos, and its place elsewhere is not infrequently taken by somewhat degenerate versions of Late Minoan I types. These considerations must always be borne in mind, but the best standard of classification is clearly to be sought on the site which supplies the most complete succession of links in the long chain of evolution.

To take one important centre like Knossos as the norm for such a stratificatory classification of the Minoan periods is advisable for another reason. Regarded as a whole, the successive human strata on a given site show in each case a certain uniformity wherever struck.

This is notably the case at Knossos, where we repeatedly find floor levels exposed in various parts of the site which exhibit a parallel series of ceramic or other remains. Such uniformity of deposit must be taken to mark a widespread change or catastrophe at the epoch to which it belongs, and recurring strata of this kind may be reasonably regarded as so many landmarks of successive historic stages.

When, again, a stratum containing ceramic or other remains of the same epoch is found to be of widespread occurrence on two or more important sites it may be taken as an indication of some general catastrophe, affecting, probably, the whole of Minoan Crete. The most striking instance of this is the evidence supplied by a well-marked deposit at Knossos and Phaistos characterized by an abundance of Middle Minoan II pottery in the same advanced stage and pointing to a more or less contemporary destruction.

   All such stratigraphical demarcations are of their nature somewhat arbitrary and any idea of Minoan civilization as divided into
so many distinct compartments must be dismissed from the minds
of students. All is, in fact, transition. What has been said above must
again be repeated. From the earliest Minoan stage to the latest there
is no real break such as might be naturally explained by conquest
from abroad. Crude foreign elements, indeed, appear at intervals,
but they are rapidly absorbed and assimilated. There are checks, it
is true, and intervals of comparative stagnation, but though its
pace occasionally varies, the course of evolution is still continuous.
One form merges into another by imperceptible gradations and
where, as is the case with a large part of the material, an object
is derived from an unstratified deposit it is at times difficult, in
default of direct evidence, to decide on which side of a more or less
artificial dividing line it should be placed. On such individual questions opinions must constantly differ. But the classification of the
Minoan Age into its Early, Middle, and Late stages, and the corresponding division of each into three periods, finds its justification
both in logic and utility.

ARTHUR EVANS

Scenes from Minoan Life

Town Houses

THE evidence from the site of Knossos discussed in the preceding
sections that relate to the acme of the Early Palace civilization has
been mainly concerned with the inner life and structural features of
the palace itself. But the remarkable remains of a faience mosaic
found on the northern border of the "Loom-Weight Basements" has
afforded an actual glimpse of a Minoan town of this epoch, situated,
moreover, it would appear, in close proximity to the sea.

Ibid., Vols. I-IV, 1921-35. "Town Houses" from Vol. I, pp. 301-3.

From the soft, perishable nature of the material, most of these inlays were in a very fragmentary state. The existing remains, striking as they are, can only represent a small proportion of the original mosaic. It is clear that many of them had been repeated from the same mould.

The central feature, as already noted, consisted of the towers and houses of a fortified town. There were, however, also abundant remains of inlays of another class, trees and water, goats and oxen, marching warriors, spearmen and archers, arms and equipments, the prow apparently of a ship, and curious negroid figures. It is suggested below that we have here the remains of a siege-scene analogous to that on the silver rhyton from Mycenae.

Unexpected as have been many of the revelations of this ancient Cretan culture the appearance of these house façades with their two and three stories and roof attics and their windows of four and even six panes of a date not later, probably, than the last half of the eighteenth century B.C. is perhaps the most astonishing. In view of the generally grandiose character of the Palace itself, the indications in it of upper stories appear natural enough. But in the houses of the mosaic we can hardly fail to recognize the dwellings of the ordinary Minoan citizens. That these should have already attained the tall proportions of a modern street-front points surely back to long generations of civic life. [Windows with wooden frames, probably similar to those pictured on the mosaic, have been discovered in the palace.]

That windows with four or even six panes, containing some substitute for window glass, should have already existed at this time is itself only another proof of the extraordinary anticipation of modern civilized usage achieved in the great days of Minoan history—an anticipation not less marked in their hydraulic and sanitary appliances. The house-fronts are clearly those of town houses, adapted to standing in rows.

The Grand Staircase of the Palace

It was in working south from the last section of the Corridor of the Bays, and thus through a blocked doorway to a threshold beyond, that the course of excavation on the palace site of Knossos took its most dramatic turn. Immediately in front of the doorway appeared the ascending steps of a flight of stairs, flanked by a stone parapet with the socketed bases of carbonized wooden columns. A couple of paces to the right, on the other hand, the paved surface

—hitherto regarded as the ground-level of this part of the building
—suddenly began to step down, and turned out to be the landing
of a descending flight of twelve steps. This led to another landing,
stepping down to a third, from which, at right angles to the left,
the head of a lower flight came into view. . . .

This part of the excavation proved to be altogether miner's work
owing to the risk of bringing down the stairway above, and necessitated a constant succession of wooden props. It was therefore a
happy circumstance that two of the workmen had worked in the
Laurion mines. Eight days of dangerous tunnelling brought us
beyond the second landing, down another flight of twelve steps,
to what, after long additional excavation, proved to be a columnar
court lighting the successive flights of the grand staircase. . . .

It would seem that the debris due to the falling in of masses of
sun-dried bricks from the upper stories had infiltrated (partly owing
to the subsequent solution of the clay) into the covered part of the
building below, and thus led to the formation of a compact filling
which had held up the floors and terraces above. The wooden
columns themselves seem to have for the most part survived awhile
in an unburnt condition. Later on, however, when owing to the
result of chemical action they had become carbonized, their function of supporting the incumbent structures above had been taken
up by this natural concretion of the fallen materials. Only in the
case of their wooden architraves and the transverse beams that
traversed the walls the carbonizing process left a certain void,
usually involving a subsidence of the overlying structures to that
extent.

Except for this slight lowering of level, however, almost the
whole floor of the first story, including pavements and door-jambs,
was found *in situ* throughout this Quarter, to a degree that seemed
little short of miraculous. But to profit by this fortunate circumstance
and to preserve the upper remains, hung thus as it were suspended,
while at the same time to lay bare the lower halls and chambers
involved a task such as never before probably has confronted excavators. It was necessary by provisional means to prop up the
upper structures while substituting more permanent materials for
the carbonized posts and columns. Simultaneously the great transverse beams, many of them 40 cm. thick, were replaced by girders
embedded in concrete, and for this part of the work the collapsed
masonry that they had supported, often weighing several tons, had
to be carefully removed block by block and replaced at its original
level. . . . Throughout the greater part of this area, indeed, the
evidence went far beyond the existence of a single upper story. It
seems certain that in the inner bay of the domestic quarter, at any

rate, there were at least three stories. In the case of the grand staircase it was possible actually to restore five flights, the uppermost
rising above the level of the central court.

The scientific skill and harmonious disposition displayed by the
structures of this quarter, the felicitous compactness of their arrangement, centring as it were round the inner private staircase,
represents a development of domestic architecture for which we
may look in vain for a parallel in Egypt or Chaldaea or any other
Oriental country. In many of its aspects, indeed, it is more modern
than anything that has come down to us from ancient Greece or
Rome.

The Mother Goddess and the Double Axe

THE Mother Goddess in her various aspects and with her various
attributes was the supreme deity of the Minoans. Her worship can
probably be traced back through Anatolia to Asiatic origins (see
also p. 127, II).

A WINDOWED structure with these sacred emblems [double axes],
served in the Mycenae wall-paintings described above as a kind of
"royal box" for lady spectators of circus sports with trained bulls
and acrobats. Among the fragments associated with those showing
the Knossian pillar shrine was one depicting dense crowds of
spectators in a walled enclosure and with it, on a larger scale, the
head of a swarthy bull and parts of the flowing locks of an acrobatic
figure. We have here new proofs of the near connexion between
the cult of the Minoan Goddess of which the Double Axes are the
outward symbols, and the bull-grappling sports.

The animal forms of the Minoan Goddess were manifold. Her
visible presence is often indicated by perched doves, as in the early
columnar sanctuary. On the painted sarcophagus they are replaced
by birds of raven-like appearance. Lions and pards are also seen in
close association, and, as we know from the contents of the temple
repositories described below, spotted snakes were her peculiar
emblem in her chthonic aspect as Lady of the Underworld.

But, taken in connexion with the traces of Minoan religion in its
prevailing aspect, not at Knossos alone, but throughout the length
and breadth of Crete, it is clear that the special aniconic form of
the supreme Minoan divinity, as of her male satellite, was the

Double Axe. The palace sanctuary itself was pre-eminently the
House of the Double Axe, and the sacred symbol formed the centre
of domestic cult in countless smaller dwellings. Even in the days
of the last Minoan decadence, when the ruins of Knossos were in
part made use of by humbler occupants, the cult of the Lady of the
Double Axe was perpetuated on the spot, and the sacral weapons
themselves found a place in her little shrine brought to light in
the south-east quarter of the site. The scene on the Sarcophagus
of Hagia Triada, however, in which, by ritual offerings before the
sacred symbols, the deceased hero is restored awhile to the upper
air, may incline us to believe that the cult of deceased and heroized
members of the line of Minoan priest-kings was associated with
that of their divine Mistress in the palace sanctuary of Knossos.

The Mother Goddess and the Snakes

THE faience figurines of the Snake Goddess and the votary date
from the Middle Minoan period (probably *c.* 1600 B.C.), and were
found in the temple repositories of the palace of Knossos. This
divinity represented the Goddess in her domestic, household aspect.
Household snakes were regarded as beneficent (p. 128, II).

THE central figure of the shrine was a Goddess—apparently the
Under-World form of the great Minoan Goddess—with a triple
group of spotted snakes twined about her. Her figure, as reconsti-
tuted, is 34.2 centimetres (13½ inches) in height. She wears a high
tiara of a purplish-brown colour with a white border, a necklace,
and a dress to be more fully described below, consisting of a richly
embroidered bodice with a laced corsage, and a skirt with a kind
of short double apron. Her hair, cut square in a fringe above her
forehead, falls behind her neck and on to her shoulders; her eyes
are black, as also her eyebrows, which are given in relief, and her
ears, partly owing to the snaky coils that surround them, appear
to be of abnormal size. Her breasts, which are almost entirely bare,
are of matronly proportions. The ground colour of the whole, including the flesh tint, is generally a milky white, the various details
being laid on in purple, purplish-brown, or black.

About the Goddess are coiled three snakes with greenish bodies
spotted with purple-brown. The head of one of these she holds out
in her right hand, its body follows the arm upwards, then descends

Ibid., Vol. I, pp. 500-3, 508-9, 510.

behind the shoulders, and ascends again to the left arm, which held
the tail. Round the hips of the Goddess, below the waist, and forming her girdle, two other snakes are interlaced. One of these, whose
head appears in the centre of this serpentine girdle, is continued
in a festoon down the front of the apron, and, thence ascending
along the edge of the bodice to the neck, coils its tail round the
Goddess's right ear. Finally, a third snake, whose tail-end forms
part of the plaitwork about the hips, runs up along the left fringe
of the bodice over the left ear and coils up round the tiara, from
the summit of which its head originally projected. . . . With the
Goddess were remains of two other figures. Of these the best preserved . . . is somewhat smaller than the other, and it seems probable from her attitude that she should rather be regarded as a
priestess or votary.

The hair, longer than that of the other figure, falls down behind
her to her hips. Though she is altogether slimmer than the Goddess,
her breasts, which are bare, are prominent . . . She wears a bracelet round the wrist of her right arm which holds out a small snake,
tail upwards. The left forearm is wanting, but doubtless also held
out a snake in a similar position. The skin here is pure white, the
bodice a dark orange with purplish-brown bands, and the rest of
the dress shows designs of the same purplish-brown on a pale
ground.

. . . The votary wears a skirt of many flounces over which is the
same double apron and the sleeved bodice, cut away so as to
expose the bosom and laced in front. Round her waist in place of
the snakes is what appears to be a tight-fitting metal belt into which
the lower border of the bodice is tucked. The lines adopted are
those considered ideal by the modern corset-maker rather than the
sculptor, and the effect is that of a fashionable Court lady.

The double apron, which in fact represents a primitive garb
common to both sexes, may perhaps be regarded as a ritual survival.
But the costume on the whole must be that of the epoch to which
these works belong. Two features that mark late Minoan fashions
are here absent—the chemise, the upper border of which is seen
beneath the neck, and the V-shaped arrangement of the flounces—
in itself suggestive of a divided skirt.

Of the latest Minoan epoch is the little shrine found at Gournia,
which contained a rude female idol rising from a cylinder below,
with a serpent coiling about her waist and over one of her raised
arms. With this, together with other cult objects, are bases, tapering
upwards and set with Sacral Horns, above which other serpents
raise their heads. Parallel with these relics and clearly contemporary
with them are the remains of similar clay objects found at Prinias,
where the female figures have snakes trailing along their forearms

like the faience Goddess of the Palace Shrine. The Gournia group is
of special interest, since there the relics dedicated to the snake cult
are associated with small clay figures of doves and a relief showing
the Double Axe.

These conjunctions are singularly illuminating since they reveal
the fact that the Snake Goddess herself represents only another aspect of the Minoan Lady of the Dove, while the Double Axe itself was
connected with both. Just as the celestial inspiration descends in
bird form either on the image of the divinity itself or on that of its
votary, or in other cases, as we have seen, upon its aniconic
columnar shape, so the spirit of the Nether World, in serpent form,
makes its ascent to a similar position from the earth itself. Nor need
this manifestation of the chthonic side of the divinity be invested
with any malignant significance. It has on the contrary a friendly
and domestic aspect with which those acquainted with primitive
ideas as they still exist on European soil must be very familiar. In
many peasant dwellings the snake, with his love of warmth which
leads him to find some cranny near the hearth, is regarded, as of old,
as a kind of good genius. To my own knowledge in Herzegovina and
the Serbian lands, East of the Adriatic, it was not an uncommon
thing for snakes, who had sought such human hospitality, to be
fed with milk and treated as domestic pets. Such a household snake
is known, indeed, as *domachitsa* or "housemother."

In its homely origin, from the religious tending of the household
snake, the cult itself may be supposed to be of old indigenous tradition. At the same time the exceptional prominence of a similar cult
in the Western Delta can hardly be left out of account. That there
was at any rate a reaction of this Nilotic cult on that of the Minoan
chthonic Goddess as finally evolved is clear from more than one
feature in her attributes and symbolism.

The snake raising its head above the tiara of the Goddess of the
Knossian shrine itself curiously recalls the uraeus in similar positions on the head of Hathor and other Egyptian Goddesses. The
Delta Goddess Wazet, in many respects the double of Hathor, the
mother of Horus, and identified in later times with Isis, could herself take the form of a serpent, and an uraeus snake is seen entwined
about her papyrus sceptre. The latter symbol of the Goddess, moreover, the *waz*, in its simpler form a papyrus stem, has been already
shown by a curious catena of evidence to have played a special part
among the borrowed materials of Cretan decorative art. Early in the
Middle Minoan Age we have seen the *waz* symbol and associated
canopy taken over as a type of Cretan signets, not, we may imagine,
without some sense of religious sanction. In derivative shapes it
continues to fulfil these sphragistic functions to the borders of the
Late Minoan Age and is interwoven with a series of fantastic seal-

types of the Zakro class. As incorporated in a decorative band we meet it again on the pedestal of a columnar lamp from the pillar crypt of the south-east house at Knossos, and it inspires a whole series of ornamental designs in Late Minoan frescoes and vase paintings. An influence productive of such continuous results cannot be lightly set aside. Considering the very ancient and intimate relations of Crete with the Nile Valley—going back to the Pre-dynastic Age, and not improbably marked by the actual settlement in the island of Egypto-Libyan elements—it was natural that the great Delta Goddess, whose chosen haunt was the papyrus thickets of Buto, should have impressed herself in an exceptional degree on the Minoan religious imagination.

How much of the spiritual being of the Egyptian Mother Goddess may not have been absorbed by her Minoan sister? How much indeed of the later traditions of Rhea and the infant Zeus may not go back to a far earlier acclimatization of the legends and the cult of Isis and Horus?

The Mother Goddess and Her Swing

PHAISTOS was situated in the southern, Mesara, region of Crete. It, too, was the site of a Minoan palace, but its rulers became subject to the supreme power of Knossos.

A REMARKABLE find made in a Phaistos shrine must be taken to show that the Minoan Goddess took delight in a much more simple, not to say childish diversion. In a deposit explored by the Italian Mission, probably belonging to a small domestic shrine like that of Gournià, was found a small female statuette, with red decoration on a white wash, in a half sitting position and bored for the insertion of a bar. With it lay remains of two posts like truncated obelisks in their general form and perforated, near their apex. It has thus needed only a little thread to restore—as has been done in the Museum of Candia—the whole group into a figure on a swing. The thread is attached to a miniature bar that serves as a seat.

The two side-posts are of special interest since they afford a near parallel to the columns of the early terra-cotta shrine from Knossos with the doves perched on their capitals, and to the palm trunks on either side of the Double Axes surmounted by birds of raven-like aspect. The settled birds that here too impersonate the alighting of

Ibid., Vol. IV, pp. 24-8.

the divine Spirit on to the baetylic pillars, though imperfectly preserved, are in this case, too, marked as doves by the remains of
one fan-tail. These settled birds define the two supports as of a
religious nature, and carry with them the conclusion that the
swinging figure was *ipso facto* possessed by the spirit of the divinity.
The archetype would clearly be the Goddess herself enjoying the
same pastime.

TERRA-COTTA REPRESENTATION OF VOTARY
SWINGING BETWEEN TWO POSTS WITH DOVES PERCHED ON THEM
AS A SIGN OF DIVINE POSSESSION

Swinging, practised as a magical and eventually a religious rite, is
known the world over. Various objects for this exercise are cited
—swinging high might produce high crops, demons could be
driven from the air, or the inspiration of spirits drawn from it. The
Attic feast of the Aiora celebrated the ripening of the grapes, and it
is noteworthy that Ikaros, the eponymus of the Deme Ikarià, to
whom, with his daughter Erigone "Child of the Spring," its origins
were ascribed, represents the pre-Hellenic, or in other words, the
Minoan, element in the population. This swinging ceremony is
further connected with the Anthesteria—the "All Souls" feast of
Ancient Greece. On vases, where Satyrs are seen swinging a Nymph,
there appears a large open rim below, like that of a large jar, such as

those from which, as is shown on a lekythos, the little ghosts or *Keres* fly out.

In Modern Greece and in Crete itself the ceremonial swinging of girls takes place on the occasion of various festivals including Easter and St. George's day.

To the Minoans, familiar with the representations of divinities descending from on high with streaming locks, the act of swinging in the air may itself have had a celestial association and might be thought to bring with it the "afflatus" of spiritual possession.

Whether the Goddess herself is to be recognized in the swinging figure before us or, as seems more probable, her votary, it is clear that she could be envisaged as herself taking delight in this airy pastime.

Might she not equally be regarded as taking part in the acrobatic feats of the arena? No impersonation of her under this aspect indeed had been hitherto brought to light. In any case it stands to reason that for such a function it would have been necessary for her to assume a special garb.

Apart from the early version of the Cretan Goddess as mothernaked inherited from Neolithic times and never, as we shall see, wholly discarded—from the beginning of the Middle Minoan Age onwards, whether in her plastic or her pictorial shape, she is consistently presented to us as following the latest styles in dress. Even the more or less cylindrical form of the lower part of the images found in her rustic shrines of the beginning of the Late Minoan Age as explored at Gournia and Prinia can be shown to be really an outgrowth of the bell-shaped skirts that were in vogue in Middle Minoan I and II. On the other hand, the splendidly executed figurines of ivory or faience from palatial shrines display in their elaborate details every item in the fashionable dress of the Court ladies of the transitional Middle Minoan III—Late Minoan I Epoch. They are seen wearing flounced skirts, shorter according to the current usage in the earlier part of that epoch, longer as a rule in the later phase and the succeeding Late Minoan Periods. Above the belt is a close-fitting, short-sleeved bodice supporting the full breasts.

So, too, among the many known impersonations of the Goddess, as seen on signet-rings and bead-seals, whatever her activities may be, she has regularly made her appearance decked out thus in the fashionable dress of contemporary female society. Her robes are as stylish when she hunts the stag or shoulders a wild-goat, as when she is receiving the adoration of her votaries. In a similar guise she is seen descending from her celestial abode, and so, too, when, assisted by a courtly attendant in her resurgence from the Underworld, she emerges from the bosom of the earth as Goddess of Spring, we see her already flounced and corseted.

It is abundantly evident that the Goddess stood in a peculiarly intimate relation to the sports of the arena, beside which, as we have seen, her columnar shrine was set up. In view of the agility displayed by her in the hunting field and apparent delight in high swinging, it might well indeed be thought by her worshippers that, in some diviner sphere, she had herself supplied an example of superhuman prowess as a taureador. It is clear, however, that the flounced attire which the Minoan artists had somehow reconciled with her other activities, was wholly incompatible with acrobatic feats.

Sport with Bulls

THERE is now a difference of opinion as to how far the famous Cretan bull-leaping, shown in many different art forms, was a sport, how far a religious rite. It may have become increasingly secularized, but there can be no doubt that there was an underlying religious significance.

THE designs [of the "Taureador Frescoes"] were originally distributed in several panels, and in the case of one of these it was possible to restore the whole composition. Here, besides the male performer, of the usual ruddy hue, who is turning a back-somersault above the bull, are two female taureadors, distinguished not only by their white skin but by their more ornamental attire. Their loincloth and girdle is identical with that of the man but of more variegated hue: his is plain yellow, theirs are decorated with black stripes and bars. They wear bands round their wrists and double necklaces—one of them beaded—and, in the case of some of the figures, blue and red ribbons round their brows. But perhaps their most distinctive feature is the symmetrical arrangement of short curls over their foreheads and temples, already noticed in the case of the female "cow-boy" of the Vapheio cup. . . . Their foot-gear consist of short gaiters or stockings and pointed mocassin-like shoes.

The girl acrobat in front seizes the horns of a coursing bull at full gallop, one of which seems to run under her left armpit. The object of her grip seems to be to gain a purchase for a backward somersault over the animal's back, such as is being performed by the boy. The second female performer behind stretches out both her hands as if about to catch the flying figure or at least to steady him when he comes to earth the right way up. The stationing of this figure handy for such an act raises some curious questions as to the arrangements within the arena.

Apart from this, certain features in the design have provoked the scepticism of experts acquainted with modern "Rodeo" performances. A veteran in "Steer-wrestling," consulted by Professor Baldwin Brown, was of opinion that any one who had anything to do with that sport would pronounce the endeavour to seize the bull's horns as a start for a somersault as quite impossible "for there is no chance of a human person being able to obtain a balance when the bull is charging full against him." The bull, as he further remarked, has three times the strength of a steer, and when running "raises his head sideways and gores any one in front of him."

"That a somersault was performed over the back of a charging bull seems evident and does not seem to present much difficulty, but surely if the bull were at full gallop the athlete would not alight on its back, but on the ground well behind it?"

All that can be said is that the performance as featured by the Minoan artist seems to be of a kind pronounced impossible by modern champions of the sport. The fresco design does not stand alone, and the successive acts that it seems to imply find at least partial confirmation in a clay seal-impression and in the bronze group where the acrobatic feat is illustrated by the diagrammatic figure.

But if the feat as thus logically developed would seem to transcend human skill, it is equally true that such scenes as are illustrated by a series of scenes on gems in which the bull wrestler seems to lift the whole mighty beast, are no less on a superhuman scale. At the same time they can be matched in this by the intaglio type given above, where the hero, armed as he is with a dirk, grips the lion's neck with his left hand.

All old African hunters know that such personal contact with a lion means nothing less than death.

The apparent action of throwing an arm over a bull's horn rather than actually gripping it is illustrated by another spirited fragment of this group of frescoes. The right hand of the female acrobat does not here seize the horn, though thrown over it, but is tightly clenched, as the result of extreme physical tension. An interesting analogy to this is supplied by the fragment of a high relief, where the hand is seen over the tip of a bull's horn similarly clenched.

Polychrome faience statuette of a Snake Goddess from the Palace of Minos at Knossos, Crete. The Great Goddess was the principal divinity of the Minoans, and the Lady of the Snakes probably represents one of her many aspects. *C.* 1600 B.C.

Small bronze statuette that gives a vigorous impression of the ritualistic bull-leaping game of the Minoans. The bronze comes from Crete, but the exact finding place is unknown.

Flying fish from the Palace of Knossos, Crete. The little faience plaques illustrate the Minoans' love of nature and the light-hearted spirit of their decorative arts. *C.* 1600 B.C.

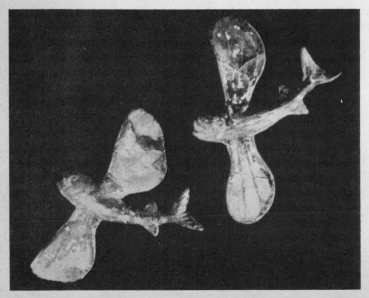

The Grand Staircase of the Palace of Minos at Knossos as reconstructed by Sir Arthur Evans. The wooden column shafts are painted red. The Palace was destroyed in about 1400 B.C.

The Throne Room of the Palace of Minos. The throne is of gypsum, and the frescoes, which show wingless griffins, are painted in green, red and blue. Probably a little before 1400 B.C.

The famous Lion Gate leading into the city of Mycenae, near Argos, Greece. The circular wall enclosing the Shaft Graves can be seen inside the gate. The Lion Gate probably dates from the fourteenth century B.C., the Shaft Graves from the sixteenth.

UPPER RIGHT: One of the gold masks that covered the faces of the dead kings buried in the Shaft Graves at Mycenae. From Grave IV, sixteenth century B.C.

LOWER RIGHT: A pot painted with octopuses and other sea creatures. Vessels of this form, known as stirrup jars, were probably used for olive oil, and were popular among the Mycenaeans after the fall of Knossos. 1230-1135 B.C.

IV

VI

A fond Etruscan couple portrayed in terracotta on the lid of a sarcophagus. Probably from Caere. 650-600 B.C.

LEFT: Late Hittite sculpture at Ivriz, on the north side of the Taurus mountains, Turkey. Urpalla, a prince of Tabal, is paying tribute to the god Tarhundas. C. 740 B.C.

An Etruscan chariot, of wood sheathed with embossed bronze, from Monteleone. Sixth century B.C.

A warrior, with a swan-crested helmet, releasing an arrow over his horse's tail. The Etruscan artist was probably portraying a Scythian rider. One of four figures on the lid of a large bronze vessel from Campagnia. *C.* 500 B.C.

It is clear that this painted relief fragment, found in the deposit of high reliefs described below, represents part of an acrobatic figure, in this case, as the red colouring shows, a man, with his arm thrown over the bull's horn and his hand not grasping it but clenched in a similar way.

In the delicately executed design, the fine lines of which recall the designs on white Athenian *lekythoi*—another female figure is seen in the act of leaping, with flying tresses, one arm held downwards and the other raised. A noteworthy feature in this representation is the strap, wound not only round the wrist but round parts of the hand. This form of *cestus* obviously had nothing to do with striking a blow, and must have been rather devised to give strength to the muscles and tendons. It recurs on the hand of the youth who is depicted flying through the air, as if in the act of alighting behind a galloping steer, whose hind legs appear below. Acrobatic feats of the same kind as the above are still said to be performed in some Portuguese *corridas*.

These highly sensational episodes are primarily exhibitions of acrobatic skill. In this respect, as already noted, they differ from the parallel performances of the Minoan cow-boys, the aim of which was rather the catching of wild or half-wild animals. That girls actually took part in this more practical side of the sport, as occasionally in the "Wild West" of America to-day, has been shown from a scene on a Vapheio Cup, but the elegance and ornaments of the female acrobats shown in the "Taureador Frescoes" belong to a different sphere. The ribbons and beaded necklaces are quite out of place in rock-set glens or woodland glades. To the palace circus they are more appropriate. The animals themselves were no doubt carefully trained. Like the bulls of the Spanish arenas they may often have been of established pedigree and reared in special herds or *ganaderias*. It is clear that in all these scenes the attention of the Minoan artist is largely centred on the animal itself, which is rendered of disproportionate size, as befitting what was to them evidently quite as much as the lion, the King of Beasts.

That the particular feat, in which a tumbler executes a back-somersault over the bull's body, to be caught by another performer behind, already formed part of the programme of the shows before the close of the Third Middle Minoan Period is attested by a clay sealing found in the Temple Repositories. A figure here turns a somersault from the beast's neck while a second behind, apparently intended for a girl, raises an arm as if to catch the other. On an agate intaglio of somewhat later date we see a curious version of a similar scene as adapted to the filling of a circular space. There are here two galloping bulls, over the back of one of which the youth turns a somersault, in this case facing towards the bull's tail. The figure behind, in which again we may recognize a girl, is placed upside down, owing to the exigencies of the circular border, and has the appearance of standing in front of the other charging animal. She holds out both hands, however, in the same manner as the figure behind the bull in the fresco.

The acrobat turning either a back-somersault or a somersault with his face towards the animal's tail occurs on a series of intaglios and sealings. At times the performer is about to gain renewed purchase off the bull's hind quarters. In another case he lands hands forward. A very fine example of this class is to be seen in the design of a gold signet-ring, recently discovered in a chamber

ACROBAT EXECUTING BACKSOMERSAULT,
TO BE CAUGHT BY FIGURE BEHIND.
TEMPLE REPOSITORY, KNOSSOS.

tomb near Arkhanes, a country town South of the site of Knossos. This, indeed, has a double interest not only as showing in front of the bull a "Sacral Knot," which brings the performance into a religious and ceremonial relation, but as indicating beneath the animal, here depicted at a flying gallop, a stepped base with iso-domic masonry. This feature, according to the conclusion drawn from other similar cases, points to a painted stucco original, per-haps in relief, on the walls of some building.

But the most remarkable illustration of such feats has now been supplied by the bronze group from Crete in the Collection of Cap-tain E. G. Spencer-Churchill. It has been already referred to above in relation to the silver figurine of a galloping bull borne by a tributary from Keftiu in the wall-painting of the Tomb of User-Amon at Thebes. This, like another representation of a standing figurine of a bull shown among these tributary gifts, attests the high esteem in which the contemporary works of Minoan toreutic Art were held by the Egyptians.

. . . That this [bronze group] represents a youth and not a girl is clear from the absence alike of formal curls or of any signs of pectoral development. The bull is splendidly modelled and the whole group, cast solid in one piece, represents the acme of Minoan metallurgic art. It is noteworthy, however, that to simplify his task the craftsman has stumped off the boy's arms at the elbows and that his head is supported in its bent-back position by the attachment of his thick flowing locks to the upper part of the bull's forehead. It was necessary to resort to this expedient to give a second support to the figure of the boy, supposed to be in the act of revolution and gaining a purchase from the animal's back by means of his feet. The hands had already released their hold of the horns and the arms could not therefore be legitimately used for attachment.

At the same time the arms, with a backward direction after losing contact with the bull's head, would have crossed the line of the connecting stem formed by the youth's hair, and this complication of the design was clearly beyond the artificer's powers. He therefore solved the difficulty by stumping off the arms at the elbows.

The idea of the performance as here conceived by the modeller of this bronze group seems to have been essentially the same as that of the fresco painter. This design, indeed, fits on to the whole series of gem types such as those illustrated above and involving three separate actions—the seizure of the horns, the landing over the head, and the final somersault behind, where timely assistance is rendered by an attendant figure.

The first part of this acrobatic cycle, as thus logically conceived, has rightly been shown to transcend the power and skill of mortal man. It may be yet worth while here to repeat a diagrammatic sketch showing the successive evolutions of the acrobatic performer as they seem to have been imaged by the Minoan artist.

(1) Shows the charging bull seized by the horns near their tips.

(2) The bull has raised his head in the endeavour to toss his assailant, and at the same time gives an impetus to the turning figure.

(3) The acrobat has released his grip of the horns, and after completing a back-somersault has landed with his feet on the hinder part of the bull's back. This is the moment in the performance of which a representation is attempted in the bronze group, but the upper part of the body is there drawn much farther back and dangerously near the bull's head, owing to the technical necessity of using the bunched locks of hair as a support.

In (4) he makes a final leap from the hind quarters of the bull—a risky plunge.

DIAGRAMMATIC SKETCH OF ACROBAT'S COURSE

Was he caught, as the youth on the fresco, by the girl performer so conveniently posted? Or did he execute another back-somersault and land on his feet in the arena? In my diagrammatic sketch as first published the first alternative is suggested. But in the painted version the boy had begun his revolution apparently as he left the animal's neck and offered an easier catch for the standing figure beyond. On the whole, therefore, the supposition that the acrobat availed himself of the purchase gained by his feet on the bull's back to make a second back-somersault seems to be the more probable.

This stationing of an assistant in a coign of vantage within the arena to catch the flying performer—as illustrated both by the wall-painting and the intaglios—is itself a remarkable feature. How could such help at need be forthcoming at the exact place and moment required?

Some enlightenment as to this problem may perhaps be obtained when we consider the probable character of the enclosure in which these circus sports took place. The traditional practice of Minoan architects leads us to assume that the walled or fenced enclosure surrounding the course would have been of rectangular shape. The "theatral stands" of the fresco form an alignment and show no trace of curving round an arena. If not in a line with one another they must at least have formed sides of a rectangular space.

But the acrobatic sports themselves were the outcome of the adventurous drives of Minoan cow-boys along the country-side, and
these, when restricted to an enclosed space, involved a round or,
more probably, elliptical course—like the arena of a Roman amphitheatre, which was originally devised to exhibit *Venationes* or
hunting scenes. It looks, therefore, as if according to the Minoan
arrangement there may have been a building for the spectators
either with a straight frontage or actually surrounding a rectilinear
space—like the central courts of the palaces—coupled with an
elliptical enclosure probably surrounded by a wooden palisade for
the performances themselves. The Spanish plazas show a space
between the ring-fence of the arena and the actual front wall below
the spectators—answering to the *podium* of the Roman Amphitheatre and giving them greater security.

If, then, we may suppose that in the case of these Minoan shows
there was an oval, fenced enclosure within a rectangular walled
space, there would have been ample facilities for the entry of assistant performers, of the kind illustrated, by means of narrow
openings at various points. They might have been posted for the
purpose and could thence rush forward to catch the flying body of
the acrobat at the critical moment.

But the whole performance was at the best a dangerous sport.
That, whether as practised in the open country or in the closed
arena, a considerable amount of risk attended these acrobatic feats,
is clear from the records that have been preserved to us. The
thrown cow-boy on the Vapheio Cup in a helpless plight with his
arms stretched out behind him, and incapable even of the endeavour to break his fall, finds his counterpart on more than one
intaglio design. What seems to be the immediately antecedent
episode occurs, indeed, on the conical steatite "rhyton" from Hagia
Triada where a figure, with outstretched arms that have clearly
missed their grasp, appears between the horns of a charging bull.
This example of the parlous plight of a performer in these sports
has a special relevance, since the two pillars of the "superposed"
type, which serve on the vase as a frame for this sensational episode, must be taken, as we have seen, for an abbreviated rendering
for the Grand Stand itself. It was part, therefore, of the spectacle
of the Minoan arena.

On the signet-ring—the subject of which, from the rocks above,
belongs to the same class as the Vapheio example—the cow-boy,
thrown on to the ground behind the bull, holds up his hands in a
similar manner. On the gold engraved bead from the "Thisbe
Treasure" the prostrate youth has one arm bent under him as if
to break his fall and holds the other to his head, as if to protect it.
From the fact that he wears a belt but no loin-clothing we may

perhaps infer that the discomfited figure is that of a comparatively young boy.

The "Sacral Knots" engraved in front of the bull in the two last examples show that they must be taken in a religious connexion. The youths laid low by the sacred animal had in a sense devoted themselves to the Minoan Goddess.

So far as our records of these ceremonial shows go, as described from the various sources above cited, their character was essentially acrobatic. They were full of thrills, however, and the Minoan on-lookers of both sexes were stirred with much the same sensational uncertainty about the fate of the performers as once excited the Roman throngs in the Amphitheatre or that still hold breathless the spectators of the Plaza de Toros.

YOUTH THROWN BY BULL   SACRIFICE OF BULL
ON GOLD BEAD-SEAL   MINOAN *Matador*

It must be borne in mind, indeed, that the Spanish *Corridas*, of their very essence, fundamentally differed from the Cretan shows. It seems to be generally agreed that they were themselves an out-growth—influenced no doubt by indigenous Iberic or Celtiberian traditions—of the sports of the Roman arena. They belong es-sentially to the category of the *tauromachia* rather than the *tauro-kathapsia*, and the object was to first wear down and finally to kill the bull. Still, the catching and overthrowing of the sacred animal that seems to have been involved in the Cretan shows may itself have had a sacrificial sequel. A noteworthy scene on a gold bead-seal from the "Thisbe Treasure," shows an obvious resem-blance to the closing episode of the *Corrida* in which the *matador* steps forward and dispatches the animal with a thrust of his sword. In the Minoan design we see a performer with a sheath slung from his shoulder who, advancing from the side, sticks his dagger into the bull's neck. The official character of the personage who thus slaughters the beast is marked not only by the fact that he is thus armed, but by two otherwise unique features—he wears a wreath on his head and a kind of chain hangs down from his shoulders terminating in star-shaped ornaments. The whole is clearly a ritual act performed by some one fulfilling priestly functions.

It was no doubt the religious character of these sports—held under the immediate patronage of the Goddess, whose pillar shrine overlooked the arena,—that made it possible and even proper for girls, apparently of high degree, to enter the ranks of these highly skilled performers.

Some of the female acrobatic figures here depicted—though otherwise attired in the ordinary manner of Minoan cow-boys— show, in fact, a special elegance in their ornaments and head-dressing; their locks are fashionably curled and they wear bright-coloured *bandeaux* above their foreheads. Not only are the upper parts of the arms encircled by broad armlets, but decidedly heavy necklaces hang down above their bosom or above the hollow of the back. The elaborate *coiffure* of the girl grappling with the bull's horns on the Vapheio Cup has already been noted. These girl performers were surely of gentle birth.

Women among the Minoans, as is well illustrated by their occupation of all the front seats of the grand stands, took the higher rank in society, just as their great Goddess took the place later assigned to Zeus.

Mutatis mutandis, then, it is allowable to compare their participation in these sports of the arena that needed such skill and strength with the appearance of personages of the highest rank as protagonists in the Spanish bull-fights. Moorish princes had adopted the native custom, and the lists of their arenas, as of that at Granada, were already famous. The Cid Campeador, who took over the sport from his "paynim" predecessors in Southern Spain, is traditionally said to have played his part as a champion in the arena. The prohibition of the sport, as barbarous, by Queen Isabella of Castile was powerless to suppress it. Later on stands out the historic episode of Charles V killing a bull with his lance in the *Plaza* of Valladolid in 1527, on the occasion of the birth of his son who was afterwards to reign as Philip II. The Spanish Grandees, encouraged by the succeeding sovereigns, continued to show a great fondness for the sport. Their participation in it, however, fell under the severe disapproval of Philip V, and from the close of the seventeenth century the professional element became gradually predominant among the *taureadors*. In a very different spirit was framed the old Spanish law that deprived of rights of citizenship the man "who, for money, should fight against a brave beast."

What the religious association had induced in ancient Crete was fostered in medieval Spain by the spirit of chivalry that led the Grandees to enter the lists against the noble animal. In Spain, indeed, as chevaleresque notions died out, and when the nobles had been forbidden to participate, the sport passed completely into the hands of professionals. But it had become a national institution, and Spanish chronicles celebrate a long list of famous *toreros*. In its minor aspects, moreover, down to quite modern times, it was supported by the example of aristocratic champions, who even included royal ladies. As late as 1893, in a trial show, or *tentadero*, of two-year old steers on the Sevillian *Vegas*, the Infanta Eulalia rode *a ancas*, or pillion fashion, with an Andalusian nobleman, while the Condesa de Paris and her daughter Princess Hélène are recorded to have each overthrown a sturdy two-year old.

In the Minoan and Mycenaean World generally the bull-grappling shows seem to have followed the fate of the whole culture, together with the religious traditions with which they were so indissolubly bound up.

Only in Northern Greece a link with the past was still preserved —under an altered form due to the use of the horse for riding purposes—in the feats of the Thessalian *taurokathaptae*.

Except for the convenient use of the horse in place of the coigns of vantage dear to the Minoan cow-boys, these feats were essentially the same. One of the particular objects of securing a good springing-off place had been to seize the bull's horns from above and to twist its head in such a way as to overthrow the mighty beast. For this the Thessalian, mounted on his fine native steed, had a great advantage and it remained one of his principal *tours de force*. It is interesting to note, moreover, that this feat—which leads us on to the performance of the Spanish *sobresalientes*—entered into the programme of the Circus sports of the ταυροκαθάπται introduced by Claudius and recorded in inscriptions. The Thessalian riders first wearied the animals by driving them round the arena and then brought them down by jumping on them and seizing their horns, in the Minoan fashion, a method still practised in the "Wild West" of America. At times the Thessalian horsemen actually broke the bull's neck by their sudden wrench. The best illustration of these circus sports is to be seen in the Greco-Roman relief from Smyrna, in the Ashmolean Museum, illustrating a scene of "the second day of the *taurokathapsia*." The riders are represented as boys, wearing round the middle part of their bodies the leather bands, or *fasciae*, that distinguished the *aurigae* of the Roman Circus. The feats here depicted, according to the expert authority quoted above, exactly answer to the throwing of steers in the modern "rodeo."

The earlier practice, however, of tackling the bull on foot was still in Hellenic times a recognized form of the sport. On the obverse of fifth-century coins of Larissa and other Thessalian cities, though the national emblem, a galloping horse, is seen on the reverse, a youth appears on foot grappling with a bull's horns and head and endeavouring to overthrow it.

What, in this connexion, is specially noteworthy in that the Greek traditions of the bull-grappling feats of Theseus and Herakles clearly acknowledge a Minoan source. It was at the behest of Eurystheus, King of Mycenae, that Herakles captured the Cretan bull, received by Minos from Poseidon. In the case of the Marathonian bull, the feat, according to the legend,—obviously out of regard for Athenian susceptibility—had been first unsuccessfully attempted by Androgeos, son of Minos, and its final achievement was reserved for the national hero, Theseus.

The metope of the Theseion, where the hero with superhuman might masters the Marathonian bull, finds its true forerunner in a series of intaglio scenes on Minoan gems. At times, as on the banded agate from Mycenae, the wrestler seems to lift the monster from the ground. A favourite feat is to seize the animal by a horn in one hand and the lower part of the jaw in the other so as to twist its neck. On a clay sealing found in the fifth magazine the champion wears the usual peaked helmet adorned, it would seem, with rows of boars' tushes, though in this case the design is somewhat marred by the barred 2 countermark. On a green jasper lentoid, where we meet with another similar design, showing surpassing strength, the youthful performer is distinguished by an exceptionally prominent nose, recalling the proto-Armenoid profile of the Minoan Priest-king on an earlier seal-impression. This feature, indeed, may have a real significance when taken in connexion with the evidence already cited for the Oriental source of this whole class of sports. Was there, perhaps, a special caste of such bull-wrestlers and acrobats belonging to the old Anatolian stock?

It has been said of bull fights that they are "in the Spanish blood." The constant recurrence of these bull-grappling scenes in paintings and painted reliefs on the walls and miniatures of porches and porticoes, palace halls and anterooms, as well as in the shrines of the divinity—in miniatures on crystal plaques, in *repoussé* designs and small reliefs on ceremonial vases, as a frequent type of intaglios and signet-rings—shows how aborbing was the interest that these sensational episodes excited in Minoan bosoms. That there was blended with this something of the fierce emotions that appealed to the spectators in the Roman Amphitheatre of the Spanish *Plaza de Toros* is probable enough. But the Cretan spectacles, even though they included this element, were on the whole devoted to the exhibition of sport and skill, and the performers— except perhaps for some act properly of a sacrificial kind—were not, as in the other case, out to kill, though often knocked out themselves.

That the painted reliefs of bull-grappling scenes such as those that remained in part at least in position above the northern entrance passage at a time when the Greek settlement was already in existence may have left their impress on later traditions of the Minotaur and of the captive boys and girls is itself, as already suggested, by no means improbable. But there is no reason to go further than this and to suppose that the acrobatic figures of either sex engaged in these dangerous feats actually represent captives, trained like the Roman gladiators to "make sport" for Minoan holidays. Still farther are we here away from any comparison with the primitive and more ferocious custom, illustrated by the monuments of prehistoric Egypt, in which prisoners of war were exposed to wild bulls.

The youthful participants in these performances,—like those of the boxing and wrestling bouts, that can hardly be separated from the same general category,—have certainly no servile appearance. They are, as we have seen, elegantly tired, and, especially in the hand-to-hand contests to be described below, often of noble mien. In these champions of either sex we must rather recognize the flower of the Minoan race, executing, in many cases under a direct religious sanction, feats of bravery and skill in which the whole population took a passionate delight.

The lithe sinewy forms of those engaged in the sports of the Minoan arena, with their violent muscular action and conventionally constricted waists, were as much the theme of the contemporary artists as were the more symmetrical shapes of her ephebi to those of classical Greece. In both cases it was the glorification of athletic excellence, manifesting itself in feats of which the Gods themselves were witnesses. So, too, the participation of women in the Minoan bull-grappling scenes can by no means be regarded as a symptom of bondage or of a perverse tyrant's whim. In was rather, as we have seen, the natural outcome of the religious organization in which the female ministers of the Goddess took the foremost place in her service. At Sparta, where the Minoan religious tradition seems to have had a considerable hold, girl athletes continued to take part in the public games.

The Palace Is Destroyed

It would seem that preparations were on foot for some anointing ceremony in the "Lustral Basin" in which the *Papa Rè* himself may well have been called on to play a leading part. For this it had evidently been found necessary to refill most of the alabaster oil vessels, usually placed, as the marks of their bases on the pave-

ment show, along the wall to the left of the entrance to the Inner
Shrine, where there was a convenient nook for this purpose. Five
out of six of these had been removed, as we have seen, from their
place of storage and set down irregularly in the area in the entrance
opening of the "Room of the Throne." One of the large oil *pithoi*
from the Magazines, the contents of which were conveniently low,
had been carried in here and laid down on its side so that the oil
could be easily ladled into the *alabastra*.

But this initial task was never destined to reach its fulfilment.
Beneath a covering mass of earth and rubble the clay oil-jar was
brought to light as it had been laid, though in a much crushed
condition, with the ritual vases on the pavement beside it as they
had been set for the filling. What happened here seems exactly
to have resembled what, as we have seen, took place in the
"Sculptor's Workshop" of the Quarter opposite, where the alabaster
and limestone "amphoras" were left unfinished on the floor.

The sudden breaking off of tasks begun—so conspicuous in the
first case—surely points to an instantaneous cause. The more
general scare occasioned by an enemy approaching the walls may
be thought a less probable cause of a violent interruption such as
that of which the signs have been here preserved for us, than another of those dread shocks that had again and again caused a
break in the palace history. The violent projection of the inlaid
casket—that had been seemingly placed on the neighbouring bench
—face downwards on to the pavement—itself fits in well with such
a seismic cause.

When we call to mind the evidence that has by now accumulated
of past experiences of this kind in this "land of earthquakes," the
last catastrophe of Knossos seems best accounted for in this way.
It must indeed be recognized that the exceptionally brilliant position at that time occupied by the palace lords, and the armaments
of which we have the records, not to speak of the generally depressed conditions elsewhere—makes a hostile attack the less
probable.

If, however, first and foremost, we have to deal with an earthquake shock, there are direct indications that the actual overthrow
(which could hardly have been so severe as some of the foregoing),
was greatly aggravated by a widespread conflagration, such as
indeed is so often the consequence of seismic destruction.

On the gypsum orthostats of the western façade of the palace
there can still be discerned what may be regarded as a clear record
of such a conflagration, which seems to have attained specially
disastrous dimensions owing to a furious wind then blowing. Here,
in the northern section of the wall the traces of smoke are visible
for a space of several metres, starting from a lighter rectangle that

evidently represents the point where a large square rafter had fallen, blazing, from the upper story.

The smoke stains here show that a wind of considerable velocity must have been blowing, since in a space of nearly five metres it rose little more than 50 centimetres. From its direction it was clearly the *Notios* or south-west wind, striking the wall across the open space of the west court. This wind, the *Gharbis* of our Moslem workmen, blowing—often for three days at a time—in an almost continuous torrent, was a constant obstacle to excavation in the spring months, attaining its maximum force in March, and often stopping all work with blinding dust clouds. The whole sky took a lurid hue, caused by the Sahara sand carried over by it, which at times even left a thin reddish deposit on house-tops and terraces, and on the palace site was blended with denser dust clouds from our own earth dumps.

The season of the *Notios'* greatest force may enable us with some probability to assign the final catastrophe of the building to the month of March, though the year can only more approximately be given as about 1400 B.C.

ARTHUR EVANS

Restorations at Knossos

AS there has been considerable criticism of Sir Arthur Evans's restorations at Knossos, this account of his problems and purposes is of interest.

IN the long work on the site of Knossos which, with some interruption caused by the Great War, has engaged my own energies for the last thirty years and the preliminaries of which go back a good deal further, it early became evident that the problem of excavation was unique in more than one respect amongst monuments of the past. The upper stories—of which in the "domestic quarter" three successive stages were encountered—had not, as in the parallel case of other ancient buildings, been supported by solid piers of masonry or brick-work, or by stone columns. They had here been held up in a principal degree by a timber framework, the huge posts and beams of which, together with the shafts of the columns, were either supplied by the cypress forests, then existing in the neighbouring glens, or by similar material imported from over sea. The reduction, either by chemical processes or by actual burning of these wooden supports to mere crumbling masses of charcoal, had thus left vast voids in the interspaces. The upper floors and structures had indeed—in a manner that sometimes seemed almost miraculous—been held approximately at their levels by the rubble formation that had insinuated itself below—due largely to the falling in of bricks of unburnt clay, partly dissolved, from the upper walls.

At the same time, whenever this intrusive material was removed, there was nothing to prevent the remains of the upper fabric from crashing down to a lower level. For the benefit of those who had not an opportunity of following in a practical capacity the long course of this arduous work, it is necessary once more to repeat that those who took part in it were confronted with only two alternatives. Either, at every step, the overlying mass had to be re-supported, or excavation itself would have reduced the remains of the upper stories—held up and preserved to us in such a marvellous fashion —to one indistinguishable heap of ruins.

Such a catastrophic result was combated at first by means of wooden beams and posts, which, however, in the Cretan climate of violent changes showed a rapid tendency to rot. These were at first replaced by piers of masonry and shafts and capitals of columns laboriously cut out of stone, while upper pavements were supported by means of brickwork arches resting on iron girders. The expense of procuring from over sea girders of a length and calibre sufficient to span the larger halls was itself prohibitive. Owing, moreover, to the exposed character of the access to Candia by sea previous to the construction of the new port, and the frequency of fierce north-westerly gales, the landing of the necessary materials was always a risky operation, and it has been already mentioned that two of the largest girders shipped from England lie at the bottom of the old harbour.

Under these circumstances the introduction of the use of reinforced concrete was a real godsend, besides ensuring the additional advantage that the new work is at once distinguishable by the spectator. Piers and columns, with their capitals superimposed, could thus be moulded and the platforms of whole floors laid on over even the largest spaces, while the floors themselves at the same time have given a much necessary compaction to the surrounding walls.

The work of reconstitution already carried out in the important blocks throughout both wings of the palace has been now tested by two earthquakes. The serious shock of June 26, 1926, that ruined houses in the neighbouring village and damaged the Museum in Candia, left even the upper structures of the Palace practically unscathed. That of February 1930, which was also severely felt on the site and throughout the neighbouring district, put a severe strain on the more recent reconstructions, which, however, they successfully resisted. It is worth remarking, moreover, that the only slight damage produced by these seismic shocks was the horizontal dislocation, to the extent of a few centimetres only, of a section of a shaft and pillar, both of masonry construction according to the earlier procedure.

It is to be observed that in the course of this work of conservation it was found advisable in places to go beyond the immediate objective and to carry up to a certain height walls and structures forming lateral supports to parts of the fabric that it seemed desirable to preserve from shocks in a special manner.

ARTHUR EVANS

Arthur Evans in an Earthquake

OCCUPIED as I largely was in the Spring of 1926 with tracing seismic action in the phenomena presented by the ancient remains at Knossos, the imminence of a fresh convulsion had become to me a kind of obsession, when on June 26 of that year, at 9:45 in the evening of a calm, warm day, the shocks began.

They caught me reading on my bed in a basement room of the

Ibid., Vol. II, 1928, pp. 315-18.

head-quarters house—the Villa Ariadne—and, trusting to the exceptional strength of the fabric, I decided to see the earthquake
through from within. Perhaps I had hardly realized the full awe-
someness of the experience, though my confidence in the strength
of the building proved justified, since it did not suffer more than
slight cracks. But it creaked and groaned, heaved, and rocked from
side to side, as if the whole must collapse. Small objects were thrown
about, and a pail, full of water, was nearly splashed empty. The
movement, which recalled to me a ship in a storm—as it had to
the Venetian Duke in 1508—though it was of only a minute and
a quarter's duration, already began to produce on me the same
effect of sickness as a rough sea. A dull sound rose from the ground
like the muffled roar of an angry bull: our single bell rang, while,
through the open window, came the more distant jangling of the
chimes of Candia Cathedral, the belfreys as well as the dome and
cupolas of which were badly damaged. As the quickly repeated
shocks produced their cumulative effects, the crashing of the roofs
of two small houses outside the garden gate made itself audible,
mingled with women's shrieks and the cries of some small children,
who, however, were happily rescued. Some guests, who were up-
stairs or on the roof, had made their way out past the lower terrace
—on which a round stone table with a thick Roman pedestal was
executing a *pas seul*—and thence to the open, between trees so
violently swayed that it looked as if they must fall. Meanwhile,
a dark mist of dust, lifted upwards by a sudden draught of air,
rose sky-high, so as almost entirely to eclipse the full moon, house
lights reflected on this cloud bank giving the appearance of a
conflagration wrapped round with smoke.

Not only did the head-quarters house resist the shocks well, but,
thanks largely to the ferro-concrete of the floors, very little damage
was done to the works of reconstitution in the upper stories of the
palace. The upper part of a masonry pillar of recent construction
which was moved bodily several centimetres due south supplied,
indeed, a good index of the prevalent direction from which the
waves of disturbance came. In neighbouring villages, however—
especially those on declivities—the destruction was great. . . . In
the town of Candia itself the damage was proportionately less and
not more than fifty houses could be described as actually reduced
to ruins, though two or three hundred suffered partial destruction,
and many more were left in a dangerous condition from the rifts
in their walls.

As on former occasions, almost the whole population, including
crowds of wailing women, poured out of the city gates and continued
for weeks to camp in the open as best they could. Happily, owing
to the early hour and the bright moonlight, the inhabitants were al-

most all up and about, and the casualties were therefore very slight.

The fabric of the Cretan Museum, containing the principal objects derived from the excavations at Knossos and elsewhere, —which in spite of the protests of the local Ephors had been built without any reference to the local conditions—suffered considerable injury. Some of the smaller relics, such as the beautiful little coloured relief known as the "Jewel Fresco," were completely pulverized, but, considering the amount of debris that was precipitated from the roof and ceilings, the damage done to the contents was almost miraculously small. Most of the breakages were found capable of being repaired, and a fortunate result of the catastrophe has been that it has stirred the Government at Athens to build a gallery constructed as far as possible to be earthquake proof.

_____

J. D. S. PENDLEBURY

Minoans—and Their Religion

THE Minoans were long-headed and such few skulls of a brachycephalic type as have been found may either be mere freaks of nature or those of actual foreigners resident in the island. In stature they were short, shorter on an average than the Cretan of the present day. Increase in height, however, with the passage of centuries is a phenomenon which appears almost universally. It cannot be said to be due to any influx of invaders, who, while responsible for shortening the skull, were certainly no taller than the aboriginal inhabitants. The present-day Cretan has, indeed, much of the Minoan in him, for the Minoan stock, like the Egyptian, was evidently one which readily absorbed new elements. All over the island to-day you see the wasp waists, no longer artificially restricted but still emphasized by the long silk girdle, the slim hips, the high square shoulders and the long legs. Many a village boy might be

From _The Archaeology of Crete_. London: Methuen & Co. Ltd.; 1939, pp. 267-74. By permission of Methuen & Co. Ltd.

the direct descendant of the Cup-Bearer or the Priest King, and who can deny the possibility that he may be? Minoan, too, is the sense of style which your modern Cretan has above all other Greeks. His very dress, the baggy breeches, the headcloth, the belt can all be paralleled in Minoan times. The Zouave jacket seems to have been confined to the women, but the well-cut riding-boots of white, red, or black leather remind us of the leggings shown on the Hagia Triada vases, on one of which the frieze cape is also shown.

It has often been said that the scanty Minoan costume is an indication of the eventual origin of the race in a warmer climate. Admittedly the codpiece has Libyan affinities, but it would be unsafe to argue from that that the Minoan stock as a whole was of Libyan origin. How far it was the artistic convention to omit everything but the simplest garb one cannot say. But their fondness for the human figure may well have caused the artists to show as much of it as they could, and it must be remembered that in Egypt men were portrayed wearing the old kilt for centuries after long robes of gauffered linen were in fashion.

One item of costume remains to be mentioned, the seal. This was probably worn in the case of a cylinder or signet, suspended round the neck, in the case of a bead-seal, lentoid or amygdaloid, round the wrist as in the Cupbearer Fresco. Finger-rings are rare and those which have survived are all of precious metals. No case is known of a stone seal set as a bezel. Such signets are particularly necessary where writing is the accomplishment of few. . . .

Throughout their history, indeed, the Minoans were worshippers of nature, who was represented from Middle Minoan times by a great Mother Goddess, Mistress of Trees and Mountains and Lady of the Wild Animals. As representing the fertility of nature she is often credited with a son—a boy-god. In Greek times her attributes were divided among a number of goddesses; Athene takes her snakes, Aphrodite her doves and her son, Artemis, her stags, and various nymphs her mountains, streams, and forests. But there was always the tendency in Crete to combine these goddesses into one, and Britomartis or Diktynna was more truly the goddess of Crete than the politely Hellenized Athene or Artemis.

When pictured on the rings and seal stones, the goddess is always bareheaded, with her long tresses floating in the wind. In the more urbane statuettes destined for palace use she wears a tiara or crown, and no doubt it is this tradition which is followed in the capped figures of Late Minoan III. In either case she follows the women's fashion of the period. Her son is shown either naked or wearing the normal loin-cloth. Occasionally he wears a peaked cap. He is one of those soulless, faun-like, heartless boys whom you meet in the wilder parts of Crete to-day.

Being divinities of the earth, the water, the air, and all that in them is, they were evidently considered to be resident in pillars, trees, or queer stones, and Evans has made out a very good case for the ritual means of evoking them by invocation, by summoning on a conch-shell, or by dancing, and for the outward manifestation of their presence by the appearance of birds perching upon the cult object.

Two objects must be mentioned in connexion with religion. The first is that known as the "horns of consecration." A detailed discussion by Nilsson shows that they mark a place of consecration where the cult objects are laid, the libation jug, the double axe, or the sacred bough. On the other hand, they may be used as an architectural decoration on buildings of a sacred character, whether actual shrines or a building like the palace at Knossos which was a kind of sanctuary itself. The double axe itself is found as a votive offering and as a cult object between the horns of consecration. On rings and seals it is seen "handled by ministers of the cult or carried by women. It is never in the hands of a male god." This makes it practically certain that it is in no sense a thunder weapon or a symbol of the male counterpart of the Mother goddess. The most likely explanation is that it was originally a sacrificial axe which had in course of time become both a cult symbol and a cult object.

The most common living creatures to appear in a religious context are the bull, the dove, and the snake. The splendid Cretan bull was a natural symbol of power and strength. We have no archaeological reason to believe that it was worshipped. It was certainly sacrificed, and if the bull-leaping sports were of a religious character at all, no doubt some of that sanctity would attach itself to the central figure, but there is no direct authority for speaking of a bull-god. On the other hand, the sky-god common to nearly all the Near East is frequently given the form of a bull. Was Crete one of the few exceptions? It is hard to think so. The doves frequently accompany the goddess and are seen perching on double axes, pillars, and trees. Again we can say that such birds are the natural attributes of a divinity of the woods. The snake, however, is in a rather different category. It seems to have been a kind of beneficent spirit looking after the welfare of the house, as it is considered in many parts of the world to this day. Mention has already been made of the paraphernalia of its cult found in a Late Minoan II house in the west court at Knossos, and in several shrines "snake tubes" have been found. It may have been actually worshipped or merely propitiated in a friendly way, but at all events it is the only living creature to which tribute was paid.

J. D. S. PENDLEBURY

The Destruction of Knossos:
Another Theory

J. D. S. PENDLEBURY here mentions Evans's theory that the destruction of Knossos was caused by an earthquake, sets out the argument of the champions of the mainland (p. 85, II), and then expounds his own view that Knosses and other Cretan cities were sacked by the Mycenaeans as a "purely political" act. Professor Palmer would agree that the Mycenaeans were the destroyers, but argues that far from withdrawing afterwards, they established a successful régime in Crete.

❧

THE catastrophe which overtook the Cretan cities at the end of Late Minoan 1b (or Late Mioan II at Knossos) was practically universal. Knossos, Phaistos, Hagia Triada, Gournia, Mokhlos, Mallia, and Zakros all show traces of violent destruction accompanied by burning. At Palaikastro, Pseira, Nirou Khani, Tylissos, and Plate there is a distinct break in the habitation, though no trace of burning was found.

This overwhelming disaster must have taken place at one and the same time and it has been attributed to a severe earthquake. Earthquakes, however, in ancient times are not liable to cause fires; these are the result of gas and electricity. It has been seen, too, that woodwork was more sparingly used at this time than before, and that previous earthquakes, which were strong enough to fling great blocks of the palace at Knosses into the houses below, had neither caused fires, though the woodwork was more extensive, nor had they caused such a complete break and set-back in the culture. Rather they had acted as a spur to fresh endeavours. Furthermore,

〰〰〰〰〰〰〰〰〰
Ibid., pp. 228-31, 267-8, 273-4.

at Knossos the first damage an earthquake of such magnitude would have done would be to shake down the domestic quarters and particularly the Grand Staircase, where four floors at least were supported on wooden columns. A very mild earthquake in 1931 snapped and shifted the upper part of a reinforced concrete column no less than 6 cm. But the Grand Staircase remained complete and practically undamaged long enough for it to be silted up with debris and earth which preserved the landing on a level with the central court to within 1½ metres of its original position. The marks of fire are most obvious on the western or official wing.

Everything, indeed, points to a deliberate sacking on the part of enemies of the most powerful cities in Crete. We have seen the prosperity of the period and it is obvious that no mere Viking raid could have accomplished such destruction. It must have been a highly organized expedition with an avowed purpose. That this purpose was not to invade and colonize the island is clear from the way in which the Minoan culture continues, though in a very minor key, without any mainland influence until the very end of Late Minoan III. The object of this thorough, relentless destruction must have been purely political.

There are two theories which will account for this. Both have much to be said for them and, curiously enough, they are diametrically opposed. According to the first theory the Minoan domination over the mainland has been grossly overestimated. It has been pointed out that if we lacked all historical documents we should, if we used similar arguments, maintain that there was an Athenian domination of Etruria in later days. On this theory the mainland and Crete were separate independent powers, the former merely adopting the outward trappings of a higher civilization. In Late Minoan II, however, the mainland was strong enough to establish control over Crete. This would account for the extremely mainland character of the palace style. In that case the destruction of the Cretan cities was due to a nationalist revolt against the foreign "harmosts." Evidence for this is the fact that in the succeeding, Late Minoan III period, the civilization of Crete has little connexion with that of the mainland; it is indeed, as will be seen, rather markedly Minoan.

The other theory, to which the present writer adheres, would regard the Minoanization of the mainland as too pronounced to be the result of mere influence. It is certainly far more complete than was the influence of Egypt in that country's highly organized empire. We would regard the archaeological results as supporting legend, the latter admittedly only referring to the Saronic Gulf, that Crete had by the end of Late Minoan I–II established a considerable domination over the rest of the Aegean. Her main dealings abroad were with Egypt and the Egyptian Empire in Syria. Egyptian objects and influence are so rare on the mainland that it would seem as if that part of the Minoan Empire was barred from direct traffic with Egypt. The presence of mainland vessels in Egypt is easily explained by the fact that they were more suitable for travelling and that therefore the tribute of the mainland to the Cretan overlord was sent direct to Egypt in payment of goods instead of being unloaded in Crete and reshipped thence.

We have seen that though superficially Minoanized, the mainland still kept a good deal of its native culture and taste. The richest market in the world was barred and we may perhaps catch an echo of the attempt to find fresh markets in the story of Jason's voyage to the Black Sea. At all events it is not hard to imagine the rebellious feelings of the dominions, and we can well imagine things getting to the pitch of a concerted effort on their part to smash the capital state of the empire.

Now there is a name which is always associated, if not with the sack of Knossos, at least with the liberation of its subjects— Theseus. Names have a habit of being remembered when the deeds with which they are associated are forgotten or garbled. Who would recognize Alexander in Iskander of the two Horns, or Virgil in the necromancer of the Middle Ages? It has already been suggested that the seven youths and seven maidens may have been the mainland quota for the bull-ring at Knossos. That is just the type of detail that would be remembered, the more so in that it may well have been the sentimental reason without which no purely commercial war can ever take place. No doubt the rape of Helen was a very good rallying cry when the Mycenaean Empire wished to break through to the Black Sea trade which Troy was keeping for itself.

And in the last decade of the fifteenth century on a spring day, when a strong south wind was blowing which carried the flames of the burning beams almost horizontally northwards, Knossos fell.

The final scene takes place in the most dramatic room ever excavated—the throne room. It was found in a state of complete confusion. A great oil jar lay overturned in one corner, ritual vessels were in the act of being used when the disaster came. It looks as if the king had been hurried here to undergo too late some last ceremony in the hopes of saving the people. Theseus and the Minotaur! Dare we believe that he wore the mask of a bull?

Such imaginings may not be suitable to archaeology but, with this possibility in mind, I defy anyone to enter the throne room without a strange thrill.

Crete had fallen and henceforward she was to be a mere satellite of the world centring round Greece, gradually drawing nearer until she was absorbed in the general Hellenic culture which she herself had done so much to found.

———

ARTHUR EVANS

Early Discoveries of Minoan Script

SIR ARTHUR EVANS here describes his classification of the three principal types of script which he had detected in Crete. First come the hieroglyphs, mostly on stone beads and seal stones, still pictorial in form. Then follows a less strictly pictographic script, best represented on the libation table from the Dictaean Cave, and to be assigned to the later Middle Minoan period. This is the script now known as "Linear A." Latest of the three is the script which Evans had found in great abundance on clay tablets in the palace at Knossos—and which has won fame as Linear B. The overwhelming majority of these he dated to the last fifty years before the destruction of Knossos in 1400, although, as appears in the last paragraph, he recognized that the use of Script B persisted in the period after the destruction. Evans did not think that there was any essential difference in the language written in Scripts A and B—nor did he doubt that it was the native tongue of his Minoans.

This division of the scripts into three successive stages, which Evans made with his quick perception, remains unquestioned. Controversy has centred round the language and age of the Linear B inscriptions.

In 1939, just before Evans's death, Professor Blegen began to

From *Scripta Minoa*. Oxford: The Clarendon Press; 1909, pp. 8-18. By permission of The Clarendon Press, Oxford.

find Linear B tablets at Pylos, a Mycenaean citadel, occupied from
1300-1200 B.C., in the south-western Peloponnese. After the war
comparable tablets turned up in buildings outside the palace at
Mycenae itself. That these archives should have been kept in what
was supposed to be a Minoan script and language was difficult
to explain, and efforts to do so (p. 151, II) were a little embarrassing. It was also puzzling that at a period when scripts might be
expected to be developing rapidly, there should be so very little
difference between Knossian tablets of 1450-1400 B.C. and Pylian
ones of two centuries later.

Then came the shock of Michael Ventris's announcement that
the language of the Linear B texts was an archaic Greek. Now, in
place of having to explain how Minoan archives got to late Mycenaean sites, it had to be explained how Mycenaean Greek archives
got to Crete at a date when nobody wanted any Greeks to be in the
island. Again explanations had to be produced (p. 85, II). Now
Leonard Palmer has dispelled both sets of difficulties (although
of course raising some new ones) by showing that several distinct
lines of reasoning (including the forms of the armour, horse-trappings and swords conventionalized in the signs themselves) point
to the Linear B tablets of Knossos being as late as those of Pylos—
or even slightly later.

As for the Linear A problem, which has hovered uncertainly in
the background of this intellectual struggle, Professor Palmer believes that the A texts are in a little-known Indo-European language
(Luvian) introduced to Crete from Anatolia by newcomers.

THE possibility that a form of writing closely resembling, or identical with, the Hittite had been introduced into prehistoric Greece
was first brought before me in a practical form in 1889. In that year
a four-sided bead-seal of cornelian, bearing on each facet a series
of figures was presented amongst other objects to the Ashmolean
Museum by that well-known antiquarian traveller, the late Mr.
Greville Chester. The stone was stated (erroneously, as it afterwards
turned out) to have been found at Sparta. That it represented some
conventionalized system of picture-writing could not be doubted.
The general resemblance of the figures upon its sides to the Hittite
characters, and in particular the identity of the wolf's (or dog's)
head showing the tongue protruding, with a not infrequent Hittite
sign, led me at the time to hesitate between the alternative hypotheses either that the inscribed seal was an imported object of
"Hittite" fabric or that a substantially identical system of conven-

tionalized pictographic writing had been introduced into prehistoric Greece under some predominant "Hittite" influence.

An objection, however, to the first alternative was to be found in the fact that no similar types of seal-stones were forthcoming from the Anatolian or Syrian side. And on the other hand, the generally independent character of the Mycenaean culture made it difficult to presuppose such an absolute indebtedness to Hittite sources in the matter of script. This high early civilization, organized as was shown by the Mycenae tombs under a succession of dynasts, presented just as favourable conditions for the rise of a conventionalized script as that of the regions to the East and South. The elaboration of a more advanced system out of the chaotic elements of primitive pictography achieved under the early monarchies in Mesopotamia, the Syro-Anatolian region, and Egypt, might with equal probability have taken place under the auspices of kings who reigned before Agamemnon on the Greek shores of the Aegean. Isolated as was this example, might it not really indicate the existence of an independent indigenous script in prehistoric Greece?

It was not long before decisive evidence came under my observation. In the course of a visit to Greece, during the early spring of 1893, I hit upon some more inscribed bead-seals of the same class as that referred to above. Like it they were perforated along their axis and presented four, in some cases three, facets engraved with signs, arranged in groups, and evidently belonging to a hieroglyphic or conventionalized pictographic system. My inquiries succeeded in tracing all of these to a Cretan source. Knowing of the considerable collection of "island" and other early gems in the Berlin Museum, I addressed myself to Dr. Furtwängler, whose catalogue of the collection was not then published, and received through his courtesy several impressions of similar seal-stones showing "hieroglyphic" characters that fitted on to and supplemented the series that I had already collected. In this case, too, the source of the stones, as far as it was known, again turned out to be Crete. The impression of a two-sided gem of another type, obtained at Athens some years earlier by Professor Sayce, and which I subsequently discovered to be also Cretan, supplied a new piece of evidence. At a meeting of the Hellenic Society, on November 27, 1893, I was thus able to make the formal announcement that I had discovered on a series of gems and seals mainly found in Crete some sixty symbols which seemed to belong to a native system of hieroglyphics distinct from the Egyptian on the one hand and from the Hittite on the other.

The evidence conclusively pointed to Crete as the principal source of these hieroglyphic forms, and it became obvious that the investigation must be followed out in that island. Various parallel researches connected with the origin of "Mycenaean" and Greek civilization had been for some time prompting me to undertake the exploration of the prehistoric remains there, as yet practically untouched, in spite of the suggestive speculations of Milchhöfer, which had already done much to stimulate my own interest in the matter. To Crete I accordingly turned. Landing at Candia early in March, 1894, I made my way round the whole Centre and East of the island, including the mountainous districts of Ida and Dicta, the extensive southern plain of Messara, and the sites of over twenty ancient cities. The number of relics illustrative of the early periods of Cretan culture that I was thus able to collect was surprisingly great, and in particular the accumulating evidence that the great days of the island lay beyond history. The Crete that thus began to open out was the Crete of the Homeric "Hundred Cities," the realm of Minos, and it soon became obvious that none of the later phases there traceable—Dorian Greek, Roman and Byzantine, Saracen or Venetian—had left such abiding records in the soil as this very ancient civilization. And in what regarded the more special object of my quest these researches were well rewarded. One of their first results had been to discover in the hands of its original owner an impression of the four-sided seal which had been erroneously labelled by Mr. Greville Chester as having been found in Sparta. This also proved to be of Cretan provenance. The net result of these investigations was to enable me to announce, as I then wrote, the discovery *in situ* of a pre-Phoenician system of writing in the island, of which two distinct phases were perceptible—one the conventionalized pictographic type represented by the seal-stones already mentioned, the other linear and quasi-alphabetic. Abundant evidence was also forthcoming of a still earlier usage of picture-signs out of which these more advanced methods of script had been successively evolved.

The more linear signs occurred on pottery as well as stone. My search for perforated seal-stones and gems was greatly helped by a piece of modern Cretan superstition, shared by other islanders of the Aegean. Such conveniently bored stones are known to the Cretan women as "milk-stones," or sometimes "milk-producers," and are worn round their necks, especially in times of child-bearing, as charms of great virtue. It was thus possible, by making a house-to-house visitation in the villages, to obtain a knowledge of a large number of early engraved stones. I was often able to purchase them from the older women, and at times I succeeded in effecting an exchange of perforated gems of the most coveted milk-white hue, but of less archaeological importance, for others of greater interest. Even in cases where, owing to the magic power that was supposed to be inherent in a stone, I could not persuade the owner to part with it, it was generally possible to secure an impression.

A summary account of the results of this first campaign in Crete was published in my "Cretan Pictographs and Pre-Phoenician Script," the principal materials of which, as better understood in view of subsequent discoveries, will be found more accurately classified in the present work. These explorations were continued during the early months of the years 1895 and 1896, and I was thus able to communicate to the Hellenic Society in November of the latter year a considerable mass of supplementary material.

Part of the material collected during these expeditions obviously belonged to a very primitive stage of Cretan culture, here referred to as "Early Minoan," including a series of bead-seals with pictographic figures. Other objects showed linear signs, probably in this case preserving ideographic values, which must thus have already existed at a time when the "conventionalized pictographic" or hieroglyphic Cretan system had not yet been developed.

The most remarkable of these that came under my notice at the time of these preliminary explorations was a steatite whorl found, together with a clay cylinder presenting linear figures, in a very early deposit at Hagios Onuphrios near the site of Phaistos, a detailed description of which, together with other examples, will be given below. Recent discoveries have left little doubt that the deposit of Hagios Onuphrios that contained these objects represented the debris of a primitive beehive tomb or ossuary of a class of which examples have now been found by Dr. Halbherr at Hagia Triada and by Dr. Xanthudides at Kumasa near Gortyna, in the same Cretan region. Here it may be sufficient to say that these early ossuaries contain ivory bead-seals and other objects attesting the influence of Sixth-Dynasty Egypt, and that, in Cretan terms, they go back in the main to the Second or Third divisions of the Early Minoan Age. According to the lowest chronological scheme advanced by any Egyptologist this would take back the date of the primitive linear seals found in these deposits to the middle of the third millennium before our era.

These early ossuaries have also been found to contain examples of a class of three-sided bead-seals of steatite engraved with figures of a primitive pictographic kind which supply the immediate antecedent stage to a similar class of seals, generally executed in hard stone, exhibiting the developed hieroglyphic script. A series of these pictographic prism-seals will be found collected in my earlier works.

Further investigations greatly added to the number of seals of the true "hieroglyphic" class, including a type curiously resembling a modern signet. Moreover, certain groups of graffito signs found on early vases already give indications of the existence of a more advanced class of linear script in which the characters seemed to have partially advanced beyond the purely ideographic stage and to have attained at least a syllabic value. The example from Prodromos Botsano is of special interest, since similar vessels, one with remains of graffito characters, have been lately found by Dr. Xanthudides on a house floor at Chamaezi in Eastern Crete, together with clay human figures of a type that characterizes the votive deposits, like Petsofa, of the earliest part of the Middle Minoan Age.

But the most remarkable example of a developed linear script that rewarded these earlier explorations belonged to an altogether different class of object.

On the steep of Mt. Lasethi, the culminating mass of the ancient Dicta, above the village of Psychro, and about four hours' mule journey from the site of the ancient Lyttos, opens a great city, which, from the abundant remains of votive and sacrificial objects discovered within it, had been evidently a principal sanctuary of the prehistoric cult of the island. There can indeed be little doubt that this was the Diktaion Antron of the Lyttian traditions, whither, according to the legend preserved by Hesiod, Rhea took refuge to give birth to the Cretan Zeus. Rhea, as we now know, represents the great Nature-Goddess of Minoan Crete, part of whose mythic being was also perpetuated under later titles as Artemis Dictynna, the "Sweet Virgin" Britomartis, the mysterious Aphaia, and Aphrodite Ariadne. With this great Minoan Goddess seems to have been associated a youthful male divinity, later identified by the Greeks with the Cretan Zeus. The aniconic or fetish forms of these, which could, through due ritual incantation, be charged, as it were, with the divinity, were the sacred Double Axes, of which numerous bronze examples were found in the Dictaean Cave, and the holy pillars of stone. A garbled reminiscence of such a stone, attaching to this very sanctuary, may be found, indeed, in the legend of the βαίτυλος swallowed by Kronos in place of his infant son.

Numerous representations of this ancient Stone and Pillar-Worship have been preserved for us in the subjects of the signets and wall-paintings both of Minoan Crete and of the Mycenaean mainland, but a special interest attaches to the discovery of a material trace of this "baetylic" cult in the Dictaean Cave itself.

In April, 1896, I obtained, from beneath a prehistoric sacrificial stratum, covering the vast "Atrium" of the Cave, part of the black steatite slab of a table that had been provided with three shallow cup-like cavities for libations. It had possessed four corner supports, and a larger central prominence below proved that it had been placed upon the top of a sacred cone or pillar. Its great antiquity is attested both by the position in which it was found and the resemblance of the cup-like cavities with their raised rims to libation cups of the same black steatite subsequently found among the fittings of a small early shrine of the Cretan Goddess in the palace at Knossos. This latter piece of evidence as well as other comparisons of an epigraphic nature, to be referred to below, carry back its date at least to the early part of the second millennium before our era. The threefold receptacle of the Dictaean Table itself, indeed, suggests interesting analogies with a ritual usage that goes back to the earliest religious stratum of Greece. In the case of such primitive worship as that of the Shades of the Departed, and again that of the Nymphs, a triple libation was frequently offered. The μελίκρητα, indeed, which, followed in turn by sweet wine and water, made up these offerings, would have been specially appropriate in the Cave Sanctuary where, according to the legend, the baby Zeus had been fed with this mingled milk and honey. We are expressly told that the ritual performed in honour of the Cretan Zeus set forth the miraculous preservation of the infant and his nourishment by Amaltheia and Melissa, personifying the goat and bee. However this may be, the Libation Table takes us back to a period when, as the concordant testimony of the early Cretan religious relics shows, the Mother-Goddess herself was the principal object of cult.

But the most remarkable phenomenon presented by the remaining portion of the Dictaean Libation Table was part of an inscription incised along its upper surface in front of the cups. The inscription was in well-defined characters belonging, as will be shown below, to an advanced type of linear script (Class A), which at Knossos is confined to the middle period of the later palace. It reads from left to right, and consists of eight or nine characters and two stops. If we may suppose it to have been symmetrically arranged, it would have originally consisted of about fifteen characters, and perhaps four words. We have here an inscription cut on stone, and probably of a dedicatory nature, which in the strictest sense of the word may be described as monumental.

The outbreak of the Insurrection in the summer of 1896 did not seriously interrupt the course of these investigations. Revisiting Crete in 1898 I was able to pursue my researches in the central and eastern parts of the island, then in Insurgent hands, and received the kindest assistance and support from the French and Italian Commanders in the districts then in their occupation. Unfortunately, however, in Candia and the adjoining districts, which had been committed to British protection, and where a large number of native Moslems were collected, the situation was very different. The policy was different, too. The complaisant attitude towards the Hamidian authorities to which it was considered necessary to resort was by no means felicitous in its results. My own guide and attendant was thrown into a noisome dungeon, from which he was with difficulty rescued. The inevitable massacre followed, directed, with every telegraphic facility, from the Palace at Yildiz; and during the burning of the Christian Quarter a series of interesting relics from the site of Knossos, including an inscribed fragment, to be described below, perished in the flames.

The advent of the new autonomous Government under Prince George of Greece, to whose friendly support I was much indebted, gave me the opportunity for which I had long been preparing of carrying out by the aid of the spade a more thorough investigation of the remains of the early civilization of the island at the spot to which all later tradition pointed as it head quarters. Knossos, the city of Minos, the legendary site of the palace wrought for him, with all the artistic wonders it contained, by his craftsman Daedalos, of the Dancing-Place of Ariadne and of the Labyrinth itself, naturally stood out as the first objective. The indications secured during a first visit to this site had themselves been of such a nature as to leave no doubt of the supreme importance of the undertaking. Fragments of painted stucco, ceramic and other relics, a gold signet ring with a religious subject, a part of a steatite vessel with spirited reliefs had rewarded my first researches on the spot. My attention had been especially turned to the hill of Kephala, where remains of early walls and of a chamber with huge store jars together with other relics had already been brought to light by a native antiquary, Mr. Minos Kalochaerinos. Certain signs already noticed by Mr. W. J. Stillman on some large blocks visible on the southern declivity of this hill might or might not be properly described as "masons' marks," but they had all the appearance of belonging to a people acquainted with the art of writing. The probability that, over and above the general artistic and architectural results, excavation here might throw a new light on the pre-Phoenician script of Crete was enhanced by more than one small find. Two seal-stones had come under my notice, picked up on or near the site by neighbouring peasants, which bore groups of hieroglyphic signs. In addition to this, however, there came subsequently to my notice a fragmentary indication the precise significance of which it was impossible at that time to appraise, but which opened out still greater possibilities. In 1895 I was shown a part of a burnt clay slip then in the possession of a Candiote, Kyrios Zachyrakis, said to have been found on the site of Kephala, presenting some incised linear signs which seemed to belong to an advanced system of writing. It had been apparently a surface find, and there was nothing by which to determine its age. The clay slip itself perished at the time of the destruction of the Christian Quarter, but I took a careful copy of it at the time. The object itself, standing as it did entirely isolated, was still of such an uncertain nature that, when publishing some supplementary materials on the Cretan script in 1896, I preferred to place this inscribed fragment, the potential significance of which might be so far-reaching, to "a reserve account."

On the Hill of Kephala therefore I resolved to dig. But, such were the local circumstances, that in order eventually to secure full freedom of action in the matter of excavation it was necessary to obtain the actual ownership of the property, which unfortunately, according to the system prevalent in Crete, was in the hands of coproprietors, who were Moslem Beys of an exceptionally intractable disposition. Already in 1895 I was able to purchase a share in the property, but it was not till six years later, after encountering every kind of obstacle and intrigue, that I finally succeeded in purchasing the whole site. This was largely owing to the assistance of Dr. Joseph Hazzidakis, now Ephor-General of Antiquities and Director of the Museum at Candia, who amidst all the obstructions to which I had been subjected had constantly seconded my efforts. Difficulties remained of a political nature, but, thanks to the goodwill of Prince George of Greece, these, too, were successfully surmounted, and at last, in March, 1900, it was possible to begin operations. The results have been such as to surpass all expectations. Aided by the Cretan Exploration Fund then started, and ably seconded by my Assistant, Dr. Duncan Mackenzie, and by the former architect to the British School of Athens, Mr. Theodore Fyfe, I was able in the course of seven campaigns to lay bare a great prehistoric palace and its dependencies. The "House of Minos," the works of Daedalos, the Labyrinth itself, have been shown to be no mere creations of ancient fancy.

On the general outcome of these excavations and the extraordinary degree of advancement exhibited by the Minoan civilization in various branches of art and of mechanical and sanitary science this is not the place to enlarge. As regards the particular subject of investigation that is the scope of the present work the results were indeed decisive.

On March 30, 1900, the exploration of the area above the southern terrace brought to light the larger part of an elongated clay tablet with signs and numbers incised upon it, which I at once recognized as presenting the same form of linear script as that of the fragmentary clay slip seen in 1895. The work of the succeeding days produced a series of these from what proved afterwards to be the second west magazine, and on April 5 there was found in a small chamber near the south propylaeum a bath-shaped vessel of terracotta containing a whole hoard of inscribed tablets, several in a perfect condition, which referred to various cereals. The tablets were arranged in rows, and from the charred wood in which they were embedded, it seems probable that their immediate receptacle had been a wooden box. From this time onwards similar finds continued at intervals throughout the whole course of the excavations. The written documents from the palace of Knossos and its immediate dependencies now amount to nearly two thousand.

The overwhelming majority of these clay documents, including the first discovered, presented an advanced type of linear script—referred to in the present work as Class B—which was in vogue throughout the whole of the concluding period of the palace history. But the course of the excavations brought out the fact that the use of this highly developed form of writing had been in turn preceded in the "House of Minos" by two earlier types—one also presenting linear characters, described below as Class A, the other, still earlier, of conventionalized pictorial aspect, recalling Egyptian hieroglyphics. The archaeological stratification of the site reveals two distinct palace eras, and, on the eastern slope, remains of a still earlier building. Beneath the most ancient remains of the Age of Palaces there came to light, moreover, layer after layer illustrating the stages of a still more primitive culture, from the earliest Neolithic times onwards. We are thus enabled to trace the whole evolution of the art of writing in a manner for which perhaps it is impossible to find an adequate parallel on any other ancient site. The consecutive phases of Minoan culture covered by the several stages in the history of the building are seen in each case to have been the gradual outgrowths of long generations of civilized life. We watch the rise, the bloom, and decadence of successive schools of art, and the fuller the volume of our detailed knowledge grows, the greater is the tale of years demanded to explain the phenomena before us. We shall not err on the side of exaggeration in estimating the period covered by the successive types of developed script on the palace site at Knossos at over a thousand years. It must at the same time be observed that the latest of the Minoan documents discovered on this site, those namely dating from the period of decline, when the palace as a palace had ceased to exist, are older by several centuries than the earliest known records of Phoenician writing. The twelfth century before our era may be regarded as their latest limit.

JOHN CHADWICK

Minoan Scripts:
Attempts at Decipherment

THE success of any decipherment depends upon the existence and availability of adequate material. How much is needed depends upon the nature of the problem to be solved, the character of the material, and so forth. Thus a short "bilingual" inscription, giving the same text in two languages, may be used as a crib, and may supply enough clues to enable the rest of the material to be interpreted. Where, as in this case, no bilingual exists, a far larger amount of text is required. Moreover, restrictions may be imposed by the type of text available; for instance, the thousands of Etruscan funerary inscriptions known have permitted us to gain only a very limited knowledge of the language, since the same phrases are repeated over and over again.

There are two methods by which one can proceed. One is by a methodical analysis, . . . the other is by more or less pure guesswork. Intelligent guessing must of course play some part in the first case; but there is a world of difference between a decipherment founded upon a careful internal analysis and one obtained by trial and error. Even this may produce the correct result; but it needs to be confirmed by application to virgin material, since it can gain no probability from its origin. A cool judgement is also needed to discriminate between what a text is likely or unlikely to contain. This faculty was notably lacking among those who risked their reputations on the conjectural method.

Evans and the more cautious of his followers had observed that with few apparent exceptions all the documents were lists or accounts. The reasons for this will be discussed later on. But this did not prevent some amateurs from venturing upon interpretations of their own. In most cases these would-be decipherers began by guessing the language of the inscriptions—most of them treated A and B and even the Phaistos Disk as all specimens of the same

From *The Decipherment of Linear B*. Cambridge: Cambridge University Press; 1958, pp. 26-39. By permission of the Cambridge University Press.

language. Some chose Greek, though the Greek which they obtained would not stand philological examination. Others chose a language with obscure affinities or one imperfectly known: Basque and Etruscan were proposed as candidates. Others again invented languages of their own for the purpose, a method which had the advantage that no one could prove them wrong. One attempt, by the Bulgarian Professor V. Georgiev, presented an ingenious *mélange* of linguistic elements, which resembled Greek when it suited his purpose and any other language when it did not. Almost all decipherers made resemblances with the Cypriot script their starting-point.

It would be tedious and unnecessary to discuss here all the attempts published up to 1950; a few samples of translations proposed should be enough to illustrate the nature of a good deal of the work on this problem.

The Czech scholar Professor Bedřich Hrozny established a deserved reputation for himself by his demonstration, about the time of the First World War, that the Hittite language written in a cuneiform script was in fact of Indo-European origin, thus opening the way to its study. His subsequent work unfortunately was not all as successful as this, and in his latter years he commenced an attack on all the unsolved scripts known to him. The Indus valley script—a prehistoric script of Northern India—was quickly "solved," he then turned to Minoan, and in 1949 produced a lengthy monograph. He collected all the inscriptions published to date, including some from Pylos, and without any discussion of method proceeded to interpret them. His method, as far as it can be observed, was to compare the Minoan signs with the signs of other scripts—not merely classical Cypriot, but Egyptian, Hieroglyphic Hittite, proto-Indian (the Indus valley script), Cuneiform, and Phoenician and other early alphabets. It is of course only too easy to find something in one of the scripts which looks vaguely like something in Linear B—and some of the resemblances are farfetched indeed. The other essential for the success of this method was that the language should turn out to be a kind of Indo-European language akin to Hittite. Without some such assumption the mere substitution of phonetic values would have been useless.

Here is his version of a Pylos text (given in English translation of the French of his publication):

Place of administration Ḥatahuâ: the palace has consumed all (?).
Place of administration Saḫur(i) ṭa (is) a bad (?) field (?): this (delivers in) tribute 22 (?) (measures), 6 T-measures of saffron capsules.

We now translate this text as follows:

Thus the priestess and the key-bearers and the Followers and Westreus (hold) leases: so much wheat 21.6 units.

The arbitrariness of Hrozny's work is so patent that no one has taken it seriously. It is a sad story which recurs too often in the world of scholarship: an old and respected figure produces in his dotage work unworthy of his maturity, and his friends and pupils have not the courage to tell him so.

In 1931 a small volume was published by the Oxford University Press entitled *Through Basque to Minoan*. Its author was F. G. Gordon, and he endeavoured to read Minoan by "assigning Basque values to the characters, on the chance that the two languages might be nearly related." The choice of Basque was dictated by the reasoning that Minoan was probably not Indo-European, and Basque is the only non-Indo-European language surviving in Europe which was not introduced in historical times.

His method is a popular one among the dilettanti. Each sign is first identified as an object, however vague the resemblance; this object is then given its name in the language assumed, and the sign is solved. Gordon was content to stay at this stage, regarding each sign as meaning a word. Others advanced further by using the "acrophonic" principle: this means that the sign may represent only the first part, or the first letter, of the word.

Gordon translated on this basis a few Knossos inventories as elegiac poems, reading the signs from left to right or right to left as suited his convenience, and even turning one tablet upside down, so that a pictogram of a chariot-frame could be misinterpreted as "an ovoid vase lying on its side, supported on two feet, and pouring out liquid." But when he turned to the Phaistos Disk he excelled himself. Here are a few lines from his translation:

. . . the lord walking on wings the breathless path, the star-smiter, the foaming gulf of waters, dogfish smiter on the creeping flower; the lord, smiter of the horse-hide (*or* the surface of the rock), the dog climbing the path, the dog emptying with the foot the water-pitchers, climbing the circling path, parching the wine-skin . . .

The same year saw another similar venture, by Miss F. Melian Stawell, in a book called modestly *A Clue to the Cretan Scripts*. Using the acrophonic principle mentioned above, she dealt with a great deal of the hieroglyphic script, the Phaistos Disk and some Linear A inscriptions. Little effort was made to interpret the Linear B tablets, except for a few formulas; she recognized that these were inventories and wisely kept to inscriptions whose sense was not obvious.

She started with the assumption that Evans was wrong and the Minoan language was in fact Greek. She named the objects in Greek, using some odd and even invented words, and extracted a syllabic value by abbreviating these. Each sign-group in the Phaistos Disk (obviously a word) is expanded to form a phrase, thus: *an-sa-kŏ-tĕ-re*. This is then expanded into what Miss Stawell thought was Greek:

> *Ana, Saō; koō, thea, Rē*
> Arise, Saviour! Listen, Goddess, Rhea!

She admitted the Greek was hardly archaic enough; clearly she knew little of what archaic Greek would look like. All her interpretations are similarly arbitrary.

Another attempt was made on the Phaistos Disk by the Greek scholar K. D. Ktistopoulos. It is only fair to say at once that he has also done some very useful statistical work on sign frequency in the Linear scripts. But here is part of his translation of the Disk, which he interprets as a Semitic language:

> Supreme—deity, of the powerful thrones star,
> supreme—tenderness of the consolatory words,
> supreme—donator of the prophecies,
> supreme—of the eggs the white. . . .

It does not need the author's apology for inexpertness in Semitic philology to make us suspect that something has gone wrong here.

One of the superficially most promising attempts at reading a Minoan text as Greek was made in 1930 by the Swedish archaeologist Professor Axel Persson. Four years earlier an expedition under his direction had found in a late Mycenaean tomb at Asine, near Nauplia in the north-east of the Peloponnese, a jar with what appears to be an inscription on the rim. He compared these signs with those of the classical Cypriot syllabary, and on this basis transcribed a few words. With one exception these looked little like Greek; but *po-se-i-ta-wo-no-se* was a plausible form, assuming the Cypriot spelling rules, for the Greek *Poseidāwōnos*, genitive of the name of the god Poseidon. Unfortunately, those expert in the Minoan scripts have been unable to share Persson's confidence in his identifications. The signs on the jar are quite unlike Linear B or any other known Bronze Age script, and it requires a good deal of imagination to see the resemblance to the classical Cypriot syllabary. In fact Ventris after a careful examination of the original came to the conclusion that the marks are not writing at all; they may be a kind of doodling, or possibly an attempt by an illiterate person to reproduce the appearance of writing. The lack of regularity and clear breaks between the signs is obvious, and at one end it tails off into a series of curves, which look more like a decorative pattern. It is interesting to observe that the form of the name read by Persson is now known to be wrong for the Mycenaean dialect, in which it appears as *po-se-da-o-no*.

Of a very different character was the work of the Bulgarian V. Georgiev, who summed up a series of earlier publications in a book entitled (in Russian) *Problems of the Minoan Language* published in Sofia in 1953. He dealt somewhat scornfully with his critics, but recognized that his theory would take a long time to perfect and could not convince everyone at once. The Minoan language was, he believed, a dialect of a widespread pre-Hellenic language spoken in Greece before the coming of the Greeks and possibly related to Hittite and other early Anatolian languages. This theory, which in one form or another has enjoyed considerable popularity, undoubtedly contains an element of truth, though we are still unable to say how much. One thing that is certain is that most Greek place-names are not composed of Greek words: there are a few that are, like *Thermopulai* "Hot-gates," but a good number, like *Athēnai* (Athens), *Mukēnai* (Mycenae), *Korinthos, Zakunthos, Halikarnassos, Lukabēttos,* are not only devoid of meaning, but belong to groups with a restricted range of endings; just as English names can be recognized by endings like *-bridge, -ton, -ford*. The preservation of place-names belonging to an older language is a common phenomenon: in England many Celtic names survive, such as the various rivers called *Avon* (Welsh *afon* "river"), though Celtic has not been spoken in the neighbourhood for more than a thousand years. The attempt has therefore been made to establish the pre-Hellenic language of Greece through the medium of these place-names; but although the fact of its existence is clear, its nature is still very much disputed.

Georgiev believed that the language of the tablets was largely archaic Greek, but containing a large number of pre-Hellenic elements. This gave him liberty to interpret as Greek, or quasi-Greek, any word which suited him, while anything that did not make sense as Greek could be explained away. It must be said that the Greek was often of a kind unrecognizable by trained philologists without the aid of Georgiev's commentary. For instance a phrase from a Knossos tablet is transcribed: *θetáaranà make* and translated "to the great grandmother-eagle," though the resemblance to Greek words is far to seek. For comparison the present version of the same phrase is: *ka-ra-e-ri-jo me-no* "in the month of Karaerios." Not a single sign has the same value. It is only fair to add that, after an initial period of hesitation, Georgiev has now fully accepted Ventris's theory.

In about 1950 a new method was tried by the German scholar

Professor Ernst Sittig. He took the Cypriot inscriptions which are not in Greek and analysed the frequency of the signs; then, assuming the affinity of this Cypriot language with Minoan, he identified the Linear B signs on a combination of their statistical frequency and their resemblance to the Cypriot syllabary. The idea was good, but unfortunately the basic assumption that the languages were related was wrong; and it would have needed more material than he had available to establish accurate frequency patterns. Of fourteen signs that he considered certainly identified by this means, we now know that only three were right. This method can in suitable circumstances offer valuable help; but there must be no doubt about the identity of the language and the spelling conventions.

There were, however, some exceptions to this catalogue of failures; notably those who confined themselves to such observations as could be made without claiming a solution of the whole problem. Evans himself set a high standard. Believing as he did that the Minoan language was not Greek and unlikely to resemble any hitherto known, he was not tempted by rash theories. He was sufficiently acquainted with other ancient scripts not to fall into some traps, though in one respect this led him astray.

A prominent feature of certain cuneiform and other scripts is the use of what are called "determinatives." These are signs which do not represent a sound but serve to classify the word to which they are added; thus the name of every town begins with the determinative sign meaning TOWN, of every man with that for MAN; similarly, all objects of wood have a special sign, and so forth. In a complicated script this is a very important clue to the meaning of a word; by classifying it the possible readings are narrowed down and it is much easier to identify. A very simple form of determinative survives in English in our use of capital letters to mark out a proper name.

Evans thought he had detected this system of determinatives in Linear B. He observed that a large number of words began with ♭, a sign resembling a high-backed chair with a crook, which his vivid imagination interpreted as a throne and sceptre. Even more words began with ⵏ, which in a stylized form was plainly descended from the double-axe sign of the hieroglyphic script. This is a frequent motif in cult scenes, and had some religious significance. The next step was to guess that these two signs, in addition to their phonetic value, were when used as initials determinatives denoting "royal" and "religious" words: the one, words connected with the palace administration; the other, with the religious practices which were of great importance to the Minoans. Although this theory had few adherents among the experts—Hrozny was one—the prestige of Evans' name gave it some authority; it was in fact totally misleading. It depended upon mere guesswork, and a full analysis of the use of the signs would have shown a much more likely theory. The true explanation will appear in the next chapter.

A luckier shot emerged from Evans' attempt at using the Cypriot clue. A remarkable tablet showed on two lines horse-like heads followed by numerals. The left-hand piece was not recorded by Evans; I identified it myself in Iraklion Museum in 1955 and joined it to the rest. One head in each line was rather smaller and had no mane, and was preceded by the same two-sign word. These were both simple signs which could fairly safely be equated with similar Cypriot signs, reading *po-lo*. Now the Greek word for a "foal" is *pōlos;* it is in fact related to the English *foal,* since by a change known to philologists as Grimm's law, *p-* in Greek is regularly represented by *f-* in certain Germanic languages including English. The coincidence was striking; but so convinced was Evans that Linear B could *not* contain Greek that he rejected this interpretation, though with obvious reluctance. It is now fashionable to give him credit for having interpreted this word; what a pity he was unwilling to follow up the clue on which he had stumbled.

Another sound piece of work was done in an article by A. E. Cowley published in 1927. Following a suggestion of Evans he discussed a series of tablets which dealt with women, since they were denoted by a self-evident pictogram. Following the entry for WOMEN there were other figures preceded by two words ⊕ ⊓ and ⊕ ⋔; it was not difficult to guess that these meant "children," that is to say, "boys" and "girls," though there was at this time no means of determining which was which—Evans and Cowley were both wrong.

In 1940 a new name appears for the first time in the literature of the subject: Michael Ventris, then only eighteen years old. His article called "introducing the Minoan Language" was published in the *American Journal of Archaeology*; in writing to the editor he had been careful to conceal his age, but although in later years he dismissed the article as "puerile," it was none the less soundly written. The basic idea was to find a language which might be related to Minoan. Ventris's candidate was Etruscan; not a bad guess, because the Etruscans, according to an ancient tradition, came from the Aegean to Italy. Ventris attempted to see how the Etruscan language would fit with Linear B. The results, as he admitted, were negative; but the Etruscan idea remained a fixation, which possessed him until in 1952 the Greek solution finally imposed itself on him. So firmly was Evans's Minoan theory based that at this date Greek seemed out of the question. "The theory that Minoan could be Greek," Ventris wrote, "is based of course

upon a deliberate disregard for historical plausibility." Hardly anyone would have ventured to disagree.

The most valuable contribution came a little later (1943-50),
from the American Dr. Alice E. Kober. She died at the early age
of forty-three in 1950, just too soon to witness and take part in the
decipherment for which she had done so much to prepare the way.
She was the first to set out methodically to discover the nature of
the language through the barrier of the script. The questions she
asked were simple ones. Was it an inflected language, using different endings to express grammatical forms? Was there a consistent means of denoting a plural? Did it distinguish genders?
Her solutions were partial, but none the less a real step forward.
She was able to demonstrate, for instance, that the totalling for-
mula, clearly shown by summations on a number of tablets, had
two forms: one was used for MEN and for one class of animals, the
other for WOMEN, another class of animals, and also for swords
and the like. This was not only clear evidence of a distinction of
gender; it also led to the identification of the means by which the
sex of animals is represented (that is, by adding marks to the
appropriate ideograms). Even more remarkable was her demonstration that certain words had two variant forms, which were
longer than the simple form by one sign. These are now commonly,
and irreverently, known as "Kober's triplets." She interpreted them
as further evidence of inflexion; but they were destined to play an
even more important role in the final decipherment. I do not think
there can be any doubt that Miss Kober would have taken a leading
part in events of later years, had she been spared; she alone of the
earlier investigators was pursuing the track which led Ventris ultimately to the solution of the problem.

At this point we must take up again the history of discovery.
Up to 1939 Linear B tablets were known only from one site,
Knossos in Crete. But a small number of vases had been found in
mainland Greece having inscriptions which had been painted on
them before they were fired. These showed some variant forms,
but had the same general appearance as Linear B. The presence of
a Cretan script was not surprising, since on Evans's theory of a
Minoan Empire Cretan imports might obviously be found at any
site under Minoan control. But just before the Second World War
the situation was suddenly and dramatically reversed.

Schliemann had been led to Mycenae by believing in the truth
of the Homeric legend; the obscure town of classical Greece, which
sent eighty men to fight the Persians at Thermopylae in 480 B.C.,
had once been the capital of a great state. Could not other Homeric
cities be located? This was the question in the mind of Professor

Carl Blegen of the University of Cincinnati, who was already recognized as one of the foremost experts on the prehistoric period in Greece, and whose careful work on the site of Troy was justly famous. He set out now to find the palace of another Homeric monarch, Nestor, the garrulous old warrior whose name was a by-word for longevity.

Nestor ruled at Pylos; but where was Pylos? Even in classical times there was a proverb which ran: "There is a Pylos before a Pylos and there is another besides." The debate over Nestor's Pylos began with the Alexandrian commentators on Homer in the third century B.C. and has continued intermittently ever since. The geographer Strabo (first century A.D.) gives a long discussion of the problem; there were three likely candidates: one in Elis (north-west of the Peloponnese), one in Triphylia (centre of west coast), and one in Messenia (south-west). For various reasons Strabo picked on the Triphylian one, and a famous German archaeologist called Dörpfeld tried to clinch the matter in the early years of this century when he located some Mycenaean tombs at a place called Kakóvatos. But although tombs usually imply a residential site in the neighbourhood, no palace could be found.

Blegen resolved to pay no attention to Strabo and to explore the Messenian area. It was here that the modern town of Pylos is situated, at the south of the bay of Navarino—the scene of the famous naval engagement of 1827, when the British, French and Russian forces destroyed the Turkish and Egyptian fleets and thus struck a decisive blow for Greek independence. The ancient town of classical times was at the northern end of the bay, the site of a famous operation by the Athenians in the Peloponnesian War (424 B.C.). But Strabo records that this was not the original site, as the inhabitants had moved there from an earlier town "under Mount Aigaleon;" unfortunately we do not know precisely which this mountain was, nor how close "under" implies. Blegen found a likely site some four miles north of the bay at a place now called Epáno Englianós, and together with the Greek Dr. Kourouniotis organized a joint American-Greek expedition to dig it in 1939. Blegen began work tentatively with the aid of one student, and by an astonishing piece of luck their first trial trench ran through what is now known as the archive room. Tablets were found within twenty-four hours, and the first season's work produced no fewer than 600 clay tablets, similar to the Knossos ones and written in the identical Linear B script. Here again war intervened and the exacavation could not be resumed until 1952, when further finds of tablets were made. Subsequent digs have continued to increase slightly the number of texts known. The war prevented study and publication of the first finds; but it was possible to photograph the

tablets before they were stored away in the vaults of the Bank of
Athens, where they remained intact throughout the occupation.
After the war Blegen entrusted their editing to Professor Emmett
L. Bennett Jr., who has now become the world expert on the
reading of Mycenaean texts. His edition, prepared from the photographs, appeared in 1951; a new edition, corrected from the original
texts and containing also the more recent discoveries, appeared at
the end of 1955. Further finds are still (1957) being made at this
site.

To complete the history of the appearance of the texts we may
anticipate a little and mention the discovery in 1952 by Professor
Wace of the first tablets from Mycenae. These were found not in
the royal palace, which had been dug by Schliemann and Tsoundas
at the end of the last century, but in separate buildings or houses
outside the walls of the acropolis or royal castle. A further find in
1954 brought the number of tablets from this site up to fifty.

Evans' reaction to the news of the tablets from Pylos is not
recorded; he was then eighty-eight and he died before the matter
could be discussed. But his followers, who included the vast
majority of archaeologists in every country, were quick to think
of explanations. "Loot from Crete" was seriously proposed; but
was it likely that a pirate or raider would carry away a bulky
collection of fragile documents that he could not read? A more
plausible theory was that the Mycenaean raiders had carried off
from Crete the scribes who had kept the accounts of the Minoan
palace and set them to work at their trade back at home. This
would explain, at need, a Greek king keeping his accounts in
Minoan, just as in the Middle Ages an English king might have his
accounts kept in Latin. But it may be doubted whether anyone
keeps accounts unless he needs to do so; an illiterate community
will not import accountants unless the economic circumstances of
its life change sufficiently to make them essential. A further idea
was also mooted: that the Mycenaeans were not Greeks at all, but
spoke some other language. The truth, that the Knossos tablets too
were in Greek, was hardly considered.

Bennett, working on the new material, proceeded with sound
sense and caution. He wrote a doctoral thesis on it, but this was
not published. His article on the different system of weights and
measures in Linear A and Linear B has been mentioned above.
But his outstanding contribution is the establishment of the
signary; the recognition of variant forms and the distinction of
separate signs. How difficult the task is only those who have tried
can tell. It is easy enough for us to recognize the same letter in our
alphabet as written by half a dozen different people, despite the
use of variant forms. But if you do not know what is the possible

range of letters, nor the sound of the words they spell, it is impossible to be sure if some of the rare ones are separate letters or mere variants. This is still the position with regard to Linear B. . . . At this time Ventris was already exchanging ideas with Bennett, and his suggestions must have contributed to the satisfactory outcome. Their correspondence laid the foundation of a friendship, which developed during Bennett's visits to Europe.

With the publication of *The Pylos Tablets* in 1951 the scene was set for the decipherment. Orderly analysis, begun by Miss Kober and Bennett, could now take the place of speculation and guesswork; but it required clear judgement to perceive the right methods, concentration to plod through the laborious analysis, perseverance to carry on despite meagre gains, and finally the spark of genius to grasp the right solution when at last it emerged from the painstaking manipulation of meaningless signs.

JOHN CHADWICK

Success with Linear B

CRYPTOGRAPHY is a science of deduction and controlled experiment; hypotheses are formed, tested and often discarded. But the residue which passes the test grows and grows until finally there comes a point when the experimenter feels solid ground beneath his feet: his hypotheses cohere, and fragments of sense emerge from their camouflage. The code "breaks." Perhaps this is best defined as the point when the likely leads appear faster than they can be followed up. It is like the initiation of a chain-reaction in atomic physics; once the critical threshold is passed, the reaction propagates itself. Only in the simplest experiments or codes does it complete itself with explosive violence. In the more difficult cases there is much work still to be done, and the small areas of sense, though sure proof of the break, remain for a while isolated; only gradually does the picture become filled out.

Ibid., pp. 67-70.

In June 1952 Ventris felt that the Linear B script had broken. Admittedly the tentative Greek words suggested in Work Note 20 were too few to carry conviction; in particular they implied an unlikely set of spelling conventions. But as he transcribed more and more texts, so the Greek words began to emerge in greater numbers; new signs could now be identified by recognizing a word in which one sign only was a blank, and this value could then be tested elsewhere. The spelling rules received confirmation, and the pattern of the decipherment became clear.

It so happened that at this moment Ventris was asked by the B.B.C. to give a talk on the Third Programme in connexion with the publication of *Scripta Minoa II* [Edited by Sir John Myres]. He determined to take this opportunity of bringing his discovery before the public. He gave first a brief historical account of the script and its discovery, and then proceeded to outline his method. Finally came the astonishing announcement:

During the last few weeks, I have come to the conclusion that the Knossos and Pylos tablets must, after all, be written in Greek—a difficult and archaic Greek, seeing that it is 500 years older than Homer and written in a rather abbreviated form, but Greek nevertheless.

Once I made this assumption, most of the peculiarities of the language and spelling which had puzzled me seemed to find a logical explanation; and although many of the tablets remain as incomprehensible as before, many others are suddenly beginning to make sense.

He went on to quote four well known Greek words which he claimed to have found (*poimēn*, "shepherd," *kerameus*, "potter," *khalkeus*, "bronze-smith," *khrusoworgos*, "gold-smith"), and to translate eight phrases. He ended on a suitably cautious note: "I have suggested that there is now a better chance of reading these earliest European inscriptions than ever before, but there is evidently a great deal more work to do before we are all agreed on the solution of the problem."

I do not think it can be said that this broadcast made a great impression; but I for one was an eager listener. In view of the recurrent claims that had been made, I did not regard Ventris's system as standing much chance; in particular I already had a pretty clear notion what Mycenaean Greek should look like, and I doubted whether Ventris had. The word *khrusoworgos*, however, was encouraging; *w* did not exist in most forms of Greek of the classical period, but should certainly appear in an archaic dialect, since its loss, as in Homer, was known to be recent. But the principles outlined by Ventris were in close agreement with those I had formulated for myself; if correctly followed the results might well be right. And I was not, as most of the archaeologists were,

prejudiced against the Greek solution; six years before I had tried
to test the few available Pylos texts on that assumption, but the
material was too scanty. I must confess that in 1952 I was ill
prepared; shortly before that I had been appointed to a post at
Cambridge, and all my spare time was devoted to writing lectures
for the following October.

The claim of Ventris, however, was too important and too relevant to my subject, the Greek dialects, to be overlooked. The first
thing was to see Sir John Myres and ask his opinion, for I knew
he was in touch with Ventris. He sat as usual in his canvas chair
at a great desk, his legs wrapped in a rug. He was too infirm to
move much, and he motioned me to a chair. "Mm, Ventris," he said
in answer to my question, "he's a young architect." As Myres at
that time was himself eighty-two, I wondered if "young" meant
less than sixty. "Here's his stuff," he went on, "I don't know what to
make of it. I'm not a philologist." On the whole he appeared sceptical, though admitting that he had not sufficient specialized
knowledge to judge if the proposed Greek was sound. But he had
some of Ventris's notes, including the latest version of the grid,
which he let me copy, promising at the same time to put me in
direct contact with Ventris.

I went home·eager to try out the new theory. I approached the
matter very cautiously, for impressed as I had been by the broadcast, I had a horrid feeling the Greek would turn out to be only
vague resemblances to Greek words, as in Georgiev's "decipherment," and wrong for the sort of dialect we expected. I set to work
transcribing words from the two sets of texts, and in four days
I had convinced myself that the identifications were in the main
sound. I collected a list of twenty-three plausible Greek words I
had found in the tablets, some of which had not then been noted
by Ventris, and on 9 July I wrote to Myres stating my conclusion.
I wrote, too, to Ventris, congratulating him on having found the
solution, and putting forward a number of new suggestions.

His reply (13 July) was typically frank and modest. "At the
moment," he wrote, "I feel rather in need of moral support. . . .
I'm conscious that there's a *lot* which so far can't be very satisfactorily explained." I had tentatively asked if I could be any help
to him; he replied: "I've been feeling the need of a 'mere philologist' to keep me on the right lines. . . . It would be extremely useful
to me if I could count on your help, not only in trying to make sense
out of the material, but also in drawing the correct conclusions
about the formations in terms of dialect and stage of development."
Thus was formed a partnership which was to last more than four
years.

A further sentence of this letter must be quoted for it introduces a crucial point. "I'm glad we coincided in some of the values which occurred to me after I wrote to Myres, though I suppose a court of law might suppose I'd pre-cooked the material in such a way that the coincidence wasn't conclusive." If we had both suggested the same values independently, only two conclusions were possible: that they were right and the decipherment was therefore proved; or that Ventris had deliberately planted the evidence for others to find. One had only to make Ventris's acquaintance to realize that the latter alternative was out of the question. Thus at the outset I felt absolutely sure that the foundation had been truly laid, whatever difficulties remained; and nothing since has shaken my faith in the least. Ventris himself had attacks of cold feet that summer; for instance he wrote on 28 July: "Every other day I get so doubtful about the whole thing that I'd almost rather it was someone else's." He was worried over some discrepancies between Mycenaean and classical Greek; on some of these points I was able to set his mind at rest. For instance, there was no reason to be bothered by the absence of the definite article; philologists had anticipated its absence in the early stages of the language. This phase of our co-operation did not last long, for in an amazingly short time Ventris had mastered the details of Greek philology for himself.

JOHN CHADWICK

Michael Ventris:
a Brief Biography

THE urge to discover secrets is deeply ingrained in human nature; even the least curious mind is roused by the promise of sharing knowledge withheld from others. Some are fortunate enough to find a job which consists in the solution of mysteries, whether it be the physicist who tracks down a hitherto unknown nuclear

Ibid., pp. 1-4.

particle or the policeman who detects a criminal. But most of us are driven to sublimate this urge by the solving of artificial puzzles devised for our entertainment. Detective stories or crossword puzzles cater for the majority; the solution of secret codes may be the hobby of a few. This is the story of the solving of a genuine mystery which had baffled experts for half a century.

In 1936 a fourteen-year-old schoolboy was among a party who visited Burlington House in London to see an exhibition organized to mark the fiftieth anniversary of the British School of Archaeology at Athens. They heard a lecture by the grand old man of Greek archaeology, Sir Arthur Evans; he told them of his discovery of a long forgotten civilization in the Greek island of Crete, and of the mysterious writing used by this fabulous people of prehistory. In that hour a seed was planted that was dramatically to bear fruit sixteen years later; for this boy was already keenly interested in ancient scripts and languages. At the age of seven he had bought and studied a German book on the Egyptian hieroglyphs. He vowed then and there to take up the challenge of the undeciphered Cretan writing; he began to read the books on it, he even started a correspondence with the experts. And in the fullness of time he succeeded where they had failed. His name was Michael Ventris.

As this book is largely the story of his achievement, it will not be out of place to begin with a short account of his life. He was born on 12 July 1922 of a well-to-do English family, which came originally from Cambridgeshire. His father was an Army officer in India, his mother a highly gifted and beautiful lady who was half-Polish; she brought him up in an artistic atmosphere, and accustomed him to spend his holidays abroad or in visiting the British Museum. His schooling too was unconventional; he went to school at Gstaad in Switzerland, where he was taught in French and German. Not content with this, he quickly mastered the local Swiss-German dialect—an accomplishment that later on endeared him at once to the Swiss scholars whom he met—and even taught himself Polish when he was six. He never outgrew this love of languages; a few weeks in Sweden after the war were enough for him to become proficient in Swedish and get a temporary job on the strength of it. Later he corresponded with Swedish scholars in their own language. He had not only a remarkable visual memory, but, what is rarely combined with it, the ability to learn a language by ear.

Back in England, he won a scholarship to Stowe School, where, as he once told me with typical modesty, he "did a bit of Greek." One cannot help thinking that his unusual interests would have made him difficult to fit into a normal school routine; but he seems to have settled down happily enough, though none would then have prophesied that his hobby would make him famous. He did not go on to a university; he had made up his mind to become an architect, and he went straight to the Architectural Association School in London. The war came to interrupt his studies, and he enrolled in the R.A.F., where he flew as navigator in a bomber squadron. Characteristically he chose navigation. "It's so much more interesting that mere flying," he remarked; and on one occasion he horrified the captain of his aircraft by navigating solely by maps he had made himself.

After the war, he returned to the study of architecture, and took his diploma with honours in 1948. Those who saw his work as a student were impressed and predicted a brilliant future for him as an architect. He worked for a time with a team at the Ministry of Education engaged on the design of new schools; and he and his wife, herself an architect, designed a charming modern house for themselves and their two children. In 1956 he was awarded the first *Architects' Journal* Research Fellowship; his subject was "Information for the Architect."

He might well have become one of the leading figures in his profession; but it was not in this way that he was to win fame. He had never lost his interest in the Minoan scripts, and with a rare concentration he devoted much of his spare time to painstaking studies of that abstruse problem. In 1952 he claimed to have found the key to its understanding, a claim which has been fully vindicated during the last five years. Honours he received included the Order of the British Empire "for services to Mycenaean palaeography," the title of honorary research associate at University College, London, and an honorary doctorate of philosophy from the University of Uppsala. These were but a foretaste of the honours that would surely have been paid to him.

"Those whom the gods love die young," said the Greek poet Menander; yet we had never dreamed that the life which had shown so much genius, and held promise of so much more, would be cut short in the very hour of triumph. On 6 September 1956, driving home alone late at night on the Great North Road near Hatfield, his car collided with a lorry, and he was killed instantly.

For me, who had the privilege of being his friend and of working closely with him for more than four years, it is hard to find words in which to describe him. I know how he would recoil from extravagant praise; yet he was a man whom nothing but superlatives fitted. His brilliance is witnessed by his achievement; but I cannot do justice to his personal charm, his gaiety and his modesty. From the beginning he advanced his claims with suitable caution and hesitancy; a promising sign to those who had repeatedly experienced the assurance of previous decipherers. But even when his success was assured, when others heaped lavish praise on him, he remained simple and unassuming, always ready to listen, to help and to understand.

If we ask what were the special qualities that made possible his achievement, we can point to his capacity for infinite pains, his powers of concentration, his meticulous accuracy, his beautiful draughtsmanship. All these were necessary; but there was much more that is hard to define. His brain worked with astonishing rapidity, so that he could think out all the implications of a suggestion almost before it was out of your mouth. He had a keen appreciation of the realities of a situation; the Mycenaeans were to him no vague abstractions, but living people whose thoughts he could penetrate. He himself laid stress on the visual approach to the problem; he made himself so familiar with the visual aspect of the texts that large sections were imprinted on his mind simply as visual patterns, long before the decipherment gave them meaning. But a merely photographic memory was not enough, and it was here that his architectural training came to his aid. The architect's eye sees in a building not a mere façade, a jumble of ornamental and structural features; it looks beneath the appearance and distinguishes the significant parts of the pattern, the structural elements and framework of the building. So too Ventris was able to discern among the bewildering variety of the mysterious signs, patterns and regularities which betrayed the underlying structure. It is this quality, the power of seeing order in apparent confusion, that has marked the work of all great men.

ALAN J. B. WACE

The Golden Ring

THE following adventure of the mythical archaeologist George Evesham is anchored on the site of ancient Mycenae, where Professor Wace was excavating during the summer of 1953.

THE tide of war carried me in 1917 to Salonica where I saw my friend George Evesham who was shortly afterwards mortally wounded in the fruitless Allied offensive in April of that year. Of his death I have written elsewhere, but what I have to tell now was also connected with his death to some extent. From Salonica I was sent on to Athens for special duty and it so happened that when Evesham was killed his colonel, whom I had met at Salonica, wrote to me once or twice about the disposal of Evesham's personal belongings. Later at the end of the summer when I thought that all Evesham's affairs had been settled, I was surprised to receive another letter from his colonel and with it a small packet.

The letter ran as follows:

"I am sending you in a separate packet something else that belonged to poor George Evesham. It is a Greek gold ring on which he set much store and always wore round his neck like an identity disk. He was not wearing it when he was killed because one night when he was asleep two subalterns cut the string and removed it for a rag. Poor Evesham was much put out, but as this happened only one of two days before the offensive he never recovered it. Of the subalterns one was killed in the same attack and the other died of wounds. The latter gave the ring and string to a chaplain in the Casualty Clearing Station. He seemed to fancy that judging by the way poor Evesham regarded the ring as a mascot he was responsible for his death, because he was not wearing it when he was killed. The chaplain went to Malta in a hospital ship and has only just returned here and that is why we did not know about the ring before. Anyway here is the ring and it is said to be Byzantine and ever so many hundred years old B.C. Still you will know all about it and what it is best to be done with it. Perhaps the Athens Museum might like it or you could give it to the British Museum. The silly bit of string to which the ring was fastened poor Evesham always wore with it and would never change. Please acknowledge on receipt. . . ."

When I opened the little packet which accompanied this rather characteristic military letter I found, in a Bryant and May match box, a worn gold ring tied to a rough piece of woolen yarn obviously hand spun and knotted thrice as though it had been cut. The ring was small and rather broad, but plain except for two bands of tiny gold pearls. It had a large almond-shaped bezel also of gold on which so far as I could see a quadruped of some kind seemed to

Reprinted from *Archaeology*, Vol. 7, 1954, with the permission of Mrs. A. J. B. Wace.

be represented in intaglio. The type of ring I recognized at once as characteristically Mycenaean and certainly ever so many centuries old, probably thirteen at least B.C., but certainly not Byzantine except to such unbelievers as told Schliemann that the royal treasures of Mycenae, which he had found, were Byzantine and therefore un-Homeric. I wondered what to do with the ring for it was so worn that it had little artistic value. Still as Evesham had always been very fond of working in the Mycenaean room of the National Museum at Athens I thought I might follow up his colonel's suggestion and see whether the museum would like it as a memorial of him.

Accordingly a few days later when I had a couple of hours free in the morning I went to the National Museum with the ring. I showed it to the then Director who was specially interested in the Mycenaean collection. After looking at it closely with a glass he said it was certainly genuine and added that the quadruped must be a bull because that was the animal most popular with the Mycenaeans for engraving on seals and gems. He promised he would have a plaster cast made so that we should be better able to judge, and then took a lump of fine beeswax from his desk and pressed the bezel of the ring into it. As he did so his fingers became entangled in the string. This annoyed him and he flew into a temper, which he did very easily, and saying that he did not want that dirty bit of string, he cut it with a pen knife from his desk. After studying the impression carefully he said he could not decide, but still was in favor of recognizing the animal as a bull. He undertook that if I would come back in two or three days he would have the plaster impression ready and that we would then go into the question more fully.

The following week when my turn for a few hours off duty came round once more I called again at the Museum. To my surprise I found it in a somewhat disturbed condition. The very day after I had seen him the Director had had a severe stroke and was now lying ill in bed at his house, speechless and helpless. The doctors said it was unlikely that he would regain the use of his faculties, but that he might survive for several months. In the meantime the assistant director had taken charge and was doing his best to cope with the situation which was made worse by the fact that one of the senior attendants had disappeared. I enquired after the ring and he called the museum technician who produced a plaster impression of the ring. We discussed the subject, but could arrive at no conclusion. I felt it was not a bull but some other animal, while both the assistant director and the technician were ready to accept the bull identification. So I asked to see the ring again. To the assistant director's horror the ring could not be found. He rummaged

through the safe and the special cupboards in the director's room
where it should have been, but there was no sign of it. Then an idea
struck him and he asked me what day it was I had brought it. When
I told him he said that on the very next day the missing attendant,
Thersites Glossopoulos, had failed to put in an appearance. It was
consequently suggested that the attendant had stolen the ring and
perhaps other things and vanished. The police were at once informed
and a strict watch was ordered to be kept on all men trying to
depart from Piraeus, Patras, or any other port whence vessels sailed
to other countries. The passport, police, and port authorities were
supplied with his name and particulars, so that if he tried to leave
even by signing on as a seaman he would be recognized and
detained.

Days, however, passed and no word came of the missing man. At
last it was discovered that he had a brother, a baker, at Chalcis and
I gladly accepted an invitation to go with the gendarmerie officer
to make enquires. When we arrived at Chalcis, the baker was
summoned to the gendarmerie station and interrogated. He said
his brother had come to see him a week or two before and stayed
a few days, but then had left suddenly, presumably to go back to his
post in Athens. We then went on to the bakery to question his wife.
She called on fire and lightning to burn her, but she knew nothing
more. She was sent into an inner room and their small daughter,
Koula, who was about ten or twelve, was called before the local
sergeant in charge of the interrogation. He pulled a tattered note-
book and a broken pencil from the lining of his cap, licked the
pencil, and looked ferociously at the girl.

"Now, tell us the truth!" he thundered in his sternest official
voice, "How many gold rings did your uncle take away with him?
Your father says he took only one, but we know better. He took six.
Now tell us the truth or you will go to prison and never come out."

The girl though obviously terrified was staunch and said simply
that her uncle had had no gold rings and that she believed he had
gone back to Athens. I felt convinced by the girl's manner that she
was telling the absolute truth and so begged the officer that the
unlucky baker and his family should be left in peace.

The railway officials said that the missing man had not gone
back to Athens by train. A boatman, however, told us that about
the time Thersites disappeared from Chalcis a Greek ship laden with
magnesite from Limne had sailed for England. Further the captain
of the vessel, also a native of Chalcis, was a godbrother of Thersites.
We jumped to the obvious conclusion. Thersites had persuaded his
godbrother to take him on as one of his crew and so had slipped
inconspicuously out of the country. On our return to Athens orders
were at once telegraphed to Gibraltar that the vessel should be

detained and searched for the man. The man, when found, was to be sent back to Greece as soon as possible for examination. Again we waited but no news came from Gibraltar and no news came from England of the ship's arrival. The vessel, the Aspasia Arabatzoglou, was never heard of again. Most probably she was sunk with all hands by the Germans somewhere in the central Mediterranean where enemy submarines were then very active.

In the winter of 1917-18 I managed to get home on leave and while in England I helped Evesham's mother to prepare the little memoir of him which was prefixed to the collected edition of his poems. I thus had the opportunity of going through his notebooks and other papers and while doing so I found his notes about the ring—how he had obtained it and some other details.

It had come into his hands in 1913. That spring he happened to be in Mycenae staying at the little inn, "The Fair Helen of Menelaus," which archaeologists always delight to patronize. One morning when he was walking up the road towards the citadel he found the road crowded with a party of shepherds who with their flocks, wives and families, dogs and cats, chickens, and other belongings were moving up into the hills for the summer. Just before Evesham reached the point where the road passes in front of the Lion Gate he overtook a group of three old women who were spinning wool as they walked along. He paid no attention to them, but one of them called him and when he turned around she showed him the ring. He took it, looked at it, and saw how worn it was and handed it back saying he did not wish to buy it. The old woman then said she did not wish to sell it, but wished to give it to him. He refused to take it because, though it had little archaeological importance, owing to its condition, it was still gold and therefore of some value. The old woman, however, insisted and so he took it and showed it would not go on his finger, as is usually the case with this type of Mycenaean ring. One of the other old women unwound a piece of the yarn from her distaff and slipped the ring on it, but she could not break the thread. So the third old woman took the scissors which were hanging by a string from her belt and cut the yarn. The first woman, the one who had produced the ring, then knotted the yarn and put it over Evesham's head.

"*Mi to khasis!* (Don't lose it!)" she said, as she did so.

"*Mi to dhosis!* (Don't sell it!)" added the second.

"*Mi to kopsis* (Don't cut it!)" concluded the third with an air of finality.

Although he thought it all sounded rather silly, Evesham to humor them said he would always wear it and thanked them very much. He then turned off to go up to the Lion Gate, but as he did so he remembered he had never asked them where it was found. He

turned back to go after them, but though he walked some distance
up the path in the direction they were going, he could not find them.
They seemed, he wrote, to have vanished.

Evesham does not seem to have shown the ring to anyone at
the National Museum or to anyone else in Athens, but on his return
to England he took the ring to the British Museum. There one of the
assistant-keepers of the Greek and Roman Department treated the
ring coldly, said it seemed genuine though a poor example, showed
he did not think much of it, but could not decide whether the quadruped was a bull or some other four-footed beast. He handed it to
one of the technicians, asking him to prepare plaster impressions
to help them to decide the nature of the animal. After two days Evesham called again and the assistant-keeper rang for his technician
to bring the ring and the impressions. An attendant came in to say
that the technician had not yet arrived that morning. Instructions
were given to telephone to his house to find out if he was ill and
to bring in the ring and impressions. A little cardboard tray was
produced and in it lay the ring, two plaster impressions of the
design on its bezel and the woolen thread which had been cut and
separated from the ring. While Evesham and the assistant-keeper
were fruitlessly debating the vexed question of the identity of the
quadruped, word was brought that the technician had left home at
his usual hour for the Museum. Hard on the heels of that message
came one from the Middlesex Hospital to say that he had been
knocked down by a car, seriously injured, and had died soon after
reaching the casualty ward.

Having failed to gain any enlightenment from the British
Museum, Evesham took the ring with him to Oxford when he went
there at the beginning of October. Oxford then boasted the possession of the chief experts in the Minoan and Mycenaean archaeology
of Greece. The three most renowned of these sat for some little time
arguing the case of the ring and its design from all aspects in the
typical Oxonian manner. The ring they all declared was not Mycenaean but Minoan, for all the civilization of Mycenae and everything
found there came from Crete. The ring therefore was Minoan,
that is to say Cretan, and since the bull, as witness the Minotaur,
was the legendary animal of Crete the quadruped on the ring must
be a bull. They further told Evesham that the ring was an inferior
specimen and obviously of late date and in such bad condition as
to be almost worthless except for its metallic value. One of the
experts began to cut the woolen thread, but Evesham checked him
just in time. He had, however, to knot the yarn to prevent a break.

Evesham, who still believed in the ring and was determined if
possible to solve the problem of the representation on it, was not
discouraged by its chilly reception both in the British Museum and

in Oxford. He wrote that he had a feeling somehow that the ring was connected with the history of Mycenae and never ceased to regret that he had not asked the old women where and how it was found. He wondered whether he would take it to Cambridge and see whether the rival university could help him, because the principal Oxford expert had been suddenly attacked by a serious infection of his eyes. He was advised, however, so Evesham noted, that no one in Cambridge was of any competence in Minoan or Mycenaean matters.

As we know, Evesham continued to wear the ring and constantly took it with him wherever he went, regarding it as a kind of mascot. Thus it happened that he had it with him when he was sent to join the Salonica army and, but for the untimely trick of the two subalterns, would have been wearing it in the Allied offensive in 1917 when he was mortally wounded.

After I read Evesham's notes about the ring and its history my interest and curiosity were still more excited and I resolved that, when I had an opportunity of revisiting Athens, I would again consult the authorities of the National Museum to see what further information could be gleaned. I even dreamed of visiting Mycenae and inquiring there whether it was possible to get into touch with the local shepherds and find the old women. For a moment I even fancied myself discovering some rich and hitherto unknown royal tomb hidden in the glens of Argolis, which would make my name as famous as that of Schliemann. Fortunately my opportunity came sooner that I could have hoped. So many British experts left the Aegean to attend the Peace Conference in Paris that their places had to be filled and so I was, much to my delight, once again sent out to Greece early in 1919.

As soon as I could after my arrival in Athens I called at the National Museum and found that my old friend, Dr. Klavdianos, had just been made director. The previous one had recently died, after being bedridden ever since the episode of Evesham's ring. Klavdianos had obtained the keys of the late director from his widow, who had been unwilling to part with them while her husband still lived and held his post. Klavdianos was thus exploring all the cupboards in the Director's office as well as the locked drawers in his desk where his private papers had been kept. I naturally asked him if he had come upon any trace of the ring.

"What ring?" he asked, and so I explained and said that the technician ought still to have one at least of the plaster impressions. Then he pulled open one of the private drawers in the director's desk which he had just unlocked to inspect and sort the contents. From this he picked out a gold ring.

"Is this it?" he asked. It was the very ring and in the same drawer we found the cut piece of woolen yarn on which it had been fastened and a wax impression of the design on the bezel. I was delighted to see the ring again and he was equally delighted that it was now proved that Thersites Glossopoulos had never stolen it. When the news spread among the other museum attendants they also were highly pleased because the honesty of their body was at last vindicated.

I then asked Klavdianos if he would like to have the ring as a gift to the Museum. He gladly accepted it and handed it at once to be numbered and entered in the inventory while we talked over other things. A small label was typed out stating that this Mycenaean ring was presented in memory of Evesham who had fallen fighting for Greece against the Bulgarians in Macedonia, and Klavdianos asked me to go with him into the Mycenaean room and select a suitable place for its exhibition. This we did and left the ring in a case containing some of the other treasures from Agamemnon's city.

We also discussed the problem of the animal represented in the intaglio on the bezel and Klavdianos said that if I would come back in a few days he would go through the collection of Mycenaean rings and engraved gems and sealstones and see if he could come to some satisfactory solution. So about a week later I visited the Museum again.

"They have taken it!" laconically remarked the chief attendant who met me and he added some derogatory remarks about "them." I failed to understand him at first, but soon elicited the fact that Evesham's ring, which Klavdianos and I had put into a locked and otherwise secure glass exhibition case not a week ago, had disappeared about three days before. In reply to my inquiries he told me that that particular day was rainy and consequently the light in the museum was not good and there were loud claps of thunder and vivid lightning. Visitors were naturally few in the Mycenaean room, only three in fact, old women wearing "Vlach" or shepherd clothing who had obviously come in to get out of the rain. The attendant on duty did not watch them very closely because they were clearly so harmless and as they moved about from case to case they exclaimed to one another in uncouth dialect about particular treasures that attracted them. His attention was distracted for a moment when the man who had repaired the roof looked in to ask whether it was watertight. When he looked round again the old women had gone and he concluded they had moved on to see the sculpture galleries. No one, however, had noticed the old women in any other gallery and no one had seen them go out, but as just at that time the sun had come out brilliantly for a brief spell, it was assumed they had taken advantage of it to go their way.

The fact that the ring was missing was not noticed until the next morning when Klavdianos came in to verify a point in connection with the comments about it he had promised me. The museum case was still locked, but the ring was gone and how it could have been abstracted no one could tell. A possible solution was that the old women were expert thieves in disguise who had taken advantage of the bad, dull weather and the thunder to employ skeleton keys on a museum case. That they had taken only the ring which was not an outstanding object was accounted for by the suggestion that they were disturbed and had just snatched at the first thing. This was the official explanation published later after a formal inquiry in which everyone was exonerated.

When I called on Klavdianos to ask if the official investigation had thrown any light on the mystery or whether he had solved the problem of the representation he turned round in his chair and took from the bookcase behind him one volume of Frazer's monumental commentary on Pausanias and turned to the page where it told the story of Atreus, Aerope, Thyestes, and the golden lamb.

Atreus vowed to sacrifice the finest animal in his flocks to Artemis. A golden lamb appeared among them, but he strangled it and kept it in a box. His wife, Aerope, granddaughter of Minos, who had been seduced by his brother Thyestes abstracted it and gave it to her lover. The Mycenaeans were told by an oracle to elect a king from the house of Pelops and sent for Atreus and Thyestes. The latter persuaded the people that the possessor of the golden lamb ought to be king. Atreus in ignorance of his betrayal agreed. Thyestes produced the golden lamb and became king. This was one of the main causes of the bitter feud between the two brothers which afterwards wrought such tragedy in the house of Atreus.

"You see this is a lamb and not a bull," explained Klavdianos. "Look at the length of the legs, the tail, and the rendering of the fleece!" As he spoke he pointed out these details on the impression, and I saw now that my original feeling that it was not a bull was perfectly correct. The Oxford and other experts to whom Evesham had shown the ring had been so convinced it must be a bull that they had not taken any other possibility seriously into consideration. Once the eye knew the solution the figure of the lamb became visible of itself.

Was this then really the golden lamb of Atreus?

Pins, Plain and Safety:
Two Elegant Scholarly Trifles

PAUL JACOBSTAHL

Greeks and Their Pins

THESE two fragments come from the carefully furnished minds of two noted scholars. Dealing with archaeological minutiae, they are included because they illustrate much that is most delightful and most irritating in high academic writing. Paul Jacobsthal left Marburg University in very early Nazi days and settled in Oxford; Miss Lorimer was an Oxford scholar who specialized in the archaeological aspects of Homeric studies.

❧

RE-READING all these pages with descriptions of petty objects and arid lists I feel that a short survey of some more relevant results, without cumbersome details, and a few remarks of more or less general nature will not be out of place.

The history of the Greek pin is an episode of five hundred years or less, the history of a dying-out Bronze Age species. In Greece pins survive just into the fifth century; in Illyria into the fourth century and even the third.

"Uncanonical" pins in Greece, as in other Iron Age civilizations, are laggards, Bronze Age fossils. In Greece they do not reappear

From *Greek Pins*. Oxford: The Clarendon Press; 1956, pp. 183-4. By permission of The Clarendon Press, Oxford.

before about 700: this and their absence in Protogeometric and Geometric Greece present a problem.

The development of the canonical pin is typically Greek. There was a small repertory of sober Geometric forms: these the Greeks worked thoroughly and patiently, and let them gradually become more ornate, but on the surface only.

There were in other countries, in Illyria, the Caucasus, and in the North, pins full of fancy, and a multitude of patterns. In the Near East, in Cyprus, at Mycenae, and in Italy pins were embellished with semi-precious stones or glass. All this did not appeal to the Greeks, and their attitude towards the figure pins of the Near East was reluctant.

This modesty and this sobriety are eminently Greek.

On the foregoing pages I have tried to solve the grave problem put by the pin from Weitgendorf. My answer, which I called rational, was half-hearted, and I shirked the problem which lies behind [it]. I now give another answer which some of my readers will call irrational and unsound.

We are wont to make trade, spreading of customs, migrations of peoples, or of artisans, accountable for the diffusion of implements, of techniques, materials, and forms. Besides these agents there is another of less rational order: those who write the history of prehistoric times should sometimes think of John 3, 8. "The wind bloweth where it listeth, and thou hearest the sound thereof, but canst not tell whence it cometh, and whither it goeth." It should also be remembered that the diffusion of plants offers similar problems. In other words, we shall not always, rarely indeed, be able to answer the question where the cradle of a given form lay, through what agents and on what routes it spread within this belt, stretching from the Near East to Scandinavia, in which from at least the Middle Bronze Age down to Hallstatt there was interchange in the sphere of arts and crafts.

When discussing the longevity of bead-and-reels and similar elements, I took it for granted that there was an uninterrupted tradition from the Middle Bronze Age to our days. A sceptic may ask, "Is what you call survival and continuity not just coincidence?" This question does not concern these patterns and pins only, but is one of principle, important for an understanding of tectonics in general. The possibilities of moulding a pin-shank or another implement of similar shape are limited, confined to projections and recessions, to those solids which I have studied in detail. The motives did not appear singly but in well-thought-out systems. Geometric two-dimensional ornament provides an analogy: its basic elements, lines, straight or broken, squares, triangles, lozenges, circles, spirals, and the like, are found singly all over the world, but sys-

tems formed of them are different in different civilizations and
ages, and if you find the same composition of units in two places
however far apart there should be connexion. The history of civilization shows that the same things and forms were hardly ever devised
independently twice. Mankind saves thought and labour and has
a long memory.

Bone pins of different ages from Ephesus, Delos, Egypt, the
Hradisht, and Britain—to mention only these—show great likeness. No doubt their patterns suited the turner, but it would be
wrong to say that the use of the lathe lead to their invention: material and tools favour certain forms—as they disfavour others—but
they do not produce them.

As long as you confine your interest to the image of man, you
divide the ancient world into an iconic and an aniconic zone, the
first comprising Egypt, the Near East, Greece, and Italy, the second
Europe. Once you have an eye to *res quae sunt infra hominem,* and
descend from the heights of imagery into the lowlands of modest
implements, tools, weapons, and ornaments of which the pin is
one, the two zones melt into one—a great problem to which this
study of pins was intended to make a small contribution.

===

H. L. LORIMER

The Doric Mode

THE subject of dress in Homer, so far at least as that of women is
concerned, is difficult and unsatisfactory. The data, archaeological
and literary, are few, and the latter at least are confusing. It is
hardly necessary to say that no actual dress has come down to us
from any date within the period concerned. Representations dating
to the Bronze Age are either irrelevant, as are almost without exception those of Late Helladic I and II, or, as is apt to be the case in Late

From *Homer and the Monuments.* London: Macmillan & Company Ltd.; 1950, pp.
336-8. By courtesy of the Governing Body of Somerville College, Oxford.

Helladic III, too summary in execution to be serviceable; in the crucial period of the Early Iron Age they are nonexistent. In the eighth century the conventions of Geometric art make the interpretation of dress as represented on Geometric monuments a hopeless task. When we turn to the poems, we find that the vocabulary, though fairly ample, is baffling, for there is almost no direct description, and many of the terms used receive little or no illumination from later Greek.

Nevertheless, many points in the interpretation of Homer were established by the fundamental studies of Helbig and Studniczka; and on one point where adequate archaeological data were lacking subsequent excavation has thrown light. This is the use of pins and fibulae respectively in connexion with the dress of women; and as both these adjuncts are found (though not necessarily associated with the dress of women) before the end of the Bronze Age, are in continuous use throughout our period, and, when representational art fails us, afford the sole evidence available for dress, it will be convenient to begin with a brief account of them. Since, however, in the matter on which Studniczka went astray and induced Helbig to change his first and better thoughts, his conclusions have been commonly accepted by editors of Homer, it will be well to clear up this point before proceeding to a chronological survey of the available material. In the first edition (1884) of *Das Homerische Epos* Helbig had declared in favour of a "one-piece" women's dress opening down the front by a slit which was fastened by a row of fibulae or clasps (*Heftel*) and was long enough to allow of the dress being pushed off the shoulders when they were undone, rightly maintaining that this alone fitted the account of Hera's dress and also squared with the way in which Athena gets rid of hers. His theory was open to criticism on the grounds that positive evidence from Greek monuments was lacking, that Etruscan material, on which he laid considerable stress, was not necessarily relevant, and that he assumed for women's dress in Homer an Oriental origin which there was at that time nothing to substantiate. These points were all made by Studniczka, who in the following year published his monograph on the early history of Greek dress, thus putting the question on a wider basis. He gave an admirable account of the historical problem as it then, in the early days of Mycenaean excavation, presented itself, and applied his solution of it to the interpretation of the Homeric text. Recognizing that the epics embody a tradition much older than Homer, whom he put in the eighth century, he rightly contended that at the time of its formation Greek women presumably wore the dress described by Herodotus as universal in Greece until the introduction of the Ionic chiton. This dress, it will be remembered, though admitting of local variations, was in essentials identical with the Dorian woman's dress in the classical age and was distinguished by the fact that, unlike the Ionic chiton, it required pins to keep it on. Accepting the criterion of Herodotus—the use of περόναι—as adequate to diagnose Doric dress, Studniczka of necessity ascribed this form to the dress of Hera and also to the peplos with twelve περόναι presented to Penelope by Antinoos, cases which will be discussed in detail later. A further consequence followed. Since Penelope's περόναι were definitely described as fibulae, it followed that fibulae were the normal fastening of the Doric peplos; and Studniczka makes the further tacit assumption that this is the only meaning of the word, not only in Homer (which is at least near the truth) but in Herodotus and Sophocles. The opinion seems to have been generally held by scholars, as will be seen on reference to the translations and editions of Rawlinson and Stein, Campbell, Jebb, and Schneidewin-Nauck. All alike appear to assume that "brooch" is the primary, if not the only meaning of περόνη, though in fact its unquestioned kinship with περαίνειν shows that its basic meaning is simply "the thing that goes through," while the verb περονᾶν is used for transfixing with a spear. Moreover, there is no other word in ordinary use to denote the straight pin, which is older in Greece than the fibula and probably in most regions commoner. Nor does it seem to have struck these eminent scholars that a safety-pin, however large, is an unhandy instrument with which to murder a man, and not particularly apt even for putting out one's own eyes. Either end would be better served by the Victorian hat-pin, a lethal weapon on occasion, of which the Greek bronze pin, with its thicker stem and blunter point, is merely a robuster and more reliable, though less obviously dangerous, version. We are now, however, in a position to put arguments from probability aside, since we have direct archaeological evidence that in most regions the normal fastening of the Doric peplos was a pair of straight pins, one on each shoulder, and that their place was but rarely taken by a pair of fibulae. Examples of both were observed by Orsi when from 1891 to 1895 he excavated at Syracuse the del Fusco cemetery, most of the graves in which dated to the late eighth or to the first half of the seventh century. Here fibulae, though slightly more numerous than in the cemetery of Megara Hyblaea, where 1,000 graves yielded a bare ten, were very few in comparison with the straight pins and did not as a rule in the women's graves take their place at the shoulders of the skeleton; they were generally an addition to the straight pins and therefore used for some other purpose. Straight pins, on the other hand, generally of bronze, sometimes of iron, occasionally of silver, were extremely common and were of familiar Greek types, having almost always disk heads and a series of globules or corrugations on the upper part of the shank; they commonly occurred in pairs, at shoulder-level, one on each side of the skeleton. The explanation was obvious and was explicitly given by Orsi in the following words: *"Le fibule in bronzo sono piuttosto rare nelle tombe greche, perchè supplivano all' ufficio di appuntar il chitone i grandi spilloni di bronzo e di argento che rivengosi sempre all' altezza delle spalle."*

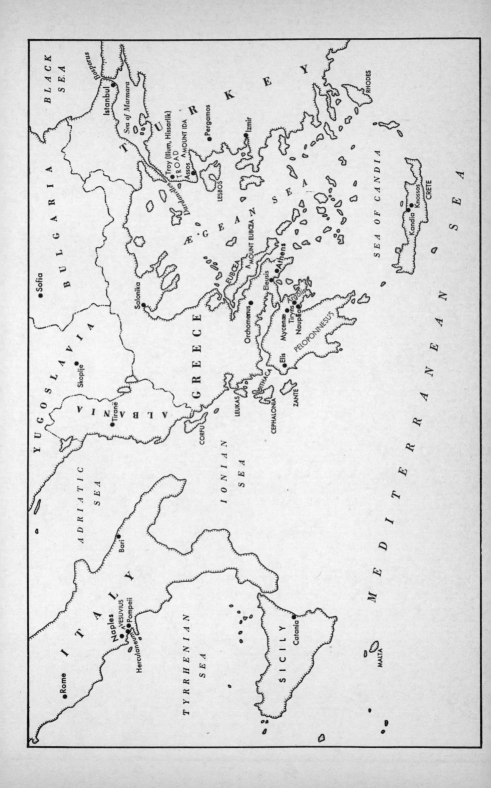

BLACK SEA

Bosporus

Istanbul

Sea of Marmara

BULGARIA

Sofia

Dardanelles

Troy (Ilium, Hissarlik)

TROAD

MOUNT IDA

Assos

LESBOS

Pergamos

Izmir

TURKEY

RHODES

SEA OF CANDIA

CRETE

Knossos

Kandia

ÆGEAN SEA

YUGOSLAVIA

Skoplje

Salonika

GREECE

EUBŒA

MOUNT EUBŒA

Orchomenus

Eleusis

Athens

Mycenæ

Tiryns

Argos

Nauplia

Elis

PELOPONNESUS

ITHACA

LEUKAS

CEPHALONIA

ZANTE

ALBANIA

Tiranë

CORFU

IONIAN SEA

ADRIATIC SEA

Bari

ITALY

Rome

Naples

VESUVIUS

Pompeii

Herculaneum

TYRRHENIAN SEA

SICILY

Catania

MALTA

MEDITERRANEAN SEA

3. *Italy*

MRS. HAMILTON GRAY

With Mrs. Hamilton Gray in Etruria

AT the height of their expansion in the sixth century B.C. the Etruscans dominated much of Italy, their territories stretching from the Po valley through Tuscany, across to eastern Corsica and down the west coast as far as Campania. Tuscany, however, was always the heart of their dominion, and it is there that most of the famous cities and cemeteries are concentrated.

As to the origin of this people, who have always been seen as somewhat mysterious foreigners in the land where they flourished, opinion is still divided. A few authorities believe that their culture was a native development of the Bronze Age Italians, merely stimulated by cultural contacts with the Mediterranean world; many more accept the traditional view, first set down by Herodotus, that there was an actual influx of people from Lydian Anatolia. It will be seen that over a century ago George Dennis saw no reason to reject this traditional account, and since then archaeological evidence has on the whole favoured it. The theory of an origin in the Rhaetian Alps was mistaken: this was a late area of Etruscan settlement.

Herodotus dated the arrival of his Lydian seafarers too early, and nineteenth century writers followed him in this. In fact the flowering of Etruscan culture begins in the middle of the eighth century B.C., when influence from the eastern Mediterranean is very strong—as for example in the magnificent Regolini-Galassi tomb (pp. 177, 200, II). This orientalizing period coincided with the foundation of the first Greek colonies in Sicily, and in the following

From *Tour to the Sepulchres of Etruria*. London: Hatchards Ltd; 1843 (3rd ed.) pp. 1-2, 24-7, 79-82, 306-11.

centuries Greek culture was profoundly to affect Etruscan—even
while politically the two peoples were bitter rivals. Etruscan merchants imported great quantities of Greek goods and works of
art, including the fine painted pottery (p. 180, II) which when it
was first unearthed was called Etruscan.

At the height of their power and prosperity, the Etruscans easily
mastered the loose confederation of Latin peoples, and the Tuscan
dynasty of the Tarquins ruled Rome during the sixth century B.C.,
turning what had been a village into a fine city. Then in 510 B.C.
came the famous expulsion of the Tarquins, and the little Roman
republic was set up. At first its citizens could not hope to turn the
tables on the stronger and more civilized Etruscans—but their time
soon came. In the course of the fourth century B.C. they conquered
the region to the west of the Tiber round Veii and Falerii, then
further to the west and north round Caere and Tarquinia. Then in
the third century they overcame Vulci and much of the territory
to the north. Meanwhile in the Po valley hordes of barbarian Celts
from across the Alps had routed the luckless Etruscans and taken
over what had been *Etruria Circumpadua*. For some time the
strongly fortified city of Volsinii and its lands held out, but its end
was hastened by a slave revolt. By the middle of the third century
B.C. Etruria submitted wholly to Rome.

Yet inevitably Etruscan civilization had permeated that of the
Latin peoples during the formative centuries of their history. As
Raymond Bloch has written, "The Etruscan influence was to live on
in Rome in her constitution and *mores*, in her religious thought
and in the arts; it was to form part of the cultural heritage which
Rome, in her turn, would leave to the West."

Although much building that is now shown as Etruscan is in
fact of Roman and later date, two fine gateways do survive, that are
known as the Porta dell' Arco at Volterra and the Porta Augusta at
Perugia. But as the following extracts show, the greatest archaeological interest has always centred on the cemeteries with their
handsomely-decorated and richly-furnished tombs, which give such
vivid pictures of Etruscan life and death. These cemeteries were
always situated outside the city walls. The simple early tombs were
quickly followed by monumental square or round chambers roofed
with false vaults like those so vividly described at Caere (p. 198, II).
Tomb chambers cut in the rock as exact copies of the homes of the
living are generally later in date. Many were painted—those of
Tarquinia admired by Dennis (p. 191, II) and D. H. Lawrence (p.
207, II) being the finest. The paintings show the Etruscans feasting
and dancing, enjoying every delight and luxury—and with a
mingling of men and women on free and equal terms. When the

tombs were sealed, the belief seems to have been that these tremendously vital scenes became the real background for the dead in Hades.

D. H. Lawrence naturally responded to their joyous life and sexual warmth. The Romans, and many since who have thought like them, were convinced that it was this shameless pleasure in living that brought the Etruscan empire so quickly to its decline and fall.

Mrs. Hamilton Gray was an English lady whose interest had been roused by Campanari's Etruscan exhibition in Pall Mall. George Dennis (p. 184, II) praises her "full and lively" account of her travels, but points out the inevitable errors resulting from her lack of proper records of what she saw.

Why Travel Ignorantly?

IT has been suggested to me, that if I wish to interest the reading public in the contents of this work, I ought first to write an introduction to the sepulchres of Etruria before describing the sepulchres themselves, on account of the very little which is as yet known in England upon the subject, and the inducements that exist to visit Etruscan remains. I have been desired to state our reasons for making this tour, and why we thought or expected such and such things at such particular places; and what other people may look for and hope to find at the same; and I the more readily comply with this suggestion, because no one has felt more acutely than myself the pain of going through a museum, or visiting a ruin, wholly ignorant of its objects and history, with an uncommunicative and learned person, or with a party of the initiated who talk to one another in a sort of free masonry, and who, even when most willing to instruct, generally suppose a vast deal of previous knowledge in the person they address—hence they refer to manners and customs of which you have never heard, prove a variety of things of which you never even suspected the existence, and use terms that convey to your mind no idea. You are accordingly obliged to admire what appears extremely ugly, to ascribe all sorts of value and merit to half-broken, tarnished, hideous things, which in your secret soul you think would have been far better thrown away, and to pretend to instruction which you never had even the opportunity of acquiring. In short, your anticipated great pleasure proves really a great bore, whilst you are ashamed to own almost to yourself that it is so, and would willingly store your mind with the information that would make it otherwise, if you could.

Etruscan Treasures for the General

THE tomb near Cerveteri was named after Archpriest Regolini (misspelled by Mrs. Gray) and General Galassi, who discovered it in 1836. A more recent account is on page 200, II.

❦

IT was about this time [1838] that we found Rome filled with amazement, and all her wise men occupied in speculations, about the stupendous discovery of the Regulini-Galassi tomb at Cerveteri. We may call it stupendous, for we may use this word to a child's toy, when upon it depends some mighty result. The Arciprete Regulini had discovered this extraordinary tomb, and General Galassi, one of the officers of highest rank in the papal army, had bought from him the articles therein found. The English used to call it "Galassi's grave." All these articles are now purchased by the government, and are to be seen properly and separately indicated in the Gregorian Museum; but in 1838 they were exhibited in the general's own house, and having obtained his permission to visit them, he was, like most of his countrymen, so polite and courteous as to explain them to us himself.

If we had been surprised at Campanari's exhibition, we were amazed almost beyond credulity at the general's. Here we saw an immense breastplate of gold, which had been fastened on each shoulder by a most delicately wrought gold fibula, with chains like those now made at Trichinopoly. The breastplate was stamped with a variety of arabesques and small patterns, as usual in the Egyptian style. The head had been crowned with fillets and circular ornaments of pure gold, and a rich mantle had covered the body, flowered with the same material. In this grave also had been found a quantity of arms, round bronze shields with a boss in the centre which was stamped, spears, lances, and arrows; a bier of bronze, as perfect as if made a year ago; a tripod, with a vessel containing some strange looking lumps of a resinous substance, and which on being burnt proved to be perfumes so intensely strong, that those who tried them were obliged to leave the room. There were many small images, perhaps of lares, or of ancestors, in terra cotta that had been ranged in double lines close to the bier; also some large common vessels for wine and oil, and some finely painted vases and tazze, with black figures upon a red ground, which had been consecrated to the dead. There were wheels of a car upon which the bier had been brought into the sepulchre, and many other things which I do not remember; but the wonder of all these treasures was a sort of inkstand of terra cotta, which had served as a schoolmaster's A B C. On it were the Etruscan letters, first in alphabet, and then in syllables, and both the letters and the syllables are the same as the oldest form of the Greek. It was deciphered by Dr. Lepsius, and is the key to all we at present know, and will be the basis of all we are ever likely to know, of the Etruscan tongue. How it came to be buried with a mighty prince, in order to teach such elements to us, the pigmies of five and twenty or thirty centuries later, it is difficult to imagine, but so perhaps it may have been ordained by Providence—

> Who sees with equal eye, as God of all,
> A hero perish or a sparrow fall.

And we reap the benefit of it. Who shall scan the counsels of him, who brings down the pride of the proudest of nations, and forces them to set a tributary people free—not by arms or battle, but by swarms of flies and lice? I confess, that along with this thought, many others of a less worthy character, and yet not inconsistent with human folly and divine overruling, came into my mind. Had it been placed there to teach Charon to spell, in case he should not understand the language of the deceased? Might it not have been to that Chief himself a foreign language, which he had mastered with difficulty, and used with triumph? Was it, perhaps, the humble memorial of some magnanimous action? or might it not have been the primer which had belonged to an only and dearly beloved child, taken from him by an early death?

We had one other idea, and it is perhaps the most probable. At the period when this tomb was constructed, Cerveteri was called Agylla, and the Agyllans were a colony of Pelasgians from Greece mingled with the aborigines. May not this mighty man have been himself a priest as well as prince? May not Pelasgian Greek have been the language consecrated to the priesthood? and may he not have desired that a specimen of that holy tongue should be laid beside his corpse? If not a priest, may he not have been some introducer or restorer of learning amongst his people? Perhaps king, priest, and historian, all in one. Certainly, an inkstand and a hornbook seem strange furniture for a warrior's grave, and would have astonished the bold barons of our Middle Ages not a little. But be this as it may, this humble article is likely to prove to Europe, what the stones of Alexandria and Rosetta have been before it, the dictionary of a lost language, and the interpreter of an extinct race.

Opening of a Tomb at Veii

In the month of February, A.D. 1839, Capranesi, the first dealer
in antiquities in Rome, and one of the first existing antiquaries for
learning and research in his own line in Europe, offered us to be
present at the opening of a tomb in the necropolis of ancient Veii.
We gladly accepted the offer, and pursued the high road to Florence,
as far as Fossa, whence we took a guide across the fields for about
two miles, pursuing a very ancient road which once led from some
minor city to the superb metropolis of Veii, and which was still in
use in the days of Tiberius; then sending our horses to the Isola
Farnese, distant by a beautiful walk of two miles further, we went
the rest of our way on foot. The spot on which we stopped was a hill
separated by a deep ravine from two others. The one in front was
once covered by the ancient and magnificent town of Veii, and the
one upon the left hand had been its chief necropolis. The site of the
graves in this hill, covering the illustrious dead of a nation now
extinct, has but lately been discovered, and the ground is hired out
to the different dealers and private antiquaries in Rome. We descended to the Formella, a brook running at the foot of the three hills
I have mentioned, and the principal branch of which turns off
through the Ponte Sodo, and washes the bottom of the front hill,
which was once entirely crowned and enclosed by the walls of
Etruscan Veii. We crossed the lesser branch upon rude stepping-
stones, not far from where the streams separate, and then ascended
a most natural and undisturbed-looking green hill, let out for pasture, where not hired for excavation. We toiled for some hundred
yards without seeing anything, and at length came upon some brushwood which concealed a party of workmen. I was startled at the
moment, for, forgetting the object of our visit, it seemed to me that
they were making a grave. They were only opening one, however,
which had been made three thousand years ago. Well does mother
Earth cover up her children upon that green hill, for not the slightest sign of the hand or foot of man is to be seen upon her surface,
save where the workmen are employed to open up afresh some
ancient tomb. Several of our party had been with the men the whole
morning, and seen the whole operation from the first disinterment.
When *we* arrived, the face of the tomb was already uncovered, and
we stood upon the brink of a deep pit, probably about ten feet deep,
looking down upon a rudely arched doorway filled up with loose
stones. It was cut in the hard tufo rock that composes the hill, very
different from the rich loose deep soil which we saw lying all around
it, and which had been brought there by the hand of ancient labour
to cover and conceal it centuries ago. On each side of this arched

door was a lesser arch leading into a small open chamber perfectly empty. The workmen made a few steps of the earth they had turned out, and I leaped down to the bottom, after their pickaxes had removed the stones from the main door. I entered the tomb, a single chamber arched in the rock, apparently ten or twelve feet square, and somewhat low; it was so dark that I was obliged to have a torch, which a labourer held within the door, that I might see by myself what was the arrangement of the tomb, and what it contained. The bottom was a sort of loose mud, both soil and wet having fallen in, through a hole which existed at top of the door, owing to the want of a closing stone. In this mud lay about twenty vases, large and small, of various forms, and two of them with four handles; but they were all of coarse clay and rude drawing, chiefly in circles or acute triangles of red and black, having fish or some simple device upon them, but no mythological subjects, and they appeared to me to be in that style which Cavaliere Manzi considers prior to all others, viz. the rude infancy of the art, and purely Etruscan, without any intermixture from Greece or Egypt. The black vases were chiefly stamped and indented, none of them rich like the Volterra vases, and none with a fine enamel; but all like the commonest of those kinds which are found in the other Etruscan cities, and the painting was such as adorned the household wine and oil vessels everywhere throughout Etruria. The tomb, which was vaulted, contained nothing else; no sarcophagus, though the place was marked where one had once stood; no gold, no bronze, no figures in stone or clay, and no marbles. It had a shelf all round it, broad enough to have held cinerary urns, or vases, or offerings for the dead, with here and there niches which went back a foot or so into the rock beyond the shelf. The tomb had evidently been rifled before, but when, who shall say?

Difficulties of Travel

MRS. GRAY describes her rather embarrassing first encounter with the great Signor Campanari—whose London exhibition had attracted her to Etruscology. He was a wealthy landowner of the region. His fine collection of Greek vases from Etruscan tombs formed the nucleus of the great series in the Gregorian Etruscan Museum in the Vatican.

THE day after our return from the plain of Vulci, where the existence of a rich and prosperous city has been in these latter times detected by its broken potsherds, we prepared to set out upon a new exploring expedition to another seat of old Etruscan greatness, Tuscania, or as it is now called Toscanella. We are, if possible, still more ignorant of the existence and fortunes of the ancient inhabitants of this city than of those of Vulci, though their abode has never been actually blotted out of the map of Italy as that of the neighbouring Vulci has been; for while the stalactyte grotto is now all that adorns the banks of the Fiora, and the ruined Cucumella stands solitary on the plain, the well-girt, turreted, and highly picturesque town of Toscanella towers over the distant landscape, and proclaims that whatever may have been the greatness of ancient Tuscania, she has left a representative not unworthy of her, at least in beauty and romantic situation.

Descending from the heights of Corneto, and winding down the valley beneath its summit, we found the road at first exceedingly pretty. It encircles the base of the hill on which stands the town, and commands a fine view of that valley which separated ancient Tarquinia from its necropolis. We admired the steep cliffs of the Monterozzi, and recognized the position of the Grotta Della Biga, and of the other sepulchres which overhang the valley, until this interesting scene was shut out from view by the rocky ridge of Turchina, once crowned by the ancient capital, and then we passed through a desolate country and along a wretched road, which I believe have never before been traversed by such a vehicle as the heavy Roman berline, which now contained the whole of our party. Not all the exertions of four excellent horses, nor the flagellations and execrations of our coachman, availed to save us from frequently sticking fast in the ground, and having to dismount ever and anon and go on foot; and from our experience, I would recommend to others a very light carriage, or if their carelessness of comfort and the season of the year permit it, an open carritella, as being the best adapted for such an excursion, unless it can be made on horseback. At length our hopes of deliverance from our unpleasant predicament were animated by the many pinnacles of Toscanella, which we descried in the distance. As we approached nearer, we saw a hill crowned with a mass of high walls, and flanked by clusters of round towers, which gave the place a very striking and fortified appearance, and recalled the middle ages, when Toscanella was long under the sway of a line of powerful feudal lords, who tyrannised over the neighbouring country.

We halted before the principal gate, and began to consult as to how and where we were to pass the night, a subject which we had omitted, in the course of conversation upon what we thought more materially concerned the objects of the expedition. We had been more occupied with sepulchres than dining-rooms, and with sarcophagi than feather beds; and now, when we awoke to our position, and considered that there was no inn here as at Corneto, and that our friends Mr. Bunsen, the Prussian minister at Rome, and his family, in a late excursion which they had made, were hospitably received by a noble family in Toscanella, and entertained by them for several nights, the question arose with disagreeable perplexity, what we were to do? We had a letter of introduction to one whom we expected to find eminently useful to us, but on whom we were fearful of trespassing too much, as his occupations were many, and his house might not be sufficiently large to contain so numerous a party, even were he hospitably disposed. This was Signor Campanari, with whose name all who have seen the beautiful antiquities which he has brought to this country, must be acquainted. We made our berline (a more capacious and heavy carriage than ever before, as I should think, traversed the *no* roads of old Etruria) wait at the city gates, whilst we held an anxious council as to the proper course to take, for the evening was rapidly turning into night, and we contemplated the possibility of either sleeping crowded in the carriage, or each on two chairs in some pot-house, the only representative of an hotel which exists in Toscanella.

At length our necessities overcame our modesty, and we desired our coachman to drive to the door of Signor Campanari, in the hope that if he did not himself take us in, he would at least put us on the way of procuring accommodation elsewhere; but as we were afraid of the carriage sticking in the narrow, twisted, and steep streets of the odd old town, we dismounted in order to walk on before, inquiring the way to the place of our destination. While yet arranging these matters before the gate, we saw a gentleman in black approaching from the country, followed by several workmen bearing shovels and mattocks. We felt a presentiment that this stranger was to have a material influence on our visit to Toscanella, which was confirmed by observing that his clothes were soiled with clay, and that he held in his hands an instrument of bronze which had evidently not seen the workshop for more than two thousand years. Following the impulse which brings "together birds of a feather," we recognised in the stranger a veteran Scavatore; and trusting that he would have a fellow feeling for us, who wished to be what he was, but lacked opportunity, and who were come for the purpose of seeing and learning that in which he was conversant —we addressed ourselves to him, inquiring the way to the house of Signor Campanari. "I am Campanari," said he, and then he explained to us that he was returning home after his day's work among the extensive excavations which he was then carrying forward.

We mentioned who we were, and by whom we were recom-

mended: and while Signor Campanari was perusing the letter which
we brought him, one of our party examined the bronze instrument
which he had brought in his hand. It was a strigil or scraping instrument used in the baths, and which had been buried in its proprietor's
tomb. As a specimen it was very fine, though extremely fragile, as
our poor friend found to his cost; for on examining it with great
curiosity, and turning it round and round in his hand, the beautiful
strigil separated in two pieces, and he remained aghast in an astonishment which produced in us feelings both of laughter and despair,
with a fragment of the strigil in each extended hand. What will Signor Campanari say, thought each one of us, when he looks up from
his letter and finds his beautiful strigil broken? Every favourable
impression will be dispelled, which may have been produced in his
mind by the energy of a large foreign party, who have come rum-
bling over the desolate and untrodden moors of Tuscania, in a vast
Roman berline, in search of the profound at the bottom of an Etruscan tomb; and every favourable sentiment produced by the recommendation of our friend, will immediately vanish when he casts
his eyes on the luckless knight of the strigil. The character of
destructiveness too justly acquired by our countrymen flashed across
our minds, and we contemplated nothing but exclusion from
museums and tombs, a melancholy evening, on our own resources,
and a night on hard boards. We were, however, speedily reassured
by the benevolent smile which crossed over Campanari's face when
he had read the letter, and which was not in the least clouded by
the discovery of the accident. He said the loss of the strigil was
of no consequence, and immediately invited us to his father's house,
regretting that it could not contain the whole party, though he
trusted to procure accommodation for the rest in the neighbourhood.
We now gave the order of march to our lumbering berline, and
preceded it in the train of our new acquaintance, under castellated
walls, and through the turreted gate of the quaint old town. After
mounting and crossing sundry steep and perplexed streets, we found
ourselves at the door of the Casa Campanari, where we were installed with such a welcome as only genuine hospitality can give,
which grudges no inconvenience, and only fears to appear sensible
of the favour which it confers.

GEORGE DENNIS

Etruria and the Etruscans

GEORGE DENNIS was a British consul in Italy who, as a cultivated amateur, visited many Etruscan sites in districts that were still half wild. His book was a great success, and went into many editions.

❦

ANTIQUARIAN research, partaking of the quickened energy of the nineteenth century, has of late years thrown great light on the early history of Italy. It has demonstrated, in confirmation of extant records, that ages before the straw hut of Romulus arose on the Palatine, there existed in that land a nation far advanced in civilization and refinement—that Rome, before her intercourse with Greece, was indebted to ETRURIA for whatever tended to elevate and humanise her, for her chief lessons in art and science, for many of her political, and most of her religious and social institutions, for the conveniences and enjoyments of peace, and the tactics and appliances of war—for almost everything in short that tended to exalt her as a nation, save her stern virtues, her thirst of conquest, and her indomitable courage, which were peculiarly her own; for verily her sons were mighty with little else but the sword—

> *Stolidum genus—*
> *Bellipotentes sunt magi' quam sapientipotentes.*

The external history of the Etruscans, as there are no direct chronicles extant, is to be gathered only from scattered notices in Greek and Roman writers. Their internal history, till of late years, was almost a blank, but by the continual accumulation of fresh facts it is now daily acquiring form and substance, and promises, ere long, to be as distinct and palpable as that of Egypt, Greece,

From *The Cities and Cemeteries of Etruria*, Vol. I. London: John Murray; 1848, pp. xxi-xxiii, xxvii-xxxvi.

or Rome. For we already know the extent and peculiar nature of their civilization—their social condition and modes of life—their extended commerce and intercourse with far distant countries—their religious creed, with its ceremonial observances in this life, and the joys and torments it set forth in a future state—their popular traditions—and a variety of customs, of all which History, commonly so called, is either utterly silent, or makes but incidental mention, or gives notices imperfect and obscure. We can now enter into the inner life of the Etruscans, almost as fully as if they were living and moving before us, instead of having been extinct as a nation for more than two thousand years. We can follow them from the cradle to the tomb,—we see them in their national costume, varied according to age, sex, rank, and office,—we learn their style of adorning their persons, their fashions, and all the eccentricities of their toilet,—we even become acquainted with their peculiar physiognomy, their individual names and family relationships,—we know what houses they inhabited, what furniture they used,—we behold them at their various avocations—the princes in the council-chamber—the augur, or priest, at the altar, or in solemn procession —the warrior in the battle-field, or returning home in triumph—the judge on the bench—the artisan at his handicraft—the husband-man at the plough—the slave at his daily toil,—we see them in the bosom of their families, and at the festive board, reclining luxuriously amid the strains of music, and the time-beating feet of dancers—at their favourite games and sports, encountering the wild-boar, or looking on at the race, at the wrestling-match, or other palæstric exercises,—we behold them stretched on the death-bed—the last rites performed by mourning relatives—the funeral procession—their bodies laid in the tomb—and the solemn festivals held in their honour. Nor even here do we lose sight of them, but follow their souls to the unseen world—perceive them in the hands of good or evil spirits—conducted to the judgment-seat, and in the enjoyment of bliss, or suffering the punishment of the damned.

We are indebted for most of this knowledge, not to musty records drawn from the oblivion of centuries, but to monumental remains—purer founts of historical truth—landmarks which, even when few and far between, are the surest guides across the expanse of distant ages—to the monuments which are still extant on the sites of the ancient cities of Etruria, or have been drawn from their cemeteries, and are stored in the museums of Italy and of Europe. . . .

It is Etruria proper alone of which I propose to treat in the following pages.

It was still an extensive region of the Italian peninsula, comprehending almost the whole of modern Tuscany, the Duchy of Lucca, and the Transtiberine portion of the Papal State; being bounded on the north by the Apennines and the river Magra, on the east by the Tiber, on the west and south by the Mediterranean. This region was intersected by several ranges of mountains, lateral branches or offsets of the great spine-bone of the peninsula—in the northern part in long chains, stretching in various directions—in the south, of much inferior altitude, lying in detached masses, and separated, not by mere valleys, but by vast plains or table-lands. The geology of the two districts differs as widely as their superficial features. In the northern, the higher mountains, like the great chain of the Apennines, are chiefly composed of secondary limestone, and attain a considerable altitude; the lower are formed of sandstone or marl. The southern district on every hand shows traces of volcanic action—in the abundance of hot springs and sulphureous waters—in vast plains of tufo and other igneous deposits, of even later date than the tertiary formations—and in the mountains which are chiefly of the same material, with beds of lava, basalt, or scoriæ, and which have been themselves volcanoes, their craters, extinct long before the days of history or even fable, being now the beds of beautiful lakes. Here and there, however, in this southern region, are heights of limestone; now, like Soracte, rearing their craggy peaks from the wide bosom of the plain; now, stretching in a con-tinuous range along the coast. On these physical differences depend many of the characteristic features of northern and southern Etruria. The line of demarcation between these two great districts of Etruria is almost that of the modern frontier between the Tuscan and Roman States—*i.e.* from Cosa north-eastward to Acquapend-ente, and thence following the course of the Paglia till it mingles with the Tiber, near Orvieto.

Of the Twelve Cities or States of Etruria proper, no complete list is given by the ancients, but it is not difficult to gather from their statements, which were the chief in the land. Foremost among them was TARQUINII, where the national polity, civil and religious, took its rise. This city was in the southern division of the land; so also were VEII and FALERII, long the antagonists, with CAERE, the ally, of Rome; and VOLSINII, one of the last to be subdued. In the northern region were, VETULONIA and RUSELLAE on the coast, CLUSIUM and ARRETIUM in the vale of the Clanis, and CORTONA and PERUSIA on the heights near the Thrasymene; while VOLATERRAE stood by herself and ruled over a wide tract in the far north. Beside these, there were many other cities, renowned in history, or remarkable for their massive fortifications still extant, for their singular tombs, or for the wondrous treasures of their sepulchral furniture—all of which will be described in the course of this work.

Etruria was of old densely populated, not only in those parts

which are still inhabited, but also, as is proved by remains of cities
and cemeteries, in tracts now desolated by malaria, and relapsed into
the desert; and what is now the fen or the jungle, the haunt of the
wild-boar, the buffalo, the fox, and the noxious reptile, where man
often dreads to stay his steps, and hurries away as from a plague-
stricken land—

> *Rus vacuum, quod non habitet, nisi nocte coacti,*
> *Invitus—*

of old yielded rich harvests of corn, wine, and oil, and contained
numerous cities, mighty, and opulent, into whose laps commerce
poured the treasures of the East, and the more precious produce
of Hellenic genius. Most of these ancient sites are now without a
habitant, furrowed yearly by the plough, or forsaken as unprofitable
wildernesses; and such as are still occupied, are, with few exceptions, mere phantoms of their pristine greatness—mean villages
in the place of populous cities. On every hand are traces of bygone
civilization, inferior in quality, no doubt, to that which at present
exists, but much wider in extent, and exerting far greater influence
on the surrounding nations, and on the destinies of the world. The
glory has verily departed from Etruria.

The sites of the cities varied according to the nature of the
ground. In the volcanic district, where they were most thickly set,
they stood on the level of the plains, yet were not unprotected by
nature, these plains or table-lands being everywhere intersected by
ravines, the cleavings of the earth under volcanic action, which
form natural fosses of great depth round the cliff-bound islands
or promontories on which the towns were built. Such was the situation of Veii, Cære, Falerii, Sutrium, and other cities of historical
renown. The favourite position was on a tongue of land at the junction of two of these ravines. In the northern district the cities stood
in more commanding situations, on isolated hills; but never on the
summits of scarcely accessible mountains, like many a Cyclopean
town of Central Italy, which—

> Like an eagle's nest, hangs on the crest
> Of purple Apennine.

Low ground, without any natural strength of site, was always
avoided, though a few towns, as Luna, Pisae, Graviscae, Pyrgi, for
maritime and commercial purposes, stood on the very level of the
coast.

The position of the cities of Etruria is in some measure a key
to her civilization and political condition. Had they been on
mountain-tops, we might have inferred a state of society little
removed from barbarism, in which there was no security or con-

fidence between the several communities. Had they stood on the unbroken level of the plains, we should have seen in them an index to an amount of internal security, such as nowhere existed in those early times. Yet is their medium position not inconsistent with a considerable degree of civilization, and a generally peaceable state of society. They are not such sites as were selected in later times, even by the Romans; but it should be borne in mind, that the political constitution of the people of early Italy, as of Greece, was entirely municipal—that cities were states, and citizens soldiers—and fortifications were therefore as indispensable to the cities of old, as standing armies and fleets are deemed to be to the states of modern Europe.

Before we consider the institutions of Etruria, it may be well to say a word on the origin of the people, and the source of their civilization.

It must be remarked, that the people known to the Romans as Etruscans were not the original inhabitants of the land, but a mixed race, composed partly of the earlier occupants, partly of a people of foreign origin, who became dominant by right of conquest, and engrafted their peculiar civilization on that previously existing in the land. All history concurs in representing the earliest occupants to have been Siculi, or Umbri, two of the most ancient races of Italy, little removed, it is probable, from barbarism, though not nomads, but dwelling in towns. Then a people of Greek race, the Pelasgi, entered Italy at the head of the Adriatic, and crossing the Apennines, and uniting themselves with the aborigines, or mountaineers, took possession of Etruria, driving out the earlier inhabitants, raised towns and fortified them with mighty walls, and long ruled supreme, till they were in turn conquered by a third race, called by the Greeks Tyrrheni, or Tyrseni, by the Romans Etrusci, Tusci, or Thusci, and by themselves, Rasena, who are supposed to have established their power in the land about 290 years before the foundation of Rome, or 1044 before Christ.

The threads of the history, however, of these races are so entangled, as to defy every attempt at unravelment; and the confusion is increased by the indiscriminate application of the word Tyrrheni, which was used by the ancients as a synonym, sometimes of Pelasgi, sometimes of Etrusci.

Amid this confusion, two facts stand out with prominence. First —that the land was inhabited before the Etruscans, properly so called, took possession of it. And secondly—that the Etruscans came from abroad. From what country, however, is a problem as much disputed as any in the whole compass of classical inquiry.

It is not compatible with the object of this work to enter fully into this question, yet it cannot be passed by in utter silence. To guide us, we have data of two kinds—the records of the ancients, and the extant monuments of the Etruscans. The native annals, which may be presumed to have spoken explicitly on this point, have not come down to us, and we have only the testimony of Greek and Roman writers. The concurrent voice of these—historians and geographers, poets and philosophers—with a solitary exception, marks the Etruscans as a tribe of Lydians, who, leaving their native land on account of a protracted famine, settled in this part of Italy. (The tradition as related by Herodotus, echoed by Servius, is this: —In the reign of Atys there was a protracted famine in Lydia; and in order to forget their misery the people had recourse to games and amusements, and invented dice, and ball, the pipes and the trumpet; abstaining from food on alternate days when they gave themselves up to these new diversions. For eighteen years they thus continued to exist, but at length, their condition being in no way improved, it was agreed that half the nation should emigrate, under the conduct of Tyrrhenus, the king's son. After various wanderings, they reached the coast of Umbria, and there established themselves, exchanging the name of Lydians for that of Tyrrhenians, in honour of their leader.) The dissentient voice, however, is of great importance—that of Dionysius of Halicarnassus —one of the most accurate and diligent antiquaries of his times, and an authority considered by many as sufficient to outweigh the vast body of opposing evidence. His objections are two-fold. First—that Xanthus, an early native historian of Lydia, "particularly well versed in ancient history," makes no mention of such an emigration. Secondly—that neither in language, religion, laws, nor customs, was there any similarity between the Lydians and Etruscans—*i.e.* as they existed in his day. He consequently broached a view entirely different from that recorded by other ancient writers, viz., that the Etruscans were an indigenous people of Italy, seeing that they were unlike every other race in language, manners, and customs. This view has been adopted by a modern Tuscan writer of celebrity, who, however, may be suspected of national prejudice, when he attempts to prove that the early civilization of Italy was indigenous.

A different opinion was held by the great Niebuhr—that the Etruscans were a tribe from the Rhaetian Alps, who conquered the Tyrrhene-Pelasgi, the earlier possessors of the land. This opinion is worthy of all respect, as coming from such a man, but seems to me to derive little support from ancient writers. Nor does the well-known fact that ancient monuments like the Etruscan, and inscriptions in a character very similar, have been found among the Rhaetian and Noric Alps, come to the aid of this theory. For though we are told that the Etruscans occupied Rhaetia, it was only when they had been driven by the Gauls from their settlements in

the plains of the Po. All history concurs in marking the emigration
to have been from the south northward, instead of the contrary.
The subjoined specimen of Rhaeto-Etruscan art confirms Livy's
testimony as to the degeneracy and semi-barbarism of these Etruscan
emigrants.

A modification of Niebuhr's view was held by Otfried Müller—
that the later element in the Etruscan nation was from Lydia, yet
composed not of natives, but of Tyrrhene-Pelasgi who had settled
on the coasts of Asia Minor; and that the earlier lords of the land
were the Rasena, from the mountains of Rhaetia, who driving back
the Umbrians, and uniting with the Tyrrheni on the Tarquinian
coast, formed the Etruscan race.

A more recent opinion, also of great weight, is that of Lepsius,—
that there was no occupation of the land by any foreign race after
its conquest by the Pelasgi, but that the Umbrians, whom they had
subdued, in time recovering strength, rebelled with success, and
that this reaction of the early inhabitants against their conquerors
produced what is known as the Etruscan people.

It would take too long to record all the opinions and shades of
opinion held on this intricate subject. Suffice it to say that the origin
of the Etruscans has been assigned to the Greeks—to the Egyptians
—the Phoenicians—the Canaanites—the Libyans—the Cantabrians
or Basques—the Celts, an old and favourite theory, revived in our
own days by Sir William Betham, who fraternises them with his
pets, the Irish—and lastly, to the Hyksos, or Shepherd-Kings of
Egypt. I know not if they have been taken for the lost Ten Tribes
of Israel, but, *certes,* a very pretty theory might be set up to that
effect, and supported by arguments which would appear all-cogent to
every one who swears by Coningsby.*

The reader, when he perceives how many-sided is this question,
will surely thank me for not leading him deeply into it, yet may
hardly like to be left among this chaos of opinions without a
guiding hand. Amid the clash and conflict of such a host of

wwwwwwwwwwwwww

* Not to mention minor analogies, there is one of so striking a character, as
satisfactorily to prove, not a descent from Abraham, but an intercourse more or
less direct with the Hebrews, and at least an oriental origin. It is in the cosmogony
of the Etruscans, who are said, on the authority of one of their own writers, to
have believed that the Creator spent 12,000 years in his operations; 6,000 of which
were assigned to the work of creation, and as many to the duration of the world.
In the first thousand he made heaven and earth. In the second, the apparent firma-
ment. In the third, the sea and all other waters. In the fourth, the great lights—
sun, moon, and stars. In the fifth, every soul of birds, reptiles, and four-footed
animals, in the air, earth, and waters. In the sixth, man. Suidas, *sub voce* Τυῤῥηνία.
To say that we recognize here a blending of Etruscan doctrines with the Mosaic
account of the Creation, as Müller observes, does not make the analogy less remarkable, for there is no proof that this mixture is not legitimate.

combatants, who shall attempt to establish harmony?—and where there are "giants in the land," who shall hope to prevail against them?

I confess I do not perceive that the crowd of authorities who maintain the Lydian origin of the Etruscans have been put *hors de combat* by the dictum of Dionysius. There seems to be life in them yet. They clearly represent the popular traditions, not of the Romans only, but of the Etruscans also, for what was current on such a matter among the former, could not have been opposed to the traditions of the latter. Nay, we have it on record that the Etruscans claimed for themselves a Lydian origin. Tacitus tells us that in the time of Tiberius, deputies from Sardis recited before the Roman senate a decree of the Etruscans, declaring their consanguinity, on the ground of the early colonization of Etruria by the Lydians. This popular tradition might not of itself be decisive of the question, but when it is confirmed by a comparison of the recorded customs and the extant monuments of the two people, as will presently be shown, it comes with a force to my mind that will not admit of rejection.

GEORGE DENNIS

Corneto and a Tarquinian Tomb

FROM Vetralla a good road leads to Corneto, eighteen miles distant. It is an instance of the imperfect system of communication in this land, that this is the high-road from Viterbo to Civita Vecchia; but in order to reach that port you must make a large angle, first westward to Corneto, and thence south to Civita Vecchia.

About three miles from Vetralla, in a glen to the right of the road,

Ibid., pp. 275-88.

may be observed many traces of sepulture, indicating the existence
of some Etruscan town, whose name and memory have utterly
perished. Six or seven miles further on the road is the village of
Monte Romano, on the hill of that name, presenting, as far as I
could perceive, no signs of antiquity.

On approaching Corneto, cultivation gives place to bare, undulating downs. The "Queen of the Maremma" comes into view at
the distance of several miles, crowned with a tiara of many towers,
and enthroned on the extremity of a long barren ridge, whose
strangely broken surface at once arrests the eye. To the right, separated from it by a deep vale, stretches a parallel ridge, browed
with white cliffs. This once bore the walls, the temples, the palaces
of ancient Tarquinii—that contained its sepulchres. The one was
the city of the living; the other the city of the dead. Once, how different! now, but too similar—rivals in desolation! The whole is a
wild and dreary scene. Not a tree on either height, or in the vale
between—wide sweeps of bare country on every hand—the dark,
serrated range of the Tolfa to the south. An aqueduct of many
arches occupies the foreground; and the sunny blue of the Mediterranean, the only cheerful feature in the landscape, gleams on the
horizon.

The road here branches to Civita Vecchia on the one hand, and
to Corneto on the other. The latter track traverses the hill of the
Necropolis, the whole surface of which is rugged with tumuli, or
what have once been such, but are now shapeless mounds of earth,
overgrown with lentiscus, myrtle, wild olive, broom, and rank grass,
and giving to the hill, even when seen from afar, a strange, pimply
appearance. Hence its appellation of "Montarozzi."

Fanno i sepolcri tutto 'l loco varo.

Towards the sea the eye passes over lower grounds, in which are
olive-groves, a farm-house or two, and several tumuli of large size.
Lower still lies the flat, barren strip of coast—the region of salt-
works and deadly fevers. Here, on the beach, stands a hamlet,
dignified with the title of Porto Clementino: a few small craft are
at anchor off shore, waiting for cargoes of corn and salt.

It is a drive of nearly three miles over the Montarozzi to the gate
of Corneto. Here a glance brings the thoughts from the most remote
antiquity, down to the days of chivalry. Long lines of yellow battle-
mented wall stretch along the crest and down the slope of the hill;
and the style of masonry, the absence of bastions and ravelins, and
of embrasures for artillery, show these fortifications to date from
the Middle Ages.

Though the chief city of the Papal Maremma, having a population of four or five thousand souls, and lying on the high-road from

Civita Vecchia to Leghorn, Corneto has, or till very recently had, no inn—none at least where the traveller, *fessus viarum*, might repose and recruit in comfort. There is a massive Gothic building in the lower Piazza, from its original application and actual condition styled Il Palazzaccio—"the great ugly Palace"—which has long served as an hostelry; but every one in quest of comfort and cleanliness has ever devoutly eschewed it, in spite of its graceful mullions and winning tracery. On my first visit to Corneto, five or six years since, the only decent *hospitium* was a private house— Casa Moirano—the resort of the few artists and antiquaries who visited the spot; its attractions lying less, it may be, in the civility and attention of the worthy hostess, than in the charms of her daughter, the pretty Gioconda. I have since learned that the Palazzaccio, having fallen into fresh hands, affords more tolerable accommodation than formerly; but I speak not from experience, for, having no great reason to quarrel with my old quarters, on subsequent visits I have returned to them. Beds may also be had at a *caffé* in the high street.

Corneto possesses little interest, save to those who love to dwell with the past. The scenery around it, though wild, and occasionally grand, is not—for Italy at least—picturesque. Bare, hog-backed heights—the broad desert strip of shore—no wood but olive plantations, dull, grey, solemn, formal, and monotonous, less cheerful even than treeless tracts, and which are to scenery what a drab coat is to humanity—these are not promising materials for the portfolio. The city itself is the finest feature in the scene, and viewed from the north, on which side the ground sinks precipitously to the banks of the Marta, it is particularly bold and imposing. With this exception, the scenic delights of Corneto may almost be summed up in what none but the determined admirer of nature will appreciate—

> Watching the ocean and the sky together,
> Under the roof of blue Italian weather.

With so little of the beautiful or picturesque around it, with dulness and dirt within its walls, the atmosphere for half the year leaden and febrile, Corneto can have charms for few. Such, however, there are—antiquaries of credit and renown—who can leave Rome and its social attractions, to pass weeks in this secluded city.

The antiquity of Corneto is very questionable. The fond pride of its citizens has assigned to it an origin in the remotest ages, identifying it, on the strength of the first syllable—on the Macedon and Monmouth principle—with the Corytus of Virgil; a pretension too absurd to need refutation. If it had an existence in Etruscan times, it were less unreasonable to suppose, with Sir W. Gell, that it occupies the site of Cortuosa, or Contenebra, towns in the territory of Tarquinii, which were captured and destroyed by the Romans, *ab urbe condita* 366. But it is not likely that either of these towns was so close to the great city of Tarquinii; and as there are no traces whatever of ancient habitation, it is more probable that this site was not occupied in Etruscan times, or at most by an outpost or fort.

There are few relics of antiquity within Corneto. In the Palazzo Bruschi are some Latin inscriptions, found on the site of the ancient city. The Palazzo Falsacappa also contains a few remains. In the Cathedral, beside some curious inscriptions of the Middle Ages, is a marble slab, forming a step in the aisle, and bearing an Etruscan epigraph, probably sepulchral.

The visitor to Corneto will do well to obtain an introduction to Signor Carlo Avvolta, once the *gonfaloniere*, or chief magistrate of the city, now a *consultore*, or counsellor, of Civita Vecchia. He is a lively, intelligent old gentleman, experienced in excavations, deeply interested in the antiquities of this site, his birthplace, ever ready to impart information, and displaying as much courtesy to strangers as cordiality to his friends. Such as feel little interest in antiquities may consult him with profit on the more rousing matters of Maremma sports. Though now nearly eighty years of age, he is still a keen sportsman, and enters on the fatigues and perils of the chase with the ardour of a man of thirty. He resides in a spacious, gloomy house, where everything breathes of antiquity; but, wherever his activity may lead him during the day, in the evening he is sure to be found at the *caffé*, or at the *spezieria*, where he will descant, with all the enthusiasm of his nature, on the last boar or roe-buck he made to bite the dust, or on the paintings and furniture of Etruscan tombs.

The Bruschi gardens, outside the city on the road to Civita Vecchia, are worthy of a visit, even from the antiquary. The parterres are adorned with altars, sarcophagi, fragments of columns, and other relics of Etruscan and Roman antiquity; and in the lower garden are some stone lions, of amusing quaintness.

But the grand lions of Corneto are the painted tombs on the Montarozzi. These, after having remained open to the wantonness of travellers and the ignorance of shepherds—in one case for nearly a century—were a few years since fitted with doors by order of the government; and the keys were intrusted to a citizen of Corneto. This man, Agápito Aldanesi, who is to be found exercising his vocation of cordwainer in the Piazza Angelica, doffs cap and apron, and comes forth a new man at the traveller's call, provided with keys and tapers to do the subterranean honours of the spot.

I shall describe these tombs in the order in which they are generally visited. More than a cursory notice may be thought super-

fluous after the full and lively descriptions of Mrs. Hamilton Gray;
but as that lady, at the time of visiting Etruria, had no intention
of writing a work on the subject, and has been obliged to depend
as much upon memory as upon notes, it is no matter of surprise
that errors have crept into her statements. The weeks I have spent
at Corneto, day after day, from sunrise to sunset,

> Hid from the world in the low-delved tombs

the paintings in most of which I have copied with the camera-lucida,
and coloured on the spot, so as to familiarise myself with all their
details, and the visits I have subsequently paid to the place, warrant me in laying claim to greater accuracy than can be attained
by the observation of a passing tourist.

About a mile from Corneto, in the heart of the Montarozzi, a deep
pit by the wayside marks the entrance to the

GROTTA QUERCIOLA

a name derived from the owner of the ground in which the tomb
lies. Agápito, "the happy man who shows the tombs" of Tarquinii,
is much dissatisfied with the nomenclature hitherto given to them,
and is wont to designate this as the Grotta della Caccia del Cignale
—"Tomb of the Boar-hunt."

A descent of about twenty steps, hewn in ancient times from
the solid rock, leads to the entrance of the tomb, which is closed
by a modern door. This opens into a spacious chamber. The first
impression is one of disappointment. The chamber is in the form
of an Etruscan tomb—but where are the paintings?—why close a
sepulchre with naked walls? Presently, however, as the eye becomes
accustomed to the gloom, figure after figure seems to step forth
from the walls, and you perceive two rows of them, separated by
a striped coloured ribbon—the upper row being nearly four feet,
the lower only half that in height. In the pediment, left at each end
of the chamber by the ceiling sloping down from the central beam,
is a third row, not more than twelve inches high.

The next impression is one of surprise. Can this be the resting-
place of the dead?—Can these scenes of feasting and merriment,
this dancing, this piping, this sporting, appertain to a tomb? There
on the inner wall, and occupying the principal row, is a banqueting
scene—figures in richly-broidered garments recline on couches,
feasting to the sound of the lyre and pipes; attendants stand around,
some replenishing the goblets from the wine-jars on a sideboard
hard by; a train of dancers, male and female, beat time with lively

steps to the notes of the instruments, on which some of them are also performing; while in the lower row are depicted field-sports, a boar-hunt being the most conspicuous.

But observe that fond and youthful pair on the central couch. The female, of exquisite beauty, turns her back on the feast, and throws her arms passionately round the neck of her lover, who reclines behind her. The other guests quaff their wine without heeding them. The elegant forms of the couches and stools, the rich drapery, the embroidered cushions, show this to be a scene of high life, and give some idea of Etruscan luxury. Even the dancers are very richly attired, especially the females, in figured robes of bright colours, with embroidered borders of a different hue. A simple mantle, either the *chlamys* or scarf, or the *pallium* or blanket, suffices for the men; but the attendants at the sideboard have unornamented tunics. The dancing-girls, like those of modern times, are decorated with jewellery—earrings, necklaces, and bracelets—and have also a frontlet on their brows; while the men wear chaplets of myrtle. A *tibicen,* or *subulo,* as the Etruscans called him, blowing the double-pipes, and a *citharista* with his lyre, stand at one end of the banqueting-scene, and a *subulo* at the other; another performer of each description mingles in the dance. All this feasting and merry-making is carried on in the open air, as is shown by the trees behind the festive couch, and alternating with the dancers; yet the *candelabrum* indicates it to be by night.

The figure over the doorway, which seems to have been a man in a *biga,* or two-horse chariot, does not belong to the foregoing scene, but seems introduced merely to fill an awkward space; though it is probable it has reference to the funeral games.

To hunt the wild boar of Etruria—*Tuscus aper*—was a favourite sport of the old Romans, as it is still of their modern representatives. From this and other ancient monuments we learn that it was also the delight of the Etruscans themselves. The bristly monster is here depicted brought to bay by the dogs. Men on foot and horseback are rushing eagerly to the attack; the former, while brandishing a spear in one hand, have an axe in the other to cut their way through the thickets, or to sever the boar's head from his carcass. Behind these figures are the nets into which it was the custom to drive the game, in order to bring it to bay. Such a scene is described by Virgil, in his usual circumstantial and picturesque manner, and with more conciseness, but not less accuracy, by Horace; and that such was the ordinary mode of hunting the boar and deer among the Greeks and Romans we have abundant evidence in ancient writers. In this lower band there seem also to have been chariot-races, but many figures have been obliterated from the wall.

In each pediment are two warriors, with short curved swords, leading their horses by the bridle; and the angles are filled by panthers—an animal frequently portrayed in Etruscan tombs, and generally over the doorway; whence it has been inferred that they were intended as figurative guardians of the dead. But their presence in tombs may be otherwise explained by their being sacred to Bacchus, who, as an infernal deity, was closely allied to, perhaps identical with, Mantus, the great god of the Etruscan Hades.

This tomb was discovered in April, 1831. It is larger and loftier than any other sepulchre in this necropolis, whose walls are completely covered with paintings, and in its original state must have been truly magnificent; but the colours have now almost faded from the walls, and it is to be feared that ere long they will vanish entirely. Agápito asserts that they have faded very much during the last few years. This is the more to be regretted, on account of the peculiar beauty of the design here exhibited, which places this at the head of the painted tombs of Tarquinii. Professor Gerhard pronounces the design to be genuinely Hellenic, of a free and perfect character, yet accompanied by features purely Etruscan; in fact, he regards it as the most instructive monument extant for the history of pictorial art in Etruria. Yet though Greek art be decidedly evident in this tomb, the subject, as in almost every other sepulchral painting, is genuinely Etruscan. The most striking peculiarity is the presence of the two sexes on the same festive couch. It is not improbable that the fair one in this scene, from her amorous attitude, and from the absence of any other of her sex at the banquet, is as frail as fair—in short, that she is a *hetæra*. But in others of these tombs females of most modest appearance are represented reclining with the males. And this is never found in Greek works of art—bas-reliefs, or even painted vases. For, with all their refinement, the Hellenes never attained to such an elevation of sentiment towards the fair sex, as to raise it to an equality with the male. In the feeling with which they regarded, and the suspicion with which they treated their females, they were half-orientals; indeed, the polished Athenians were in this respect behind their ruder Dorian rivals. Their wives and daughters were never suffered to share the festive couch with their lords. *Hetæræ* alone were admitted to that equivocal honour. The superiority of the Romans in this point, there is little doubt was owing to the example of the Etruscans, who, as is abundantly proved from their monuments, as well as from history, admitted their females to an equal place at the board. Such, however, was not the custom of the early Romans, for they reclined at table, while their women sat on chairs; and so also they used to represent their deities in the *lectisternia,* or sacred feasts, for the statue of Jupiter was laid on a couch, while those of Juno and Minerva, his sister-wife and daughter, be it remembered, were placed in a sitting posture.

One peculiarity of this tomb is, that the sexes are not distinguished by their colour, as is always the case in the early and purely Etruscan tombs, where the males are coloured a deep-red, but the females left white. Another peculiarity is, that there are no chaplets represented, either suspended from the walls, or in the hands of the dancers. The colours used in these paintings are red, yellow, blue, grey, black, and white. It is said that when the tomb was opened, an Etruscan inscription was legible near the principal figures of the banquet; but it has completely disappeared, the surface of the wall in this part being sadly dilapidated.

———

SIBYLLE VON CLES-REDEN

Caere, a City of the Dead

BARELY twenty-five miles separate Caere from Rome. Yet it is as if one were at the beginning of an entirely different world, infinitely strange. The red volcanic soil of what was once the Tyrrhenian coastline still bears the indelible stamp of the Etruscan character branded on it. Nowhere else is the Etruscan mystery so inscrutable and oppressive, seemingly so near to a solution and yet so incomprehensible, as here in Caere: not so much in those parts of it which were once inhabited by the living Tyrrhenians, but in Caere's city of the dead—the necropolis which grew up like a ghostly twin beside the living town, and never stopped growing as the other died.

On a rocky ridge of red tufa-stone, which protrudes down to the bare seashore like a bastion of the wooded mountains, stood the ancient Chisra of the Etruscans, which the Romans later called Caere. A last echo of the name is still to be heard in that of the somnolent, dreamy village of Cerveteri, or *Caere Vetus*, whose

From *The Buried People, a Study of the Etruscan World*. Translated from the German by C. M. Woodhouse. London: Rupert Hart-Davis Ltd.; 1955, pp. 29-30, 33-4, 35-9. By permission of Rupert Hart-Davis Ltd.

crumbling mediaeval walls stand on the outer limits of what was once the Tyrrhenian township. As in the case with most Tyrrhenian settlements, a gorge separates it from a parallel ridge on which stands the city of the dead. But the wealthy, sophisticated town of Caere, where young Roman nobles used to be sent to acquire a veneer of culture and refinement, never occupied more than about seventy acres even in its most brilliant period; whereas the necropolis expanded insatiably over a thousand years. So the bright green plain by the sea gradually changed into a monstrous landscape of the dead, the appearance of which can still be detected today.

They were a strange people, the Etruscans. They generally built houses for their gods and their living out of wood or baked clay; but for their dead they carved stone mansions out of the rock, as though building them for eternity, as though only the dead were real in this world of illusion.

The mounds containing the Etruscan tombs, large and small, cover some 140 acres. They protrude above ground level like a gigantic silent city stretching from the sea to the hills; and the round summits of the hills seem like nothing so much as a magnified repetition of the same shapes on a larger scale. Where the necropolis of Caere ends, those of its harbours begin: Pyrgi, Alsium and Punicum. It seems almost incredible that this land still had room for the living, together with their fields and pastures.

Long before the dun-coloured eyrie of Cerveteri becomes visible, the road is lined on the right by the tumuli of these Tyrrhenian sepulchral monuments. Many of them have been explored, but many more are still unopened. Only a small area of the necropolis of Caere—about six acres out of 140—has been systematically excavated and restored.

The ancient cemetery road, with its deeply indented tracks made by the two-wheeled wagons which once carried the splendid funeral processions of the Etruscans to the city of the dead, still leads into the home of long-forgotten shades, as it has done for thousands of years. In long rows stand the vast and silent mounds, rising to 130 feet in height. They are made of earth heaped up on drum-shaped bases, which are carved out of the solid tufa-stone: magnificent survivals from the eighth, seventh and sixth centuries B.C. At that date, when almost the whole of Italy was under Etruscan domination, the builders disdained to inscribe the names of those buried on the walls of their tombs, for it was unthinkable to them that their fame should ever come to be forgotten. . . .

But the true aspect of Caere is not to be found in these melancholy graves of a defeated people, a dying epoch, their gloomy depths gleaming with stagnant water. It lies rather in the paintings of the dead which the mighty Etruscans produced at the date

when, in Livy's words, they controlled Italy "from sea to sea." In
the scale of these there can still be seen the extravagance of a
nation intoxicated by its youthful strength. The thirty centuries
through which their secret has endured still lie heavy on the land,
like a magic spell. We know very little, indeed practically nothing,
of that cult of the dead whose regulations imposed the round shape
of the universe on these funeral mounds. But we can detect in them
the passionate character of the life lived by the Etruscans in their
archaic period, which led them to glorify death as the highest
pinnacle of happiness. In this great period death was overshadowed
by no regrets or fears for these bold seafarers, these dauntless conquerors, these epicures in love with beauty.

In the dark bosom of the red tufa-stone, under the rounded domes
of the funeral mounds, their dead dwelt in habitations faithfully
modelled on the homes of the living. The larger tumuli often housed
several of them, each having their separate entrance in the form
of a high, narrow slit, tapering at the top and leading down to a
low doorway into the underground house.

Beyond the entrance to the habitation of the dead a larger ante-
room opens out, followed by smaller rooms which connect with this
atrium through openings shaped like doors or windows. Stone slabs
line the walls, many of them in the shape of beds; and on them
rested the embalmed bodies of the dead, as if asleep, hung with
jewellery, exquisitely dressed, with laurel-wreaths of gold on their
brows. There are also sometimes sarcophagi of earthenware, stone
or wood standing on pedestals. Sometimes the dead were laid out
on the slabs with their beds, as witness the notches into which the
legs of the beds were fitted. The smaller chambers were reserved
for married couples in their last sleep, the wife on the left of her
husband: her position is still indicated by a stone triangle, the
sign of womanhood. The other members of the family generally
rested in the ante-room. Only the children were left out of this
community; their little bodies were buried outside, in the stone in
front of the mounds, presumably because the Etruscans' faith did
not permit them to share the other world of the grown-ups. In front
of the entrance stood other crude stone symbols: a phallic column
for the man, and for the woman again the triangle shaped like the
pediment of a building, which could be interpreted either as a sexual symbol or as the sign of the house, the domain of the woman.
The number and size of these symbols show the number and age
of the dead in each particular tumulus. . . .

In 1836 a priest and a general discovered in a vineyard, at some
distance from the real necropolis of Caere, a tomb of the middle
of the seventh century B.C., which has since become famous as the
"Regolini-Galassi" tomb, so called after them. It lies in the heart of

a mound whose periphery contains five more graves. Within are two chambers forming a gallery, which indicates the great antiquity of the construction. The lower part of their walls is cut directly out of the solid tufa-stone, while the upper part is built of stone blocks gradually overlapping each other to form a rough kind of vault. Constructions of this kind, with primitive vaults formed of overlapping masonry over square or round chambers, are characteristic of the prehistoric Mediterranean culture, extending from the Aegean to Sardinia; and they were often used in Etruscan mausoleums of the early period. It was only in the course of the sixth century B.C. that the Tyrrhenians began to carve the habitations of their dead entirely out of the solid rock and to make their ceilings flat.

It is not recorded whether these two discoverers had the same strange and frightening experience that befell some others at the opening of Etruscan tombs; whether, in fact, at the moment when the dark shaft of the desecrated grave was opened to the light, they caught one startled glimpse of the motionless figures of the dead royal couple, luxuriously clothed and perfectly preserved as if alive —only to see them a moment later dissolve into dust, like ghostly apparitions, at the first breath of air from without.

At any rate, the Regolini-Galassi tomb had been fortunate in being spared the vandalism suffered by the five outer funeral chambers. So its discoverers found almost intact in it all the treasures with which the princely Etruscan couple—for such they were, to judge from the richness of the gifts accompanying them —had been equipped in their last dwelling-place thousands of years before. These treasures which thus emerged again out of the darkness of the centuries, a ghostly vision in the faint light of their torches, today fill an entire hall of the Vatican Museum.

When the tomb was opened, the body of a man was found in the front room on a bronze bed; in the room to the rear was a woman, covered all over in jewellery. A vessel containing ashes stood in a niche near the exit; there were also weapons and the charred remains of a war-chariot. No doubt a soldier was stationed there to guard the dead couple. The royal occupants of the tomb remain without name or history so far as we are concerned, but the things they loved and had with them in their life and round them in their death speak eloquently to us of the splendor of the young Etruscan nation.

The extravagant taste for luxury which the Etruscans developed at the dawn of Tyrrhenian greatness has little in common with the frugal simplicity of their previous period. The princess wears on her breast, like a religious pectoral, a large round sheet of gold plate covered with an intaglio design of plants and animals in imitation of the Greek orientalising style. The fine, closely worked pattern gives an impression not unlike an exquisite embroidery. Her cloak was held together by a gold clasp made in two sections, one of the masterpieces of the goldsmith's craft from the ancient world. The first section consists of a large oval plate with five lions on it, surrounded by embossed lotus-flowers. Two hinged joints connect the larger plate with a smaller oval plate, which has minute golden ducklings marching across its curved surface in two rows. Between these little figures, which stand out vertically, the surface is further decorated with embossed lions, their shapes outlined with a microscopic *appliqué* of little gold points. This extraordinary attractive technique of granulation, which seems to give an extra glitter to the gold ornamentation, is an achievement unique to Etruscan craftsmanship, unrivalled before or since. It is only within recent years that German goldsmiths have succeeded in rediscovering the lost secret of these tiny points of gold, as practised by the Tyrrhenian goldsmiths.

Apart from the clasp of the mantle, which was twenty inches in length, the queen also wore two arm-bands, spreading out like ruffles and lavishly decorated with human and animal shapes in embossed and granulated work. The almost barbaric extravagance of design is continued into the decoration of the inside of the arm-bands. Finally, the priceless collection is completed by two neck-laces—a simple one of heavy, engraved beads of beaten gold, and another consisting of pendants of gold and ambergris—together with ear-rings, spiral finger-rings, brooches and pins of gold. In spite of the quantity, the whole collection weighs hardly more than a heap of rose-petals. With a mastery unrivalled even by Benvenuto Cellini, the Etruscan goldsmiths knew how to work the precious metal to a fineness and delicacy so incredible that their master-pieces seem to be practically without weight. Caere was evidently a centre of this highly developed craftsmanship in gold from an early date; and her products soon displaced the foreign works of art which had originally served as models.

Apart from the gold-work, the dead king and his queen were further equipped with a great number of articles of everyday use. There were hemispherical bronze vessels on raised pedestals, with the heads of imaginary animals leaning over their rims; and round ornamental discs, with panthers' faces glaring like spectres out of the centre, their eyes enamelled and their jaws agape; and em-bossed silver bowls and great earthenware jars, which were filled with grain, oil, honey and even eggs for the dead; and many smaller vessels of bronze and terracotta. All these bear witness to the artistic care and taste with which even the simplest (not to mention the more expensive) articles of everyday use in the house were designed. There is even a bronze bed in the Regolini-Galassi tomb, made of rough lattice-work supported by six legs, with a head-rest; and the dead ruler was not deprived in the underworld even of his throne, the symbol of his rank. The austerity of the lines of this bronze-plated armchair with its high, straight back, and the stiff row of stylised lotus-flowers forming its head-piece, is strongly reminiscent of the throne of a mediaeval prince. Finally, we find among the funerary gifts the remains of a wide triumphal chariot, also exquisitely plated in bronze. On this we can imagine the Lucumon driving through his city, crowned with a golden laurel-wreath, dressed in his embroidered tunic and his mantle of purple, preceded by his heralds and lictors carrying the double axe in its bundle of rods before him as the sacred symbol of power; and we can see in him the forerunner of the Roman emperors of a later day. The bronze plating of this magnificent vehicle, like all other articles of the period, is decorated with a curvilinear design of plants, vulture-headed lions and sphinxes, winged horses, grinning Gorgons—all motives derived from Egypt, early Greece, Babylonia and Crete. The grotesquely extravagant splendour of these orientalising designs reflects a naïve longing for luxury on the part of the youthful Etruscan nation, which was still groping eagerly for a style of its own.

J. D. BEAZLEY

Etruscan Life in Vase-Painting

SIR JOHN BEAZLEY, perhaps the world's greatest authority on Greek vases, looks with understanding on their Etruscan counterparts.

GREEK vases used to be called Etruscan: but there are plenty of Etruscan vases. They have not received much attention, and this is

From *Etruscan Vase Painting.* Oxford: The Clarendon Press; 1947, pp. 1-3. By permission of The Clarendon Press, Oxford.

intelligible, for few of them are works of art. The Etruscans were
gifted artists, but clay vases were not their forte. Bronze was their
favourite material, and their best achievements were in bronze:
statues and statuettes, candelabra, mirrors, and the rest. Yet many
of their clay vases have great interest of subject. In style, they imitate Greek models, but they have a characteristic flavour which is
sometimes agreeably racy.

I shall say nothing about the earliest Etruscan or Italic imitations
of Greek vases, in the eighth and seventh centuries, and the first
part of the sixth; the importance of these has been shown by Blake-
way, Payne, and Mrs. Dohan. Let us begin with an Etruscan black-
figured vase from the middle of the sixth century, a neck-amphora
in Munich of the so-called Pontic class ("Pontic" is only a conventional term). It is a gay lively piece in an eclectic style with the
Eastern Greek element predominating. The Judgment of Paris, one
half of the picture on each side of the vase. Hermes is conducting
the three goddesses to Paris, and he turns to give his last instructions. Hera, Athena, and Aphrodite are all well differentiated. Priam
has guided the party to Paris. Here is Paris's dog with lolling tongue,
Paris's herd, and their familiar, the raven. The photograph shows
that the modern copyist has not got the expression of number one,
Hera, perfectly right: till now she has been smiling and chattering
like the others; but when Hermes gives the word she becomes suddenly serious. These "Pontic" vases were made in Etruria, but
they are very Greek, and it is possible that the fabric was founded
by a Greek immigrant. Another vase by the Paris Painter, as he has
been called from the Munich vase, is a neck-amphora of the same
shape in the Vatican. This picture, too, is divided between the two
sides of the vase: a cavalry engagement: on the one hand, Oriental
archers, with high felt caps, using the Parthian shot; on the other,
Western javelin-throwers. Hounds and hares form a kind of under-
plot. This is lively too, though it pales a little if it is compared with
the sort of original from which it was imitated, an Attic vase-
picture of about 560.

In the later stage of the "Pontic" fabric the non-Hellenic element,
as might be expected, becomes somewhat stronger: but that need
not be illustrated, and instead let us pass to a black-figure fabric
which succeeds the Pontic and is the most important group of
Etruscan vases in the last quarter of the sixth century and the early
part of the fifth. The chief artist may be named the Micali Painter
in honour of an Italian scholar who published some of the vases
a hundred years ago. This painter has a jolly, slogging style, and
must have enjoyed himself. A neck-amphora of his in Baltimore
immediately transports us into what has been called "that wonder-
world of rushing men, women, satyrs, maenads, amidst all sorts

of plants, trees, weeds, birds, beasts real and fantastic, in which
the Etruscan, especially the earlier Etruscan, delights." The chief
picture on his hydria [a water jar] in the British Museum represents
a dead man lying in state with the mourners about him, but the
artist has not let that cast him down. There is nothing funereal
about the winged youth, or the Pegasus, or the capering centaur.
Big ugly birds like those that jostle the youth and the centaur are
great favourites in Etruria and you find them everywhere in Etruscan art. Here is a late work by the same painter, a neck-amphora
in the Vatican with a battle of gods and giants: Herakles, Athena,
and Ares on the gods' side; the giants assisted by a winged goddess
—Eris or the like—and also by a second Athena, due to the excessive
love of symmetry sometimes found in Etruria: the style is coarser
and the movement more lumbering but there is still plenty of life.
A hideous bird has already alighted on one of the giants. A fourth
work by this painter, one of his earliest, is worth looking at more
closely. A neck-amphora in the British Museum presents a sports
meeting in the Etruria of the late sixth century B.C. There are
several scenes. First scene, a boxing-match. There are many such
pictures on Greek vases, and amusing ones, but here it is not so
much of Greek vases that we think as of those rude old prints,
from the classic era of English boxing, in which the heroes of the
prize-ring are shown confronting each other in bellicose attitudes:
Tom Cribb, Jem Belcher, or Molyneux the Moor. The boy looks
like a bottle-holder, but although he has the sponge in one hand, it
is an oil-flask, a lekythion, that he holds in the other, and the water
—or wine—is in a jug on the ground. They box to the flute, in
Etruscan fashion. Then comes the umpire with his wand. This
scene, and others on the vase, reappear on the walls of the Tomba
della Scimmia at Chiusi. Second scene, climbing the greasy pole.
Third scene, at the end of the picture-band, under the handle:
I always took these to be spectators, the countryman bringing his
old father to see the fun; but there is a similar scene in the Tomba
della Scimmia, where the couple seem to be performers, and it has
been suggested that they are acrobats, and the little man a child in
disguise. Fourth scene, pentathlon—discus-thrower, javelin-thrower.
Fifth scene, dance in armour: the youth is leaping up, on a springy
platform. Sixth scene, chariot-race, the winner passing the post.
Seventh scene, satyrs dancing. Are they real satyrs, in which case
the artist in his excitement has left the sports ground and soared
into another sphere? Or are they performers dressed as satyrs?—If
so, the artist has used his privilege of making the performer more
like what he is intended to be than would be possible in real life,
and has depicted not the actors but the characters they represent.
Eighth scene, a second team of dancers, veiled women. One of them

turns and looks at you; and if we were told that these were modern Italian women, in local costume, from the Abruzzi or Sardinia, I believe we should agree. Ninth scene, a third team, boys dancing in pairs and playing the castanets.

───────

D. H. LAWRENCE

D. H. Lawrence and the Etruscans

D. H. LAWRENCE went to live near Florence in 1926. Although he was already seriously ill, and was several times near death, he found the energy, in addition to his purely literary work, to visit Etruscan sites and to write the unfinished *Sketches of Etruscan Places*.

❧

An Etruscan Mood

THERE is a queer stillness and a curious peaceful repose about the Etruscan places I have been to, quite different from the weirdness of Celtic places, the slightly repellent feeling of Rome and the old Campagna, and the rather horrible feeling of the great pyramid places in Mexico, Teotihuacan and Cholula, and Mitla in the south; or the amiably idolatrous Buddha places in Ceylon. There is a stillness and a softness in these great grassy mounds with their ancient stone girdles, and down the central walk there lingers still a kind of

From *Etruscan Places* by D. H. Lawrence. Reprinted by permission of The Viking Press, Inc., New York; 1932, pp. 24, 62-5, and by permission of Laurence Pollinger Limited and the Estate of the late Mrs. Frieda Lawrence, for the publication by William Heinemann Ltd., London.

homeliness and happiness. True, it was a still and sunny afternoon in April, and larks rose from the soft grass of the tombs. But there was a stillness and a soothingness in all the air, in that sunken place, and a feeling that it was good for one's soul to be there.

The same when we went down the few steps, and into the chambers of rock, within the tumulus. There is nothing left. It is like a house that has been swept bare: the inmates have left: now it waits for the next comer. But whoever it is that has departed, they have left a pleasant feeling behind them, warm to the heart, and kindly to the bowels.

They are surprisingly big and handsome, these homes of the dead. Cut out of the living rock, they are just like houses. The roof has a beam cut to imitate the roof-beam of the house. It is a house, a home.

The Painted Tombs of Tarquinia

We come up the steps into the upper world, the sea-breeze and the sun. The old dog shambles to his feet, the guide blows out his lamp and locks the gate, we set off again, the dog trundling apathetic at his master's heels, the master speaking to him with that soft Italian familiarity which seems so very different from the spirit of Rome, the strong-willed Latin.

The guide steers across the hilltop, in the clear afternoon sun, towards another little hood of masonry. And one notices there is quite a number of these little gateways, built by the Government to cover the steps that lead down to the separate small tombs. It is utterly unlike Cerveteri, though the two places are not forty miles apart. Here there is no stately tumulus city, with its highroad between the tombs, and inside, rather noble, many-roomed houses of the dead. Here the little one-room tombs seem scattered at random on the hilltop, here and there: though probably, if excavations were fully carried out, here also we should find a regular city of the dead, with its streets and crossways. And probably each tomb had its little tumulus of piled earth, so that even above-ground there were streets of mounds with tomb entrances. But even so, it would be different from Cerveteri, from Caere; the mounds would be so small, the streets surely irregular. Anyhow, to-day there are scattered little one-room tombs, and we dive down into them just like rabbits popping down a hole. The place is a warren.

It is interesting to find it so different from Cerveteri. The Etruscans carried out perfectly what seems to be the Italian instinct: to have single, independent cities, with a certain surrounding territory, each district speaking its own dialect and feeling at home in its own little capital, yet the whole confederacy of city-states loosely linked together by a common religion and a more-or-less common interest. Even to-day Lucca is very different from Ferrara, and the language is hardly the same. In ancient Etruria this isolation of cities developing according to their own idiosyncrasy, within the loose union of a so-called nation, must have been complete. The contact between the plebs, the mass of the people, of Caere and Tarquinii must have been almost null. They were, no doubt, foreigners to one another. Only the Lucumones, the ruling sacred magistrates of noble family, the priests and the other nobles, and the merchants, must have kept up an intercommunion, speaking "correct" Etruscan, while the people, no doubt, spoke dialects varying so widely as to be different languages. To get any idea of the pre-Roman past we must break up the conception of oneness and uniformity, and see an endless confusion of differences.

We are diving down into another tomb, called, says the guide, the Tomb of the Leopards. Every tomb has been given a name, to distinguish it from its neighbours. The Tomb of the Leopards has two spotted leopards in the triangle of the end wall, between the roof-slopes. Hence its name.

The Tomb of the Leopards is a charming, cosy little room, and the paintings on the walls have not been so very much damaged. All the tombs are ruined to some degree by weather and vulgar vandalism, having been left and neglected like common holes, when they had been broken open again and rifled to the last gasp.

But still the paintings are fresh and alive: the ochre-reds and blacks and blues and blue-greens are curiously alive and harmonious on the creamy yellow walls. Most of the tomb walls have had a thin coat of stucco, but it is of the same paste as the living rock, which is fine and yellow, and weathers to a lovely creamy gold, a beautiful colour for a background.

The walls of this little tomb are a dance of real delight. The room seems inhabited still by Etruscans of the sixth century before Christ, a vivid, life-accepting people, who must have lived with real fullness. On come the dancers and the music-players, moving in a broad frieze towards the front wall of the tomb, the wall facing us as we enter from the dark stairs, and where the banquet is going on in all its glory. Above the banquet, in the gable angle, are the two spotted leopards, heraldically facing each other across a little tree. And the ceiling of rock has chequered slopes of red and black and yellow and blue squares, with a roof-beam painted with coloured circles, dark red and blue and yellow. So that all is colour, and we do not seem to be underground at all, but in some gay chamber of the past.

The dancers on the right wall move with a strange, powerful alertness onwards. The men are dressed only in a loose coloured scarf, or in the gay handsome chlamys draped as a mantle. The *subulo* plays the double flute the Etruscans loved so much, touching the stops with big, exaggerated hands, the man behind him touches the seven-stringed lyre, the man in front turns round and signals with his left hand, holding a big wine-bowl in his right. And so they move on, on their long, sandalled feet, past the little berried olive-trees, swiftly going with their limbs full of life, full of life to the tips.

This sense of vigorous, strong-bodied liveliness is characteristic of the Etruscans, and is somehow beyond art. You cannot think of art, but only of life itself, as if this were the very life of the Etruscans, dancing in their coloured wraps with massive yet exuberant naked limbs, ruddy from the air and the sea-light, dancing and fluting along through the little olive-trees, out in the fresh day.

The end wall has a splendid banqueting scene. The feasters recline upon a checked or tartan couch-cover, on the banqueting couch, and in the open air, for they have little trees behind them. The six feasters are gold and full of life like the dancers, but they are strong, they keep their life so beautifully and richly inside themselves, they are not loose, they don't lose themselves even in their wild moments. They lie in pairs, man and woman, reclining equally on the couch, curiously friendly. The two end women are called *hetaerae*, courtesans, chiefly because they have yellow hair, which seems to have been a favourite feature in a woman of pleasure. The men are dark and ruddy, and naked to the waist. The women, sketched in on the creamy rock, are fair, and wear thin gowns, with rich mantles round their hips. They have a certain free bold look, and perhaps really are courtesans.

An Anonymous Translator (Preface) and
JOHANN WINCKELMANN

Winckelmann
and Herculaneum

THE unknown English translator of this minor work of Johann
Winckelmann has made a excellent job both of the Preface and of
the translation. He describes in some detail the brutal murder of
the great pioneer art historian at Trieste. Winckelmann's own witty
account of various scandals—follies, forgeries and obscenities—
connected with Herculaneum reveals a different side of his mind
from that lofty enthusiasm associated with his famous *History of
Ancient Art* (1764).

❦

THE present century has had the advantage of discovering the ruins
of three ancient towns, covered by the eruptions of Mount Vesuvius,
and of having what they contained laid open to the inspection of the
curious, who by these means have obtained a vast field for the gratification of curiosity, and of that inextinguishable thirst of knowledge, which is one of the principal characteristics of rational beings.
These towns were Herculaneum, Pompeii, and Stabia.

The city of Herculaneum first suffered by an earthquake, which
happened on the 5th of February, in the year 63, and continued to
waste the neighbouring country during many days. Pompeii was
entirely swallowed up, great part of Herculaneum was reduced to
ruin, and the rest so shattered that it must have fallen, had it not
been repaired after the people had recovered from their fright. Sixteen years after this accident, on the first of November, 79, in the
first year of the Emperor Titus, Herculaneum, was totally over-

From *Critical Account of Herculaneum, Pompeii and Stabia*. London: Carnan &
Newberg; 1770, pp. i-vi (by an anonymous translator), 20-3, 25-6, 29-32, 37-8, 39-43.

whelmed by an irruption of Mount Vesuvius. Uncommon heats, and many shocks of an earthquake, had been felt for some days, accompanied with a noise like thunder, not only in the air, but under the ground, and upon the sea. This noise, which seemed to be the groan of Nature, increased in a moment, like a cry extorted by some sudden pang; and there issued from all the apertures of the mountain, a prodigious quantity of stones and ashes, which were thrown to an incredible height. These were followed by a stream of fire which spread like a sheet, and a thick smoke, which totally intercepted the light of Heaven, and produced an unnatural night of tremendous darkness, which the flames of the Volcano in a manner rendered visible. With the fire issued an astonishing quantity of cinders, ashes, and stones, which filled not only the air and the earth, but the sea. Pompeii which had just been rebuilt, was totally destroyed, and was buried with Stabia and Herculaneum, under the lava of Vesuvius.

The dreadful circumstances which attend the destruction of these cities, are worthy of being prefixed to a work which treats of the antiquities they contained, since these melancholy events were attended with a circumstance that will be of advantage to mankind. By their being thus overflowed by the lava of Vesuvius, they were locked up and secured from the ravages of the Goths and Vandals, who destroyed most of the vestiges they found of the arts, and were preserved through a long series of barbarous ages for the improvement of very distant times. By their being thus secluded from public view for near seventeen hundred years, by the hand of Providence, it seems as if they were reserved by the Omnipotent Disposer of all things, for the instruction and improvement of the present century, in which the arts are cultivated throughout all Europe, and are gradually rising to perfection, particularly in this kingdom, where a gracious Prince has taken them under his peculiar protection.

The study of antiquities is one of the most pleasing, and the most instructive of those in which the curiosity of man can be engaged. These are of the greatest consequence in elucidating history, particularly such antiquities as these, which afford a distinct knowledge of the furniture, domestic utensils, sacred vessels, paintings, statutes, intaglios, seals, &c. found at Herculaneum, many of which are amazingly beautiful, and superior to any antiquities before discovered. By these discoveries we are introduced, as it were, into the age in which the ancient Romans flourished; and enter more minutely into their public and domestic life.

At the time when the above cities were destroyed, the arts flourished, and were carried to the greatest height. The cities of Italy were embellished with the works of the greatest masters of Greece, and contained the most finished and most perfect works in

painting, statuary, and engraving of seals; works that will ever be
the admiration of mankind, and are worthy of being transmitted
as models to be carefully studied by the artists of all future ages,
wherever there is a desire of carrying the arts to the utmost perfection. This renders the present work both interesting and highly
necessary at the present time, when by the study of nature and her
finest models produced by the ancients, our artists are exerting all
their abilities to arrive at perfection.

After all, these antiquities afford the most striking moral reflec-
tions to the mind of the contemplative; when we consider that the
objects here exhibited belonged to the mighty empires of Greece
and Rome, long since destroyed, and were part of the furniture of
the ancient Romans, so celebrated in history, and of their towns; we
see the transitory glory of all earthly objects, that empires, however
firmly founded, and that cities, however embellished, are like man,
subject to mortality, and liable to dissolution. This thought naturally
humbles the mind in the dust, and we learn to know our own insignificance, the vanity of our pretensions, and the futility of all
earthly glories.

The Abbé Winckelmann, the learned author of this work, acquired
a very great reputation, by his various researches into the Grecian
and Roman Antiquities. Being at Vienna in the Year 1768, he met
with a most honourable reception from all persons of distinction,
and was particularly loaded with favours by the Empress Queen,
who amongst other presents gave him three valuable gold medals,
which had the impressions of the late Emperor Francis, of her imperial and royal majesty, and of the reigning Emperor, which soon
after unhappily proved the cause of his death; for arriving at Trieste
in order to return by sea to Rome, he was murdered in the chamber
of the inn where he lodged, by a passenger, who, desiring to see the
three medals, while he was opening the box in which they were contained, threw a cord with a running knot round his neck; and the
knot stopping at the chin, he gave him seven stabs with a knife.
Thus, to the regret of all Europe, died this ingenious and learned
gentleman on the 9th of August, 1768, by the hand of a villain, after
having been distinguished not only by his learning, but by his can-
dour, his love of liberty, and the most amiable virtues.

This work was originally written in German, the Author's native
language, and the Translator begs leave to observe, that he did not
take upon him to translate it, till he had long waited for some indications of its being undertaken by a better pen, though in point of
faithfulness he flatters himself that none can exceed him.

[*End of Preface by translator*]

. . . A well dug for the prince of Elbeuf, at a small distance from his house, was the first thing that gave occasion to the discovery they are now pursuing [at Herculaneum]. The prince had built this house in order to make his constant residence in it. It lay behind the Franciscan convent, at the extremity of, and upon, a rock of lava near the sea. It afterwards fell into the hands of the house of Falletti of Naples, from whom the present king of Spain purchased it, in order to make a fishing seat of it. The well in question had been sunk near the garden of the barefooted Carmelites. To form it, they were obliged to dig through the lava to the live rock, where the workmen found, under the ashes of mount Vesuvius, three large clothed female statues. These the Austrian viceroy very justly laid claim to, and, keeping part of them in his hands, ordered them to Rome, where they were repaired. They were then presented to Prince Eugene, who placed them in his gardens, at Vienna. On his death, his heiress sold them to the king of Poland for six thousand crowns or florins; which, I cannot positively say. Seven years after my setting out for Italy, they stood in a *pavillon* of the great royal garden, without the city of Dresden, along with the statues and busts of the palace of Chigi, for which the late Augustus, king of Poland, had given sixty thousand crowns. This collection was added to some ancient monuments, which cardinal Alexander Albani had ceded to the same prince for ten thousand crowns.

On the discovery of these antiquities, orders were given to the prince of Elbeuf, not to dig any further. Thirty years, however, were suffered to elapse, before any more notice was taken of them. At length, the present king of Spain, as soon as by the conquest of Naples he found himself in peaceable possession of it, chose Portici for his spring residence; and, as the well was still in being, ordered the works begun at the bottom of it to be continued, till they reached some buildings. This well still subsists. It runs down perpendicularly through the lava to the middle of the theatre, (the first building discovered,) which receives no light but by it. Here an inscription was found containing the name of Herculaneum, which, by giving room to guess what place they had hit upon, determined his majesty to proceed further.

The direction of this work was given to a Spanish engineer, called Roch Joachim Alcubierre, who had followed his majesty to Naples, and is now colonel, and chief of the body of engineers at Naples. This man, who, (to use the Italian proverb,) knew as much of antiquities as the moon does of lobsters, has been, through his want of capacity, the occasion of many antiquities being lost. A single fact will be sufficient to prove it. The workmen having discovered a large public inscription, (to what buildings it belonged,

I can't say) in letters of brass two palms high; he ordered these letters to be torn from the wall, without first taking a copy of them, and thrown pell mell into a basket; and then presented them, in that condition, to the king. They were afterwards exposed for many years in the cabinet, where every one was at liberty to put them together as he pleased. . . .

The happy issue of the works undertaken at Herculaneum proved a motive for opening the earth in other places; and the doing this soon enabled them to ascertain the situation of the ancient Stabia, and led them, at Pompeii, to the vast remains of an amphitheatre, built on a hill, part of which, however, had been always visible above ground. The diggings in these places proved far less expensive than the diggings in Herculaneum, as there was no lava to dig through. The subterraneous works at Pompeii are those which promise most; for here they are not only sure of proceeding step by step in a great city, but have found out the principal street of it, which runs in a strait line. But, notwithstanding all this certainty of their being able to find treasures unknown to our ancestors, the works for that purpose are carried on in a very slow and indolent manner; there being but fifty men, including the Algerine and Tunisian slaves, employed in all these subterraneous places. Great a city as Pompeii is known to have been, I, in my last journey, found but eight men at work on the ruins of it.

To compensate this neglect, the method observed in digging is such, that it is impossible the least spot should escape unnoticed. On both sides of one principal trench, carried on in a right line, the workmen alternately hollow out chambers, six palms in length breadth, and height; removing the rubbish, as they proceed, from every one of these chambers, to the chamber opposite it, that was last hollowed out. This method is taken, not only with a view of lessening the expence, but of supporting the earth over one chamber, with the rubbish taken out of another.

I know that strangers, particularly travellers, who can take but a cursory view of these works, wish that all the rubbish was entirely removed, so as to give them an opportunity of seeing, as in the plan of which I have been speaking, the inside of the whole subterraneous city of Herculaneum. They are apt to impeach the taste of the Court, and of those who direct these works. But this is a mere prejudice, which a rational examination of the nature of the spot, and other circumstances, would soon conquer. I must, however, agree with foreigners in regard to the theatre; for it might have been entirely cleared; and it was, certainly, a thing well worth the expence. I am, therefore, very far from being satisfied with their just disencumbering the seats, the form of which could be so easily gathered from the many other ancient theatres still in being; whereas they have left the stage as they found it, though the most essential part of the whole building, and the only one, of which we have no clear and precise ideas. They have, it is true, done something towards giving this satisfaction to the curious and the learned, having cleared the steps leading from the Arena, or Pit, to the stage, so that we may hope to enjoy, one day or another, though under ground, a sight of the whole theatre of Herculaneum.

As to the whole town, I must beseech those who long for a free view of it, to consider that, the roofs of the houses having given way under the enormous weight of the superincumbent lava, nothing could be seen in that case but the walls. Besides, as those walls which had paintings on them have been cut out, and carried off, that such inestimable pieces might not suffer by the air or rain, no walls, but those of the poorest and meanest houses, would appear entire. Now, I leave any one to judge, how excessively expensive it would be to blow up such a thick and extensive crust of lava, and remove the vast quantity of ashes accumulated under it. And, after all, what would the advantage of it be? That of laying bare a parcel of old ruinous walls, merely to satisfy the ill-judged curiosity of some virtuosi, at the expence of a well built and very populous city. The theatre, indeed, might be entirely laid open at no expence but that of the garden belonging to the barefooted Carmelites, under which it lies.

Those who have a mind to see the walls of ancient buildings formerly buried in the same manner, may satisfy their curiosity at Pompeii. But few persons, except Englishmen, have resolution enough to go so far on that account. At Pompeii the ground may be dug up, and turned topsy-turvy, without any risk, and at a small expence, the land lying over it being of little value. Formerly, indeed, it used to produce the most delicious wine; but that it now produces is so middling, that the country would suffer very little by the entire destruction of its vineyards. I must add that this country is more subject than any other to those dangerous exhalations called *Muffeta* by the inhabitants, which burn up all the productions of the earth. This I had an opportunity of observing on a great number of elms, which, six years before, I had seen in a very thriving way. These exhalations generally precede an eruption, and are first felt in places under ground. Accordingly, a few days before the last eruption, some of the inhabitants dropt down dead on entering their cellars.

It appears by the indolent manner in which these works are conducted, that a fine field of discovery must remain to posterity. As great treasures might, perhaps, be discovered at the same expence, by digging at Pozzuoli, Baiae, Cuma, and Misenum, where the Romans had their finest country seats. But the court is so well

satisfied with the discoveries now making, that it has forbid the earth to be dug any where else below a certain depth. Certain it is that, in the districts I have been mentioning, there are ancient buildings, hitherto little, or not at all, noticed, as appears by what I am going to relate. An English Captain, whose ship lay at anchor two years ago in these parts, discovered under Baiae a spacious and beautiful hall, accessible only by water, in which there still remained very fine ornaments in stucco. It is only since my return from Naples that I heard of this discovery, of which, however, I have seen the drawing. Mr. Adams, of Edinburgh in Scotland, gave me a circumstantial account of it. He is a lover of the arts, particularly architecture, and intends to visit Greece, and Asia Minor.
. . . The theatre of Herculaneum, whether we consider the date of its discovery, or the magnificence of its structure, is, of all the immoveable monuments, the first to challenge our attention. It has twenty-four rows of seats, each four Roman palms broad, and one high. These seats are hewn out of the live rock, which is of free-stone, and not formed of hard stones, as Martorelli pretends. Above these seats is a portico, under which there were three more rows of seats. Amongst the lower seats there are seven flights of stairs, of a particular form, for the conveniency of the spectators. These are what they called *Vomitoria*. The seat next the pit forms a semi-circle of sixty-two Neapolitan palms diameter; from which, and the dimensions and number of the other rows, it has been calculated that, allowing a palm and a half to every spectator, this theatre could give seats to thirty thousand five hundred persons, exclusive of those in the *Arena* or *Platea*. This interior space was anciently paved with very thick squares of antique yellow marble, the remains of which are still to be seen in several parts of it. The porticos scooped out in the story under the seats were paved with squares of white marble. The cornish, that runs round the upper portico, and which is still in being, is likewise marble.

This vast building was surmounted by a quadriga, or four-horse chariot, with its charioteer, as big as life; the whole of gilt bronze. The base of white marble, on which it stood, is still to be seen. Some persons affirm that, instead of one four-horse chariot, there were three two-horse chariots; a disagreement sufficient to prove the little skill and care of those, who first conducted the works. These pieces of statuary were, as we may easily imagine, overturned by the lava; however, none of them could be wanting. Yet, how were these precious remains treated by those, who then presided over the works? They were thrown pell-mell into a cart; brought in that manner to Naples; and shot down into a corner of the court belonging to the castle. Here they remained for a long time in the character of old iron; and it was not till several pieces that had been stolen were missed, that a resolution was taken to make an honourable use of what remained. This honourable use consisted in melting down great part of it into two busts of the king and queen. One may easily guess, what has been the fate of these two pieces, which I could never get a sight of. In fact, they are become invisible. Care was taken to bury them in some hole, as soon as the shameful neglect, of which they were the monuments, came to be taken notice of. The remains of the chariot, the horses, and the driver, were then, at length, sent to Portici, and deposited in the cellars of the castle, where nobody was permitted to see them. A long time after this, the inspector of the cabinet proposed, that one horse, at least, should be made out of the pieces which still remained; and, his scheme being approved, some founders, sent for from Rome to be employed in works of that kind, were set about it. As several of the pieces requisite to compose an entire horse were wanting, there was a necessity for casting others to supply the place of them. By so doing, however, a tolerably fine horse was at last formed. . . .

This horse, thus patched up, appeared, at first, as if formed at a single cast. But, as it is no easy matter to make new-cast metal take well with pieces of metal that have been long broken, the joints have given way, so that, on the falling of a great rain in March, 1759, (I was then on the spot) so much water made its way through the openings, as to give the poor horse the dropsy. No stone was left unturned to hide the disgrace of so wretched a piece of patchwork. The gates of the cabinet were kept shut for three days together, that the workmen spent in tapping the dropsical animal, which was all the relief they could give him, so that he still remains with all his blemishes, in a manner, about him. Such is the history of the famous four-horse chariot, in gilt bronze, which originally crowned the theatre of Herculaneum. . . .

As to the different curiosities preserved in the cabinet of Portici, they may be divided into two classes. In the first, I shall include every thing relating to the arts, and the different kinds of furniture and utensils; and, in the second, the manuscripts. The pictures, big and little, with which I shall begin my observations, may amount to about a thousand They are all framed and glazed, except those which, being too large to be kept and shewn in that manner, such as the Theseus, the Telephus, the Chiron, and others, are enclosed in glass presses. Most of them are painted in distemper, as has already been taken notice by the learned men, who have given descriptions of them; and but a few in fresco. But, as it was so generally thought in the beginning, that all the paintings on the walls were executed in the last manner, that is to say, in fresco, they never gave themselves the trouble to examine if the thing was really so; so

that somebody having offered a varnish, which, he said, would infal-
libly preserve these paintings, they laid it, without farther enquiry,
on all those which had been discovered; thereby rendering it impossible to discover the methods used in executing them by the ancient
artists. The finest of these paintings [from the walls of houses in
Herculaneum] represent dancing women, and centaurs, about a
span in height, on a black ground; and must have been the work of
some great master, for they are as light as thought itself, and as
beautiful as if they had been done by the hands of the Graces. The
paintings worthy of being placed in the next, or even the same,
rank with the dancing women, are two pieces, the figures of which
are somewhat larger than those of the preceding. One of these
pieces represents a young satyr attempting to kiss a young nymph;
and the other, an old faun in love with an hermaphrodite. It is impossible to conceive any thing more voluptuous, or painted with
more art. There are, likewise, a great many fruit and flower-pieces,
all most exquisite in their kind.

If, in such a town as Herculaneum, and even on the walls of
its houses, such fine paintings were to be found, to what a degree
of perfection may we not conclude that fine art was carried in the
brilliant ages of Greece? . . .

I must here take notice, that all the paintings on pieces of wall,
which from *Italy* have spread beyond the Alps, into England, France,
or Germany, are to be considered as spurious. The Count de Caylus
got one of them engraved; and has given it as an antique, in his
collection of antiquities, because it had been sold to him for a piece
found at Herculaneum. The Margrave of Bareith was imposed upon
in the same manner, during his stay at Rome, where he bought
several of these pieces; and I have been since informed, that several
other German Princes have been equally duped with these wretched
performances; for they were all painted at Rome by Joseph Guerra,
a Venetian painter of very slender abilities, who died but last year.
It is not, after all, any way surprising, that strangers should have
been thus mistaken, since a man of great learning, and a very able
antiquary, Father Contucci, a Jesuit, director of studies and the
cabinet in the Roman college, purchased above forty of these pieces,
as so many jewels brought from Sicily, and even Palmyra. Nay,
several of these pictures were sent to Naples, and from thence
brought back to Rome, to give a greater air of genuineness to them;
and some of them were likewise decorated with characters, in nothing resembling those of any known language. Who knows but
another Kircher might have started up to explain them, if the imposture had not been timely discovered. Men of taste, acquainted
with the arts, and skilled in antiquities, need only examine them
with a little attention, to discover the fraud; for Guerra has not

shewn in them the least knowledge of the manners and customs of the ancients. It plainly appears by them, that he was an ignorant fellow, who drew every thing from his own imagination, so that allowing the honour of being an antique to a single piece of his would be sufficient to contradict and overturn all our notions of antiquity. Amongst the pieces of his doing, purchased by the Jesuits, there is an Epaminondas, carried off from the field of Mantinea, in which Guerra has represented that Grecian captain, completely armed in steel, as our knights used to be in their tournaments. In another piece, representing a combat of wild beasts exhibited in an amphitheatre, we see a pretor or emperor, who presides at it, with his hand resting on the guard of a naked sword, like those in use during the thirty years war. This forgerer made genius consist in representing Priapuses of an immoderate size, and beauty in slenderness, so that all his figures look like so many spindles. About two years ago, long after these pieces had been generally acknowledged at Rome for what they really are, an Englishman, who happened to be in that city, was, notwithstanding, fool enough to give six hundred crowns for some of them. So much for the pictures. . . .
. . . the order from his majesty, by which I had special admittance to the cabinet [of Portici], was confined to those things, which it was lawful to shew. I did not enquire into the reasons of this restriction, as I could not but know it regarded the antiquities stored up in the cellars of the castle, particularly an obscene figure, which has been condemned to them. However, having acquired the confidence of the inspector, I had the good fortune to be admitted to see them all, except this obscene one, which was not to be seen without a special licence signed by his majesty, and for which, as it had not been solicited by any one else, I thought it did not become me to be the first to apply. This piece, which is in marble, represents a Satyr about three Roman palms in height, and a she-goat; and is said to be of most admirable workmanship. As soon as found, it was sent, well wrapped up, to his majesty, then with his court at Caserta, who immediately sent it back with the same precautions, to be put into the hands of Joseph Canart, his sculptor, at Portici, with express orders not to let any one see it. We are not, therefore, to believe some English travellers, who tell us they have been allowed that favour.

CHARLES WALDSTEIN

Herculaneum and
Its Destruction

PROFESSOR WALDSTEIN'S style is ornate, but his book is probably the best account of the site from the period before 1914.

THUS the sudden destruction of Herculaneum resulted in the arrestation of the life of that ancient community in its full vigour and completeness—it was, as it were, hermetically sealed and preserved; and while in other sites we may have an illustration of the one or the other side of ancient life and of man's work, we can never hope to find a picture of life from all sides and in its organic completeness. Moreover, every ancient city, excepting those of Campania grouped round Vesuvius, has passed through the vicissitudes which centuries of eventful history entail, and those consequent changes which cause the complete destruction or the long transformation of its life and monuments during the Middle Ages down to modern times. The inroads of the barbarous hordes which usher in the Decline of the Roman Empire continue in devastating frequency throughout the Middle Ages down to the very threshold of our own day, when, even in the early nineteenth century, Moorish pirates made raids on the seaport towns of the Mediterranean coast. The changes of rulers—not only Christian and Mohammedan, but among the Christians themselves—and the iconoclastic activity of each successive dominion; the wars and sieges; the sacking and burning and all the wanton destruction in their wake—when we remember these, we must ask how much of the ancient splendour were we justified in expecting to find under the ruins of modern Rome, the Forum, Athens, Delphi, and Olympia? Think of the

From *Past, Present and Future Herculaneum*. London: Macmillan & Company Ltd.; 1908, pp. 2-6. By permission of Macmillan & Company Ltd.

wealth of classical treasure massed within the walls of the ancient Byzantium: and what may we hope to find remaining there even if we could level modern Constantinople and dig beneath its ruins? How much would remain of Alexandria, that metropolis of classical culture in later times, even if we could raze the modern city to the ground and dig down (often below sea-level) beneath its soil, where in the mud the ancient remains lie buried?

Even without the destructive hand of man, envious Time of itself sees that its own soul of change should feed on the death of the spirit of each age of man and on his works, perennial as bronze, on which he has imprinted his living spirit. Exposed to the vicissitudes of weather, cold and heat, storm and sunshine, they crumble away and lose the clearness and beauty of their features and form. What is upright is levelled to the ground by slow waste and corrosion or by sudden earthquake, and what is hollow is filled in; dust storms and streaming water soon choke and bury what has not crumbled away. When once these works of man are below the covering dust, and vegetable and animal life is buried with them, the organic matter, the biting acids of the earth, eat into the hard bronze to the very heart of its beauteous shape, rasp the smoothly modelled marble, and destroy its subtle grace of line. The dry sands of Egypt are kinder. Yet the sands of Egypt had not to nurse Hellenic Beauty and Truth but as rare and exotic intruders into its ancient life.

But our Herculaneum died young and in full vigour, and its embalmed body was hidden away beyond the hands of all rapacious men, excepting those who long lovingly to restore it to the pristine beauty of its early life. Here Vesuvius, as it were, arrested Time, arrested the hand of man bent on ravage or raised in internecine warfare. Thus were the towns of Campania preserved for posterity by the very agencies which of old caused their destruction.

Among these cities, again, Herculaneum holds a unique position, and has preserved what neither Neapolis, Cumae, Stabiae, nor even Pompeii can ever yield. For the entombment of Herculaneum was both sudden, complete, and secure, and this was not the case with the other Campanian cities nor with Pompeii. A glance at the map of Campania will show that Pompeii is about five and three-quarter miles from the foot of Vesuvius, while Herculaneum is considerably nearer, a distance of only four and a half miles. From the account of the catastrophe in the letter of the younger Pliny we learn that Pompeii was ultimately buried by the rain of ashes which the wind, blowing from the north-west, gradually sent over the distant city. The process, though more destructive and terrible, was very similar to that which was seen during the most recent eruption. The inhabitants had every reason to hope that their city might be saved from total destruction; so that many of them lingered on, hiding in cellars and elsewhere for some time. Even ultimately the city was not completely buried, the ashes not reaching a greater height than 20 feet, so that the upper storeys of the houses projected after the eruption had ceased. The result was that there was ample time to save and remove all valuables. No doubt the inhabitants returned immediately after the destruction and entered almost every house, clearing it of nearly all furniture and all that was valuable and portable. Even in later times the city was continually approached by easy passages dug into the friable covering, so that hardly a house remains the walls of which were not broken into so as to admit those who were bent upon carrying off its contents. The number of statue-bases that remain, the statues themselves having disappeared, show how even heavy articles were taken from the public places.

In Herculaneum, on the other hand, there is no evidence that there was time to save the valuables; the statues remain on their bases or are found in close proximity to them. In the lower portions, where the covering was not so thick (nearer the sea, where the newer excavations are now to be seen), there is evidence that attempts were made to excavate and save what was buried. In later times also the workers in the field and those who dug down for wells—as in 1709 such digging led to the finds which initiated the first excavations—were casually and sporadically led to seek for treasure in the buried remains. But the mass of ancient Herculaneum was completely buried to a depth of about 80 feet, which made it impossible for the inhabitants to recover what they had lost. The city was not gradually covered by the rain of ashes lasting for days; but suddenly there appeared the torrent of liquid mud, of ashes mixed with water from the torrential rains or from the lakes and rivulets, along the courses of which it moved down the slope, and this swept all before it. The danger was imminent and unmistakably recognisable by the inhabitants. There could be no hesitation, no wavering or faltering, no hope such as kept the dwellers of Pompeii in their homes for days praying for the cessation of the catastrophe. Thus it was a general *sauve qui peut*, the stream of mud advancing with terrible, relentless slowness, so that there was time to escape from the town, though most of those who could not flee by the sea must have found their death in the fields of the neighbouring country. These conditions explain the circumstance—at first striking us as singular and unexpected—that comparatively so many bodies were found at Pompeii and so few at Herculaneum. The one fact, so important for the question we are considering, remains: that Herculaneum differs from Pompeii in that the treasures and all portable objects, including works of art, remained securely buried at Herculaneum and were not disturbed in later times, while this is not the case at Pompeii.

CHARLES WALDSTEIN

International Excavation:
a Dream

IN 1904 Professor Waldstein campaigned both in Europe and the United States for international collaboration in a thorough excavation of Herculaneum. After long negotiations, it had to be agreed that the Italians alone should be responsible. In the end even this scheme came to nothing, owing to obstruction by the landowners at Lerici. Here Waldstein expounds his idea for the international project.

MOREOVER, while the excavation was proceeding, the constant presence at every point of experts supervising the work became in my conception of the reformed methods an absolute necessity. At the same time, the care and elaboration of the objects discovered required the presence of an equal number of experts. I should roughly estimate that the staff should consist of at least a hundred experts and students. Now, apart from the enormous financial sacrifice, it seemed impossible for any one country—even one so rich in the experts required as is Italy—to provide this large number, and to support them while at work. More and more the only conceivable way by which Herculaneum could be restored to the light of day which presented itself to my mind was that of international cooperation under the predominant guidance of Italy, and in accordance with Italian laws.

This international aspect of the undertaking necessarily arose out of the exceptional conditions which would make the excavation of Herculaneum possible. But for itself and in itself it appeals to the ardent and enthusiastic support of the best that is in all thoughtful

Ibid., pp. 17-19.

and honest men who can look further and rise higher than their own immediate hearthstone, whether personal, communal, or national; it became inextricably interwoven with the whole idea of the excavation of Herculaneum, an essential feature in the whole plan. And how worthy of such enthusiastic acceptance and support is the idea of international co-operation in the cause of science and art! Who will gainsay what is constantly repeated by leaders of politics and of thought all over the world, that Science and Art know no national boundaries? Here, moreover, we have the type for this unifying element of Science and Art: for we should be working together on the very soil on which our common civilisation rests, and our object would be to restore the living testimonies of culture which belong to us all. We may differ in language (even here the roots or essential elements have been taken from the same sources by most of us), in religion, in political institutions and aims, in customs, in manners, and in material interests; but we all have—in our best moments—the same ideas of the value of Art and Science, the same ideals as to the pursuit of the Beautiful and the True out of which, or on which, our conceptions of the Good must grow, or by which they must be tested and modified. They have come to us from Hellas, to a great extent as they have passed through Rome or the Italian land.

Such a united effort of civilised nations would become the type for other co-operation in the domain of Science and Art where now there is wastefulness—often ineffectiveness—of national or individual effort, sometimes even leading to antagonism where there ought but to be union. In this time of the maleficent recrudescence of Chauvinism, as stupid and as vapid in its argument and claim to racial or historical foundation as it is baneful to the best that is in man and in men, to have before the eyes of the world such a scene of common labour in an ideal cause, actually to see, and to have our interest aroused and kept alive by, the representatives of all nations toiling together on that ancient site, with the most modern appliances and the ingenuity born of modern discovery—to see this peaceful co-operation of the peoples of the world to effectuate our common ideals, this would do more for the advance of mankind and the peace of the world than all the Hague Conferences, noble as their task is.

PAUL MACKENDRICK

A Tiberian Fantasy:
the Grotto at Sperlonga

IN August, 1957, road improvements near Sperlonga, on the coast, about sixty-six miles southeast of Rome, offered G. Iacopi of the Terme Museum the opportunity for partially restoring, and closely examining, the ruins of a well-known villa there, commonly called the Villa of Tiberius. Making soundings near the villa in a wide, lofty cave fronting on the beach, partly filled with sea-water, Iacopi discovered that the natural cave had been made over into a *nymphaeum* or *vivarium,* a round artificial fish-pool, with a large pedestal for statuary in the middle, and artificial grottoes opening behind. In the pool and the grottoes, buried under masses of fallen rock, Iacopi and his assistants found an enormous quantity—at last accounts over 5,500 fragments—of statuary. The fallen rock gave a clue for dating at least one phase of the cave's existence, and a possible confirmation of the popular name for the adjoining villa. For the historian Tacitus mentions that in A.D. 26, Tiberius, dining in a natural cave at his villa at Spelunca, was saved from being crushed under falling rock by the heroism of his prefect of the praetorian guard, Sejanus, who protected him with his own body. This is very likely the actual cave which Iacopi explored, though his discoveries suggest that there were additions after Tiberius's time.

The exploration was carried on under difficulties of several kinds. The Italian budget for archaeology is notoriously inadequate; the cave was subject to flooding from springs, and lashing by winter storms; and it contained a dangerous quantity of ammunition and explosives stored there in World War II. The first difficulty was temporarily overcome by the generosity of the engineer in charge of the road-building nearby; the second by installing three pumps and building a dike; the third by keeping an ordnance expert constantly on duty.

From *The Mute Stones Speak.* London: Methuen & Co. Ltd.; 1962, pp. 173-8. By permission of Methuen & Co. Ltd. and St. Martin's Press, Inc., New York.

When the finds from the cave were first reported in the press, great excitement was caused by the announcement—premature, as it turned out—that among the fragments of sculpture were some resembling the Laocoön group. The original Laocoön group had been described by Pliny the Elder as carved out of a single block, probably with the sculptors' names on the base, whereas the famous Vatican Laocoön is not monolithic and is unsigned. Among the Sperlonga finds, on the other hand, were fragments of a Greek inscription giving the names of the three Rhodian sculptors mentioned by Pliny (but not in the precise form transcribed by him: in the Sperlonga inscriptions, their fathers' names are recorded, in Pliny not), plus some colossal pieces (the central figure would have been nineteen feet eight inches tall) including parts of two snake-like monsters, presumably the serpents sent by Athena to punish Laocoön and his sons for resisting the proposal to drag the Wooden Horse within the walls of Troy. This great group, much larger, earlier (according to Iacopi, on the somewhat doubtful evidence of the letter-styles of the Greek inscription, which he would date in the second or first century B.C.) than the Vatican version, and different in conception, fits the pedestal in the middle of the circular pool.

Another inscription goes some way to explain both the quantity and the arrangement of the sculpture in the grotto. In ten lines of Latin verse it describes how a certain Faustinus adorned the cave with sculpture for the pleasure of his Imperial masters, choosing subjects which, Vergil himself would admit, outdid his own poetry. One of the subjects mentioned is Scylla, the fabulous cave-dwelling sea-monster, with a girdle of dogs' heads about her loins, who guarded the straits of Messina. Now in the cave, carved in the living rock, at the right of the entrance, is the prow of a ship set with blue, green, yellow and red mosaic, and presenting some evidence of having once had a marble superstructure. To this ship Iacopi would assign some of his key figures: a bearded Ulysses in a seaman's cap, his face expressing horror; a lovely archaic statuette of Athena, grasped by a huge hand (Athena might be the figurehead); Scylla's gigantic hand seizing a seaman by the hair, and a terrified mariner who has taken refuge from Scylla at the ship's prow. A niche carved in the rock above the ship would be an appropriate vantage-point for Scylla herself: in one fragment one of her dog's heads has bitten deep into a sailor's shoulder. It is true that the mosaic names the ship *Argo*, but Iacopi explains this as a generic name for a ship, not necessarily referring to the one that bore the Argonauts.

If Iacopi is right about this group, it was a baroque or even rococo effect that Faustinus arranged for his Imperial masters. But the Laocoön and Scylla groups by no means exhausted his fancy or his pocketbook: there was Menelaus with the body of Patroclus, Ganymede borne to heaven by an eagle (carved so as to be seen to best effect from below, and therefore possibly belonging to a pedimental treatment of the cave façade). There are heads of gods and heroes, satyrs and fauns, a charming Cupid trying on a satyr's mask, a delightful head of a baby with ringlets over the ears—all in the fanciful, complex, sometimes tortured baroque style of Hellenistic Pergamum and Rhodes. These are all of fine crystalline Greek island marble, so that they may be Greek originals. The soapy native Carrara stone is normally used in Roman copies—and in too much modern American church sculpture.

At the present writing the Sperlonga cave cannot be said to have yielded up all its secrets. It is not even certain that the equipping of Tiberius's outdoor dining-room as a lavish baroque museum took place in Tiberius's lifetime, for the donor, Faustinus, may be the rich villa-owner of that name who was a friend of the poet Martial, and therefore of Domitianic date. The residents of Sperlonga want the sculpture kept where it was found, to entice tourists; the archaeologists want to take it to Rome for analysis and reconstruction. Meanwhile, definitive conclusions are impossible. But one thing is certain: the bizarre taste of the place, whether Tiberius's or Domitian's, is characteristic of the first century of the Empire, and reflects the gap between the ostentatious rich and the church-mouse poor which was one day to contribute to the Empire's fall.

PAUL MACKENDRICK

The Houseboats of Lake Nemi

THE same fantastic extravagance marks our next finds. Seventeen miles southeast of Rome, cupped in green volcanic hills, lies the beautiful deep blue Lake of Nemi, the mirror of Diana. Here divers,

Ibid., pp. 178-82.

as long ago as 1446, reported, lying on the bottom in from sixteen to sixty-nine feet of water, two ships, presumably ancient Roman. A descent was made in a diving bell in 1535. Another attempt in 1827 used a large raft with hoists and grappling irons, and an art dealer tried again in 1895, but all three efforts were chiefly successful in damaging the hulls, tearing away great chunks without being able to raise the ships to the surface. The 1895 attempt did, however, produce a mass of tantalizing fragments: beams; lead waterpipe; ball-bearings; a number of objects in bronze, including animal heads holding rings in their teeth, a Medusa, and a large flat hand; terracotta revetment plaques, a quantity of rails and spikes, and a large piece of decking in mosaic. This treasure-trove, displayed in the Terme Museum, naturally whetted appetites, not least Mussolini's. He determined to get at the ships by lowering the level of the lake, a colossal task undertaken eagerly by civil and naval engineers enthusiastic about classical civilization. The job was made easier, but no less expensive, because there existed an ancient artificial outlet, a tunnel a mile long, dating from the reign of Claudius, which could be used to carry off the overflow. The pumps were started on October 20, 1928, in the presence of the *Duce*. After various vicissitudes over a space of four years, the lake level was lowered seventy-two feet, and by November, 1932, the first ship was installed in a hangar on the shore, and the second lay exposed in the mud.

The ships proved to be enormous by ancient standards, of very shallow draft, very broad in the beam (one was sixty-six feet wide, the other seventy-eight) and respectively 234 and 239 feet long. They were larger than some of the early Atlantic liners. Their 1100 tons burden gave them ten times the tonnage of Columbus's largest ship.

The task of freeing the ships of mud and debris, recording the finds level by level, reinforcing the hulls with iron, shoring them up, raising and transporting them to the special museum built for them on the lake shore proved in its way to be as great a challenge to Italian patience and ingenuity as the job of excavating the slabs and fragments of the Altar of Peace from under the Palazzo Fiano. There was always the danger of the ships' settling in the mud in a convex curve, springing the beams. The excavating tools used were made entirely of wood; iron would have damaged the ancient timbers. As each section of the hull emerged from the water that had covered it for so many centuries, it was covered with wet canvas to keep it from deteriorating.

The hulls proved to be full of flat tiles set in mortar. These overlaid the oak decking, and over these again was a pavement in polychrome marble and mosaic. Fluted marble columns were found in the second ship, suggesting a rich and heavy superstructure. A round pine timber from the first ship, thirty-seven feet long and sixteen inches in diameter, with a bronze cap ornamented with a lion holding a ring in its teeth, proved to be a sweep rudder, one of a pair. It showed that these enormously heavy vessels (the decking material alone must have weighed 600 or 700 metric tons) were actually intended to be practicable, and to move about in the waters of the lake.

Clay tubes, flanged like sewer-pipe to fit into each other, were arranged in pairs to make an air-space between one level of deck and another. This suggests radiant or hypocaust heating, as in a Roman bath: these floating palaces, or temples, or whatever they were—perhaps both—had bathing facilities. Wooden shutters warrant the inference that the ships were provided with private cabins. A length of lead water-pipe stamped with the name of Caligula has been used to date the ships to that reign (and indeed in some ways they accord well with Caligula's reputation for madness), but of course there is nothing to prevent lead pipe of Caligula's short reign (A.D. 37-41) from being used in Claudius's, and many scholars, on the evidence of the art objects found, would date the ships in the latter reign.

Boards in the bottom of the hold were removable to facilitate cleaning out the bilge. This was done with an endless belt of buckets, some of which were found, and are on display, restored, in the museum. Over the ribs of the hull was pine planking, then a thin coating of plaster, then a layer of wool treated with tar or pitch, finally lead sheathing clinched with large-headed copper nails.

The second ship had outriggers supporting a platform for the oarsmen, and a bronze taffrail decorated with herms—miniature busts tapering into square shafts. A number of mechanical devices of great technical interest was found: pump-pistons; pulleys; wooden platforms (use unknown), one mounted on ball-bearings, another on roller-bearings; a double-action bronze stem-valve (perhaps for use in pumping out the bilge), which had been welded at a high temperature (1800° Fahrenheit); anchors, one with the knot tied by a Roman sailor still intact, another with a moveable stock, anticipating by over 1800 years a similar model patented by the British Admiralty in 1851. Its use is to cant the anchor, giving it a better bite in the mud.

In 1944 the retreating Germans wantonly burned the ships in their museum. Their gear, stored in a safe place, survived. From careful drawings made at the time the ships were raised, models were made to one-fifth scale. They are now on display in the re-stored museum.

The ships did not contain within themselves clear evidence about what they were used for. Whether they had some religious purpose in connection with the nearby Temple of Diana, or were used as pleasure-craft, or both, they reflect, like the cave at Sperlonga, the mad extravagance which increasingly characterized the Roman Empire on its road to absolutism.

II

India, China and Elsewhere

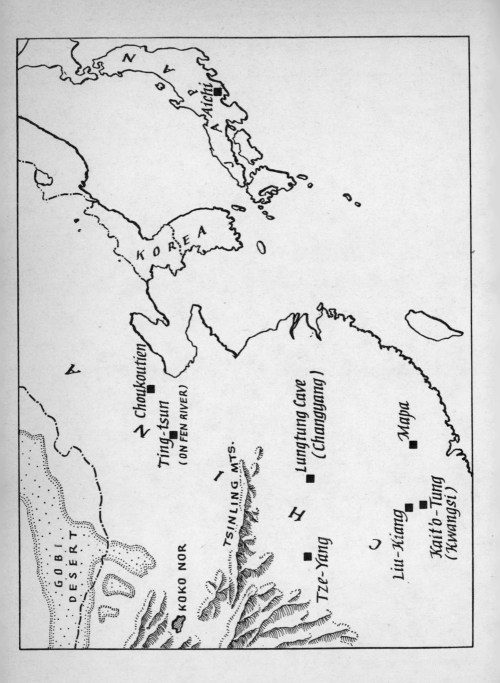

GOBI DESERT

KOKO NOR

TSINLING MTS.

Choukoutien

Ting-tsun
(ON FEN RIVER)

Tze-Yang

Lungtung Cave
(Changyang)

Liu-Kiang

Mapa

Kait'o-Tung
(Kwangsi)

KOREA

Aichi

INTRODUCTORY

The Indus Civilization

THE oldest civilization of India flourished in the Indus valley between 2500 and 1500 B.C. Its rapid rise and fall and something of its character are outlined in the following extracts. As Sir Mortimer Wheeler says, "the Indus civilization appears to spring into being fully grown." Its antecedents are probably in fact to be sought in the Neolithic and Chalcolithic villages that spread across the Iranian plateau and Baluchistan. Upland villagers may have moved down into the valley, just as they did much earlier in Mesopotamia, and there responded to the challenge to their farming skill. The conditions at first would have been difficult, but, once they were cultivated, the silts were fertile enough to support the development of great cities.

Mohenjo-Daro and Harappa, the two chief cities, have much in common. Both have walled circuits of about three miles, a citadel dominating a lower town, and streets laid out on a grid plan. They were excavated during the 1920's and '30's (p. 96, I).

JOHN MARSHALL

Mohenjo-Daro

Soil and Climate

THE richest grain-lands of Sind in the days before modern irriga-
tion were the broad plains of Lārkāna between the Indus and the
Kohisthān or Kirthar hills. Nowadays their fertility is much enhanced by the network of artificial canals and protective "bands"
along the banks of the river, but, even without these, this tract
must always have been an exceptionally productive one, since it
was watered not only by the main stream of the Indus but by the
long and winding loop that now functions as the Western Nāra
Canal, as well as by a multitude of other natural waterways and
lakes that take the drainage of the western mountains. Round
Lārkāna itself the country is known as the Garden of Sind, and
compared with many parts of the Province it may well be likened
to a garden. At the best, however, the term is a relative one. For
in spite of its natural advantages, there are still many patches of
salt wilderness or stretches of unreclaimed jungle interrupting the
cultivation.

It is in this district and in one such small patch of barren land
that Mohenjo-Daro, the "Mound of the Dead," is situate. It stands
on what is known locally as "The Island"—a long, narrow strip of
land between the main river bed and the Western Nāra loop, its
precise position being 27° 19′ N. by 68° 8′ E., some 7 miles by road
from Dokri on the North-Western Railway, and 25 from Lārkāna
town. The mounds which hide the remains of the ancient city, or
rather series of cities (since there are several of them superimposed one upon the other) are conspicuous from afar in the riverine
flat, the highest of them, near the north-west corner, rising to a
height of some 70 feet, the others averaging from 20 to 30 feet
above the plain. The actual area covered by the mounds is now

no more than about 240 acres, but there is little doubt, as we shall
presently see, that floods and erosion have greatly diminished their
extent, and that the deep alluvium deposited by the river has
covered all the lower and outlying parts of the city. Floods, too, and
erosion, accelerated by the extreme aridity of the climate, have
worked much havoc in the mounds that have survived, cutting them
up into hillocks, furrowing their sides, and widening and deepening
the long depressions that mark the lines of the ancient streets. The
salts also which permeate the soil of Sind have hastened the decay
of the site. With the slightest moisture in the air, these salts crystallize on any exposed surface of the ancient brickwork, causing it
to disintegrate and flake away, and eventually reducing it to powder. So rapid is their action that within a few hours after a single
shower of rain newly excavated buildings take on a mantle of
white rime like freshly fallen snow. The desolation that thus distinguishes this group of mounds is shared by the plain immediately around them, which for the most part is also white with salt
and sustains little besides the dwarf tamarisk and the babul, the
camel-thorn, and tussocks of coarse *kanh* grass. Add to this that
the climate of the locality is one of the worst in India; that the
temperature ranges from below freezing point to 120 degrees
Fahrenheit; that there are bitterly cold winds in winter, frequent
dust storms in summer; that the average rainfall is not more than
6 inches, but occasionally (as in 1929) varied by torrential down-
pours; that clouds of sandflies and mosquitoes increase the dis-
comforts of life—and it will be found hard to picture a less
attractive spot than Mohenjo-Daro is to-day. Nevertheless, it would
be wrong to assume that the conditions now prevailing were necessarily the same five thousand years ago, when Mohenjo-Daro was a
flourishing city. On the contrary, there are reasons for believing
that both the climate and physical aspects of the country have
undergone material changes since then. Thus, that the rainfall used
to be substantially heavier than it is at present, may be inferred
from the universal use of burnt instead of sun-dried bricks for the
walls of dwelling houses and other buildings. From the earliest
times at Mohenjo-Daro with which we are as yet acquainted, its
builders were just as familiar with sun-dried as with kiln-burnt
bricks, and habitually employed the former for foundations and
infillings, wherever they were protected from the elements. Had the
climate been as dry and the rainfall as scanty as it is to-day, it can
hardly be doubted that they would have used sun-dried bricks
(which are far cheaper than burnt ones) in exposed parts of the
buildings as well, just as builders use them to-day, not only in Sind
but in every other arid country of the Orient.

Austere Architecture

Anyone walking for the first time through Mohenjo-Daro might fancy himself surrounded by the ruins of some present-day working town of Lancashire. That is the impression produced by the wide expanse of bare red brick structures, devoid of any semblance of ornament, and bearing in every feature the mark of stark utilitarianism. And the illusion is helped out, or perhaps rather the comparison is prompted, by the fact that the bricks themselves of which these buildings are composed are much of a size with modern English bricks, but differ conspicuously from any used during the historic period in India. This workaday appearance of the buildings and signal absence of decoration is the more remarkable, because Indian architecture is notorious for the rich exuberance of its ornament, and the art of brick carving itself was developed to a wonderful pitch as far back even as the Gupta Age. It may be, of course, that originally there was ornament in plenty but that it was confined to the woodwork only, and has, therefore, inevitably perished. The woodcarver's craft was one of the most ancient in India, and nowhere did his skill show itself more than in the fashioning of architectural members into appropriate shapes and the embellishing of them with pleasing devices. We know, moreover, from the evidence of the fires which consumed many of the Mohenjo-Daro buildings, that wood must have been freely used in their superstructures, and we cannot, therefore, ignore the likelihood that they were just as effectively decorated as the early rock-cut temples, for example, which for the most part were replicas of wooden structures, or as those half-timbered houses and temples which are portrayed in the reliefs of the Early Indian School. For the present, however, we must take the Indus buildings as we find them, and not assume the existence of ornament of which there is now no visible proof.

Works of Art: Two Statuettes

THE age of these two little naturalistic sculptures from Harappa is still in dispute. There is nothing else like them known within the Indus civilization, yet it is difficult to see how they and they alone could have made their way into the mound—also it is far from clear to what later culture they could have belonged. Better known, and certainly authentic, are the small bronze of a dancing girl and the stylized figure of a bearded man, both from Mohenjo-Daro. There are also some excellent studies of bulls—some modelled in

terra cotta, some engraved on stone seals. In general, however, the
people of the Indus civilization failed to produce a distinguished art.

∾❦∾

AND now we come to two small statuettes . . . found in strata
of the Chalcolithic Age at Harappa. When I first saw them I found
it difficult to believe that they were prehistoric; they seemed so
completely to upset all established ideas about early art. Modelling such as this was unknown in the ancient world up to the
Hellenistic age of Greece, and I thought, therefore, that some mistake must surely have been made; that these figures belonged to
the Indo-Greek, Scythian, or Parthian period in the Punjab, and
somehow or other had found their way into levels some 3,000
years older than those to which they properly belonged. This, too, I
expect, will be the first idea of everyone else who is familiar with
the history of early sculpture. Let us, however, look at the facts.
One of these statuettes was unearthed by Mr. M. S. Vats among
remains of the third or fourth stratum in a part of the site where
no objects whatever of the historic age have appeared. The other
was discovered by Rai Bahadur Daya Ram Sahni in the fourth or
fifth stratum in a different part of the site, but, again, at a spot
where none but prehistoric remains have come to light. Now it is
possible, though the possibility is remote, that one of these two
statuettes might at some time or other have worked its way down
through 6 to 10 feet of ruined masonry and pottery into the older
strata; but that two should have done this in different parts of the
site, and that these two should be the only objects of a later age
found under the layers of prehistoric debris, is well-nigh incredible.
    Let us consider, further, the internal evidence afforded by the
statuettes themselves. And first as to their materials. The [torso]
statuette is of fine red stone, the other of dark grey slate. Now, there
was no stone obtainable at Harappa or anywhere near it. Whatever
stone was needed there had to be brought from great distances.
Where the particular kinds of stone we are discussing came from
we do not know, but we do know that during the prehistoric age
they were being imported and used for other objects besides the
statuettes, while on the other hand there is no evidence to suggest
that they were still being imported here 3,000 years later. Moreover, among the multitudes of Indo-Hellenistic sculptures in the
Punjab and on the north-west frontier there is not one, so far as I
am aware, that is made from either of these stones. Then, as
to technique. In both statuettes there are socket-holes in the neck

and shoulders for the attachment of the head and arms, which were made in separate pieces; and in both, moreover, the nipples of the breasts were made independently and fixed in with cement. So far as I know, this technique is without parallel among stone sculptors of the historic period, whether of the Indo-Hellenistic or any other school. On the other hand, it is also unexampled at Mohenjo-Daro, though this in any case would hardly surprise us, since the technique in question is one that is specially suited to small statuettes rather than to larger images like those of Mohenjo-Daro, which offer much less risk of breakage. There is another point of technique that is also significant. In the red stone statuette, there is a large circular depression in front of each shoulder, with a smaller circular protuberance broken off in the middle of it. What these depressions were for is not clear. They look as if they were intended to be inlaid with circular ornaments something like the circlets in the same position on the prehistoric terra-cotta figurine from Baluchistan. This, however, is beside the point. What I wish to draw attention to is that these depressions were made with a tubular drill, and that the tubular drill was habitually used by stoneworkers in the prehistoric, but rarely, if ever, in the historic age.

Thirdly, as to style. The treatment of the red stone torso could hardly be simpler or more direct. The pose is a frontal one with shoulders well back and abdomen slightly prominent; but the beauty of this little statuette is in the refined and wonderfully truthful modelling of the fleshy parts. Observe, for example, the subtle flattening of the buttocks and the clever little dimples of the posterior superior spines of the ilium. This is work of which a Greek of the fourth century B.C. might well have been proud. And yet the set of the figure, with its rather pronounced abdomen, is characteristically Indian, not Greek; and even if Greek influence could be proved, it would have to be admitted that the execution is Indian. The other statuette is of an entirely different order. It is the figure of a dancer standing on his right leg, with the body from the waist upwards bent well round to the left, both arms thrown out in the same direction, and the left leg raised high in front. Although its contours are soft and effeminate, the figure is that of a male, and it seems likely that it was ithyphallic, since the *membrum virile* was made in a separate piece. I infer, too, from the abnormal thickness of the neck, that the dancer was three-headed or at any rate three-faced, and I conjecture that he may represent the youthful Siva Natarāja. On the other hand, it is possible that the head was that of an animal. Whatever it may have been, no parallel to this statuette is to be found among Indian sculptures of the historic period. Indeed, what we have to try and realize, not only about this but about the other

statuette as well, is that, altogether apart from the circumstances
of their finding, it is almost as difficult to account for them on the
assumption that they belong to the historic as it is on the assumption that they belong to the prehistoric age. Of the influence exerted
by Greek art in the north-west of India, there are hundreds of examples among the sculptures of the Scytho-Parthian and Kushān
periods; but one and all are radically dissimilar from these two statuettes. They give us the form, not the substance, of Greek art.
Superficially, they call to mind the Hellenistic prototypes of which
they are to some extent transcripts; and they possess besides many
merits of their own in which Hellenic inspiration had no part. But
they miss altogether that characteristic genius of the Greek which
delighted in anatomical truth and took infinite pains to express it
convincingly. Now, in these two statuettes it is just this anatomical
truth that is so startling; that makes us wonder whether, in this all-
important matter, Greek artistry could possibly have been anticipated by sculptors of a far-off age on the banks of the Indus. We
know definitely that the Indus engraver could anticipate the Greek
in the delineation of animal forms: and if we compare the statuette with [certain seals], we must admit that there is a certain kinship between the two, both in the "monumental" treatment of the
figures as a whole and in the perfection of their anatomical details.
Experienced sculptors whom I have consulted on the subject take
the view that an artist who could engrave the seal in question would
have had little difficulty in carving the statuette; archaeologists will
probably take another view and prefer to wait for further discoveries
before committing themselves.

MADHO SARUP VATS

Everyday Life in the Indus Civilization

THE following picture of the life that was led by the Indus peoples of the third and fourth millenia B.C. who were in possession of a highly developed culture, in which no vestige of Indo-Aryan influence is to be found, is drawn by Sir John Marshall and is based on the discoveries made at Mohenjo-Daro and Harappa. "Like the rest of Western Asia, the Indus Country is still in the Chalcolithic Age— that age in which arms and utensils of stone continue to be used side by side with those of copper or bronze. Their society is organized in cities; their wealth derived mainly from agriculture and trade, which appears to have extended far and wide in all directions. They cultivate wheat and barley as well as the date-palm. They have domesticated the humped zebu, buffalo, and short horned bull, besides the sheep, pig, dog, elephant, and camel; but the cat and probably the horse are unknown to them. For transport they have wheeled vehicles, to which oxen doubtless were yoked. They are skilful metal workers, with a plentiful supply of gold, silver, and copper. Lead, too, and tin are in use, but the latter only as an alloy in the making of bronze. With spinning and weaving they are thoroughly conversant. Their weapons of war and of the chase are the bow and arrow, spear, axe, dagger, and mace. The sword they had not yet evolved; nor is there any evidence of defensive body armour. Among their other implements, hatchets, sickles, saws, chisels, and razors are made of both copper and bronze; knives and celts sometimes of these metals, sometimes of chert or other hard stones. For the crushing of grain they have the muller and saddle-quern but not the circular grindstone. Their domestic vessels are commonly of earthenware turned on the wheel and not infrequently painted with encaustic designs; more rarely they are of copper, bronze, or silver. The ornaments of the rich are

From *Excavations at Harappa*. Government of India Press, 1940, pp. 5-6.

made of the precious metals or of copper, sometimes overlaid with gold, of faience, ivory, carnelian, and other stones; for the poor, they are usually of shell or terracotta. Figurines and toys, for which there is a wide vogue, are of terracotta, and shell and faience are freely used, as they are in Sumer and the West generally, not only for personal ornaments but for inlay work and other purposes. With the invention of writing the Indus peoples are also familiar, and employ for this purpose a form of script which, though peculiar to India, is evidently analogous to other contemporary scripts of Western Asia and the Nearer East."

Besides the cultivation of wheat, barley, and date-palm, evidence of which has also been found at Mohenjo-Daro, the inhabitants of Harappa cultivated peas and sesanum too. Nevertheless, for their food they were not dependent entirely on agriculture, for it is notorious that there is hardly a place at Harappa where bones are not upturned by the spade. Moreover, the numerous sling balls of clay, the copper fish hooks, the arrow-heads, the flaying knives, constitute sufficient proof, if proof were needed, of the extent to which the inhabitants of Harappa depended for their food on birds and beasts and fish. Among the animal remains from Harappa Dr. Baini Prashad has identified several fragments of hyoplastron, hypoplastron and xiphiplastron species of turtle which were caught for food. . . .

MORTIMER WHEELER

The Beginning and the End of the Indus Civilization

IN volume 1 of the *Cambridge History of India,* published in 1922, Sir John Marshall introduced his chapter on the monuments of ancient India with the observation that "before the rise of the

From *The Indus Civilization.* Cambridge: Cambridge University Press; 1953, pp. 1, 14-15, 90-5. By permission of Sir Mortimer Wheeler and the Cambridge University Press.

Maurya Empire a well-developed and flourishing civilization had existed in India for at least a thousand years; yet, of the structural monuments erected during those ages not one example has survived save the Cyclopean walls of Rajagriha" (of the sixth century B.C.). Too late to modify this established view, in the previous year a member of Sir John's own Indian staff, Rai Bahadur Daya Ram Sahni, had already in fact nullified it. Sealstones bearing animal-designs in intaglio and inscribed in an undeciphered pictographic script had long been known from ancient city-mounds at Harappa, a small town in the Montgomery district of the Punjab, and a trial excavation in 1921 had quickly established their chalcolithic context. What that implied in terms of absolute chronology was still undetermined, but it was clear enough that an urban culture appreciably earlier than the Maurya Empire, or indeed than Rajagriha, had now been identified. And in 1922 another member of Sir John's staff, Mr. R. D. Banerji, was already finding similar remains beneath a Buddhist stūpa which crowned the highest of a large group of mounds known as *Mohenjo-Daro* (possibly = "the hill of the dead") nearly 400 miles away in the Lārkāna district of Sind. Within a few weeks of publication, it was abundantly clear that a new chapter would have to be added to the prehistory of India and to the record of civilization.

Now, a generation later, the time has come to attempt the missing chapter. Much that is essential to an understanding of this ancient Indian civilization, both in detail and in general context, still eludes us. We do not know the processes of its early growth and but vaguely understand its evolution and its decay. Certain possibilities as to the circumstances of its end have begun to crystallize under recent reviews of the evidence, but here too conjecture is still preponderant. On the other hand, the first active phase of exploration has now been completed and it is unlikely that large-scale excavation will be resumed in the near future. . . .

At present, the Indus civilization appears to spring into being fully grown, and, though further exploration . . . must tell us much, we may still expect a high measure of suddenness in the actual genesis of the great cities. The geographical opportunities to which reference has been made were an immediate challenge to any folk sufficiently gifted with the creative imagination to take it up, and *without* that creative imagination no stretch of time could have provided a substitute. The Indus civilization, like other great revolutions, may best be visualized as the sudden offspring of opportunity and genius, and much playing with potsherds and culture-spreads may help a little to define the opportunity but cannot explain the genius. As the evidence stands, civilization emerged in Mesopotamia before it emerged in the Punjab or Sind, though, be it added, we still know little enough of the beginning of Harappa and nothing of the beginning of Mohenjo-Daro. It is difficult to suppose that, in spite of the parallelism of opportunity, so complex a conception can have arisen independently in both regions, related as they are to a common stem on the Irano-Afghan plateau. On the other hand, contacts between the two civilizations—and then of a commercial rather than a cultural kind—are rare before the Sargonid period, about 2300 B.C., and notable differentiations in script, metalwork and pottery indicate an essentially divergent development. A partial resolution of the problem may perhaps be found by analogy with another transfer of ideas in the full light of the historic period. The *idea* of the Islamic mosque and domed tomb and diwan came to India largely from Persia; but a comparison, for example, of the Isfahan of Shah Abbas with the contemporary Fathpur Sikri of Akbar the Great reveals the almost fantastic extent to which the same idea, even at a time of close political interchange, may be differentiated in its local manifestation. On this showing a far closer and more persistent interrelationship between the Indus and Meso-potamia than appears actually to have obtained might be postulated without the necessary implication of anything approaching cultural identity. It is legitimate to affirm that the *idea* of civilization came to the land of the Indus from the land of the Twin Rivers, whilst recognizing that the essential self-sufficiency of each of the two civilizations induced a strongly localized and specialized cultural expression of that idea in each region. . . .

Altogether, the archaeological evidence, though of varying value in detail, supports a continuation of the Indus civilization well into the first half of the second millennium B.C. Considered in the light of the civic structure as revealed by the excavations at Harappa and Mohenjo-Daro in 1946 and 1950, this revised dating has justified a fresh assessment of the literary tradition regarding the Aryan immigrations into India. It has long been accepted that that tradition is incorporated in the older hymns of the Rig-Veda, the compo-sition of which is attributed to the second half of the second millen-nium. It can now be seen that the literary (or, rather, oral) tradition and archaeological inference have apparently more in common with each other than was previously suspected.

It is not necessary here to reopen the question as to the probable date of the initial Aryan invasion of the land of the Seven Rivers, the Punjab and its environs. Discussion has ranged widely and has not always been immune from tendentious enthusiasm. To-day it is generally accepted that the fifteenth century B.C. is a reasonable approximation, likely if anything to be on the conservative side. In the Rig-Veda, the invasion constantly assumes the form of an onslaught upon the walled cities of the aborigines. For these cities, the term used is *pur*, meaning a "rampart," "fort," "stronghold." One is called "broad" (*prithvī*) and "wide" (*urvī*). Sometimes strongholds are referred to metaphorically as "of metal" (*āyasī*). "Autumnal" (*śāradī*) forts are also named: "this may refer to the forts in that season being occupied against Aryan attacks or against inundations caused by overflowing rivers." Forts "with a hundred walls" (*śatabhuji*) are mentioned. The citadel may be of stone (*aśmamayī*): alternatively, the use of mud-bricks is perhaps alluded to by the epithet *āmā* ("raw," "unbaked"). Indra, the Aryan war-god, is *puraṁdara*, "fort-destroyer." He shatters "ninety forts" for his Aryan protégé, Divodāsa. The same forts are doubtless referred to where in other hymns he demolishes variously ninety-nine and a hundred "ancient castles" of the aboriginal leader Sambara. In brief, he "rends forts as age consumes a garment."

Where are—or were—these citadels? It has until recently been supposed that they were mythical, or were "merely places of refuge against attack, ramparts of hardened earth with palisades and a ditch." The discovery of fortified citadels at Harappa and Mohenjo-Daro, supplemented by the already identified defences of the Harrappan sites of Sutkagēn-dōr in Makrān, Ali Murād in Sind and others of more doubtful period, have changed the picture. Here we have a highly evolved civilization of essentially non-Aryan type, now known to have employed massive fortifications, and known also to have dominated the river system of north-western India at a time not distant from the likely period of the earlier Aryan invasions of that region. What destroyed this firmly settled civilization? Climatic, economic, political deterioration may have weakened it; certainly there was a marked degeneration in civic standards during the later phases of Mohenjo-Daro, where the evidence has been most abundantly recoverable. To a height of 20 ft. or more, the great brick podium of the granary on the citadel there was engulfed in debris interleaved with small, untidy buildings. Everywhere the houses, mounting gradually upon the remains of their predecessors or on platforms of baked and unbaked brick which raised them above the floods, were carved up by new partitions into warrens for a swarming, lower-grade population. Streets were encroached upon, lanes wholly or partly choked with mean structures or even with kilns such as would in better times have been excluded from the residential area. Latter-day Mohenjo-Daro, and by inference Harappa and the rest, were poor shadows of their former selves. Nevertheless, the ultimate extinction of such a society would be expected to have come from without. And so it was. In the last phase of Mohenjo-Daro, men, women, and children were massacred in the streets and houses, and were left lying there or, at the best, crudely covered without last rites. Thus in (one) room the skeletons of thirteen adult males and females and a child, some wearing bracelets, rings and beads, were found in attitudes suggesting simultaneous death. The bones were in bad condition, but it was noted that one of the skulls bore "a straight cut 146 mm. in length" which "could only have been done during life with a sharp and heavy weapon, such as a sword, and that this was in all probability the cause of death"; and another skull showed similar signs of violence. In a lane lay a group of six skeletons, including a child. In another lane lay a single skeleton, though the circumstances of death and burial, in any, are obscure. [Elsewhere] was found a group of nine skeletons, amongst them five children, "in strangely contorted attitudes and crowded together." They seem to have lain in a shallow pit, and with them were two elephant tusks. Their exacavator suggested that they were "the remains of a family who tried to escape from the city with their belongings at the time of a raid but were stopped and slaughtered by the raiders. One or more of the family may have been ivory-workers, and only the tusks for which the raiders had no use were not taken as loot." And yet again, in the same last phase, a public well-room was the scene of a tragedy which involved four deaths. The well was approached from the higher level of the adjacent "Low Lane" by a short flight of brick steps. "On the stairs were found the skeletons of two persons, evidently lying where they died in a vain endeavour with their last remaining strength to climb the stairs to the street." One of them was probably a woman. It appears that the "second victim fell over backwards just prior to death." Remains of a third and a fourth body were found close outside. "There seems no doubt that these four people were murdered. . . . It can be regarded as almost certain that these skeletal remains date from the latter end of the occupation of Mohenjo-Daro and are not later intrusions. The facts that some of the bones of one of these skeletons rested on the brick pavement of the well-room and that the skull of another lay on the floor of a (brick-lined) sediment-pit (adjoining the entrance) prove beyond doubt that both well-room and pit were in actual use when the tragedy took place.

On circumstantial evidence such as this, considered in the light of the chronology as now inferred, Indra stands accused. Alternatively, if we reject the identification of the fortified citadels of the Harappans with those which he and his Vedic Aryan following destroyed, we have to assume that, in the short interval which can, at the most, have intervened between the end of the Indus civilization and the first Aryan invasions, an unidentified but formidable civilization arose in the same region and presented an extensive fortified front to the invaders. This second assumption is more difficult than the first; it seems better, as the evidence presents itself, to accept the identification and to suppose that the Harappans in their decadence, in the sixteenth or fifteenth century B.C., fell before the advancing Aryans in such fashion as the Vedic hymns proclaim: Aryans who nevertheless, like other rude conquerors of a later age, were not too proud to learn a little from the conquered. A provisional dating of 2500-1500 B.C. for the Indus civilization responds consistently to the current tests.

Any attempt to appreciate the general position of the Harappans in the history of civilization as a whole must be based on an evaluation of three factors: the contribution of the seemingly earlier civilization of Mesopotamia, the initiative of the constituent Indus population, and the debt of both to a pre-existing or underlying continuum of ideas. The civilizations alike of the Twin Rivers and of the Indus converge retrospectively in the vast massif which extends from the Himalaya and the Hindu Kush westwards across Iran into Anatolia. In this mountainous zone, broken by patches of steppe and stony plateau, a great variety of small related cultures developed in the fifth millennium to the capacity of a restricting environment; and from that zone in the fourth millennium certain of the more enterprising of them began to escape southwards and south-westwards into the riverine plains, there to encounter simultaneously unprecedented problems and opportunities. The rapid consequence was a social co-ordination which by the latter half of the millennium was already, in Mesopotamia, worthy of the name of civilization.

It is to be supposed that the Indus civilization, too exotic to be regarded merely as a Mesopotamian colony, was essentially the parallel product of similar stimuli at a somewhat later date. It is equally to be supposed that the primary struggles of the proto-Sumerians towards civilization had provided a pattern which was now ready to the hands of the evolving Harappans and helped them to an early and easy maturity. For it is the likelihood of an early and easy maturity that has, above all things, impressed the excavators of the Harappan sites. True, there are matters which require further examination before this impression hardens. There is that unknown quantity, the unsounded depths of Mohenjo-Daro and Chanhu-Daro. There is the suspicion that the citadel-builders of Mohenjo-Daro and of Harappa were innovators, arriving with architectural traditions founded elsewhere upon the manipulation of mud-brick and timber, and imposing themselves upon a pre-existing urban population. The high-built citadels seem indeed to be frowning upon their cities with a hint of alien domination. If so, at Mohenjo-Daro that domination must have been dynastic rather than cultural, for the excavations of 1950 indicated a substantial continuity of culture from the pre-citadel into the early citadel phase. These and other possibilities must be given provisional weight without undue emphasis. But it can at least be averred that, however translated, the *idea* of civilization came to the Indus from the Euphrates and the Tigris, and gave the Harappans their initial direction or at least informed their purpose.

Between the two civilizations ensued a sufficiently active inter-relationship to carry seals and other knick-knacks westwards to Sumer and, more rarely, Sumerian or Iranian objects eastwards to the Indus. At the back of this trifling interchange was presumably a more ample trade in perishable commodities such as incense, cotton, perhaps slaves and timber; the unsuitability of both climates for the preservation of organic material prevents certainty. But the surviving evidence of this interchange is not impressive in bulk, and it is likely enough that many of the inter-regional resemblances, particularly in matters of religion, owe more to community of inheritance than to trade. It is improbable that Gilgamesh, for example, was carried from Sumer to Mohenjo-Daro like so much merchandise and there equipped, as we seem to find him, with adopted tigers instead of lions; certainly it is easier to postulate an ancestral Gilgamesh native to both civilizations and absorbed independently into the two environments. For there is on the whole a notable absence of intellectual borrowing between the material cultures of the two regions. In a vague sense the artificial mountain of the ziggurat and the artificial mountain of the Indus citadel may be thought to reflect a comparable hierarchical polity. The regimented cantonment of Harappa may suggest the priest-controlled industries of Sumer. It may even be permissible to propose a priest-king for Mohenjo-Daro. But all these points of resemblance, real or imagined, may be ascribed rather to the inherent cousinship of a social phase than to literal, local interchange. They are common generalities, the product of stray seeds readily fertilized in similar historical and geographical settings. The particularities, on the other hand, show abundant and significant local variation. In such sculptural art as the Indus has produced there is no real affinity with the sculpture of Sumer. No one would mistake a stone carving from Mohenjo-Daro for one from Tell Asmar. The Indus terra-cottas are in a different world from those of Mesopotamia. The art of the Harappan seals has no close parallel in the whole history of glyptic. And the Indus language, in so far as its features may be dimly determined through the veil of its unread script, differed as its script differed from that of Sumer and owed no more to this than the basic *idea*, perhaps, of written record. The integrity of the Indus civilization stands unchallenged.

Such integrity itself, however, implies an isolation which raises the further and final question: How far did the Indus civilization contribute to the enduring sum-total of human achievement? It is not difficult to relate the civilization of Mesopotamia to the general development of civilization in the West. There the Harappans have at present small claim to partnership. Nor at first sight have they any great claim to their own sub-continent. Their cities decayed and were, it seems, obliterated in their decadence by an insurgent barbarism, instinct with the heroic qualities which barbarism is liable to assume but not sympathetic to the vestiges of urban discipline. Slaughtered Harappans lay unburied amidst their streets and drains. Did all that they represented perish with them? Their plumbing at least and their special artistry they failed to bequeath to later ages. What of their less tangible qualities, their philosophy and their beliefs? Here archaeology is of necessity an insensitive medium. But reason has been shown to suspect that the later Hinduism, in spite of its Aryan garb, did in fact retain not a little of the non-Aryan, Harappan mentality and relationships, perhaps to a far greater extent than can now be proved. The recurrent figures of a proto-Siva, seated in sinister state or possibly dancing as triumphant Natarāja, the evidence of phallic worship, of reverence paid to animals, particularly of the cult of the bull, have nothing to do with Vedic faith but anticipate dominant elements of the historic Brahmanism. Paradoxically it would appear that the Indus civilization transmitted to its successors a metaphysics that endured, whilst it failed utterly to transmit the physical civilization which is its present monument. Our appreciation of its achievement must in the end depend upon a marshalling of values which lies outside the scope of this chapter.

MORTIMER WHEELER

From Hertfordshire
to Coromandel

THERE may be many people who do not admire Roman civilization, but there are few who do not respond to the idea of an empire stretching from Scotland to the Persian Gulf. Roman trade went far beyond the imperial frontiers, and the discovery by the Bay of Bengal of sherds of the red Arretine ware mass-produced in Italy just before the time of Christ, makes the exploits of these traders seem very real.

❦

THIS little book first took shape on a hot May morning in 1945, when an Indian student of mine emerged excitedly from a deep trench beside the Bay of Bengal waving a large slice of a red dish in his hand. Removal of the slimy sea-mud revealed the dish as a signed work of a potter whose kilns flourished nearly 2,000 years ago and 5,000 miles away, on the outskirts of Arezzo in Tuscany. Were drama admissible to the archaeological scene, I should have been tempted to describe the moment as dramatic. In that moment the pages of the historians and the geographers leapt to life; the long, acquisitive arm of imperial Rome became an actuality. . . .

The discovery of Arikamedu is in more than one respect a landmark in the study of Indo-Roman relations. For the first time it gives a habitation and a name to one of the *emporia* with which the literature and the coinage had in a more general way familiarized us. The quantity of the Mediterranean material produced by comparatively trifling excavation is a suggestive index of the extent of the international trade which used the place. This fact, with the early

From *Rome Beyond the Imperial Frontiers*. London: G. Bell & Sons Ltd.; 1954, pp. v, 150. By permission of Sir Mortimer Wheeler and G. Bell & Sons Ltd.

date of some of the material and the suddenness with which it is superimposed upon a purely native and local culture, has substantiated the essentially Augustan organization of regulated monsoon traffic; whilst the remoteness of the site, on the further side of India, emphasizes the range of this new organization, the powerful purpose with which it was reaching out eastwards to the sources of pearls and silk. The imagination of the modern enquirer kindles as he lifts from the alluvium of the Bay of Bengal sherds bearing the names of craftsmen whose kilns lay on the outskirts of Arezzo. From the woods of Hertfordshire to the palm-groves of the Coromandel, these red-glazed cups and dishes symbolize the routine adventures of tradesmen whose story may be set only a little below that of King Alexander himself.

A. PITT-RIVERS

A Capture of Benin Art

THE great English excavator and anthropologist, General Pitt-Rivers (p. 87, I), wrote this account of an unhappy episode in British imperial history because he himself acquired many of the works of art pillaged from Benin and put them in his museum at Farnham in Dorset. In his day such works were no more than anthropological specimens, but now Benin bronzes and ivories command the highest esteem—and prices.

BENIN is situated on the Guinea Coast, near the mouth of the Niger, in latitude 6°12′ north, and longitude 5° to 6° east.

It was discovered by the Portuguese at the end of the fourteenth or commencement of the fifteenth centuries. The Portuguese were followed by the Dutch and Swedes, and in 1553 the first English

From *Antique Works of Art from Benin.* Privately printed, 1900, pp. iii-iv.

expedition arrived on the coast, and established a trade with the king, who received them willingly.

Benin at that time appears by a Dutch narrative to have been quite a large city, surrounded by a high wall, and having a broad street through the centre. The people were comparatively civilized. The king possessed a number of horses which have long since disappeared and become unknown. Faulkner, in 1825, saw three solitary horses belonging to the king, which he says no one was bold enough to ride.

In 1702 a Dutchman, named Nyendaeel, describes the city, and speaks of the human sacrifices there. He says that the people were great makers of ornamental brass work in his day, which they seem to have learnt from the Portuguese. It was visited by Sir Richard Burton, who went there to try to put a stop to human sacrifices, at the time he was consul at Fernando Po. In 1892 it was visited by Captain H. L. Galloway, who speaks of the city as possessing only the ruins of its former greatness; the abolition of the slave trade had put a stop to the prosperity of the place, and the king had prohibited any intercourse with Europeans. The town had been reduced to a collection of huts, and its trade had dwindled down to almost nil. The houses have a sort of impluvium in the centre of the rooms, which has led some to suppose that their style of architecture may have been derived from the Roman colonies of North Africa.

In 1896 an expedition, consisting of some 250 men, with presents and merchandise, left the British settlements on the coast, and endeavoured to advance towards Benin city. The expedition was conducted with courage and perseverance, but with the utmost rashness. Almost unarmed, neglecting all ordinary precautions, contrary to the advice of the neighbouring chiefs, and with the express prohibition of the King of Benin to advance, they marched straight into an ambuscade which had been prepared for them in the forest on each side of the road, and as their revolvers were locked up in their boxes at the time, they were massacred to a man with the exception of two, Captain Boisragon and Mr. Locke, who, after suffering the utmost hardships, escaped to the British settlements on the coast to tell the tale.

Within five weeks after the occurrence, a punitive expedition entered Benin, on 18th January, 1897, and took the town. The king fled, but was afterwards brought back and made to humiliate himself before his conquerors; and his territory annexed to the British crown.

The city was found in a terrible state of bloodshed and disorder, saturated with the blood of human sacrifices offered up to their Juju, or religious rites and customs, for which the place had long been recognised as the "city of blood."

What may be hereafter the advantages to trade resulting from this expedition it is difficult to say, but the point of chief interest in connection with the subject of this paper was the discovery, mostly in the king's compound and the Juju houses, of numerous works of art in brass, bronze, and ivory, which, as before stated, were mentioned by the Dutchman, Van Nyendaeel, as having been constructed by the people of Benin in 1700.

These antiquities were brought away by the members of the punitive expedition and sold in London and elsewhere. Little or no account of them could be given by the natives, and as the expedition was as usual unaccompanied by any scientific explorer charged with the duty of making inquiries upon matters of historic and antiquarian interest, no reliable information about them could be obtained. They were found buried and covered with blood, some of them having been used amongst the apparatus of their Juju sacrifices.

A good collection of these antiquities, through the agency of Mr. Charles Read, F.S.A., has found its way into the British Museum; others no doubt have fallen into the hands of persons whose chief interest in them has been as relics of a sensational and bloody episode, but their real value consists in their representing a phase of art—and rather an advanced stage—of which there is no actual record, although no doubt we cannot be far wrong in attributing it to European influence, probably that of the Portuguese some time in the sixteenth century.

GUNNAR ANDERSSON

A Rich Grave in Kansu: Excavation and Opposition

NEOLITHIC village communities flourished on the loess soil of central China from perhaps as early as the fourth millennium B.C. until the middle of the second millennium. The grave described here represents the Pan Shan variant of the widespread Yang Shao culture which prevailed in the Kansu region. It is distinguished by its magnificent painted pottery. Gunnar Andersson was a pioneer of Chinese Neolithic sites (p. 96, I).

✤

WE had now arrived at midsummer, 1924. We had already spent two months in the T'ao valley, working eagerly to establish order in the confusion of prehistoric sites, of varying age, which we here encountered. During the whole of this time as we worked up from site to site, I had always in mind the recollection of Chuang's lively account of the remarkable cemeteries from which we had purchased such quantities of large and magnificent painted urns in Lanchow. It was only on June 26th that I had an opportunity of myself visiting the sites.

We left our quarters at P'ai Tzŭ P'ing down on the Ma Lan terrace early in the morning, accompanied by Chuang and two Mohammedan porters and guides. All the cemeteries of the prehistoric period in question which we had hitherto examined had been situated close to their respective dwelling-sites, or in other words, the prehistoric habitations and cemeteries had lain side by side. It therefore seemed to us most surprising when our guides led us out of the valley higher and higher up the western slopes. We ascended hun-

From *Children of the Yellow Earth.* London: Kegan Paul Trench & Trübner; 1934, pp. 267-71. By permission of Routledge & Kegan Paul Ltd.

dreds of metres. The fertile valley bottom now lay far below us like
a deep green ribbon, and the view began to extend over distant valleys which I had not seen before. I asked the men if we should soon
arrive at the graves.

"No," they answered, "higher, much higher, up."

Two hundred metres higher up we rode along paths which wound
in sharp curves up the steep valley side. We had now reached an
entirely different landscape. There was an open view for 50 km. on
all sides. I looked out upon a number of hills and ridges, all of about
the same height, and thus constituting an old, but now broken,
plateau, which in the east continued unbroken as far as the horizon,
but on the south and west at a distance of about 30 miles was
bounded by a high dark wall of mountains which marks the boundary of the Tibetan highlands. We were now 2,200 metres above the
sea and the mountain wall to the south-west was between three and
four thousand metres high.

We had reached a height from which we had a completely open
view in all directions. Here I saw the traces of extensive excavations,
and in the earth thrown up were visible everywhere fragments of
painted vessels of the same kind as the magnificent, intact vessels
which we had bought at Lanchow. It was evident that many vessels
had been crushed in the graves by the pressure of the earth and that
others had been broken in the competition of the villagers to despoil
the old graves of their treasures.

The extent of the cemetery was clearly indicated by the recent
excavations, which had fairly completely plundered the whole
of the site. The cunning Mohammedans had made yard-long iron
probes, with which they had dragged the ground and with striking
accuracy localized every burial urn which was not more than one
metre below the surface.

After we had hastily examined this first site, my guides conducted me to a second cemetery of the same kind, and it soon became clear to me how many hundreds of graves containing burial
ware of unique size and beauty had been looted by a desecration
which had for all time rendered impossible a scientific investigation
of the connection between the various objects in the graves. It was
poor comfort that we had been able to acquire by purchase almost
all the more interesting burial urns. It is more important that, but
for the large scale urn business in Lanchow, we should not have
known at all of the existence of these remarkable sites.

When I had thought out, with very mixed feelings, the course of
events, I sat down and tried to reconstruct the conditions under
which these in many respects unique accumulations of graves had
come into existence. Each of the five grave sites is situated on one
of the highest hills in the district, surrounded by steep and deep

ravines, 400 metres above the floor of the neighbouring T'ao valley. Continued investigation fully confirmed my first surmise that these cemeteries, situated on the highest hill-tops, must have belonged to the habitations of the same period down on the valley terraces. It then became clear that the settlers in the T'ao valley of that age carried their dead 10 km. or more from the villages up steep paths to hill-tops situated fully 400 metres above the dwellings of the living to resting places from which they could behold in a wide circle the place where they had grown up, worked, grown grey and at last found a grave swept by the winds and bathed in sunshine.

It must indeed have been a strong, virile and nature-loving people which was at pains to give to its departed such a dominating resting place, and as I sat there on a grave mound that sunlight day in June I tried in imagination to reconstruct the funeral procession which assuredly slowly wound its way with great pomp and now for ever forgotten ceremonies up the mountain sides.

It was now a question of saving what remained of undisturbed evidence of the old graves, and in order to facilitate my work, I removed the whole of my staff to the nearest farm where suitable quarters could be obtained.

This farm happened to belong to a rich young Mohammedan of the name of Ma, who was so exceedingly kind as to place his best house at my disposal and another at that of my servants and soldiers. He himself had previously lived in the large house with his two young wives and a whole bunch of little children, but he now removed the whole family to another much smaller house, and I greatly appreciated his kindness in giving up the best premises to me.

Ma's two wives were quite young and, as far as I could judge, of about the same age. They wcre pretty little creatures, but extremely shy. I only saw them properly on two occasions, once when I came home unexpectedly and found them in my house examining my things, and the second time when we left the place and they came out to nod farewell to us. But their seemly modesty was combined with considerable curiosity. The little ladies' window was diagonally opposite mine, and whenever I looked out in their direction I always saw a pair of interested eyes seeking a glimpse of the curious foreign devil. We used to call them Huang-Yang, gazelles, because they were so shy.

But there was another woman in Ma's house who was not at all timid, and that was his old grandmother. Ma's parents were dead, but his grandmother lived, and although she was old and wrinkled and hobbled about on a stick, she ruled the whole household. Not only did the two wives and the small children obey her least sign, but my men and my soldiers stood to attention when granny was

hobbling around. She ruled and ordered even in my house, with
the consequence that I had to pack up all my collections so that the
old lady might not mix up my labels, for which she had very little
respect.

For a long time we sought for graves which had escaped the
ravages of the villagers. For several days it looked as if the whole
district had been completely plundered, but finally Chuang made a
magnificent discovery at Pien Chia Kou. It was, in fact, the most
splendid grave which we found during the whole of the Kansu expedition.

One exquisitely painted jar after another was laid bare during
our careful excavations, and in the end we beheld twelve burial
urns placed round the skeleton of a full-grown man, who lay on his
left side with his knees drawn up. Two polished stone axes and two
whetstones close to his head completed the ample equipment of the
grave.

It was not possible to complete the major excavation the same
day as we made the discovery, so I had one of our small tents pitched
on the spot and left the two soldiers to guard the site. Early the
following morning I was up on the mountain, but found the situation changed in an alarming way. The whole slope was swarming
with Mohammedans. One of the soldiers met me a short distance
down the slope, evidently much perturbed.

"Anlaoyeh," he said, "many Mohammedans have come, more than
200. I am afraid they will make war on us. Cannot Anlaoyeh make
haste with the old man's bones so that we can go back to Titao? I
think that would be best."

We had now reached the cemetery and I saw to my indescribable
joy that nothing had been touched in the grave. But round about sat
a couple of hundred men from the villages, looking very serious.

In the middle of the crowd, on one of our tarpaulins, which one
of the soldiers had laid out, sat an old Mohammedan with large
horn spectacles on his nose. He looked very venerable and pleasant.
He rose up and advanced to meet me. We saluted each other according to all the rules of Chinese etiquette. Then we sat down together on the tarpaulin and began to talk.

He explained that our excavations had aroused general hostility
in the neighbourhood and that he expected serious difficulties if I
did not kindly abandon the work and leave the district.

I saw that there was little prospect of defying such a widely held
opinion. I therefore decided to concentrate entirely on the unique
grave which was for the most part laid bare before our eyes.

I told him that I was quite willing to agree with him and to undertake not to look for any more graves, but I made clear to him at the
same time that under all circumstances and without regard to what

the villagers proposed to do, I was resolved to complete the excavation which we had begun the previous day.

He explained that he fully understood my point of view and promised to order the men present to give me every assistance during the day on condition that this would be the last excavation. Thus we became good friends and in the end I took a photograph of the original old gentleman.

Towards midday we had the grave so cleaned up that I could take my photographs and make the necessary detailed measurements. Whilst I was doing this I saw a dark bank of cloud mounting up in the west and I knew only too well what that meant. We hurried on our work as much as possible, and just as we had collected the last bones of the skeleton the first raindrops fell. We then hastily retreated to the little tent, where we sat for several hours, packed like sardines in a box, among urns and packages of bones, with a torrent of rain streaming down around us. At dusk the rain abated somewhat and we wandered back to Ma's house over steep mountain paths, which were now so slippery from the rain that the men had to dig down to dry earth with their spades in the most difficult streams.

AUREL STEIN

A Desert Expedition: Giant Statues of Rawak Stupa

AUREL STEIN, the indefatigable Anglo-Hungarian traveller and archaeologist, made this visit from Khotan, in the extreme southwest corner of China near the Indian and Tibetan frontiers, in the spring of 1901.

From *Sand-buried Ruins of Khotan*. London: Fisher Unwin; 1903, pp. 446, 449-52, 457-9, 463-8. By permission of Ernest Benn Ltd.

ON the 6th of April [1901] I halted in Yurung-kash, where fresh supplies and labourers had to be secured, and many repairs to be effected in our equipment. Increasing heat by day and recurring dust storms warned me that the season was close at hand when work in the desert would become impossible. Instead of taking the rest we all by this time felt much in need of, I hastened to set out for the ancient sites which still remained to be explored in the desert north-east of Khotan. So after discharging Ibrahim Akhun, our worthy Darogha, with a liberal reward in glittering gold rubles for himself and an ample supply of specially desired medicines for his Amban, the caravan was set in march again on the morning of April 7th. . . .

On the 10th of April I left Ak-sipil, and marching due north for about fourteen miles, partly over dunes of coarse grey sand, partly along a pebble-covered "Sai" clearly recognisable as an ancient river-bed, arrived in the evening at the ruins called "Rawak" ("High Mansion") by Turdi and the men of his craft. Here an unexpected and most gratifying discovery awaited me. Our honest old guide had spoken only of "an old house" to be seen there half buried in the sand, but in reality the first glimpse showed a large Stupa with its enclosing quadrangle, by far the most imposing structure I had seen among the extant ruins of the Khotan region. Large dunes of coarse sand, rising over 25 feet in height, covered the quadrangle and part of the massive square base of the Stupa on the north-west and north-east faces. But towards the south the drift sand was lower, and there great portions of the Stupa base, as well as the lines of masonry marking the quadrangular enclosure of the Stupa court, could be readily made out. Near the south corner of the enclosing wall fragments of the heads of colossal stucco statues, the spoil of casual diggings by "treasure-seekers," were lying on the surface. I realised at once that there was scope here for extensive excavations, and accordingly lost no time in sending back urgent orders for a reinforcement of labourers.

Fortunately the position of the ruin, within a day's march of the oasis, enabled me to secure a large number of willing workers from the nearest villages of the Jiya tract. A favourable factor of still greater importance was the relative ease with which the question of water supply for such a number of men was solved. For though the sand dunes surrounding us looked more formidable than at any ancient site previously explored, it was possible to dig a well in a depression within two miles of the Stupa, and there the labourers' camp was conveniently established. A look at the map shows that the distance from the Rawak site to the bank of the Yurung-kash is only about seven miles. In fact, to this comparative proximity of the present river-bed were due both the forbidding height of the dunes and the slight depth of subsoil water.

The season of Burans had now fully set in, and the gales that were blowing daily, though from different quarters and of varying degrees of violence, carried along with them a spray of light sand that permeated everything. I noticed the frequency with which the wind would shift round to almost opposite directions on successive days, sometimes even between morning and evening—a feature of Burans well known to all natives living near the Taklamakan and observed also by former travellers. To the discomfort which the constant drifting of sand caused, and which we naturally felt in a still more irritating fashion while engaged in excavation, was added the trying sensation of glare and heat all through the daytime. The sun beat down with remarkable intensity through the yellowish dust-haze, and the reflection of its rays by every glittering particle of sand made the heat appear far greater than it really was. The quick radiation that set in as soon as the sun had gone down caused rapid and striking variations in the temperature at different portions of the day, and I have little doubt that the agues and fevers, from which all my own followers began to suffer after our start from Yurung-kash, were mainly brought on by these sudden changes. It was impossible for me to escape exposure to these adverse atmospheric influences; but luckily the chills I caught freely could be kept in check by liberal doses of quinine until my work at these fascinating ruins was done.

The excavations, which I commenced on the morning of the 11th of April in the inner south corner of the quadrangle, soon revealed evidence that the enclosing wall had been adorned with whole rows of colossal statues in stucco. Those on the inside face of the wall could still be expected to be in a fair state of preservation owing to the depth of the sand, which was in no place less than 7 feet, greatly increasing towards the west and east corners. But I realised that great masses of sand would have to be shifted before these sculptures could be systematically unearthed and examined in safety. For the heavy earthwork implied by this task it was necessary to await the arrival of the reinforcements already summoned. But in the meantime I was able to utilise the dozen labourers already at hand for such clearings as the preliminary survey of the structural remains demanded. . . .

It is possible that originally a wooden gallery or some similar structure projecting from the top of the enclosing wall offered shelter to the sculptures. But this, if it really existed, must have been systematically removed even before the sand had completely invaded the Stupa court, for only in one place near the inner south-east face did my excavations bring to light some pieces of timber, about 4 inches thick, that might have served for such a structure. Considering how comparatively expensive an article building timber is to this day in the immediate vicinity of a large Turkestan town, we could scarcely be surprised at the early removal of this, the most useful material the deserted shrine could offer.

The total number of individual relievos of large size, which were unearthed along the cleared portions of the south-west and south-east walls, amounted to ninety-one. In addition to these the finds included many small relievos forming part of halos, etc., or deposited as ex-votos before the main images. The position of all statues was carefully shown in the ground-plan and a detailed description of every piece of sculpture, with exact measurements, duly recorded. In addition, I obtained a complete series of photographs of whatever sculptural work appeared on the excavated wall faces, the aggregate length of which amounted in the end to more than 300 feet. It was no easy task to collect all these records with the needful accuracy while directing the successive stages of the excavation in atmospheric conditions trying alike to eyes, throat, and lungs. Though Ram Singh and Turdi rendered, each in his own way, very intelligent assistance, I had myself to remain in the trenches practically from sunrise until nightfall. I could judge from the dust-laden look of the men what an appearance I presented during those days. Needless to say that the notebook used at this site feels gritty with sand to this day! . . .

Want of space does not permit further details about other remarkable pieces of statuary. But I may briefly mention the discovery of remains of gold-leaf stuck originally in small square patches to the left knee of the colossal image. I could not have wished for a better illustration of the quaint custom which Hiuen-Tsiang records of a miracle-working Buddha figure of colossal size he saw at Pi-mo. "Those who have any disease, according to the part affected, cover the corresponding place on the statue with gold-leaf, and forthwith they are healed. People who address prayers to it with a sincere heart mostly obtain their wishes." From the number of gold-leaf plasters of which the marks remain on this Rawak image, it would seem as if it had enjoyed particular fame for healing power in affections of the knee.

But more important and fascinating than any such details was the very close affinity in style and most details of execution which every single find revealed with the so-called Graeco-Buddhist sculptures of the Peshawar valley and the neighbouring region. Whether that sculptural art, mainly of classical origin, had been brought direct from the Indus or from Bactria, there can be no further doubt, in view of these discoveries, that at an early date it found a true home and flourished in Khotan. The close study of this wealth of sculpture is a task of great historical and artistic interest. . . .

Our data for the chronology of Graeco-Buddhist art in India are as yet too scanty to permit any safe conclusion as to the date of the Rawak relievos. No epigraphical finds of any kind were made in that part of the ruins which could be cleared, but I was fortunate enough to secure *in situ* numismatic evidence of distinct value. While cleaning the pedestals of various statues along different portions of the enclosure as well as while examining the wall where the wooden gate had once been fixed, we came again and again upon Chinese copper coins bearing the "Wu-tchu" symbols and belonging to issues of the Han dynasty, just like the coins I had discovered below mouldings at the foot of the great Stupa. These coins were invariably found within small cavities or interstices of the plaster or brickwork, into which they must have been slipped as votive offerings. Subsequently, when a detached base only eight feet square, probably once surmounted by a small votive Stupa, was excavated near the inner south corner of the quadrangle, many more coins of the same type came to light between the masonry of the base and a much-decayed wooden boarding which encased it.

With this discovery the total number of such coins rose to close on a hundred. Most of them are in good preservation and do not show any marks of long circulation. Only current coins are likely to have been used for such humble votive gifts, and as no finds of a later date were made, there is good reason to believe that the latest known date of these issues marks the lowest chronological limit for the Rawak sculptures. The rule of the Later Han dynasty extended over the period 25–220 A.D., but the issue of some of its coin-types appears to have continued to the close of the fourth century. So far as minor antiquarian indications, derived from the construction, the materials, etc., of the ruined Stupa and its adornments, permit us to judge at present, the date of its erection may well fall near the period to which the ruins of the ancient settlement beyond Imam Jafar Sadik have proved to belong.

I soon realised with regret that, owing to the extremely friable condition of the stucco and the difficulties of transport, the removal of the larger relievos was impracticable. Those pieces of the colossal images which were found already detached, such as portions of arms, projecting drapery, etc., usually broke when lifted, whatever care was used. An attempt to move the complete statues or torsos from their places would have meant only vandal destruction, unless elaborate appliances, including perhaps specially constructed coffin-like cases made to measure, as it were, could be provided. To improvise these I had neither time nor the technical means, and in any case it would have been a practical impossibility to arrange for the safe transport of such loads over the mountains, whether to India or Europe.

All that could be done in the case of these large sculptures was to bury them again safely in the sand after they had been photographed and described, and to trust that they would rest undisturbed under their protecting cover—until that time, still distant it seems, when Khotan shall have its own local museum. But of the smaller relievos and sculptural pieces already detached, I succeeded in bringing away a considerable number. I felt greatly relieved when I found on my arrival at Kashgar, and later also in London, that the great trouble and labour which the safe packing of these extremely fragile objects had cost me was rewarded by their having accomplished the long journey—some six thousand miles by camels, ponies, railway and steamer—without any serious damage. The two heads of saints in alto-relievo still retaining part of their colouring, illustrate types frequently recurring in this collection.

By April 18th those portions of the Stupa court which were not actually buried under sand dunes had been explored. The proper excavation of the other parts could not have been accomplished without months of labour and proportionately heavy expenditure. A careful examination of the surrounding area revealed no other structural remains: broken pottery found here and there on some narrow patches of ground between the swelling sand dunes was the only trace left of what probably were modest dwelling-places around the great shrine. The sand-storms, which visited us daily and the increasing heat and glare, had made the work very trying to the men as well as myself. It was manifestly time to withdraw from the desert. Before, however, leaving the ruins I took care to protect the sculptures which could not be moved, by having the trenches that had exposed them filled up again. It was a melancholy duty to perform, strangely reminding me of a true burial, and it almost cost me an effort to watch the images I had brought to light vanishing again, one after the other, under the pall of sand which had hidden them for so many centuries.

Jumbe-kum, some four miles beyond Rawak to the north-east, was the only remaining desert site around Khotan from which occasional finds had been reported to me. I took occasion to visit it from Rawak and convinced myself that this debris-strewn "Tati" contained no remains capable of excavation. Thus, when on the 19th of April I started back to Khotan, I had the satisfaction of knowing that the programme of my explorations in the desert was completed.

AUREL STEIN

An Ingenious Forger Unmasked

IT had become obvious that a variety of forged texts was emanating from somewhere round Khotan and Kashgar: they had been sold to English, Russian and other collectors. Learned and ignorant had been hoodwinked alike. Aurel Stein went to investigate.

❧

BUT in the matter of the "old books" he for a long time protested complete innocence. He [Islam Akhun] pretended to have acted merely as the Kashgar sale agent for certain persons at Khotan, since dead or absconded, who, rightly or wrongly, told him that they had picked them up in the desert. When he found how much such "old books" were appreciated by Europeans, he asked those persons to find more. This they did, whereupon he took their finds to Kashgar, etc. Now, he lamented, he was left alone to bear the onus of the fraud—if such it was. Muhammad Tari, one of those who gave the "books," had previously run away to Yarkaud; Muhammad Sidiq, the Mullah, had absconded towards Aksu; and a third of the band had escaped from all trouble by dying.

It was a cleverly devised line of defence, and Islam Akhun clung to it with great consistency and with the wariness of a man who has had unpleasant experience of the ways of the law. I had thought it right to tell him from the first that I was not going to proceed against him at the Amban's Yamen in the matter of these happily ended forgeries; for I was aware that such a step, in accordance with Chinese procedure, was likely to lead to the application of some effective means of persuasion, *i.e.*, torture. This, of course, I would not countenance; nor could a confession as its eventual result be to me of any value. Whether it was from Islam Akhun's reliance on these scruples of mine, or from his knowledge that direct evidence could not easily be produced within the time available,

Ibid., pp. 474-9.

two long cross-examinations, in the interval of which I had Islam Akhun's wants hospitably looked to by my own men, failed to bring a solution. However, in the course of his long protestations of complete innocence, Islam Akhun introduce a denial which seemed to offer some chance of catching my wary defendant. He emphatically denied having seen any of the alleged find-places himself, in fact having ever personally visited any ancient site in the desert.

I had purposely refrained at the time from showing any special interest in this far-reaching disclaimer. Consequently I had no difficulty in inducing him to repeat it with still more emphasis and in the presence of numerous witnesses when he was brought up "on remand" for a third time. Whether encouraged by his apparent success so far or by the forbearing treatment I had accorded to him, it was evident that the sly, restless-looking fellow was for the time being off his guard. So I promptly confronted him, from the detailed account printed in Dr. Hoernle's Report, with an exact reproduction of the elaborate stories which he had told, in the course of depositions made on different occasions before Mr. Macartney, about his alleged journeys and discoveries in the Taklamakan during the years 1895–98.

The effect was most striking. Islam Akhun was wholly unprepared for the fact that his lies told years before, with so much seeming accuracy of topographical and other details, had received the honour of permanent record in a scientific report to Government. Hearing them now read out by me in re-translation, he was thoroughly startled and confused. He appeared also greatly impressed by the fact that, with the help of the exact information recorded by Mr. Macartney and reproduced by Dr. Hoernle, I could enlighten him as to what "old books" he had sold at Kashgar on particular occasions, what remarkable statements he had made about the manner of their discovery by himself, etc. He was intelligent enough to realise that he stood self-convicted, and that there was nothing to be gained by further protestations of innocence. He now admitted that he had seen manuscripts being written by his above-named employers (recte accomplices) at a deserted Mazar near Sampula. Little by little his admissions became more detailed, and ultimately, when assured that no further punishment awaited him, he made a clean breast of it.

Islam Akhun's subsequent confessions proved perfectly correct on many important particulars when checked from the records kept at Kashgar, as well as from the evidence of a number of independent witnesses. He showed himself to be possessed of an excellent memory, and readily recognised among the numerous photogravure plates accompanying Dr. Hoernle's Report those representing specimen pages from the "block-printed" books in "unknown characters" which formed his own manufacture. He had, previous to 1894, been engaged at times in collecting coins, seals, and similar antiques from Khotan villages. About that time he learned from Afghan traders of the value which the "Sahibs" from India attached to ancient manuscripts. Genuine scraps of such had indeed been unearthed by Turdi and some other "treasure-seekers" at Dandan-Uiliq. But the idea of visiting such dreary desert sites, with the certainty of great hardships and only a limited chance of finds, had no attraction for a person of such wits as Islam Akhun. So in preference he conceived the plan of manufacturing the article he was urged to supply the Sahibs with.

In this enterprise he had several accomplices, among whom a certain Ibrahim Mullah was the leading man. This person appears to have made it his special business to cultivate the Russian demand for "old books," while Islam Akhun attended chiefly to the requirements of British officers and other collectors. Ibrahim Mullah, from whom the Russian Armenian I met on my first arrival at Khotan had purchased his forged birch-bark manuscript, was credited with some knowledge of Russian, a circumstance which explains the curious resemblance previously noticed between the characters used in some of the "block-prints" and the Greek (*recte* Russian) alphabet. Ibrahim Mullah gave proof of his "slimness," as well as his complicity, by promptly disappearing from Khotan on the first news of Islam Akhun's arrest, and could not be confronted with him.

The first "old book" produced in this fashion was successfully sold by Islam Akhun in 1895 to Munshi Ahmad Din, who was in charge of the Assistant Resident's Office at Kashgar during the temporary absence of Mr. Macartney. This "book" was written by hand, and an attempt had been made, as also in some others of the earliest products of the factory, to imitate the cursive Brahmi characters found in fragments of genuine manuscripts which Ibrahim was said to have secured from Dandan-Uiliq. Though the forgers never succeeded in producing a text showing consecutively the characters of any known script, yet their earliest fabrications were executed with an amount of care and ingenuity which might well deceive for a time even expert scholars in Europe. This may be seen by referring to the facsimiles which are given in Dr. Hoernle's Second "Report on Central-Asian Antiquities," from "codices" belonging to the early output, now deposited with so many other products of Islam Akhun's factory in the "forgery" section of the Manuscript Department of the British Museum. The facsimile of an "ancient Khotan manuscript" which appears in the German

edition of Dr. Sven Hedin's work *Through Asia*, is a conveniently
accessible illustration of the factory's produce in a somewhat later
and less careful phase of its working.

Seeing that remunerative prices could be obtained for such
articles at Kashgar and, through Badruddin's somewhat careless
mediation, also from Ladak and Kashmir, the efforts of the forgers
were stimulated. As Islam Akhun quickly perceived that his "books"
were readily paid for, though none of the Europeans who bought
them could read their characters or distinguish them from ancient
scripts, it became unnecessary to trouble about imitating the characters of genuine fragments. Thus, apparently, each individual
factory "hand" was given free scope for inventing his own "unknown characters." This explains the striking diversity of these queer
scripts, of which the analysis of the texts contained in the "British
collection" at one time revealed at least a dozen—not exactly to the
assurance of the Oriental scholars who were to help in their
decipherment.

The rate of production by the laborious process of hand-writing
was, however, too slow, and accordingly the factory took to the
more convenient method of producing books by means of repeated
impressions from a series of wooden blocks. The preparation of
such blocks presented no difficulty, as printing from wooden blocks
is extensively practised in Chinese Turkestan. This printing of
"old books" commenced in 1896, and its results are partly represented by the forty-five "block-prints" which are fully described and
illustrated in Dr. Hoernle's First Report. These, too, showed an
extraordinary variety of scripts in their ever-recurring formulas,
and were often of quite imposing dimensions in size and bulk.

Islam Akhun, when once his defence had collapsed, was not
chary about giving technical details about the forgers' methods of
work. In fact, he seemed rather to relish the interest I showed in
them. Thus he fully described the procedure followed in preparing
the paper that was used for the production of manuscripts or
"block prints," as well as the treatment to which they were subjected in order to give them an ancient look. The fact of Khotan
being the main centre of the Turkestan paper industry was a great
convenience for the forgers, as they could readily supply themselves
with any variety and size of paper needed. The sheets of modern
Khotan paper were first dyed yellow or light brown by means of
"Toghrugha," a product of the Toghrak tree, which, when dissolved
in water, gives a staining fluid.

When the dyed sheets had been written or printed upon they
were hung over fireplaces so as to receive by smoke the proper hue
of antiquity. It was, no doubt, in the course of this manipulation
that the sheets occasionally sustained the burns and scorchings of

which some of the "old books" transmitted to Calcutta display evident marks. Afterwards they were bound up into volumes. This, however, seems to have been the least efficiently managed department of the concern, for the coarse imitation of European volumes which is unmistakable in the case of most of the later products, as well as the utter unsuitability of the fastenings employed (usually pegs of copper or twists of paper), would *à priori* have justified grave suspicions as to their genuineness. Finally the finished manuscripts or books were treated to a liberal admixture between their pages of the fine sand of the desert, in order to make them tally with the story of their long burial. I well remember how, in the spring of 1898, I had to apply a clothes brush before I could examine one of these forged "block-prints" that had reached a collector in Kashmir.

All the previously suspected details of this elaborate and, for a time, remarkably successful fraud were thus confirmed by its main operator in the course of a long and cautiously conducted examination. It was a pleasure to me to know, and to be able to tell fellow-scholars in Europe: *habemus confitentem reum*—and that without any resort to Eastern methods of judicial inquiry. Yet possibly I had reason to feel even keener satisfaction at the fact that the positive results of my explorations were sufficient to dispose once for all of these fabrications so far as scholarly interests were concerned, even if Islam Akhun had never made his confession. In the light of the discoveries which had rewarded my excavations at Dandan-Uiliq and Endere, and of the general experience gained during my work in the desert, it had become as easy to distinguish between Islam Akhun's forgeries and genuine old manuscripts as it was to explode his egregious stories about the ancient sites which were supposed to have furnished his "finds." Not only in the colour and substance of the paper, but also in arrangement, state of preservation, and a variety of other points, all genuine manuscripts show features never to be found in Islam Akhun's productions. But apart from this, there is the plain fact that the forgers never managed to produce a text exhibiting consecutively the characters of any known script, while all ancient documents brought to light by my explorations invariably show a writing that is otherwise well known to us. There is, therefore, little fear that Islam Akhun's forgeries will cause deception hereafter.

MRS. S. ROUTLEDGE

The Routledge Expedition to Easter Island

THE extreme isolation of Easter Island—two thousand miles west from the Chile coast and fourteen hundred miles east of Pitcairn Island—its small size (48,000 acres) and its huge, startling and unique monuments, have inevitably inspired some imaginative speculations concerning its history. The most persistent is that this small volcanic island is the only surviving fragment of a great lost continent.

In comparison the interpretations of the scientists are dull: nor are they altogether in agreement. It seems to be generally accepted that the present people and their culture and language are predominantly, if not wholly, Polynesian. Most authorities therefore believe that the peopling must have taken place during the known Polynesian settlement of the Pacific, and have dated it to various times between the twelfth and fifteenth centuries A.D. Others insist upon an Easter Island connection with South America, seeing likenesses between the two both in building and in sculpture. Thor Heyerdahl, who led an expedition to the island in 1955-6, claims to have secured Carbon-14 dating evidence for a settlement of the island as early as the fourth century A.D. Such a date would certainly make some pre-Polynesian contact with South American civilization more possible.

However this may be, there seems no doubt that most of the famous statues are very much more recent. Probably many of them were not very old when they were looked on for the first time by a European—the Dutch admiral Roggeveen who landed in the island on Easter Day, 1722. The practice of carving them may have been brought to an end only by the inter-tribal wars that began the destruction of Easter Island society some little time before the nineteenth century slave-traders came to finish it off.

Nearly all the giant statues were quarried from the volcanic tufa of the Rano Raraku crater towards the eastern end of the island. (A few, however, including one specimen in the British Museum, are of basalt.) Scores of them still stand or lean inside the crater and down its external slopes, while a number lie unfinished in the quarry, still attached to the rock face. Among these incomplete, rock-bound figures is one monster sixty feet in length.

From Rano Raraku some of the statues were taken to be lined up, facing inland, on the stone-built *ahu* platforms that are set on shores and cliffs all round the island. The *ahu* (p. 273, II) were mausolea belonging to the many sub-tribes into which the population was divided. They continued in use until about a century ago, although nearly all the statues had been overthrown during the tribal struggles. Other statues again were set up in irregular lines on the central plain of the island and by the south coast. It seems to have been only the *ahu* figures that were crowned with red top-knots (p. 299, II).

The expedition led by Mrs. Scoresby Routledge was the first to attempt a scientific study of Easter Island; it remained there for seventeen months. Unhappily the field notes and much other material were destroyed on Mrs. Routledge's death, so that her book is almost the sole record of the expedition.

The Decision to Go

"ALL the seashore is lined with numbers of stone idols, with their backs turned towards the sea, which caused us no little wonder, because we saw no tool of any kind for working these figures." So wrote, a century and a half ago, one of the earliest navigators to visit the Island of Easter in the south-east Pacific. Ever since that day passing ships have found it incomprehensible that a few hundred natives should have been able to make, move, and erect numbers of great stone monuments, some of which are over thirty feet in height: they have marvelled and passed on. As the world's traffic has increased, Easter Island has still stood outside its routes, quiet and remote, with its story undeciphered. What were these statues of which the present inhabitants know nothing? Were they made by their ancestors in forgotten times or by an earlier race? Whence came the people who reached this remote spot? Did they arrive from South America, 2,000 miles to the eastward? Or did they sail against the prevailing wind from the distant islands to

From *The Mystery of Easter Island*. London: Sifton Praed & Company Ltd; 1919, pp. 3-4, 124-5, 151-4, 164-74, 175-99, 352-66. By permission of Sifton Praed & Company Ltd.

the west? It has even been conjectured that Easter Island is all that remains of a sunken continent. Fifty years ago the problem was increased by the discovery on this mysterious land of wooden tablets bearing an unknown script; they too have refused to yield their secret.

When, therefore, we decided to see the Pacific before we died, and asked the anthropological authorities at the British Museum what work there remained to be done, the answer was, "Easter Island." It was a much larger undertaking than had been contemplated; we had doubts of our capacity for so important a venture; and at first decision was against it, but we hesitated and were lost. Then followed the problem how to reach the goal. The island belongs to Chile, and the only regular communication, if regular it can be called, was a small sailing vessel sent out by the Chilean Company, who use the island as a ranch; she went sometimes once a year, sometimes not so often, and only remained there sufficient time to bring off the wool crop. We felt that the work on Easter ought to be accompanied with the possibility of following up clues elsewhere in the islands, and that to charter any such vessel as could be obtained on the Pacific coast, for the length of time we required her, would be unsatisfactory, both from the pecuniary standpoint and from that of comfort. It was therefore decided, as Scoresby [Mr. Routledge] is a keen yachtsman, that it was worth while to procure in England a little ship of our own, adapted to the purpose, and to sail out in her. As the Panama Canal was not open, and the route by Suez would be longer, the way would lie through the Magellan Straits. . . .

Arrival and Early Days

Easter Island at last! It was in the misty dawn of Sunday, March 29th, 1914, that we first saw our destination, just one week in the year earlier than the Easter Day it was sighted by Roggeveen and his company of Dutchmen. We had been twenty days at sea since leaving Juan Fernandez, giving a wide berth to the few dangerous rocks which constitute Salo-y-Gomez and steering directly into the sunset. It was thirteen months since we had left Southampton, out of which time we had been 147 days under way, and here at last was our goal. As we approached the southern coast we gazed in almost awed silence at the long grey mass of land, broken into three great curves, and diversified by giant molehills. The whole looked an alarmingly big land in which to find hidden caves. The hush was broken by the despairing voice of Bailey, the ship's cook. "I don't know how I am to make a fire on that island, there is no wood!" He spoke the truth; not a vestige of timber or even brushwood was to be seen. We swung round the western headland with its group of islets and dropped anchor in Cook's Bay. A few hundred yards from the shore is the village of Hanga Roa, the native name for Cook's Bay. This is the only part of the island which is inhabited, the two hundred and fifty natives, all that remain of the population, having been gathered together here in order to secure the safety of the livestock, to which the rest of the island is devoted. The yacht was soon surrounded by six or seven boat-loads of natives, clad in nondescript European garments, but wearing a head-covering of native straw, somewhat resembling in appearance the high hat of civilisation.

The Manager, Mr. Edmunds, shortly appeared, and to our relief, for we had not been sure how he would view such an invasion, gave us a very kind welcome. He is English, and was, to all intent, at the time of our arrival, the only white man on the island; a French carpenter, who lived at Hanga Roa with a native wife, being always included in the village community. His house is at Mataveri, a spot about two miles to the south of the village, surrounded by modern plantations which are almost the only trees on the island; immediately behind it rises the swelling mass of the volcano Rano Kao. The first meal on Easter Island, taken here with Mr. Edmunds, remains a lasting memory. It was a large plain room with uncarpeted floor, scrupulously orderly; a dinner table, a few chairs, and two small book-cases formed the whole furniture. The door on to the veranda was open, for the night was hot, and the roar of breakers could be heard on the beach; while near at hand conversation was accompanied by a never-ceasing drone of mosquitoes. The light of the unshaded lamp was reflected from the clean rough-dried cloth of the table round which we sat, and lit up our host's features, the keen brown face of a man who had lived for some thirty years or more, most of it in the open air and under a tropical sun. He was telling us of events which one hardly thought existed outside magazines and books of adventure, but doing it so quietly that, with closed eyes, it might have been fancied that the entertainment was at some London restaurant, and we were still at the stage of discussing the latest play. . . .

We had just begun the week's work on Monday, October 12th, when word was brought that some steamers had appeared. The whole of the native staff, of course, at once departed to see what could be begged from the ships. The vessels turned out to be a German squadron, going, they said, "from the China station to Valparaiso." Some more turned up later, till there were twelve in all, four or five of the number being warships, and the remainder colliers or other smaller vessels. They kept entire silence on the European situation. We had not, of course, the slightest idea that war had broken out, still less that our lonely island was the meeting-place, cleverly arranged by Admiral von Spee, for his ships from Japan—the *Scharnhorst* and *Gneisenau*—with the other German warships in this region; the *Nürnberg* and *Leipzig* had turned up from the west coast of Mexico, and the *Dresden* from the other side of South America. A writer in the *Cornhill* (August 1917) states "there happened to be upon it [Easter Island] a British scientific expedition, but busied over the relics of the past, the single-minded men of science did not take the trouble to cross the island to look at the German ships." S. was, as a matter of fact, twice over at Mataveri while they were in Cook's Bay, but it is true of this "single-minded" woman, who felt she had something else to do than to ride for some four hours to gaze at the outside of German men-of-war. What did interest us was that presumably, after the usual manner of passing ships, the officers would come over to Raraku, and being intelligent Germans, would photograph our excavations. We therefore turned to, and with our own hands covered up our best things.

We seized the opportunity to write letters, which were posted on the ships, and one of our number went to see the doctor. To the credit of the enemy be it said, that almost all the letters subsequently arrived, a sad exception being a butterfly, addressed to Professor Poulton at Oxford, which, if, as may have been the case, it was retained as something valuable, presumably went down off the Falkland Islands. Mr. Edmunds, meanwhile, had not unnaturally rejoiced at having his market brought to his door, and sold the ships nearly £1,000 worth of meat. They offered to pay for it in gold, but it seemed common prudence to ask instead for an order, a decision which was later sadly lamented.

On Thursday some of our staff returned: the Germans were, it seemed, most unpopular; they did not come on shore and had given no food, clothes, or soap. Kanaka sentiment at this moment would have been certainly pro-Ally.

On Friday rumours reached us that there was something mysterious going on. Why, it was asked, did the Germans say they had no newspapers, so rarely come on shore, and go out at night without lights? and why did one officer say that "in two months Germany would be at the top of the tree"? We discussed the matter and passed it off as "bazaar talk." On Sunday, however, news came from Mataveri which we could no longer wholly discredit. The German tobacco planter had been on board, and the crew had disobeyed orders and disclosed to their countryman the fact that there was a great European war; the combatants were correctly stated, but much detail was added. Two hundred thousand men were, it was said, waiting at Kiel to invade England; the war had taken our country by surprise, and the German ships had already made a sudden raid and sunk eight or nine Dreadnoughts in the Thames; the Emperor was nearly at Paris, though the French continued to fight on most bravely. It was a terrible war as neither side would show the white flag. An army had been sent from England to the assistance of the French, but it had been badly defeated. The English Labour Party had objected to troops being sent out of the country, in consequence of which the Asquith ministry had fallen, the House of Lords came in somehow; anyway, England was now a Republic, and so were Canada and Australia; India was in flames, and two troopships had been sunk on the way there from Australia.

We are still inclined to think that the Germans themselves believed all these things; they had so often been told, by those in authority, that such would occur on the outbreak of war with England, that wishes had become facts. As a small mercy we got the news of the loss of the German colonies, but the *Scharnhorst,* which had just come from the French possession of Tahiti, said that the natives there having risen and killed the Germans, the warships had therefore bombarded the town of Papette, which was now "no more." The reason given for keeping us in the dark so long was, that hearing there were foreigners on the island, they thought that we might fight amongst ourselves. Von Spee made exact inquiries as to the number of whites in the place, and told the Kanakas that when he returned he would hold them responsible for our safety. The real reason of the silence maintained was most probably to prevent any question being raised of their use of the island as a naval base. When the news could no longer be concealed, the officers gave it as their opinion, that "when Germany had conquered France, peace would be made with England, in which case Britain would probably gain some territory as she had such good diplomatists," a compliment at least for Lord Grey. The reality of the war was brought home by the concrete fact that the ships were reliably reported to be in fighting trim, with no woodwork visible. That Sunday evening one of us saw the squadron going round in the dusk, the flagship leading. They had said that they would come again, but they never did. They went on their way to Coronel and the Falklands. . . .

[Von Spee went down with his flagship in the battle of the Falkland Islands.]

The Ahu and the Statues

In many places it is possible in the light of great monuments to reconstruct the past. In Easter Island the past is the present, it is impossible to escape from it; the inhabitants of to-day are less real than the men who have gone; the shadows of the departed builders still possess the land. Voluntarily or involuntarily the sojourner must hold commune with those old workers; for the whole air vibrates with a vast purpose and energy which has been and is no more. What was it? Why was it? The great works are now in ruins, of many comparatively little remains; but the impression infinitely exceeded anything which had been anticipated, and every day, as the power to see increased, brought with it a greater sense of wonder and marvel. "If we were to tell people at home these things," said our Sailingmaster, after being shown the prostrate images on the great burial place of Tongariki, "they would not believe us."

The present natives take little interest in the remains. The statues are to them facts of every-day life in much the same way as stones or banana-trees. "Have you no *moai*" (as they are termed) "in England?" was asked by one boy, in a tone in which surprise was slightly mingled with contempt; to ask for the history of the great works is as successful as to try to get from an old woman selling bootlaces at Westminster the story of Cromwell or of the frock-coated worthies in Parliament Square. The information given in reply to questions is generally wildly mythical, and any real knowledge crops up only indirectly.

Anyone who is able to go to the British Museum can see a typical specimen of an Easter Island statue, in the large image which greets the approaching visitor from under the portico. The general form is unvarying, and with one exception, which will be alluded to hereafter, all appear to be the work of skilled hands, which suggests that the design was well known and evolved under other conditions. It represents a half-length figure, at the bottom of which the hands nearly meet in front of the body. The most remarkable features are the ears, of which the lobe is depicted to represent a fleshy rope, while in a few cases the disc which was worn in it is also indicated. The fashion of piercing and distending the lobe of the ear is found among various primitive races. The tallest statues are over 30 feet, a few are only 6 feet, and even smaller specimens exist. Those which stood on the burial-places, now to be described, are usually from 12 to 20 feet in height, and were surmounted with a form of hat.

Position and Number of Ahu.—In Easter Island the problem of the disposal of the dead was solved by neither earth-burial nor cremation, but by means of the omnipresent stones which were built up to make a last resting-place for the departed. Such burial-places are known as "ahu," and the name will henceforth be used, for it signifies a definite thing, or rather type of thing, for which we have no equivalent. They number in all some two hundred and sixty, and are principally found near the coast, but some thirty exist inland, sufficient to show that their erection on the sea-board was a matter of convenience, not of principle. With the exception of the great eastern and western headlands, where they are scarce, it is probably safe to say that, in riding round the island, it is impossible to go anywhere for more than a few hundred yards without coming across one of these abodes of the dead. They cluster most thickly on the little coves and their enclosing promontories, which were the principal centres of population. Some are two or three hundred yards away from the edge of the cliff, others stand on the verge; in the lower land they are but little above the sea-level, while on the precipitous part of the coast the ocean breaks hundreds of feet below.

It was these burial-places, on which the images were then standing, which so strongly impressed the early voyagers and whose age and origin have remained an unsolved problem.

During the whole of our time on the island we worked on the ahu. . . . Those which happened to lie near to either of our camps were naturally easy of access, but to reach the more distant ones, notably those on the north shore, involved a long expedition. Such a day began with perhaps an hour's ride; at noon there was an interval for luncheon, when, in hot weather, the neighbourhood was scoured for miles to find the smallest atom of shade; and the day ended with a journey home of not less than two hours, during which an anxious eye was kept on the sinking sun. The usual method, as each ahu was reached, was for S. to dismount, measure it and describe it, while I sat on my pony and scribbled down notes; but in some manner or other every part of the coast was by one or both of us ridden over several times, and a written statement made of the size, kind, condition, and name of each monument.

Unfortunately there is in existence no large-scale plan of the coast, a need we had to supply as best we could; map of Easter Island there is none, only the crude chart; the efforts of our own surveyor were limited, by the time at his disposal, to making detailed plans of a few of the principal spots. The want is to be regretted geographically, but it does not materially affect the archæological result. We were always accompanied by native guides in order to learn local names and traditions, and it was soon found necessary to make a point of these being old men; owing to the concentration of the remains of the population in one district, all names elsewhere, except those of the most important places, are speedily being forgotten. The memories of even the older men were sometimes shaky, and to get reasonably complete and accurate information the whole of a district had, in more than one case, to be gone over again with a second ancient who turned out to have lived in the neighbourhood in his youth and hence to be a better authority.

Original Design and Construction of Image Ahu.—The burial-places are not all of one type, nor all constructed to carry statues; some also are known to have been built comparatively recently, and will therefore be described under a later section. The image ahu are, however, all prehistoric. They number just under a hundred, or over one-third of the whole. The figures connected with them, of which traces still remain, were counted as 231, but as many are in fragments, this number is uncertain.

A typical image ahu is composed of a long wall running parallel with the sea, which, in a large specimen, is as much as 15 feet in height and 300 feet in length; it is buttressed on the land side with a great slope of masonry. The wall is in three divisions. The main or central portion projects in the form of a terrace on which the images stood, with their backs to the sea; it is therefore broad enough to carry their oval bed-plates; these measure up to about 10 feet in length by 8 feet or 9 feet in width, and are flush with the top of the wall. On the great ahu of Tongariki there have been fifteen statues, but sometimes an ahu has carried one figure only.

The wall which forms the landward side of the terrace is continued on either hand in a straight line, thus adding a wing at each end of the central portion which stands somewhat farther back from the sea. Images were sometimes placed on the wings, but it was not usual. From this continuous wall the masonry slopes steeply till it reaches a containing wall, some 3 feet high, formed of finely wrought slabs of great size and of peculiar shape; the workmanship put into this wall is usually the most highly finished of any part of the ahu. Extending inland from the foot of this low wall is a large, raised, and smoothly paved expanse. The upper surface of this, too, has an appreciable fall, or slope, inland, though it is almost horizontal, when compared with the glacis.

By the method of construction of this area, vault accommodation is obtained between its surface pavement and the sheet of volcanic rock below, on which the whole rests. In the largest specimen the whole slope of masonry, measured that is from either the sea-wall of the wing or from the landward wall of the terrace to its farthest extent, is about 250 feet. Beyond this the ground is sometimes levelled for another 50 or 60 yards, forming a smooth sward which much enhanced the appearance of the ahu. In two cases the ahu is approached by a strip of narrow pavement formed of water-worn boulders laid flat, and bordered with the same kind of stone set on end; one of these pavements is 220 feet in length by 12 feet in width, the other is somewhat smaller.

The general principle on which the sea or main walls are constructed is usually the same, though the various ahu differ greatly in appearance: first comes a row of foundation blocks on which have been set upright the largest stones that could be found; the upper part of the wall is composed of smaller stones, and it is finished with a coping. The variety in effect is due to the difference in material used. In some cases, as at Tongariki, the most convenient stone available has consisted of basalt which has cooled in fairly regular cubes, and the rows are there comparatively uniform size; in other instances, as at Ahu Tepeu on the west coast, the handiest material has been sheets of lava, which have hardened as strata, and when these have been used the first tier of the wall is composed of huge slabs up to 9 feet in height. Irregularities in the shape and size of the big stones are rectified by fitting in small pieces and surmounting the shorter slabs with additional stones until the whole is brought to a uniform level; on the top of this now even tier horizontal blocks are laid, till the whole is the desired height. The amount of finish put into the work varies greatly: in many ahu the walls are all constructed of rough material; in others, while the slabs are untouched, the stones which bring them to the level and the cubes on the top are well wrought; in a very few instances, of which Vinapu is the best example, the whole is composed of beautifully finished work. Occasionally, as at Oroi, natural outcrops of rock have been adapted to carry statues.

The study of the ahu is simplified by the fact that they were being used in living memory for the purpose for which they were doubtless originally built. They have been termed "burial-places," but burial in its usual sense was not the only, nor in most cases their principal, object. On death the corpse was wrapped in a tapa blanket and enclosed in its mattress of reeds; fish-hooks, chisels, and other objects were sometimes included. It was then bound into a bundle and carried on staves to the ahu, where it was exposed on an oblong framework. This consisted of four corner uprights set up in the ground, the upper extremities of which were Y-shaped, two transverse bars rested in the bifurcated ends, one at the head, the other at the foot, and on these transverse bars were placed the extremities of the bundle which wrapped the corpse. The description and sketch are based on a model framework, and a wrapped-up figure, one of the wooden images of the island, prepared by the natives to amplify their verbal description. At times, instead of the four supports, two stones were used with a hole in each, into which a Y-shaped stick was placed. While the corpse remained on the ahu the district was marked off by the péra, or taboo, for the dead; no fishing was allowed near, and fires and cooking were forbidden within certain marks—the smoke, at any rate, must be hidden or smothered with grass. Watch was kept by four relatives, and anyone breaking the regulations was liable to be brained. The mourning might last one, two, or even three years, by which time the whole thing had, of course, fallen to pieces. The bones were either left on the ahu, or collected and put into vaults of oblong shape, which were kept for the family, or they might be buried elsewhere. The end of the mourning was celebrated by a great feast, after which ceremony, as one recorder cheerfully concluded, "Papa was finished."

Looked at from the landward side, we may, therefore, conceive an ahu as a vast theatre stage, of which the floor runs gradually upwards from the footlights. The back of the stage, which is thus the highest part, is occupied by a great terrace, on which are set up in line the giant images, each one well separated from his neighbour, and all facing the spectator. Irrespective of where he stands he will ever see them towering above him, clear cut out against a turquoise sky. In front of them are the remains of the departed. Unseen, on the farther side of the terrace, is the sea. The stone giants, and the faithful dead over whom they watch, are never without music, as countless waves launch their strength against the pebbled shore, showering on the figures a cloud of mist and spray.

Reconstruction and Transformation.—Those which have been described are ideal image ahu, but not one now remains in its original condition. It is by no means unusual to find, even in the oldest parts now existing, that is in walls erected to carry statues, pieces of still older images built into the stonework; in one case a whole statue has been used as a slab for the sea-wall, showing that alteration has taken place even when the cult was alive. Again, a considerable number of ahu, some thirteen in all, after being destroyed and terminating their career as image-terraces, have been rebuilt after the fashion of others constructed originally on a different plan. This is a type for which no name was found: it is in form that of a semi-pyramid, and there are between fifty and sixty on the island, in adition to those which have been in the first place image ahu. A few are comparatively well made, but most are very rough. They resemble a pyramid cut in two, so that the section forms a triangle; this triangle is the sea-wall; the flanking buttress on the land side is made of stones, and is widest at the apex or highest point, gradually diminishing to the angles or extremities. The greatest height, in the centre, varies from about 5 feet to 12 feet, and a large specimen may extend in length from 100 feet to 160 feet. They contain vaults. In a few instances they are ornamented by broken pieces of image-stone, and occasionally by a row of small cairns along the top, which recall the position of the statues on the image-platform; for these no very certain reason was forthcoming, they were varyingly reported to be signs of "péra" or as marking the respective right of families on the ahu. As image-terraces may be found reconstructed as pyramid ahu, the latter form of building must have been carried on longer than the former, and probably till recent times, but there is nothing to show whether or not the earliest specimens of pyramid ahu are contemporary with the great works, or even earlier.

Overthrow of the Images and Destruction of the Ahu.—The only piece of a statue which still remains on its bed-plate is the fragment already alluded to at Tongariki. In the best-preserved specimens the figures lie on their faces like a row of huge nine-pins; some are intact, but many are broken, the cleavage having generally occurred when the falling image has come in contact with the containing wall at the lower level. The curious way in which the heads have not infrequently turned a somersault while falling and now lie face uppermost is shown in the eighth figure from the western end on Tongariki ahu.

No one now living remembers a statue standing on an ahu; and legend, though not of a very impressive character, has already arisen to account for the fall of some of them. An old man arrived, it is said, in the neighbourhood of Tongariki, and as he was unable to speak, he made known by means of signs that he wished for chicken-heads to eat; these were not forthcoming. He slept, however, in one of the houses there, and during the night his hosts were aroused by a great noise, which he gave it to be understood was made by his feet tapping against the stone foundations of the house. In the morning it was found that the statues on the great ahu had all fallen: it was the revenge of the old man. Such lore is, however, mixed up with more tangible statements to the effect that the figures were overthrown in tribal warfare by means of a rope, or by taking away the small stones from underneath the bed-plates, and thus causing them to fall forward. That the latter method had been used had been concluded independently by studying the remains themselves. It will be seen later, that other statues which have been set up in earth were deliberately dug out, and it seems unnecessary to look, as some have done, to an earthquake to account for their collapse.

Moreover, the conclusion that the images owed their fall to deliberate vandalism during internecine warfare is confirmed by knowledge, which still survives, connected with the destruction of the last one. This image stood alone on an ahu on the north coast, called Paro, and is the tallest known to have been put up on a terrace, being 32 feet in height. The events occurred just before living memory, and, like most stories in Easter Island, it is connected with cannibalism. A woman of the western clans was eaten by men of the eastern; her son managed to trap thirty of the enemy in a cave and consumed them in revenge; and during the ensuing struggle this image was thrown down. The oldest man living when we were on the island said that he was an infant at the time; and another, a few years younger, stated that his father as a boy helped his grandfather in the fight. It is not, after all, only in Easter Island that pleasure has been taken during war-time in destroying the architectural treasures of the enemy.

While, therefore, the date of the erection of the earliest image ahu is lost in the mists of antiquity, nor are we yet in a position to say when the building stopped, we can give approximately the time of the overthrow of the images. We know, from the accounts of the early voyagers, that the statues, or the greater number of them, were still in place in the eighteenth century; by the early part of the middle of the nineteenth century not one was standing.

The destruction of the ahu has continued in more modern days. A manager, whose sheep had found the fresh-water springs below high water, thinking they were injuring themselves by drinking from the sea, erected a wall round a large part of the coast to keep them from it. For this wall the ahu came in of course most conveniently; it was run through a great number and their material used for its construction. One wing of Tongariki has been pulled down to form an enclosure for the livestock. In addition to the damage wrought by man, the ocean is ever encroaching: in some cases part of an ahu has already fallen into the sea, and more is preparing to follow; statues may be found lying on their backs in process of descending into the waves. One row of images, on the extreme western edge of the crater of Rano Kao, which were visible, although inaccessible, at the time of the visit of the U.S.A. ship *Mohican* in 1886, are now lying on the shore a thousand feet below. As the result of these various causes the burial-places of Easter Island are, as has been seen, all in ruins, and many are scarcely recognisable; only their huge stones and prostrate figures show what they must once have been.

Rano Raraku and the Statues in the Quarries

Strange as it may appear, it is by no means easy to obtain a complete view of a statue on the island: most of the images which were formerly on the ahu lie on their faces, many are broken, and detail has largely been destroyed by weather. Happily, we are not dependent for our knowledge of the images on such information as we can gather from the ruins on the ahu, but are able to trace them to their origin, though even here excavation is necessary to see the entire figure. Rano Raraku is, as has already been explained, a volcanic cone containing a crater-lake. It resembles, to use an unromantic simile, one of the china drinking-vessels dedicated to the use of dogs, whose base is larger than their brim. Its sides are for the most part smooth and sloping, and several carriages could drive abreast on the northern rim of the crater, but towards the south-east it rises in height, and from this aspect it looks as if the circular mass had been sliced down with a giant knife forming it into a precipitous cliff. The cliff is lowest where the imaginary knife has come nearest to the central lake, thus causing the two ends to stand out as the peaks already mentioned.

The mountain is composed of compressed volcanic ash, which has been found in certain places to be particularly suitable for quarrying; it has been worked on the southern exterior slope, and also inside the crater both on the south and south-eastern sides. With perhaps a dozen exceptions, the whole of the images in the island have been made from it, and they have been dragged from this point up hill and down dale to adorn the terraces round the coast-line of the island; even the images on the ahu, which have fallen into the sea on the further extremity of the western volcano, are said to have been of the same stone. It is conspicuous in being a reddish brown colour, of which the smallest chips can be easily recognised. It is composite in character, and embedded in the ash are numerous lapilli of metamorphic rock. Owing to the nature of this rock the earliest European visitors came to the conclusion that the material was factitious and that the statues were built of clay and stones; it was curious to find that the marooned prisoners of war of our own time fell into the same mistake of thinking that the figures were "made up."

The workable belt, generally speaking, forms a horizontal section about half-way up the side of the mountain. Below it, both on the exterior and within the crater, are banks of detritus, and on these statues have been set up; most of them are still in place, but they have been buried in greater or less degree by the descent of earth from above. Mr. Ritchie made a survey of the mountain with the adjacent coast, but it was found impossible to record the results of our work without some sort of plan or diagram which was large enough to show every individual image. This was accomplished by first studying each quarry, note-book in hand, and then, with the aid of field-glasses, amalgamating the results from below; the standing statues being inserted in their relation to the quarries above. It was a lengthy but enjoyable undertaking. Part of the diagram of the exterior has been redrawn with the help of photographs; the plan of the inside of the crater is shown in what is practically its original form.

Quarries of Rano Raraku.—Leaving on one side for the moment the figures on the lower slope, let us in imagination scramble up the grassy side, a steep climb of some one or two hundred feet to where the rock has been hewn away into a series of chambers and ledges. Here images lie by the score in all stages of evolution, just as they were left when, for some unknown reason, the workmen laid down their tools for the last time and the busy scene was still. Here, as elsewhere, the wonder of the place can only be appreciated as the eye becomes trained to see. In the majority of cases the statues still form part of the rock, and are frequently covered with lichen or overgrown with grass and ferns; and even in the illustrations, for which prominent figures have naturally been chosen, the reader may find that he has to look more than once in order to recognise the form. A conspicuous one first strikes the beholder: as he gazes, he finds with surprise that the walls on either hand are themselves being wrought into figures, and that, resting in a niche above him, is another giant; he looks down, and realises with a start that his foot is resting on a mighty face. To the end of our visit we occasionally found a figure which had escaped observation.

The workings on the exterior of Raraku first attract attention; here their size, and incidentally that of many of the statues, has largely been determined by fissures in the hillside, which run vertically and at distances of perhaps 40 feet. The quarries have been worked differently, and each has a character of its own. In some of them the principal figures lie in steps, with their length parallel to the hill's horizontal axis; one of this type is reached through a narrow opening in the rock, and recalls the side-chapel of some old cathedral, save that nature's blue sky forms the only roof; immediately opposite the doorway there lies, on a base of rock, in quiet majesty, a great recumbent figure. So like is it to some ancient effigy that the awed spectator involuntarily catches his breath, as if suddenly brought face to face with a tomb of the mighty dead. Once, on a visit to this spot, a rather quaint little touch of nature supervened: going there early in the morning, with the sunlight still sparkling on the floor of dewy grass, a wild-cat, startled by our approach, rushed away from the rock above, and the natives, clambering up, found nestling beneath a statue at a high level a little family of blind kittens.

In other instances the images have been carved lying, not horizontally, but vertically, with sometimes the head, and sometimes the base, toward the summit of the hill. But no exact system has been followed, the figures are found in all places, and all positions. When there was a suitable piece of rock it has been carved into a statue, without any special regard to surroundings or direction. Interspersed with embryo and completed images are empty niches from which others have already been removed; and finished statues must, in some cases, have been passed out over the top of those still in course of construction. From all the outside quarries is seen the same wonderful panorama: immediately beneath are the statues which stand on the lower slopes; farther still lie the prostrate ones beside the approach; while beyond is the whole stretch of the southern plain, with its white line of breaking surf ending in the western mountain of Rano Kao.

The quarries within the crater are on the same lines as those without, save that those on the south-eastern side form a more continuous whole. Here the most striking position is on the top of the seaward cliff, in the centre of which is a large finished image; on one side the ground falls away more or less steeply to the crater-lake, on the other a stone thrown down would reach the foot of the precipice; the view extends from sea to sea. Over all the most absolute stillness reigns.

The statues in the quarries number altogether over 150. Amongst this mass of material there is no difficulty in tracing the course of the work. The surface of the rock, which will form the figure, has generally been laid bare before work upon it began, but occasionally the image was wrought lying partially under a canopy. In a few cases the stone has been roughed out into preliminary blocks, but this procedure is not universal, and seems to have been followed only where there was some doubt as to the quality of the material. When this was not the case the face and anterior aspect of the statue were first carved, and the block gradually became isolated as the material was removed in forming the head, base, and sides. A gutter or alley-way was thus made round the image, in which the niches where each man has stood or squatted to his work can be clearly seen; it is, therefore, possible to count how many were at work at each side of a figure.

When the front and sides were completed down to every detail of the hands, the undercutting commenced. The rock beneath was chipped away by degrees till the statue rested only on a narrow strip of stone running along the spine; those which have been left at this stage resemble precisely a boat on its keel, the back being curved in the same way as a ship's bottom. In the next stage shown the figure is completely detached from the rock, and chocked up by stones, looking as if an inadvertent touch would send it sliding down the hill into the plain below. In one instance the moving has evidently begun, the image having been shifted out of the straight. In another very interesting case the work has been abandoned when the statue was in the middle of its descent; it has been carved in a horizontal position in the highest part of the quarry, where its empty niche is visible, it has then been slewed round and was being launched, base forward, across some other empty niches at a lower level. The bottom now rests on the floor of the quarry, and the figure, which has broken in half, is supported in a standing fashion against the outer edge of the vacated shelves. The first impression was that it had met with an accident in transit, and been abandoned; but it is at least equally possible that for the purpose of bringing it down, a bank or causeway of earth had been built up to level the inequalities of the descent, and that it was resting on this when the work came to an end; the soil would then in time be washed away, and the figure fracture through loss of support.

In the quarry . . . the finished head can be seen lying across the opening, the body is missing, presumably broken off and buried; the bottom of the keel on which the figure at one time rested can be clearly traced in a projecting line of rock down the middle of its old bed, also the different sections where the various men employed have chipped away the stone in undermining the statue. In the quarry wall the niches occupied by the sculptors are also visible, at more than one level, the higher ones being discarded when the upper portion of the work was finished and a lower station needed.

The tools were found with which the work has been done. One type of these can be seen lying about in great abundance. They are of the same material as the lipilli in the statues, and made by flaking. Some specimens are pointed at both ends, others have one end more or less rounded. It is unlikely that they were hafted, and they were probably held in the hand when in use. They were apparently discarded as soon as the point became damaged. There is another tool much more carefully made, an adze blade, with the lower end bevelled off to form the cutting edge. In the specimen shown, the top is much abraded apparently from hammering with a maul or mallet. These are rarely found, the probability being that they were too precious to leave and were taken home by the workmen. The whole process was not necessarily very lengthy; a calculation of the number of men who could work at the stone at the same time, and the amount each could accomplish, gave the rather surprising result that a statue might be roughed out within the space of fifteen days. The most notable part of the work was the skill which kept the figure so perfect in design and balance that it was subsequently able to maintain its equilibrium in a standing position; to this it is difficult to pay too high a tribute.

It remains to account for the vast number of images to be found in the quarry. A certain number have, no doubt, been abandoned prior to the general cessation of the work; in some cases a flaw has been found in the rock and the original plan has had to be given up—in this case, part of the stone is sometimes used for either a smaller image or one cut at a different angle. In other instances the sculptors have been unlucky enough to come across at important points one or more of the hard nodules with which their tools could not deal, and as the work could not go down to posterity with a large wart on its nose or excrescence on its chin, it has had to be stopped. But when all these instances have been subtracted, the amount of figures remaining in the quarries is still startlingly large when compared with the number which have been taken out of it, and must have necessitated, if they were all in hand at once, a number of workers out of all proportion to any population which the island has ever been likely to have maintained. The theory naturally suggests itself that some were merely rock-carvings and not intended to be removed. It is one which needs to be adopted with caution, for more than once, where every appearance has pointed to its being correct, a similar neighbour has been found which was actually being removed; on the whole, however, there can be little doubt that it is at any rate a partial solution of the problem. Some of the images are little more than embossed carvings on the face of the rock without surrounding alley-ways. In one instance, inside the crater, a piece of rock which has been left standing on the very summit of the cliff has been utilised in such a way that the figure lies on its side, while its back is formed by the outward precipice; this is contrary to all usual methods, and it seems improbable that it was intended to make it into a standing statue. Perhaps the strongest evidence is afforded by the size of some of the statues: the largest is 66 feet in length, whereas 36 feet is the extreme ever found outside the quarry; tradition, it is true, points out the ahu on the south coast for which this monster was designed, but it is difficult to believe it was ever intended to move such a mass. If this theory is correct, it would be interesting to know whether the stage of carving came first, and that of removal followed, as the workmen became more expert; or whether it was the result of decadence when labour may have become scarce. It is, of course, possible that the two methods proceeded concurrently, rock-carvings being within the means of those who could not procure the labour necessary to move the statue.

Legendary lore throws no light on these matters, nor on the reasons which led to the desertion of this labyrinth of work; it has invented a story which entirely satisfies the native mind and is repeated on every occasion. There was a certain old woman who lived at the southern corner of the mountain and filled the position of cook to the image-makers. She was the most important person of the establishment, and moved the images by supernatural power (*mana*), ordering them about at her will. One day, when she was away, the workers obtained a fine lobster, which had been caught on the west coast, and ate it up, leaving none for her; unfortunately they forgot to conceal the remains, and when the cook returned and found how she had been treated, she arose in her wrath, told all the images to fall down, and thus brought the work to a standstill.

Standing Statues of Rano Raraku.—Descending from the quarries, we turn to the figures below. A few at the foot of the mountain have obviously been thrown down; one of these was wrecked in the same conflict as the one on Ahu Paro, and one is shown where an attempt has been made to cut off the head. Another series of images have originally stood round the base on level ground, extending from the exterior of the entrance to the crater to the southern corner; these are all prostrate. On the slopes there are a few horizonal statues, but the great majority, both inside the crater and without, are still erect.Outside, some forty figures stand in an irregular belt, reaching from the corner nearest the sea to about half-way to the gap leading into the crater. The bottom of the mountain is here diversified by little hillocks and depressions; these hillocks would have made commanding situations, but rather curiously the statues, while erected quite close to them, and even on their sides, are never on the top. Inside the crater, where some twenty statues are still erect, the arrangement is rather more regular; but, on the whole, they are put up in no apparent order. All stood with their backs to the mountain.

They vary very considerably in size; the tallest which could be measured from its base was 32 feet 3 inches, while others are not much above 11 feet. Every statue is buried in greater or less degree, but while some are exposed as far as the elbow, in others only a portion of the top of the head can be seen above the surface; others no doubt are covered entirely. The number visible must vary from time to time, as by the movement of the earth some are buried and others disclosed. An old man, whose testimony was generally reliable, stated, when speaking of the figures on the outside of the mountain, that while those nearer the sea were in the same condition as he always remembered them, those farther from it were now more deeply buried than in his youth.

Various old people were brought out from the village at Hanga Roa to pay visits to the camp, but the information forthcoming was never of great extent; one elderly gentleman in particular took much more interest in roaming round the mountain, recalling various scenes of his youth, than in anything connected with the statues. A few names are still remembered in connection with the individual figures, and are said to be those of the makers of the images, and some proof is afforded of the reality of the tradition by the fact that the clans of the persons named are consistently given. Another class of names is, however, obviously derived merely from local circumstances; one in the quarry, under a drip from above, is known by the equivalent for "Dropping Water," while a series inside the crater are called after the birds which frequent the cliff-side, "Kia-kia, Flying," "Kia-kia, Sitting," and so forth. A solitary legend relates to an unique figure, resembling rather a block than an image, which lies on the surface on the outside of the mountain. It is the single exception to the rule mentioned above, that no evolution can be traced in the statues on the island. The usual conception is there, and the hands are shown, but the head seems to melt into the body and the ear and arm to have become confused. It is said to have been the first image made and is known as Tai-haré-atua, which tradition says was the name of the maker. He found himself unable to fashion it properly, and went over to the other side of the island to consult with a man who lived near Hanga Roa, named Rauwai-ika. He stayed the night there, but the expert remained silent, and he was retiring disappointed in the morning, when he was followed by his host, who called him back. "Make your image," said he, "like me,"—that is, in form of a man.

On our first visit to the mountain, overcome by the wonder of the scene, we turned to our Fernandez boy and asked him what he thought of the statues. Like the classical curate, when the bishop inquired as to the character of his egg, he struggled manfully between the desire to please and a sense of truth; like the curate, he took refuge in compromise. "Some of them," he said doubtfully, he thought "were very nice." If the figures at first strike even the cultured observer as crude and archaic, it must be remembered that not only are they the work of stone tools, but to be rightly seen should not be scrutinised near at hand. "Hoa-haka-nanaia," for instance, is wholly and dismally out of place under a smoky portico, but on the slopes of a mountain, gazing in impenetrable calm over sea and land, the simplicity of outline is soon found to be marvellously impressive. The longer the acquaintance the more this feeling strengthens; there is always the sense of quiet dignity, of suggestion and of mystery.

While the scene on Raraku always arouses a species of awe, it is particularly inspiring at sunset, when, as the light fades, the images gradually become outlined as stupendous black figures against the gorgeous colouring of the west. The most striking sight witnessed on the island was a fire on the hill-side: in order to see our work more clearly we set alight the long dry grass, always a virtuous act on Easter Island, that the live-stock may have the benefit of fresh shoots; in a moment the whole was a blaze, the mountain, wreathed in masses of driving smoke, grew to portentous size, the quarries loomed down from above as dark giant masses, and in the whirl of flame below the great statues stood out calmly, with a quiet smile, like stoical souls in Hades.

The questions which arise are obvious: do these buried statues differ in any way from those in the workings above, from those on the ahu or from one another? were they put up on any foundation?

and, above all, what is the history of the mountain and the *raison d'être* of the figures? In the hope of throwing some light on these problems we started to dig them out. It had originally been thought that the excavation of one or two would give all the information which it was possible to obtain, but each case was found to have unique and instructive features, and we finally unearthed in this way, wholly or in part, some twenty or thirty statues. It was usually easy to trace the stages by which the figures had been gradually covered. On the top was a layer of surface soil, from 3 to 8 inches in depth; then came debris, which had descended from the quarry above in the form of rubble, it contained large numbers of chisels, some forty of which have been found in digging out one statue; below this was the substance in which a hole had been dug to erect the image, it sometimes consisted of clay and occasionally in part of rock. Not unfrequently the successive descents of earth could be traced by the thin lines of charcoal which marked the old surfaces, obviously the result of grass or brushwood fires. The few statues which are in a horizontal position are always on the surface, and at first give the impression that they have been abandoned in the course of being brought down from the quarries; as they are frequently found close to standing images, of which only the head is visible, it follows that, if this is the correct solution, the work must still have been proceeding when the earlier statues were already largely submerged. The juxtaposition, however, occurs so often that it seems, on the whole, more probable that the rush of earth which covered some, upset the foundations of others, and either threw them down where they stood or carried them with it on top of the flood. These various landslips allow of no approximate deductions as to the date, in the manner which is possible with successively deposited layers of earth.

To get absolutely below the base of an image was not altogether easy. The first we attempted to dig out was one of the farther ones within the crater; it was found that, while the back of the hole into which it had been dropped was excavated in the soft volcanic ash, the front and remaining sides were of hard rock. This rock was cut to the curvature of the figure at a distance of some 3 inches from it, and as the chisel marks were horizontal, from right to left, the workmen must have stood in the cup while preparing it: in clearing out the alluvium between the wall of the cup and the figure, six stone implements were found. The hands, which were about 1 foot below the level of the rim, were perfectly formed. The next statue chosen for excavation was also inside the crater; it was most easily attacked from the side, and this time it was possible to get low enough to see that it stood on no foundation, and that the base instead of expanding, as with those which stood on the ahu, contracted in such a manner as to give a peg-shaped appearance; this confirmed the impression made by the previous excavation, that the image was intended to remain in its hole and was not, as some have stated, merely awaiting removal to an ahu.

The story was shown not only in the sections of the excavation, but in the degrees of weathering on the figure itself: the lowest part of the image to above the elbow exhibited, by the sharpness of its outlines and frequently of the chisel cuts also, that it had never been exposed, the other portions being worn in relative degrees. Traces of the smoothness of the original surface can still be seen above-ground in the more protected portions of some of the statues, such as in the orbit and under the chin, but a much clearer impression is of course gained of the finish and detail of the image when the unweathered surface is exposed. The polish is often very beautiful, and pieces of pumice, called "punga," are found, with which the figures are said to have been rubbed down. The fingers taper, and the excessive length of the thumb-joint and nail are remarkable. The nipples are in some cases so pronounced that the natives often characterized them as feminine, but in no case which we came across did the statues represent other than the nude male figure; the navel is indicated by a raised disk. On the statue with the contracting base, which is one of the best, the surface modelling of the elbow-joint is clearly shown. The orbital cavity in the figures on Raraku is rather differently modelled from those on the ahu; in the statues on the mountain the position of the eyeball is always indicated by a straight line below the brow, the orbit has no lower border. On the terraces the socket is constantly hollowed out as in the figure at the British Museum.

The eye is the only point in which the two sets vary, with the important exception that some on the mountain have a type of back which never appears on the ahu. This question of back proved to be of special interest: in some images it remained exactly as when the figure left the quarry, the whole was convex, giving it a thick and archaic appearance, particularly as regards the neck; in other instances, the posterior was beautifully modelled after the same fashion as those on the terraces, the stone had been carefully chipped away till the ears stood out from the back of the head, the neck assumed definite form, and the spine, instead of standing out as a sharp ridge, was represented by an incised line. This second type, when excavated, proved, to our surprise, to possess a well-carved design in the form of a girdle shown by three raised bands, this was surmounted by one or sometimes by two rings, and immediately beneath it was another design somewhat in the shape of an M. The whole was new, not only to us, but to the natives, who greatly admired it. Later, when we knew what to look for, traces of the girdle could be seen also on the figures on the ahu where the arm had protected it from the weather. It was afterwards realised with amusement that the discovery of this design might have been made before leaving England by merely passing the barrier and walking behind the statues in the Bloomsbury portico. One case was found, a statue at Anakena, where a ring was visible, not only on the back but also on each of the buttocks, and in view of subsequent information these lower rings became of special importance. The girdle in this case consisted of one line only; the detail of the carving had doubtless been preserved by being buried in the sand. The two forms of back, unmodelled and modelled, stand side by side on the mountain.

The next step was to discover where and when the modelling was done. Certainly not in the original place in the quarry, where it would be impossible from the position in which the image was evolved; generally speaking there was no trace of such work, and it was not until many months later that new light was thrown on the matter. Then it was remarked that in one of the standing statues on the outside of the hill, which was buried up to the neck, while the right ear was most carefully modelled, showing a disk, the left ear was as yet quite plain, and that the back of the head also was not symmetrical. Excavations made clear that the whole back was in course of transformation from the boat-shaped to the modelled type, each workman apparently chipping away where it seemed to him good. Two or three similar cases were then found on which work was proceeding; but on the other hand, some of the simpler backs were excavated to the foot, and others a considerable distance, and there was no indication that any alteration was intended. There are three possible explanations for these erect and partially moulded statues: Firstly, it may have been the regular method for the back to be completed after the statue was set up, in which case some kind of staging must have been used; one of our guides had made a remark, noted, but not taken very seriously at the moment, that "the statues were set up to be finished"; some knowledge or tradition of such work, therefore, appeared to linger. Secondly, the convex back may be the older form, and those on which work was being done were being modelled to bring them up to date. Alteration did at times take place; a certain small image presented a very curious appearance both from the proportion of the body, which was singularly narrow from back to front, and because it was difficult to see how it remained in place as it was apparently exposed to the base; it turned out that the figure had been carved out of the head of an older statue, of which the body was buried below. Thirdly, these particular figures may have been erected and left in an unfinished condition; if so, their deficiencies were high up and would be obvious.

Scamping did not often occur, and when it did so it was in the concealed portions. In one case the left hand was correctly modelled, but the right was not even indicated beyond the wrist. The statue which rejoices in the name of Piro-piro, meaning "bad odour," stands at the foot of the slope, and appears to remain as it was set up without further burial. It is a well-made figure, probably one of the most recent, and the upper part of the back is carefully moulded, but on digging it out it was found that the bottom had not been finished, but left in the form of a rough excrescence of stone; there was no ring, but a girdle had been carved on the protruding portion, so that this was not intended to be removed. In another instance a large head had fallen on a slope at such an angle that it was impossible to locate the position of the body; curiosity led to investigation, when it was found that the thing was a fraud, the magnificent head being attached to a little dwarf trunk, which must have been buried originally nearly to the neck to keep the top upright. These instances of "jerry-building" confirm our impression that at any rate a large number of the statues were intended to remain *in situ*.

Indications were found of two different methods of erection, and the mode may have been determined by the nature of the ground. By the first procedure the statue seems to have been placed on its face in the desired spot, and a hole to have been dug beneath the base. The other method was to undermine the base, with the statue lying face uppermost; in several instances a number of large stones were found behind the back of the figure, evidently having been used to wedge it while it was dragged to the vertical. The upright position had sometimes been only partially attained; one statue was still in a slanting attitude, corresponding exactly to the slope of a hard clay wall behind it; the interval between the two, varying from three yards to eighteen inches, had been packed with sub-angular boulders which weighed about one hundredweight, or as much as a man could lift.

A few of the figures bear incised markings rudely, and apparently promiscuously, carved. This was first noted in the case of one of two statues which stand together nearest to the entrance of the crater; here it has been found possible to work the rock at a low level, and in the empty quarry, from which they no doubt have been taken, two images have been set up, one slightly in front of the other; six still unfinished figures lie in close proximity. The standing figure, nearest to the lake, bore a rough design on the face, and when it was dug out the back was found to be covered with similar incised marks. The natives were much excited, and

convinced that we should receive a large sum of money in England
when the photograph of these was produced, for nothing ever dispelled the illusion that the expedition was a financial speculation.
It was these carvings more especially that we ourselves hastily
endeavoured to cover up when, on the arrival of Admiral von Spee's
Squadron, we daily expected a visit from the officers on board. The
markings have certainly not been made by the same practised hand
as the raised girdle and rings, and appear to be comparatively recent. Other statues were excavated, where similar marks were noticed, but, except in this case, digging led practically always to
disappointment. It was the part above the surface only which had
been used as a block on which to scrawl design, from the same
impulse presumably as impels the school-boy of to-day to make
marks with chalk on a hoarding. On one ahu the top of the head
of a statue has been decorated with rough faces, the carving evidently having been done after the statue had fallen.

In digging out the image with the tattooed back, we came across
the one and only burial which was found in connection with these
figures; it was close to it and at the level of the rings. The long
bones, the patella, and base of the skull were identified; they lay
in wet soil, crushed and intermixed with large stones, so the attitude could not be determined beyond the fact that the head was
to the right of the image and the long bones to the left. These bones
had become of the consistency of moist clay, and could only be
identified by making transverse sections of them with a knife, after
first cleaning portions longitudinally by careful scraping.

In several other instances human bones were discovered near
the statues, but, like the carvings, they appeared to be of later
date than the images. One skull was found beneath a figure which
was lying face downwards on the surface; another fragment must
have been placed behind the base after the statue had fallen forward. The natives stated that in the epidemics which ravaged the
island the statues afforded a natural mark for depositing remains.
In the same way a head near an ahu, which was at first thought
to be that of a standing statue, turned out to be broken from the
trunk and put up pathetically to mark the grave of a little child.
There is a roughly constructed ahu on the outside of Rano Raraku
at the corner nearest to the sea, of which more will be said hereafter, and a quarried block of rock on the very top of the westerly
peak was also said to be used for the exposure of the dead. Close
to this block there are some very curious circular pits cut in the
rock; one examined was 5 feet 6 inches in depth and 3 feet 6 inches
in diameter. It is possible they were used as vaults, but, if so, the
shape is quite different from those of the ahu. The conclusion
arrived at was that the statues themselves were not directly con-

nected with burials. There seems also no reason to believe that they are put up in any order or method; they appear to have been erected on any spot handy to the quarries where there was sufficient earth, or even, as has been seen, in the quarry itself when circumstances permitted.

The South-Eastern Side of Rano Raraku is a problem in itself. The great wall formed by the cliff is like the ramparts of some giant castle rent by vertical fissures. The greatest height, the top of the peak, is about five hundred feet, of which the cliff forms perhaps half, the lower part being a steep but comparatively smooth bank of detritus. Over the grassy surface of this bank are scattered numerous fragments of rock, weighing from a few pounds to many tons, which have fallen down from above. The kitchen tent in our camp at the foot had a narrow escape from being demolished by one of these stones, which nearly carried it away in the impetus of its descent. It has never been suggested that this face of the mountain was being worked; nevertheless, it was subsequently difficult to understand how we lived so long below it, gazing at it daily, before we appreciated the fact that here also, although in much lesser degree, were both finished and embryo images. At last one stone was definitely seen to be in the form of a head, and excavation showed it to be an erected and buried statue. A few other figures were found standing and prostrate, and some unfinished images; these last, however, were in no case being hewn out of solid rock, but wrought into shape out of detached stones. On the whole, it is not probable that this portion was ever a quarry, in the same way as the western side and the interior of the crater. It is, of course, impossible to say what may be hidden beneath the detritus, but the lower part of the cliff is too soft a rock to be satisfactorily hewn, and the workmen appear simply to have seized on fragments which have fallen from above. "Here," they seem to have said, "is a good stone; let us turn it into a statue."

One day, when making a more thorough examination of the slope, our attention was excited by a small level plateau, about half-way up, from which protruded two similar pieces of stone next to one another. They were obviously giant noses of which the nostrils faced the cliff. Digging was bound to follow, but it proved a long business, as the figures it revealed were particularly massive and corpulent. Their position was horizontal, side by side, and the effect, more particularly when looking down at them from the cliff above, was of two great bodies lying in their graves. The thing was a mystery; they were certainly not in a quarry, but if they had once been erect, why had they faced the mountain, instead of conforming to the rule of having their back to it? Orientation could not account for it, as other statues on the same slope were differently placed. Then again, if they had once stood and then fallen, and in proof of this one head was broken off from the trunk, how did it come about that they were lying horizontally on a sloping hill-side? The upper part of the bodies had suffered somewhat from weather, and a small round basin, such as natives use for domestic purposes, had been hollowed out in one abdomen, but the hands were quite sharp and unweathered. We used to scramble up at off moments, and stand gazing down at them trying to read their history.

It became at last obvious they had once been set up with the lower part inserted in the ground to the usual level, and later been intentionally thrown down. For this purpose a level trench must have been cut through the sloping side of the hill at a depth corresponding to the base of the standing images, and into this the figures had fallen. While they lay in the trench with the upper part of the bodies exposed, one had been found a nice smooth stone for household use. A charcoal soil level showed clearly where the surface had been at this epoch, which must have been comparatively recent, as an iron nail was found in it. Finally, a descent of earth had covered all but the noses, leaving them in the condition in which we found them.

This, though a satisfactory explanation as far as it went, did not account for the fact that the figures were facing the mountain, and here for once tradition came to our help. These images had, it was said, marked a boundary; the line of demarcation led between them, from the fissure in the cliff above right down to the middle statue in the great Tongariki terrace. To cross it was death; but as to what the boundary connoted no information was forthcoming; there seemed no great tribal division—the same clans ranged over the whole of the district. When, however, the line is followed through the crevice into the crater, it is found to form on both sides the boundary where the image-making ceased and was probably the line of taboo which preserved the rights of the image-makers. I was later given the cheering information that a certain "devil" frequented the site of my house, which was just on the image side of the boundary, who particularly resented the presence of strangers, and was given to strangling them in the night. The spirits who inhabit the crater are still so unpleasant that my Kanaka maid objected to taking clothes there to wash, even in daylight, till assured that our party would be working within call.

Isolated Statues.—The finished statues, as distinct from those in the quarries, have so far been spoken of under two heads, those which once adorned the ahu and those still standing on the slope of Raraku; there is, however, another class to consider, which, for want of a better name, will be termed the Isolated Statues. It has already been stated that, as Raraku is approached, a number of figures lie by the side of the modern track, others are round the base of the mountain, and yet other isolated specimens are scattered about the island. All these images are prostrate and lie on the surface of the ground, some on their backs and some on their faces. These were the ones which, according to legend, were being moved from the quarries to the ahu by the old lady when she stopped the work in her wrath; or, according to another account, quoted by a visitor before our day, "They walked, and some fell by the way."

There must, we felt, have been roads along which they were taken, but for long we kept a look-out for such without success. At last a lazy Sunday afternoon ride, with no particular object, took one of us to the top of a small hill, some two miles to the west of Raraku. The level rays of the sinking sun showed up the inequalities of the ground, and, looking towards the sea, along the level plain of the south coast, the old track was clearly seen; it was slightly raised over lower ground and depressed somewhat through higher, and along it every few hundred yards lay a statue. Detailed study confirmed this first impression. At times over hard stony ground the trail was lost, but its main drift was indisputable; it was about nine feet or ten feet in width, the embankments were in places two feet above the surrounding ground, and the cuttings three feet deep. The road can be traced from the south-western corner of the mountain, with one or two gaps, nearly to the foot of Rano Kao, but the succession of statues continues only about half the distance. It generally runs some few hundred yards further inland than the present road, but a branch, with a statue, leads down to the ahu of Teatenga on the coast, and, another portion, either a branch or a detour of the main road, also with a statue, goes to the cove of Akahanga with its two large image ahu. There are on this road twenty-seven statues in all, covering a distance of some four miles, but fourteen of them, including two groups of three, are in the first mile. Their heights are from fifteen feet to over thirty feet, but generally over twenty feet.

As a clue had now been obtained, it was comparatively simple to trace two other roads from Raraku. One leads from the crater, and connects it with the western district of the island. It commences at the gap in the mountain wall, in the centre of which an image lies on its face with weird effect, as if descending head foremost into the plain; and runs for a while roughly parallel to the first road but about a mile further inland. It is not quite so regular as the south road, and is marked for a somewhat less distance by a sequence of images, some fourteen in number, which in the same way grow further apart as the distance from the mountain increases. When the succession of statues ceases, the road divides; one track turns to the north-west, and reaches the sea-board through a small pass in the western line of cones; the other continues as far as a more southerly pass in the same succession of heights. In each pass there is a statue.

The third road, which runs from Raraku in a northerly direction, is much shorter than those to the south and west. It has only four statues covering a distance of perhaps a mile, and it then disappears; if, however, the figures round the base of the mountain belonged to it, and they lie in the same direction, it started from the southern corner of the mountain, led in front of the standing statues and across the trail from the crater, before taking its northward route up the eastern plain. The furthest of the images is the largest which has been moved; it lies on its back, badly broken, but the total of the fragments gives a height of thirty-six feet four inches. In addition to these three avenues, there are indications that some of the statues on the south-eastern side of Raraku may have been on a fourth road along that side beneath the cliff.

So far the matter was sufficiently clear, but another problem was still unsolved: if the images were really being moved to their respective ahu all round the coast, how was it that, with very few exceptions, they were all found in the neighbourhood of Raraku? If also they were being moved, what was the method pursued, for some lay on their backs and some on their faces? With the hope of elucidating this great question of the means of transport, we dug under and near one or two of the single figures without achieving our end—nothing was found; but the close study which the work necessitated called attention to the fact that on one of them the lines of weathering could not have been made with the figure in its present horizontal attitude. The rain had evidently collected on the head and run down the back; it must therefore have stood for a considerable time in a vertical position. It was again a noticeable fact that, though some single figures are lying unbroken, others, like the large one on the north road, proved to be so shattered that no amount of normal disintegration or shifting of soil could account for their condition—they had obviously fallen. So wedded, however, were we at this time to the theory that they were in course of transport, that it was seriously considered whether they could have been moved in an upright position. The point was settled by finding one day by the side of the track, some two miles from the mountain, a partially buried head. This was excavated, and a statue found that had been originally set up in a hole and, later, undermined, causing it to fall forward. This was the only instance of an isolated figure where the burial had been to any depth, but in various other cases it was then seen that soil had been removed from the base, and one or two more of the figures had not quite fallen.

When the whole number of the statues on the roads were in

imagination re-erected, it was found that they had all originally stood with their backs to the hill. Rano Raraku was, therefore, approached by at least three magnificent avenues, on each of which the pilgrim was greeted at intervals by a stone giant guarding the way to the sacred mountain (map of roads). One of the ahu on the south coast, Hanga Paukura, has been approached by a similar avenue of five statues facing the visitor. These five images when first seen were a great puzzle, as some of them are so embedded in the earth that their backs are even with the levelled sward in front of the ahu; later there seemed little doubt that, like the two giants on the southeast side of Raraku, trenches had been dug into which they had fallen. Subsequently, a sixth statue was discovered, the other side of a modern wall, weathered and worn away, but of Raraku stone and still upright. This is the only instance of an erect figure to be found elsewhere than on the mountain.

In addition to the images which have stood in these processional roads, there are, excluding one or two figures near the mountain whose *raison d'être* is somewhat doubtful, fourteen isolated statues in various parts of the island, for whose position no certain reason could be found. Some of these may have belonged to inland ahu which have disappeared, or they may be solitary memorials to mark some particular spots, but the greater number appear to have stood near tracks of some sort. Some of these last may have been boundary stones, and in this class may perhaps fall the smaller statue now at the British Museum, which is a very inferior specimen. According to local information it stood almost half-way on the track leading from Vinapu to Mataveri along the bottom of Rano Kao; the hole from which it was dug was pointed out, and our informant declared that he remembered it standing, and that the people used to dance round it. The larger figure at the British Museum was in a unique position, which will be spoken of later.

No statues were, therefore, found of which it could be said that they were in process of being removed, and the mode of transport remains a mystery. An image could be moved down from the quarry by means of banks of earth, and though requiring labour and skill, the process is not inconceivable. Similarly, the figures may have been, and probably were, erected on the terraces in the same way, being hauled up on an embankment of earth made higher than the pedestals and then dropped on them. Near Paro, the ahu where the last statue was overthrown, there is a hillock, and tradition says that a causeway was made from it to the head of the tall figure which stood upon the ahu, and along this the hat was rolled, a piece of lore which seems hardly likely to have been invented by a race having no connection with the statues. But the problem remains, how was the transport carried out along the level? The weight of some amounted to as much as 40 or 50 tons. It would simplify matters very much if there were any reason to suppose that the images were moved, as was the case with the hats, before being wrought, merely as cylinders of stone, in which case it would be possible to pass a rope under and over it, thus parbuckling the stone or rolling it along, but the evidence is all to the contrary. There is no trace whatever of an unfinished image on or near an ahu, while, as we have seen, they are found at all stages in the quarry. Presumably rollers were employed, but there appears never to have been much wood, or material for cordage, in the island, and it is not easy to see how sufficient men could bring strength to bear on the block. Even if the ceremonial roads were used when possible, these fragile figures have been taken to many distant ahu, up hill and down dale, over rough and stony ground, where there is no trace of any road at all.

The natives are sometimes prepared to state that the statues were thrown down by human means, they never have any doubt that they were moved by supernatural power. We were once inspecting an ahu built on a natural eminence; one side was sheer cliff, the other was a slope of 29 feet, as steep as a house roof; near the top a statue was lying. The most intelligent of our guides turned to me significantly. "Do you mean to tell me," he said, "that that was not done by *mana*?" The darkness is not rendered less tantalising by the reflection that could centuries roll away and the old scenes be again enacted before us, the workers would doubtless exclaim in bewildered surprise at our ignorance, "But how could you do it any other way?"

Besides the ceremonial roads and their continuations, there are traces of an altogether different track which is said to run round the whole seaboard of the island. It is considered to be supernatural work, and is known as Ara Mahiva, "ara" meaning road and "Mahiva" being the name of the spirit or deity who made it. On the southern side it has been obliterated in making the present track—it was there termed the "path for carrying fish"; but on the northern and western coasts, where for much of the way it runs on the top of high cliffs, such a use is out of the question. It can be frequently seen there like a long persistent furrow, and where its course has been interrupted by erosion, no fresh track had been made further inland; it terminates suddenly on the broken edge, and resumes its course on the other side. It is best seen in certain lights running up both the western and southern edges of Rano Kao. Its extent and regularity appeared to preclude the idea of landslip. There is no reason to suppose that it is due to the imported livestock, and it has no connection with ahu, or the old native centres of population, yet to have been so worn by naked feet it must constantly have been used. This silent witness to a forgotten past is one of the most mysterious and impressive things on the island.

Mention must finally be made of the crowns or hats which adorned the figures on the ahu. Their full designation is said to be "Hau (hats) hiterau moai," but they are always alluded to merely as "hiterau" or "hitirau."

These coverings for the head were cylindrical in form, the bottom being slightly hollowed out into an oval depression in order to fit on to the head of the image; the depression was not in the centre, but left a larger margin in front, so that the brim projected over the eyes of the figure, a fashion common in native head-dresses. They are said by the present inhabitants to have been kept in place by being wedged with white stones. The top was worked into a boss or knot. The material is a red volcanic tuff found in a small crater on the side of a larger volcano, generally known as Punapau, not far from Cook's Bay. In the crater itself are the old quarries. A few half-buried hats may be seen there, and the path up to it, and for some hundreds of yards from the foot of the mountain, is strewn with them. They are at this stage simply large cylinders, from 4 feet to 8 feet high, from 6 feet to 9 feet across, and they were obviously conveyed to the ahu in this form and there carved into shape. An unwrought cylinder is still lying at a hundred yards from the ahu of Anakena. The finished hats are not more than 3 feet 10 inches to 6 feet in height, with addition of 6 inches to 2 feet for the knob; the measurement across the crown is from about 5 feet 6 inches to 8 feet. The stone is more easily broken and cut than that of the statues, and while many crowns survive, many more have been smashed in falling or used as building materials.

It is a noteworthy fact that the images on Raraku never had hats, nor have any of the isolated statues; they were confined to those on the ahu.

The Script

THE possession of a hieroglyphic script is another Easter Island peculiarity. Today the material is limited to inscriptions on twenty-one wooden tablets, a staff and three or four breastplates. Yet nineteenth century missionaries recorded that inscribed tablets and staves existed in almost every house. The highly stylized hieroglyphs represent such things as birds, fish, plants—and numerous human figures; they are exquisitely cut. Most authorities agree that the islanders had long used the signs only as a form of mnemonic; yet it seems there must have been a time when they formed a true script.

The greatest religious festival in Easter Island was that of

the bird man described in detail by Mrs. Routledge. It was closely
linked with the cult of the god Maké-maké. Usually only war
chiefs competed for the extraordinary privilege of being bird man,
and the successful were allowed to exercise a kind of holy tyranny.
The elaborate rites and the passionate feeling concentrated on the
laying of a sea-bird's egg seem fantastic or absurd. Yet as Alfred
Mértaux says, "The egg was the incarnation of the god Maké-maké
and the tangible expression of religious and social forces of great
intensity. The stake in this struggle for the possession of an egg
was nothing less than divine favour and the sanction of political
power." Many students have commented that archaeology and
anthropology, the past and the present, come together in Easter
Island. This account of a ritual (equally with that in the following
extract) have been included to suggest the nature of emotions,
strange to the modern world, that may have played upon many
of the dumb and lifeless monuments and objects of the prehistoric past.

A GREAT effort was subsequently made to get further information
from Tomenika, more particularly as to the exact method of writing, but he was back in his hut very ill, and all conversation had
once more to be done through the doorway. Every way that could
be thought of was tried to elicit information, but without real success. He did draw two fresh symbols, saying first they were "new"
and then "old," and stating they represented the man who gave
the koro [a feast] but "there was no sign meaning a man." "He did
not know that for ariki [nobility], the old men did," "the words
were new, but the letters were old," "each line represented a koro."
An attempt to get him to reproduce any tau [a kind of tablet] made
by himself was a failure. The answers, on the whole, were so
wandering and contradictory, that after a second visit under those
conditions, making five in all, the prospect of getting anything further of material value did not seem sufficient to justify the risks
to others, however slight. As the last interview drew to a close, I left
the hut for a moment, and leant against the wall outside, racking
my brains to see if there was any question left unasked, any possible
way of getting at the information; but most of what the old man
knew he had forgotten, and what he dimly remembered he was
incapable of explaining. I made one more futile effort, then bade
him good-bye and turned away. It was late afternoon on a day
of unusual calm, everything in the lonely spot was perfectly still,
the sea lay below like a sheet of glass, the sun as a globe of fire

was nearing the horizon, while close at hand lay the old man gradually sinking, and carrying in his tired brain the last remnants of a once-prized knowledge. In a fortnight he was dead.

No detailed systematic study of the tablets has as yet been possible from the point of view of the Expedition, but it seems at present probable that the system was one of memory, and that the signs were simply aids to recollection, or for keeping count like the beads of a rosary. To what extent the figures were used at will, or how far each was associated with a definite idea it is impossible to say. Possibly there was no unvarying method; certain ones may conveniently have been kept for an ever-recurrent factor, as the host in the tau, and in well-known documents, such as "he timo te ako-ako," they would doubtless be reproduced in orthodox succession. But in the tablets which we possess the same figures are continually repeated, and the fact that equivalents were always having to be found for new names, as in that of the fish-man, or ika, suggest that they may have been largely selected by the expert haphazard from a known number. As Tomenika said, "the words were new, but the letters were old," or to quote Kapiera to the same effect, they were "the same picture, but other words." It will be noted how few men are reported to have known each variety of rongo-rongo, and that while Ngaara looked at the tablets of the boys, apparently to see if they were properly cut, it was in the recitation only of the older men that accuracy was insisted on. The names which Bishop Jaussen's [Bishop of Tahiti. He had been sent an inscription as part of a gift from newly converted Easter Islanders] informant assigned to some five hundred figures may or may not be accurate, but whether the native or anyone else could have stated what the signs conveyed is another matter. It is easy to give the term for a knot in a pocket-handkerchief, but no one save the owner can say whether he wishes to remember to pay his life insurance or the date of a tea-party.

In trying to enter into the state of society and of mind which evolved the tablets there are two points worth noticing. Firstly, the Islanders are distinctly clever with their hands and fond of representing forms. Setting aside the large images, the carving of the small wooden ones is very good, and the accuracy of the tablet designs is wonderful. Then they have real enjoyment in reciting categories of words; for example, in recounting folk-tales, opportunity was always gleefully taken of any mention of feasting to go through the whole of the food products of the island. In the same way, if a hero went from one locality to another, the name of every place *en route* would be rolled out without any further object than the mere pleasure of giving a string of names. This form of recitation appears to affect them aesthetically, and the mere continuation of sound to be a pleasure. Given, therefore, that it was desired to remember lists of words, whether categories of names or correct forms of prayer, the repetition would be a labour of love, and to draw figures as aids to recollection would be very natural.

Nevertheless, the signs themselves have no doubt a history, which as such, even apart from interpretation, may prove to be signposts in our search for the origin of this mysterious people.

The Bird Cult

Knowledge of the tablets was confined to a few, and formed a comparatively small element of life in the island; the whole of social existence revolved round the bird cult, and it was the last of the old order to pass away. The main object of the cult was to obtain the first egg of a certain migratory sea-bird, and the rites were connected with the western headland, Rano Kao. Little has yet been said of this volcano, but, from the scenic point of view, it is the most striking portion of the island. Its height is 1,300 feet, and it possesses a crater two-thirds of a mile across, at the bottom of which is a lake largely covered with weeds and plant-life. On the eastward, or landward face, the mountain, as already explained, slopes downward with a smooth and grassy incline, and the other three sides have been worn by the waves into cliffs over 1,000 feet in height. On the outermost side the sea has nearly forced its way into the crater itself; and the ocean is now divided from the lake at this point by only a narrow edge, along which it would be possible but not easy to walk with safety. At some near date, as geological ages reckon, the island will have a magnificent harbour. Off this part of the coast are three little islets, outlying portions of the original mountain, which have as yet withstood the unceasing blows of the ocean. Their names are Motu Nui, Motu Iti, and Motu Kao-kao, and on them nest the sea-birds which have for unknown centuries played so important a part in the history of the island. On the mainland, immediately opposite these islets, there is on the top of the cliff a deserted stone village; it is known as Orongo, and in it the Islanders awaited the coming of the birds. It consists of nearly fifty dwellings arranged in two rows, both facing the sea, and partly overlapping; the lower row terminates just before the narrowest part of the crater wall is reached. The final houses are built among an outcrop of rocks; they are betwixt two groups of stones, and have in front of them a small natural pavement. The stones nearest the cliff look as if at any moment they might join their brethren in headlong descent to the shore below. Both the upstanding rocks and pavement are covered with carvings; some of them are partly obliterated by time, and can only be seen in a

good light, but the ever-recurrent theme is a figure with the body
of a man and the head of a bird; portions of the carvings are
covered by the houses, and they therefore antedate them.

The whole position is marvellous, surpassing the wildest scenes
depicted in romance. Immediately at hand are these strange relics
of a mysterious past; on one side far beneath is the dark crater lake;
on the other, a thousand feet below, swells and breaks the Pacific
Ocean; it girdles the islets with a white belt of foam, and extends, in
blue unbroken sweep, till it meets the ice-fields of the Antarctic.
The all-pervading stillness of the island culminates here in a silence
which may be felt, broken only by the cry of the sea-birds as they
circle round their lonely habitations.

The stone village formed the scene of some of our earliest work
during our first residence at the Manager's house; for some weeks.
weather permitting, we rode daily up the mountain, an ascent
which took about fifty minutes, and spent the day on the top
studying the remains, and picking the brains of our native companions. Some of the houses have been destroyed in order to obtain
the painted slabs within, but most are in fair, and some in perfect,
preservation. The form of construction suitable to the low ground
has perhaps been tried here and abandoned, for some of the foundation-stones, pierced with the holes to support the superstructure of
stick and grass, are built into the existing dwellings. The present
buildings are well adapted to such a wind-swept spot; they are
made of stone laminae, with walls about 6 feet thick; the inside
walls are generally lined with vertical slabs, and horizontal slabs
form the roof.

The greater number are built at the back into rising ground,
and their sides and top are covered with earth; the natives call
them not "haré," or houses, but "ana," or caves. Where space per-
mits it, the form is boat-shaped, but some have been adapted to
natural contours. The dwellings vary in shape and size, from 52
feet by 6 feet to 8 feet by 4 feet; the height within varies from 4
feet to over 6 feet, but it is the exception to be able to stand upright.
In some cases they open out of one another, and not unfrequently
there is a hatch between two through which food could be passed.
The doorway, with its six foot of passage, is just large enough to
admit a man. Into each of them, armed with ends of candles, we
either crawled on hands and knees, or wriggled like serpents, according to our respective heights. The slabs lining the wall, which
are just opposite the doorway, and thus obtain a little light, are
frequently painted; some of them have bird and others native
designs, but perhaps the most popular is a European ship, sometimes in full sail, and once with a sailor aloft in a red shirt. Inside
the houses we found the flat, sea-worn boulders which are used

as pillows and often incised with rough designs; there were also a
few obsidian spear heads, or mataa, and once or twice sphagnum
from the crater, which was used for caulking boats, and also as
a sponge to retain fresh water when at sea. Outside many of the
doors are small stone-lined holes, which we cleared out and examined. They measure roughly rather under 2 feet across by some
15 inches in depth. Our guides first told us that they were "ovens,"
but, as no ash was found, it seems probable that their second
thoughts were right, and they were used to contain stores.

The groups of dwellings have various names, and are associated
with the particular clans, who, it is said, built them. One house,
which stands near the centre of the village, Taurarenga by name,
is particularly interesting as having been the dwelling of the
statue Hoa-haka-nanaia, roughly to be translated as "Breaking
Wave," now resident under the portico of the British Museum. Lying
about near by were two large stones, which had originally served
as foundations for the thatched type of dwelling, but had apparently
been converted into doorposts for the house of the image; on one
of them a face had been roughly carved. The statue is not of Raraku
stone, and it will be realised how entirely exceptional it is to find a
statue under cover and in such a position. The back and face were
painted white, with the "tracings" in red. The bottom contracts, and
was embedded in the earth, though a stone suspiciously like a
pedestal is built into a near wall. The house had to be broken down
in order to get the figure out. According to the account of the missionaries, three hundred sailors and two hundred Kanakas were
required to convey it down the mountain to H.M.S. *Topaze* in Cook's
Bay. The memory of the incident is fast fading, but our friend Viriamo repeated in a quavering treble the song of the sailors as they
hauled down their load. The figure is some eight feet high and
weighs about four tons.

Day by day, as we worked, we gazed down on the islets. The
outermost, which, as its name Motu Nui signifies, is also the largest,
is more particularly connected with the bird story, which we were
gradually beginning to grasp, and at last the call to visit it could no
longer be resisted. It was not an easy matter, for *Mana* was away;
the boats of the natives left a good deal to be desired in the way of
seaworthiness, and it was only possible to make the attempt on a
fine day. Finally, on arrival at the island, it required not a little
agility to jump on to a ledge of rocks at the second the boat rose
on the crest of the waves, before it again sank on a boiling and
surging sea till the heads of the crew were many feet below the
landing-place. We managed, however, between us to get there three
times in all. Once, when I was there without S., there was an anx-

ious moment on re-embarking. No one quite knew what happened. Some of the crew said that the gunwale of the boat, as she rose on a wave, caught under an overhanging shelf of rock, others were of the opinion that the sudden weight of the last man, who at that moment leapt into the boat, upset her balance; anyway, this tale was very nearly never written. Once landed on the island, the surface is comparatively level and presents no difficulties; it is about five acres in extent, the greater part is covered with grass, and in every niche and cranny of the rock are seabirds' nests. By a large bribe of tobacco one of the most active old men was induced to accompany us, and to point out the sites of interest. Later, we followed up the story at Raraku, and so little by little at many times, in divers places, and from various people was gathered the story of the bird cult which follows.

Not many sea-birds frequent this part of the Pacific, but on Motu Nui some seven species find an abiding-place. Some stay for the whole year, some come for the winter, and yet others for the summer. Among the last is a kind known to the natives as manu-tara [sooty-tern]; it arrives in September, the spring of the southern hemisphere. The great object of life in Easter was to be the first to obtain one of the newly laid eggs of this bird. It was too solemn a matter for there to be any general scramble. Only those who belonged to the clan in the ascendancy for the time being could enter on the quest. Sometimes one group would keep it in their hands for years, or they might pass it on to a friendly clan. This selection gave rise, as might be expected, to burnings of hearts; the matter might be, and probably often was, settled by war. One year the Marama were inspired with jealousy because the Miru had chosen the Ngaure as their successors, and burnt down the house of Ngaara. This was, perhaps, the beginning of the fray when the old Ariki was carried off captive.

The fortunate clan, or clans, for sometimes several combined, left nothing to chance; in fact, as soon as one year's egg had been found, the incoming party made sure of their right of way by taking up their abode at the foot of Rano Kao—namely, at Mataveri. Here there were a number of the large huts with stone foundations; in these they resided, with their wives and families. One of our old gentlemen friends first saw the light in a Mataveri dwelling, when his people were in residence, or, to use the proper phraseology, when his clan were "the Ao." This name "ao" is also given to a large paddle, as much as 6 feet in length, used principally, if not exclusively, in connection with bird rites and dancing at Mataveri. In some specimens a face is fully depicted on the handle; in others the features have degenerated to a raised line merely indicating the eyebrows and nose. There are pictures of it on slabs in the Orongo houses, in which the face is adorned with vertical stripes of red and white after the native manner, as described by the early voyagers.

Naturally the months passed at Mataveri were occupied by the residents in feasting as well as in dancing, and equally naturally the victims were human. It was to grace one of these gatherings, when the Ureohei were the Ao, that the mother of Hotu, the Miru, was slain in a way which he considered outraged the decencies of life, and it was in revenge for another Mataveri victim that the last statues were thrown down. It is told that the destined provender for one meal evaded that fate by hiding in the extreme end of a hut, which was so long and dark that she was never found. Some of these repasts took place in a cave in the sea-cliff near at hand. Here the ocean has made great caverns in a wall of lava, into which the waves surge and break with booming noise and dashing spray. The recess which formed the banqueting-hall is just above high-water mark, and is known as "Ana Kai-tangata," or Eat-man Cave. The roof is adorned with pictures of birds in red and white; one of these birds is drawn over a sketch of a European ship, showing that they are not of very ancient date.

When July approached, the company, or some of them, wound their way up the western side of the hill, along the ever-narrowing summit to the village of Orongo; the path can just be traced in certain lights, and is known as the "Road of the Ao." They spent their time while awaiting the birds in dancing each day in front of the houses; food was brought up by the women, of whom Viriamo was one. The group of houses at the end among the carved rocks was taboo during the festival, for they were inhabited by the rongo-rongo men, the western half being apportioned to the experts from Hotu Iti, the eastern to those from Kotuu. "They chanted all day; they stopped an hour to eat, that was all." They came at the command of Ngaara, but it is noteworthy that he himself never appeared at Orongo, though he sometimes paid a friendly call at Mataveri.

A short way down the cliff immediately below Orongo is a cave known as "Haka-rongo-manu," or "listening for the birds"; here men kept watch day and night for news from the islet below.

The privilege of obtaining the first egg was a matter of competition between members of the Ao, but the right to be one of the competitors was secured only by supernatural means. An "ivi-atua," a divinely gifted individual, of the kind who had the gift of prophecy, dreamed that a certain man was favoured by the gods, so that if he entered for the race he would be a winner, or, in technical parlance, become a bird-man, or "tangata-manu." The victor, on being successful, was ordered to take a new name, which formed part of the revelation, and this bird-name was given to the year in which victory was achieved, thus forming an easily remembered system of chronology. The nomination might be taken up at once or not for many years; if not used by the original nominee, it might descend to his son or grandson. If a man did not win, he might try again, or say that "the ivi-atua was a liar," and retire from the contest. Women were never nominated, but the ivi-atua might be male or female, and; needless to say, was rewarded with presents of food. There were four "gods" connected with the eggs—Hawa-tuu-také-také, who was "chief of the eggs," and Maké-maké, both of whom were males; there were also two females, Vie Hoa, the wife of Hawa, and Vie Kenatea. Each of these four had a servant, whose names were given, and who were also supernatural beings. Those going to take the eggs recited the names of the gods before meat, inviting them to partake.

The actual competitors were men of importance, and spent their time with the remainder of the Ao in the stone houses of the village of Orongo; they seleced servants to represent them and await the coming of the birds in less comfortable quarters in the islet below. These men, who were known as "hopu," went to the islet when the Ao went up to Orongo, or possibly rather later. Each made up his provisions into a "pora," or securely bound bundle of reeds; he then swam on the top of the packet, holding it with one arm and propelling himself with the remaining arm and both legs. An incantation, which was recited to us, was said by him before starting. In one instance, the ivi-atua, at the same time that he gave the nomination, prophesied that the year that it was taken up a man should be eaten by a large fish. The original recipient never availed himself of it, but on his death-bed told his son of the prophecy. The son, Kilimuti, undeterred by it, entered for the race and sent two men to the islet; one of them started to swim there with his pora, but was never heard of again, and it was naturally said that the prophecy had been fulfilled. Kilimuti wasted no regret over the misfortune, obtained another servant, and secured the egg; he died while the Expedition was on the island.

The hopu lived together in a large cave of which the entrance is nearly concealed by grass. The inside, however, is light and airy; it measures 19 feet by 13, with a height of over 5 feet, and conspicuous among other carvings in the centre of the wall is a large ao more than 7 feet in length. A line dividing the islet between Kotuu and Hotu Iti passed through the centre of the cave, and also through another cave nearer the edge of the islet; in this latter there was at one time a statue about 2 feet high known as Titahanga-o-te-henua, or The Boundary of the Land. As bad weather might prevent fresh consignments of food during the weeks of waiting, the men carefully dried on the rocks the skins of the bananas and potatoes which they had brought with them, to be consumed in case of necessity. It was added with a touch appreciated by those acquainted with Easter Island, that, if the man who thus practised foresight was not careful, others who had no food would steal it when he was not looking.

The approach of the manu-tara can be heard for miles, for their cry is their marked peculiarity, and the noise during nesting is said to be deafening; one incised drawing of the bird shows it with open beak, from which a series of lines spreads out fanwise, obviously representing the volume of sound; names in imitation of these sounds were given to children, such as "Piruru," "Wero-wero," "Ka-ara-ara." It is worth noting that the coming of the tara inaugurates the deep-sea fishing season; till their arrival all fish living in twenty or thirty fathoms were considered poisonous. The birds on first alighting tarried only a short time; immediately on their departure the hopu rushed out to find the egg, or, according to another account, the rushing out of the hopu frightened away the birds. The gods intervened in the hunt, so that the man who was not destined to win went past the egg even when it lay right in his path. The first finder rushed up to the highest point of the islet, calling to his employer by his new name, "Shave your head, you have got the egg." The cry was taken up by the watchers in the cave on the mainland, and the fortunate victor, beside himself with joy, proceeded to shave his head and paint it red, while the losers showed their grief by cutting themselves with *mataa*.

The defeated hopu started at once to swim from the island to the shore, while the winner, who was obliged to fast while the egg was in his possession, put it in a little basket, and, going down to the landing-rock, dipped it into the sea. One meaning of the word hopu is "wash." He then tied the basket round his forehead and was able to swim quickly, as the gods were with him. At this stage sometimes accidents occurred, for if the sea was rough, an unlucky swimmer might be dashed on the rocks and killed. In one instance, it was said, only one man escaped with his life, owing, as he reported, to his having been warned by Maké-maké not to make the attempt. When the hopu arrived on the mainland, he handed over the egg to his employer, and a tangata-rongo-rongo tied round the arm which had taken it a fragment of red tapa and also a piece of the tree known as "ngau-ngau," reciting meanwhile the appropriate words. The finding was announced by a fire being lit on the landward side of the summit of Rano Kao on one of two sites, according to whether the Ao came from the west or east side of the island.

It will be remembered that on the rocks which terminate the settlement of Orongo the most numerous of the carvings is the figure of a man with the head of a bird; it is in a crouching attitude with the hands held up, and is carved at every size and angle according to the surface of the rock. It can still be counted one hundred and eleven times, and many specimens must have disappeared: all knowledge of its meaning is lost. The figure may have represented one of the egg gods, but it seems more probable that each one was a memorial to a birdman; and this presumption is strengthened by the fact that in at least three of the carvings the hand is holding an egg. The history of another figure, a small design which is also very frequent, still survives and corroborates this by analogy; within living memory it was the custom for women of the island to come up here and be immortalised by having one of these small figures ("Ko Mari") cut on the rock by a professional expert. We know, therefore, that conventional forms were used as memorials of certain definite persons.

The bird-man, having obtained the egg, took it in his hand palm upwards, resting it on a piece of tapa, and danced with a rejoicing company down the slope of Rano Kao and along the south coast, a procedure which is known as "haka epa," or "make shelf," from the position of the hand with regard to the egg. If, however, the winner belonged to the western clans, he generally went to Anakena for the next stage, very possibly because, as was explained, he was afraid to go to Hotu Iti; some victors also went to special houses in their own district, otherwise the company went along the southern shore till they reached Rano Raraku.

Amongst the statues standing on its exterior slope, there is shown at the south-west corner the foundations of a house. This is the point which would first be approached from the southern coast, and here the bird-man remained for a year, five months of which were spent in strict taboo. The egg, which was still kept on tapa, was hung up inside the house and blown on the third day, a morsel of tapa being put inside. The victor did not wash, and spent his time in "sleeping all day, only coming out to sit in the shade." His correct head-dress was a crown made of human hair; it was known as "hau oho," and if it was not worn the aku-aku would be angry. The house was divided into two, the other half being occupied by a man who was called an ivi-atua, but was of an inferior type to the one gifted with prophecy, and apparently merely a poor relation of the hero; there were two cooking-places, as even he might not share that of the bird-man. Food was brought as gifts, especially the first sugar-cane, and these offerings seem to have been the sole practical advantage of victory; those who did not contribute were apt to have their houses burnt. The bird-man's wife came to Raraku, but dwelt apart, as for the first five months she could not enter her husband's house, nor he hers, on pain of death. A few yards below the bird-man's house is an ahu consisting merely of a low rough wall built into the mountain, the ground above it being levelled and paved. It was reserved for the burial of bird-men; they were the uncanny persons whose ghosts might do unpleasant things—they were safer hidden under stones. The name Orohié is given to the whole of this corner of the mountain, with its houses, its ahu, and its statues. To this point the figures led which were round the base of the hill. If they were re-erected, they would stand with their backs not to the mountain, but to Orohié. As the bird-man gazed lazily forth from the shade of his house, above him were the quarries with their unfinished work, below him were the bones of his dead predecessors, while on every hand giant images stood for ever in stolid calm. It is difficult to escape from the question, Were the statues on the mountain those of bird-men?

The hopu also retired into private life; if he were of the Ao, he could come to Orohié, but he might, if he wished, reside in his own house, which was in that case divided by a partition through which food was passed; it might not be eaten with his right hand, as that had taken the egg. His wife and children were also kept in seclusion and forbidden to associate with others.

The new Ao had meanwhile taken up their abode at Mataveri. From here a few weeks after their arrival they went formally to Motu Nui to obtain the young manu-tara, known from their cry as "piu." After the brief visit of the birds when the first egg was laid, they absented themselves from the islet for a period varyingly reported as from three days to a month. On their return they laid plentifully, and, as soon as the nestlings were hatched, the men of the celebrating clan carried them to the mainland, swimming with them in baskets bound round the forehead after the manner of the first egg. They were then taken in procession round the island, or, according to another account, only as far as Orohié. If was not until the piu had been obtained that it was permissible to eat the eggs, and they were then consumed by the subservient clans only, not by the Ao. The first two or three eggs, it was explained, were "given to God"; to eat them would prove fatal. Some of the young manu tara were kept in confinement till they were full grown, when a piece of red tapa was tied round the wing and leg, and they were told, "Kaho ki te hiva," "Go to the world outside." There was no objection to eating the young birds. The tara departed from Motu Nui about March, but a few stragglers remained; we saw one bird and obtained eggs at the beginning of July, but the natives failed to get any for us in August. When in the following spring the new bird-man had achieved his egg, he brought it to Orohié and was given the old one, which he buried in a gourd in a cranny of

Rano Raraku; sometimes, however, it was thrown into the sea, or kept and buried with its original owner. The new man then took the place of his predecessor, who returned to ordinary life.

The last year that the Ao went to Orongo, which is known as "Rokunga," appears to have been 1866 or 1867. The names of twelve subsequent years are given, during which the competition for the egg continued, and it was still taken to be interred at Raraku. The cult thus survived in a mutilated form the conversion of the island to Christianity, which was completed in 1868; it is said that once the missionaries saw the Ao dancing with the egg outside their door in Hanga Roa and "told the people it was the Devil." It must have been celebrated even after the assembly of the remains of the clans into one place, which occurred about the same time, but it was finally crushed by the secular exploiters of the island, whose house at Mataveri, that of the present manager, rests on the foundation-stones of the cannibal habitation. The cult admittedly degenerated in later years. A new practice arose of having more than one bird-man, with other innovations. The request to be given the names of as many bird-years as could be remembered met with an almost embarrassing response, eighty-six being quoted straight away; some of these may be the official names of bird-men and not represent a year, but they probably do so in most cases; chronological sequence was achieved with fair certainty for eleven years prior to the final celebration at Orongo. In addition to the bird-name, the names of both winner and hopu were ascertained, with those of their respective clans.

T. G. STREHLOW

The Past in the Present: Caves and Hunters

THE Aranda is a large aboriginal tribe of central Australia. This description of a visit by Aranda hunters to one of their sacred caves is included here because it concerns a living people of the Pacific. No one, however, can read it without recalling the hunters and artists of the Upper Palaeolithic Age of Europe (p. 204, I).

❧

ARANDA myths are rarely elaborate in form. They are simple and brief accounts of the lives of the totemic ancestors of a given group in the tribe. They are handed down through word of mouth by the old leaders of a group to the younger generation of initiated men, usually on the occasion of a visit to the local sacred cave where the *tjurunga* sticks and stones are kept.

A brief description of such a visit may throw some light on the importance of this totemic ceremonial centre in helping to preserve the original myth in its traditional form through the passing centuries.

Let us suppose the scene of such a visit to be the sacred cave of Ulamba, an isolated mountain formation several miles north-east of the highest peaks in the Western MacDonnell system. A party of men is ready to set off for the cave. Spears and all other chattels are left behind at a small soak near the edge of the plain and the men move off in silence towards the steep peak on whose slopes the cave is situated. There is only one correct track by which it may be approached, a track which through long disuse has become almost invisible; hence the oldest and most experienced man of

From *Aranda Traditions*. Carlton: Melbourne University Press; 1947, pp. 1-4. By permission of G. H. Strehlow and the Melbourne University Press.

the totemic group leads the way, while the remainder follow in
single file. All are silent; for the cave must be approached with awe
and reverence.

From time to time the leader halts, points out rocks and trees
which figure in the legend of the Ulamba ancestor, and neatly explains their significance by means of sign-language. No questions
may be asked, the young men must be content with such explana-
tory remarks as the leader is prepared to give them. If these are
insufficient for a complete grasp of the myth, the young men must
wait respectfully until another of these rare opportunities presents
itself.

After half an hour's steep climbing the leader stops. He points
towards a huge round boulder which is resting on a smooth ledge
of rock above them. The boulder has an opening in it; and the
leader signals that it was from this rock and through this very
opening that the Ulamba ancestor first burst into life. Still higher
up another rock represents the body of a bird-totem ancestor who
used to hide there, afraid lest the Ulamba chief should kill him. A
little further on the party comes upon a confused heap of rocks
which marks one of the night camps of the Ulamba ancestor: the
fallen rocks are the bodies of his human victims whom he had
killed with his spears in order to make a meal of their "sweet"
flesh. A magnificent view can be gained from here of Mt. Hay,
whose blue mass dominates the dark sea of mulga in the east; of
Mt. Sonder and Mt. Zeil, the two highest peaks in Central Australia,
which raise their pale blue summits on the western horizon; and
of the long line of massed parallel ranges to the south which constitute the Western MacDonnells. The leader explains that, in the
beginning, the Ulamba ancestor often used to stand here on cold
mornings, and scan the horizon around with his keen eyes for
human victims. Finally he had set out over the low pass in the first
range to the south towards the territory now held by the Western
Aranda; but before plunging down to the basin of the Upper Ormis-
ton on the other side, he had paused on the saddle of the mountain
for a brief moment and looked back regretfully towards his native
Ulamba. Finally, the leader directs the gaze of his followers to a
prominent conical hill just below the narrow pass: this represents
the body of the ancestor when he returned to his home from his
last trail.

The party is now close to the cave. At a signal from the leader
every man stoops down and picks up a handful of sticks, stones,
or pine needles. They turn around a sharp corner; the cave suddenly bursts into view; stones and sticks and pine needles are flung
towards it: the spirits of the ancestors must be warned of the approach of human visitors, for to disturb them rudely means to

court their displeasure, and this may result in a sudden death in the near future.

The cave itself consists of two huge boulders piled high upon each other. The dark bottom mass is the body of the Ulamba ancestor himself: thus had he stretched himself out for his final sleep when he returned home from his last venture. Mortally wounded by his victim, he had struggled back to his own home; nowhere else would he close his death-dim eyes. His father had awaited him here and had cast himself down in grief over the prostrate body of his son. They had changed into great rocks, filled with the seeds of life.

The party halts. In the narrow cleft between the two boulders rest the sacred *tjurunga*. At a signal from the leader, the party sits down in a half-circle on a convenient ledge of rock at the base of the cave. Two hundred feet below them, at the bottom of a steep ravine, several slender white-barked gums are to be seen pointing upwards towards the cave: they represent spears which the Ulamba ancestor had once hurled at his victims.

The leader raises himself to the level of the cave by climbing up on three little stone steps in the lower of the two great boulders. He removes the stones with which the narrow opening has been skilfully blocked up to keep out rain-storms from the south, and also to prevent animals from entering the cave. These stones, it should be added, also serve the purpose of hiding the cave from the eyes of strangers and robbers. He takes out several bundles of *tjurunga*, closely wrapped around with hair-string, and hands them to the men waiting below, who place them on a bed of grass and leaves so that they shall not touch the ground.

Then the leader steps down, takes up each bundle in turn, unwinds the hair-string, and chants the song which relates the wanderings of the Ulamba ancestor. Gradually the party takes up the verses of the chant; and in low, hushed voices their song bursts upon the silence that has enfolded the cave up to this moment. The *tjurunga* have now been unwrapped. They are spread out side by side; each represents the ancestor at a different stage of his career, and hence has a special verse of the chant assigned to it. The leader takes up each *tjurunga* in turn, chants the words appropriate to it, and hands it around for inspection. Each man presses the *tjurunga* affectionately to his body, and then passes it on to his neighbour.

III

*Britain
and Europe*

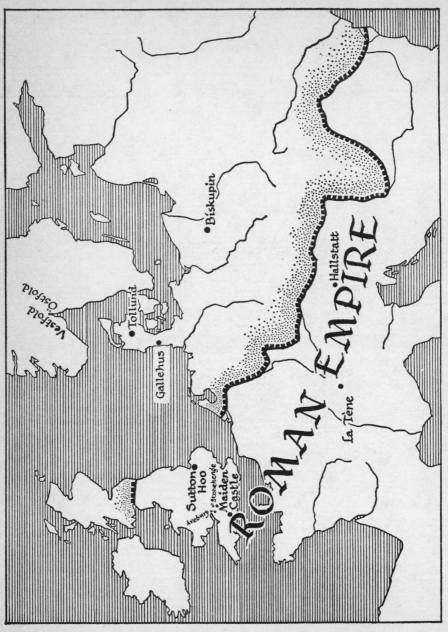

ROMAN EMPIRE

Biskupin

Vestfold
Osfold

Tollund

Gallehus

Hallstatt

La Tène

Sutton
Hoo

Avebury
Stonehenge
Maiden
Castle

INTRODUCTORY

BY the beginning of the second millennium B.C. there had been a thousand years of urbanized civilization in south-west Asia and Egypt, and five hundred years in India. Civilization had also taken root in Asia Minor and south-eastern Europe, and was even beginning to spread westward along the Mediterranean. But Europe to the west and north of these advanced areas remained in the hands of Neolithic farmers living in steadings, hamlets and villages. In the second millennium, probably due at first to the influence of traders from more civilized lands seeking for metal and other raw materials, these Europeans began to use copper and bronze, and in time to develop a stratified type of society, with ruling élites dominating the old peasantries. It was these rulers who acquired the bronze ornaments and weapons. The process was probably encouraged by the spread into Europe, perhaps from southern Russia, of various of the early Indo-European-speaking peoples whose expansion also took them to Greece, Asia Minor and India (pp. 61, I, 243, II).

Britain was by no means so far behind in this development as her outlying position might lead one to expect. This was because there were valuable sources of gold and copper in Ireland, and, more important still, of tin (needed for bronze) in Cornwall. (Other important sources of European ores lay in Austria, Hungary and Bohemia.) The early Indo-European intrusion into Britain is thought to be represented by an element in the various invading groups known as the Beaker peoples (p. 403, II). They introduced the practice of burial under circular mounds—or round barrows—which continued in slightly varying forms through most of the Bronze Age.

For some centuries the amount of bronze in use was small, but by 1500 B.C. some of the more successful pastoral and trading societies had build up what can rank as a true Bronze Age culture.

One of the most prosperous occupied the good light pasture of the chalk country of southern England. These Wessex people, who made Stonehenge the greatest piece of prehistoric architecture in Europe, had trading contacts with much of Europe and the Mediterranean—including Mycenaean Greece (p. 387, II).

Meanwhile, although Scandinavia had lagged behind Britain at the beginning of the Bronze Age, Denmark and adjacent territories began to prosper—chiefly as a result of the demand for Baltic amber. The Danish peoples grew very prosperous indeed, and during the end of the second millennium B.C. and the beginning of the first, decked themselves with ornate and often massive ornaments of bronze and gold, and carried handsome weapons.

During the European Late Bronze Age of this last millennium B.C. supplies of bronze became more abundant, techniques for working it more proficient, and its distribution by travelling merchants better organized. It was during this period that Britain began to be invaded by Celtic-speaking peoples, more dependent on agriculture than their predecessors. These invasions continued after the adoption of iron—a far more abundant metal which, once its smelting had been mastered, at last made it possible for quite humble people to have good metal implements.

I. *Early Antiquaries and Their Work*

MUCH of the interest in this field of British and European archaeology lies not so much in the remains of antiquity themselves, but
in the antiquaries who delighted in them. The progress of their
knowledge and skills has already been quite fully described (pp.
14, 24, I), but is better appreciated at closer quarters.

T. D. KENDRICK

John Leland—and the Thieving Franciscans

HE [Leland] describes the library at Wells as notably rich in ancient
books, and another library that he sincerely admired was that of
the Abbey of Glastonbury. He began his stay by resting, for he
arrived tired by his studies; but when Richard Whyting, the last
Abbot of Glastonbury, showed him the library, as a great privilege,
Leland's enthusiasm at once returned. "It contained, I suppose,
the richest collection in Britain of books on our church history; the

From *British Antiquity*. London: Methuen & Co. Ltd.; 1950, pp. 51-2, 55. By permission of Methuen & Co. Ltd.

mere sight of this incredible series of most ancient books inspired
me, and for a while I stood lost in wonder on the threshold. I spent
days examining the shelves." This was a happy experience; but
there were others of a different kind, such as his visit to the library
of the Franciscans at Oxford, where he wanted to see the books
left by Robert Grosseteste. He said: "I was at once obstructed by
some asses who brayed about nobody being able to see the library
except the Warden and the Bachelors of the college; but I persisted,
and waived my royal commission in their face, and came very
near to using force. Then one of the asses, grumbling a good deal,
at last reluctantly opened the doors for me. Ye Gods! What did I
find there! Dust, cobwebs, moths, cockroaches, mould, and filth. I
even found some books, but I wouldn't willingly have given three-
pence for the lot! And it is this wonderful mass of rubbish that
the Oxford Franciscans guard so jealously; for, needless to say, all
Grosseteste's books, once a most valuable collection, have gone,
stolen by the monks themselves. This will show bishops how foolish
it is to bequeath important books to friars of this sort." . . .

Leland did not look at the antiquities of pre-Conquest Britain
with more than the ordinary interest he took in everything else. A
few Arthurian sites, of course, like the camp of Camelot (Cadbury)
seemed to him to be of special significance, because they had a
bearing on the veracity of the British History; other archaeological
remains he took as he found them. He visited the Roman wall and
noted the existence of the turf wall; he describes Caerleon, Caer-
went, Richborough, and Cirencester, and finds in many other
Roman towns are recorded; he made a long and most delightful
list of the Romano-British sculptures he saw at Bath; he was interested in Roman coins. He recognized Roman tiles, which he called
"long Briton bricks," in masonry, that therefore seemed to him to
be early. He knew Watling Street was used as a Roman highway,
but he probably regarded it as of British origin, as he did the
Fosseway. He recognized Offa's Dyke at several points of its course,
and he visited the group of menhirs known as the Devil's Arrows
near Borough Bridge in Yorkshire, which he thought to be a Roman
trophy by the side of Watling Street. He took considerable interest
in hill-forts, the camps "of the men of war," and realized that some
of them were pre-Roman. Silbury Hill did not arouse his curiosity,
and he did not mention a visit to Stonehenge, though he passed
close by and knew the legend about it. He recorded chance discoveries reported to him; the gold sword, sword-harness and spurs
from Kyloe, Northumberland, the monks' garments dug up at
Bangor-on-Dee, and the wonderful gold helmet studded with gems
found at Harlaxton, Lincs.

T. D. KENDRICK

William Camden

THERE can be no doubt that the first man possessed of the requisite
generalship and judgment was William Camden, the great antiquary whose name is as familiar as that of Leland. Camden rejected
the discursive Harrisonian model, and in setting himself the task
of succeeding where Leland had failed [p. 15, I] he saw that what
was needed was not a mass of miscellaneous information, but the
systematic handling of the material, whether it were already familiar or the results of new fieldwork. By one book, while still a
young man, he raised topographical studies in Britain to a new
dignity and usefulness.

William Camden (1551-1623) was a young schoolmaster at
Westminster, aged thirty-five, when he published the *Britannia,*
his first book. His father came from the Midlands and his mother
of a Cumberland family, and he had been educated at Oxford.
He tells us that between leaving Oxford and taking up his master-
ship at Westminster at the age of twenty-four he had travelled
over a considerable part of Britain in order to visit antiquities,
for he had been interested in the past ever since he had been a
schoolboy. He was able to continue his investigations in the Westminster holidays, and it seems that even in these early days he
had acquired a knowledge of Anglo-Saxon and Welsh. His talents
as an antiquary were recognized when he was still a very young
man, but the visit of Abraham Ortelius to England in 1577 was
the most important event of his first years at Westminster, for it
was Ortelius who advised him "to restore Britain to Antiquity, and
Antiquity to Britain" by editing his topographical collections in
the form of an antiquarian survey of the whole country, just as
Ortelius also urged Humphrey Lhuyd to use his equally valuable
place name and historical material.

Camden's *Britannia* is not an easy book to discuss because
even in the author's lifetime it changed from a small octavo volume to a robust and copiously illustrated folio of 860 pages, and
~~~~~~~~~~~~~~~~~~
Ibid., pp. 143-5.

we to-day who use the great three- or four-volume editions of 1789
and 1806 with their heavy apparatus of supplements and ad-
denda of all kinds, have naturally enough almost lost sight of
the book's beginnings. The scope of Camden's survey was, however, from the start ambitious. Leland had confined himself to
England and Wales; Camden included Scotland and Ireland, and
outlying islands from the Shetlands (his Ultima Thule) to the
Scilly Islands and the Channel Islands, and to Ushant and Oleron,
and the islands of the Frisian coast. It was not possible for him
to see all these places for himself, and he depended on others for
help; indeed, at his fame grew, he found himself in touch with
such a useful band of local correspondents that, even though he
sometimes edited their work without actual reference to the monuments they were describing, the *Britannia* has throughout to a most
creditable extent the appearance of being work done on the spot.
But Camden was himself a very experienced traveller, and he had
seen much of England, certainly the eastern counties and Lancashire and Yorkshire, before the *Britannia* was published; before
his last edition he had been to Wessex, and Wales, and to the
north midlands, and to Cumberland. He was therefore not merely
an efficient organizer, but a practical man undertaking the antiquarian description of a land that he had taken the trouble to
know very well.

It is possible that a first reaction on its publication in 1586
was that antiquarian interests were obscuring the learning expected
of a sixteenth century schoolmaster, for Camden expanded the
second edition not only with new topographical information but
with additional references to the classics and appropriate samples
of a schoolman's wisdom. Nevertheless, the topographical theme
prevailed, and, the plan of his book being clear to him from the
start, Camden made no important alterations in its essential structure. It opened with a general geographical note on the British
Isles that was followed by a discussion of their first inhabitants
and of the origin of the name *Britain*; then came historical notices
of the Romans in Britain, the Britons in Armorica, the Picts and
Scots, the Saxons, the Danes, and the Normans; Camden then
discussed the Roman and Saxon "divisions" of Britain and the creation of the shires; he next described the social orders and the
government of the English, and included an apologetic note on
the astrological sign under which Britain lies; then he proceeded
to his detailed antiquarian account of the shires, which, in England and Wales, he arranged in groups that he thought represented
the areas occupied by the ancient British tribes.

Before beginning the section *Danmonii* (Cornwall and Devon),
Camden stated his general aim: "in each county I mean to describe

its antient inhabitants, estymology of its name, its limits, soil, re-markable places both ancient and modern, and its dukes or earls from the Norman Conquest." And then he says: "Aggreably to my principal design, I proceed now to describe the promontories, cities, and rivers, mentioned by the antients," and thereby he de-clared the central theme of his book; it was to be in the main an account of British antiquities written for antiquaries, and though Camden did not deny himself the pleasure of recording that which seemed delightful and interesting to him in Tudor England, whatever its age or nature, he was much more sparing in this matter than Leland had been, and on the whole the infor-mation he gave about the (in his day) present state of the country is a kind of stage-setting for the parade of antiquities he had in mind.

RICHARD COLT-HOARE

In Praise of
Wiltshire Antiquities

It is somewhat singular, that amongst our numerous writers on the subject of English Topography, no one should have employed his pen in the description of Wiltshire; and that a county so abun-dant in British and Roman Antiquities, and so interesting in a more modern point of view, should have been so very imperfectly illus-trated; for, if I except the writings of Dr. Stukeley and others on our celebrated temples at Abury [Avebury] and Stonehenge, nothing important has been added to the ample store of county history which our topographical libraries have collected.

The ancient stone temples at Abury and Stonehenge stand un-rivaled, not only in our own dominions, but even in Europe: traces

From *The Ancient History of South Wiltshire*. London: William Miller; 1812, pp. 1-2.

of British population are every where apparent upon our extensive downs; and numerous Roman roads, towns, villas, &c. mark the power and residence of that conquering and civilizing nation. And if we descend to the antiquities of the succeeding era, our county is equally fertile and interesting; for the Abbey of Malmsbury presents the richest specimen of Saxon architecture; and the Cathedral Church of Salisbury the purest example of the Pointed architecture existing in England.

My present researches will commence with the most early period of British history, and will terminate with the Roman era. I can neither flatter my readers or myself with the hopes of ascertaining the origin of those stupendous temples at Abury and Stonehenge, which for ages past have attracted the curiosity of every passenger; but I hope to throw some new light on the history of those Britons who formerly resided on our hills; to point out the sites they selected for habitation and to mark their gradual progress from the bleak hill to the fertile valley, and from barbarism to civilization.

RICHARD COLT-HOARE

A Very Low View of the Ancient Britons

SIR RICHARD COLT-HOARE quotes an account of the German tribe of the Fenni from what he calls "the masterly hand of the historian Tacitus" as providing a likely analogy for the ancient inhabitants of Wiltshire. It is surprising that he should wish to liken the Bronze and Iron Age farmers of his county to a people so obviously far more primitive, but perhaps as an intelligent antiquary of his day he wished to make his readers think of the

Ibid., pp. 15-16.

ancient Britons as barbarians, or even savages, rather than as English or Trojan gentlemen.

❦

"NOTHING can equal the ferocity of the *Fenni*, nor is there any thing so disgusting as their filth and poverty. Without arms, without horses, and without a fixed place of abode, they lead a vagrant life; their food the common herbage; the skins of beasts their only cloathing; and the bare earth their resting place. For their chief support they depend on their arrows, to which, for want of iron, they prefix a pointed bone. The women follow the chase in company with the men, and claim their share of the prey. To protect their infants from the fury of wild beasts, and the inclemency of the weather, they make a kind of cradle amidst the branches of trees interwoven together, and they know no other expedient. The youth of the country have the same habitation, and amidst the trees old age is rocked to rest. Savage as this way of life may seem, they prefer it to the drudgery of the field, the labour of building, and the painful vicissitudes of hope and fear, which always attend the defense, and the acquisition of property. Secure against the passions of men, and fearing nothing from the anger of the gods, they have attained that uncommon state of felicity, in which there is no craving left to form a single wish." [From Tacitus' *Germania*]

Such, probably, was the way of life, and such the habits of those Britons who, in ancient times, resided upon our Wiltshire downs; and in treating of their towns and *tumuli*, I shall have an opportunity of marking the strong resemblance between them and the *Fenni*. The numerous and diversified *mausolea* of their dead are every where apparent on the high grounds throughout England; but the habitations of the living have hitherto escaped unnoticed, and their discovery and investigation have, fortunately, been reserved for us. To the learned Dr. Stukeley we are much indebted for many interesting particulars respecting the stone temples at Abury and Stonehenge; but practical experience has shewn us in how imperfect and unsatisfactory a manner his researches on barrows were conducted. He has said but little on the fortresses and earthen works of the Britons, and the sites and remains of their towns have totally escaped his observation. These will form a very prominent feature in my work, and must naturally excite the curiosity of the historian, and of every lover of antiquity. To the general eye of observation, our Wiltshire downs appear as uninteresting as the moors in Yorkshire, or the fens in Lincolnshire; bleak, desolate, and shelterless; and affording only a scanty subsistence to the numerous flocks that are pastured on them: yet on these apparently barren and uninteresting spots we find the traces of an extensive British and Roman population; and the modern agriculturist confesses the superior excellence of those districts, heretofore inhabited, and which are still decidedly marked by a more verdant and fertile soil.

To the investigating eye and persevering hand of Mr. Cunnington, the discovery of these British towns is justly and solely due; a discovery totally new, and highly interesting; as by a certain and infallible index, we are enabled to trace the progress of British population from the rudest to the most civilized era.

In traversing the extensive downs of Wiltshire, our attention is continually arrested by the works of the ancient Britons; strong fortresses, circles, barrows, and other inequalities in the ground, which are evidently contrary to nature. Whoever has studied attentively the formation of our chalk hills, will observe, that all maiden downs, by which I mean all land untouched by the plough, bear a most even and smooth surface; and whenever we find the appearance of that surface altered by excavations and other irregularities, we may there look with a prospect of success for the habitations of the Britons; and especially if the herbage is of a more verdant hue, and the soil thrown up by the moles of a blacker tint. There, on turning up the soil, will be found convincing proofs of ancient residence, such as animal bones, pottery, brick tiles, and coins of the lower Empire. Such are the certain *indicia* which have led us to the discovery of numerous British towns and settlements; and I flatter myself that the same *indicia* will lead to equally important discoveries in other counties where the plough has not annihilated them.

C. ROACH SMITH

The British Museum and British Government Attacked

BRYAN FAUSSETT wrote his account of his excavations of Anglo-Saxon cemeteries in Kent between 1757 and 1773, but did not publish it. At the time he believed that the graves belonged to the Roman period. In 1856 the antiquary Roach Smith edited his work and published it privately under the title of *Inventorium Sepulchrale*. The folly of the British Museum in refusing the Faussett Collection, and the general failure of the authorities to recognize the importance of the study of British, as opposed to classical and biblical, antiquities, roused his indignation. It cannot be said that the Trustees of the British Museum have since become much more forward-looking.

ALTHOUGH I could not be ignorant of the indifference with which our national antiquities have been and are regarded by the Government, I thought it possible that what could not be looked for from good taste, or from patriotism, might be conceded to dictation or to interest; and I advised that the collection should be offered to the Nation, through the Trustees of the British Museum. This was done; and an extremely moderate sum was asked. To any private individual the price proposed would have been moderate; so much so, that no less than three persons were willing to purchase in the event of the Trustees declining—a contingency not calculated on. The Trustees, however, did refuse the offer. The leading metropolitan antiquarian societies now came forward, to back the recommendation of the officers of the depart-

From *Inventorium Sepulchrale*, ed. by C. Roach-Smith. Privately published in 1856. Pp. v-vi, ix-x, xii-xiv.

ment of antiquities in the British Museum: Mr. Wylie offered to present to the Nation, free of any cost, the valuable Saxon antiquities discovered by him at Fairford, in Gloucestershire, provided the Faussett collection were secured in the British Museum; and Dr. Faussett's executors extended the time afforded for the consideration and decision of the Trustees over several months. But it was said, "the Trustees were not to be persuaded"; "the Trustees were not to be compelled"; and "the Trustees were not to be dictated to"; and the Nation, consequently, was not to possess a most extraordinary collection of the rarest monuments, which is in every point of view truly valuable, and which, as purely national remains of historical importance may be considered priceless. Mr. Wylie's antiquities were, as a matter of course, also lost to the Nation. The particulars of this exposure of the lamentable construction of the Board of Trustees are sufficiently public; but the responsibility must rest with the Government; and be reckoned among the numerous inconsistencies and deficiencies which it has manifested, and for which it will have to answer to all who desire to see our country respected and honoured. When our Government shall be composed of statesmen instead of placemen; of men who look to the credit, the prosperity, and the glory of the country, more than to the maintenance of themselves in power, and their connexions in places and in pensions; then, and then only, may it be expected that our national antiquities will be cared for and protected; and that, at the same time, the ancient national literature will be appreciated and its students encouraged.

The real value of antiquities should be determined by the extent to which they are capable of being applied towards illustrating history. The farther they are removed from the probability of throwing some faint light on the state of man in past ages, the more they become depreciated for all useful purposes; but in proportion as they serve to supply greater evidence on the manners or on the arts of the ancients, so must they rise in the estimation of all whose education has directed them to engage in a comprehensive examination of the past. It is no longer necessary to make an apology for the study of antiquities when undertaken in such a spirit; defence or excuse is to be made by those who deny its utility, or who undervalue it; for every man is now expected to be educated; and he who is ignorant of his antecedents, whatever may be his worldly condition, cannot be called properly educated. The English archaeologist can select no worthier course of study than that which directs him to the history of those from whom he inherits not only his material existence and the language he speaks, but also many of the civil and political institutions under which he lives in freedom, and surrounded with advantages and privileges unknown to many nations and countries. Nothing that relates to the knowledge of the human race, can, indeed, be unworthy the consideration of man; and the antiquities of all parts of the globe claim, more or less, to be understood and brought to bear upon historical evidence in every possible way. But those of our own land appeal first to our regard and challenge our sympathy, because they once belonged to those from whom we spring; and because they teach us something, at least, of the habits, customs, and arts of our forefathers. The colossal wonders and hieroglyphic literature of Egypt; the monuments of Nineveh and Babylon; the architecture and sculpture of Greece and Rome, and all the various artistic productions of classical antiquity, are not to be the less appreciated, because we look to our native country first, and contemplate the remains of those who bequeathed to us our island home, and with it, laws and institutions which have founded or regulated our manners and our national character.

It need never be apprehended, that where, as in this country, refinement of taste and a sound system of education prevail, classical antiquities will ever be neglected, or be in danger of being superseded; it would be as unreasonable to dread such a result as to fear decadence of esteem for the noble literature of Greece and Rome. Yet not only does the Government begin with gathering the monuments, ancient and modern, of all foreign countries, but it ends there also. Our national antiquities are not even made subservient and placed in the lowest grade; they are altogether unrecognized and ignored; and that, too, with an English metropolitan museum, surrounded by an English population, and paid for, with no stinted liberality, by English money. When those who are not ashamed of their parentage; whose patriotism is not ostentatious but deep; who do not reverence their country less because they know it more:—when those persons expostulate, and protest against this repudiation of National Antiquities, they are answered by some dogma about "fine art", and by unphilosophical axioms of mere *dilettanteism*. The same spirit, applied to literature, would exclude *Beowulf* and Bede, because they are not the *Iliad* and Tacitus. But in spite of an unfostering and undiscerning Government, England has produced scholars worthy of her ancient literature and students devoted to her antiquities.

A. PITT-RIVERS

The Father of
Modern Excavation

GENERAL PITT-RIVERS' work at the Romano-British villages of
Woodcuts and Rotherley show him as a pioneer in the extensive
excavation of prehistoric sites (p. 87, I).

❧

IN issuing the first volume of records of my excavations near Rushmore, which is intended, if I live, to be followed by others of the
same kind, it may be desirable to say something of the circumstances under which they were undertaken, and of the manner in
which they have been executed; to state how I came to be connected
with the particular district in which the excavations have been
made; and to explain more especially the reason for my change
of name to Pitt Rivers instead of Lane Fox, under which latter
designation I am perhaps better known to anthropologists, having
made some previous contributions to anthropological science.

I inherited the Rivers estates in the year 1880, in accordance
with the will of my great uncle, the second Lord Rivers, and by
descent from my grandmother, who was his sister, and daughter
of the first lord. The will was excessively binding, and provided
amongst other things that I was to assume the name and arms of
Pitt Rivers within a year of my inheriting the property, in default
of which it was to pass without reserve to the next in the entail.
It had been equally binding on my predecessors, who were
descended from the eldest sister, and who in accordance with its
provisions had relinquished the name of Beckford and taken that
of Pitt Rivers some fifty years ago

The title of Baron Rivers, which would naturally have died out

From *Excavations in Cranbourne Chase*. Privately printed in 1887. Pp. xi-xv, xvi-
xviii.

with the second lord, who had no children, was, by an alteration in the patent of the first lord before his death, made to pass by descent to the children of the eldest sister, who were at that time the heirs apparent of the property. In this way the title became extinct on the death of my immediate predecessor, the sixth lord, who was related to my great grandfather, the first lord, and his successor precisely in the same degree as myself. Even if the will had not been so imperatively binding, my own feeling would have strongly inclined me to preserve the name of Pitt in connection with the property, parts of which had been associated with it since the 16th century. No considerations of personal discomfort ought, in my judgment, to be allowed to sever old connections when they are legitimately and reasonably maintained in a direct line of family descent, and in conformity with established precedents. In my own case the only inconvenience I can be said to have suffered by it has been the severance of my name from previous publications of the same character as the present, which had obtained for me the honour of being elected a fellow of the Royal Society.

Having retired from active service on account of ill health, and being incapable of strong physical exercise, I determined to devote the remaining portion of my life chiefly to an examination of the antiquities on my own property. Of these there were a considerable number, especially near Rushmore, consisting of Romano-British villages, tumuli and other vestiges of the bronze and stone age, most of which were untouched and had been well preserved.

Many circumstances had combined to preserve the ancient monuments in this neighbourhood. The soil on the southern slopes of the Wiltshire downs, though possessing many excellent agricultural qualities, cannot be said to be of the most fertile description, and on this account large tracts had retained their original forest character, and had been untouched by the plough. Amongst other things which had also contributed in no small degree to the preservation of these relics and the suppression of cultivation must be mentioned the existence of Cranbourne Chase, with the somewhat barbarous rights and privileges attached to it. This Chase had been the possession of my great grandfather, the first Lord Rivers, who inherited it from his great grandfather, Mr. Thomas Pile, of Beverstock, Wilts, in the year 1714. It assured to its possessor the right of pasturing fallow deer, of which about 12,000 were preserved, over the whole extent of country between Salisbury on the east and Blandford on the west, Semley and Tisbury on the north, and Fordingbridge and Ringwood on the south, including in the outer bounds between 700,000 and 800,000 acres, although the whole of this was not actually overrun by the deer. In this district the owners were bound to preserve *vert* [cover] for the deer. Not only was considerable damage done to the existing crops, but it appears by Mr. West's *History of the Chace,* published in 1816, that the Chase laws forbade the conversion of the land into arable. On this account, and also by reason of the lawlessness which arose from the presence of numbers of persons who lived by deer stealing, and the frequent battles between them and the keepers, resulting in some instances in loss of life, an agreement was come to between the second Lord Rivers and the owners of the several properties within the Chase boundaries, to abolish the Chase in consideration of certain sums to be paid as compensation for the loss of the Chase rights. It was, therefore, disfranchised in the year 1830 and the deer destroyed.

Since then many of the parts marked on the old Ordnance Survey as forest have been converted into pasture, and in more prosperous times for agriculture into arable, to be again laid down into grass in consequence of the depression of the agricultural interest at the present time. Much of the land around Rushmore, however, still retains all the beauty of its original forest scenery; the tumuli and other vestiges of antiquity still remain uninjured save by the roots of trees, which were often found to have done much damage to the fragile urns and skulls contained in them.

I had an ample harvest before me, and with the particular tastes that I had cultivated, it almost seemed to me as if some unseen hand had trained me up to be the possessor of such a property, which, up to within a short time of my inheriting it, I had but little reason to expect. I at once set about organising such a staff of assistants as would enable me to complete the examination of the antiquities on the property within a reasonable time, and to do it with all the thoroughness which I had come to consider necessary for archaeological investigations.

A permanent residence in the district to be explored is almost necessary for a satisfactory investigation of its ancient remains, and it is needless to say that ownership adds greatly to the power of carrying out explorations thoroughly, for although I have found my neighbours at all times most obliging in giving me permission to dig, it requires some assurance so far to trespass on a friend's kindness as to sit down and besiege a place on another man's property more than a year, which is not at all too long a time to spend in the excavation of a British village.

Whilst living at Kensington I had carefully examined the drift gravels near Acton and Ealing, and by constantly watching the excavations for buildings made at no great distance from my place of abode, I had been able to make the first carefully recorded discovery of palaeolithic implements in association with the remains of extinct animals that had been made in the Thames Valley near

London up to that time. These researches have been successfully followed since my departure from that district by Mr. Worthington Smith, Mr. J. Allen Browne, and others. In Sussex also I had made some more or less lengthy excavations, in camps at Mount Caburn, Cissbury, and other places, dating from the late Celtic period, the value of which would certainly have been much increased if a permanent residence in the neighbourhood had enabled me to devote more time to them. At Thebes, in Egypt, I had discovered palaeolithic implements in the gravels of the Nile Valley, embedded in them in the sides of Egyptian tombs, a discovery the interest of which consisted in finding these implements for the first time *in situ*. But anthropology has no pet periods, all ages have afforded materials of nearly equal value for the history of the human race, and in the region around Rushmore my attention has been drawn more especially to the Romanised Britons, as being the race for whose study the district appears capable of affording the greatest facilities.

In any part of the east or north of Britain, an archaeologist who attempts to deal with the ethnological characters of people of the Roman era is met with the difficulties which Mr. Wright has so well pointed out in his "Celt, Roman, and Saxon." It is impossible to say to what nationality or to which of the Roman auxiliary races a skeleton found in association with Roman antiquities may have belonged. It may be a Briton or a Roman, a Fortensian from Asiatic Sarmatia, a Tungrian, a Gaul from Tournay, a Vetasian from Belgic Gaul, a Moor, a Spaniard, or a Thracian. But in the west of England, where the Romans colonised less frequently, this difficulty in a great measure disappears, and in ancient villages and farm homesteads upon the Wiltshire hills, remote from the great centres of Roman occupation, the evidence that we are dealing with a genuine Briton when the associated remains are such as to show that he had lived during the Roman period, becomes fairly reliable. The importance of the investigation as evidence of the condition and physical peculiarities of the Romanised Britons is in an inverse proportion to the importance of the site in which the remains are found, and in the ancient villages which form the subject of this memoir, there can be little doubt from the coins and other relics discovered, that we have to do with Britons of the latest period of the Roman dominion, or that which immediately succeeded it, a race about whom less is known to anthropologists than of those which preceded and followed it.

It is to investigations of sites such as these that we must look for a solution of the problem which has so largely occupied the attention of historians, viz., to what extent were the Britons exterminated (as some authors have supposed) by the Saxons after their abandonment by the Romans, in what proportion does Celtic blood circulate in the veins of the existing population of England, and to what class and description of people are we to look as the survivors of the Celtic population at the present time.

Whatever importance may attach to an examination of the form and arrangement of the Romano-British villages, the first of which is described in the following pages, or to the relics of human industry found in them, there can be no doubt that the chief interest of this investigation will be found to consist in the discovery of the remarkably small race of people that were buried in its pits and ditches. It is this which gives value to the relics associated with them, as evidence of the time and condition of civilisaton in which they lived.

It was known by an examination of the "long barrows" by Thurnam, Greenwell, and others, that a long-headed race of small stature, whose average height is estimated at 5 feet 6 inches, inhabited Britain in the Stone Age. These were succeeded by a tall, round-headed people of larger size, estimated at 5 feet 8 inches, and these again were replaced in after times by the Saxons, whose stature was also large. But of the peculiarities of the Romanised Britons little as yet is known. Professor Rolleston examined a number of skeletons from Frilford, believed to be Roman Britons, whose average height amounted for the males to 5 feet 8.4 inches, and for the females 4 feet 10.5 inches. But the present discovery of a race of Britons whose stature in the two villages at Woodcuts and Rotherley and in the pit near Park House does not exceed 5 feet 2.6 inches for the males and 4 feet 10.9 inches for the females, is, so far as I know, quite new to anthropologists. What race can these people be taken to represent? Are they the survivors of the Neolithic population, which, after being driven westward by successive races of Celts and others, continued to exist in the out-of-the-way parts of this region up to Roman times, for which hypothesis the crouched position of the interments and their markedly dolichocephalic and hyperdolichocephalic skulls appears to afford some justification, or are they simply the remnants of a larger race of Britons, deteriorated by slavery and reduced in stature by the drafting of their largest men into the Roman legions abroad? Perhaps the comparatively large size of the females may be taken to support this latter view. . . .

It will, perhaps, be thought by some that I have recorded the excavations of this village and the finds that have been made in it with unnecessary fullness, and I am aware that I have done it in greater detail than has been customary, but my experience as an excavator has led me to think that investigations of this nature

Young Etruscan couple confronted in a ritual dance. They express the zest for physical life, and the freedom between the sexes, characteristic of the Etruscans. Wall painting from the Tomb of the Lioness, Tarquinia. *C.* 520 B.C.

The Via di Stabia, a street in Roman Pompeii. Ruts worn by wheeled traffic can be seen between the blocks of the pedestrian crossing. Pompeii was destroyed by an eruption of Vesuvius in A.D. 79.

UPPER RIGHT: The citizens of Mohenjo-Daro in the Indus valley of India used engraved stone seals to mark their goods. Pictographs, still undeciphered, probably represent owners' names. The Indus civilization lasted from 2500-1500 B.C.

CENTER RIGHT: A dancing girl from Mohenjo-Daro clad only in armlets and necklace. This little bronze figurine together with the seal engravings are the best achievements of a civilization poor in the visual arts. C. 1500 B.C.

LOWER RIGHT: A small steatite sculpture of a bearded man from Mohenjo-Daro. The trefoil was a widespread religious symbol and may indicate that the figure represents a priest-king or a divinity. C. 1500 B.C.

Three of the great Easter Island statues standing at the foot of Rano Raraku volcano. They are choked with rubble from the quarries which lie above them.

Beakers from burials in Berkshire, southern England.
These vessels, the distinctive possession of various groups
of invaders reaching Britain from the Continent, were the
subject of one of the first exact typological studies. 1900-
1700 B.C.

An aerial view of the sanctuary of Stonehenge, Wiltshire, England, showing the circular bank, probably delimiting the sacred area, and the beginning of the Avenue opening to the left. A Bronze Age burial mound appears in the background. Enclosure bank *c.* 2000 B.C.; stone structure, sixteenth century B.C.

UPPER RIGHT: Stone carving of a lion, excavated by Leonard Woolley at the Roman depot of Corstopitum (Corbridge), Northumberland, England, just to the south of Hadrian's Wall. Something of the Celtic spirit survives in this sculpture. Second or third century A.D.

LOWER RIGHT: The most northerly frontier between Roman and Barbarian. Hadrian's Wall near Borcovicus (Housesteads), Northumberland. A.D. 122-28.

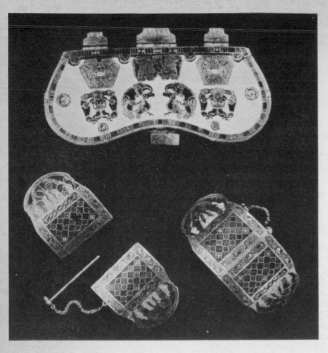

Superb examples of the Anglo-Saxon goldsmith's art. Mounts for a purse and a pair of belt clasps, inlaid with garnets and coloured glass. From the Sutton Hoo ship-burial, Suffolk, England. Seventh century A.D.

The stern of the Sutton Hoo ship after the removal of the treasure. All wood had perished, but the excavators followed the lines of iron rivets and the discoloration of the sand. Seventh century A.D.

are not generally sufficiently searching, and that much valuable evidence is lost by omitting to record them carefully. That this has been so in the present instance is proved by the fact that this village had before been examined and reported upon in the XXIVth. Vol. of the *Journal of the Archaeological Institute*, and not a single pit or skeleton had been found; whilst I have discovered 95 pits and 15 skeletons.

Excavators, as a rule, record only those things which appear to them important at the time, but fresh problems in Archaeology and Anthropology are constantly arising, and it can hardly fail to have escaped the notice of anthropologists, especially those who, like myself, have been concerned with the morphology of art, that, on turning back to old accounts in search of evidence, the points which would have been most valuable have been passed over from being thought uninteresting at the time. Every detail should, therefore, be recorded in the manner most conducive to facility of reference, and it ought at all times to be the chief object of an excavator to reduce his own personal equation to a minimum.

I have endeavoured to record the results of these excavations in such a way that the whole of the evidence may be available for those who are concerned to go into it . . .

Another circumstance which makes the relics found in these villages valuable for reference, is the fact of their being entirely of one continuous period. The ground never having been cultivated since Roman times, and the spot having always been, as it is at present, remote from human habitation, there is little probability of their having become mixed with relics of a later date.

I have placed all the relics discovered in the ancient villages and tumuli in a Museum near the village of Farnham, Dorset, where each object is carefully ticketed and described. Accurate models have been made of the villages, and models on a larger scale of the particular finds. In the case of Rotherley, I have a model of the ground, both before and after excavation, by means of which the results of the exploration are explained in such a way as to require the least possible effort of attention. The Museum also includes other objects of husbandry and peasant handicraft, calculated to draw the interest of a purely rural population, 10 miles distant from any town or railway station, and I am glad to say the interest it has attracted amongst the working men of the neighbourhood has exceeded my utmost expectations. On Sunday afternoons the visitors' book often records more than 100 visitors; and on special holidays, between 200 and 300 frequently visit the Museum. It is about a mile and a half distant from the old wych-elm, at the Larmer boundary above-mentioned, which was traditionally the spot where king John used to meet for hunting in the chase, where I have established a pleasure ground and built a temple in the woods, with a private band, and where upwards of 1,000 of the villagers and neighbours frequently congregate with their wives and families, between the hours of divine service upon Sunday afternoons.

All the villages and tumuli, after being excavated, have been restored and turfed over, leaving sufficient indication to mark the various parts discovered in the villages, and at the bottoms of the principal excavations I have placed the medallet . . . to show future explorers that I have been there.

2. Britain and the Bronze Age

IN the following section, first the general background of prehistoric Britain, its peoples and their principal monuments are sketched. Then accounts of the greatest Bronze Age monument of all—Stonehenge—are followed from Tudor times to the present. Finally, the same development of knowledge for the Bronze Age as a whole is followed—inevitably with special emphasis on the burial mounds that the old antiquaries most liked to excavate, and on the Beaker people whose pottery made them conspicuous.

CYRIL FOX

The Pattern of British Prehistory

CYRIL FOX was one of the first British archaeologists to study the effect of geographical and ecological factors on early human settlement and cultural development (p. 88, I). The appearance of his *Personality of Britain* is said to have caused a "minor earthquake" in geographical thinking. It certainly had a stimulating effect on British archaeology.

From *The Personality of Britain*. Cardiff: National Museum of Wales; 1932. The following citations from pp. 86-9 of the fourth edition, 1943, by permission of the National Museum of Wales.

I. Position, outline, relief and structure are involved in this study of the island of Britain; the climate resulting from position and relief, and the soil related to structure, determine the vegetable life which she nourishes and the animal life which she harbours. The whole represents Man's environment, and Britain's personality.

II. The position of Britain adjacent to Europe renders her very liable to invasion therefrom; her indented outline offers convenient harbourage for invaders, her deep estuaries and slow-moving rivers invite penetration.

III. Embarkation points for those to whom the sea is a barrier have extended for 500 miles, from Finistère (Brittany) to the Rhine-mouths; from such points settlement along the whole length of the south coast, and the east coast to the Humber and beyond have taken place. Embarkation points for those to whom the sea is a highway have extended from the Spanish peninsula to Brittany on the west, and from the Rhine-mouths to Norwegian fiords on the north; to such the west and north coasts of Britain from Lands End to Caithness, and the east coast from Caithness to the Humber, have also lain open.

IV. In the earliest times under review (c. 2400 B.C.) the land of Britain was higher than at present—in south-east Britain not less than 25 feet. Extensive alluvial and marshy flats fringed much of the coast. The Straits of Dover were narrower, the southern part of the North Sea probably a complex of sandbanks and tidal channels. Little, if any, traffic followed the Channel–North Sea route; by contrast, entry into southern Britain offered little difficulty to landsmen such as the Neolithic "A" and "B2" Beaker peoples. When subsidence and sea erosion had moulded Britain into the now familiar outline, oversea invasion tended to concentrate on the continental angle (Kent) and the Thames estuary.

V. One reservation is, however, necessary. Brittany, a peninsula within easy distance of Britain, with marked physiographic individuality, metalliferous, eminently suitable for early man's occupation, situated at the Atlantic-Channel angle and so stimulated by cultural ideas both seaborne and landborne, has exercised both by invasion and commerce, an influence localized indeed, but disproportionate to its area.

VI. European civilization has its source in the Near East, and Mediterranean societies thereafter are in the van of continental progress. Other things being equal, the nearer the Mediterranean the higher the culture in early times. The further north the homeland of invaders of Britain, then, the greater the likelihood that invasion will lower the level of our insular culture.

VII. Goods reach Britain in the way of trade from both northern and southern Europe. But since traders transmit ideas as well as goods, the products of higher civilizations arriving in this manner are doubly significant for the cultural development of an island in a state of barbarism. In general, then, the further south the port of entry in Britain, the more important culturally was the trade.

VIII. The commercial activity of higher civilizations may, under certain circumstances, be almost as powerful an instrument of cultural change in Britain as is invasion.

IX. While the Atlantic sea-way from Spain northwards was in full use in Megalithic and Early Bronze Age times, Britain was in the van of western European progress. But in the Middle Bronze Age land routes ("amber routes") which had been developing across Europe sapped the European importance of Atlantic commerce. Britain thenceforward tended more and more to occupy a position historically familiar; a country on the edge of the known world, the last to receive and absorb cultures moving from east to west. But the Atlantic routes never fell into complete disuse, and were indeed revivified by an increased demand for Cornish tin.

X. The structure of Britain has exerted a powerful influence on her prehistory. South of the Forth-Clyde isthmus the island consists of two parts, the Highland Zone to the west and the Lowland Zone to the east. A diagonal line drawn from Teesmouth (Durham) to Torquay (Devon) roughly indicates the boundary of the two areas. In the Highland Zone, high plateaux and mountains are characteristic; in the Lowland Zone, such hills as occur are usually of slight elevation. Stone suitable for tombs, for defensive structures, for dry-walled dwellings, occurs everywhere in the Highland; it is localized in the Lowland. The Lowland provides the largest area of fertile and habitable ground, and hence it nourishes wealthier populations than the Highland.

XI. The portion of Britain adjacent to the continent being Lowland, it is easily overrun by invaders, and on it new cultures of continental origin brought across the narrow seas tend to be imposed. In the Highland, on the other hand, these tend to be absorbed. Their manifestations are, then, later and less distinctive in the Highland than in the Lowland. There are areas (intermont and coastal) of lowland in the Highland Zone, and in some of these undifferentiated cultures of lowland origin may establish themselves. But no such area in Britain south of the Forth-Clyde isthmus is large enough for such cultures to develop therein an independent character.

XII. There is greater *unity* of culture in the Lowland Zone, but greater *continuity* of culture in the Highland Zone. A tendency to unity of culture is sometimes seen in the Highland Zone south of the Forth-Clyde isthmus; the Highland north of the Forth-Clyde isthmus, on the other hand, tends, by reason of its remoteness, to develop unique cultures.

XIII. The ultimate expression of any continental culture in Lowland Britain tends to possess individual characters. The sea barrier inhibits mass movement and encourages independent adventure; Lowland culture at any given period thus tends to represent the mingling of diverse continental elements rather than the extension beyond the Straits of a single continental culture.

XIV. New cultures of continental origin coming across the high seas tend to impinge on the Highland Zone rather than on the Lowland. Again, the heavy (orographic) rainfall of the Highland increases the contrast between it—as an environment for Man— and the Lowland. These factors intensify the cultural differentation between the two Zones already examined.

XV. Britain is subjected to influences from a quarter other than those mentioned—Ireland. These influences, though persistent and important, are, owing to the comparative smallness of the exportable surplus of men therein and to the existence of the Highland Zone as a wall protecting the Lowland, not very extensive culturally; the more permanent effects of this Irish contact are usually limited to the Highland Zone. The existence of the Highland Zone tends to isolate the inhabitants of the British coast-lands facing St. George's Channel and the Irish Sea; the lands fronting Channel and Sea thus tend to cultural unity.

XVI. The influence of Ireland during one of the periods under review (the Bronze Age) was greatly strengthened by her importance as a gold and copper producing centre; Britain, lying between Ireland and the continent, benefited by trade created by this exportable wealth.

XVII. Deposits of all the metals important in the Bronze Age, copper, tin, and gold, are present in Britain; only those of tin, in Cornwall, are considered to have been worked throughout that Age. The influence of the tin industry on the cultural history of Britain, then as later, is held to be very great.

XVIII. The distribution of population in Britain in prehistoric times is controlled by physiographical conditions. In the Lowland Zone a pervious subsoil, resulting in open country, parkland, scrub, or forest with not too dense undergrowth, is the chief factor. Low hills of easy contour and plateaux possessing such subsoil (chalk and limestone) form the framework of lowland Britain and thus provide the main field for Man's activities; but gravel terraces by rivers are equally suitable, sandy heaths are sometimes occupied, and harbours offering opportunities for commerce are not neglected.

xix. The areas shunned by Early Man in the Lowland Zone are the impervious clay-lands, which are very extensive; these tend to be waterlogged and to carry dense forest—"damp" oakwood.

xx. In the Highland Zone also soils exert a powerful influence on distribution, but this influence is masked by another factor peculiar to the Zone—elevation. Above a certain level, whatever the soil may be, Man cannot comfortably live in our wet and cold winters.

xxi. Hence we may say that *soil character* is' the controlling factor in lowland distribution, *elevation* in highland distribution; also that Early Man tends to fit himself *into the mountain pattern* of the Highland Zone, *on to the hill pattern* of the Lowland Zone.

xxii. The type of country which Early Man preferred, open or lightly forested with pervious soil, is comparatively infrequent in Britain. Moreover, a great deal of such country was not available, since the range within which he could live in reasonable comfort was limited to about 1,000 feet—from sea-level upwards. Now the most extensive of the areas fulfilling the required conditions happen to be hills or plateaux from 200 to 700 or 800 feet in height. On these he is accordingly in greater evidence (taking all prehistoric periods, Neolithic, Bronze, and Iron into consideration) than in the equally suitable (intrinsically) but restricted low-lying areas, in the Highland and the Lowland Zones alike; there is little or no difference between the two zones in this respect. But whereas this serviceable upland country *dominates* the pattern of the Lowland Zone, it is for the most part *recessive* in the pattern of the Highland Zone. The psychological effect of this difference in environment can hardly be other than profound.

xxiii. The most complete and full manifestation of any *primitive* culture entering eastern or southern Britain from the continent will come to be in the Lowland Zone. The centre and focus in the Lowland Zone of such culture will tend to be the Salisbury Plain region ("Wessex"), because it has the largest area of habitable country, is close to south-coast seaports conveniently reached by Atlantic and Armorican trade, and is the meeting point of the (natural) traffic routes of the Lowland Zone.

xxiv. As civilization developed, and overseas trade growing more important tended to concentrate at the Thames estuary, an economic change began to make itself felt, a change in the type of country and of soil desired by inhabitants and invaders.

xxv. Pervious soils are more easily worked, but clay-lands are more fertile. Hence the progress from subjection to, to control of, environment, which is that from barbarism to civilization, is expressed

physiographically by the utilization of the "damp" oakwoods and
their gradual replacement by arable fields. Though this change
made but little progress save in Roman and late Anglo-Saxon times,
it is probable that the preponderance of heavy soils in south-eastern
Britain as contrasted with that of pervious soils in south-western
Britain (Salisbury Plain region) influenced the transfer of the
chief cultural area to the neighbourhood of the lower Thames in
the late La Tène period. The absence hereabouts of any spot com-
bining geographic and economic suitability resulted in varied choice
of a centre—St. Albans, Colchester; but these both lay at no great
distance from the Thames estuary, the physiographic disadvantages
of which for concentrated settlement were overcome when the
Roman civilization was established—they recurred when it decayed.

JACQUETTA HAWKES

Early Britain:
Peoples and Monuments

AFTER the present chapter this book will be devoted to a description of the traces of prehistoric man still to be seen in the countryside of England and Wales. They must be described region by region
as the traveller is likely to visit them. Just as I wanted to give some
account of the whole country before dismembering it, so now I want
to tell as a continuous narrative the history of the various peoples
who left these remains behind them. When visiting a region all
its monuments of whatever age must be looked at together; here
I wish to arrange them in due order in their historical setting.

Very many people take it for granted that by scrutinizing a

From *A Guide to Prehistoric and Roman Antiquities of England and Wales*. London:
Chatto and Windus Ltd.; 1952, pp. 13-35. By permission of Chatto and Windus
Ltd. and the Harvard University Press, Cambridge, Massachusetts.

building, whether it is a cathedral, castle or cottage, they will be able to judge within a century or so when and in what conditions it was built. So, too, though with much wider margins of error, it is possible to date the more remote antiquities, the part of our inheritance which has fallen into disuse, and to understand something of the ways of life which produced them. It is perhaps the greatest wonder of human life to be always changing; ants have been unshaken conservatives for many millions of years, men change everything they do, everything they make from year to year and millennium to millennium. Because of this restlessness, this perennial dissatisfaction with things as they are, it is always possible to distinguish between the products of every age.

No doubt there are plenty of people, and intelligent ones, who believe the present thirst for factual knowledge to be misguided, holding it to be much better to enjoy birds and flowers without asking all their names, to feel the awe inspired by ancestral monuments without wishing to assign them to precise dates or peoples. I myself have always given delighted approval to Shakespeare's eternal condemnation:

> These earthly godfathers of heaven's lights
> That give a name to every fixed star
> Have no more profit of their shining nights
> Than those that walk and wot not what they are.
> Too much to know is to know nought but fame;
> And every godfather can give a name.

Nevertheless few of us are always in that mood, and I know that I have sometimes enjoyed my shining nights the more for being able to name some of the stars and constellations, and my country days the more when I could distinguish chiffchaff from willow warbler and wild bryony from old man's beard. So, too, while a general sense of the past is exciting, as it excited the eighteenth century, most people find it more satisfying if they can give it sharper definition through factual knowledge. They like to picture it with the perspective given by chronology, and with the colour that intensifies with our understanding of the quality and character of life at different times and among different peoples.

One of the pleasures of historical associations we shall have to forswear in our excursions into prehistory. St. Thomas à Becket adds something to Canterbury cathedral, there is Wordsworth at Dove Cottage and on Westminster Bridge, and even the least credulous look with an added appreciation at all the beds dinted by Queen Elizabeth or the lacy gloves worn by Charles the First on the scaffold at Whitehall. The first individuals to emerge in British history, Cassivellaunus, Cunobelin and Caractacus and the other princes of the Belgic royal house ruling just before and after the beginning of our era, suggest that there must have been plenty of strong personalities among their prehistoric forbears; Boudicca shows that they need not always have belonged to men. But they have been forgotten for ever. Without the written letters which Celts, Anglo-Saxons, Danes were so understandably to regard as magical, there was nothing to hold their names or their exploits in the flux of time. It is a grievous loss. I personally feel sure that behind every monument of outstanding character and originality— Stonehenge and Avebury, Silbury Hill, Maiden Castle and the White Horse—we can assume the inspiration, the ruthlessness perhaps, of some individual of extraordinary vitality and imagination.

I am writing now for the traveller who has no desire to make an expert study of field archaeology but wishes to flavour his enjoyment of the countryside by visiting its antiquities, or who may even be inclined to make special pilgrimages to prehistoric sites just as he would to famous cathedrals, castles and mansions. It may always happen, I cannot promise it will not, that a few of these carefree dilettanti will become so infected by such visits that they will begin to study field archaeology in earnest, to survey and make discoveries. For this is one of the delights of the subject—it still offers opportunity to amateurs, though some regions have been thoroughly worked, others, having failed in the past to produce their local historians, remain almost uncharted.

Though it may help to ensnare them, this book will be of no help to those who wish to undertake original work, for it will include only monuments too conspicuous to have escaped general attention. I shall confine my descriptions to sites striking enough either in themselves or in their situation to rouse the imagination and to repay, if need be, a walk across a ploughed field or wet grass, a bitter conflict with brambles or nettles. I shall not send my readers to those faint shadows or tussocks, those dubious piles of stone or dark depressions in gravel-pits which rouse the enthusiasm of the true addict.

The first human inhabitants of Britain have left no visible monuments. As hunters and gatherers of wild foods, the Old Stone Age peoples had neither leisure nor social organization to dig or build on the scale necessary to leave any mark after the passage of at least ten thousand years. Their relics cannot be visited but must be sought after with patient and expert care. Their stone implements are found in the gravel terraces of some of our rivers, particularly in the south of England; many of these must have been lost on hunting expeditions, sometimes perhaps carried off by wounded animals, sometimes thrown and lost among the riverside vegetation.

Patient collectors may acquire these implements by years of

watching in gravel-diggings, where they may also find the bones of the elephants, hippopotami, mammoths, bears and other great beasts that lived in England during the alternating warm and arctic phases of the Ice Age. Very rarely such watchers may find bones of another species among the gravels, human fragments which give a sudden clue to the appearance of the Old Stone Age hunters and the evolutionary history of *Homo sapiens*.

The discovery of the Piltdown skull by a local Sussex amateur geologist is well known; not very many years ago the skull fragments of Swanscombe Man, the second oldest European, were found by a dentist who for long had given his spare time to collecting implements and fossil fauna in the huge gravel-pits of the Thames estuary.

Such adventures are not for ordinary visitors, though they may care to vary a journey by persuading the passing scenery to revert to what it was when the hunters knew it—seeing either a landscape of grey, scrub-grown tundra with an edge of ice in the wind, or, with the abrupt transition allowed only to the inner eye, a lush, semi-tropical jungle.

The only places associated with the Old Stone Age which reward a visit are the natural caves where the hunting families took shelter during the winter months when they could not be out, following the trail of the game herds. There on the floor they left a litter of food bones, lost or discarded implements and flint chippings, and occasionally their own bodies. Such cave dwellings are rare in England and Wales, but we shall find a few of them in Devon and Somerset, South Wales, Derbyshire and Yorkshire. Most of these were occupied only towards the very end of the Old Stone Age or in the succeeding Middle Stone Age, but two or three were already inhabited before the last cold phase of the Ice Age when the Neanderthal type of man was dominant in Europe.

Apart from the caves there are no Middle Stone Age sites, either, which are worthy of a visit. This was the time when milder weather allowed first pine and then oak forests to spread across Europe and when the native peoples, still dependent on wild foods, often lived by the sea shore or river bank where they could supplement their diet with substanial quantities of fish and molluscs. Such a way of life could hardly produce lasting monuments, and in fact we know only of a few huts and marsh-side dwellings of a kind which can be excavated but not preserved.

During the Middle Stone Age, about eight thousand years ago, Britain began to assume its present familiar shape as the North Sea broke through to the Channel and turned what had been a West European peninsula into an island. This was an event whose future significance for human history could hardly have been appreciated by the fishers and fowlers who gradually settled the new coast-lines, struggling with their primitive nets and hooks, their bows and arrows, to win a livelihood from a damp and still chilly land.

It was when men began to raise their own food supplies that they developed the power to construct substantially, so to cut about the land on which they lived as to leave enduring scars. The first farming peoples were crossing to Britain between four and five thousand years ago; they not only themselves practised husbandry but their example taught its rudiments to the native Middle Stone Age hunters. Though they still had no more than stone tools, immediately, if slowly, the newcomers made their mark on the countryside. Inevitably they changed its natural face by a clearance of trees on the uplands and other light soils, by the cultivation of corn plots and the pasturing of large flocks and herds. But beyond this, the New Stone Age farmers built for their practical life and, far more nobly, for their religious life; they were responsible, too, for the earliest industrial litter.

They have left four principal kinds of remains behind them— ditched and banked enclosures connected with stock-breeding, flint-mines, earthen burial-mounds, and tombs with sepulchral chambers built of massive stones.

The first three of these were all the work of invaders who crossed from France and the Low Countries to our south and south-east coasts bringing with them domestic cattle, sheep and pigs and the seed grain of wheat and barley. Probably their earliest building enterprise, and the earliest in Britain on a scale larger than that of wattle huts and animal traps, were the embanked compounds which have sometimes been called "causewayed camps". These enclosures have been identified in some numbers between Sussex and Devonshire, but they are generally inconspicuous, so much worn away by time as to be hardly deserving of a visit. Of them all only the enclosure crowning Windmill Hill above the Bronze Age sanctuary of Avebury has been excavated in such a way that the ditches remain open, and even here they are overgrown and forlorn. Nevertheless as our first buildings they have a claim on our interest.

These compounds are roughly circular, with from one to four rings of ditches which are not dug continuously but interrupted at frequent intervals by causeways. When they were in commission the banks behind the ditches may have been reinforced with stockades or thorn hedges, and some at least of the causeways were fitted with wooden gates.

There is nothing to suggest that the causewayed camps were in fact built for military purposes—indeed, their builders may have been the only entirely peaceable people this country has ever known. Rather they are likely to have been designed to protect the livestock against the wolves and other wild beasts that must still have been a constant menace, always ready to leave the forests and dispute the man's still insecure possession of the land. It is believed that the causewayed camps were used only seasonally when the approach of winter made it necessary to reduce the stock. We can guess how, when the tops of the oak-trees were showing yellow and the pigs were out after acorns, the tribal groups made for their pounds, mended fences and gates and perhaps put up some flimsy shelters. Then they would round up the cattle from their whole territory until the herds of sturdy, wide-horned beasts flowed through the entrances, jostling and butting. Scores of the young animals of the year had to be slaughtered; they were probably tied with sinew ropes and then poleaxed, a flint point being driven in above the left eye.

The carcasses were flayed, the skins perhaps going to the women for flensing and dressing, while the flesh, cut up with flint knives, may either have been smoked or cut in strips to dry in the air. Once in Mexico when I entered a village I thought a fiesta was going on, for the whole place appeared to be decorated with red flags and streamers. On going nearer I found the decorations to be strips and sheets of drying meat.

Flint-mining is the industrial enterprise of the New Stone Age which has left noticeable if unattractive traces behind it—most frequent on the chalk downs of southern England. In one place only, at Grimes Graves in Norfolk, an excavated shaft has been kept open and there visitors are able to gain a most lively impression of a highly specialized aspect of Stone Age life. The greatest practical need of the farmers of the time was for good axes for forest clearance, and for making the fences and more advanced works of carpentry of which we know they were capable. For axe-manufacture the nodules of fresh flint to be found bedded in layers in the chalk were greatly superior to surface flint, and that was why these primitive engineers were ready to sink shafts through the chalk and often to tunnel along the seams with antler picks and bone shovels and with no stronger source of light than a moss wick floating in animal fat. When the flint was exhausted, or the galleries had become so long that hauling out the nodules was becoming burdensome (need I say when the mine was becoming uneconomic?), a new shaft was sunk, the rubble from it being thrown into the old one. As anyone who has experience of refilling holes could guess, not all of the up-cast could be got back into the ground and so chalk dumps were formed, miniature white counterparts of the mountainous slag-heaps of our own coal-mines. After a time, too, the filling of the old shafts subsided leaving hollows at their mouths.

In many areas the mines still throve in the earlier part of the Bronze Age when metal remained scarce, but as gradually they were abandoned, grass and weeds grew over the broken chalk and thickened into turf, until these first industrial scars were softened into the mounds and hollows which are all that show to-day.

The remains of cattle-pounds and flint-mines are, then, the most ancient imprint of human economic activity left on the face of this country. Both are feeble imprints, mere unevenness of the turf unless excavated; exactly the kind of antiquity which should make any sane visitor forswear his interest in the past. Yet there are monuments of the New Stone Age capable of exciting the eye and quickening the imagination. In most of our towns and villages the religious buildings still dominate houses and even factories. We take this for granted, yet since in the nineteenth century we allowed ourselves to be caught up in an insane passion for the production of material goods, we simultaneously assume that art, ritual and the religious life are minor concerns on the fringe of real life. The small funds spent on such things are the first to be subjected to economy cuts by a State which spends thousands of millions on material ends. This assessment of values is exceptional in human history. Most societies from the most primitive to the most highly civilized have chosen to devote wealth, labour and genius to the service of their ritual life. In this our earliest agricultural population certainly conformed. For them the ritual centre of each community was the sepulchre built for its dead. In the south and east of England these tombs took the form of the long mounds or "barrows" which are still to be seen lying on or just below the crest of the chalk downs. They were far more impressive when four thousand years ago they stood contained within wooden or turf walls with flanking ditches magnifying their apparent height. One can imagine, too, that they may have had near them the strange magical furnishings and religious symbols which so often accompany primitive ritual.

Even more impressive were the tombs raised by distinct, though probably related, peoples who came not across the narrow seas from France and the Low Countries but made far longer voyages right up our rocky western coasts from Cornwall to the Orkneys. Their burial-chambers were built with large stone slabs and hidden by long or round cairns. In our area the finest examples of this megalithic architecture occur in the south-western peninsula, in the Cotswolds and round the coasts of Wales. There are outlying tombs in Wiltshire, and even a little isolated group in Kent. Abroad these megaliths find parallels in Brittany, Spain and Portugal and even in the eastern Mediterranean—though here very often the chambers are not megalithic but hewn in the solid limestone. Like our own family vaults, the burial-chambers might be used again and again for successive generations. Occasionally they have been found containing large numbers of skeletons and with clear signs that old corpses have been pushed aside to make room for new ones.

These tombs were far more than burial-places. It is interesting to speculate how much a future excavator of Christian churches might over-estimate the importance of the churchyard and tombs. Comparison is hardly just, for the megalithic chambers were opened only to receive the dead, yet on the other hand, there is little doubt that the monuments must have served as religious meeting-places, the scenes of the season festivities of a simple agricultural people. This becomes more acceptable when it is remembered that the cult associated with the tombs seems to have been no cult of the dead of a necrophilous kind but on the contrary one very much concerned with ideas of rebirth. In Britain we do not find the sculptured goddesses and female symbols which occur in some French megaliths, but all cult objects belonging to our New Stone Age are female figurines and phalli, both surely attributable to the Earth-Mother and her fertility rites. I do not think it is allowing the imagination too great liberty to say that the faith, for it is very truly a faith, which made the New Stone Age communities labour to drag, raise, pile thousands of tons of stone and earth, was in resurrection, the resurrection of their corn and beasts, of themselves. They laid their dead in the dark, earth-enclosed chamber with something of the same conviction with which they cast the seed corn into the soil.

In the character of the visible remains left in the countryside the break between the New Stone Age and the ensuing Bronze Age is almost complete. The embanked cattle enclosures were no longer dug, and megalithic funerary architecture and long barrows soon went out of use. Such an abrupt change in the remains of both secular and religious life is the material expression of the history of those days. After some five hundred years, the New Stone Age was brought to an end in about 1900 B.C. by the arrival of fresh invaders who steered their boats to good landing-places all along our southern and eastern coasts. In contrast with the New Stone Age peoples these invaders appear from the first to have introduced a martial tradition, which was indeed already characteristic of their continental ancestors. They were powerful bowmen, and though in early days when bronze was hard to get their chief metal weapons were small daggers, the British bronze-smiths in time developed a powerful armoury of halberds, rapiers and spears.

It was sometimes well-armed and richly-dressed chiefs, the embodiment of such a warlike ideal, who were buried under the round barrows which took the place of the long burial-mounds of the New Stone Age. These round barrows, so familiar from the old Ordnance Survey maps as *tumuli*, are by far the most widespread, abundant and characteristic of the Bronze Age con-tributions to our landscape. It is a remarkable fact that until late

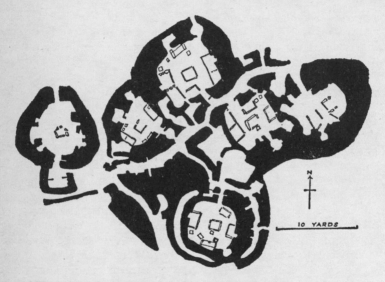

SIX OF THE FURNISHED STONE AGE COTTAGES OF SKARA BRAE.
THE CENTER RECTANGLE IS THE HEARTH, FLANKED BY TWO BEDS,
WITH THE "DRESSER" IN BETWEEN FACING THE DOOR.
THE SMALLER SQUARES ARE STONE-LINED PITS SUNK IN THE FLOOR.

in the period when a new form of agriculture was introduced, there are practically no traces of settlements or indeed of any substantial remains connected with mundane affairs. A few flimsy huts of the earlier part of the Bronze Age have been detected by excavation, while a small proportion of the moorland hut-circles in the southwest and in Yorkshire may have been built in the middle and later phases. Otherwise there is nothing, and it has been suggested that these invaders with traditions inherited in part from the European and Asiatic steppes may often have used the skin or felt tents characteristic of nomadic pastoralists. The light frameworks of such tents and the thorn hedges or other trans-ient defences would have left no mark that we could expect to see after the passage of well over three thousand years. On the other hand some round barrows have been found to cover ritual houses of the dead which suggest a more substantial architecture.

There is no doubt, at least, about the solidity and durability of the round barrows piled for the dead; they are immensely common both on the English uplands and the moors of the west and north. It is hardly surprising that they should be so numerous, for they remained the usual form of grave for more than a millennium of steadily mounting population. Then, too, they were normally raised over one or two bodies, other burials might occasionally be added in the material of the mound, but there was never the communal burial associated with megaliths and long barrows.

The first invaders introduced the simplest kind of round barrow, a pudding-shaped mound often closely surrounded by a ditch, and in many parts of the country this form lasted almost as long as the Bronze Age. These barrows may remain as lofty and steep-sided as the fine specimen many visitors have noticed on their way into Maiden Castle near Dorchester, or they may be reduced to no more than a faint swelling in a ploughed field—a swelling which in chalk country is usually emphasized by a scatter of white chips. In stone country the smooth contours of the chalk mounds are replaced by the roughness of a naked or heather-covered cairn.

In the downland areas of Dorset, Wiltshire and Hampshire, which is conveniently described by the title of the later Anglo-Saxon kingdom of Wessex, a further foreign influence made itself felt after about 1500 B.C. This was of great significance for the Bronze Age monuments of the area, for the Wessex chieftains patronized a new and more sophisticated form of funerary architecture. These can still be classified as round barrows, but one of the two main innovations is very distinctive. This is the so-called disk barrow in which a circular ditch with a small external bank is the most conspicuous feature; inside this ring the burial is usually covered by a tump hardly larger than an ambitious ant-heap; occasionally there are two or even three of these little mounds. The second new type is more like the ordinary round barrow, except that the mound does not run right to the edge of the ditch but is separated from it by a level platform. It would be more accurate to say "was originally separated" for in the course of time the central pile has normally slipped and splayed out over the platform; the resulting shape has given this variety the name of bell barrow. Both the disk and the bell barrows of Wessex are distinguished by a remarkable perfection in their building; seen from the air the geometrical precision of mound, bank and ditch makes them stand out sharply—an assertion of the human mind among the natural curves of the downland.

Any observer of these graves, whether they lie beside one of the broad green ridgeways which make walking on the downs so pleasurable, whether they are seen, more substantial but functionless among shooting-butts on the moors, or are briefly noticed from motor-car or train, may ask what is likely to lie concealed below their smooth or broken domes. The answer is that only rarely are they undisturbed. Very few have been scientifically excavated, but during the eighteenth and nineteenth centuries barrow-digging became a gentlemanly pastime. Landowners who did not wish to hunt the fox might instead enjoy the milder excitement of hunting their forbears. The usual method was to set some stout gamekeepers or labourers to work with spades while the gentry picnicked *al fresco*. The sole object was to reach the burial, assumed to be at the centre of the mound, and to remove the urns and weapons, ornaments and other grave-goods which might lie beside the dead. Very many *tumuli* still show an irregular dent in their crowns as the results of these forays, but most of the plunder seems to have vanished, often no doubt thrown away by reforming widows, or even at spring cleanings, when the objects had grown dusty and lost the glamour of new discovery.

Although, after the recent assaults of romance and science, few of the dead still lie in their graves, we have learnt what structures and what forms of burial the mounds originally covered, and were able to preserve through thousands of years of quiet, uncurious peasant life. The earlier Bronze Age conquerors did not burn their corpses, but dug pits in the chalk or constructed boxes of stone slabs in which they were laid with knees drawn up towards the chin. The dead, whether men or women, were buried fully dressed and wearing their ornaments—which among the wealthy might be of gold, amber or jet. Women had their hair properly dressed, the prevailing fashion being to fasten it on the back of the head with a long bone pin. Warriors might be furnished with bow and arrows, a flint or bronze dagger and a heavy axe of polished stone. It was also customary to stand beside the dead pottery vessels containing food and drink.

In the middle of the Bronze Age, after about 1500 B.C., this simple conception of burying the dead as they had lived and supplying them with the needs of physical existence was completely changed. More than half the round barrows were raised over cremation burials, after a funeral at which the body was burned on a huge pyre of faggots, and the ashes placed in a clay urn. The practice of urn-burial brought to an end the old custom of provisioning the grave and furnishing it with possessions. So the traveller must accept the improbability of any barrow he passes containing a rich burial. If it has escaped the various threats of man and nature, the chances are it covers only an earthenware urn full of charred bones. Yet of course there is always a possibililty, however slight, that the remains of some nobleman of the early Bronze Age are waiting there in the earth, the gold bright but unseen, bronze staining the soil with green, and roots pushing and twining round the skeleton.

If round barrows and cairns are the most characteristic and common of the Bronze Age features in our rural landscape, there is another type of monument which can be far more imposing. This is the embanked sanctuary or temple, an architectural form which includes two of our most famous prehistoric sites, Avebury and Stonehenge. These sanctuaries can be recognized by a circular enclosing bank and ditch, usually with one or two entrances and with the bank placed outside the ditch—an arrangement unthinkable in a military or defensive work. Inside this ring, which presumably marked off the sacred area, the temple consisted of settings of upright stones or massive wooden posts arranged either in circles or on the horseshoe plan so splendidly represented by the gigantic inner trilithons at Stonehenge. Occasionally the sanctuary may be approached by an avenue or holy way; at Stonehenge the course of such a way is defined only by an inconspicuous bank and ditch, but at Avebury we shall find an impressive avenue of standing stones.

Although of their nature these monuments could not be very numerous, they are remarkably widespread; in England we shall encounter them as far apart as in Somerset, Norfolk and Derbyshire, while fine examples exist as far north as the Orkney islands. This architectural form may have inherited something from the native New Stone Age peoples; but certainly it owed its main inspiration to the Bronze Age invaders. Avebury and many other of the simpler temples seem to have assumed their final shape quite early in the Bronze Age, but Stonehenge was added to and altered over as long a period as our Gothic cathedrals. While its foundation was probably as early as that of Avebury, the unique trilithons and the lintelled outer circle were added perhaps four centuries later by the builders of the bell and disk barrows. An equivalent to the Victorian additions to our cathedrals is provided by some remodeling in the Iron Age, though it was certainly less harmful than brass furnishings and encaustic tiles.

As their tombs were for the New Stone Age communities, these sanctuaries must have been the centres of religious life for the peoples of the Bronze Age. The fact that they are larger, fewer and more widely spaced suggests that they served much more extensive social groups. Beyond that, it is a kind of penance for the imagination to look at them, so impossible is it to recreate for oneself any satisfying picture of what went on in them. We are grown so rational (in some directions) that the vast irrational imaginative creations of peoples living for their emotions and intuitions elude our understanding. We watch films of modern primitives performing their dances; we read about or look at pictures of the gorgeous cruelties of the Aztecs and Incas, but we do so as anthropologists, as historians, and cannot participate. Indeed, few of us can any longer truly participate in the rituals of Christianity. Yet if nearly two thousand years later the Druids, a philosophical priesthood, could still cram great wicker effigies with living animals and men and set fire to them, we should avoid English moderation in thinking of what may have been enacted among those sarsen stones which now stand so quiet and grey in our temperate countryside.

Round barrows and temples, together with the simple forms of stone circle and avenue which lack the sanctuary enclosures, are the only conspicuous marks of their presence left by the increasingly prosperous generations who lived in Britain for the thousand years of the Bronze Age between about 1900 and 900 B.C. They followed their flocks and herds, they raised a little corn, became increasingly skilful as metallurgists; they traded and fought. Yet none of these activities has left a lasting impression on their land. The results are to be seen in museum cases, but not in our fields or on our hills. Even more than in the New Stone Age, it was the energy generated by transcendental presentiments that was great enough to move earth and stone into enduring forms.

The end of the Bronze Age and the beginning of the Iron Age were of great importance in our prehistory. It was then that wave after wave of Celtic-speaking immigrants made a solid contribution to our racial stock and introduced a language parental to the Gaelic now spoken by millions of Scots and Irishmen. It was then, too, that these Celtic settlers began revolutionary changes in agriculture which affected the relationship between the people and the land, and their whole way of life. Regular and permanent fields cultivated with ox-drawn ploughs now took the place of the shifting corn plots turned by hand with hoe or digging-stick. From this change it followed that the farmers and their households gave up their partially nomadic life to settle beside their fields, living sometimes in clusters of huts, sometimes in relatively spacious single farmsteads. The improvement in agriculture and all the associated crafts of carpentry, building and the making of farm implements, was greatly helped at this same period by an increase in the available supplies of metal. At first the production of bronze mounted sharply, probably because the trade in copper and tin was better organized; then, in about 450 B.C., iron began to be worked in Britain and very rapidly outstripped bronze. It appears that the earliest mining was in the Forest of Dean, but it has left no certain traces; the earliest striking remains of what was to become one of our greatest industries are in the Sussex Weald where we shall find a system of roads largely surfaced with iron slag from the mines which they served.

I have said that cheap metal encouraged the manufacture of more and better-designed tools for the use of craftsman; this was certainly so, but at the same time, then as to-day, this technological advance went together with a lavish expense of resources on instruments of war. In the Late Bronze Age, from about 900 to 450 B.C., more bronze was used for making swords, spears and fine shields than went into axes, sickles, gouges and saws, while in the Iron Age long swords were the finest product of the blacksmith. The Celtic peoples were already showing the passion for fighting which in the end was to bring about their subjection.

The beginnings of military architecture are, indeed, the only noticeable remains of the later Bronze and earliest Iron Ages, and even these are still very modest in scale. Of all periods in British prehistory since the first introduction of farming, it has left least that is worth seeing out of doors. No great ceremonial seems to have been allowed to death; urn-burial in flat cemeteries was the common practice and where in the Late Bronze Age barrows were raised they were so low-pitched as to be unimpressive. Nor, evidently, did other religious rites demand elaborate or substantial settings; the building of stone circles and sacred enclosures came to an end.

Some of the huts, walled plots and enclosures on Dartmoor and other moorlands in the south-west date from these centuries of transition from the Bronze to the Iron Age, and there are traces of settled farms of the same age on the Sussex Downs. In the stone country of the north, too, there are Late Bronze Age huts and other remains among the many antiquities scattered over the north Yorkshire moors. But these sites are both local and unremarkable.

The earliest military architecture of the Iron Age is represented by a number of simple earthworks in the south of England; the crown of a hill was defended by a single line of bank and ditch following along the natural contour; often this was no more than a trench with a stockade which would have disappeared but for the fact that they were sometimes covered by the massive ramparts of the later Iron Age and can be recovered by excavation.

Very few of the monuments of the period from 1000 B.C. to 300 B.C. are of even the second rank as spectacles and not many of them will be found to deserve mention in later chapters. When set beside the great megalithic tombs, barrows, long and round, Silbury

Hill, Stonehenge, Avebury, and all the other fine monuments of earlier times, the survivals from this age are paltry indeed. Perhaps our conclusion should be that such momentous works are only created when human imagination is unbalanced, run riot after one aim so that men are happy to fling a disproportionate amount of effort into its service.

It has already appeared how in early days the imagination and its creative powers had been engaged in religious enthusiasm, but now, as the Celtic Iron Age progressed, it found a new obsession, a new madness, to divert it alike from religion and from the dull sensible pursuit of economic well-being. This obsession was war. From about 250 B.C. there were continued Celtic immigrations into various parts of the island, among the most important being those which affected Yorkshire and the south-west—where the trade in Cornish tin was always a powerful lure. These later invaders, like their immediate precursors, spoke the Celtic tongue which has survived in Welsh and Cornish. As conquerors imposing themselves upon the less vigorous, less well armed and equipped natives they remained in many regions as a warrior aristocracy. In Yorkshire, for example, small barrows were found to cover the graves of such fighting chiefs, some of whom had been buried with their weapons and their battle chariots in a fashion well known in their homelands in northern France. Both the new leadership itself and the effort to resist the invaders served to heighten the warlike qualities of the Celts. All historical records of this virile and gifted people both on the Continent and in Britain itself show them as prone to inter-tribal warfare and dynastic feuds. From petty cattle raiding to struggles between the princes of powerful royal families, we see them squandering their force in an endless competitiveness.

Without the testimony of history, there is striking evidence of the military spirit of the Celts to be found among the hills and mountains of Britain. No class of prehistoric monument is at once so numerous, widespread and conspicuous as the forts of the Celtic Iron Age whose ramparts show against the sky on many downland summits, and on the more jagged crests of the mountain country. Whether the ramparts were of chalk rammed behind wooden palisades or of rough stone masonry (sometimes bonded with timber) they were both more massive and far more elaborate than the embankments and stockades of the earlier Iron Age. Often there were two, three or even four lines of rampart, and outworks and other devices for the defence of the gates.

Taking the country at large, the bulk of chalk laboriously dug, shovelled into baskets, carried and piled, the tonnage of stone blocks lifted and built, the vast number of trees felled and baulks of timber shaped, make a staggering total of human effort. It is a remarkable

proof of the fertility of the island even at a time when so much of
the richest land was still forested that enough grain and meat could
be raised to support the labourers—in addition to the riches, time
and human life sacrificed to war itself.

Some of the forts were built against the invaders of the middle
of the third century B.C., being rushed up in a spirit of emergency
akin to that of 1940. Others were built as tribal strongholds, places
of retreat where cattle and other property could be defended in
time of danger, whether the threat was a raid from a neighbouring
tribe or one of military conquest. Not very many of them were
permanently occupied by any number of people and we must
beware of thinking of them all as towns. Although I am still fond
of Kipling's lines:

> Oh, they are the walls the flint men made
> To guard their wondrous towns

he was wrong not only about the age of the earthworks but also
about their usual purpose.

In Cornwall the promontory forts whose strong ramparts run
from cliff to cliff to fortify a headland, as well as perfectly circular
forts such as Chun Castle, were probably built by invaders who,
as I have said, came to the peninsula to control the tin trade with
the Continent. Some of the most striking of the Wessex forts, on the
other hard, including the final elaboration of the extraordinary
maze of ramparts at Maiden Castle, Dorchester, are believed to
have been the work of the Venetic Celts of Brittany, who fled to
Britain after their utter rout on land and sea by Julius Caesar.

We can imagine disorganized parties of refugees fleeing across
the Channel in their shallow-draft, leather-sailed ships and dropping anchor off the Dorset beaches. The Veneti were famous for
their skill as slingers, and it may have been as a defence against
this long-range weapon that they had devised and adopted the type
of fort with many lines of rampart. At Maiden Castle itself over
twenty thousand slingstones were found in a single arsenal, all of
them natural pebbles brought from Chesil Beach.

There were other movements into Britain during this restless
time at the close of our prehistoric era which led to yet more fort-
building and to a widespread refurbishing of neglected defences.
As we know from his own mention of it in the *Gallic War* there
had been an invasion of south-eastern England from Gaul not very
many years before Caesar's expeditions to this island in 55 and
54 B.C. We now understand that a second, lesser, invasion followed
soon after. Both movements were of Belgic tribes, a stock of mixed
Celtic and Teutonic origin coming from the territories round the
lower Rhine which still form the borderland between these two

great peoples. That the Belgae were at least as martial in their ideals as any of their Celtic precursors in Britain is shown accurately enough by the name of their most powerful tribe. The opposition to Caesar, and later to the legions of Claudius, was led by the princes of the Catuvellauni, a title which may be translated Mighty Warriors. The Mighty Warriors called their capital Camulodunum after Camulos, god of War. After their conquest and settlement in the south-east and south, the Belgae began to fight their way westward, and their ruthless campaigning led to the strengthening of fortifications both by and against them. When we reach Wessex we shall encounter a line of very strong hill forts which held the Belgic advance for a number of years; we shall also meet the relics of the destruction wrought when the advance went on—for example in the storming and reduction of the fort on Bredon Hill.

It is not to be expected that the arrival of such a people as the Belgae would reduce the preponderance of martial remains among the monuments of the Iron Age. We do know of some most remarkable burial-vaults where the dead, though their bodies were cremated, were buried with the complete furnishings for a luxurious feast by a rite which recalls the graves of early Bronze Age warriors more closely than those of the intervening centuries. However, these vaults have been closed and the traveller will generally look in vain for remains left by the Belgae other than their fortifications. On the other hand they began an agricultural revolution which was to transform the landscape of Britain. Coming themselves from heavily forested country on the Continent, their first contingents found it natural to use the river valleys of south-east England for their lines of communication and to begin their clearance and cultivation. In short it was the Belgae who were the pioneers in the movement down from the hills and on to the rich but hitherto heavily encumbered lowland soils which was described at the end of the last chapter.

They, therefore, have left the oldest monuments to survive on these heavier soils. To the west of modern Colchester we shall presently discover the lines of massive banks and ditches, many miles long, with which they defended their capital of Camulodunum —a scattered settlement occupying a gravel promontory between two rivers. There is another, much smaller dyke system just outside the Roman town of Verulamium, but more significant, if they are indeed Belgic, are the similar dykes on the Sussex coastal plain near Chichester. These Sussex earthworks are more significant because they may be an instance of a direct movement down from the hills. The old Celtic tribal stronghold of the Regni had been the fort now known as the Trundle near the Goodwood racecourse; the Belgic conquerors destroyed the place and shifted

the capital down to the neighbourhood of Chichester, protecting
it, perhaps, with these dykes and giving it the title of Noviomagus—
the New Settlement on the Plain.

It must have been noticed how in this account of the later Iron
Age the names of peoples, places and at last even of individuals
have begun to assert their definite shapes against the vast anonym-
ity of prehistoric times. This last century before our era is in
fact the period of transition when the literacy which was spreading
west and north with the soldiers and traders of Rome first begins
to cast a few sparks of historical light as far as this island.

There had been the visit of the Greek traveller Pytheas in the
fourth century B.C., but apart from the tantalizing scraps of his
story which are all that survive, we owe our first news of ourselves
to the Romans. The earliest invaders whose tribal name we have
been able to identify are the Parisii of Yorkshire, the earliest name
of an individual, Cassivellaunus. As for literacy in Britain itself,
the oldest lettering is found on Belgic coins, the oldest handwriting
is scratched on potsherds from the quayside at Camulodunum. So
words begin to assert their authority beside the evidence of things,
and the archaeologist must work in co-operation with the historian.

After the successful conquest which began in 43 A.D., England
and Wales were, of course, drawn within the limits of a fully
historic Empire and their prehistory was brought at least temporarily
to an end. There is no need for me to recall in detail the familiar
story of that conquest. The Roman armies had little trouble in
subduing the English lowlands; the open country was itself vulner-
able and its peoples betrayed one another through inter-tribal feuds.
When, however, the human resistance was stiffened by the highland rocks, by the ancient hills and mountains of west and north,
the advance was slowed. Wales and the north gave trouble, and
meanwhile Queen Boudicca had raised her savage forces, her
infantry and chariots, and sacked the new towns at Colchester,
London and St. Albans, before she herself was killed and her rebellion most brutally put down. It is worth remarking that this
fiery, tragic and finally unsuccessful woman is the only native of
Britain before King Alfred to have made a deep enough impression
on the imagination of the more recent population to have been
honoured by a statue. At the end of Westminster Bridge trams
grind round the bend within a few feet of the forehoofs of her
horses; decorously and even voluminously dressed she is driving
her chariot towards Parliament Square. Although not allowed the
protection of a work of art, this Victorian rendering of an indomitable and virtuous, if bloodthirsty, queen survived all the bombs
aimed at Westminster and Whitehall.

The rebellion was the end of resistance in England, and the

Province of Britannia may be said to have reached stability when by the early second century Wales was easily controlled from Caerleon and Chester, while Hadrian's Wall had just been built from the Tyne to the Solway, to hold the untamed northern barbarians at bay. The Wall, one of our most commanding relics of antiquity, stands as a fine achievement of rational planning and of orthodox military engineering to set beside the strange imaginative creations of Avebury and Stonehenge.

In this it clearly exemplifies the change which all travellers will expect to find when they turn from prehistoric remains to those of Roman Britain. They represent the first surviving marks on the face of Britain of intellectual planning imposed from a distant centre of control. The like is hardly to be seen again before the eighteenth century. First there are the roads, primarily military in purpose, and the lightly built marching camps of the Roman army; then the more substantial garrison forts and the big legionary fortresses of the permanent military areas of the west and north. There is Hadrian's Wall itself. It is certainly true to say that in spite of the *Pax Romana* military monuments are still dominant.

We shall, however, come across plentiful reminders of Roman civil life: the towns that were founded and at first carefully fostered as a part of the Imperial policy for Romanization of the native Britons, and the villas where the successfully romanized aristocrats of the Province lived in comfort on their well-cultivated estates. The towns were of various kinds; tribal capitals, smaller country towns and the *coloniae* where retired soldiers were settled and given small holdings. There were certain semi-military centres, the chief being York, and there was London, the trading emporium which after Boudicca's revolt seems to have become the capital of the Province. Even in the towns the remains of the civic architecture—the forum with its basilica and other public buildings, the bath-houses and amphitheatres—have hardly survived so well as the military defences. Though generally unwalled in the earlier years, by the third century most of the towns had secured themselves behind stout walls and gateways. It is their massive masonry, often stripped of its smooth stone facings, which we shall find standing in many of our modern towns, sometimes clear to see, sometimes incorporated in the medieval walls. Here and there, when exceptionally the sites were not chosen for later towns, we shall see their ruins looking still a little incongruous in the rural landscape. The most famous of these urban ghosts is at Silchester in Hampshire where the complete circuit of the city walls still stands—enclosing arable fields and a diminutive parish church.

For many people the most characteristic remains of Roman Britain are the villas—the country houses of well-to-do farmers and the upper class. The villas flourished long after the Roman towns began to decline in the late second century, but with the Anglo-Saxon conquest they and all that they stood for were completely obliterated.

The barbarian raiders had no sympathy for their civilized life, central heating, baths, and quotations from Virgil in mosaic on the drawing-room floor. They decayed or were destroyed, but their floors and foundations often survive, protected by the accumulations of nearly two thousand years. When uncovered, they are, I think it is true to say, the flimsiest of our antiquities. Only too often visitors will find them under dilapidated or downright ruinous roofs, the mortar of foundations and hypocausts slowly disintegrating, perhaps with vegetation sprouting through the mosaic floors. Yet they are always popular, these earliest traces of a domestic life already very like our own.

When the Roman Province began to be seriously threatened by raids from barbarian pirates in the Channel and North Sea, the authorities responded vigorously. They built the so-called forts of the Saxon Shore to protect the whole eastern angle of England from the Wash to the Solent. These forts, of which nearly a dozen survive, are the latest buildings with which I am properly concerned; their long curtain walls and projecting bastions have endured remarkably well. All were originally on the sea, but several we shall find now to be standing among fields well away from the water, a reminder of how greaty silt has accumulated round the Kentish and Sussex coasts.

The Forts of the Saxon Shore symbolize the impossibility of turning back the great tides of history. The Empire was crumbling; it lacked the vitality to hold out for long against the violently fluctuating yet persistent pressure of the northern peoples who for so many centuries had lived as free barbarians in the prehistoric darkness beyond the Roman frontiers. The Anglo-Saxon invasions soon swept round these forts leaving them at once as the meaningless shells which we ourselves have inherited.

For a time after the withdrawal of the Romans in the fifth century, Britain returned to what were virtually prehistoric conditions. Yet it was in truth a very brief relapse into darkness. With extraordinary speed the roving bands of freebooters turned into settlers—clearers of the land, builders of strong kingdoms—until, in less than two hundred years after the legions sailed away to Rome, St. Augustine was returning from the holy city, and a Christian England was in sight. Soon we shall find that the monuments are no longer deserted antiquities but still a functioning part of our national life. Bradford-on-Avon and many less excellent examples of Saxon churches still serve their congregations and indeed in most villages if we cannot see any traces of the pre-Norman church, it is because the existing one is built upon it. The present pattern of rural England, its villages, country towns and even many of its county divisions, was already established before the Normans came; very many of the names now marked on Ordnance Survey maps are to be identified in Domesday Book. Saxon life has been wholly absorbed into our own.

WILLIAM CAMDEN

Stonehenge and Avebury in Tudor Times

THE original Latin edition of Camden's *Britannia* was published in 1586. This is one of the earliest accounts of Stonehenge and Avebury. The idea that the huge blocks at Stonehenge are synthetic is, of course, as fanciful as the references to notions borrowed from the *British History*.

TOWARD the North, about six miles from Salisburic, in these plaines before named, is to bee seene a huge and monstrous piece of worke, such as Cicero termeth *insanam substructionem*. For, within the circuit of a Ditch, there are erected in manner of a Crowne, in three rankes or courses one within another certaine mightie and unwrought stones, whereof some are 28 foote high, and seven foote broad, upon the heads of which, others like over-thwart pieces do beare and rest cross-wise, with a small tenents and mortescis, so as the whole frame seemeth to hang: whereof

From *Britannia*, 1637, pp. 251-5.

wee call it *Stonehenge,* like as our old Historians termed it for the greatnesse *Chorea Gigantum; The Giants Daunce.* The description, or draught whereof, such as it is, because it could not be so fitly expressed in words, I have caused by the gravers helpe to bee portraied . . . as it now standeth weatherbeaten, and decaied.

Our countrie-men reckon this for one of our wonders and miracles. And much they marvaile: from whence such huge stones were brought, considering that in all those quarters bordering thereupon, there is hardly to be found any common stone at all for building: as also by what meanes they were set up. For mine own part, about these points I am not curiously to argue and dispute, but rather to lament with much griefe that the Authors of so notable a monument are thus buried in oblivion. Yet some there are, that thinke them to bee no naturall stones hewne out of the rocke, but artificially made of pure sand, and by some glewie and unctuous matter knit and incorporate together, like as those ancient Trophies or monuments of victorie which I have seene in Yorkshire. And what marvaile? Read we not, I pray you, in Plinie, that the sand or dust of *Puteoli* being covered over with water, becommeth forthwith a very stone: that the cesternes in Rome of sand digged out of the ground, and the strongest kind of lime wrought together grow so hard, that they seeme stones indeede and that Statues and images of marble chippings, and small grit grow together so compact and firme, that they are deemed entire and solid marble: The common saying is, that *Ambrosius Aurelianus,* or his brother *Uther* did reare them up by the art of *Merlin* that great *Mathematician,* in memorie of those Britaines who by the treachery of Saxons were there slaine at a parley. Whereupon *Alexander Necham,* a Poet of no great antiquitie, in a poeticall fit, but with no speciall grace, and favour of *Apollo,* having instructions out of *Geffreys* British historie, come out of these verses:

> The Giants Daunce, a famous stone-worke stands
> Art did her best in bringing it to passe,
> Vain prating fame, reports by Merlins hands
> In manner strange this worke effected was.
>> The stones (men say) in their land first did lie,
>> Whence Cranes in flocks so many use to flie.
> From thence conveied, as things of charie price,
> The Irish soile received them with joy.
> For why? their vertue in a wondrous wise,
> Oft cures the griefe that doth sicke folke annoy.
>> For, waters cast and sprinckled on these stones
>> Their vertue take, and heale the grieved ones.
> The noble Uther that Pendragon hight,
> Them over seas to Ambresburie brought;
> Returning thence, where he by martiall might,

Had quel'd his foes in Battel fiercely foughte.
O worthy Wight, how many on that Plaine
Of you lie dead by Hengist treason slaine!

[The rest of the verse is too absurd to reproduce.]

Others say that the Britaines erected this for a stately sepulchre of the same Ambrose in the very place where hee was slaine by his enemies sword that hee might have of his countries cost such a piece of worke, and the tombe set over him as should for ever be permanent as the altar of his vertue and manhood.

True it is that mens bones have many times beene digged up heere and the village lying now on Avons side is called Ambresburie [now Amesbury], that is to say Ambrose his town: where certain ancient Kings, by the report of the British Historie, lay interred. . . .

More somewhat into the East, the River *Cunetio*, . . . commonly *Kenet* [the River Kennet] ariseth neere unto a little Village of the same name, which some would have to be that Cunetio mentioned by Antoninus: but the distance of both sides gainsaieth it. Heere Selburie [Silbury Hill, a huge artificial mound probably dating from the Bronze Age] a round hill mounteth up aloft, to a great height, which by the forme of the hill it selfe, and the outward settling of the earth beneath, may seeme to have beene cast up by mans hand. And many of that sort, round and with sharpe tops are to bee seene in this tract: *Burrowes* they call them and *Barrowes*, raised, happily in memoriall of Souldiers there slaine. For bones are found in them, and read I have, how an usuall thing it was with the Northerne nations, that every souldier remaining alive after a foughten field, should carry his head-piece full of earth toward the making of their fellowes tombes that were slaine. Although I am of opinion rather, that this of Selburie, was set there in stead of a limit, if not by the Romans, then certainly by the Saxons: Like as that fosse called *Wodensdike*, considering that betweene the Mercians and the West-Saxons there was much bickering in this Shire many a time, about their Marches: and both Boetius and the Grammaticall Writers have made mention of such Mounts raised for bounds. Within one mile of Selburie, is Aiburie [Avebury], an up-landish village built in an old Campe as it seemeth, but of no large compasse, for it is environed with a faire trench, and hath foure gappes as gates, in two of the which stand huge Stones as jambes, but so rude, that they seem rather naturall than artificiall, of which sort, there are some other in the said village. This River Kenet runneth at the first Eastward, through certaine open fields, out of which there stand up aloft every where stones like rockes. . . .

RICHARD COLT-HOARE

Stonehenge in the Early Nineteenth Century

THIS extract contains the first intelligent observations concerning the two kinds of stones employed at Stonehenge—the huge sarsens, coming from no great distance, and the much smaller "blue-stones" (mostly of spotted dolerite) which we now know to have been brought from western Wales. Cunnington was right in thinking that they might represent different building periods, but the story is infinitely more complicated than he could have imagined—as modern archaeology has discovered.

❦

LET us now approach this mysterious building, and enter within its hallowed precincts. "When you enter the building, "says STUKELEY," whether on foot or horseback, and cast your eyes around upon the yawning ruins, you are struck into an extatic *reverie*, which none can describe, and they only can be sensible of, that feel it. Other buildings fall by piecemeal, but here a single stone is a ruin, and lies like the haughty carcase of Goliath. Yet there is as much of it undemolished, as enables us sufficiently to recover its form, when it was in its most perfect state: there is enough of every part to preserve the idea of the whole. When we advance further, the dark part of the ponderous imposts over our heads, the chasm of sky between the jambs of the CELL, the odd construction of the whole, and the greatness of every part, surprizes. We may well cry out in the poet's words, 'Tantum religio potuit.' If you look upon the perfect part, you fancy entire quarries mounted up into the air; if upon the rude havock below, you see, as it were, the bowels of a

From *The Ancient History of South Wiltshire*, 1812, pp. 145-6, 151-3.

mountain turned inside outwards." At first sight all is amazement
and confusion; the eye is surprised, the mind bewildered. The
stones begin now, and not before, to assume their proper grandeur;
and the interior of the temple, hitherto blinded by an uniform
exterior, displays a most singular variety and gigantic magnificence.
But such is the dilapidation, and such the confusion of the displaced
fragments, that no one, who has not, as I may say, got the plan
by heart, can possibly replace them in imagination according to
their original destination. To obviate these difficulties, and assist
the antiquary in developing this labyrinth of stones, I have annexed a correct plan of them as they now stand, which would be
rendered more perspicuous at first sight, if each circle, as well as
each oval, were distinguished by a separate colour. . . .

[Colt-Hoare here quotes a letter from his fellow Wiltshire antiquary,
William Cunnington]

"ON viewing the remains of this monument of the Britons, I have
been surprized that the following question never occurred to those
writers who have considered this subject, viz. 'Why did the Britons,
in erecting STONEHENGE, make use of two kinds of stone, which
are totally dissimilar to each other?' Any person versed in
mineralogy, will perceive that the stones on the outside of the work,
those composing the outward circle and its imposts, as well as the
five large trilithons, are all of that species of stone called *sarsen,*
which is found in the neighbourhood; whereas the inner circle of
small upright stones, and those of the interior oval, are composed
of granite, horn-stone, &c., most probably brought from some part of
Devonshire or Cornwall, as I know not where such stones could be
procured at a nearer distance."
    "In considering the subject, I have been led to suppose that
STONEHENGE was raised at different aera; that the original work
consisted of the outward circle and its imposts, and of the inner
oval of large trilithons; and that the smaller circle and oval, of
inferior stones, were raised at a later period; for they add nothing
to the general grandeur of the temple, but rather give a littleness
to the whole; and more particularly so, if, according to SMITH, you
add the two small trilithons of granite."
    I am much pleased with this new idea respecting STONEHENGE,
which, to use a well known Italian proverb, "*Se non è vero, è ben
trovato.*" *If not true, is well imagined;* for it is not, like many others,
founded on idle conjecture, but has some rational ground to rest
upon. In erecting this mighty structure, its builders would naturally
select for that purpose the materials nearest at hand; such were the
sarsens, which compose the grandest part of the work, viz. the

outward circle, and large oval; and why, with these materials, ac-
quireable at no great distance (for at that early period, the plains
adjoining STONEHENGE might very probably have furnished stones
sufficiently large), should the architects have sought materials for
the small circle and small oval, in such distant counties? This difference in the stones is a strong argument in favour of Mr.
CUNNINGTON'S conjecture; for had the Britons erected the temple
at one and the same period, they would most naturally have made
use of the native, not foreign materials. And in viewing this new
supposed plan of STONEHENGE, divested of its unmeaning pigmy
pillars of granite, and diminutive trilithons, we behold a most
majestic and mysterious pile, unconfused in its plan, simple and
grand in its architecture, most awful and imposing in its effect.
Such indeed is the general fascination imposed on all those who
view it, that no one can quit its precincts, without feeling strong
sensations of surprize and admiration. The ignorant rustic will with
a vacant stare attribute it to the giants, or the mighty archfiend;
and the antiquary, equally uninformed as to its origin, will regret
that its history is veiled in perpetual obscurity. The artist, on viewing
these enormous masses, will wonder that art could thus rival nature
in magnificence and picturesque effect: even the most indifferent
passenger over the plain must be attracted by the solitary and
magnificent appearance of these ruins; and all with one accord will
exclaim, "HOW GRAND! HOW WONDERFUL! HOW INCOMPREHEN-
SIBLE!"

RICHARD ATKINSON

Stonehenge According to Modern Archaeology

FROM 1950 for several seasons Stuart Piggott, Richard Atkinson and their assistants carried out excavations to try to piece together a coherent history of this much altered—and much excavated—monument. Their findings can be roughly summarized. Stonehenge I: The earliest sanctuary was constructed at the very end of the Neolithic period and the beginning of bronze-using times: about 1900–1700 B.C. The main features were a circular embanked enclosure with one entrance and with a ring of ritual pits following the inside of the bank. Some of the pits contained cremation burials. The only important stone feature was the standing monolith now known as the Heel Stone just outside the entrance. Stonehenge II: During the next two centuries the bluestones were brought from Wales and set up in two concentric circles in the middle of the old enclosure. The embanked ceremonial way known as the Avenue, which leads past the Heel Stone in the direction of the midsummer sunrise, was added at this time. The Beaker people played some part in this phase. Stonehenge III: Between 1500 and 1400 B.C. the sanctuary was raised to its greatest grandeur by the pastoral chieftains of the Wessex culture (p. 384, II). The huge sarsens were brought from the Marlborough district (*c.* twenty-four miles) and set up in their present positions: an outer ring of uprights supporting a continuous lintel, and an inner horseshoe setting of trilithons (two uprights and one lintel). Meanwhile the bluestones had been taken down. There were changes of plan over their re-use, but finally they were. set up as at present—a circle inside the sarsen circle and a horseshoe setting inside the horseshoe of trilithons. The open ends of the horseshoes faced down the Avenue towards

wwwwwwwwwwwww

From *Stonehenge*. London: Hamish Hamilton Ltd.; 1956, pp. 1-5, 94, 98-100, 105, 106-111, 114-16, 127-33, 134-5, 158-65. By permission of Hamish Hamilton Ltd.

the sunrise, helping to confirm the supposition that sun worship played an important part in Stonehenge rituals. There is evidence for some deliberate destruction during Roman times.

⚜

Description and Outline of History

STONEHENGE stands on Salisbury Plain, about eight miles north of Salisbury and a little more than two miles west of Amesbury. To the visitor who approaches the monument for the first time, particularly from the direction of Amesbury, the first glimpse is often keenly disappointing, for the stones, vast though they are, seem entirely dwarfed by the even vaster background of rolling Wiltshire downland. It is not until one approaches more closely, so that the stones are silhouetted against the sky, that the true size of the place becomes apparent, and begins to communicate to even the most casual and unfeeling visitor something of the awe and wonder with which it has for so many centuries been invested.

The monument stands on a slight eminence of the chalk downs, but its position was evidently not chosen to command a particularly wide view. To the west the ground rises slightly; in all other directions it falls, though gently, the steepest slope being on the east, where the surface declines to the floor of a dry valley. In the immediate neighbourhood of the stones the ground is almost level.

The details of the surrounding landscape are almost wholly manmade: the buildings of Larkhill Camp to the north; the sunlit hangars of Boscombe Down aerodrome on the eastern skyline; the massed birch trees of Fargo Plantation to the north-west; the long wind-break of conifers north-eastwards towards Durrington; and the two plantations of beeches, north of the Amesbury road, which conceal the cemetery of Bronze Age burials known as the Old and New King Barrows. Only to the south does something of the primitive landscape remain, where the skyline of Normanton Down is punctuated by the barrows of another cemetery. Happily, however, all the more obtrusively modern elements in the landscape lie at a moderate distance, so that even today the visitor, especially if he is fortunate enough to have the place to himself, can still sense something of that wild and treeless isolation which even the least sensitive observer must feel to be the proper setting for Stonehenge.

Of the nature of the original landscape of Stonehenge, at the time the monument was erected, we know nothing directly. We can be fairly sure, admittedly, that the actual conformation of the ground, the shapes of the skylines, the hills and the valleys, have not changed appreciably. But of the vegetation, the grass, the bushes, the kinds and disposition of the trees, which clothe the bare bones of a landscape and give it its essential character, we have no evidence. The most one can say is that probably the ground was a good deal less bare than today, broken by at least occasional thickets of thorn, juniper and gorse, and possibly by scattered but isolated trees. Even then, however, the effects of human occupation may have been apparent, though in a form less obtrusive than bricks and mortar. For nothing is more effective in clearing and keeping in check the natural vegetation than the continuous browsing of sheep and cattle; and it may well be that Stonehenge was originally set not in a thorny wilderness, but amid a carpet of short springy turf, even as it is today, created and maintained by the ceaseless wandering of prehistoric herdsmen and their flocks.

Of the stones themselves no words of mine can properly describe the suble varieties of texture and colour, or the uncountable effects of shifting light and shade. From a distance, they have a silvery grey colour in sunlight, which lightens to an almost metallic bluish-white against a background of storm clouds, an effect so notably recorded by Constable in his well-known water-colour. When the ground is covered in snow in midwinter, with a dull leaden sky threatening further falls, they seem nearly black; and at sunset in midsummer their surfaces glow, as if from within, with a soft warm pinkish-orange light.

At a nearer view, each stone takes on its own individual pattern of colour and texture. Some are almost white, like coarse marble, with the sparkling grain of white lump sugar, and so hard that even thirty-five centuries of weathering has not dimmed the irregular patches of polishing executed so laboriously by the original builders. Others are a dull mat grey, streaked and lined by close-set vertical cracks and fissures, like the grain of some vast stump of a petrified tree; and others again are soft, buff or even pink in colour, and deeply eroded into hollows and overhangs in which a man may crouch, the compact curves of his limbs and the rounded thrust of shoulder and hip matching the time-smoothed protuberances of the stone around him. Here and there, the fine smooth grain of the stone is broken by small nodules of creamy or pinkish flint. And in places patches of a natural siliceous cement, like a thick weathered layer of amber lacquer, marks where the rock has split along a natural plane of cleavage.

On many of the surfaces, particularly on the lee side protected from the scouring force of wind and rain, there is a light growth of fluffy grey-green lichen, accented here and there by vivid patches of scaly yellow, which softens the contours of the stone, and half conceals, like a growth of fur, the scars left by those who have sought a little squalid immortality by the laborious incision of name or initials.

The huge mass of the stones, their upward taper, and the uncompromising four-squareness of the lintels which they support, together give an impression of forceful upward growth combined with an immense solidity and security. There is no top-heaviness, no feeling of impending ruin, even where an upright now leans from the perpendicular. Nor do the many stones which have fallen, and now lie half buried in the soil, give one any sense of cataclysmic destruction. Even their fall seems to have had a ponderous and purposeful deliberation.

To the inquiring observer the signs of man's handiwork are everywhere apparent: the squared and tapering forms of the stones; the severely functional shapes of the mortice and tenon joints on uprights and lintels; and the delicate rippled fluting of their tooled surfaces, like wave-patterns left on the sand by an ebbing tide. Yet these things, though they betray the hand of the mason, and alone allow us to confer upon Stonehenge the dignity of architecture, are nowhere obtrusive. Everywhere these specifically man-made forms are being etched and gnawed by remorseless time, so that the stone, having once yielded itself to the builders and suffered shaping to their purpose, now seems to be reasserting its own essential nature by the gradual obliteration of their handiwork. To me at least this stubborn yet imperceptible battle between the works of man and of nature, in which nature must inevitably triumph in the end, gives to Stonehenge a quality of immemorial antiquity and, at the same moment, of timeless permanence, that is lacking from all our other early prehistoric monuments, whose stones have only been chosen, but not shaped, by man.

All this, admittedly, is a private and personal vision, and some at least of my more austere colleagues would say that it has nothing whatever to do with the archaeology of Stonehenge. True enough, each man's vision of Stonehenge is particular, and none, perhaps, will much resemble my own. Yet even the archaeologist (perhaps, indeed, the archaeologist more than others) must look at his monuments not merely with a professional eye (an eye which too often is buried, ostrich-like, below the ground), but also with that wandering and passively receptive regard which, with practice, can penetrate beyond the surface to an inwardness which is none the less real or significant for being personal and, in part at least, incommunicable. For who is to say that for the ultimate understanding of Stonehenge, not in terms of the categories of archaeological research, but as part of our human inheritance, and to that degree as part of ourselves, the aesthetic experience must play a lesser part than the precise and academic dissection of the evidence we recover from its soil?

Transport and Erection of the Stones: The Bluestones

The source of the majority of the bluestones has been narrowed down, by petrological identifications, to an area of about one square mile at the eastern end of the Prescelly Mountains in north Pembrokeshire. There can be no question of the stones having been carried even part of the way towards southern England by ice during the Pleistocene period, and their appearance at Stonehenge can only be explained as the result of deliberate transport by man. The question to be answered is therefore quite clear: by what route, and by what means, were these eighty-odd stones, weighing up to four tons apiece, brought from Prescelly to Stonehenge, a distance as the crow flies of some 135 miles? Of the alternative answers of a land and a water route, it is safe to say that the second is overwhelmingly the more probable.

The enormous growth of rail and road transport in the last half-century has tended to obscure the fact that carriage by boat, either coastwise or on inland waterways, is by far the most economical means of moving bulky material from one place to another. The decline in such traffic (neglect of our inland waterways apart) is due chiefly to the fact that it is much slower than the alternatives of road and rail. In prehistoric times the undoubted advantages of water transport would have been even more apparent, for not only was time, relatively speaking, of little importance, but in addition there were no alternatives, as there are today. During the second millennium B.C., at any rate, there were no wheeled vehicles or even pack-animals. The only beast of burden was man himself. Under these circumstances water transport was the sole means of moving goods, and above all heavy goods, with relative speed and economy. That this was widely realized in prehistoric times is amply demonstrated by the relation of the pattern of settlement to the river systems of the country, and more particularly by the very large numbers of objects, of all dates from the Neolithic onwards, which have been dredged in modern times from the rivers themselves. . . .

If it is accepted that the bluestones were brought to Wiltshire by water, what type of craft was used? The alternatives are rafts, made of suitable solid logs lashed together, or true boats, either dug-outs hollowed out from the solid or composite boats formed of a skin hull stretched on an articulated wooden frame. For the sea journey the raft has some marked advantages over the boat, in that it is unsinkable and cannot be swamped in rough weather. On the other hand a raft to support a given weight is very much larger and heavier than a boat, or composite vessel of several boats lashed together, to carry the same burden, and is therefore more difficult to propel by paddling, and far less manœuvrable in an emergency. Moreover, while it is possible that rafts were used at sea, it is very doubtful if they would be practicable for the inland part of the journey. . . .

For the inland part of the journey . . . boats must have been used. What kind of boats were they? Fortunately we have plenty of evidence, in the form of actual remains dredged from the beds of rivers, for the use of dug-out canoes in Britain from Neolithic times onwards, and indeed before. It is not impossible that skin boats were used as well, though no actual remains survive. The Eskimo *umiak*, the Irish curragh and on a smaller scale the Welsh coracle are all modern representatives of the type. It need not be considered further here, however, as it is structurally unsuitable for carrying the loads envisaged.

The dug-out canoes were made by splitting a large tree trunk longitudinally and hollowing out the interior, probably with the help of fire in the initial stages, until a one-piece hull was obtained with walls some 2–3 ins. thick. The size and shape of such boats is determined by the available raw material, which is usually oak. Exceptional examples have been recorded with a total length of 55 ft., but for present purposes it will be wise to assume a maximum length of 35 ft., a beam of 4 ft., and a depth of 2 ft. The shape of these vessels resembles that of an unusually deep punt, with a more or less flat bottom and vertical sides.

Theoretically a single canoe of this size will carry a weight of about 8,700 lbs. with a displacement of half its depth. Two such boats lashed side by side could therefore support the Altar Stone and a crew of at least ten men, with a freeboard of 1 ft. In fact, however, three or more boats would make a more satisfactory composite vessel. With two boats only the load on each gunwale would be of the order of 1¾ tons, and this load would be concentrated in the central half of the vessel, measured longitudinally, so that there would be a tendency both for the sides of the individual canoes to spread or buckle and for the vessel as a whole to break its back in the middle. Three canoes, each of the same beam and draught, but only 24 ft. in length, would carry the same weight far more safely distributed. The stone would rest, of course, on bearers extending the full width of the vessel, so that the load was evenly divided between the six gunwales. These same bearers would also serve to lock the three canoes together, and if they were notched to fit over the gunwales would at the same time act as stretchers preventing the sides from spreading under the applied load.

The practicability of this arrangement was proved in an experiment devised by the writer and his colleagues in collaboration with Mr. Paul Johnstone of the B.B.C. Television Service, which formed part of a television programme on Stonehenge broadcast in July 1954. Three "canoes," built of elm boarding and measuring 12 ft. by 2 ft. 3 ins. by 1 ft. 6 ins., were fixed together by four transverse bearers and floated on the River Avon near Salisbury. A replica of a bluestone in reinforced concrete, measuring 7 ft. 6 ins. by 2 ft. by 1 ft. 6 ins., was lowered on to the vessel by a mobile crane. The total load, including a crew of four boys from Bryanston School, was about 3,600 lbs. and gave a draught of 9 ins. The crew punted the loaded vessel up and down a stretch of the Avon with the greatest ease, and it was clear that it could have been propelled, at least in slow-flowing water, by a single man. Indeed, the operation had much in common with the pleasant pastime of punting agreeable companions (built happily upon less uncompromisingly monolithic lines) upon the quiet waters of the Cherwell or the Cam.

This practical trial leaves very little doubt that some such arrangement of dug-out canoes was used for the inland part of the voyage from Prescelly. The possibility of using the same craft *at sea* is another matter, and has not so far been put to the test. There is every reason to suppose that such canoes were used at sea in prehistoric times, though not usually with so heavy a load. But in any case, as we have seen, rafts could have been used for this part of the journey, and would have some advantages over boats.

The route suggested above includes at least twenty-four miles of land transport: sixteen miles from Prescelly to Canaston Bridge, six miles between Frome and Warminster, and two miles up the Avenue from the Avon to Stonehenge. Over these distances the stones must have been dragged on sledges.

The almost universal use of wheeled vehicles today makes us forget that sledges are not merely for use in snow, but are also by far the best way of carrying heavy or bulky goods over dry ground, where wheeled vehicles or pack-animals are not available. Indeed there are still farms in Wales and Ireland today where the horse-drawn sledge is the main and sometimes the only vehicle. One can safely assume the existence of such dry-ground sledges in prehistoric Britain (though drawn by men, not animals), though owing to the perishable nature of their timbers no certain example has survived. What may be the remains of such a sledge, however, were found by the writer, in a condition so decayed as to render identification uncertain, in a grave near Dorchester-on-Thames, where it had apparently been used to transport the body of the dead man from a distance. Significantly, perhaps, he belonged to the Beaker culture, to which the earliest bluestone structure should probably be assigned.

The practicability of sledging the bluestones was also tested successfully in the television programme referred to above. A sledge was made to the writer's specification of roughly squared 6 in. timbers, with an overall length of 9 ft. and a width of 4 ft., and the replica of the bluestone was lashed in place upon it. The loaded sledge was then dragged over the down immediately south of Stonehenge by a party of thirty-two schoolboys, arranged in ranks of four along a single hauling-rope, each rank holding at chest level a wooden bar to whose centre the rope was fastened. It was found that this party could just haul the sledge, weighing some 3,500 lbs. in all, up a slope of about 4° (1 in 15), though it is doubtful whether they could have continued this effort for long. The sledge slid easily over the long rank grass, and left no sign of its passage apart from some slight crushing.

The use of wooden rollers under the runners of the sledge allowed the hauling-party to be reduced from thirty-two to fourteen, that is, by 56 per cent., and it is certain that if the rollers had been more carefully selected for roundness a further reduction to a dozen or even less could have been made. The saving in man-power is not quite as great as it looks, however, because a separate party is needed to shift the rollers as they emerge from behind the sledge, and lay them again some distance in front of it, so that there is always a sufficient number in place to form a track. Moreover as soon as rollers are used the problem of steering the sledge arises, as especially when climbing a slope obliquely it has a natural tendency to slip sideways off the rollers. To counteract this, guide-ropes were fixed to the four corners of the sledge and each was manned by two people. These ancillary tasks occupied at least a dozen people, so that the total number required to move the stone *with rollers* would be twenty-four, against thirty-two *without rollers*.

The experiment was carried out with senior schoolboys from Canford School, who were naturally unaccustomed to this particular activity; and the figures given are critical figures, that is, the *minimum* number necessary to move the stone. It seems safe to assume, however, that if the same numbers of *trained and experienced men* were employed, the stone could be moved continuously for several miles a day without undue exertion. The total required is thus in the region of sixteen men per ton weight, or about 110 men for the Altar Stone, the heaviest of the foreign stones.

There is no means of telling, of course, how many of the bluestones were transported at one time, nor how long a journey took.

But for the sea and river voyage, at least, it is probable that there were convoys of perhaps up to a dozen vessels, whose crews would provide a body of men sufficiently large to ensure that help could rapidly be given to any individual vessel that found itself in difficulties.

The Sarsens

It is now generally agreed by archaeologists and geologists that the origin of the Stonehenge sarsens must lie on the Marlborough Downs, in the area where sarsen blocks still litter the surface in many places today. In the past it has been suggested that the stones came from some other and smaller deposit of sarsen on Salisbury Plain, much closer to Stonehenge, which has since been entirely worked out. There is no evidence to support this. It is inconceivable that this hypothetical deposit should have consisted entirely of blocks of just the right size and number for the building of Stonehenge, for even in the thick concentrations of boulders near Avebury examples comparable in size with even the smaller uprights at Stonehenge are very rare. Had this deposit existed, it must have contained many smaller boulders suitable for modern building, and some of these at least would now be incorporated in the houses and barns of the neighbouring villages. In fact, it is only around Avebury that sarsen is used for building at all. In the villages of the Pewsey Vale, east of Devizes, in the upper valley of the Avon and on the Plain itself, sarsen in buildings is unknown. This in itself is sufficient to disprove the notion that the Stonehenge sarsens came from anywhere nearer than the Marlborough Downs.

The method of transport to Stonehenge must certainly have been by sledge-hauling overland all the way, for there is no possible water route. The difficulties of this operation must have been enormous, for though the total distance, about twenty-four miles, is almost exactly the same as for the haulage of the bluestones, the weights involved are about seven times as great, both for the heaviest stones and for the aggregate of them all. Moreover, the shortest route involves a river crossing and the negotiation of a steep escarpment of the chalk. . .

For the actual methods used in hauling the stones we must fall back once more upon conjecture aided by common sense. Clearly rollers must have been used to reduce friction, and the stones must have been cradled in massive timbers, or bound on to enormous sledges, in either case to provide uniform runners to rest on the rollers and a means of attaching the hauling-ropes, which could not be fixed to the stone itself. The operation must therefore have necessitated the cutting and dressing of very considerable quantities of timber, almost certainly oak.

The ropes were probably of twisted or plaited hide thongs, such as were in use in cart-horse harness at least until the early nineteenth century; for it is doubtful if any native vegetable fibre existed capable of being fabricated into ropes of the required diameter and breaking strain. This in turn must have involved the preparation of enormous lengths of narrow thong, from hides either collected over a long period beforehand, or very likely from beasts specially slaughtered for the purpose. Huge amounts of animal fat must also have been prepared for keeping the leather ropes supple and waterproof.

We have seen that the comparatively light bluestones required a hauling-party of some sixteen men per ton weight. To arrive at the minimum numbers for hauling the sarsens (that is, sufficient to haul the heaviest stone) it is not sufficient, however, merely to scale up this figure by the appropriate factor. The far greater weight of the sarsens, for instance, would require both a closer setting of the rollers, in order to distribute the weight and prevent their being driven into the ground, and a larger diameter of roller as well, to avoid breaking them when passing over irregularities of the surface. Since the weight of a hardwood roller measuring 12 ft. by 9 ins. is in the region of 300 lbs., at least two men would be required to lift and move it; and the rate of progress of the stone would be limited by the speed at which the re-laying of the rollers could be carried out. The proportion of the total party engaged on shifting the rollers would thus have to be doubled at least, and the overall total of men for a given weight increased accordingly.

For purposes of estimating the *minimum* labour force required we may therefore take a figure of twenty-two men per ton weight and an average rate of progress of half a mile per day. The heaviest stones, which weigh about fifty tons, would therefore need some 1,100 men to move them, one at a time, over the twenty-four miles to Stonehenge, and would take about seven weeks for the journey. But even this is not enough, for it allows only for hauling up gentle slopes. To negotiate the steep escarpment at Redhorn Hill would certainly require a substantial addition, bringing the total up to perhaps 1,500 men. Moreover, some time must be allowed for the return journey from Stonehenge, presumably with the cradles or sledges, now empty, and the rollers; and even more for very necessary rest and recuperation. It would not be too much, therefore, to allow nine weeks for the round trip.

On this basis it can be calculated that the smallest requirements for the transport of the eighty-one sarsens to Stonehenge would be 1,500 men working for five and a half years, and working, moreover, without more than a few days' rest between trips. In fact, of course, it would have been impossible to maintain continuous working in this way for so long. Not only would there be interruptions owing to bad weather, but at certain seasons of each year the workers would perforce have to return home to attend to their crops and herds. It is thus safe enough to assume that the transport of the stones, all told, took upwards of ten years, unless the number of men employed was far larger than there is any reason to suppose.

Even in these days of dense populations and large-scale works of civil engineering, the employment of so many men upon a single project for so long would be worthy of remark. In prehistoric Britain, a land by modern standards extremely sparsely populated, the withdrawal of so many farmers and shepherds from their normal occupations for parts of the year, and their concentration in a single area upon a task of unwonted physical difficulty, must have been an entirely revolutionary proceeding, whose repercussions on the daily life of the countryside must have extended for many score miles beyond Stonehenge and Avebury. One has only to think of the problems of feeding and sheltering this number of people today to realize how profound must have been the upheaval thus occasioned in a society of so much simpler structure and communications, living so much nearer the borderline of subsistence. . . .

The Erection of the Uprights

The first task was to dig the stone-holes, whose depths must have been carefully adjusted to the variable lengths of the stones, so that when upright their tops were at the correct level. These holes have an approximately rectangular plan, matching that of the stones but some 9 inches to a foot wider all round. Three sides are steep, but the fourth, towards the centre of the site in the case of the trilithons and away from it in the circle, is in the form of a ramp sloping from the base of the hole proper to the surface, at an angle of about 45°. Against the back of the hole (that is, opposite the ramp) a number of wooden stakes, 4–6 inches in diameter, were set in a row, their purpose being to protect the chalk side from being crushed by the toe of the stone as it was raised, thus bringing down on to the bottom a mass of loose rubble which would make an unsuitable foundation and upset the levels. This device of anti-friction stakes (the decayed remains of the stakes themselves survive in a number of instances) had already been used in the erection of the Heel Stone in period I at Stonehenge, and in the great stone circles at Avebury.

The stone to be erected was then aligned radially upon the stone-hole, supported horizontally on rollers of large diameter, so as to raise it as far as possible above the surface. It was then dragged forward, still on a radial line, so that the front end, that is, the base, began to overhang the ramp. By previous trial and error the rollers would have been positioned so that as the centre of gravity of the stone passed over the leading roller (which would be checked at this point by stakes driven into the ground) it overbalanced, tipping the base squarely into the hole, the lower part of the outer face resting on the ramp. This manœuvre raised the stone half-way to the upright position by the force of gravity alone, and substantially diminished the effort required to bring it from the horizontal to the vertical position.

The final stage of the operation could doubtless have been achieved merely by attaching ropes to the top of the stone and hauling it upright by brute force. The direction of the pull would necessarily be at an acute angle to the length of the stone, however, and for that reason inefficient. Mr. E. H. Stone has pointed out that the use of a large pair of timber shear-legs located behind the stone-hole would greatly diminish the effort required. A cross-bar at the base of the legs prevents them from spreading or closing, and another nearer the apex forms an anchorage for ropes attached to the top of the stone and is positioned so that the initial pull is at right-angles to its length, the most efficient direction; the ropes used by the hauling-party are attached at the apex, the difference in height between it and the upper cross-bar providing some multiplication of leverage. Experiments with scale models showed that with this device the pull required to raise a stone of the outer circle, weighing 26 tons, would be 4½ tons, representing a force of 180 men each exerting a pull of 56 lbs.

Once approximately upright the stone would require final adjustment to bring it truly vertical, a process which it is difficult to believe could be carried out without the use of a plumb-line. Doubtless with this purpose in view, the bases of all the uprights have been left roughly pointed, so that a movement of a degree or two in any direction could fairly easily be obtained. Once the position of the stone was considered satisfactory, the space between its base and the sides of the hole was packed tightly with stones and boulders, many of them being discarded mauls, used in the dressing of the surfaces previously. The presence among these packing-stones of fragments of rock from Chilmark, eleven miles away to the south-west, has never been satisfactorily explained, though it suggests a local scarcity of suitable material, perhaps because so many local sarsen boulders had already been used up as mauls.

Once the ramps had been filled with tightly rammed chalk rubble, it seems probable that the uprights were then left alone, perhaps for a year or more, before any further work was done. It would certainly be desirable to leave an interval during which any instability could manifest itself and be corrected; and more particularly it would be necessary to let the uprights settle in the relatively soft chalk foundation in which they stood, for until all settlement had ceased the work of fashioning seatings for the lintels at a uniform level could not be begun.

The Raising of the Lintels

It is probable that the work of preparing the tenons and dished seatings for the lintels was done first, the mortices being sunk in the undersides of the lintels to match them afterwards, the necessary dimensions being transferred by measurement from one to the other. This seems the most satisfactory way of minimizing errors of fit, and of avoiding the necessity of frequent trial fittings, which would obviously occasion much difficulty. Even so, however, errors did occur, as is shown by the fact that at one end of lintel 102 there are two adjacent mortices, with centres differing by about 9 inches.

The problem of how the lintels were raised into position is one which most frequently troubles the visitor to the site, and has taxed the imagination of archaeologists for many years. The solution most commonly propounded (among others by Mr. E. H. Stone) is that of an earthen ramp built against the pair of uprights on which the lintel was to be placed, up which it was hauled, or perhaps rolled in a timber cradle, much as barrels of beer are today parbuckled up a pair of planks into a brewer's lorry. The origin of this notion, as applied to Stonehenge, seems to lie in the belief (almost certainly correct) that this method was used in dynastic Egypt for the erection of colossal stone statues, and indeed of the Pyramids themselves.

So far as Stonehenge is concerned, there are two main objections to this otherwise plausible theory. The first is the effort and time involved in digging away and rebuilding the ramp for each fresh lintel to be raised. The second is the absence of any evidence for the origin of such a ramp (which must have had a volume of not less than 10,000 cubic feet for the sarsen circle lintels alone, to say nothing of the much higher trilithons) in the form of a quarry, even refilled, in the vicinity of the site. It can safely be said that neither the material of the bank nor the silting of the ditch has been re-used in this way.

The alternative of a timber ramp, or scaffolding with one sloping side, is more feasible, and a working model of such a structure was demonstrated by the writer in the television programme on Stonehenge mentioned above, and is now in the Salisbury Museum. To a lesser extent, however, the same objections apply to this solution as to that of an earth ramp, namely the labour of repeatedly assembling and dismantling the framework for each fresh operation of raising a lintel; for such a structure would necessarily have its component beams fixed together either by tree-nails (wooden pegs) or by lashings. Moreover, the erection of such a timber structure would involve the sinking of a considerable number of post-holes to support its vertical members, and its repeated construction around the circle would produce a recognizable and recurrent pattern of post-holes. No such pattern was revealed by Colonel Hawley's extensive excavations, and such post-holes as he did find were too few and too irregular in their spacing to represent a timber structure of the kind envisaged.

There remains, however, a third method of raising the lintels, originally mentioned as a possibility, though an improbable one, by Colonel R. H. Cunnington in his *Stonehenge and Its Date* (1935), and since convincingly urged upon the writer and his colleagues in correspondence by Mr. G. A. Gauld, B.Sc., M.I.C.E., an engineer with practical experience of raising heavy weights by primitive means. This method involves the building of a timber "crib," that is, a structure of alternate layers of parallel timbers laid horizontally, the direction of the timbers in one layer being at right-angles to that in the layers above and below it. As Mr. Gauld points out, this means is still commonly used today for raising or lowering massive pieces of machinery on to their foundations where cranes and other mechanical lifting devices are not available.

The procedure suggested is as follows. The lintel is first positioned on the ground a few feet from its uprights and parallel to the position which it is ultimately to occupy. By means of a long wooden lever one end of the stone is then raised a few inches, and a short packing-piece of squared timber is inserted beneath it, close to the end. The other end is then lifted and packed up in the same way, and the process repeated alternately at each end until the stone is raised on two piles of packing a foot or two above the ground. At this stage the packing tends to become unstable, and the construction of the crib is accordingly started. A row of longer timbers is laid down, parallel to each other and to the existing packing-pieces, at intervals of a foot or two both under the raised stone and beyond its ends. On these a second layer of timbers is laid at right-angles, that is, parallel to and outside the longer sides of the lintel. A third layer is then laid parallel to the first, and so on until the top of the crib is close beneath the lower surface of the stone. The top of the crib is then decked over with planks to form a working platform, and the stone is again lifted by levering so that its weight is transferred from the original piles of packing to new packing-pieces resting alongside the old on the decked surface. The old packing is then lifted out, the decking completed, and the whole process started again from the beginning.

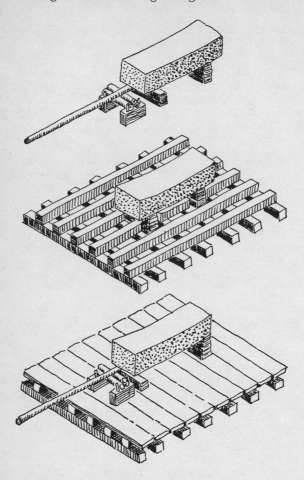

THREE STAGES IN THE RAISING OF A LINTEL BY MEANS OF A CRIB.

One problem posed by the raising of the lintels still requires discussion, namely how was their levelling achieved. We have already seen that the builders achieved a surprisingly close approximation to a true horizontal plane in the setting of the lintels, and it seems inconceivable that this was done by eye alone. If instruments were used, as they must surely have been, what were they?

There appear to be two possible answers to this question. The first is some form of water-level, akin to the modern builder's spirit-level and used in the same way. This might well have taken the form of a narrow trough of wood, or more probably of sheet bronze, with vertical sides very carefully worked to exactly the same height above the base all round. If this tray were filled with water to just below the edge, and rested on the edge of a suitable rigid wooden bar of uniform depth, levels could be transferred from one point to another with considerable accuracy, particularly if the modern practice was followed of reversing the actual instrument end for end for each reading, and taking a mean.

The second type of instrument that could have been used is a large wooden square, shaped like the letter L on its side, like an enlarged version of the modern joiner's square, with a plumb-line suspended from the apex. Provided that the angle of the two sides was a true right-angle, a matter which can very easily be checked, the long side would necessarily be horizontal when the plumb-line hung in coincidence with the edge of the short side. Such an instrument could equally well have been used to transfer levels from one point to another, and its use at Stonehenge is perhaps rather more probable than that of the water-level. In either case, however, the degree of accuracy with which the lintels have been levelled, both in the circle and on the trilithons, makes it morally certain that some device of this kind was known to and employed by the builders.

The Historical Background of Stonehenge:
Was There a Mycenaean Architect?

There are similarities between the classification of archaeological material and the taxonomic arrangement of the various forms of living creatures. This biological analogy can usefully be extended to the study of the growth, change and decay of archaeological cultures, for these too, like the men and women which they represent, are dynamic rather than static in their nature.

In the evolution of living creatures, the high road of biological development is peopled with life-forms whose survival has been assured by lack of specialization and by a genetical vigour expressed in prolific variation. The side roads, ending ultimately in cul-de-sacs, are filled with forms which have become adapted, through a greater degree of specialization of function, to one particular mode of existence. Being thus more sensitive to changes of environment, such forms are the more liable to extinction.

The history of the Neolithic cultures of Britain suggests an analogous process of natural selection. The Primary Neolithic cul-

tures arrived in these islands already fully formed, with a pattern
of economic life based upon husbandry which implies some degree
of physical immobility and of adaptation to a particular environment of climate and vegetation. On the other hand, the Secondary
Neolithic and Beaker cultures (that of the Necked-Beakers in particular) are largely native growths within these islands, whose relative lack of economic specialization permitted them more freely to
adapt themselves to contemporary changes of physical environment, and more readily to exploit to their own advantage such
technological innovations as the introduction of metallurgy. Moreover, the greater physical mobility of these communities made for
more frequent opportunities for contact between them, and thus
for the development of that "hybrid vigour" which in the biological
field so frequently results from the cross-fertilization of different
strains.

It would be unwise to push this biological analogy too far. None
the less it may serve to illumine, even if it does not accurately
describe, the course of British prehistory towards the close of the
first half of the second millennium B.C. For already before 1500 B.C.
the Primary Neolithic cultures were in decline, and indeed, so far
as southern England is concerned, almost extinct; whereas the
Secondary Neolithic and Beaker cultures still flourished vigorously,
no longer, it is true, in their original forms, but as a single new
culture partaking of both, yet also transcending both in enterprise
and in its level of material wealth. One may hazard the guess that
the main causes of this decline and growth were, on the one hand,
a gradual drying-up of the climate, doubtless intensified by the
deforestation brought about by Neolithic pastoralism; and on the
other the growth of Irish metallurgy, which was radically to transform the part played by Britain in the economic structure of prehistoric Europe and create opportunities of quite exceptional
advancement for the peoples of southern England, lying on the
trade-routes from Ireland to the Continent.

The growth of this new culture, known as the Wessex culture
of the Early Bronze Age, is marked in the archaeological record by
the appearance of numerous burials of exceptional richness and
elaboration; for here too, as in the earlier Beaker cultures, evidence
of the living comes almost entirely from the tombs of the dead.
The barrows themselves are of specialized form, which illustrates
very well the hybrid and yet unitary character of the new culture.
For though the body is still placed singly beneath a round mound,
the mound itself is commonly surrounded by a ditch with an external bank. We thus have here the apparent fusion of two traditions: the round barrow appropriate to the Beaker cultures, and
the circular embanked enclosure of the Secondary Neolithic henge

monuments. These two elements are combined in various forms
to make a group of types, known collectively as "circle-barrows."
They range from bell-barrows, in which the mound is of considerable height and occupies almost the whole of the enclosed area,
leaving only a narrow strip between its edge and the ditch; to disk-
barrows, in which the burial lies beneath an insignificant tump [or
mound] in the centre of an otherwise flat circle like a small henge
monument, though without entrances. Between these two extremes
there are a number of intermediate types.

It is significant too that bell-barrows, whose large mounds must
surely represent the earlier traditions of the Necked-Beaker culture,
commonly contain the burials of men accompanied by objects of
martial panoply such as battle-axes; whereas the disk-barrows, to
judge from the associated objects, are the graves of women. Moreover, whereas men were sometimes buried by the Beaker rites, as
crouched inhumations in a proper grave, the women were invariably
cremated and their bones placed merely in a shallow pit, an old
Secondary Neolithic rite which gradually became universal during
the *floruit* of the Wessex culture.

The burials thus give us a picture of a culture in which earlier
traditions have fused into a distinctive form, and in which the
warrior-chieftain element, already discernible in embryonic form
in the Necked-Beaker culture, now achieves a dominant place,
though ultimately to be absorbed, in the decline of the culture, by
the less spectacular but more persistent heritage of the Secondary
Neolithic.

The occurrence in the graves, particularly of men, of rich assemblages of bronze tools and weapons and of gold ornaments
implies that we are dealing here with a "heroic" society in which
the ordinary population is dominated and controlled by a caste of
warrior-chieftains, essentially the same type of society, that is to
say, as those of the Homeric epics, of the Norse sagas and of the
early literature of Wales and Ireland. But it is clear that in spite
of the element of martial display represented by skilfully wrought
battle-axes and mace-heads of stone, and by bronze daggers with
hilts richly ornamented in gold, the fundamental feature of the
Wessex culture is commercial success. Whatever their pretensions
to warlike valour, the dead buried in the Wessex circle-barrows
were essentially hard-headed and successful business men, who
had made the best of their position as middle-men in the metal
trade between Ireland and the Continent.

The evidence for this commercial activity is chiefly in the form
of metal tools and weapons. Not only, for instance, are bronze axes
and halberds known from European finds, whose distinctive form
and decoration mark their Irish origin; but also in the graves of

the Wessex culture itself there appear objects which are either direct imports, or close native copies of such imports, from the principal continental centre of metallurgy in South Germany and Bohemia. It is thus clear that the Wessex culture played an integral part in a commercial system which now, for the first time in European prehistory, achieved a truly international character. The complexity of this system is nowhere better illustrated than in a couple of Wessex graves which yielded complex necklaces of amber beads. These had clearly been obtained, not directly from the sources of amber in Scandinavia, but from *entrepots* far to the south in Central Europe, on the long overland route by which amber was traded to the Mediterranean from the north.

Indeed the Mediterranean itself was not outside the orbit of trade from Wessex, for in each area there occur gold objects which must have originated in the other. Here, however, it is likely that it was the south that played the active and the north the passive role in the exchange. For at this time there flourished in the central Mediterranean the great maritime empire of Minoan Crete, and its offshoot and competitor on the Greek mainland, centred upon Mycenae, the city of Agamemnon. It has long been recognized that the stories of Odysseus and of the Argo enshrine in legendary and heroic form the more prosaic commercial exploits of merchant-venturers from these two great centres, within the limits of the tideless Inland Sea. From Britain there is most suggestive evidence that exceptionally perhaps, but none the less successfully, they dared to voyage beyond the Pillars of Hercules into the inhospitable waters of Ocean, no longer wine-dark, but grey beneath anything but a halcyon sky.

Among the most exotic of the objects found in Wessex graves, chiefly those of women, are small ribbed beads of blue faience, often fragmentary with their brilliant colour dulled by fire and by the stains of time, which clearly had sometimes been handed down as treasured heirlooms before their final burial. Careful examination leaves little doubt that these beads are of Egyptian manufacture, and their sporadic occurrence both in Crete and on the Atlantic coasts of Iberia and France suggests forcibly that they reached Britain by sea. It is difficult not to see in them the exact counterparts of those gaudy glass beads, strung on lengths of copper wire, which were carried as trade goods by the Western explorers of Africa in the nineteenth century A.D. Is it then too fanciful to regard this handful of trinkets, insignificant in themselves, as the tangible relics of some unsung Odyssey? And may not the Golden Fleece have been fetched from the Island of the Hyperboreans, no less than from Colchis?

Whatever may have been the precise part played by the Wessex culture in this widespread network of European trade, it is clear that here, and here alone in Britain, have we a community able to command the immense resources of labour and craftsmanship necessary for the building of Stonehenge III. This conclusion is confirmed by the very notable concentration of burials of the Wessex culture close to Stonehenge, where they cluster in great barrow-cemeteries on the crests of the neigbouring downs. When one stands within the stones looking out over their ruins southwards to the barrows on the skyline of Normanton Down, one can be sure that in them the builders of Stonehenge themselves now rest from their labours.

And yet were these Wessex chieftains *alone* responsible for the design and construction of this last and greatest monument at Stonehenge? For all their evident power and wealth, and for all their widespread commercial contacts, these men were essentially barbarians. As such, can they have encompassed unaided a monument which uniquely transcends all other comparable prehistoric buildings in Britain, and indeed in all Europe north of the Alps, and exhibits so many refinements of conception and technique? I for one do not believe it. It seems to me that to account for these exotic and unparalleled features one *must* assume the existence of influence from the only contemporary European cultures in which *architecture*, as distinct from mere construction, was already a living tradition; that is, from the Mycenaean and Minoan civilizations of the central Mediterranean. Admittedly not all the refinements of Stonehenge can be paralleled in detail in Mycenaean or Minoan architecture, though it is noteworthy that the structure of the Postern Gate at Mycenae is very similar to the trilithons at Stonehenge, even to the use of mortice-and-tenon joints to hold the lintel in place. But even without this specific parallel, the architecture of the central Mediterranean provides the only outside source for the sophisticated approach to architecture exhibited at Stonehenge. We have seen that through trade the necessary contacts with the Mediterranean had been established. The Stonehenge dagger too may be seen, if one wishes, to point more directly at Mycenae itself. We know from Homer that architects, like the poets of whom he himself was one, were homeless men, wandering from city to city. Is it then any more incredible that the architect of Stonehenge should himself have been a Mycenaean, than that the monument should have been designed and erected, with all its unique and sophisticated detail, by mere barbarians?

Let us suppose for a moment that this is more than mere conjecture. Under what circumstances, then, could a man versed in the traditions and skills of Mediterranean architecture find himself working among barbarians in the far cold North? Only, surely, as the skilled servant of some far-voyaging Mycenaean prince, *fortis ante Agamemnona;* or at the behest of a barbarian British king, whose voice and gifts spoke loudly enough to be heard even in the cities of the Mediterranean. Have we then any evidence in Britain for the concentration of power in the hands of a single overlord, native or foreign?

Here too, I believe, Stonehenge itself provides the answer. For one must remember that Stonehenge is not only unique in the refinement of its details; it is unique also as the *only* monument, great or small, which can be assigned to the Wessex culture, apart, of course, from the barrows. The great sanctuaries such as Avebury all belong to an earlier age, and by the time Stonehenge was built there can have been no living and active tradition of communal building of this kind. The building of Stonehenge is thus unlikely to have been the expression of the common will, but rather the fulfilment of a purpose imposed from above. Now in the rich and martially furnished Wessex graves we can admittedly see evidence for chieftainship, and the grouping of the graves in cemeteries may imply whole dynasties of chiefs. Yet the pattern of society which they represent is surely that of so many other heroic societies, in which clan wars with clan, and rival dynasties carry on a perpetual struggle for power. Under such conditions, can the construction of Stonehenge, involving the displacement of so many hundreds of men from their homes for so long, have been attempted, still less achieved? Surely not; for such great works can only be encompassed by a society at peace within itself. And in such a society of conflicting factions, how is peace imposed except from above?

I believe, therefore, that Stonehenge itself is evidence for the concentration of political power, for a time at least, in the hands of a single man, who alone could create and maintain the conditions necessary for this great undertaking. Who he was, whether native-born or foreign, we shall never know; he remains a figure as shadowy and insubstantial as King Brutus of the medieval British History. Yet who but he should sleep, like Arthur or Barbarossa, in the quiet darkness of a sarsen vault beneath the mountainous pile of Silbury Hill? And is not Stonehenge itself his memorial?

JOHN EVANS

The Bronze Age in Britain

JOHN EVANS (the father of Sir Arthur) was a versatile archaeologist. He had already made a useful contribution to knowledge concerning ancient British coins and the Palaeolithic and Neolithic periods before publishing his book dealing with the Bronze Age. His summary of the period is remarkably good for the time, for his three periods very nearly correspond (in a simplified form) to the Early, Middle and Late phases of the modern classification of the British Bronze Age. The very beginning of the bronze-using period is now known to be a few centuries earlier than Evans thought— about 1900-1800 B.C.

❧

NOTWITHSTANDING all [the] historical testimony in favour of the prior use of bronze to that of iron, there have been not a few authors who have maintained that the idea of a succession of stone, bronze, and iron is delusive when applied to Western Europe. Among these was the late Mr. Thomas Wright, who has gone so far as to express "a firm conviction that not a bit of bronze which has been found in the British Islands belongs to an older date than that at which Caesar wrote that the Britons obtained their bronze from abroad, meaning of course from Gaul." "In fact these objects in bronze were Roman in character and in their primary origin." As in the same page he goes on to show that two hundred years before Christ the swords of the Gauls were made of iron, and as his contentions have already been met by Sir John Lubbock, and will, I think, be effectually disposed of by the facts subsequently to be mentioned in this volume, it seems needless to dwell on Mr. Wright's opinions. I may, however, mention that, while denying the antiquity of British, German, and Scandinavian weapons and tools of bronze,

From *Ancient Bronze Implements of Great Britain*. London: Longmans, Green & Co.; 1881, pp. 20-1, 473, 488.

he admits that in Greece and Italy that metal was for a long period the only one employed for cutting instruments, as iron was not known in Greece until a comparatively late date.

About one hundred and thirty years ago, in 1751, a discussion as to the date of bronze weapons took place among the members of the Académie des Inscriptions et Belles Lettres of Paris, on the occasion of some bronze swords, a spear-head, and other objects being found near Gannat, in the Bourbonnais. Some antiquaries regarded them as weapons made for use; others as merely made for show. The Count de Caylus considered that the swords were Roman, though maintaining that copper or bronze must have been in earlier use than iron. Lévesque de la Ravalière maintained, on the contrary, that neither the Greeks, Romans, Gauls, nor Franks had ever made use of copper or bronze in their swords. The Abbé Barthélemy showed from ancient authors that the earliest arms of the Greeks were of bronze; that iron was only introduced about the time of the siege of Troy; and that in later times among the Romans there was no mention of bronze having been used for weapons of offence, and therefore that these swords were not Roman. Strangely enough, he went on to argue that they were Frankish, and of the time of Childeric. Had he been present at the opening of the tomb of that monarch in 1653 he would, however, have seen that he had an iron sword.

A still warmer discussion than any which has taken place in England or France, one, in fact, almost amounting to an international war of words, has in more recent times arisen between some of the German antiquaries and those of the Scandinavian kingdoms of Denmark and Sweden. . . .

The Bronze Age of Britain may, therefore, be regarded as an aggregate of three stages: the first, that characterized by the flat or slightly flanged celts, and the knife-daggers frequently found in barrows associated with instruments and weapons formed of stone; the second, that characterized by the more heavy dagger-blades and the flanged celts and tanged spear-heads or daggers, such as those from Arreton Down; and the third, by palstaves and socketed celts and the many forms of tools and weapons, of which fragments are so constantly present in the hoards of the ancient bronze-founders. It is in this third stage that the bronze sword and the true socketed spear-head first make their advent. The number of these hoards, and the varieties in the forms of these swords and spear-heads, as well as in the socketed celts and other tools, would, I think, justify us in assigning a minimum duration of some four or five centuries to this last stage. The other two stages together must probably have extended over at least an equal lapse of time; so that for the total duration of the Bronze Period in Britain we cannot greatly err in attributing eight or ten centuries. This would place the beginning of the Period some 1,200 or 1,400 years B.C.—a date which in many respects would seem to fit in with what we know as to the use of bronze in the southern parts of Europe. . . .

So far as the general interest attaching to the Bronze Period is concerned, it may readily be conceded that it falls short of that with which either of the two stages of the Stone Period which preceded it must be regarded. The existence of numerous tribes of men who are, or were until lately, in the same stage of culture as the occupants of Europe during the Neolithic Age, affords various points of comparison between ancient and modern savages which are of the highest interest, while there exists at the present day not a single community in which the phases of the Bronze culture can be observed. The Palaeolithic Age has, moreover, a charm of mysterious eld attaching to it as connected with the antiquity of the human race, which is peculiarly its own.

The Bronze Age, nevertheless, from its close propinquity to the period of written history, is of the highest importance to those who would trace back the course of human progress to its earliest phases; and though in this country many of the minute details of the picture cannot be filled in, yet, taken as a whole, the broad lines of the development of this stage of civilisation may be as well traced in Britain as in any other country. It has been a pleasure to me to gather the information on which this work is based; and I close these pages with the consolatory thought that, dry as may be their contents, they may prove of some value as a hoard of collected facts for other seekers after truth.

WILLIAM GREENWELL

British Barrows
and Their Builders

WILLIAM GREENWELL was a minor canon and librarian of Durham cathedral. He very well typifies the more energetic and able
type of Victorian antiquary—and his *British Barrows* is a classic
of British archaeology. He started barrow digging and collecting
bronze implements in about 1858. His large collection finally went
to the British Museum. "The Canon" was born in 1820, and lived to
be ninety-eight.

❧

Barrow Burial

THE almost universal custom of raising a mound, the so-called
barrow, over the buried dead, to mark the place where they were
laid in the grave, has been variously discussed, and by many different writers. Notices of the practice have been so often collected
from the works of Greek and Latin authors and other sources, that
it is not necessary for me to enter upon any general consideration
of the subject, except in very brief terms.

This form of memorial, *monumentum ære perennius*, as ancient
as it has been lasting, is found in almost all parts of the globe,
from the extreme west of Europe to the eastern limit of the continent of the New World. Barrows, under diverse names, line the
coasts of the Mediterranean, the seats of ancient empires and
civilisations, before whose rise they were in existence, and whose
decay they have witnessed and outlived. So numerous are they, that
they spread like a covering over the wide plains, the Steppes of

From *British Barrows*. London: Oxford University Press; 1877, pp. 1-2, 116-20, 121-3,
232-4.

Northern Asia, from the Euxine almost to the Icy Sea, where a few wandering nomads now feebly represent a population which was once large, wealthy, and powerful. The continent of India possesses them in abundance, and their buried contents present an identity in many particulars so close with those of Britain, that some have considered it as affording a proof of a near connection between the two peoples who erected them. Egypt knows them as the sepulchres of her early kings, and the Pyramids have remained, an unchanging legacy from the dead, when the wisdom of her learned exists only in the oft transmuted knowledge of many an alien race, and when her religion, her literature, her art, almost her language, the living expressions of a nation's being, have all but passed away and been forgotten. The red man of America still places his dead beneath them, and the huge mounds, so common in some parts of that continent, are the evidences of an early civilisation, to which the marvellous ruined cities of Central America bear a stronger witness; cities which, in their elaborate and profuse though strange sculpture, give indications of an art development so distinctive in its character, that it could scarcely have had its origin in the mind of any of the races of the Old World.

They abound in Great Britain and Ireland, differing in shape and size, and made of various materials; and are known as barrows (mounds of earth), and cairns (mounds of stone), and popularly in some parts of England as lows, houes, and tumps. They vary in size from a few feet in diameter to a miniature mountain, like Silbury Hill in Wiltshire, which covers above five acres of ground, and measures 130 ft. in perpendicular height. . . .

Life of the Barrow Builders

Their dress, the use of metal, their weapons, implements, ornaments, and pottery have already been treated of at some length, so that it is only necessary here to give a slight account of them. That woollen, and probably linen, fabrics were manufactured is evident from the remains of such which have been discovered. The evidence is indeed but scanty, as might be expected, on account of the perishable nature of the material; portions, however, of woven stuffs have been found with deposits of burnt bones, either the remainder of the dress of the person or of some wrapping in which the bones had been collected from the funeral pile. In one of the barrows at Weaverthorpe, the half of a clay spindle-whorl was met with, which may be supposed to indicate a knowledge of spinning. They further appear to have been clothed in garments which had made some considerable advance beyond such as were merely wrapped round the body; for, in a grave at Butterwick, six buttons of jet and stone were found placed in a line in front of the chest of the buried man, showing that the vestment was to some extent fitted to the form of the wearer, and had been fashioned into shape with somewhat of sartorial skill. Their dress appears to have been fastened in a variety of ways. Buttons and pins have occurred in many instances; and a ring with perforations on the side has sometimes been met with, usually in connection with buttons. An oblong narrow article, made of jet or other lignite, having a slit, which widens towards the middle, and occupies about two-thirds of the whole length, has been found on the wolds accompanying a body; and also in other places in Britain. They have probably been used in some way for fastening the dress, a belt perhaps having been passed through the slit. A ring of jet from a barrow at Rudstone, which is too small for an armlet, had possibly been made for the same purpose, though its form is not quite so suitable as the oblong one would be. Sir R. Colt-Hoare discovered, in a barrow at Upton Lovell, what he considered to be gold boxes; and somewhat similar objects, though smaller, were found in a barrow at Cressingham in Norfolk; but they may very possibly have been buttons, the more solid part having been made of wood upon which the thin gold plating was laid; what are undoubtedly buttons, of a conical form, and made in the way I have suggested, of wood and gold, have occurred in the Wiltshire barrows. What may be called a fibula of bone has also been found, and always, so far as I know, with burnt bodies. No bronze fibulæ or any fastenings of that nature have been discovered in barrows of the bronze age, though they occur in those of the early time of iron; but a few buckles, small and of a simple form, show that, as might be expected, so very natural a mode of connection was known. The dress was no doubt fastened more commonly by tags or laces, but of such things it is not to be expected that any trace would be left.

The implements and weapons of bronze show that they had attained to a high perfection in the process of casting, and give evidence of no little progress in metallurgy; whilst the pottery is quite equal to what has been discovered in other parts of Britain, though perhaps the designs upon some of the vessels do not show so much artistic skill as is seen upon those from the south-west of Scotland. It manifests, however, a long-continued experience in the manufacture of fictile ware. The ornamentation upon the vases and urns is not wanting in a certain tasteful arrangement, but in the ignorance of the use of the wheel, in the imperfect firing, in the absence of glazing, and of any other form of design in the patterns than simple combinations of lines or of circular markings, it cannot be said that they had attained to any great perfection in the art of the potter.

The personal ornaments, which have however occurred in a very few instances, give indications of some artistic power, though developed after a simple fashion. They have consisted of necklaces, generally made of jet, or other and inferior lignite; of buttons and rings of jet, in some cases tastefully decorated, and therefore having a claim to be classed under the head of ornaments; of ear-rings of bronze; of beads and pendants of bone, jet, and other substances, not found in sufficient numbers to constitute a necklace; and of some humbler articles, such as perforated teeth.

The whole evidence of the barrows appears to show that the people living on the wolds were, to some extent, isolated from the rest of the country, with which they seem to have held little intercourse; this state of things originating partly in the natural features of the district in which they dwelt, surrounded, as it was on all sides, by low-lying ground, swampy and largely covered with wood. They were apparently not possessed of much in the shape of gold, bronze, amber, or glass. Their condition may perhaps be described as that of people who were living in the pastoral state, but at the same time cultivating grain, though probably not extensively. Their clothing no doubt consisted largely of skins, though they certainly used textile fabrics; and such ornaments as they possessed were of a simple, though by no means of an unartistic, description. The presence of a lump of ochre, which has been found in more than one instance associated with the body, may perhaps be considered as affording some evidence of the use of colour as a means of personal adornment; nor is it easy to account for its occurrence on any other supposition. When these people are compared with the inhabitants of some other districts in Britain, as for instance of Wiltshire, and even of Derbyshire, who, to judge by the pottery, implements, and ornaments, must have been occupying the country at the same time, they cannot be regarded as having been in possession of the same amount of wealth of various kinds, as of bronze and other materials, or to have arrived at quite the same height of cultivation.

It cannot be expected that the contents of the burial mounds should give much information upon the social relations of these people, the position the wife occupied in the family, and questions akin to this. Some few inferences may, however, be drawn from the facts which the barrows have disclosed. For instance, the central and indeed the sole burial in a barrow upon Heslerton Wold, was that of a very young child, placed in a grave sunk in the chalk; and in the largest barrow I have opened on the wolds, at Rudstone, the primary burial, over which the whole mound had been raised, was that of an infant. Numerous other instances have occurred where quite young children had been buried with associ-

ated vases, and in a manner which betokens that much care was
bestowed upon the burial, as in a barrow at Rudstone, where the
grave had been lined out with wood. I have met with other cases
elsewhere; for instance, the central cist in a barrow at Ford,
Northumberland, was occupied by the skeleton of an infant, having
a "food vessel" with it, whilst round the cist were seven burnt
bodies, deposited in as many cinerary urns, in one of which was a
flint implement.

From these and similar instances we may gather that the family
tie had much influence with these people, and that the child of the
chief or other person of distinction held an important position in
the estimation of the tribe. The affection of the father might prompt
him to honour with the full ceremonial of the burial rites the child
whose early death he mourned, but unless the social importance
of the infant had been likewise recognised in the eyes of the people,
it is scarcely likely that so high a mark of consideration as a separate barrow implies would have been accorded to so young a member of the community. Perhaps it may not be considered to be an
unfair inference to regard a circumstance like this as indicating
that something like an hereditary headship prevailed amongst them.

The great labour and pains bestowed upon the burial of the dead,
the large mound, the deep grave, the various attendant ceremonies
of the funeral, may not necessarily show any high advance in
civilisation, for in very rude conditions of society the disposal of
the body after death has generally been attended with somewhat
of care, and regarded as requiring the presence of some rites of
burial. But, making allowance for this, we cannot look upon the
barrows and their varied contents without being impressed with
the belief that the semi-savage state had been well-nigh passed,
and that the dawn of an advanced civilisation was approaching.
The pottery, with its simple and yet effective ornamentation, the
bronze knife-dagger and awl, the necklace of jet, the buttons tastefully decorated, the ear-ring of metal, may all be regarded as
heralds of cultivation and refinement, even as the east is flecked
with streaks of gold and crimson before the morning sun breaks
forth in all his splendour.

There are, on the other hand, some features pointing to a condition of things which ill accords with much advance beyond
savagery, though to the practices these would seem to indicate we
might find a parallel amongst people who, in some of the processes
of mental development, have been second to few. It can scarcely be
questioned that it was the habit to slay at the funeral and to bury
with the dead man, wives, children, and others, probably slaves.
The frequent occurrence of several bodies, all certainly interred at
the same time, the finding of a man and woman in adjoining

graves, which must have been excavated together, or of two persons of different sexes in the same grave, with the remains of children, or with deposits of burnt bones, are incidents difficult to interpret in any other way. Nor has the practice been so uncommon that we need feel much hesitation in attributing it to the ancient dwellers upon the wolds. The custom of suttee which still, in spite of the most stringent enactments, lingers in India, shows that, under an elaborate religious system and in highly organised communities, a habit so repugnant to our ideas has nevertheless prevailed. That it was in use amongst the ancient Scythians, the account of the burial of their kings given by Herodotus (and amply confirmed by the examination of the burial mounds of the countries occupied by that people) abundantly proves. That women, however, were not in the condition of slaves, but held a position of trust as the equals in some degree of the husband, may perhaps be considered as not improbable, when the manner in which they seem to have received burial in the barrows is remembered. They have been found interred apart from any male, and occupying an important position in the burial mounds, in some cases a woman being the sole tenant of a barrow,—a circumstance which is quite inconsistent with their place in the house being merely a servile one.

Physical Types

One of the most important and interesting subjects of enquiry which a knowledge of the contents of the barrows has enabled us to discuss is that of the people themselves, with reference to their physical characteristics. Some description therefore of their form, stature, and general appearance is necessary to complete, as far as is possible, the imperfect picture we have hitherto been able to present. There are, as has already been mentioned, two classes of barrows upon the wolds, so different in their appearance and construction, as to suggest at once, without any further investigation of their contents, that they belong to different periods of time, and the probability that they are the burial-places of different peoples. The one is eminently a long mound, the other is circular in its outline; the former being the grave-hills of a markedly dolichocephalic (long-headed) people, the latter producing skulls both dolichocephalic and brachycephalic (round-headed). . . .

The round barrows, then, contain two very distinct forms of skull, a long and a round one, together with other less characteristic forms which may be supposed to have belonged to people who were descended from inter-marriages between persons whose heads were of the two different types in question. The dolichocephalic head of the round barrows does not differ from the dolichocephalic head of the long barrows. It would appear from this that if, as there is every reason to believe is the case, the long barrows are the burial-places of the oldest occupants of the wolds (at all events in Neolithic times), the long-headed people of the round barrows are the representatives of those persons who buried in the earlier long-shaped mounds. This people was probably intruded upon and conquered by the more powerfully made round-headed folk, who, as is nearly always found to be the case, would in course of time become intermixed with them, and with whom in the end they would become identified as one people. This appears to be the most reasonable, in fact the only, way of accounting for the finding of the bones of the long-headed people in the round barrows.

Monuments at Rudstone

On the ridge of the wolds, where the chalk range slopes sharply away to the flat land of Holderness, and near the division between the parishes of Rudstone and Burton Agnes, is a group of barrows which follows more or less the line of the crest of the hill. There are first three, very near together and standing the furthest to the west, then a single one, and still more to the east another. Somewhat to the south-east of the last are two long mounds, almost parallel, their northern ends gradually losing themselves in the surface-level, but connected together at their southern ends by another long mound. Then about half a mile to the east-north-east is a very large barrow, while other three are placed at considerable intervals still further to the east. One of this group, that the most towards the west, was almost entirely removed many years ago, when bones are said to have been found in large quantities: part also of one of the long mounds was taken away fifty years since in order to fill in a neighbouring chalk-pit, but finding some human bones, the workmen were stopped, leaving it little disturbed except at one end. I opened seven of the round barrows which remained untouched, and also the long mounds.

The position which the barrows occupy is a very striking one, and must always have been so. The men who raised these funeral mounds looked on the one side over the swelling upland of the wold, bleak, grey, and treeless, their eye taking in on many a distant ridge the burial-places of chiefs of other, though perhaps kindred, tribes; whilst upon an outcrop of rock, lifting itself out of the valley just beneath them, rose the lofty monolith which now stands in Rudstone churchyard, even then it may be hoar and lichen-covered, and to them equally speechless, as to its origin and meaning, as it is to ourselves at the present day. Or possibly they might look upon it with traditionary knowledge of its purport, or even have helped

to raise it from its bed, where, laid ages before, it told of a mighty
cataclysm, and how it had wandered far from its original home,
borne over the waves on some buoyant ice ship. There it stood, telling them perchance that at its base was laid to his rest a mightier
warrior than him they were entombing on the height above; or it
may have spoken to them as the symbol of a belief, according to
which their lives were regulated, and marked the place it stood
upon as holy ground. If they looked to the south there was nothing
but a dreary tract of marsh-land, which seemed almost interminable,
wherein however, amidst the coarse vegetation and brushwood, the
deer and the wild swine had their haunt, and where the beaver made
a habitation almost equal in point of construction to those they had
themselves the skill to form. Beyond was the sea, as yet enlivened
by no sail.

A very different sight met our eye, when on a bright frosty day
in November, with a strong north-east wind sweeping over the
hills, we commenced opening the barrows. Below us was, as of
old, the mighty stone, ancient of days; but side by side with it stood
the shrine of a purer faith, a more humane teaching; whilst round
it rose in the clear air from many a chimney the pale blue line of
smoke, suggestive of comforts those older people never dreamed of.
The cold and cheerless wold, with its flocks of bustards and flights
of dotterel, had given place to bright-green cultured fields, and
flocks of sheep, and teams of horses turning up the rich brown
mould in preparation for the golden sheaves of the next coming
harvest. And just as great a change had taken place in the other
direction, in what had been the dreary swamps of the old days.
There the rough sedges, and rank growth of rush and reed, and the
thickets of the water-loving alder and the willow were replaced by
fields teeming with agricultural wealth, and diversified by hedgerows
broken up by the varying forms of oak and ash and elm-tree. Far
away rose the towers of Beverley, the beautiful minster, the creation
of a belief and culture which, unlike that of the people who raised
the Rudstone, has not died away. Still further in the distance, and
dimly seen in the haze of the far-off horizon, were tall chimneys,
and the smoke which marked where Hull, with its commerce and
manufactures, was in itself more stirring and changing than was all
the world with which these ancient wold-dwellers were acquainted.
In the distance still, but nearer to us, was the Bay of Bridlington,
where hundreds of ships were lying at anchor, kept there by the
wind which forbade a course to the north. There they were, laden
with the products and goods of many a land, manned by the sons of
many a clime, making the whole world akin in purpose and pursuit.
As we looked, the thought could not but be stirred—How much have
we changed from those who, in the dark past, raised the mound on

which we are standing, and which they thought would speak with
no faltering tongue to all future time! How much more from us will
those have changed who, thousands of years hence, may stand on
the self-same spot, and to whom our boasted knowledge may seem
as feeble and as strange as we think theirs who laid beside the
ashes of the departed the food they thought he needed for the journey to the unknown land.

JOHN ABERCROMBY

The Beaker Folk

LORD ABERCROMBY'S book is as much a classic of British archaeology as Canon Greenwell's, but for a different reason. It represents
one of the first attempts to make a thorough typological study of a
large category of prehistoric artifacts, and to use it to reconstruct
the history of a period. His classification of the different types of
beaker was particularly valuable in leading to a new understanding
of the beginning of the British Bronze Age. Here, however, he is
discussing more general aspects of the "Beaker Folk."

THE pottery used by the new invaders of Britain having been examined, classified, and arranged in such a manner as to exhibit the
relative chronology of the different sections into which it has been
divided, it remains to take a glance at the newcomers themselves,
to learn what manner of men they were. The Neolithic men whom
they were to encounter were of comparatively refined appearance,
with oval faces, regular features, and the type of skull known as
dolichocephalic; all or most of them belonged to the Mediterranean

From *Bronze Age Pottery of Great Britain*. London: Oxford University Press; 1912,
pp. 64, 70-1.

race of Sergi, with an average height of about 5 ft. 5½ in.-5 ft. 6½ in., and a physique not remarkable for its strength. To these men some of the new invaders offered the greatest contrast. The skull was short and square, the general aspect of the face rugged and forbidding owing to the great development of the superciliary ridges and of the eyebrows. The cheekbones were prominent and the nose projected much beyond the prominent eyebrows; the lower jaw was square, massive, often prognathous, and terminated in a prominent chin. Coupled with teeth often of extraordinary size many of these invaders must have presented the appearance of great ferocity and brutality, in a degree which far surpasses our modern conventional representation of the criminal of the type of Bill Sikes. They were rather taller than the old inhabitants and had the advantage of a powerful build, and great muscular development. Their women were less ill-favoured; the superciliary ridges were much less developed and the facial outlines being on finer lines gave them a softer and less repelling appearance. . . .

If all the men led the same sort of life, which was mainly pastoral, and only the fittest children survived, one man would be as good as another and the social body would be essentially democratic, although ruled by a council of elders who were well versed in tribal custom and on emergency by an elected chief. In this rather early stage of civilization the hereditary principle would hardly come into play, especially if the family was of a very primitive type. . . . The chief occupation of the men would be to look after the cattle, the swine, and the domestic animals, and to protect them from the attacks of wolves and other rapacious animals. Others would hunt or trap the deer and the wild boar that frequented the forests and swampy ground. And if the invaders on first arrival were few in numbers they would have to make friends with the natives they found in the country rather than to fight them, although encounters between them must sometimes have taken place. It was the same when the colony at the Cape was first founded; the Dutch settlers made friends with the Hottentots, who at that time were vastly superior in numbers and warlike into the bargain. And as white women were scarce, they sometimes took Hottentot wives.

Although the status of women was such that after death they were accorded the same honourable burial as men, during their lifetime they had to work. The manufacture of domestic and sepulchral pottery would be left to them; the little agriculture that was practised would certainly be their business, and they probably dug or helped to dig the graves. Canon Greenwell records the finding of a pick, made from the shed antler of a red deer, near the knees of a skeleton, probably that of a woman. The preparation of skins and sewing them into garments was undoubtedly left to the women, and this accounts for the small bronze prickers or awls occasionally found with female skeletons. Between cooking, looking after their children, and the tasks above mentioned their day was fully occupied.

Although it is to be supposed that the invaders lived chiefly on their flocks and herds, yet they developed a taste for shell-fish. Perhaps in winter when shell-fish are in season, and the rigour of the climate was tempered by the superior temperature of the sea, the new settlers sometimes congregated on the sea-shore to feast on the products of the sea. Mr. A. Curle has recently found the sites of small kitchen-middens at Gullane Bay in East Lothian. They were composed of heaps of shells of whelks, limpets, oysters, and mussels, mixed with crabs' claws and animals' bones, and the sand among which they lay had been blackened by the decomposition of animal matter. Dispersed through the mass lay a few flint scrapers and flakes, a bone pin and fragments of 27 beakers. In two other kitchen-middens at North Berwick, found by Mr. J. Cree, one of which measured about 150 ft. by 36 to 45 ft. wide and from 10 to 12 inches deep and lay 8 ft. below the surface, large numbers of shells and other objects were picked up. These consisted of whelks, limpets, a few oysters, crabs' claws and fish bones, a few well-worked flints, stone pounders, and fragments of beakers. At the bottom of a potsherd—not a beaker—were seen the impressions of grains of wheat. That no such kitchen-middens have been noticed on the East coast of England is to be attributed to the extensive erosion by the sea, which has swept away all trace of such sites.

Old men, at least some of them, were respected and held in honour. In Wilts a patriarch of from 70 to 80 years of age had been buried with a bronze dagger—the largest found with any beaker—a stone bracer, and a beaker the ornament of which had been filled with a white substance. As his stature had been about 6 ft., he must have been a man of mark in his day and a chief elected for his size and strength.

Both Canon Greenwell and Mr. Mortimer came to the conclusion which can scarcely be questioned that it was the habit to bury with the dead chief his wives, children, and probably slaves. In arriving at this result, both drew their conclusions from a survey of the interments of the whole Bronze Age, but here I expressly limit my observations to the earliest phase of it, to the time when beakers were in use. I have had moreover to exclude examples, which perhaps illustrate their inference, because no pottery happened to accompany the interments. In the Iron Age, when society was on a large scale and the power of certain individuals had much increased, it was possible and even customary for wives and slaves to be put to death at the funeral of a Scythian king or of a Gaulish or Teutonic chieftain. But it does not follow that such a practice was compatible with society on a small—perhaps very small—scale, many centuries earlier, when the population was scanty and the power of the chiefs, for all we know, was of a limited nature. If the custom existed among the invaders, it was not habitual. For instance, the barrow raised over the grave of the patriarch mentioned above, who was undoubtedly a man of note, contained no other interment.

STUART PIGGOTT

The Beaker Folk in Modern Archaeology

FROM Holland and the Rhineland the Beaker people invaded Britain in a succession of movements and landings spread over a century or so round about 1900–1800 B.C. The landings were mainly made along the east coast, from Kent and Sussex to Yorkshire, and again in Aberdeenshire; one group came in to Dorset and may have started from Brittany, where descendants of the Spanish Beaker folk had established themselves fairly early in the eastward spread of the culture. We shall see that the evidence suggests that at least the first landings were spear-heads of invasion, though certainly followed by a settlement phase, and the characteristics of the Battle-axe folk seem to have permeated the racially mixed Beaker invasion of Britain. Not only is there a clearly perceptible fusion of pottery styles and modes of burial, there is also an unmistakable hint of warrior chieftains imposing new ideas and planting new colonies of foreigners among the old Neolithic stock.

For the Beaker invasion of Britain cuts across the whole complex of Neolithic society as we can see it in the archaeological record.

From *British Prehistory*. London: Oxford University Press; 1949, pp. 109-19. By permission of Oxford University Press.

There is the novel racial element—tall, heavy-boned, rugged, and round-headed—and there is an organization of society which is reflected not in the custom of collective burial without much regard for the trappings of the corpses, but in single graves, often under conspicuous mounds, where a man may lie in the clothing and armament of life ready to reassume in the next world his individual personality and status. More than this, the Beaker people brought to England, as they had to other European regions, the first knowledge of and demand for metal tools and weapons, even if at first actual metal-smiths did not set up workshops in the newly settled areas.

The maximum incidence of the Beaker invasion was in the Lowland Zone of Britain—the south-east—which, while an area of agricultural fertility, had no natural sources of metal ores. These lay to the west—the copper ores of Ireland and of Weardale, the tin of Cornwall—and there is no evidence of direct Beaker immigration to these regions, only a late and sporadic eventual colonization of west Britain after the south-east had been intensively settled, and there is even less evidence of Irish settlement. Two things seem reasonably clear, therefore, when we come to consider the presence of copper or bronze daggers, axes, or other tools in the areas of maximum Beaker settlement, mainly if not exclusively of types familiar in Ireland and Atlantic Europe, and not likely to have been brought by the new arrivals from the Rhineland. The first is that a practical knowledge of metallurgy in Ireland and west Britain generally must have been established before or contemporaneously with the arrival of the Beaker folk in eastern Britain, but hardly by them; the second is that adequate trade routes between the areas of production and the areas of purchasing power must have been worked out at an early stage in the Beaker settlement phase.

The second of these factors—the routes to the west—we have already seen as existing as part of the foreign-stone axe trade late in the neolithic and before the arrival of the first Beaker contingents: routes to Cornwall, to North Wales, and to north-west England from the good pasturage of the Wessex chalk and the Thames Valley gravels. The first and more crucial factor in the case raises many points at present unsolved in British prehistory, and discussion had best be postponed until we have further considered the complex nature of the Beaker immigrations themselves.

The new colonists can be recognized from a very large number of burials (between six and seven hundred in Britain, and a few in Ireland) and a smaller number of habitation sites, in all of which the characteristic, well-made, reddish or buff pots, ornamented with zones or panels of fine impressed cord or a very distinctive notched technique, have been found. A consideration of the types of these vessels suggests a division into two main groups (one again divisible itself into two), and the associated metal and stone types in the tombs confirm the essential duality of the Beaker invasion of Britain. The current nomenclature of the pots still continues to use a nineteenth-century typology which implied a sequence we now know to be inverted, so we start with the makers of beakers of type B.

These pots, with a curved profile and zonal ornament, come nearest to the assumed Spanish prototypes (though equally found in the Rhineland), and with them in graves may be associated copper daggers held in the haft by a tang (characteristic of all European Beaker peoples), and little stone plaques which, strapped on the left wrist, protected it against the flick back of the bow-string. A subgroup of pottery has a distinctive Wessex distribution and may represent a Breton contribution to the complex (or the Breton pots may come from Wessex): the daggers may have been imported from that region, though at least one mould shows them to have been cast in Ireland. In general, however, the B Beaker folk colonized the same areas of south-eastern England as did the makers of A type pots described below (and also made landings in eastern Scotland), and the evidence of the submergence of the Essex coast shows that this geological event occurred after the arrival of the B folk, but before that of the A group. This evidence for priority of arrival is confirmed by archaeological stratigraphy in eastern England.

The A Beaker invasion made its main impact on East Anglia and Yorkshire, and certainly came from the Rhineland area. The pots show panel as well as zonal ornament and their profiles reflect the contribution of the potters of the Battle-axe people. It is hardly surprising that stone battle-axes are in fact found in graves with A beakers in Britain, and there are also daggers with riveted-on hilts (a Mediterranean type), or copies of these in flint. The evidence of physical anthropology confirms these Battle-axe elements in the British Beaker population, for a number of skulls from A Beaker graves belong to a dolichocephalic type associated with this culture on the Continent, but dissimilar from the old Neolithic long-headed stock of these islands.

In Scotland, apart from specific direct colonization probably from Holland, and in other parts of north Britain, the Beaker types are represented by degenerate forms grouped together as type C— minute analysis can assign these to ultimate B or A origins in many instances, but their significance is clearly that of local degeneration or of secondary colonization from England and Wales after the first force of the invasions was spent.

The burial rite was inhumation for all groups (a few exceptional cremations are known), and graves, dug into the subsoil, may be without any covering mound and either isolated or grouped into small cemeteries of up to about twenty graves, or may be under conspicuous round barrows or cairns. Such barrow-burial is characteristic of the Battle-axe element in the Beaker culture in Europe, and in the British tombs we find accessory ritual features such as circular ditches or stone settings, or wooden structures, and the use of stone-built cists.

Numerically, the actual metal objects found in graves with Beaker burials are very few. Of 650 or rather more graves known, four have yielded tanged copper daggers with B Beakers, and eight, riveted daggers with those of type A or C. Other metal types found with Beaker burials include copper or bronze awls (about a dozen or so in England and Wales), while ring-bracelets or broad armlets of bronze are known from a few graves, bringing up the total to about thirty objects. While there is no up-to-date collation of the whole Beaker material of Britain to work on, and figures must be approximate pending detailed research, the number of Beaker graves containing copper or bronze objects must be rather under 5 per cent. of the total. This figure is quite comparable with that for Holland, a convenient area for comparison, where slightly over 4 per cent. of Beaker graves had metal objects in them. We shall see that similar figures obtain for Early Bronze Age graves in Britain not directly attributable to the Beaker colonists, and that 5 per cent. seems a very good average, on available evidence, for the proportion of the population able to acquire copper or bronze in the earliest metal-using communities in England, Scotland, or Wales.

The Beaker folk were not the only group intrusive to the old Neolithic stock that can be traced taking a part in the early development of metallurgy in Britain, and before we can discuss this extremely important phase in our prehistory we shall have to consider the problems presented by those who are known, again from a pottery type, as the Food-vessel people. But with whatever group or groups we are dealing, the ultimate problem remains the same—the relationship of the areas in the west containing the natural metal lodes, which must have been exploited on the spot by persons well knowing the requirements of metal-smiths, if not smelting and founding themselves, and those who seem to have been the first in Lowland Britain to appreciate the value of metal tools, and to stimulate their production by purchase. The old foreign-stone axe routes might lead towards Irish copper or direct to the Cornish tin areas (a Beaker chieftain was buried on Salisbury Plain with a splendid battle-axe of rose-pink Land's End granite); but without tin-streamers working there, or Irish tinkers already trading at North Welsh ports, the Neolithic Peterborough folk or their immediate successors in the trade, however knowledgeable in greenstone, could hardly of themselves have discovered the complex techniques of metallurgy and ore prospecting. Perhaps we have for too long looked only at the front door of Britain—the invasion coast of the Lowland Zone, with the Beaker chieftains leading in the little fleets of canoes to East Anglian creeks and harbours—and forgotten that the longer sea-routes of the west, that had brought the Neolithic colonists and builders of megalithic tombs from Iberia and Brittany to the Irish Sea, still led to the back door in the Highland Zone—a back door that so well might be a tradesmen's entrance!

Though metal tools and weapons reached many of the main areas of Beaker colonization in England—Derbyshire, Yorkshire, Wessex —yet such areas of primary settlement as East Anglia suffered by the capture of the trade in more westerly regions, and bronze daggers were imitated in flint by the less fortunate Beaker chieftains in these parts. Mining for flint and the production of axes certainly continued after the advent of Beaker people in Sussex and Wiltshire, and in the latter county a mining village of rather flimsy hurdle-work huts, partly dug into the ground, was built and occupied by users of Beaker pottery on Easton Down near Salisbury. A few domestic sites are known elsewhere, in the Highland Zone with circular stone-built hut foundations, or on the coast in an almost Mesolithic manner. Grain impressions on pottery show that barley was the staple crop, as it continued to be throughout the Bronze Age in Britain.

The graves beneath barrows and cairns, often conspicuous on the crest-lines of hills, show that men, women, and children were entitled to a form of individual burial that might be monumental in character. In the area of dense Beaker occupation in Yorkshire the proportions of the sexes (where ascertainable or recorded) are almost equal; several barrows cover the grave of a man, a woman, and a child, or of a man and woman. The burials lay on one side, lightly crouched in the natural posture of sleep, though sometimes forcibly bound into a tight bundle. One skull from Crichel Down in Dorset had been trepanned before death, following a practice known on the Continent; on another the pathological erosion of the bone affords one of the earliest known examples of the deficiency disease, rickets. The warrior status of many male burials is shown by the accompanying dagger of stone or bronze, or a battle-axe, and the archery implied by the wrist-guards already mentioned is also suggested by the barbed flint tips that survived from a sheaf of half a dozen arrows in more than one man's grave, while the hawks' heads found in a couple of male burials look like evidence of falconry. A few ornaments were also acquired from the Irish gold-fields: a young archer buried at Radley near Oxford was wearing gold ear-rings. There is evidence of finely woven fabric, not likely to be linen, as flax seems to have been hardly known in Britain until later in the Bronze Age, but more probably woven from the fibres of nettles—a technique and fabric which survived in Scandinavia until the last century.

The most striking monuments of the Beaker people in Britain are, however, neither domestic nor directly sepulchral. In many of the Dutch barrows, where the Battle-axe element in the Beaker culture is strong, there is evidence of complex circular structures built around the grave with upright wooden posts, which may sometimes belong to roofed buildings, sometimes to fences or settings of posts with a structural or ritual significance. In general terms there is evidence of a probable Battle-axe, rather than true Beaker, ancestry for such complicated adjuncts to the tomb. In Britain there is some evidence for similar if simpler structures in Early Bronze Age barrows (a couple of small square wooden "mortuary-houses" are known as well, from Beaulieu in the New Forest), but what appears to be an insular development takes place, whereby an open circular sanctuary, occasionally dedicated by a burial but not primarily designed as a tomb, is enclosed by structures of earthwork, timber settings, or upright stones. We have already seen that some such monuments may be attributable to the Peterborough-Skara Brae group of late Neolithic cultures, perhaps in pre-Beaker times.

These circular sanctuaries seem to fall into three main classes. The first consists of a ditched enclosure with a single entrance, with or without a setting of wooden posts within the earthwork ditch and bank. This type of monument is known in East Anglia (Arminghall near Norwich), at Dorchester in Oxfordshire, in Dorset, and at Gorsey Bigbury on Mendip in Somerset; in Wiltshire the well-known "Woodhenge" belongs to this group, and near this the more famous Stonehenge seems to have been such a sanctuary in its earliest phase, when it consisted of a ditch, a bank, and the "Aubrey Holes" holding timber uprights [this had now been disproved. The "Aubrey Holes" were ritual pits], and had as yet no stone structure. At Stonehenge in this first phase and in a group of similar though smaller sites near Dorchester (Oxon) cremation burials were made within the sacred area. The evidence for dating shows that some of these monuments belong to late Neolithic cultures and may date from before the advent of the B Beaker folk, and the association of others with certain specialized types of A Beaker ware may stress their Battle-axe connexions.

The second group also has an enclosing bank and ditch, but with two entrances, diametrically opposed. None are known with timber uprights (though some of the many unexcavated examples might show they existed), but several have standing stones within the earthwork. Direct or inferential evidence associates the excavated monuments of this class with the A Beakers, and they are widely distributed from Wessex to Yorkshire, and in Scotland. Arbor Low in Derbyshire is one of the finest of these sites, though its stones are now all fallen.

There remains the third group, of very wide distribution and a variety of type which reflects multiple origins and dates. Free-standing circles of upright stones are frequent all over the Highland Zone of Britain, varying considerably in size, and some or many of them must belong to later phases of the Bronze Age rather than the Beaker period. But at Avebury in Wiltshire such circles seem to have been erected by the B Beaker folk (the sub-group possibly derived from Brittany, where comparable structures occur), and the associated double lines, or avenues, of stones (again known from Brittany, and in England at Stanton Drew in Somerset) were certainly put up by these people. At Avebury the great bank and ditch is demonstrably a later feature than the B Beaker constructions, and may therefore be attributed to our second class of monument, although with four instead of two entrances.

It is suggested that the ditched elements and the use of wooden posts are early features in this series of monuments, harking back to a stoneless lowland country, and probably to Holland and the Battle-axe element in the mixed Beaker culture there, and their inception in Britain may antedate even the main B Beaker invasions, since, as we have seen, they have some significant associations with the late Neolithic grooved ware described in Chapter III. The double-entrance monuments, so often with contained stone circles (two single-entrance sanctuaries with stone circles only are known, both in the Highland Zone), are likely to be attributable to the A Beaker folk, and seem to contain two distinct traditions—the stone circle, proper to the Highland Zone and perhaps having one of its origins in the free-standing curbs round some passage-graves, or a development of the crescentic forecourt, and the earthwork, essentially Lowland. Can we then see in these impressive structures an indirect expression of that linking of Highland to Lowland Zone that the early metal trade implies? The stones and the ditches of Arbor Low in Derbyshire or the Devil's Quoits at Stanton Harcourt in the Upper Thames valley would then symbolize the fusion of east and west as clearly as the Irish metal-work in the graves of the Dutch or Rhenish invaders who lie grouped around the sacred centres of their cult.

Of the nature of this cult we can only guess by analogy that an open sanctuary is appropriate to a sky-god, and that some may have been planned in relation to a celestial phenomenon such as sunrise at the summer solstice. Woodhenge may have been a roofed temple of some kind, as may another site at Avebury, and the circular-house type which on the Continent is characteristic of the western cultures (including the Beaker folk) rather than those of central Europe, may well have played a part in deciding the formal plan of these monuments. But it is interesting that the simple stone circles of the British types are scarcely known on the European mainland outside Brittany, and the ditched sanctuaries as a group are a unique British phenomenon, and stand as a tribute to the inventive genius of our Early Bronze Age population.

3. *Iron Age and Roman Britain*

THE Iron Age in Britain, which can be taken as covering the last five centuries B.C. and lasting until the Roman Conquest in A.D. 43, saw the arrival of many distinct groups of Celtic-speaking invaders. Some formed relatively peaceful farming communities, others (like those whose chieftains were buried with their chariots in north-east England) brought more warlike traditions. They came from various points on the continental coast from the Rhine southward at least as far as Brittany. Their settlements led at last to the pattern of Celtic tribes which the Romans found and made use of in their conquest and colonization of Britain. One of the last invasions, that of the Belgae (p. 424, II) from the Rhine region, was recorded by Julius Caesar.

The Celts were much given to inter-tribal wars, and some of the hillforts (such as Maiden Castle), which are the most conspicuous monuments they have left behind them, were built as tribal strongholds. Others were intended to repel new invaders. From about the third century B.C. onwards the British Celts, like their continental kinsmen in Gaul and elsewhere, developed a magnificent decorative art. It survives today mainly in metal work—shields, swords, helmets, horse-trappings, flagons, hand mirrors and personal ornaments.

CYRIL FOX

A Glimpse of Early
Iron Age Britain

ONE task remains; it is to present a sketch of the essential Britain, wherein Man ensconced himself so snugly. The picture must be imperfect: on no one canvas can we depict "her infinite variety"; and since her character changed in the course of centuries some one date must be chosen. Let us select the dawn of the Iron Age, 500–400 B.C.

The trader in iron and bronze, and the iron-using invader, coasting along the beaches and the cliffs of southern Britain, found by experience that, though sheltered anchorages, creeks, and landing places were numerous, only those where chalk downs or heaths were visible offered the opportunity they sought for barter or for entry. Where estuary or harbour was fringed with forest, the mud-flats and beaches were deserted and no trackways led inland.

To these intruders, as to the native, southern Britain presented an illimitable forest of "damp" oakwood, ash and thorn and bramble, largely untrodden. This forest was in a sense unbroken, for without emerging from its canopy a squirrel could traverse the country from end to end; but in another sense it was limited, for the downs and heaths which here and there touched the sea or navigable rivers, and where the overseas adventurers beached their oaken ships, were the terminals of far-reaching stretches of open and semi-open country, grassland and parkland. These zones it was that nourished much of the human life of the time; here were flocks and herds and patches of corn, groups of thatched huts with trails of smoke, and the palisaded banks of the new and strange fortresses; manifestations which all became scantier as parkland merged into woodland.

This open country was sometimes at valley level, but more often consisted of low hills, plateaux, or ridges of moderate elevation but dominant; so that Man moved on his vocations above the environing forest, and his eye ranged over wide spaces.

From *The Personality of Britain*, 4th ed. 1943, pp. 90-1, by permission of the National Museum of Wales.

Lowland Britain then, to most natives in the dawn of the Iron Age took shape as an environment in which Man's life was canalized, and movement shepherded, along belts of open country which, here expanding into wide acreage, there contracting into a narrow ridge, and occasionally gapped by river valleys, ended either at the sea or in the mountains; the memory of movement along them took the form of a succession of great landscapes—the Weald of Sussex seen from the South Downs; the lower Severn and the hills of Wales from the Cotswolds; the Fenland from the Icknield Way; the Vale of Trent from Lincoln Edge. The bad lands were crossed only when unavoidable, and by the narrowest gaps. Just as we moderns, reviewing our journeys in Britain along our valley roads, identify our routes by the towns passed through, so they, moving along the now deserted ridgeways, recalled the forms of the higher hills— Chanctonbury, Leith Hill, the Wrekin, their landmarks on long journeys.

The man through whose eyes we see may have witnessed the beginning of encroachment on the "damp" oakwoods, at first shunned and feared. They were haunted by lynx, wolf and boar, bear and fighting ox; and were hostile in themselves to Man, his flocks and herds. The transformation by which these areas became, in historic times, centres of agricultural life, had its small beginnings at this time, for the bronze-founders of the Late Bronze Age were located in such forest near Cambridge, and burnt its oaks for charcoal.

Occasionally our Lowlander might make a long journey to the west. The more mountainous the part visited, the less it is changed to-day from what it was then. Though forest may have clothed the high plateaux originally, he saw in 500 B.C., I think, as we see, country "waste as the sea, red with heather, with the moorfowl and the peewits crying." As he approached the Highland Zone from the lowland, the character thus represented in extreme form slowly became apparent to him. The landscape became wilder, the forest more restricted as the valleys became narrower; moorland replaced grassland, the life of his fellows thinned out along the traffic ways and was to be found, sometimes in strange guise, in the hollows of the hills rather than on the crests. Still, however, the keys to the understanding of this high country, as of the lowlands, were the major landmarks; our traveller steered his way along plateau and spur, past barrow and cairn and stone circle, by the sight of successive mountain tops. So guided he reached his goal, the shore of a now forgotten harbour, and saw against the sunset the black ships of the Irish.

JULIUS CAESAR

The Britons and
Their Chariots

IN Caesar's day the Gauls had given up the use of chariots in warfare, but the Britons still retained them.

❦

THEIR mode of fighting with their chariots is this: firstly, they drive about in all directions and throw their weapons and generally break the ranks of the enemy with the very dread of their horses and the noise of their wheels; and when they have worked themselves in between the troops of horse, leap from their chariots and engage on foot. The charioteers in the meantime withdraw some little distance from the battle, and so place themselves with the chariots that, if their masters are overpowered by the number of the enemy, they may have a ready retreat to their own troops. Thus they display in battle the speed of horse, [together with] the firmness of infantry; and by daily practice and exercise attain to such expertness that they are accustomed, even on a declining and steep place, to check their horses at full speed, and manage and turn them in an instant and run along the pole, and stand on the yoke, and thence betake themselves with the greatest celerity to their chariots again.

From *De Bello Gallico and Other Commentaries*, translated by W. A. Macdevitt. Written in the first century B.C.

J. R. MORTIMER

Chariot Burials in Britain

THE Celtic people responsible for the Yorkshire chariot burials came from the Seine region of France (Gaul) during the third century B.C. Mortimer, who opened so many Yorkshire barrows, learnt much from Canon Greenwell. He seems also to have criticized him, for the Canon refers in a letter to "that scoundrel Mortimer" who had been spreading "calumnious reports" about his methods of excavation.

NOT until towards the close of my work amongst the barrows, viz., in 1887, had I the good fortune to find any remains of a British chariot, although such had been found on the Wolds. The first two discoveries of this kind of which I have any knowledge were made by the late Rev. E. W. Stillingfleet, Vicar of South Cave, during the years 1816-17. One of these was at Hessleskew, and the other at Arras, both places being about three miles east of Market Weighton, and both were with inhumed interments. One chariot was accompanied with the bronze boss and iron rim of a shield, and with the other were the skulls of two boars and the bones of two small horses. Both chariots were accompanied by rings, buckles, and two snaffle-bits, belonging to the horses' bridles—one of iron, the other of iron coated with bronze. Portions of some of these objects are in the York Museum; the others are, as far as I know, lost. The wheels from the Hessleskew barrow measured rather more than 2 feet 11 inches in diameter; and the diameter of the iron hoops covered with copper, which had encircled the naves, was very nearly 6 inches. The wheels from the Arras barrow were only about 2 feet 8 inches in diameter, and the iron hoops of the naves were about 5 inches in diameter.

On December 15th, 1879, the guard to a North Eastern Railway

From *Forty Years' Researches in British and Saxon Burial Mounds of East Yorkshire.* London: A. Brown & Son; 1905, pp. 358-9, 361-2.

ballast train informed me that he was present at the finding of the large granite boulder in the ballast pit of Seamer Station, near Scarborough, which is now set up in the station-master's garden at Seamer. It was found at about half the depth of the face of the pit, and about one-third the distance from the Scarborough end of the pit. He also said he was present when the remains of what he called a small horse and cart were found in the pit, about the year 1862. On being questioned, he stated that the horse and cart were found in a quantity of dark soily matter, which, as far as he could remember, filled a hole 4 to 5 feet in depth, that had been dug into the clean gravelly material forming the upper part of the pit. He added that one of the workmen made his long smock-frock into a sack by tying up the neck, in which he carried away the bones and bits of iron, and afterwards sold them. The hoops of the wheels were broken and much rusted, and all the wood had disappeared.

This appears to be a discovery worthy of being recorded, as it seems to have been nothing less than a British interment, consisting of the remains of a chariot, with the bones of the horse and probably those of the charioteer, which would not be recognised by the workmen.

In 1875 a fourth discovery was made by two labourers digging for chalk at Arras. A very small barrow was then encroached upon, under which a grave had been sunk into the chalk rock. It was circular, 12 feet in diameter, and 3 feet deep. At the bottom was a skeleton, accompanied by the remains of a chariot. The iron hoops of the wheels measured about 3 feet in diameter. The hoops of the naves were of bronze, or were plated with bronze. Accompanying these were two bridle-bits of bronze, or plated with bronze; and a circular mirror of iron, 8 to 9 inches in diameter, the handle of which is slightly ornamented with bronze.

A mirror of iron was found with the chariots discovered by the late Rev. E. W. Stillingfleet in one of the barrows on Arras, which he opened in 1816.

The fifth discovery was made by Canon Greenwell in a barrow on Westwood, Beverley, in 1875, and consisted of the hoops of two chariot wheels, about 3 feet in diameter, and what was almost certainly an iron bit or bits.

Still later, the remains of a chariot were found in No. 13 of the "Danes' Graves," which I excavated during the first fortnight in July, 1897. These consisted of the iron hoops of the wheels and naves, and rings of bronze and iron belonging to the chariot and the trappings of the horses. In the grave with these were two adult skeletons, probably the remains of the owner of the chariot and his charioteer.

In the North Riding the late Thomas Kendal, of Pickering, about

the year 1849, found the remains of a British chariot, in a barrow
close to the Cawthorne Camps, north of Pickering, the wheels and
other parts of which are now in the possession of Thomas Mitchel-
son, Esq., of Pickering. I well remember Mr. Kendal naming this
find to me many years ago, and he much regretted that he was not
able to sketch, so as to give the shape and position of the chariot.
He described the mound as being mainly composed of light-coloured
sand, and said that the position and, in the main, the form of the
chariot was clearly visible. The tyres of the wheels were well preserved, whilst the pole (which had measured about 7 feet) and
other woodwork was shown by dark lines of decayed wood, clearly
defined in the clean light-coloured sand. It is much to be regretted
that so good an opportunity of obtaining a restoration of the chariot
was lost.

On April 2nd, 1894, I interviewed Mr. Thomas Dowson, of Pickering, who was Kendal's foreman in all his barrow-digging. Though
he was about seventy-eight years of age he retained a vivid recollection of the barrow openings at which he had assisted. He fully
confirmed what Kendal had told me about the chariot, and added
that the mound is situated very near the south-eastern corner of the
most easterly of the three Cawthorne Camps, and that at the time
its height would be a little over 3 feet. One of the chariot wheels
was pressed down nearly flat, and the decayed wood of the spokes,
which numbered only four, was shown very clearly. The other wheel
stood upright, and nearly reached to the top of the barrow. The
diameter of these wheels, judging from the tyre now preserved,
was about 3 feet; and from preserved portions of the tyre of the
naves they seem to have been hooped with iron plated with thin
bronze. Mr. Dowson said the pole reached eastwards about 7 feet
from the body of the chariot, and at the terminal end were decayed
hooks and rings of iron and brass (bronze).

In reply to further inquiry, he said there were no human or animal bones, or any other article, with the chariot, which seemed
to have been placed on the old surface line under the barrow. Unless
the interment was a cremated one simply placed in a heap at the
base of the barrow, and not observed by Mr. Kendal, I am inclined
to think that the owner of the chariot may have been buried in a
grave somewhere under the mound, and that after his body was
covered up the chariot was placed upon or near the grave, and then
covered with the mound. If so, the grave yet remains unexplored,
and the mound should, if possible, be traced and carefully reopened.

This chariot is the only one I know of as having been found in
the North Riding of Yorkshire. It is, however, highly probably that
in both Ridings others have been accidentally unearthed by persons
who were ignorant of the nature of the finds.

Chariots have been found in various districts throughout England, Scotland, and Ireland; but in no district of the same area have a greater number of them been found than in the barrows of the East Riding of Yorkshire. They have been found also throughout Europe, and three hundred years before Christ chariots were extensively used by the Gauls.

In every instance the remains are those of the two-wheeled war chariot, which probably was drawn by two horses, and which I believe is the only kind that has ever been found in connection with an interment.

At what period the chariot was first introduced into the British Isles, and whether by the Phoenicians, Gauls, or other nation, may probably never be ascertained. That it must have been a period long previous to Caesar's invasion is evident from the great numbers which were then brought together to oppose him, and from their remains having been found in tumuli so widely scattered throughout the country.

TACITUS

The Britons and Their Conquest

TACITUS wrote his account of the Britons and their conquest mainly to magnify the achievements of his father-in-law, the great Agricola. Agricola was appointed to command the Twentieth Legion in Britain in A.D. 70 and campaigned there with success for about three years, subduing the stubbornly resisting tribes of Wales, the north of England and southern Scotland. The events Tacitus refers

From *Agricola*, 1st century A.D. In *On Britain and Germany*, translated by H. Mattingly. Harmondsworth: Penguin Books Ltd; 1948, pp. 61-3, 72-4, 113-15, 122-3, 133-4, 137-9. By permission of Penguin Books Ltd.

to therefore occurred after the storming of Maiden Castle (p. 421, II), but his account is put first because it serves as a general introduction to the Britons of the time of the Roman Conquest.

WHO the first inhabitants of Britain were, whether natives or immigrants, remains obscure; one must remember we are dealing with barbarians. But physical characteristics vary, and that very variation is suggestive. The reddish hair and large limbs of the Caledonians proclaim a German origin, the swarthy faces of the Silures, the tendency of their hair to curl and the fact that Spain lies opposite, all lead one to believe that Spaniards crossed in ancient times and occupied the land. The peoples nearest to the Gauls are correspondingly like them. Perhaps the original strain persists, perhaps it is climatic conditions that determine physical type in lands that converge from opposite directions on a single point. On a general estimate, however, we may believe that it was Gauls who took possession of the neighbouring island. In both countries you will find the same ritual, the same religious beliefs. There is no great difference in language, and there is the same hardihood in challenging danger, the same subsequent cowardice in shirking it. But the Britons show more spirit; they have not yet been softened by protracted peace. The Gauls, too, we have been told, had their hour of military glory; but then came decadence with peace, and valour went the way of lost liberty. The same fate has befallen such of the Britons as have long been conquered; the rest are still what the Gauls used to be.

Their strength is in their infantry. Some tribes also fight from chariots. The nobleman drives, his dependents fight in his defence. Once they owed obedience to kings; now they are distracted between the jarring factions of rival chiefs. Indeed, nothing has helped us more in war with their strongest nations than their inability to cooperate. It is but seldom that two or three states unite to repel a common danger; fighting in detail they are conquered wholesale. The climate is objectionable, with its frequent rains and mists, but there is no extreme cold. Their day is longer than is normal in the Roman world. The night is bright and, in the extreme North, short, with only a brief interval between evening and morning twilight. If no clouds block the view, the sun's glow, it is said, can be seen all night long. It does not set and rise, but simply passes along the horizon. The reason must be that the ends of the earth, being flat, cast low shadows and cannot raise the darkness to any height; night therefore fails to reach the sky and its stars. The soil can bear all produce, except the olive, the vine, and other natives of

warmer climes, and it is fertile. Crops are slow to ripen, but quick
to grow—both facts due to one and the same cause, the extreme
moistness of land and sky. Britain yields gold, silver and other
metals, to make it worth conquering. Ocean, too, has its pearls,
but they are dusky and mottled. Some think that the natives are
unskilful in gathering them. Whereas in the Red Sea the oysters
are torn alive and breathing from the rocks, in Britain they are
collected as the sea throws them up. I find it easier to believe in a
defect of quality in the pearls than of greed in us. . . .

The following winter was spent on schemes of the most salutary
kind. To induce a people, hitherto scattered, uncivilized and therefore prone to fight, to grow pleasurably inured to peace and ease,
Agricola gave private encouragement and official assistance to the
building of temples, public squares and private mansions. He
praised the keen and scolded the slack, and competition to gain
honour from him was as effective as compulsion. Furthermore, he
trained the sons of the chiefs in the liberal arts and expressed a
preference for British natural ability over the trained skill of the
Gauls. The result was that in place of distaste for the Latin Language came a passion to command it. In the same way, our national
dress came into favour and the toga was everywhere to be seen.
And so the Britons were gradually led on to the amenities that make
vice agreeable—arcades, baths and sumptuous banquets. They
spoke of such novelties as "civilization," when really they were
only a feature of enslavement.

  The fourth summer was spent in securing the districts already
overrun, and, if the valour of our armies and the glory of Rome
had not forbidden a halt, a place for halting was found inside Britain itself. Clyde and Forth, carried inland to a great depth on the
tides of opposite seas, are separated only by a narrow neck of land.
This neck was now secured by garrisons, and the whole sweep of
country to the south was safe in our hands. The enemy had been
pushed into what was virtually another island.

MORTIMER WHEELER

The Romans Storm
Maiden Castle

AT the time of the Claudian invasion of A.D. 43, the part of the
army responsible for the conquest of southern Britain was commanded by the future emperor Vespasian. He is known to have
captured as many as twenty Celtic strongholds, and excavation has
shown that the massively fortified Maiden Castle was among them.
It must have fallen between A.D. 43 and 47.

❧

APPROACHING from the direction of the Isle of Wight, Vespasian's
legion may be supposed to have crossed the River Frome at the only
easy crossing hereabouts—where Roman and modern Dorchester
were subsequently to come into being. Before the advancing troops,
some 2 miles away, the sevenfold ramparts of the western gates
of Dunium towered above the cornfields which probably swept,
like their modern successors, up to the fringe of the defences.
Whether any sort of assault was attempted upon these gates we
do not at present know; their excessive strength makes it more
likely that, leaving a guard upon them, Vespasian moved his
main attack to the somewhat less formidable eastern end. What
happened there is plain to read. First, the regiment of artillery,
which normally accompanied a legion on campaign, was ordered
into action, and put down a barrage of iron-shod ballista-arrows
over the eastern part of the site. Following this barrage, the infantry
advanced up the slope, cutting its way from rampart to rampart,
tower to tower. In the innermost bay of the entrance, close outside

From *Maiden Castle*. London: Society of Antiquaries at the Oxford University Press;
1943, pp. 61-3. By courtesy of Sir Mortimer Wheeler and The Society of Antiquaries
of London.

the actual gates, a number of huts had recently been built; these were now set alight, and under the rising clouds of smoke the gates were stormed and the position carried. But resistance had been obstinate and the fury of the attackers was roused. For a space, confusion and massacre dominated the scene. Men and women, young and old, were savagely cut down, before the legionaries were called to heel and the work of systematic destruction began. That work included the uprooting of some at least of the timbers which revetted the fighting-platform on the summit of the main rampart; but above all it consisted of the demolition of the gates and the over-throw of the high stone walls which flanked the two portals. The walls were now reduced to the lowly and ruinous state in which they were discovered by the excavator nearly nineteen centuries later.

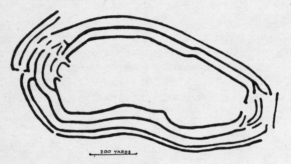

THE DEFENSE WORKS OF MAIDEN CASTLE.

That night, when the fires of the legion shone out (we may imagine) in orderly lines across the valley, the survivors crept forth from their broken stronghold and, in the darkness, buried their dead as nearly as might be outside their tumbled gates, in that place where the ashes of their burned huts lay warm and thick upon the ground. The task was carried out anxiously and hastily and without order, but, even so, from few graves were omitted those tributes of food and drink which were the proper and traditional perquisites of the dead. At daylight on the morrow, the legion moved westward to fresh conquest, doubtless taking with it the usual levy of hostages from the vanquished.

Thereafter, salving what they could of their crops and herds, the disarmed townsfolk made shift to put their house in order. Forbidden to refortify their gates, they built new roadways across the sprawling ruins, between gateless ramparts that were already fast assuming the blunted profiles that are theirs to-day. And so, for some two decades, a demilitarized Maiden Castle retained its inhabitants, or at least a nucleus of them. Just so long did it take the Roman authorities to adjust the old order to the new, to prepare

new towns for old. And then finally, on some day towards the close
of the sixties of the century, the town was ceremonially abandoned,
its remaining walls were formally "slighted," and Maiden Castle
lapsed into the landscape amongst the farm-lands of Roman Dorchester.

So much for the story; now for its basis. First, scattered over the
eastern end of Maiden Castle, mostly in and about the eastern
entrance and always at the same Romano-Belgic level, were found
upwards of a dozen iron arrow-heads of two types: a type with a
pyramidal point, and the simple flat-bladed type with turn-over
socket. Arrow-heads occurred at no other Iron Age level, but both
types are common on Roman military sites where *ballistae* but not
hand-bows are to be inferred. There, then, in the relatively small
area uncovered, are the vestiges of the bombardment.

Secondly, the half-moon bay which represents the Iron Age B
adaptation of the Iron Age A barbican, close outside the portals
of the eastern entrance, was covered with a thick layer of ash associated with the post-holes of three or more circular or roundish
huts. In and immediately below this ash were quantities of late
Belgic or "Belgicizing" pottery. In the surface of the ash was similar
pottery with scraps of pre-Flavian Samian. There are the burnt
Belgic huts, covered by the trodden vestiges of the continued post-
conquest occupation for which more tangible evidence will be
offered shortly.

Thirdly, into this ash a series of graves had been roughly cut,
with no regularity either of outline or of orientation, and into them
had been thrown, in all manner of attitudes—crouched, extended,
on the back, on the side, on the face, even sitting up—thirty-eight
skeletons of men and women, young and old; sometimes two persons were huddled together in the same grave. In ten cases extensive
cuts were present on the skull, some on the top, some on the front,
some on the back. In another case, one of the arrow-heads already
described was found actually embedded in a vertebra, having
entered the body from the front below the heart. The victim had
been finished off with a cut on the head. Yet another skull had been
pierced by an implement of square section, probably a ballista-bolt.
The last two and some of the sword-cuts were doubtless battle-
wounds; but one skull, which had received no less than nine savage
cuts, suggests the fury of massacre rather than the tumult of battle—a man does not stay to kill his enemy eight or nine times in
the mêlée; and the neck of another skeleton had been dislocated,
probably by hanging. Nevertheless, the dead had been buried by
their friends, for most of them were accompanied by bowls or, in
one case, a mug for the traditional food and drink. More notable,
in two cases the dead held joints of lamb in their hands—joints

chosen carefully as young and succulent. Many of the dead still wore their gear: armlets of iron or shale, an iron finger-ring, and in three cases bronze toe-rings, representing a custom not previously, it seems, observed in prehistoric Britain but reminiscent of the Moslem habit of wearing toe-rings as ornaments or as preventives or cures of disease. One man lay in a double grave with an iron battle-axe, a knife and, strangely, a bronze ear-pick across his chest. The whole war cemetery as it lay exposed before us was eloquent of mingled piety and distraction; of weariness, of dread, of darkness, but yet not of complete forgetfulness. Surely no poor relic in the soil of Britain was ever more eloquent of high tragedy, more worthy of brooding comment from the presiding Spirits of Hardy's own *Dynasts*.

CHRISTOPHER HAWKES

The Britons in Subjection and Revolt

BETWEEN Caesar's campaigns in Britain and the final Roman Conquest, a king from one of the royal houses of the Belgic tribes in Britain had established his capital outside modern Colchester (Essex)—on a site now known as Sheepen. This man was Cuno belin, the Cymbeline of Shakespeare. The capital he founded in about A.D. 10 came to be known as *Camulodunum*—after the Celtic god Camulos. He was a strong and aggressive ruler and had soon extended his kingdom over much of south-east and south central England. Cunobelin died in A.D. 40, and his son Caratacus was one of the kings who tried unsuccessfully to oppose the Romans. *Camulodunum*, which had been protected by massive embankments, or "dykes," seems to have fallen without resistance. The excavation described here revealed what happened to the site of the old town when the Romans set up their Colonia nearby (in the heart of

modern Colchester). The new town became for a time the capital
of the Roman province—until it was succeeded by *Londinium*. It
was among the places sacked by Queen Boudicca (Boadicea). As
even this fragment can show, the excavation of *Camulodunum* is
an outstanding instance of what archaeology can do to fill in and
humanize a scanty historical record.

THAT the Sheepen population still for the most part consisted of
natives, now reduced to a subject working-class for the Roman
citizens of the Colonia, is made absolutely clear by the dwellings.
A new and more numerous series of huts was established over the
ditch-filling of the old dyke, of which about a dozen were either
cleared or sectioned by excavation, and over the whole area within
twenty more were found occupied in this period: six entirely new,
three rebuilt on period III sites, ten or eleven continuing from
period III, and one the large hut mentioned above as lasting on from
period I. In addition there were the large and intensively occupied
industrial quarters along and mainly north of the contemporary
road. Altogether, the hut-dwelling population was evidently at least
double what it had been in period III. And everywhere the huts were
of the same old native type, modified only in some rare cases by the
addition of dug post-holes for sturdier roof-ridge supports. Even
that addition had appeared at least as early as period III, and cannot
be called specifically Roman. Otherwise, the greater frequency and
thickness of clay flooring and clayey wall-banks is the only sign of
improvement. In one case the hardening of this clay in the Boudic-
can conflagration enabled us to recognize the six driven stake-holes,
4 in. square and 9 in. deep, that had supported the wattle-and-daub
walling: the hut had only been 8 ft. across. In such hovels (though
this one was exceptionally small) lived the native working-class.
On the other hand, the buildings of more civilized type which now
appear on the site are much rarer and wholly distinctive, and the
two best preserved examples prove them to have been of oblong-
rectangular plan, with uprights set in dug post-holes and vertical
wattled walls bedded in gullies between. Iron nails from woodwork
and remains of roof-tiles were found in quantity on these sites, and
the plan of at least one of them recalls the regular barrack-building
of Roman camps or forts. That this was a centre of specifically
Roman occupation is shown by the differential distribution of Ro-

From *Camelodunum*. London: The Society of Antiquaries at the Oxford University
Press; 1947, pp. 53-6. By courtesy of Christopher Hawkes and The Society of Antiquaries of London.

man coins, Decorated and Plain Terra Sigillata, and other wholly
Roman pottery, as between it and the crowded native huts along
the old ditch-line near by. There was no mistaking conquerors and
conquered.

Against this harsh background of Roman and barbarian, which
fits Tacitus' account of the times so well, we have to interpret the
massed evidence of industrial activity and material culture. And here
our finds when studied in abstraction present a much more evenly
toned picture, of a steady romanization in which native tradition
blended with what Rome imposed. While the workers dug clay and
sand and gravel, and stacked and carried brick and tile and stone,
to build what seemed to them a citadel of eternal domination over
their country, clay from the same ground was serving a pottery
industry in which Roman and native elements had begun to merge
into truly Romano-British work. Rather over a century later even
the mass of imported Sigillata was to meet competition in its own
kind here from these potters' descendants, and the same is probably
true of the imported glass. Meanwhile this period's Romanization of
unglazed potting is only the intensified sequel to more than a generation of pre-conquest influence on the native craft. Similarly in
metal-work, native and imported brooch-types now begin to coalesce
in new Romano-British models owing features to both. Native ena-
mel-working was not wholly dead, and its practitioners could take
ideas from the polychrome work introduced from the Continent.
In ironwork, too, new types appear; and if we had the evidence of
perishable substances no doubt the tale could be extended. Behind
the bitter hatred of subjects for new masters a material matrix was
being formed for the cultural amalgam of Roman Britain. But
before that amalgam could harden, the political atmosphere had
to be cooled by the gathering and clearing of the storm of revolt.

Boudicca's rising [of A.D. 61] found Roman Colchester unprepared, and our site has brought telling evidence of a desperate
effort to rearm. Yet there was no effective resistance when her
onslaught came, and Sheepen and its industries, the Colonial and
its temple, met a common ruin. But when the flames died down the
significance of the Sheepen site may have been asserted in a new
way. If its refortification was indeed taken in hand by her, the
ditch and palisaded rampart were to redraw the lines of Cunobelin's
mightier defences. Boudicca will have aimed not only at fortifying
a base for her campaign, but at strengthening her cause by founding afresh—and no doubt re-dedicating to Camulos the war-god—
the capital of the old Belgic king. Her defeat and death quickly
followed. If the refortifying works are not hers, they can only be
attributed to the victorious Romans. They will then represent a
project for turning the site into a large base-camp, which was

countermanded before they had been finished. In either case they
were very quickly levelled; and the Roman authorities decided to
abandon the site altogether. While the Colonia was rebuilt, the
wreckage Boudicca had left behind her here was decently buried
in rubbish-pits and under spreads of gravel; the road was made up;
and a sizable hut of the old type was built in one place over the
newly filled-in ditch, for someone—perhaps a native overseer of
these humble works—whose family possessions suggest an old
loyalty to Rome. Soon the works were done and the hut demolished;
and but for some continued quarrying, and a shack or two on the
eastern outskirts with a little metal-working, nothing was left.

F. HAVERFIELD

How Far Was
Britain Romanized?

THE question as to how far the native Celtic culture survived
Roman conquest and rule has always been an interesting one—
particularly in the light of the wonderful flowering of late Celtic
art in Christian times. Haverfield, an eminent Roman historian at
Oxford, was one of the first to examine it in some detail.

Language

FIRST, in respect of language. Even before the Claudian conquest
of A.D. 43, British princes had begun to inscribe their coins with
Latin words. These legends are not merely blind and unintelligent

From *The Romanization of Roman Britain*. Oxford: The Clarendon Press; 4th ed.,
rev. by George MacDonald, 1923, pp. 29-31, 50-1, 53-4. (1st ed., 1906). By permission
of The Clarendon Press, Oxford.

copies, like the imitations of Roman legends on the early English *sceattas*. The word most often used, REX, is strange to the Roman coinage, and must have been employed with a real sense of its meaning. After A.D. 43, Latin advanced rapidly. No Celtic inscription has been detected, I believe, on any monument of the Roman period in Britain, neither cut on stone nor scratched on tile or potsherd, and this fact is the more noteworthy because Celtic inscriptions are not unknown in Gaul. On the other hand, Roman inscriptions occur freely in Britain. They are less common than in many other provinces, and they abound most in the northern military region. But they appear also in towns and country-houses of the lowlands, and some of the instances are significant.

The town site which we can best examine for our present purpose is Calleva Atrebatum (Silchester), ten miles south of Reading, which has been completely excavated within the circuit of its walls. It was a small town in a stoneless country; it can never have had many lapidary inscriptions, and such as there were must have been eagerly sought by later builders. Nevertheless, a few fairly perfect inscriptions on stone and many fragments have been found here and prove that the public language of the town was Latin. The speech of ordinary conversation is equally well attested by smaller inscribed objects, and the evidence is remarkable, since it plainly refers to the lower class of Callevans. When a weary brickmaker scrawls SATIS (enough) with his finger on a tile, or some prouder spirit writes FECIT TVBVL(*um*) CLEMENTINVS (Clementinus made this box-tile); when a bit of Samian is marked FVR (thief), presumably as a warning from the servants of one house to those of the next, or a brick shows the word PVELLAM, part of an amatory sentence otherwise lost, or another brick gives a Roman date, the "sixth day before the Calends of October," we may be sure that the lower classes of Calleva used Latin alike at their work and in their more frivolous moments. When we find a tile scratched over with cursive lettering—possibly part of a writing lesson—which ends with a tag from the Aeneid, we recognize that not even Vergil was out of place here. The examples are so numerous and remarkable that they admit of no other interpretation.

I have heard this conclusion doubted on the ground that a bricklayer or domestic servant in a province of the Roman Empire would not have known how to read and write. The doubt rests on a misconception of the Empire. It is, indeed, akin to the surprise which tourists often exhibit when confronted with Roman remains in an excavation or a museum—a surprise that "the Romans" had boots, or beds, or waterpipes, or fireplaces, or roofs over their heads. There are, in truth, abundant evidences that the labouring man in Roman days knew how to read and write at need, and there is reason to believe that in the lands ruled by Rome education was better under the Empire than at any time since its fall till the nineteenth century.

It has, indeed, been suggested by doubters, that these *graffiti* were written by immigrant Italians, working as labourers or servants in Calleva. The suggestion does not seem probable. Italians certainly emigrated to the provinces in considerable numbers, just as Italians emigrate to-day. But we have seen above that the emigrants of the Imperial age were not labourers, as they are to-day. They were traders, dealers in land, money-lenders, or other "well-to-do" persons. The labourers and the servants of Calleva must be sought among the native population, and the *graffiti* testify that this population wrote Latin.

Art

Castor ware was decorated by the method often called "barbotine"; the ornament was in relief and was laid on by hand in the form of a semi-liquid "slip" with the aid of a tube or other tool—just as in the later Roman Empire the ornament was laid on glass, or as in our own day it is put on sugar-cakes. Every piece is, therefore, the individual product of a potter, not a mechanical cast from a mould. From this point of view it is noteworthy that the British Castor ware directly embodies the Celtic tradition. If it was copied from the Continent, the island potters either took over with it an element which has all but disappeared from the Gaulish work, or else they added that element. Castor ware is based, indeed, on classical patterns—foliated scrolls, hunting scenes, gladiatorial combats, even now and then a mythological representation. But it recasts these patterns in accordance with its own traditions and also with the vigour of a true art. Those fantastic animals with strange outstreched legs and back-turned heads and eager eyes; those tiny scrolls scattered by way of background above and below them; the rude beading which serves, not ineffectively, for ornament or for dividing line; the suggestions of returning spirals; the manifest delight of the artist in plant and animal forms—all these things are Celtic.

When we turn to the scenes in which man is prominent—a hunting picture in which (exceptionally) the huntsman appears, or a chariot race, or a gladiatorial show, or Hesione fettered naked to a rock and Hercules saving her from the sea-monster—we do not always find the same skill and vigour. From of old the Celtic artist had been averse to representations of the human form. When with an initiative lacking in his continental rival—an initiative which it is fair to recognize—he added this to his repertory, he passed beyond his proper bounds. Now and then he succeeded; more often he failed; his Hercules and Hesione are not fantastic but grotesque. In taking in new Roman elements, his Celtic art lost its power and approximated to the conventionalism of Samian ware.

Perhaps it is to this survival of the Celtic spirit in a Romanized Britain that we should ascribe two remarkable sculptures found at Bath and at Corbridge. The Spa at Bath (Aquae Sulis) contained a stately temple to Sul or Sulis Minerva, goddess of the hot springs. The pediment of this temple, partly preserved by a lucky accident and unearthed in 1790, was carved with a trophy of arms—in the centre a round wreathed shield upheld by two Victories, and below and on either side a helmet, a standard (?), a cuirass, besides other details now lost. It is a classical group, such as occurs on other Roman reliefs. But its treatment breaks clean away from the classical. The sculptor placed on the shield a Gorgon's head, as suits alike Minerva and a shield. But he gave to the Gorgon a beard and moustache, almost in the manner of a head of Fear, and he wrought its features with a fierce virile vigour that finds no kin in Greek or Roman art. I need not here discuss the reasons which may have led him to add male attributes to a female type. For our present purpose the important fact is that he could do it. Here is proof that, for once at least, the supremacy of the dominant conventional art of the Empire could be rudely broken down.

Another example is supplied by the Corbridge Lion, found among the ruins of Corstopitum in Northumberland in 1907 [p. 444, II]. It is a sculpture in the round showing a nearly life-sized lion standing above his prey. The scene is common in provincial Roman work, and not least in Gaul and Britain. Often it is connected with graves; sometimes (as perhaps here) it served for the ornament of a fountain. But if the scene is common, the execution of it is not. Technically, indeed, the piece is open to criticism. The lion is not the ordinary beast of nature. His face, the pose of his feet, the curl of his tail round his hind leg, are all untrue to life. The man who carved him knew perhaps more of dogs than lions. But he fashioned a living animal. Fantastic and even grotesque as it is, his work possesses a wholly unclassical fierceness and vigour, and not a few observers have remarked when seeing it that it recalls not the Roman world but the Middle Ages.

IAN RICHMOND

Country Life in Roman Britain

ROMAN villas are so old and well-established a part of Romano-British archaeology that they require, paradoxically, some explanation. Most have been recognized, and many rendered famous, through the discovery of their mosaic pavements, which by modern standards would belong to sumptuous country houses. But while country houses erected for pleasure existed in the Roman world, they were almost exclusively the privilege of the very wealthy. The normal Roman villa was not a liability of this kind but a profit-making farm, and the very richest villas in Roman Britain show no departure from this economic basis. Comfortable on the average, luxurious at best, and squalid at worst, the Romano-British villas ranged in size from cottage to mansion, and the associated acreage varied accordingly. Nor are villas to be connected with Roman immigrants rather than native Britons. Roman settlers there were, retired soldiers or administrators, but these were very much in a minority compared with the native British land-owners, the principal farmers and notables of the tribes. In short, the villas mostly represent the adoption of Roman standards in greater or lesser degree by natives of substance.

But it is hardly to be considered that in building villas, any more than in erecting towns, the native began on a sumptuous scale. The first villas, like the first towns, must have been, with due exceptions, simple and unpretentious houses; and three examples, two from the territory of the Catuvellauni and one from among the Belgae, will serve to illustrate the point. Park Street near St. Albans and Lockleys near Welwyn began their existence as a single range of four or five rooms, divided by a passage from back to front. Park Street had a basement storehouse at one end, but neither building appears to have had a substantial upper storey. Catsgore (Somersetshire) is even simpler, comprising little more than a couple of detached barns, perhaps sub-divided in timber. In this it closely resembles

From *Roman Britain*. Harmondsworth: Penguin Books Ltd.; 1955, pp. 109-22. By permission of Penguin Books Ltd.

the earliest Roman buildings at Langton (E. Yorks). But all three houses were erected on the site of earlier native huts, two of oblong plan at Park Street, and single round huts at Lockleys and Catsgore. Thus, however simple the new houses of Roman structure, there was a profound difference in solidity and comfort between them and the native buildings whose place they took, and the cost of making the change doubtless represented a considerable capital expenditure in the owners' eyes. As for standards, it is instructive to compare these plans with that of the smaller English farm-house of the sixteenth or seventeenth century. The types compare so closely that the known simple standards of the English example might serve as a pattern for those of earlier days. The important point about all these villas is that Roman building fashions, though not yet Roman luxury, had been adopted within a generation of the conquest.

The materials used in such houses were not necessarily the most solid and permanent. Stone foundations may connote half-timber superstructures rather than a building wholly of stone. At Ditchley (Oxfordshire), the timber posts forming a colonnade in front of the earliest house plainly indicate this type of modest structural programme, comparable with the now rare but once common timber arcades of Norman domestic architecture, of which carpentry made a delightful thing. Behind this front the Ditchley house differed little from Lockleys or Park Street, and it is probable that only a loft-like first floor rose above the colonnade. But about the turn of the first century A.D. there were added a new stone-built veranda and projecting end rooms which gave to the establishment both privacy and a new elegance. There was now room for recreation and entertainment in what had been previously a workaday farm, wherein the whole household lived together. Socially speaking, the new plan divided the household and accentuated the position of master and mistress. In Britain this type of house became widespread, and it brought the new province into touch with the mainstream of contemporary West-European domestic architecture. For in Gaul or the Rhineland the design was generally common, and went with a sizeable farm. And so it was in Britain, for on the basis of its granary accommodation the Ditchley villa has been related to an estate of some thousand acres. This supplies, then, a kind of yardstick, however rough, by which the size and standing of different kinds of villas can be gauged. Even allowing for the fact that, on the ancient system of crop-rotation, one-third of the arable lay fallow each year, it becomes clear that by this standard the numerous bigger villas must have been related to very substantial estates indeed. Not enough is known about the social organization of such larger estates to say whether they were run by slaves or by crofter-labourers. But where a resident staff of labourers appears, their accommodation nearly always takes the form of a barn-dwelling, frequently ranged on one side of a farmyard or court. This structure, convenient for so many purposes, is planned with nave and aisles divided by timber columns. As in Friesian farm-houses to-day, the nave served for stores, tools, and livestock, while the aisles or the whole of one end of the building were partitioned to house the workers. In the form of a subsidiary building essential to the working of a farm this type of house was so general, even in the largest establishments, that its prototype has been sought in the pre-Roman days. But no proof of such antecedents has yet appeared, and it may well be that the type is borrowed from the Italian *villa rustica*. There are some villas also in which this type of house is the only domestic accommodation present, as for example Clanville (Hampshire) or Denton (Lincolnshire). These represent either small tenant farms or bailiff-run establishments, where the distinction between tenant or supervisor and workers was less sharply defined. Some, as at Castlefield (Hampshire), are so primitive in their arrangements that any distinction seems out of the question.

The planning of the houses so far described is determined by work. No mention has been made of bath-houses, because in the earlier Romano-British villas of this class they are a luxury rarely supplied. It is, indeed, one of the evidences of advancing civilization that in most later villas a bath-house, however simple, is an essential part of the plan. The next class of house on the upward scale, the so-called corridor-house, is a development of the Park Street type of house, by adding to the number of rooms, and linking them with a front corridor. A bath-house was often attached to one end, or set closely adjacent to avoid the risk of fire. In such houses there is a tendency for the main rooms to lie at the end of the range, but a single large central room also tends to come into prominence. This is the dining-room, the social centre of Roman private life, bracketed by Tacitus with baths as the hallmark of civility; and it must be understood that in educated Roman circles the meal was savourless without good conversation and literary entertainment. A plan of this kind is accordingly the silent witness of the adoption of such standards by British well-to-do circles. But there are also corridor-houses of which the planning is still more deliberately balanced, with rooms disposed in relation to garden or landscape. Such villas, as at Folkestone with its Channel view, though not necessarily very large, evoke a picture of yet another kind of sensibility.

The conversion of a corridor-house into a courtyard-house is dictated by size of household and estate rather than by other cultural or aesthetic considerations. The courtyard-house always gives an impression of great size, and it is possible nowadays to exaggerate this, when so much that would now be arranged in storeys was in

Roman Britain spread out upon the ground floor. Nevertheless, the biggest of these villas are large indeed, and it must be borne in mind that in a society based upon slavery or small tenants, even moderately wealthy folk tended to accumulate large households. Britain has not furnished such scenes of daily life as grace the funeral monuments of the Moselle valley in lively variety. But there is no reason to think that the life of the wealthy in the provinces differed in its essentials. So the kitchen scenes of Gallia Belgica, with their cooks and scullions; the hunting scenes, with grooms and estate lads, or the boudoir scenes, with mistress and maids, might be applied to the world of the large Romano-British villas almost without observing the change of locality. What must be emphasized, however, as a social fact, upon which stress has already been laid, is that a villa so large as Woodchester, where by no means all the remains have yet been uncovered, comprises both residential and workaday quarters. The inner garden court, with its vast house, enormous central dining-room and imported marble sculptures, is reached through an outer courtyard flanked by a pair of barn-dwellings of the type associated with farm-workers and farm-stock. The direct connexion of this richest of houses with the development of an estate is thus demonstrated by the plan.

Woodchester was uncovered and published in an age when evidence for the growth or evolution of villas was not sought. To perceive such a phenomenon it is necessary to go to a later excavation at Northleigh (Oxfordshire). This great house in its final form comprised a vast courtyard-house of many rooms, with servants' quarters and baths occupying the two wings. The farm buildings have been descried by air-photography on a site outside the courtyard. But excavation further demonstrated that the house began its existence as a simple corridor-house with modest bath-house adjoining, covering about one-third of the later area but plainly connected with the farm. This change in the character of the main house is important as indicating the growing wealth and prosperity of the estate and its owners. The process is matched in greater or lesser degree in many villas. There are few which did not grow in prosperity, even from small beginnings: and this is something to put beside the decay of cultivated town life, which appears to blight the province and to stamp it as unfruitful.

But not all villas passed through the same kind of development. An instructive contrast is provided by Llantwit Major, in the Glamorganshire sea-plain. This estate developed in the second century A.D., administered from a simple courtyard-house with modest farm-buildings attached, of which the most important was a barn-dwelling for the estate staff. At the beginning of the fourth century A.D. the main house was deserted, and fell into ruin. The barn-dwelling, on the other hand, functioned actively for another century; and it becomes evident that the estate continued to exist as an economic unit, but that its owners no longer dwelt there. Whether they had migrated behind town walls in times of uncertainty, or whether, for example, failure in the male line had transferred the estate to another family, cannot be revealed by the plan. The modifications evident in the plan of Chedworth (Gloucestershire) reveal that something like the second event certainly happened there: for this large and comfortable villa, delightfully situated and handsomely planned, was converted in its latest days into a manufactory, engaged partly in fulling cloth and partly in the production of wrought-iron agricultural tools. Such a revolution in the function of the building must have coincided with the passing of the estate into the hands of an owner who lived elsewhere and was no longer interested in its residential possibilities. The very existence of such manufacturing processes, on the other hand, is intimately connected with servicing the surrounding arable estates and the sheep-farms producing woollen cloth; and it is a likely assumption that the property had fallen into the hands of a magnate connected with one side or the other and possessed of the capital required to reap advantage from both. Comparable conversions of good farming property into manufacturing concerns have been noted at Titsey (Surrey) and Darenth (Kent); and both of these establishments are somehow connected with processing in vats, though the exact nature of the operation remains uncertain.

Normally the social picture implied by the planning of large villas is not unkindly. The master's house is flanked with quarters for servants or slaves which were not so sordid as to merit concealment. Nearly all, however, are associated with the practice of infant exposure, repellent to modern civilized folk, to a degree suggestive of a slave or serf population whose increase was harshly limited. This phenomenon is particularly marked at Hambledon (Buckinghamshire), where a small but comfortable farm overlooks an area honeycombed with successive corn-drying ovens in every variety of form, and flanked by simple barn-dwellings. The occupants of the house later reversed its main front, so that it now looked away from the work-yard, as if this had become too much of an eye-sore. It is tempting to recognize here a slave-run establishment engaged in corn-production on a large scale and managed, whether for a rich proprietor or for the Imperial Government, by a prosperous freedman bailiff.

It would be difficult in the present state of knowledge to say where villa-life first began to flourish on a widespread scale, but it may be recognized that in some districts its beginnings came much later than in others. A remarkable case of a late start occurs in the territory of the Parisi in east Yorkshire. Here, at the excavated villas of Langton and Rudston, the agricultural ditches which marke the first phase in the history of the site are strewn with pottery belonging to the late first century A.D. In other words, they mark the new phase of activity in cultivation stimulated by the *pax Romana* and by the demands of taxation or levies in kind made upon an allied community by the Roman government. But the first modest buildings in the Roman manner at both sites do not come into existence until the third century A.D. This again marks the incorporation of the tribe within the newly constituted province of Britannia Inferior and the more insistent development of the natural resources within easy range of its new capital at York. But amenities can hardly be said to exist until the fourth century A.D., by which time the still greater insistence upon the development of local economy and the ever-growing tendency to levy taxation in kind rather than in money, caused a rise in values and prices of agricultural produce and increased the wealth of farming folk. The two villas could then be furnished with mosaic pavements and bath-houses, the latter of real luxury at Rudston. Vigorous local schools of mosaic workers, copying classical models with enthusiastic infidelity, grew up to meet the demand. A house of considerable architectural pretensions at Harpham belongs to this period, though its beginnings were earlier.

A second area where development came late is the north-east corner of the territory of the Brigantes, now County Durham. The villa at Old Durham has a bath-house which belongs to the fourth century A.D., and large threshing-floors of the same date. But the agricultural ditches which, as at Langton or Rudston, mark the earliest dated phase of activity on the site, yielded Antonine pottery. This is interesting because it marks a forward movement of Romanized property-holders in correspondence with the advance of the Roman frontier from the Tyne to the Forth.

There is no indication that the Old Durham site outlasted the severe troubles of A.D. 367–9, when Hadrian's Wall fell and was reorganized in so different a fashion from ever before. Open settlements so far north hardly seem to have been regarded as safe. But the villas of the Yorkshire Wolds lasted, behind their new coastal signal-stations and naval protection, until at least the opening of the fifth century A.D.: and the silver hoards of clipped *siliquae* which formed the money of account in the first decades of that century reach as far north as the Fylde and the Tees. The peasant militia of Hadrian's Wall may have faded out as an effective frontier force, but the inner territory of the Brigantes was still intact and Roman, although the central government of the Empire was no longer in control of it. The same can be said of the coin evidence from Britain further south, and there is a very large number of villas

which have produced coinage as late as the close of the fourth
century A.D. The Somersetshire villas have long been cited as
productive of a striking number of late fourth-century silver coin-
hoards; and this special phenomenon has a special explanation related to the silver-lead mines. But the association of late coinage with
villas is not confined to Somersetshire and is true of many sites
south-east of a line drawn from east Yorkshire to Devon.

This evidence may seem to disregard or contradict the fact that
a considerable number of sites cannot be shown to have survived for
so long. There are numerous villas, widely dispersed, from which
the recorded coins do not go beyond the fifties and sixties of the
fourth century A.D.; and, while negative evidence of this kind may
always lie open to revision, there must be some substantial truth
behind this apparent termination of activity, as Haverfield long ago
perceived. It must in fact have a connexion with the troublous
years which culminated in the invasions of A.D. 367–9, when the
province was beset on all sides by raiders from overseas and much
damage was done. It would, however, be a mistake to exaggerate
the permanent effect of these years of ill fortune. In east Yorkshire,
for example, the damage done at Langton was repaired and an age
of prosperous activity ensued. In Lincolnshire an entirely new villa
at East Denton came into being after A.D. 369, and although it is
of the barn-dwelling type and therefore perhaps a bailiff-run farm
rather than an owner's residence, its creation nevertheless attests
that confidence in the peace and potential prosperity of the countryside still reigned. At Great Casterton a villa in open country was
being actively reconstructed in the eighties. It might be guessed that
what caused the ultimate collapse of the villa system was not the
insecurity of the countryside so much as the collapse of the world
upon whose markets they had depended.

No consideration of villas as a whole is complete without some
reference to those mosaic pavements which have so often indicated
their existence. The most famous and most evocative are those
decorated with figure-scenes from mythology. But when an attempt
is made to estimate the position of the patron in the choice of
pattern, it must be borne in mind that the range of patterns available will have depended upon the pattern-book of the firm which
laid the pavement. Again, the execution of the work might vary
sharply according to the competence of the worker. A striking
example of this is furnished by the Cirencester pavement of the
Four Seasons, of which, out of three surviving, two are fashioned
with sensitive grace while the third is a coarse and clumsy rendering
of the same subject, wholly lacking in deftness of line or subtlety of
colour-blending. Entire compositions, based upon original designs of
obvious breadth or delicacy, could become mere caricatures in the

hands of inexperienced or over-ambitious workmen. Such are the
Wolf and Twins pavement from Alborough, now at Kirkstall
Museum, Leeds, the Venus pavement at Rudston (E. Yorks), and
the Apollo and Marsyas pavement, from Lenthay Green, Sherborne
(Dorset). A comparable failure in detail marred the Horkstow
pavements, though in some reproductions of lost examples the
copyist must bear his share of the blame. The fact that such
standards of workmanship passed muster serves as a check upon
the sensibility of Romano-British patrons. It is clear that many
were about as far from an appreciation of classical taste as a
worker of samplers from a designer of Gobelins tapestry. What is
remarkable is that they should have wanted such things at all,
particularly when a rich and attractive variety of conventional
patterns in abstract design was also available, which native instinct
would have prompted them to choose. The choice then becomes
something purposeful, as deliberate as Chaucer's choice of classical
legend and interpreted in as crude an idiom. It becomes a reflection,
however pale, of classical culture.

There is no doubt, then, that the richer villa-owners appreciated
classical themes, and it is certain that many of their choices were
directly linked with classical habits of mind or behaviour. The Dido
pavement from Low Ham need not mean that its owner was an
enthusiast for Vergil, but its existence does mean that this was the
idiom of his choice; while the style of the design suggests that an
African workshop may have produced the pattern. The Otford
(Kent) wall-plaster, with its Vergilian scenes and quotations, attests
that same feeling in a kindred field. No less striking are the dining-
room pavements from Aldborough and Lullingstone. In the former
house, the undecorated semicircular margin which, in the Roman
manner, held the three couches for diners, looked on to a rich
panel, now vanished, which formed a complementary centre-piece
to the nine standing figures of the Muses with Greek inscription.
In the latter villa a well-drawn and spirited scene of Europa and the
bull forms the centre-piece and is embellished by a verse couplet
which has the amateurish ring of an impromptu production of
the dining-table. These pavements and their planning reflect good
cheer and good company in the Roman style: what was mannered
in the first century A.D. had become manners in the fourth.

R. G. COLLINGWOOD

Some Means
of Communication

Roman Roads

"TRANSPORTATION is civilisation"; and no one ever knew this better than the Romans. Of all the remains that they have left behind them, their roads are the most familiar and the most impressive. But Roman roads are not so uniform in character as we are apt to think. It is a mistake to suppose that a Roman road always has the same features and the same structure. Some were elaborately metalled highways laid out in straight lines; others were more simply made and less rigidly laid out; others, again, were mere tracks with little or no metal and little or no definite design. Of the last class, which were probably the most numerous, it is naturally difficult to quote instances; but the disposition of farms and villages is clear enough proof of their existence. It is only the most elaborate that can now be traced with any certainty.

Signal Stations

The ancients were well acquainted with the art of transmitting news by means of visible signals. As early as 458 B.C. Aeschylus, in the *Agamemnon*, could represent the news of the fall of Troy as having come to Greece by way of a chain of beacons; and, in Rome, Polybius (x, 44 *seqq.*) describes methods of sending elaborate messages by light-signals as actually used in the second century B.C. The late military writer Vegetius (iii, 5) says that fire, smoke, and semaphore codes were in use in his time.

Archaeological evidence confirms the general sense of these statements. Early in the second century we find signal-stations

From *Roman Britain*. London: Methuen & Co. Ltd.; 1930, pp. 1, 56, 61-3. By permission of Methuen & Co. Ltd.

depicted on Trajan's Column. They are wooden towers two storeys high, surrounded by palisades; the upper storey has a balcony, and from its window projects a stick like a barber's pole, which must be a torch for sending fire-signals. Late in the same century we see them again on the Column of Marcus. They have undergone a certain development. They are now, sometimes at least, built of stone and provided with tiled, instead of thatched roofs; the palisade round them has become stouter, and the opening in it is closed with a gate.

Lighthouses

Lighthouses, consisting of towers on whose summit a fire could be lit, were in use among the ancients from the Hellenistic period onwards; the famous Pharos of Alexandria was built in the third century B.C. They served not to mark headlands and dangerous rocks, but to show the entrance to a harbour.

There may have been many Roman light-houses in Britain; but we have certain knowledge only of two, one on each side of the harbour at Dover. That on the east side, on Castle Hill, is still standing to a height of 62 feet, of which only 43 feet are Roman work, the rest, together with most of the external face, being medieval. It is octagonal in plan, each side 15 feet long at the base; internally it is 13 feet 10 inches square. The sides rose vertically and were stepped back at each storey, giving the tower a profile like that of an open telescope. Judging by the known dimensions, the original height must have been about 80 feet; for at that height the walls, 12 feet thick at the bottom, would have been diminished by the successive offsets to between 3 and 4 feet. The core of the walls is concrete, the faces ashlar, and at every seven courses there is a bonding-course of tile. The doorway, and the recesses and windows which occur at each storey, are mostly arched with blocks of tufa alternating with pairs of tiles. Each storey had a wooden floor, the first floor being 17½ feet above ground, the others at intervals of 7½ to 8 feet. In the main, this tower must have resembled the Roman light-house at Boulogne, which like it was octagonal in plan and telescopic in profile, but was 200 feet high.

GEORGE BOON

Romans at the Baths

ALL towns of any size boasted suites of public baths, and those of
Calleva [In Hampshire, now Silchester. It was a provincial town of
some importance.] lie in Insula XXXIII, south-east of the Forum, on
the south side of a declivity which exists in that part of the town.
The building was excavated in 1903–4. Reasons have been given
above for believing it to be the earliest large structure of the town,
and the only one of importance constructed so near the "Belgic"
enceinte, which probably runs hard by its eastern side and conditions
its somewhat curious alignment. The need for copious water supplies
and easy drainage obviously governed the choice of site.

Bath-buildings everywhere show signs of constant alteration and
improvement, and so provide their own evidence of the value set
upon cleanliness and the social amenities which they offered. The
Baths of Calleva are no exception. The original plan was overlaid
by numerous additions which W. H. St. J. Hope was able to ration-
alize into five groups, making six structural periods in all. From the
first the accommodation (later extended) comprised (*a*) an entrance portico; (*b*) an exercise-yard or *palaestra;* (*c*) an undressing-
room, as the Romans called it, or *apodyterium;* (*d*) a cold-bath
room, *frigidarium;* (*e*) a warm room with sweating-chamber
annexed, *tepidarium* and *sudatorium;* (*f*) a hot-bath room, *calidarium.* The building was set north and south, with these chambers
arranged in an orderly row leading one into the other, and in the
first period covered about 7,500 square feet; the plan is a very
common one, especially on military sites. The heating was by the
hypocaust system, in which a cavity is constructed below the floor
and connected to a furnace built in an outside wall at foundation-
level. The heat and hot gases generated here circulated under the
floor, warmed it, and passed up small chimney-flues embedded in
the walls. The flues were made of box-shaped tiles cramped to the
walls and covered by a plaster rendering. How the flues terminated

From *Roman Silchester*. London: Max Parrish & Co. Ltd.; 1957, pp. 101-6. By permission of Max Parrish & Co. Ltd.

is uncertain, but it seems possible that they were led at right-angles through the walls to debouch under the broad eaves of the roof.

The elaborate nature of the accommodation makes it clear that the procedure of bathing was on the Turkish plan and did not resemble the humble domestic routine of today. The so-called Turkish bath is in fact an adaptation of such baths as those under discussion, visible in cities of the Eastern Roman Empire with which the Turks were in contact. Since Turkish baths are no longer very popular in this country, and the public swimming-baths of modern towns have neither gymnasia nor heated rooms, a brief description of the ordinary method of bathing may be useful. The *palaestra* was available for preliminary exercises, such as ball games, of which the Romans were very fond, and for social intercourse generally. After their fill of this, the bathers proceeded to the *apodyterium,* undressed, and walked straight through to the first heated room, the *tepidarium.* The raised temperature promoted the perspiration induced by exercise, and the process was completed in the adjoining, very hot *sudatorium.* There, or in the *calidarium* the sweat, dead skin and dirt were scraped off with a strigil. Several of these have been found at Calleva, notably an iron specimen placed conveniently for the stoker's use by the furnace of a domestic hypocaust. After a dip in the hot bath, the bathers returned to the *frigidarium,* and freshened up by a turn in the cold bath or by a shower, either of which served to close the pores of the skin. An apartment added to the *apodyterium* has been identified as an *unctorium* for massage with olive oil, as a final touch. Many pieces of small spherical glass oil-bottles, with little handles from which they might be suspended by a cord, have been found at Silchester. Soap had probably not been invented. Even shaving, when popular in the first and fourth centuries, was done with the aid of water only. Tedious and uncomfortable the process must have been—especially with razors like those found on our site—as we can infer from references to it in writers such as Martial. A clean shave must have been a rarity without the brutal help of tweezers.

The most common toilet articles of all betoken a widespread attention to personal hygiene. These are bronze nail-cleaners, tweezers and ear-picks, found singly and in sets. Double-sided bone and wooden combs and fragments of white-metal mirrors have also been found, as well as numerous surgical or quasi-surgical instruments and accessories, such as would have been used by barber-surgeons congregating at the baths for custom. They include spatula-probes, scalpels, forceps, a retractor for pulling back the edge of a wound for inspection, and an artery forceps with serrated jaws and a sliding ring to hold them tightly in place. Among the accessories may be mentioned a little bronze pharmaceutical mortar and balances, Purbeck, green porphyry and greenstone palettes with bevelled edges, and a compartment-lid from a medicine-chest.

Since the baths were supported by local taxation, admission was either free or for an insignificant sum. The travellers who stayed at the Mansio in Insula VIII, however, were provided with their own accommodation. Public baths were in general use amongst town-dwellers, rich and poor alike, and came perhaps to be the most democratic institution of the Empire. At Calleva, few houses had bath-suites, for everyone expected to use the public accommodation, and thought it no disgrace to do so. No more illuminating sidelight could be thrown upon the difference between public life then and now. How the habit of bathing became ingrained is exemplified by the dozens of country villas far from any town. Nearly all had their little suites modelled upon those of the great cantonal edifices, with all the necessary accommodation in miniature, decorated with mosaics and frescoes.

IAN RICHMOND

Drought Reveals a Temple

MITHRAIC sanctuaries are not uncommon either in the great commercial centres or in the military centres of the later Roman Empire, their heyday being the third century A.D., though the religion first came westwards in the later first century B.C. In Britain three temples are known upon Hadrian's Wall, and there is the evidence of inscriptions for at least three more. But in no case was the discovery more dramatic or more rewarding than at Carrawburgh, the sixth fort from the east along the line of the Wall. It happened on a sunny evening in the summer of 1949, memorable for its long drought, that Mr. Noel Shaw of Haydon Bridge was walking across

From *Recent Archaeological Excavations in England*, ed. by Rupert Bruce-Mitford. London: Routledge & Kegan Paul; 1956, pp. 69-70. By permission of Penguin Books Ltd.

the site. In a normal year he would have seen an expanse of green pasture, light-hued on the hill-top occupied by the fort, dark and sombre in the marshy valley which flanks the fort to west. In 1949 the scene was different. The long drought had parched to a bright yellow or rich brown the grass which covered masonry or streets, and the buried foundations of the fort and surrounding settlement stood out as if a poker-worker had traced their outlines. In the valley bottom, where the Well of Coventina still bubbles up in its cistern of Roman masonry, the marsh which the ancient waters have fed and formed was unusually dry, and the border had shrunk. On its eastern fringe a long and narrow building, in most summers hardly visible in quaking bog, lay high and dry above the shrunken surface, and at one end of it a carved stone was visible. Closer inspection assured Mr. Shaw that it was the top of a Roman altar, apparently standing in its original position.

When permission to examine the stone had been obtained from the owner of the site, Mrs. W. J. Benson, it became clear that Mr. Shaw's powers of observation had been rewarded threefold. Three altars stood side by side at the end of the building, all inscribed to Mithras.

LEONARD WOOLLEY

Young Woolley
Discovers a Lion

LEONARD WOOLLEY found the Corbridge Lion in 1907, during one of his earliest excavations (p. 89, I). It was in the ruins of Roman *Corstopitum,* in Northumberland. The beast is bent over its prey, and the "orange" is its tongue. This sculpture is discussed by Professor Haverfield on p. 430, II.

From *Spadework*. London: Lutterworth Press; 1953, p. 16. By permission of Lutterworth Press.

THE most dramatic discovery was that of the Corbridge Lion. We had found a stone cistern attached to a large Roman building and in the course of the morning had cleared about half of the earth filling. It happened to be a Saturday and after my lunch I went to the bank to draw money for the men's wages, and as I was kept waiting for some while, the interval was over and work had started again before I got back to the site. As I came near I saw all the men crowded closely together by the side of the cistern, and wondered what had happened; only when I was close up did they separate this way and that, and between the two groups of them I saw the stone lion grinning over the fallen stag. They had lifted it out of the cistern (which of course was wrong of them) and had deliberately staged a surprise for me, and a fine surprise it was, but what struck me at once was that the men were even more excited than I was. The actual finder, who was not Tyneside but a "foreigner," an East Anglian curiously unlike his fellow miners, a big fellow with a round fair face and a fair round belly, was shaking as if with an ague and quite incoherent; when he recovered enough to speak at all in answer to my question "Did *you* find that?" he could only stammer "Yes, sir, and you'll never believe me, but it's God's own truth, when I first saw that there lion he had a blooming orange in 'is mouth!"

4. *The Anglo-Saxons*

BRYAN FAUSSETT

A Famous Brooch Discovered

GREAT numbers of Anglo-Saxon cemeteries, both pagan and Christian, have been excavated in England. Some of the richest were found in Kent, within the area settled by the Jutes. Bryan Faussett was an east Kent parson who explored many graves between 1757 and 1773. The magnificent circular gold brooch inlaid with garnets was the finest single object he unearthed.

THIS tumulus exceeded the middle size. The grave far exceeded any which I have before opened, both in depth, length, and width; it being full six feet deep, and ten feet long, and eight feet broad. The coffin, which seemed to have been much burnt, and very thick, appeared to have been equal to the dimensions of the grave; and had been strongly bound and secured at its corners with large clasps and riveted pieces of iron. The bones were much decayed; the skeleton did not appear to have borne any proportion to the dimensions either of the grave or coffin. The skull was remarkably small, and seemed to have had what we call a very low or short forehead. Near the neck, or rather more towards the right shoulder, was a most surprisingly beautiful and large fibula subnectens: it is entirely of gold; and is most elegantly and richly set with garnets and some pale blue stones, the name of which I am at present a stranger to; it is three and a half inches in diameter, a quarter of an inch in thickness, and weighs 6 oz. 5 dwt. [pennyweight] 18 gr. The acus on the under side is quite entire, and is also beautifully ornamented

Written in 1757-73. From *Inventorium Sepulchrale*, 1856, pp. 77-9.

with garnets. I flatter myself it is altogether one of the most curious and, for its size, costly pieces of antiquity ever discovered in England; with it was found a golden amulet, or ornament for the neck: it is one-eighth of an inch in diameter, and weighs 2 dwt. 7 gr. Here were also two very neat silver fibulas, of an ingenious contrivance, and different from any I have yet seen described. Montfaucon has some a little like them. These were found near the bone of the left thigh; here was also just such an iron instrument as that described before. It plainly appeared to have been riveted to some wood; it was found at the feet, and certainly belonged to a box; but its particular use I cannot guess at. Along with it were found two small hinges: an iron chain like those mentioned before; it consisted of about twenty links, each about two inches long, and about the size of a crow quill; each link was twisted a little way at each end, for forming the eyes. Here was a wrought urn of coarse red earth; two brass kettles, or pans; one of them is in shape pretty much like that described, but is much larger than that, being thirteen inches wide, and four and a half inches deep; it has two handles also on the outside, and appears to have been gilded in the inside. The other was much smaller, and was found in the great one. This, which has three little handles, appears also to have been gilded on the inside, and has three flat coin-like pieces of copper soldered on its outside. So that, it is plain, it was not intended for any use over a fire, which would immediately have melted them off; under the large pan was a *small brass trivet,* about four inches diameter. All these things, I think, were in the coffin; and beyond the coffin, and at the foot of it, were the bones of a child; they were very fresh, white, and sound; and lay altogether in a heap. These, doubtless, had been buried previous to the interment of the mother, (for so I think I may venture to call the person here deposited), and were at that time taken up and placed at her feet in the manner we found them. What should make them so much sounder than those of the mother, I do not pretend to give any guess. Here was also a beautiful green glass urn, finely coated both inside and outside with armatura or electrum. Certainly the grave of a woman.

THOMAS GODFREY FAUSSETT

And a Comment
on the Discovery

THOMAS GODFREY FAUSSETT was the great-grandson of the
Reverend Bryan Faussett.

HIS son, Henry Godfrey Faussett, was born at the vicarage of Ab-
berbury in 1749, a short time only before the return of his family
into Kent. Companion from his childhood in all his father's
archaeological rambles and researches, he may be said to have been
born and bred an antiquary; and it was his boast through life that
he had himself discovered, as he superintended the opening of one
of his father's barrows on Kingston Down, that famous fibula, which
was the gem of his collection, as it still is, I believe, of all Anglo-
Saxon tumular antiquities. The story of its discovery, by the way,
will give some idea of the astonishment and prejudice which antiquaries of that day had to encounter. On finding it, he carried it with
great glee to his father, who was in his carriage hard by, suffering
under an attack of his old enemy [gout]; his father drove off with
it; and next day a report was spread that the carriage had been so
full of gold that the wheels would scarcely turn; and the lord of the
manor prohibited all further excavations on these downs.

Ibid., pp. 205-6.

C. W. PHILLIPS

A Royal Treasure:
the Sutton Hoo Ship-burial

THE Sutton Hoo treasure is easily the richest Anglo-Saxon find ever made. It was also one of the most unexpected, for burials from mounds adjacent to this one had been humbly furnished. Nor were the rulers of East Anglia (Sutton Hoo is near Woodbridge in Suffolk) previously known to have had such splendid possessions. No bones were found in the ship, so it can be assumed that it was the cenotaph of some king whose body was either lost or buried elsewhere. The monument certainly dates from near the middle of the seventh century A.D., when East Anglia was passing from paganism to Christianity. Several different candidates have been advanced as the king commemorated. The latest is Ecgric, who died in the early 640's.

WHEN I crossed the short stretch of heath from Mrs. Pretty's house and saw the large dump of sand that had already been moved out of the excavation I had no clear idea of what I was going to see in a few moments. When it came the sight was a shock. There, slightly adumbrated by the removal of the greater part of the middle of the overlying mound, was more than half of a boat which seemed unlikely to be less than 100 feet long overall. In the event its length proved to be 89 feet, but the first impact was staggering. . . .

Put simply, the stern end of the chamber, to the west, was the most important area with symbols and accoutrements of royalty placed close together in a group. The chief objects were: an iron

From *Recent Archaeological Excavations in England*. London: Routledge & Kegan Paul Ltd.; 1956, pp. 150-8, 160-2. Ed. by Rupert Bruce-Mitford. Reprinted by permission of Routledge & Kegan Paul Ltd.

standard and ceremonial whetstone; a splendid helmet, sword and shield, with the jewelled fittings of the sword belt; jewelled epaulettes for a cuirass; a set of seven assorted spears and a dirk; an exotic bronze Coptic bowl from Egypt containing the finest example of a "hanging bowl" yet known, in which in turn were the remains of a harp; a matched set of ten silver bowls imported from the Byzantine Empire and two silver spoons, one with the name of Saul and the other with the name of Paul on it in Greek letters. Setting off from this group along the keel line of the boat towards the bow was first a group of decayed and crushed drinking horns with silver mounts, and then a great silver dish which had been placed on the top of a pile of miscellaneous objects containing, among many other things, decayed clothing, shoes, a lesser silver dish, and a coat of mail. Finally, across the bow end of the chamber were disposed in line a great iron-hooped wooden tub and three bronze cauldrons placed in descending order of size. Near these was some complex ornamental iron tackle which is regarded as being used to hang these vessels over a fire. If any wooden furniture had been placed to fill up the spaces along each side of the chamber, it had entirely disappeared and could have had no metal elements in its construction. No sign of a bedstead was present, and the remains of sacrificed animals were entirely wanting, either as bones or teeth or, by implication, through harness or other gear. . . .

A number of remarkable moments stand out in the memory. The first was on July 22nd, when the main treasure of jewellery was found. This requires no further comment, except that it was here that a find of the greatest scientific importance vital to the whole excavation was made in the shape of 37 gold coins in the purse, all of them struck in the kingdom of the Merovingian Franks in France. There has been argument about the precise dating of these, but one thing appears to be certain. On the evidence provided by their presence in the grave it cannot be older than A.D. 650. Another climax was on July 26th, when the big silver dish was lifted. It was clear that this was partly covering at least one other silver vessel, and we could not guess what else might be found. As a precaution a considerable preparation was made of bowls of water, wet moss, cotton wool, and boxes, etc., to deal with any fragile objects which might appear. Arrangements were also made to photograph every phase of the proceedings, and the assorted mass of decayed cloth, pillow-down, shoes, gourd cups, etc., which was revealed justified our care. Another dramatic moment was when the great whetstone began to emerge from the sand. It was projecting upwards, and the sinister-looking bearded human heads carved on the emergent end gave it a daunting look. The first guess was that it was a sceptre. When removed from the ground it proved to be in form a whetstone, but it is interesting to note that the best opinion now considers that it was indeed a symbol of power. . . .

Since the great find at Sutton Hoo had all the form and trappings of a royal grave, it was with some surprise that the excavators early became aware that it had never contained a body. The absence of obvious human remains did not of itself provoke comment, because the conditions of this grave set deep in damp sand were most unfavourable to the survival of any organic remains. But no cremated bones were found, and all the other evidence on the way of the disposition and character of the finds pointed in the same direction. There was really no room for the proper laying out of a body at the more honourable end of the grave, nor were there any of those smaller, more personal objects found which would have been on a clothed body. Chemical tests later carried out on the grave goods have gone far to prove that no body was ever placed in any attitude in this part of the grave. Thus the most remarkable burial assemblage in Britain has proved to have been almost certainly a cenotaph, and this fact has posed a nice problem for those whose task it is to interpret the results of the excavation. Theories which have been advanced to account for it include the suggestion that the man commemorated was lost at sea, that his body was lost beyond recovery on a stricken field, or that he was in fact a Christian and was buried elsewhere in consecrated ground, though family custom and public policy still required this expensive and essentially pagan monument to his memory. Here we have no time to probe further into the enigma of these pagan rites in an East Anglia which, by A.D. 650, was substantially Christian. Some of the objects found have certainly had a Christian origin, like the silver spoons, and others are capable of a Christian interpretation, but the whole taken together is still the provision for the passage to Valhalla.

T. D. KENDRICK

The End of
Anglo-Saxon Art?

IN our survey we have been mainly concerned with Saxon art at the
time of its greatest strength and of its most daring imaginings, and
it is sufficient to have discovered that its spirit survived to endow
with its peculiar graces some of the manuscripts and monuments
of a later age. We find, which is the important thing, that the
Conquest itself and the settlement here of influential foreign patrons
of art did not operate as an instant death-blow to the brilliantly
idiomatic native taste; but we also discover that after the Conquest,
as is natural enough, the Saxon style is only infrequently expressed
in its original manner, and the lesson of this and the previous
chapter is that on the whole Saxon art as a period-style must be held
to have dissolved itself somewhat rapidly in the newly created
Anglo-Norman Romanesque styles. Yet the tradition of Saxon drawing remained, and, as a last imponderable, we must reckon with the
apparently unimportant fact that we are not dealing only with an
unconscious transmission of the Saxon temper and feeling, some
dim inherited aptitude for sensitive drawing, but with a real and
discernible legacy. After all, in their book-illuminations the Saxons
gave us one of the noblest collections of works of art that England
has ever produced, and this did not vanish from the land. On the
contrary, it survived in part throughout the Middle Ages and could
be seen in its original form in full and unfaded glory in many of
the large monastic libraries. This great corpus of remarkable paintings and drawings must assuredly have been an ever-present
inspiration to the artists who in the later centuries worked in the
same monasteries. Times change and fashions alter, and there was
no reason for copying the old pictures in the books that the Church
still treasured; but this national example cannot have been entirely

From *Late Saxon and Viking Art*. London: Methuen & Co. Ltd; 1949, pp. 147-8. By
permission of Methuen & Co. Ltd.

negligible. The significance of Saxon art, then, lies not only in its own great achievement, but also in the possibility that it remained long after its own day was over as a force sufficient to quicken the imagination of the Englishmen who were the heirs of the Saxons, a force perhaps potent enough even to guide the later artist's hand.

5. Europe

HERODOTUS

The Burial of Scythian Kings

THE Scythians formed the main clan of an enormously widespread group of nomads, whose territories may at times have stretched as far east as the Yenisei. Although there was no political unity among them, these nomadic tribes shared much in common in their way of life and in their art. The Scyths proper occupied the more westerly part of the range. By the seventh century B.C. they were established in southern Russia, the Kuban and the Crimea, and in time they pushed further into eastern Europe—into Roumania, Bulgaria, Hungary and Prussia. At various points, and particulaly along the Black Sea, they came into contact with the Greek colonists. Nomadic chiefs employed Greek craftsmen to work for them, and some Scythic art shows a blending of Hellenic with Persian and other oriental elements.

The Scyths were so powerful in the fifth century B.C. that Herodotus devoted an entire Book to them. To collect material he went to Olbia, a Greek commercial outpost on the Black Sea by the mouth of the Bug. Some of the information he recorded was fanciful, but much has been proved correct. In particular his description of the burial of Scythic kings has been supported even in detail by graves excavated in south Russia and elsewhere. (p. 457, II)

THE burial-place of the Scythian kings is in the country of the Gerrhi, near the spot where the Borysthenes first becomes navigable.

From *The Histories*, Book IV. 5th century B.C. London: Martin Secker & Warburg Ltd; 1954, pp. 264-5. By permission of David Higham Associates, Ltd.

When a king dies, they dig a great square pit, and, when it is ready, they take up the corpse, which has been previously prepared in the following way: the belly is slit open, cleaned out, and filled with various aromatic substances, crushed galingale, parsley-seed, and anise; it is then sewn up again and the whole body coated over with wax. In this condition it is carried in a wagon to a neighbouring tribe within the Scythian dominions, and then on to another, taking the various tribes in turn; and in the course of its progress, the people who successively receive it, follow the custom of the Royal Scythians and cut a piece from their ears, shave their hair, make circular incisions on their arms, gash their foreheads and noses, and thrust arrows through their left hands. On each stage of the journey those who have already been visited join the procession, until at last the funeral cortège, after passing through every part of the Scythian dominions, finds itself at the place of burial amongst the Gerrhi, the most northerly and remote of Scythian tribes. Here the corpse is laid in the tomb on a mattress, with spears fixed in the ground on either side to support a roof of withies laid on wooden poles, while in other parts of the great square pit various members of the king's household are buried beside him: one of his concubines, his butler, his cook, his groom, his steward, and his chamberlain—all of them strangled. Horses are buried too, and gold cups (the Scythians do not use silver or bronze), and a selection of his other treasures. This ceremony over, everybody with great enthusiasm sets about raising a mound of earth, each competing with his neighbour to make it as big as possible. At the end of a year another ceremony takes place: they take fifty of the best of the king's remaining servants, strangle and gut them, stuff the bodies with chaff, and sew them up again—these servants are native Scythians, for the king has no bought slaves, but chooses people to serve him from amongst his subjects. Fifty of the finest horses are then subjected to the same treatment. The next step is to cut a number of wheels in half and to fix them in pairs, rim-downwards, to stakes driven into the ground, two stakes to each half-wheel; then stout poles are driven lengthwise through the horses from tail to neck, and by means of these the horses are mounted on the wheels, in such a way that the front pairs support the shoulders and the rear pairs the belly between the thigs. All four legs are left dangling clear of the ground. Each horse is bitted and bridled, the bridle being led forward and pegged down. The bodies of the men are dealt with in a similar way; straight poles are driven up through the neck, parallel with the spine, and the lower protruding ends fitted into sockets in the stakes which run through the horses; thus each horse is provided with one of the young servants to ride him.

When horses and riders are all in place around the tomb, they are left there, and the mourners go away.

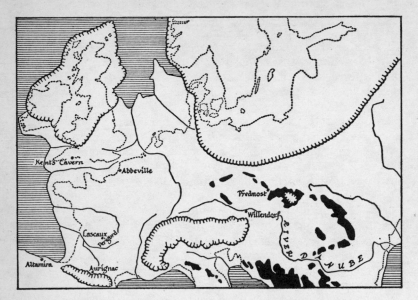

NORTHERN EUROPE AT THE HEIGHT OF THE LAST ICE AGE

TAMARA TALBOT RICE

A Royal Scythian
Tomb Excavated

CHERTOMLYK is near Nikopol in the southern Ukraine. The burial
dates from the fourth century B.C.

THE SCYTHIANS, as we learn from their own proud and defiant
retort to the taunts of Darius, valued their burial grounds above all
their possessions, venerating them with a passion that was perhaps
increased by their lack of temples and holy sites. To them the
burial ceremony was an intensely mystical and august ritual, but
it was also a singularly costly affair, not only in labour, material
and worldly goods, but also in life. The loss in horses was especially
high. Recent discoveries show that orthopaedically faulty animals
were sometimes killed off in Hungary and a proportion of those
buried in Altaian graves suffered from similar defects, but many of
the horses found at Pazirik were in excellent condition at the time
of their death. Information on this point is lacking with regard to
the Kuban and south Russian burials, but the numbers of horses
killed at important funerals in the Kuban was tremendous. There
the figures varied from a score to several hundred, the highest to be
recorded being at Ulski, where some four hundred had been buried.
    The most important and impressive of the Scythian burials are
the royal tombs of southern Russia, and of them all Chertomlyk is
perhaps the richest, both in the variety and artistic quality of
the objects found in it and also in the well-nigh fabulous intrinsic
value of the gold-work. Like so many other burials, Chertomlyk

From *The Scythians*, Vol. II in the series *Ancient Peoples and Places*, ed. by Dr.
Glyn Daniel. London: Thames and Hudson Ltd; 1957, pp. 92-5. By permission of
Thames and Hudson Ltd.

had attracted the attention of thieves, but in this instance a fall of earth in the entrance shaft they had dug trapped and killed at any rate one of the gang, leaving the objects he had amassed piled up in a corner of the tomb. Since this robber was unlikely to have dug the trench single-handed, it is probable that his companions escaped with some of the booty. Nevertheless, the archaeologists

FELT AND LEATHER HORSE'S HEAD-DRESS FROM PAZIRIK

who opened the tomb some two thousand years later still found in it much that was of considerable monetary value and a great deal more that was of absorbing interest.

The barrow was unusually elaborate in plan, for it contained a central burial chamber with four minor ones radiating from it. The first chamber to be entered by the excavators contained a small Scythian cauldron, a magnificent gorytus [bow-case] complete with arrows, and five knives with bone handles and iron blades. In the main chamber they found fragments of a carpet, but these were too decayed to give any idea of its pattern. Hooks for clothes to hang on were still in place on the walls and ceilings, but the garments which had once hung there had perished, and only the stamped golden plaques with which they had been trimmed lay in heaps where they had fallen to the ground. Placed in niches set at floor level in the walls were further personal belongings and some gold vases. In the north-eastern chamber stood six amphorae still holding the dregs of the wine and oil that had once filled them and also a bronze mirror mounted on an ivory handle.

DETAIL ON THE FRIEZE ON THE CHERTOMLYK KUMIS JUG

The dead man lay on his back, facing east. The setting in which he took leave of this world was of extraordinary opulence. A fine bronze torque encircled his neck, a gold ear-ring had been placed in one ear and there were gold rings on all his fingers. According to custom, an ivory-handled knife lay within easy reach of his left hand, together with a gorytus containing sixty-seven bronze arrow-heads and an ivory-handled riding whip laced with gold. Fragments of an ivory casket, a silver spoon, numerous gold plaques from his clothes, pendants, gold tubes, beads and buttons were also found here. In the third small chamber lay two bodies, each adorned with a gold torque, gold bracelets and rings, and a belt decorated with gold plaques, together with the gold plaques which had trimmed the clothing strewn about their bare bones. Beside them stood a bronze cup, a silver ewer, a gorytus containing arrows, and a whip. In the fourth chamber were fragments of a bronze bier that had once been decorated with an elaborate design carried out in dark and light blue, green and yellow paint. A woman's body lay on it, still wreathed in gold bracelets, finger-rings and ear-rings. Twenty-nine stamped gold plaques, twenty gold roundels and seven gold buttons lay intermingled with her bones. On her head were the remnants of a purple veil with the fifty-seven gold plaques which had formed its trimming still in place. Within her reach was a bronze mirror set in blue paste. Nearby lay a man's body, probably an attendant's, with a bronze bracelet on his arm, his knife and arrow-heads within grasp of his left hand. Between the bodies stood an elaborately ornamented silver dish, and it was there that the famous Chertomlyk vessel itself was found. A large bronze cauldron, measuring three feet in height, with six splendidly modelled goats ranged round its rim to serve as handles, was also found in the tomb, as well as a smaller bronze cauldron, numerous minor objects in gold, a great ornamented sheet of gold which had been ripped off the king's gorytus, five splendid swords, and numerous fragments of delicate Greek pottery. Ten horses lay fully caparisoned outside the burial chamber, but in the same compound. The trappings of five were embellished with gold decorations, those of the rest with silver.

THE GREAT GODDESS FLANKED BY ATTENDANT BEASTS.
DETAIL FROM THE GILT AND ENGRAVED SILVER
MIRROR FROM KELERMES IN THE KUBAN. VII-VI B.C.

HERODOTUS

Tin, Amber
and One-Eyed Men

So much for the countries at the furthest limits of Asia and Libya. About the far west of Europe I have no definite information, for I cannot accept the story of a river called by non-Greek peoples the Eridanus, which flows into the northern sea, where amber is supposed to come from; nor do I know anything of the existence of islands called the Tin Islands, whence we get our tin. In the first place, the name Eridanus is obviously not foreign but Greek, and was invented by some poet or other; and, secondly, in spite of my efforts to do so, I have never found anyone who could give me first-hand information of the existence of a sea beyond Europe to the north and west. Yet it cannot be disputed that tin and amber do come to us from what one might call the ends of the earth. It is clear that it is the northern parts of Europe which are richest in gold, but how it is procured is another mystery. The story goes that the one-eyed Arimaspians steal it from the griffins who guard it; personally, however, I hesitate to believe in one-eyed men who in other respects are like the rest of us. In any case it does seem to be true that the countries which lie on the circumference of the inhabited world produce the things which we believe to be most rare and beautiful.

J. M. DE NAVARRO

Celtic Art and Celtic Thirst

THE art developed by the Celtic peoples from the fifth century B.C. onwards is known as La Tène. In its early stages it made use of many classical Greek motifs—such as the palmette—though the brilliant barbarian artists soon changed them almost beyond recognition. The western Celts were in touch with the Greeks principally through the colony of Massilia and through Italy, where the Etruscans acted as middlemen.

CLASSICAL writers speak of the Celtic peoples' great love of wine, and the evidence of archaeology not only bears out what they have to say on this point, but shows that there is a long history behind these references. Most of the imported vessels, whether pottery or bronze, were ultimately connected with the carrying, storing, mixing and drinking of wine. If, as in the case of the La Motte St. Valentin *stamnos,* they were used for cinerary urns, it does not mean that they were imported for that purpose, nor does it follow that they were all imported solely as *objets d'art.* In the "Chieftains' Graves," we sometimes find a regular table service of bronze vessels; while the fragments of undecorated *amphorae* from other than sepulchral sites prove that the vessels can hardly have been imported as anything else than receptacles for the produce of the South. But is this true for such works of art as some of the bronze vessels or the decorated Greek pottery? In the "Chieftains' Grave" at Weisskirchen (Rheinprovinz) the bronze *stamnos* was found to contain a resinous substance. This, on chemical analysis, proved to be white pitch. We know from classical sources that the ancients sometimes pitched their wines. Pliny (*Hist. nat.* XIV, 24) tells us that the Greeks, to give briskness to their wines when too flat, mixed them with potters'

From "Massilia and Early Celtic Culture" in *Antiquity*, Vol. II. 1928, pp.434-5. By permission of Dr. Glyn Daniel and *Antiquity*, where it first appeared.

earth, pounded marble, salt or sea-water, the Italians with *brown* pitch, and that it was "the universal practice both there (in Italy) and in the neighbouring provinces to season their wine with resin." But later in the same work (XIV, 25), still speaking of wine, he tells us that the best quality of pitch is that from Mount Ida, though Vergil (*Georgic* II, 498) speaks of Narycian pitch. The latter reference is of interest. Narycia is the poetical name for the Greek colony Locri in southern Italy, and it has lately been suggested that many of the archaic Greek bronze vessels may have been made at Locri rather than, as hitherto supposed, at Tarentum. Locri was in Bruttium, a region according to Pliny (*l.c.*, XIV, 25) that produced the most highly esteemed pitch in Italy in preparing vessels for the storing of wine.

The contents of the Weisskirchen *stamnos* not only shows that this practice dates back to the fifth and possibly even into the sixth century, but that those vessels were used by the Celts for wine, and seem, originally, to have owed their introduction into the Celtic area to the wine trade, which, as the *amphorae* from the Camp de Château and other sites show, probably started in phase D of the Hallstatt Period. If this conjecture is correct, the La Tène art may largely have owed its existence to Celtic thirst.

JULIUS CAESAR

Julius Caesar on Gallic Forts

THIS type of stone and timber rampart observed by Caesar in Gaul was also employed by some British Celts, particularly in Scotland.

BUT this is usually the form of all the Gallic walls. Straight beams, connected lengthwise and two feet distant from each other at equal

From *De Bello Gallico and Other Commentaries*, translated by W. A. Macdevitt. 1st century B.C.

intervals, are placed together on the ground; these are mortised on
the inside, and covered with plenty of earth. But the intervals
which we have mentioned, are closed up in front by large stones.
These being thus laid and cemented together, another row is added
above, in such a manner that the same interval may be observed,
and that the beams may not touch one another, but equal spaces
intervening, each row of beams is kept firmly in its place by a row
of stones. In this manner the whole wall is consolidated, until the
regular height of the wall be completed. This work, with respect
to appearance and variety, is not unsightly, owing to the alternate
rows of beams and stones, which preserve their order in right lines;
and, besides, it possesses great advantages as regards utility and
the defence of cities; for the stone protects it from fire, and the
wood from the battering ram, since it [the wood] being mortised
in the inside with rows of beams, generally forty feet each in length,
can neither be broken through nor torn asunder.

TACITUS

Tacitus on the Germans

WHEN not engaged in warfare, they spend some little time in hunting, but more in idling, abandoned to sleep and gluttony. All the
heroes and grim warriors dawdle their time away, while the care
of house, hearth and fields is left to the women, old men and
weaklings of the family. The warriors themselves lose their edge.
They are so strangely inconsistent. They love indolence, but they
hate peace. It is usual for states to make voluntary and individual
contributions of cattle or agricultural produce to the chiefs. These
are accepted as a token of honour, but serve also to relieve essential

From Tacitus: *On Britain and Germany*. Harmondsworth: Penguin Books Ltd.;
1960, pp. 113-15, 122-3, 133-4, 137-9. Translated by H. Mattingly. Reprinted by
permission of Penguin Books Ltd.

needs. The chiefs take peculiar pleasure in gifts from neighbouring states, such as are sent not only by individuals, but by the community as well—choice horses, splendid arms, metal disks and collars; the practice of accepting money payments they have now learnt—from us.

It is a well-known fact that the peoples of Germany never live in cities, and will not even have their houses set close together. They live apart, dotted here and there, where spring, plain or grove has taken their fancy. Their villages are not laid out in Roman style, with buildings adjacent or interlocked. Every man leaves an open space round his house, perhaps as a precaution against the risk of fire, perhaps because they are such inexpert builders. They do not even make any use of little stone blocks or tiles; what serves their every purpose is ugly timber, both unimpressive and unattractive. They smear over some parts of their houses with an earth that is so pure and brilliant that it looks like painting or coloured mosaics. They have also the habit of hollowing out caves underground and heaping masses of refuse on the top. In these they can escape the winter's cold and store their produce. In such shelters they take the edge off the bitter frosts; and, should an invader come, he ravages the open country, but the secret and buried stores may pass altogether unnoticed or escape detection, simply because they have to be looked for.

The universal dress is the short cloak, fastened with a brooch or, failing that, a thorn. They pass whole days by the hearth fire wearing no garment but this. The richest are not distinguished, like the Persians and Sarmatians, by a long flowing robe, but by a tight one that shows the shape of every limb. They also wear the pelts of wild animals, the tribes near the Rhine without regard to appearance, the more distant peoples with some refinement of taste, for there is no other finery that they can buy. These latter peoples make careful choice of animal, then strip off the pelt and mottle it with patches of the spotted skins of the beasts that live in the outer ocean and the unknown sea. The dress of the women differs from that of the men in two respects only. The women often wear undergarments of linen, embroidered with purple, and, as the upper part does not extend to sleeves, forearms and upper arms are bare. Even the breast, where it comes nearest the shoulder, is exposed too. . . .

There is no pomp about their funerals. The one rule observed is that the bodies of famous men are burned with special kinds of wood. When they have heaped up the fire they do not throw robes or spices on the top; but only a man's arms, and sometimes his horse, too, are cast into the flames. The tomb is a raised mound of turf. They disdain to show honour by laboriously rearing high monuments of stone; they would only lie heavy on the dead. Weeping and wailing are soon abandoned—sorrow and mourning not so soon. A woman may decently express her grief in public; a man should nurse his in his heart.

Such is the general account that we find given of the origin and customs of the Germans as a whole. . . .

The Langobardi are distinguished by the fewness of their numbers. Ringed round as they are by many mighty peoples, they find safety, not in obsequiousness but in battle and its perils. After them come the Reudigni, Aviones, Anglii, Varini, Eudoses, Suarini and Nuitones behind their ramparts of rivers and woods. There is nothing particularly noteworthy about these people in detail, but they are distinguished by a common worship of Nerthus, or Mother Earth. They believe that she interests herself in human affairs and rides through their peoples. In an island of Ocean stands a sacred grove, and in the grove stands a car draped with a cloth which none but the priest may touch. The priest can feel the presence of the goddess in this holy of holies, and attends her, in deepest reverence, as her car is drawn by kine. Then follow days of rejoicing and merry-making in every place that she honours with her advent and stay. No one goes to war, no one takes up arms; every object of iron is locked away; then, and then only, are peace and quiet known and prized, until the goddess is again restored to her temple by the priest, when she has had her fill of the society of men. After that, the car, the cloth and, believe it if you will, the goddess herself are washed clean in a secluded lake. This service is performed by slaves who are immediately afterwards drowned in the lake. Thus mystery begets terror and a pious reluctance to ask what that sight can be which is allowed only to dying eyes. . . .

Passing the Suiones, we find yet another sea that is sluggish and almost stagnant. The reason why this sea is believed to be the boundary that girds the earth is because the last radiance of the setting sun lasts here till dawn, with a brilliance that dims the stars. Rumour adds that you can hear the sound he makes as he leaves the waves and can see the shape of his horses and the rays on his head. At this point our real knowledge of the world ends. However, turning to the right shore of the Suebian sea, we find it washing the territories of the Aestii, who have the religion and general customs of the Suebi, but a language approximating to the British. They worship the Mother of the gods. They wear, as emblem of this cult, the masks of boars, which stand them in stead of armour or human protection and ensure the safety of the worshipper even among his enemies. They seldom use weapons of iron, but cudgels often. They cultivate grain and other crops with a patience quite unusual among lazy Germans. Nor do they omit to ransack the sea;

they are the only people to collect the amber—*glaesum* is their own word for it—in the shallows or even on the beach. Like true barbarians, they have never asked or discovered what it is or how it is produced. For a long time, indeed, it lay unheeded like any other jetsam, until Roman luxury made its reputation. They have no use for it themselves. They gather it crude, pass it on unworked and are astounded at the price it fetches. Amber, however, is certainly a gum of trees, as you may see from the fact that creeping and even winged creatures are often seen shining in it. They got caught in the sticky liquid, and were imprisoned as it hardened. I imagine that in the islands and lands of the West, just as in the secret chambers of the East, where the trees sweat frankincense and balm, there must be woods and groves of unusual fertility. Their gums, drawn out by the rays of their near neighbour, the sun, flow in liquid state into the sea and are finally washed by violent storms on to the shores opposite. If you care to test the properties of amber by applying fire to it, you will find that it lights like a torch and gives off a thick and heavily scented flame; it then cools into a sticky solid like pitch or resin.

Continuous with the Suiones are the nations of the Sitones. They resemble them in all respects but one—woman is the ruling sex. That is the measure of their decline, I will not say below freedom, but even below decent slavery.

J. J. A. WORSAAE

Denmark and the Three Age System

WORSAAE'S book was first published in Denmark (as *Danmarks Oldtid*) in 1842. It was very influential in inducing the acceptance of the Three Age System (p. 31, I) by other European archaeologists.

As collections of antiquities were intended to afford illustrations of history, it followed as a natural consequence, that as soon as a few objects were collected, attempts were made to explain them. The course which was at first pursued was, however, obviously incor-

THE MOST IMPORTANT OF THE SEVERAL HUNDRED KITCHEN MIDDENS OF DENMARK. THE SOLID LINE IS THE COASTLINE OF SOME 5000 YEARS AGO, THE DOTTED LINE THAT OF TODAY. THE SEA IS ENCROACHING IN THE SOUTH AND RECEDING IN THE NORTH, SO THAT THE MIDDENS IN THE NORTH ARE THE ONLY ONES NOW ABOVE SEA-LEVEL. BARKÆR (SHOWN IN BRACKETS) IS THE SITE OF ONE OF THE FIRST COLONIES OF FARMERS IN DENMARK, FOUNDED WHILE THE KITCHEN MIDDENS WERE STILL INHABITED.

rect: for example, it was at once perceived that the antiquities which had been discovered differed materially from each other, since some were carved from stone, while others were beautifully

From *The Primeval Antiquities of Denmark*, translated by W. J. Thomas. London: John Henry Parker; 1849, pp. 7-9.

formed of metal. Although it was now generally acknowledged that our native land had been inhabited by several distinct races, still it was supposed that all these antiquities must have belonged to one and the same people, namely, those who were the last that found their way into our country, the Goths of Scandinavia, from whom we derive our descent. By this means, objects appertaining to the most different times were naturally mingled together. We will quote a striking instance of this fact, and we do so because the view which is here maintained is one which is still not unfrequently expressed both in writing and in conversation.

It is well known that stones shaped by art into the form of wedges, hammers, chisels, knives, &c., are frequently exhumed from the earth. These, in the opinion of many, could certainly never have served as tools or implements, since it was impossible either to carve or cut with a stone; hence it was concluded, that they had formerly been employed by our forefathers in those sacrifices which were offered to idols, during the prevalence of heathenism. Thus it was said the hammers of stone were used to strike the sacrifice on the forehead; and after the sacrificing priest with a chisel, likewise formed of stone, had stripped off the skin, the flesh was cut to pieces with knives of stone, &c. The Cromlechs, Cairns, and Barrows in which such objects are found, were conceived to have been partly places of sacrifice, partly temples and seats of justice. But when amidst the vast mass of antiquities of stone which had been gradually collected, several shewed obvious marks of having been much used and worn, doubts began to be entertained whether they really had been employed as instruments of sacrifice. At length attention was directed to the fact that even at the present day, in several of the islands of the South seas and in other parts, there exist races of savages who, without knowing the use of metals, employ implements of stone which have the same shape and adaptation as those which are discovered in the earth in such quantities in Denmark, and further, it was shewn in what manner those savages made use of such simple and apparently such useless implements. No one after this could longer remain in doubt that our antiquities of stone were also actually used as tools in times when metals were either unknown, or were so rare and costly, that they were only in the possession of very few individuals. That this could not have been the case in this country while inhabited by our forefathers the Goths, is evident from all historical records, we must therefore seek for the origin of the antiquities of stone in an earlier time, in fact, as we shall soon perceive, among the first inhabitants of our native land.

As soon as it was once pointed out that the whole of these antiquities could by no means be referred to one and the same period, people began to see more clearly the difference between them. We are now enabled to pronounce with certainty, that our antiquities belonging to the times of paganism may be referred to three chief classes, referable to three distinct periods. The first class includes all antiquarian objects formed of stone, respecting which we must assume that they appertain to the stone-period, as it is called, that is, to a period when the use of metals was in a great measure unknown. The second class comprises the oldest metallic objects; these however were not as yet composed of iron, but of a peculiar mixture of metals, copper and a small portion of tin melted together, to which the name of "bronze" has been given; from which circumstance the period in which this substance was commonly used has been named the Bronze Period. Finally, all objects appertaining to the period when iron was generally known and employed, are included in the third class, and belong to the Iron Period.

OWL'S HEAD CARVED IN THE ROUND
IN BRONZE ON A LA TÈNE CALDRON
FROM BRAA IN JUTLAND

OSCAR MONTELIUS

Swedish Prehistory

OSCAR MONTELIUS did much to perfect the Three Age System by sub-dividing its Ages on the basis of typology (p. 76, I). The marvellous finds of men's and women's clothes in the Danish bogs give the only reliable picture of Bronze Age dress in Europe. It is fair to assume that very much the same kind of garments would have been worn in southern Sweden.

The Three Age System in Sweden

THE history of the earliest inhabitants of the North was till about fifty years ago shrouded in obscurity. It was not till then that antiquarians began generally to recognize that the antiquities which are dug up from time to time, and the barrows and stone monuments which still abound throughout the country, do not all belong to that part of heathen times which immediately preceded the introduction of Christianity, and of which the Icelandic sagas relate. When Ansgar first came to Sweden in the ninth century, the use of iron was universal in the country, and had been so for a long time. A careful investigation of the antiquities has shown however that before that period, now usually known as the Iron Age, there was another, when iron was altogether unknown, in which weapons and tools were made of bronze, a mixture of copper and tin. This period, called the Bronze Age, had, as well as the Iron Age, continued for many centuries. But before the beginning of the Bronze Age, Sweden had for a very long time been inhabited by people who lived in entire ignorance of the use of the metals, and were therefore compelled to make their instruments and weapons of such materials as stone, horn, bone, and wood. This last period is known therefore as the Stone Age.

From *The Civilization of Sweden in Heathen Times*. London: Macmillan & Co. Ltd.; 1888, pp. 1-6, 42-7, 59-62.

This division of heathen times in the North into three great periods was already made and published as long ago as the last century, but it was not till 1830-40 that it had any special importance in antiquarian researches. The honour of developing a scientific system based upon this triple division—a work so important for gaining an insight into the earliest condition of the whole human race—belongs to the *savants* of the North. The first place among them is occupied by Councillor Christian Jürgensen Thomsen (died 1865), to whose labours we are mainly indebted for the celebrated Museum of Northern Antiquities in Copenhagen. Next to him we must place as the founders of the prehistoric archaeology of the north Professor Sven Nilsson of Lund (died 1883), and Chamberlain J. J. A. Worsaae (died 1885). Thomsen's system was soon taken up by the Royal Antiquary Bror Emil Hildebrand (died 1884), who did the greatest service by his development of the National Historical Museum at Stockholm. The "Three Age System" was also quickly adopted in almost every other country. The attack long made against it in Germany may now be regarded as ceased, and the correctness of this division has been generally recognized even in that country.

The thousands of finds which have come to our knowledge since this system was published, have not only proved in a striking manner that the outline of the earliest history of Northern culture which antiquarians endeavoured to draw more than fifty years ago was correct, but have also opened a new and wide field for further research. We can now form a very clear idea of the circumstances under which the first settlers in our land lived, and we can follow, step by step, the slow but sure development whereby the inhabitants of Sweden, once a horde of savages, have reached their present condition.

It is true that we meet with no line of kings, no heroic names dating from these earliest times. But is not the knowledge of the people's life, and of the progress of their culture, of more worth than the names of saga heroes? And ought we not to give more credence to the contemporary, irrefutable witnesses to whom alone archaeology now listens, than to the poetical stories which for centuries were preserved only in the memory of skalds?

It might seem unnecessary at present to give any special proof of the correctness of this threefold division of heathen times in the North, inasmuch as the whole account we shall give may be regarded as proving it. But as the present position of Northern archaeology depends so peculiarly upon this division, we shall now point out some circumstances which show how well grounded the opinion is, at least so far as Scandinavia is concerned.

That there was a time when all metals were entirely unknown

is clearly seen from the many large finds and the hundreds of remarkable graves containing numerous relics of stone, bone, &c.,
but no trace of metal. That there was another period when the use
of bronze, but not of iron, was known, is equally clear from the
large number of hoards and graves which contain weapons, ornaments, &c., of bronze, but no trace of iron; while on the other hand
bronze implements are hardly ever found with those of iron. That
there was a third period in heathen times when iron was in general
use we can see by the first glance at any large collection of antiquities. From this is follows of necessity that the earliest history of
Northern culture—the time antecedent to the establishment of
Christianity—actually embraces the three great periods which derive their names from the most important material in use during
each of them.

And there can hardly be any doubt of the order in which these
periods followed each other. That the Stone Age must be older than
the Bronze Age is self-evident, and is further proved by the fact that
we often find graves of the Bronze Age in the upper part of barrows
which have been raised over a grave chamber of the Stone Age
which usually lies at the bottom in the centre of the barrow, while
the converse has never occurred. And our earliest sources of history which throw light on the conditions of life during the last
part of heathen times point only to a period when iron was in general use. It follows therefore that the Iron Age must be the last of
these three periods.

How far the beginning of each period coincides with the appearance of a new race which subdued the earlier settlers in the country,
is a further question which we must for the present distinguish
from that which concerns only the order in which the several
heathen periods followed each other.

Before we now make an attempt to set before our readers a picture of the life in Sweden during heathen times, we must observe
that if that picture shall prove imperfect and blurred, it is partly
perhaps owing to the insufficiency of our sources of information
about a period so wanting in written historical materials. It is doubtless true, and should be gladly acknowledged, that we have discovered much richer documents dating from heathen times than
we had any right to expect; but by far the majority of the antiquities
preserved to our own day are naturally works of stone, metals, and
the like, while it is only by an exceptional conjunction of specially
favourable conditions that such perishable materials as wood, bone,
leather, cloth, &c., have been able to survive. It follows that we
must have a very imperfect knowledge of furniture, stuffs, and
clothes made out of such materials; and yet these formed incomparably the greater part of the belongings of the heathen Northmen.

But even of metal and stone objects used in those days our knowledge is very imperfect. Only a small part of what once existed was
buried in the ground; only a part of what was buried has escaped
the destroying hand of time; of this part all has not yet come to
light again; and we know only too well how little of what has come
to light has been of any service for our science. Almost all the finds
of past centuries have disappeared without a trace, and even much
of what has been discovered in the present century has been
destroyed.

We can easily realize the importance of these facts if we imagine
that an antiquarian some thousand or two thousand years hence
should attempt to represent our own manner of life, and yet had
scarcely any other material for the purpose beyond the verdigrised
and rusty remains of our metal works, and so could not complete
the picture of the nineteenth century by the help of works of literature and art. This comparison shows how cautious we should be in
our attempt to trace the civilisation of heathen times, the earliest
part of which was several thousand years before our day.

The Bronze Age and Bronze Age Costume

BEFORE the Stone Age ended the inhabitants of Sweden had raised
themselves considerably above the savage state; but, so long as
they were completely ignorant of metals, it was impossible for them
to reach a higher degree of civilisation. But at last the fruits of the
civilisation attained by the cultured races of the East spread to the
distant regions of the North; and through the knowledge of metals,
at first only bronze and gold, there began for those lands a new
era known as the Bronze Age.

By these words is understood that period in the earliest civilisation of the Northern races, when they made their weapons, tools,
&c. of bronze, a mixture of copper and tin. Besides bronze, they
knew only of one metal, namely, gold. Iron, steel, silver, and all
other metals were still completely unknown in these countries.

Before we go further we must call attention to the inaccuracy
of an opinion which not unfrequently finds expression, that all
antiquities of bronze should be referred by antiquarians to the
Bronze Age. Vessels, rings, buckles, needles and the like were, as
we might have supposed, still made of bronze after the end of this
period, just as they are even in our own day, but generally of a
somewhat different composition from that used in the Bronze Age.
To this age belong only weapons and edge-tools made of bronze,
and such vessels and ornaments as are usually found with them.

With respect to the important question *how* the Bronze Age
began in the North, different opinions have been expressed. Some

have supposed that it was due to the immigration of a Celtic race, others to a Teutonic immigration. Professor Nilsson has endeavoured to show that the North is indebted to Phoenician colonists for the earliest knowledge of metals, while Herr Wiberg, in Gefle, regarded the Bronze Age to have begun in the North through the influence of the Etruscans. Also Professor Lindenschmit of Mainz, who does not believe in the existence of a Bronze Age in the sense understood by the Northern antiquarians, considers that most of the bronze works in question were Etruscan.

THE PLOW COMES TO EUROPE. BRONZE AGE ROCK CARVING FROM SWEDEN.
A MAN, CARRYING A BAG OF SEED CORN AT HIS BELT
AND A BRANCH IN HIS HAND, IS DRIVING A TWO-OX PLOW.

It seems to us that there are strong grounds for the opinion that the beginning of the Bronze Age in Scandinavia was not connected with any great immigration of a new race, but that the people of the North learnt the art of working bronze by intercourse with other nations. The resemblance of the graves during the last part of the Stone Age and the early part of the Bronze Age, as well as other circumstances, point to such a conclusion. From Asia the "Bronze Culture," if we may so express the higher civilisation dependent on the knowledge of bronze, had gradually spread itself over the continent of Europe in a northerly and north-westerly direction, until at last it reached the coasts of the Baltic.

We have already mentioned that the end of the Stone Age, and therefore the beginning of the Bronze Age, in the North, must be regarded as having taken place 3,500 years ago. The latest investigations have shown that the Bronze Age proper came to an end in these regions in the beginning of the fifth century B.C. It lasted therefore about a thousand years.

As the Bronze Age comprises so long a period, attempts have

naturally been made to distinguish the antiquities belonging to its earlier and later parts. Such attempts might have been supposed almost useless, when we consider that among the thousands of finds of the Bronze Age in the North as yet known, there is not a single coin, or any other object, with an inscription, either native or foreign. Nevertheless, by a careful and thorough examination of the many antiquities and graves of the Bronze Age now known, it has fortunately proved possible to distinguish in it six consecutive periods. But as it would take us too long to describe separately each

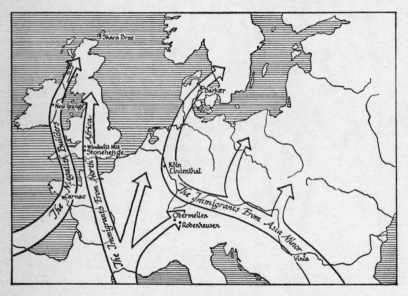

THE SPREAD OF FARMER-SETTLERS OVER VIRGIN EUROPE
IN THE PERIOD FROM 3000 TO 2000 B.C.

of these periods, we must restrict ourselves to mentioning which of the antiquities belong to the earlier, and which to the later, portion of the Bronze Age.

The works of the earlier part—the Earlier Bronze Age as it is called—are decorated with fine spiral ornaments and zigzag lines. The graves generally contain remains of unburnt bodies. The antiquities of this period found in the North (which appear to be almost without an exception of native workmanship) are distinguished by artistic forms, and point to a highly developed taste in the working of bronze. They generally surpass in this respect the relics of the Bronze Age found in almost all other European countries.

On the other hand, the works belonging to the latter part of the period, the so-called Later Bronze Age, are characterized by a very different taste and style of ornamentation, though even they are often the result of great skill. We do not find in them spirals, of the same shape as in the Earlier Bronze Age, engraved or beaten in with a punch; but the ends of rings, knife-handles, and the like, are often rolled up in spiral volutes. During this period the dead were always burnt.

Still more surprising are some discoveries made in Denmark. In 1861, in the so-called "Treenhöi," a barrow at Havdrup in Ribe amt, a coffin was found made out of a cloven and hollowed trunk of an oak. In this coffin, which fortunately was examined by experts, a warrior had been buried with his sword and with all his clothes. The still perfectly preserved clothes of simply woven wool consist of a high cap, a wide, roundly-cut mantle, a sort of tunic, and two small pieces of wool, which probably covered the legs; at the feet were seen some small remains of leather, which were possibly once shoes. The cap, which had no shade, was made of thick woven wool, and the outside was covered with projecting pieces of worsted, all ending in a knot. The inside of the mantle also was covered with pendent worsted threads. The tunic was kept together by a long woollen belt, which went twice round the middle, was knotted in front, and had two long ends hanging down and decorated with fringes. They also found in the grave a second woollen cap and a woollen shawl decorated with tassels; half of the latter lay rolled up as a pillow under the head. The whole contents of the coffin were inclosed in a hide, probably that of a cow. Although the woollen clothes were so remarkably well-preserved the body had almost completely perished; even the skeleton had crumbled away. Only the black hair and the brain protected by the cap were preserved; the form of the brain could still, curiously enough, be easily recognized. By the left side of the body lay a bronze sword in a wooden sheath lined with skin. At the foot stood a round wooden box containing a smaller box of the same kind, in which lay the last-mentioned woollen cap, as well as a horn comb and a bronze knife. The knife, which in shape is like a modern razor, had possibly been used for the same purpose.

The value of this remarkable find—and others like it have since been made—is greatly increased by the discovery ten years later in 1871, of a complete woman's dress of the same period, in another Danish barrow, Borum-Eshöi, near Aarhus in Jutland. In this case also the body was buried in a coffin made out of a cloven and hollowed trunk of an oak. An untanned hide, probably of a cow or an ox, inclosed the contents of the coffin. The body had been wrapped in a large mantle, woven with a mixture of coarse wool and cow hair. That it was a woman who was here buried, was

clearly shown by the well-preserved skeleton. The very long hair
had probably been fastened up by a horn comb which was found
in the grave. Upon the head was a well-knotted worsted net. There
were also found remains of a second similar net. The body too was
clad in a complete dress of woollen stuff, consisting of a jacket
with sleeves and a long robe. The weaving was of precisely the same
kind as that of the clothes found in the graves of Dömmestorp and
Treenhöi. The jacket was sewn together under the arms and upon
the back, and open in front, where it had probably been fastened
with a string or a little bronze *fibula* found in the coffin, unless the
latter had been used for the mantle. The coarse seam on the back
of the jacket shows that it used to be covered by the mantle. The
robe was kept together round the body by two woollen bands, one
of coarser, the other of finer work. The latter band, or rather belt,
was of wool and cowhair mixed, woven in three rows, of which the
middle appeared to have been of a different colour from those on
the sides. It ended in thick ornamental tassels.

The other bronze ornaments taken out of the coffin, besides the
fibula already mentioned, were a spiral finger-ring, two bracelets, a
torque, and three round, beautifully decorated plates of different
sizes with points projecting in the middle. A comparison with
similar ornaments recently found in other graves proves that they
were decorative plates belonging to belts. Strangely enough there
lay by the side of this woman's body a bronze dagger with a horn
handle.

GEOFFREY BIBBY

Bodies from the Bogs

BOGS can be even more effective than a totally dry atmosphere for
the preservation of normally perishable substances. Fully clothed
bodies dating from the Bronze Age came to light in Danish bogs
during the nineteenth century (p. 72, I), and in the twentieth naked

From *The Testimony of the Spade*. New York: Alfred A. Knopf; 1956, pp. 397-401.
By permission of Alfred A. Knopf, Inc. and William Collins Sons & Co. Ltd. © 1956 by
Geoffrey Bibby.

bodies dating from the beginning of our era have been found in the bogs of Denmark and the adjacent part of Germany. These men and women had all been violently done to death. In an account of the tribes inhabiting north Germany and Jutland, Tacitus describes a rite celebrating the fertility goddess, Nerthus, that involved some of the attendants being killed and thrown into a lake. This may explain the bodies in the bogs. On the other hand Tacitus also records that throughout the Germanic area traitors were hanged, while cowards and perverts were drowned in swamps.

IT was perhaps too much to ask for individual portraits of the warrior-farmers of northern Europe's Iron Age. Extension after extension of the technique of extracting new information from excavation material have not yet cured archaeologists of the frequent use of the phrase "We shall never know . . . ," but surely here was a pipe-dream that could never be realized. We could never know what a race with no knowledge of naturalistic portraiture looked like.

And then in May 1950 an archaeologist looked upon the face of a man who had lived in northern Europe two thousand years ago. And in the past five years two hundred thousand people have seen in person two men and a girl who were contemporaries, approximately, of Julius Caesar and of Christ Himself.

It was Peter Glob, the discoverer of the settlement of the first Danish farmers at Barkaer, who dug up both Tollund man and Grauballe man. He tells how, in May 1950, he was lecturing to students at Aarhus University in Jutland when he was called away with the news that the police wished to speak to him. It was a telephone call from the police station at Silkeborg, twenty-five miles away. The superintendent explained that he had just received word that peat-cutters at a little peat bog at Tollund a few miles out had come across the body of a man in the peat.

Now, many works of man are dug up from the Danish peat bogs, and they prove, almost without exception, to be of prehistoric date. Nor, as we shall see, are remains of human bodies from these periods any unusual phenomenon. The superintendent of police acted, therefore, with some insight in enrolling a professor of archaeology as his adviser before going out to view the reported body.

Professor Glob has described in his own words the events of the day. "I started at once for Tollund Mose, a narrow peat bog among high, steep hills in a wild region of central Jutland.

"In the peat cut, nearly seven feet down, lay a human figure in a crouched position, still half buried. A foot and a shoulder protruded, perfectly preserved but dark brown in colour like the surrounding peat, which had dyed the skin. Carefully we removed more peat, and a bowed head came into view.

"As dusk fell, we saw in the fading light a man take shape before us. He was curled up, with legs drawn under him and arms bent, resting on his side as if asleep. His eyes were peacefully shut; his brows were furrowed and his mouth showed a slightly irritated quirk as if he were not overpleased by this unexpected disturbance of his rest.

"That this rest had lasted 2000 years was clearly shown by the seven feet of peat which had gradually formed above him throughout the centuries . . .

"Now it was necessary to act swiftly to prevent the air from destroying this rare relic and to bring it as soon as possible under the care of a skilled conservator.

"Careful hands covered the body again with peat, cut free the section in which it lay, and placed it in a wooden case. Thus the body was transported to the National Museum in Copenhagen."

On examination beneath the arc lights in Cophenhagen the body of Tollund man was seen to be naked, save for a leather belt around his waist and a leather cap, formed of eight pieces of skin sewn together, upon his head. There was one other item. Still around his neck was the braided leather rope with which they had hanged him.

Two years later, almost to the day, Peter Glob was again called out to a body found in the peat. The site was only a few miles from Tollund, a little sphagnum bog near the village of Grauballe. Here workmen cutting peat one Saturday morning came, six feet below the surface, upon the head of a man and, realizing this time that their discovery must be prehistoric, they sent word posthaste to the Prehistoric Museum at Aarhus.

Glob drove out at once, to find the perfectly preserved head of a man exposed in the peat. Excavating only enough to show the lie of the body, he spent the rest of the day cutting, drawing, and photographing a section through the peat from the surface to below where the body lay. After taking a series of samples of the peat for pollen-analysis he cut out the block in which Grauballe man lay and, sliding a zinc sheet under the block, succeeded in hoisting it on to a truck for transport to the museum in Aarhus.

There in the following days the peat was inch by inch removed from the body, samples being taken every few centimetres and the work photographed at every stage. The complete and perfectly preserved body of a man, stained a dark brown by the peat water, was gradually exposed to view. He lay prone and at full length, with

an arm twisted behind him and one knee drawn up. He was completely naked.

A plaster cast was made of the body while it still lay on its bed
of peat and, with the cast still in position to ensure that the body
was not disturbed a hair's breadth from its original position, the
whole block was turned upside down. The underlying peat, now
on top, was then equally carefully removed, so that the underside
of the body was exposed. The cause of death could now be clearly
seen. The man's throat had been cut from ear to ear.

In the meantime, experts from the Peat Geological Laboratory
in Copenhagen had been at work in the bog at Grauballe, cutting
sections and taking samples and working out the history of the bog
from its formation to the present day. They gave it as their opinion
that peat had been anciently cut there and that the body had been
laid in the bottom of one of the then open cuts. The samples of the
later peat formed within the cut and lying immediately around the
body suggested a date of round about the commencement of the
Christian era.

The environs of the body had now been thoroughly examined. It
was time to turn to the body itself.

The medical faculty of Aarhus University was recruited for the
task. The body was X-rayed from all angles, and an autopsy was
then performed by one of the professors. The teeth were examined
by a committee of three dental surgeons, and a regulation dental
card filled out in the name of Grauballe man. They gave a unani-
mous opinion that the man had been about forty years old at death,
but for this age his teeth were well preserved. Only one had been
lost in life and only one showed signs of caries. All the teeth, however, showed considerable wear, a not uncommon phenomenon
among primitive agricultural peoples whose stone querns introduce a quantity of grit into the flour. The teeth were then sent for
more detailed examination to the University College of Dentistry.
In the course of the autopsy the stomach was removed, in order
that its contents might be examined, and the liver excised for age-
determination by the radioactive-carbon process. The fingerprint
department of the police took records for their files of one of the
earliest Danes known. The fingerprints were beautifully clear and
showed no characteristics to distinguish them from those of anyone now living.

Between the finding of Tollund man and of Grauballe man a
discovery of the same nature and of even greater interest had been
made in a peat bog in Schleswig-Holstein in northern Germany.
Here again, peat-cutters discovered a body, but this time of a
fourteen-year-old girl. The body was naked, apart from a collar of
oxskin, and perfectly preserved. Dr. Karl Schlabow of the Schleswig-

Holstein museum was called out to the site and removed the body to the museum in a block of peat, using, appropriately enough, a motor hearse for the transport. The body was freed from peat in the museum and examined. No cause of death could be ascertained, but one circumstance made it certain that death had been violent. A woven band was still in position, blindfolding the eyes of the victim. The left side of the girl's head had been shaved. Pollen-analysis placed the death at about two thousand years ago.

Not far away from the girl a second body was discovered, that of a man of about forty, strangled with a hazel wand. This body, however, was in a poor state of preservation and could not be recovered.

The finding of the girl from Schleswig and the two men from central Jutland was a world sensation. The grave intellectual features of Tollund man, the quizzical, rather impish expression of Grauballe man, and the pathetic figure of the dead girl became known far beyond the sober pages of the journals of prehistory. Here, better preserved than any Egyptian pharaoh, was, as it were, a personal delegation from the ancestors of the European peoples, bridging with their common humanity and obvious individuality a gap of sixty generations. Looking upon the man from Tollund, you knew that he would have, and probably had, discussed reports of a bald-headed general from Italy, called Caesar, who was gobbling up the nations between the Alps and the Rhine at an alarming rate —and discussed them with the same resolute shrewdness as his descendants two thousand years later discussed the moves of an Austrian ex-corporal.

And then, in addition to the human interest, here was a murder mystery second to none. Four people had come to a violent end under approximately the same circumstances and at approximately the same time. Was there a common motive behind the killings? And if so, what was it?

H. SHELELIG AND H. FALK

Runic Writing

THE ancient Germanic letters, the runes, are among the most interesting cultural phenomena which come to light in Scandinavia
during the Roman period. Runes appear among the Germanic
peoples about the same time in the north as in the south, roughly
A.D. 200; that is, at a time when the barbarians were receiving a
multitude of strong impulses from classical culture: it is important
to remember that this was the situation when the art of writing
first appeared among the Germans. It is therefore quite certain
that the runes were not formed spontaneously, without any earlier
prototype; but it is also characteristic of the Germans that they did
not immediately adopt either of the existing alphabets which they
would meet with in Roman use, Latin and Greek: on the contrary, they formed a set of letters which is independent in many
particulars, in form, in sound-value, in the names given to the
individual runes, and in the fixed position of the letters in the
series. The study of runes and their origins accordingly involves a
number of problems which are always tempting to investigators,
but are as yet a long way from any certain solution. Runes have
preserved their old attraction of mystery even to this day.

To the popular consciousness runes have always been something
more than an ordinary form of writing. Even in recent times popular belief has endued runes with mysterious magical attributes;
the runic art was a form of wizardry which conferred powers of
protection or injury, and this conception appears still more clearly
in the older sources. In the Edda poems, which still present an
almost wholly heathen way of thought, there is valuable information about runes. A myth about the origin of runes is inserted in
Hàvamàl, where Othin himself relates it (*Hàvamàl*, stanza 140):

nam ek upp rúnar,	*I caught up the runes,*
œpandi nam:	*crying aloud I took them:*
fell ek aptr þaðan.	*down I fell from there.*

From *Scandinavian Archaeology*, translated by E. V. Gordon. Oxford: The Clarendon
Press; 1937, pp.212-15. By permission of The Clarendon Press, Oxford.

The runes come from the highest of the gods:

Rúnar munt þú finna	Runes shalt thou find
ok ráðna stafi,	and letters bearing meaning.
mjǫk stóra stafi,	letters most mighty,
er fáði fimbulþulr	which the Great Counsellor coloured
ok gørðu ginnregin	and most holy gods devised
ok reist hroptr rǫgna.	and the spokesman of the gods had carved.

In *Sigrdrifumál* the valkyrie gives a complete set of instructions for the use of all kinds of runes which fulfil wishes and protect against evil, beginning with runes for victory:

Sigrúnar skaltu kunna,	Runes of victory shalt thou know,
ef þú vilt sigr hafa,	if thou wilt have the victory,
ok rísta á hialti hiǫrs,	and cut them on thy sword-hilt,
sumar á véttrimum,	some on the hilt-rings,
sumar á valbǫstum,	some on the plates of the handle,
ok nefna tysvar Tý.	and twice name the name of Týr.

So also there were runes for women in labour, runes against poison in drink, against distress at sea, runes to heal wounds, and runes that produce eloquence and wisdom. Many traces are preserved also of rites belonging specially to the employment of runes; for example, the runes were coloured red with blood, and when the letters which had been cut were shaved off, the chips could be used in various ways with far-reaching magical power. The valkyrie Sigrdrifa tells how runes originally got their magical virtue in this way:

Allar váru af skafnar	All (the runes) were shaved off
þær er váru á ristnar	that had been cut,
ok hverfðar við inn helga miǫð	and mixed with the holy mead (of inspiration)
ok sendar á víða vega.	and sent upon far ways.

The saga of Egill Skalla-Grímsson shows us the old runic art still undiminished in power at the beginning of the historical period; the saga even implies that Egill's runes were the real cause of Eirik Bloodaxe's loss of his kingdom in Norway (A.D. 947). Runic monuments bear witness to the same traditions in older times. The most important monument of the kind is the Eggjum stone from about the seventh century, bearing a long inscription in which the language and the poetic style are nearly related to the Edda poems. This inscription consists of two stanzas of definitely magical purport, intended to protect the grave and secure vengeance for the man slain. This example provides the key to the general nature of runic documents in early times: the purpose of the runes was not to make statements of fact; their significance was contained in themselves. For this reason the old inscriptions have only a poor and meagre content, according to our ideas. We are most anxious for information about the life of the time, but all we find are names of individual persons and brief formalized phrases. It was not the sense of what was written that held the primary significance: the runes themselves were to have an effect, if correctly used and arranged in certain numerical combinations. The gold ring from Petroassa in Roumania is hallowed by a runic inscription, of which only one word can be interpreted with certainty: *hailag,* "holy." Runes on a spearhead give the weapon power, and they are cut on small implements to secure fortune and efficiency in their use. Runes on a trinket make it an amulet which protects its owner.

From all that we know about the magical use of runes, it was comparatively rarely that the runic art was employed in a way that would leave traces lasting into future ages; the runes had their use as an aid to sorcery to obtain immediate results on particular occasions, cut in perishable material, often obliterated again as part of the same magical rite. In the *Edda* (in *Sigrdrifumál*) part of the precaution against treachery was to mark runes on the back of the hand and scratch *Nauð* (the rune for N) on the nail, so that in this instance the runes were written on the actual person. The runes were generally not intended to be read by others. A certain number of Norwegian runic stones, among them the Eggjum stone mentioned above, were buried in a grave mound with the notion that they would never again be brought to light; the hidden runes would fulfil their magical purpose. This circumstance is given special emphasis in order to make it clear that the surviving records do not give any reliable indication of the actual extent and use of runes in the oldest times. . . .

H. SHELELIG AND H. FALK

Royal Ship-Burials in Viking Times

THE great ships from Oseberg and Gokstad and their contents—
exquisite works of art and craft and all kinds of everyday objects—
are displayed in a museum of their own at Oslo.

THE custom of burial in a vessel was itself not limited to royal
persons, as we have already seen; on the contrary, it was very common in Norway and Sweden at this time to bury the dead in a
boat, usually in one that was not very large, but not in the smallest.
The custom is remarkable, and, so far as we know, without any
analogue in prehistoric Europe; the nearest parallels must be sought
in ancient Egypt, where examples are known of graves with ships
and also a grave built of stone in the form of a boat. We have
described earlier an interesting group of grave-monuments on Got-
land, constructed with ship-formed rows of stones, which can be
traced back as far as the fourth and fifth phases of the Bronze
Age. All are agreed that this form of grave expresses the same idea
as the ship-graves of the Viking period, that the symbolical rows of
stones represent an actual vessel, and go back to a time when it is
not inconceivable that there might be some connexion with the
similar forms of grave in Egypt. In these forms we have to reckon
with the belief about the dead journeying in a ship, and the function ascribed to the ship in the cult of the dead, which we have
already discussed in connexion with the Bronze-Age rock-carvings,
and we discovered from some of the Norwegian carvings and
Swedish sculptured stones that pictures of this kind, representing
ships, were still executed in the early Iron Age. Accordingly, it

wwwwwwwwwwwww

Ibid., 280-3, 425-30.

seems probable that the boat-graves and ship-graves, as we encounter them in the Viking period, have their roots in a very ancient
Norse survival, and that the vessel in the grave has a more specific
symbolism than the rest of the grave-goods. The most natural interpretation of the boat-graves must be that the vessel was to serve
for the journey over the sea to the kingdom of the dead.

We have other traces also of this belief in the Iron Age in
Scandinavia: there is a certain number of examples from the
Roman period and the migration period of a gold coin or a small
cut piece of gold being put into the dead man's mouth as he lay
in the grave, or into the urn when the body was cremated. These
are "Charon's pennies" following the true classical example, which
also originated in the belief that mankind after death must make a
journey across a river or the sea: this is clearly the same notion
that is at the root of the boat-graves. Graves with vessels are also
undoubtedly in evidence some time before the Viking period. In the
years round about A.D. 500 some examples of boat-graves appear
on the coasts of Norway in Nordland, near Bergen, and near
Arendal; the boat is sometimes burned on the pyre, sometimes
buried unburned. To the same period belongs the only boat-grave
known from Anglo-Saxon times in England; it was found on Snape
Common near Aldeburgh in Suffolk. The contents of this grave had
not been burned; the boat was a good 14 metres long, and contained, among other articles, a gold finger-ring of fifth-century
Italian make and fragments of a glass vase. Mr. Reginald A. Smith
has dated the grave *c.* 500, and it is thus completely parallel with
the oldest boat-graves known in Norway. But it is by no means
certain that the oldest boat-graves which we know are the oldest
that existed. In earlier times the boats were made entirely of perishable material, without even iron nails, so that they would disappear
on the pyre or in the earth without leaving a trace, and it is accordingly quite possible that the boat-graves represent a much older
custom than we now have evidence of.

What is certain is that graves containing vessels first become
apparent in Scandinavia in the migration period, *c.* A.D. 500. In
the seventh century they are more widely distributed through Norway, Sweden, and Finland, and are then represented with unusual
richness in the royal graves in Uppland which have already been
described. In the Viking period, from the beginning of the ninth
century, this form of burial reached its greatest extent and popularity, and at the same time achieved its highest development in
the graves of the Norwegian kings. All of them exhibit a constant
arrangement which in this particular group of royal graves can be
described as a general feature. The king's own ship in which he
regularly made his journeys, as a rule a vessel of something over

20 metres in length, was set up in the place which had been selected for the grave. A burial chamber of boards or of thick oak planks was erected amidships, but in the form of a ship's tent with a sharp gable, and there the dead man was laid to rest on a bed of down and pillows. Remains of clothing are found worked with gold and with embroidery and *appliqués* of vari-coloured silks; there are cloths woven in patterns and long friezes of tapestries woven in pictures. The personal equipment was the richest possible, we must believe, though practically all the ship-graves were plundered in ancient times, so that now very little in the way of ornaments and weapons is found. In Storhaugen on Karmøy, the only grave of this type which had not been touched, were found a gold ring, playing-pieces of glass and amber, and all the usual weapons.

The whole ship was freighted in the same luxurious fashion. We need only mention the Oseberg grave, where the conditions were so exceptionally favourable that everything was preserved complete; in addition to all the gear of the ship, the mast, oars, anchor, gang-plank, &c., there were two large tents, a four-wheeled wagon, four sledges, three or four beds, a large number of chests, buckets and pails, implements for weaving and other handcrafts, and much else. There was also an offering of many kinds of animals at the burial. In the Oseberg ship were found thirteen horses, six dogs, a whole young ox, and a severed ox-head; in the Gokstad ship a similar number of horses and dogs and also a peacock. Finally there was in the Oseberg grave a very interesting feature, the remains of skeletons of two women, one elderly and one young, one of them (but it is uncertain which) in all probability a serving-woman sacrificed in order that she might accompany her mistress. When everything was disposed in order, an immense mound was raised over the grave and the ship, composed for the most part either of thick clay or of grass turf alone, a solicitude which we have to thank for several of these ships being found in a remarkably well-preserved state. The ship-graves unroll to our gaze a complete picture of the life of the time, ranging from all kinds of everyday things for household work up to the highest forms of decorative art in woodcarving and weaving. Scarcely anywhere else in Europe is the whole inventory of the early Middle Ages known in such complete detail as in Norway. . . .

Of the conceptions which the inhabitants of the north entertained at different periods of the places where the dead had their dwelling, only the manner of burial can give us information. We have seen above how the Scandinavians at all periods must have believed that death consisted in the desertion of the man by the spiritual being which controlled him, in order to live elsewhere. The mode of burial may be judged to be very near the base of this belief. From the early stone age no graves are known; but in the Danish kitchen middens the bodies lie among the remains of provisions. The significance of this can hardly be anything else than an intention that the soul, which was believed to require sustenance, might find it as near as possible and remain in a dwelling-station near the survivors. The open tombs of the late stone age with their furnishing were undoubtedly regarded as a place of resort or refuge for the soul, in the same way that a house is for men. At the close of the stone age the dead were placed in completely closed stone tombs or coffins. The explanation of this form of burial must be that men now had the notion of a kingdom of the dead to which the soul went immediately after death. The same idea must lie beneath the cremation of the bronze age, which for a long period went side by side with burial in closed graves. In both of these methods of burial, however, there seems to have been another motive present, a precaution due to the belief, so strongly developed in the north, in the hauntings of the dead. Both the tightly closed graves and, still more, cremation (which was introduced from the south) gave security against the dead man's walking again. In heathen society it was a duty to give certain attentions to corpses immediately after death; these offices to the dead were called *nābjargir*, the most important of which seems to have been the closing of the nostrils, a custom which must be regarded in the light of the ancient belief that the soul passes through the nose and mouth. When these openings were stopped the soul was prevented from returning to the body, that is, the dead man was prevented from walking again as a spook. From the same motive the body of any one who walked after death was dug up and burned.

The megalithic graves of the Stone Age may be regarded as the starting-point of the belief in larger realms of the dead. And just as the megalithic tomb must have been the burial place of a family, we know examples from Iceland of noble families who had a special hill which they entered after death. The common Germanic name for the subterranean abode for all the dead appears in Old Norse as Hel (etymologically "Covering"). Common Germanic also was the belief that the dead must wander a long way before they find their appointed resting-places. When in Norse sources a journey over a river or the sea is indicated, this may be connected with the mighty river Gjǫll which divided the realm of Hel from the world of the living, or it may be a poetic tradition from the Skjǫld story, in which the hero also comes as an infant in a ship to this world. These myths are undoubtedly connected with the idea that the dead had to make a journey over the sea to the other world. The same conception finds expression in the custom of burying the dead in a ship, described in an earlier chapter. We may also recall Balder's funeral, where his body was actually placed in a ship that was launched out to sea. The same sort of ship-funeral appears again in Snorri's account of King Haki in Uppsala (*Ynglinga saga*, ch. 27) and in Scyld's obsequies in *Beowulf*.

CHRISTOPHER HAWKES

The Prehistoric Roots of European Culture and History

WHAT is characteristic of Europe is not its internal complexities of race so much as its attainment already by the Middle Bronze Age of so large a measure of a cultural unity and coherence absolutely distinctive of itself. Therein lie the prehistoric foundations of European history.

We have repeatedly spoken of this as a cultural balance, and the metaphor applied to our foundations is just, for equilibrium is never far from instability, and instability and movement, elasticity and change, have been of the essence of the European endeavour to "live well." We have long ago seen that the dawn of civilization broke in the East, and that from the earliest Neolithic onwards its spread westward over Europe was an affair of Oriental influence, the West receiving, tardily and in comparative poverty, what the East was only giving after long familiarity within its own borders. But we have never found it possible to call this reception merely passive. The peoples of Europe already had developed cultural traditions within the limits imposed by their Mesolithic economy, and the spontaneity and adaptive vigour with which they took to themselves

From *The Prehistoric Foundations of Europe*. London: Methuen & Co. Ltd.; 1940, pp.381-4. By permission of Methuen & Co. Ltd.

the elements of Oriental culture that reached them typify not passive reception but positive reaction. From the Danubian Neolithic to the Mycenaean Bronze Age, the result was characteristically not second-hand reflexion of Eastern achievement, but integration of Eastern with native elements in something essentially new. And the very remoteness and poverty that divided Europe from Mesopotamia or Egypt was a naturally imposed safeguard against Orientalization. For, above all, it kept most of Europe for thousands of years free of the "urban revolution" which set in so early in the history of the Near East and set its magnificent achievement of initial civilization in a rigid framework of conservatism under the absolute rule of priest and king. Writing and numeration, astronomy and mathematics, were all invented in the East to be pinned to the service of a static civilization dominated by the temple and the court, and it was the hard mould of urban culture that kept that civilization static. When the culture of cities came to Europe, it was taken into a social tradition already matured on other lines, and the ancient inventions and discoveries of Sumer, Babylon, and Egypt were vitalized by the Greeks, in whom the European dawn of civilization passed into bright morning. The culture of the Greek city-states absorbed what it drew from the Orient only to withstand and finally to transform the mass of what the Orient retained, and the tradition of the Greek people went back far beyond their Orientalizing period to the Mycenaean Bronze Age of which we have here written, in the literature of their mythology and above all in the unique possession of the Homeric poems. It is in Homer that the citizens of ancient and modern Europe alike come closest to their culture's prehistoric foundations, and the moderns have what the ancients had not, the clue of archaeology not only to the Cretan labyrinth of the Aegean world of which Homer kept the memory, but to the whole maze of prehistoric civilization in Europe. In this book we have tried to follow that clue through the many meanderings that have led to the point at which the Minotaur was slain, and with the Fall of Knossos the culture of the European Bronze Age stands free of the Oriental debt whence for two thousand years its independence had been slowly matured.

Its foundations were formed of a balance of cultures, in which Mediterranean and Western, Alpine and Danubian, Nordic and East European elements of Stone Age inheritance were poised against the civilizing influence of the Orient, in an equilibrium dominated by the peoples of Aryan speech and warrior tradition, who from the years before and after 2000 B.C. onwards have given so much to the moving pattern of European achievement. The movement of the pattern, the instability of the balance, seem throughout characteristic of historic process in Europe, as against the "changeless

East," which invented civilization only to stagnate in it. In particular, our balance of 1400 B.C. proved as unstable as the balance of the Antonine Age from which Gibbon traced the Decline and Fall that was the counterpart of the rise of mediaeval and modern Europe. For the Mycenaean supremacy, spreading out to its share in the great age of land-raids and sea-raids, the Trojan War, and the whole turmoil in which the Bronze Age of the Near East during the next three centuries or so sank to its end, collapsed in exhaustion, and its seats of power in the Peloponnese fell before the Dorian invasion from the hinterland of North Greece where Mycenaean culture had stopped short, leaving the fatal blank we marked at the beginning of this chapter. And the Oriental reaction to its down-

THE UNKNOWN BEAST OF LASCAUX

fall brought the Phoenicians on to the seas, to reach as far west as Carthage and Spain, and in due course the Etruscans from Asia Minor to Italy, while the Greek world emerged from this Dark Age with the walled cities and the alphabetic writing of the Near East, painfully rebuilding a new cultural poise of its own, in which Hellenism set its citizens in antithesis to the "barbarians" of Europe, even while colonizing their shores. And from that antithesis sprang the division of Europe between the Graeco-Roman world and the peoples beyond, whom it could never conquer, so that it was not till the centuries of its Decline and Fall, of the Germanic migrations, and of the rise of Christendom, that a balance of cultures could again be struck, in which European civilization could again be at one. And thereafter the balance has changed into a Balance of Power. Yet the instability of Europe's equilibrium has been not its weakness but its strength: its safeguard against Oriental stagnation, and perhaps of an inner virtue of its own which possesses absolute value for human progress. For we saw in our prologue that change and adaptiveness seemed the grand biological condition of survival in evolution, and suspected that of human progress the same was true. And the Europeans, who from their Palaeolithic past made a Mesolithic background ready for civilization, and thereon fashioned civilization into a thing of their own, have throughout our story kept that adaptiveness alive, and so have built on foundations whose instability of balance has been the measure of their success under the law of all life.

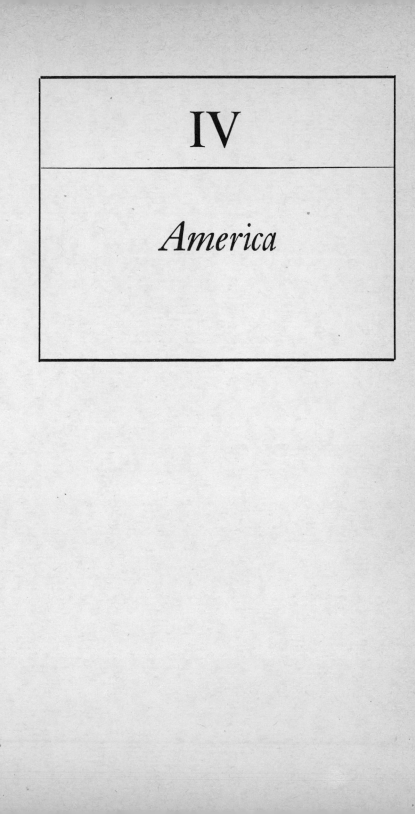

IV

America

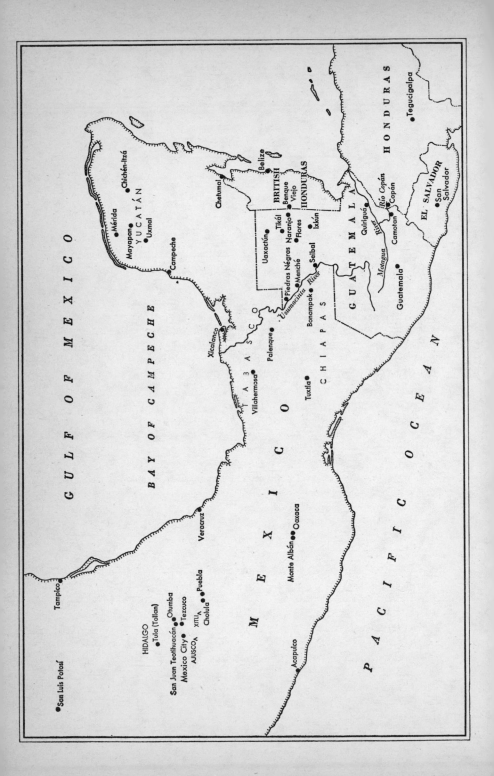

GULF OF MEXICO

BAY OF CAMPECHE

PACIFIC OCEAN

HONDURAS

Tegucigalpa

BRITISH

HONDURAS

Belize

Benque
Viejo

Chetumal

EL SALVADOR

Río Copán

San
Salvador

Copán

Chichén-Itzá

Mérida

Mayapan

YUCATÁN

Uxmal

Tikal

Naranjo

Ixkún

Flores

Quiriguá

GUATEMALA

River

Camotan

Uaxactún

Campeche

Piedras Negras

Menché

Seibal

Usumacinta

River

Bonampak

Guatemala

Motagua

Xicalanco

T A B A S C O

Palenque

CHIAPAS

Tuxtla

Villahermosa

M E X I C O

Veracruz

Monte Albán

Oaxaca

Otumba

HIDALGO

Tula (Tollan)

Tezcuco

San Juan Teotihuacán

XITLA

Puebla

Mexico City

AJUSCO

Cholula

Tampico

Acapulco

San Luis Potosí

INTRODUCTORY

THE American hemisphere saw nothing of the slow, distressful evolution of man. The men-apes and ape-men in all their uncouth variety never set foot there. This seems fitting for continents that were to be known as the New World. *Homo sapiens* arrived in America ready made. That is accepted—and also that his first representatives entered from eastern Asia, probably by way of the Bering Straits. The date at which this peopling began is still uncertain, but at least it is now very generally agreed that it was during the latter part of the final glaciation—say between 10,000 and 20,000 B.C.

A far more significant subject of disagreement concerns the possibility of there having been later immigrations. Did further groups arrive after the spread of farming in Asia, or even within historical times? This is a question of quite exceptional interest from the point of view of innate cultural tendencies in man. It is true that the civilizations which developed in the New World had striking differences from those of the Old, but essentially they were very much the same. Did they grow up from foundations laid by humble hunters and food gatherers in complete independence of Asia?

Most people think that they did, or at the most with the help of some faint idea of the existence of Asian civilization spread by wandering hunters or traders. Yet others are convinced that there must have been later contacts. Eric Thompson, for example, believes that considerable numbers of immigrants arrived by the same Bering Strait route during the last two millennia B.C., bringing with them the crafts of potting, spinning and weaving and a knowledge of agriculture. The very latest arrivals, he thinks, may have "left Siberia as late as the beginning of the Christian era," and have introduced certain religious concepts that seem to be shared by American and Asian cultures.

The strongest arguments against this point of view are found in the absence of either Asian domestic plants and animals, or of pre-Columbian Asian artifacts, on American soil. It also seems difficult to explain why, if peoples of higher culture kept entering through Alaska, the high civilizations developed thousands of miles to the south.

If the orthodox belief in independent development is the true one, it is still difficult enough to explain why high civilizations grew up in Central and South America and not in the more temperate lands to the north. The south-west of the United States was well to the fore in the early days of farming, yet the step towards civilization was not taken there. Much later the Pueblo Indians again seemed about to take it (in the creation of little towns such as Mesa Verde), but again they failed. It is particularly hard to account for the birth of Maya civilization in a region of bad climate and poor natural resources. It just has to be accepted that these things came to pass—and the fact that they did bursts the seams of the strait jacket of geographical determinism.

What happened, then, was that more than six thousand years after men had first reached the southern extremity of America and more than two thousand years after the beginning of farming in Middle America, advances towards higher civilization began to be made at various points along a relatively narrow strip of country between the Valley of Mexico and Peru. Many different cultural groups arose, became more or less powerful and prosperous, influenced one another, changed, competed and often dominated one another. This process was still going on when the Europeans arrived and native American civilization in all its variety collapsed fast and horribly.

The Inca, Maya and Aztec peoples were dominant at the time of the Spanish conquest, and it is largely for this reason that their names have always been given very great prominence in American history. It is now known that they were surrounded and preceded by numbers of other peoples of equal, and often higher, cultural distinction, even if usually of less political power. Yet it is justifiable to arrange the literature under their names, partly because of the nature of that literature itself, partly because the civilizations of the Inca, Maya and Aztecs did to some extent reflect that of their neighbours and embody that of their predecessors.

I. *The Maya*

THE Maya civilization was the only one in America to possess a developed hieroglyphic writing. For this reason, and because of its achievements in astronomy and mathematics and the excellence of its architecture and sculpture, it is usually judged to be supreme. It first assumed its distinctive "form" in the rain-soaked lowland jungle country lying north and north-west of the Guatemalan highlands and in the adjoining uplands of Chiapas. The heart of this formative region of Mayan culture is the Peten district of Guatemala and the adjoining parts of British Honduras and Mexico. It contains Tikal and many of the greatest cities—and today is almost uninhabited.

Here the civilization took shape during the early centuries of our era. Already its learned men were preoccupied with time and the calendar cult—an obsession which inspired so much of Mayan life. In the so-called Classic period from the fourth to the ninth centuries A.D., very many ceremonial centres with their great courts, temple pyramids and other religious buildings came into being all the way from the Pacific to Yucatan; hundreds of calendar stones (stelae) were set up. Then, during the ninth and tenth centuries, one after another these centres were abandoned (p. 647 ff., II) and the Maya returned to a much simpler way of life. Meanwhile, Mexican influence made itself felt in the Yucatan peninsula, and in about A.D. 1000 the Itza people established themselves at Chichen Itza (already an important ceremonial centre in Classic times), introducing Mexican artistic and religious forms—including the worship of the feathered serpent, Quetzalcoatl. Later the main centre of power shifted to the city of Mayapan to the west of Chichen Itza, but a few decades before the Spaniards arrived it had been overthrown by a successful revolt and centralized government brought to an end. Thus, unlike the Incas and the Aztecs, the Maya were far gone in decline before the Conquistadors came to dispatch them.

JOHN L. STEPHENS

The Travels of
John Lloyd Stephens
and Frederick Catherwood
and Their Explorations
of the Maya Ruins

Voyage and Impressions of Belize

BEING intrusted by the President with a Special Confidential Mission
to Central America, on Wednesday, the third of October, 1839, I
embarked on board the British brig Mary Ann, Hampton, master,
for the Bay of Honduras. The brig was lying in the North River,
with her anchor apeak and sails loose, and in a few minutes, in company with a large whaling-ship bound for the Pacific, we were
under way. It was before seven o'clock in the morning: the streets
and wharves were still; the Battery was desolate; and, at the moment
of leaving it on a voyage of uncertain duration, seemed more beautiful than I had ever known it before.

Opposite the Quarantine Ground, a few friends who had accompanied me on board left me; in an hour the pilot followed; at dusk
the dark outline of the highlands of Neversink was barely visible,
and the next morning we were fairly at sea.

My only fellow-passenger was Mr. Catherwood, an experienced
traveller and personal friend, who had passed more than ten years
of his life in diligently studying the antiquities of the Old World;
and whom, as one familiar with the remains of ancient architectural

From *Incidents of Travel in Central America, Chiapas and Yucatan*, Vol. I. London:
John Murray; 1842, pp. 9-16, 86-109, 115-16, 117-29.

greatness, I engaged, immediately on receiving my appointment, to accompany me in exploring the ruins of Central America.

Hurried on by a strong northeaster, on the ninth we were within the region of the trade-winds, on the tenth within the tropics, and on the eleventh, with the thermometer at 80°, but a refreshing breeze, we were moving gently between Cuba and St. Domingo, with both in full sight. For the rest, after eighteen days of boisterous weather, drenched with tropical rains, on the twenty-ninth we were driven inside the Lighthouse reef, and, avoiding altogether the regular pilot-ground, at midnight reached St. George's Bay, about twenty miles from Belize. A large brig, loaded with mahogany, was lying at anchor, with a pilot on board, waiting for favourable weather to put to sea. The pilot had with him his son, a lad about sixteen, cradled on the water, whom Captain Hampton knew, and determined to take on board.

It was full moonlight when the boy mounted the deck and gave us the pilot's welcome. I could not distinguish his features, but I could see that he was not white; and his voice was as soft as a woman's. He took his place at the wheel, and, loading the brig with canvas, told us of the severe gales on the coast, of the fears entertained for our safety, of disasters and shipwrecks, and of a pilot who, on a night which we well remembered, had driven his vessel over a sunken reef.

At seven o'clock the next morning we saw Belize, appearing, if there be no sin in comparing it with cities consecrated by time and venerable associations, like Venice and Alexandria, to rise out of the water. A range of white houses extended a mile along the shore, terminated at one end by the Government House, and at the other by the barracks, and intersected by the river Belize, the bridge across which formed a picturesque object; while the fort on a little island at the mouth of the river, the spire of a Gothic church behind the Government House, and groves of cocoanut-trees, which at that distance reminded us of the palm-trees of Egypt, gave it an appearance of actual beauty. Four ships, three brigs, sundry schooners, bungoes, canoes, and a steamboat, were riding at anchor in the harbour; alongside the vessels were rafts of mahogany; far out, a negro was paddling a log of the same costly timber; and the government dory which boarded us when we came to anchor was made of the trunk of a mahogany-tree.

We landed in front of the warehouse of Mr. Coffin, the consignee of the vessel. There was no hotel in the place, but Mr. Coffin undertook to conduct us to a lady who, he thought, could accommodate us with lodgings.

The heavy rain from which we had suffered at sea had reached Belize. The streets were flooded, and in places there were large puddles, which it was difficult to cross. At the extreme end of the principal street we meet the *"lady,"* Miss——, a mulatto woman, who could only give us board. Mr. Coffin kindly offered the use of an unoccupied house on the other side of the river to sleep in, and we returned.

By this time I had twice passed the whole length of the principal street, and the town seemed in the entire possession of blacks. The bridge, the market-place, the streets and stores were thronged with them, and I might have fancied myself in the capital of a Negro republic. They were a fine-looking race, tall, straight, and athletic, with skins black, smooth, and glossy as velvet, and well dressed, the men in white cotton shirts and trousers, with straw hats, and the women in white frocks with short sleeves and broad red borders, and adorned with large red earrings and necklaces; and I could not help remarking that the frock was their only article of dress, and that it was the fashion of these sable ladies to drop this considerably from off the right shoulder, and to carry the skirt in the left hand, and raise it to any height necessary for crossing puddles.

On my way back I stopped at the house of a merchant, whom I found at what is called a second breakfast. The gentleman sat on one side of the table and his lady on the other. At the head was a British officer, and opposite him a mulatto; on his left was another officer, and opposite him also a mulatto. By chance a place was made for me between the two colored gentlemen. Some of my countrymen, perhaps, would have hesitated about taking it, but I did not; both were well dressed, well educated, and polite. They talked of their mahogany works, of England, hunting, horses, ladies, and wine; and before I had been an hour in Belize I learned that the great work of practical amalgamation, the subject of so much angry controversy at home, had been going on quietly for generations; that colour was considered mere matter of taste; and that some of the most respectable inhabitants had black wives and mongrel children, whom they educated with as much care, and made money for with as much zeal, as if their skins were perfectly white.

I hardly knew whether to be shocked or amused at this condition of society; and, in the mean time, joined Mr. Catherwood, to visit the house offered by Mr. Coffin. It was situated on the opposite side of the river, and the road to it was ankle deep in mud. At the gate was a large puddle, which we cleared by a jump; the house was built on piles about two feet high, and underneath was water nearly a foot deep. We ascended on a plank to the sill of the door, and entered a large room occupying the whole of the first floor, and perfectly empty. The upper story was tenanted by a family of negroes; in the yard was a house swarming with negroes; and all over, in the yard and in front, were picturesque groups of little negroes of both sexes, and naked as they were born. We directed the room to be swept and our luggage brought there; and, as we left the house, we remembered Captain Hampton's description before our arrival, and felt the point of his concluding remark, that Belize was the last place made.

We returned; and, while longing for the comfort of a good hotel, received through Mr. Goff, the consul of the United States, an invitation from his excellency, Colonel McDonald, to the Government House, and information that he would send the government dory to the brig for our luggage. As this was the first appointment I had ever held from government, and I was not sure of ever holding another, I determined to make the most of it, and accepted at once his excellency's invitation.

There was a steamboat for Izabal, the port of Guatemala, lying at Belize; and, on my way to the Government House, I called upon Señor Comyano, the agent, who told me that she was to go up the next day; but added, with great courtesy, that, if I wished it, he would detain her a few days for my convenience. Used to submitting to the despotic regulations of steamboat agents at home, this seemed a higher honour than the invitation of his excellency; but, not wishing to push my fortune too far, I asked a delay of one day only.

The Government House stands in a handsome situation at the extreme end of the town, with a lawn extending to the water, and ornamented with cocoanut-trees. Colonel McDonald, a veteran six feet high, and one of the most military-looking men I ever saw, received me at the gate. In an hour the dory arrived with our luggage, and at five o'clock we sat down to dinner. We had at table Mr. Newport, chaplain, and for fifteen years parish clergyman at Belize; Mr. Walker, secretary of the government, and holding, besides, such a list of offices as would make the greatest pluralist among us feel insignificant; and several other gentlemen of Belize, office-holders, civil and military, in whose agreeable society we sat till eleven o'clock.

The next day we had to make preparations for our journey into the interior, besides which we had an opportunity of seeing a little of Belize. The Honduras Almanac, which assumes to be the chronicler of this settlement, throws a romance around its early history by ascribing its origin to a Scotch buccaneer named Wallace. The fame of the wealth of the New World, and the return of the Spanish galleons laden with the riches of Mexico and Peru, brought upon the coast of America hordes of adventurers—to call them by no harsher name—from England and France, of whom Wallace, one of the most noted and daring, found refuge and security behind the keys and reefs which protect the harbour of Belize. The place where he built his log huts and fortalice is still pointed out; but their site is now occupied by warehouses. Strengthened by a close alliance with the Indians of the Moscheto shore, and by the adhesion of numerous British adventurers, who descended upon the coast of Honduras for the purpose of cutting mahogany, he set the Spaniards at defiance. Ever since, the territory of Belize has been the subject of negotiation and contest, and to this day the people of Central America claim it as their own. It has grown by the exportation of mahogany; but, as the trees in the neighbourhood have been almost all cut down, and Central America is so impoverished by wars that it offers but a poor market for British goods, the place is languishing, and will probably continue to dwindle away until the enterprise of her merchants discovers other channels of trade.

At this day it contains a population of six thousand, of which four thousand are blacks, who are employed by the merchants in gangs as mahogany cutters. Their condition was always better than that of plantation slaves; even before the act for the general abolition of slavery throughout the British dominions, they were actually free; and, on the thirty-first of August, 1839, a year before the time appointed by the act, by a general meeting and agreement of proprietors, even the nominal yoke of bondage was removed.

The event was celebrated, says the Honduras Almanac, by religious ceremonies, processions, bands of music, and banners with devices: "The sons of Ham respect the memory of Wilberforce"; "The Queen, God bless her"; "McDonald forever"; "Civil and religious liberty all over the world." Nelson Schaw, "a snowdrop of the first water," continues the Almanac, "advanced to his excellency, Colonel McDonald, and spoke as follows: 'On the part of my emancipated brothers and sisters, I venture to approach your Excellency, to entreat you to thank our most gracious Queen for all that she has done for us. We will pray for her; we will fight for her; and, if it is necessary, we will die for her. We thank your Excellency for all you have done for us. God bless your Excellency! God bless her Excellency, Mrs. McDonald, and all the royal family! Come, my countrymen, hurrah! Dance, ye black rascals; the flag of England flies over your heads, and every rustle of its folds knocks the fetters off the limbs of the poor slave. Hubbabboo Cochalorum Gee!' "

Journey to Copan. First View of the Ruins, and Reflections on Their Origins

COPAN, in Honduras and very much an eastern outpost of high Maya culture of the Classic period, was a ceremonial city of great distinction. It seems to have been a seat of scientific studies, its astronomers leading the way in solving problems concerning the exact length of the tropical year and other matters important for religious observances and divinations. It also had excellent architects and sculptors. The stelae, so many of which were drawn by Frederick Catherwood, are noteworthy for the way that the subjects are sculptured to stand out boldly from the shaft.

TURNING away from the church, we passed the brow of a hill, behind which was a collection of huts almost concealed from sight, and occupied by our friends of the night before. Very soon we commenced ascending a mountain. At a short distance we met a corpse borne on a rude bier of sticks, upon the shoulders of Indians, naked except a piece of cotton cloth over the loins, and shaking awfully under the movements of its carriers. Soon after we met another, borne in the same way, but wrapped in matting, and accompanied by three or four men and a young woman. Both were on their way to the graveyard of the village church. Ascending, we reached the top of a mountain, and saw behind us a beautiful valley extending toward Jocotan, but all waste, and suggesting a feeling of regret that so beautiful a country should bc in such miserable hands.

At half past twelve we descended to the banks of the Copan River. It was broad and rapid, and in the middle was a large sandbar. We had difficulty in fording it; and some of the baggage, particularly the beds and bedding, got wet. From the opposite side we again commenced ascending another ridge, and from the top saw the river winding through the valley. As we crossed, by a sudden turn it flowed along the base, and we looked directly down upon it. Descending this mountain, we came to a beautiful stream, where a gray-haired Indian woman and a pretty little girl, pictures of youth and old age, were washing clothes. We dismounted, and sat down on the bank to wait for the muleteer. I forgot to mention that he had with him a boy about thirteen or fourteen years old, a fine little fellow, upon whom he imposed the worst part of the burden, that of chasing the mules, and who really seemed, like Baron Münchhausen's dog, in danger of running his legs off.

Our breach with the muleteer had not been healed, and at first we ascribed to him some agency in our troubles at Comotan. At all events, if it had not been for him, we should not have stopped there. All day he had been particularly furious with the mules, and they had been particularly perverse, and now they had gone astray; and it was an hour before we heard his spiteful voice, loading them with curses. We mounted again and at four o'clock saw at a distance a hacienda, on the opposite side of a valley. It stood alone, and promised a quiet resting-place for the night. We turned off from the *camino real* into a wild path, stony, and overgrown with bushes, and so steep that we were obliged to dismount, let the mules go ahead, and hold on ourselves by the bushes to descend. At the foot of the hill we mounted and crossed a stream, where a little boy, playing in the water, saluted me by crossing his arms upon his breast, and then passed on to Mr. Catherwood. This was a favourable omen; and, as we climbed up a steep hill, I felt that here, in this lonely spot, away from the gathering-places of men, we must meet kindness. On the top of the hill a woman, with a naked child in her arms and a smile on her face, stood watching our toilsome ascent; and when we asked her if we could make *posada* there, she answered, in the kindest phrase of the country, with a face that spoke even a warmer welcome than her words, *"como non?"* "Why not?" and when she saw that our servant had pineapples in his *alforjas,* she asked why he brought them, and if he did not know that she had plenty.

The situation of the hacienda of San Antonio was wildly beautiful. It had a clearing for a cowyard, a plantation of corn, tobacco, and plantains, and the opening gave a view of the high mountains by which it was surrounded. The house was built of poles plastered with mud, and against the wall in front of the door was a figure of the Saviour on the cross, on a white cotton cloth hung round with votive offerings. The naked child which the mother carried in her arms was called Maria de los Angeles. While supper was in preparation the master of the house arrived, a swarthy, grim-looking fellow, with a broad-brimmed sombrero and huge whiskers, and mounted on a powerful young horse, which he was just breaking to the mountain-roads; when he knew that we were strangers asking hospitality, his harsh features relaxed, and he repeated the welcome the woman had given us.

Unfortunately, the boy of the muleteer was taken very ill; his master paid no attention to him, and, while the poor little fellow was groaning under a violent fever, ate on with perfect indifference. We made him a comfortable bed on the piazza, and Mr. Catherwood gave him a dose of medicine. Our evening passed very differently from the last. Our host and hostess were a kind-hearted and simple couple. It was the first time they had ever met with men from another country, and they asked many questions, and examined our little travelling apparatus, particularly our plated cups, knives, forks, and spoons; we showed them our watches, compass, sextant, chronometer, thermometer, telescope, &c., and the woman, with great discernment, said that we must be very rich, and had *"muchos ideas,"* "many ideas." They asked us about our wives, and we learned that our simple-minded host had two, one of whom lived at Hocotan, and that he passed a week alternately with each. We told him that in England he would be transported, and in the North imprisoned for life for such indulgences, to which he responded that they were barbarous countries; and the woman, although she thought a man ought to be content with one, said that it was no *pecado* or crime to have two; but I heard them say, *sotto voce*, that we were "mas Christianos," or better Christians than they. He assisted us in swinging our hammocks, and about nine o'clock we drove out the dogs and pigs, lighted cigars, and went to bed. Including servants, women and children, we numbered eleven in the room. All around were little balls of fire, shining and disappearing with the puffs of the cigars. One by one these went out, and we fell asleep.

In the morning we all rose together. The boy was much better, but we did not think him in a condition to travel. His brutal master, however, insisted upon his going. For all that our kind friends had done for us, they would have charged us nothing; but, besides compensating them in money, we distributed among them various trifles, and, when bidding them farewell, I saw with regret a ring which I had given her sparkling on his finger. After we had mounted, the little boy whom we had met at the stream came staggering under a load of six freshly-cut pineapples; and even when we had started, the woman ran after me with a piece of fresh sugar-cane.

All parted at the hacienda of San Antonio with kind feelings except our surly muleteer, who was indignant, as he said, that we made presents to everybody except to him. The poor boy was most grateful, and, unfortunately for him, we had given him a knife, which made the muleteer jealous.

Almost immediately from the hacienda we entered a thick wood, dense as that of the Mico Mountain, and almost as muddy. The ascent was toilsome, but the top was open, and so covered with that beautiful plant that we called it the Mountain of Aloes. Some were just peeping out of the ground, others were twenty or thirty feet high, and some gigantic stalks were dead; flowers which would have kindled rapture in the breast of beauty had bloomed and died on this desolate mountain, unseen except by a passing Indian.

In descending we lost the path, and wandered for some time before we recovered it. Almost immediately we commenced ascending another mountain, and from its top looked completely over a third, and, at a great distance, saw a large hacienda. Our road lay directly along the edge of precipice, from which we looked down upon the tops of gigantic pines at a great distance beneath us. Very soon the path became so broken, and ran so near the edge of a precipice, that I called to Mr. Catherwood to dismount. The precipice was on the left side, and I had advanced so far that, on the back of a perverse mule, I did not venture to make any irregular movement, and rode for some moments in great anxiety. Somewhere on this road, but unmarked by any visible sign, we crossed the boundary-line of the state of Guatemala and entered Honduras.

At two o'clock we reached the village of Copan, which consisted of half a dozen miserable huts thatched with corn. Our appearance created a great sensation. All the men and women gathered around us to gaze. We inquired immediately for the ruins, but none of the villagers could direct us to them, and all advised us to go to the hacienda of Don Gregorio. We had no wish to stop at a village, and told the muleteer to go on, but he refused, and said that his engagement was to conduct us to Copan. After a long wrangle we prevailed, and, riding through a piece of woods, forded once more the Copan River, and came out upon a clearing, on one side of which was a hacienda, with a tile roof, and having cosina and other outbuildings, evidently the residence of a rich proprietor. We were greeted by a pack of barking dogs, and all the doorways were filled with women and children, who seemed in no small degree surprised at our appearance. There was not a man in sight; but the women received us kindly, and told us that Don Gregorio would return soon, and would conduct us to the ruins. Immediately the fire was rekindled in the cosina, the sound of the patting of hands gave notice of the making of tortillas, and in half an hour dinner was ready. It was served up on a massive silver plate, with water in a silver tankard, but without knife, fork, or spoon; soup or caldo was served in cups to be drunk. Nevertheless, we congratulated ourselves upon having fallen into such good quarters.

In a short time a young man arrived on horseback, gaily dressed, with an embroidered shirt, and accompanied by several men driving a herd of cattle. An ox was selected, a rope thrown around its horns, and the animal was drawn up to the side of the house, and, by another rope around its legs, thrown down. Its feet were tied together, its head drawn back by a rope tied from its horns to its tail, and with one thrust of the machete the artery of life was severed. The pack of hungry dogs stood ready, and, with a horrible clicking, lapped up the blood with their tongues. All the women were looking on, and a young girl took a puppy dog and rubbed its nose in the crimson stream, to give it early a taste for blood. The ox was skinned, the meat separated from the bones, and, to the entire destruction of steaks, sirloins, and roasting-pieces, in an hour the whole animal was hanging in long strings on a line before the door.

During this operation Don Gregorio arrived. He was about fifty, had large black whiskers, and a beard of several days' growth; and, from the behaviour of all around, it was easy to see that he was a domestic tyrant. The glance which he threw at us before dismounting seemed to say, "Who are *you?*" but, without a word, he entered the house. We waited until he had finished his dinner, when, supposing that to be the favourable moment, I entered the house. In my intercourse with the world I have more than once found my overtures to an acquaintance received coldly, but I never experienced anything quite so cool as the don's reception of me. I told him that we had come into that neighbourhood to visit the ruins of Copan, and his manner said, What's that to me? but he answered that they were on the other side of the river. I asked him whether we could procure a guide, and again he said that the only man who knew anything about them lived on the other side of the river. As yet we did not make sufficient allowance for the distracted state of the country, nor the circumstance that a man might incur danger to himself by giving shelter to suspected persons; but, relying on the reputation of the country for hospitality, and the proof of it which we had already met with, I was rather slow in coming to the disagreeable conclusion that we were not welcome. This conclusion, however, was irresistible. The don was not pleased with our looks. I ordered the muleteer to saddle the mules; but the rascal enjoyed our confusion, and positively refused to saddle his beasts again that day. We applied to Don Gregorio himself, offering to pay him; and, as Augustin said, in the hope of getting rid of us, he lent us two, on which to ride back to the village. Unfortunately, the guide we sought was away; a brisk cockfight was then pending, and we received no encouragement, either from the appearance of the people or from invitation, to bring back our luggage to that place. And we learned, what was very provoking, that Don Gregorio was the great man of Copan; the richest man, and the petty tyrant; and that it would be most unfortunate to have a rupture with him, or even to let it be known at the village that we were not well received at his house. Reluctantly, but in the hope of making a more favourable impression, we returned to the hacienda. Mr. C. dismounted on the steps, and took a seat on the piazza. I happened to dismount outside; and, before moving, took a survey of the party. The don sat on a chair, with our detestable muleteer by his side, and a half-concealed smile of derision on his face, talking of "idols," and looking at me. By this time eight or ten men, sons, servants, and labourers, had come in from their day's work, but not one offered to take my mule, or made any of those demonstrations of civility which are always shown to a welcome guest. The women turned away their heads, as if they had been reproved for receiving us; and all the men, taking their cue from the don, looked so insulting, that I told Mr. Catherwood we would tumble our luggage into the road, and curse him for an inhospitable churl; but Mr. Catherwood warned me against it, urging that, if we had an open quarrel with him, after all our trouble we would be prevented seeing the ruins. The don probably suspected something of what passed; and, fearing that he might push things too far, and bring a stain upon his name, pointed to a chair, and asked me to take a seat. With a great effort, I resolved to smother my indignation until I could pour it out with safety. Augustin was very indignant at the treatment we received; on the road he had sometimes swelled his own importance by telling of the flags hoisted and cannon fired when we left Belize; and here he hoisted more flags and fired more guns than usual, beginning with forty guns, and afterward going on to a cannonade; but it would not do. The don did not like us, and probably was willing to hoist flags, and fire cannons too, as at Belize, when we should go away.

Toward evening the skin of an ox was spread upon the piazza, corn in ears thrown upon it, and all the men, with the don at their head, sat down to shell it. The cobs were carried to the kitchen to burn, the corn taken up in baskets, and three pet hogs, which had been grunting outside in expectation of the feast, were let in to pick up the scattered grains. During the evening no notice was taken of us, except that the wife of the don sent a message by Augustin that supper was preparing; and our wounded pride was relieved, and our discontent somewhat removed, by an additional message that they had an oven and flour, and would bake us some bread if we wished to buy it.

After supper all prepared for sleep. The don's house had two sides, an inside and an out. The don and his family occupied the former, and we the latter; but we had not even this to ourselves. All along the wall were frames made of sticks about an inch thick, tied together with bark strings, over which the workmen spread an untanned oxhide for a bed. There were three hammocks besides ours, and I had so little room for mine that my body described an inverted parabola, with my heels as high as my head. It was vexatious and ridiculous; or, in the words of the English tourist in Fra Diavolo, it was "Shocking! positively shocking!"

In the morning Don Gregorio was in the same humour. We took no notice of him, but made our toilet under the shed with as much respect as possible to the presence of the female members of the family, who were constantly passing and repassing. We had made up our minds to hold on and see the ruins; and, fortunately, early in the morning, one of the crusty don's sons, a civil young man, brought over from the village José, the guide of whom we stood in need.

By reason of many vexatious delays, growing out of difficulties between José and the muleteer, we did not get away until nine o'clock. Very soon we left the path or road, and entered a large field, partially cultivated with corn, belonging to Don Gregorio. Riding some distance through this, we reached a hut, thatched with corn-leaves, on the edge of the woods, at which some workmen were preparing their breakfast. Here we dismounted, and, tying our mules to trees near by, entered the woods, José clearing a path before us with a machete; soon we came to the bank of a river, and saw directly opposite a stone wall, perhaps a hundred feet high, with furze growing out of the top, running north and south along the river, in some places fallen, but in others entire. It had more the character of a structure than any we had ever seen, ascribed to the aborigines of America, and formed part of the wall of Copan, an ancient city, on whose history books throw but little light.

I am entering abruptly upon new ground. Volumes without number have been written to account for the first peopling of America. By some the inhabitants of this continent have been regarded as a separate race, not descended from the same common father with the rest of mankind; others have ascribed their origin to some remnant of the antediluvian inhabitants of the earth, who survived the deluge which swept away the greatest part of the human species in the days of Noah, and hence have considered them the most ancient race of people on the earth. Under the broad range allowed by a descent from the sons of Noah, the Jews, the Canaanites, the Phoenicians, the Carthaginians, the Greeks, the Scythians in ancient times; the Chinese, the Swedes, the Norwegians, the Welsh, and the Spaniards in modern, have had ascribed to them the honour of peopling America. The two continents have been joined together and rent asunder by the shock of an earthquake; the fabled island of Atlantis has been lifted out of the ocean; and, not to be behind-hand, an enterprising American has turned the tables on the Old World, and planted the ark itself within the State of New York.

The monuments and architectural remains of the aborigines have heretofore formed but little part of the groundwork for these speculations. Dr. Robertson, in his History of America, lays it down as "a certain principle, that America was not peopled by any nation of the ancient continent which had made considerable progress in civilization." "The inhabitants of the New World," he says, "were in a state of society so extremely rude as to be unacquainted with those arts which are the first essays of human ingenuity in its advance toward improvement." Discrediting the glowing accounts of Cortez and his companions, of soldiers, priests, and civilians, all concurring in representations of the splendour exhibited in the buildings of Mexico, he says that the "houses of the people were mere huts, built with turf, or mud, or the branches of trees, like those of the rudest Indians." The temple of Cholula was nothing more than "a mound of earth, without any steps or any facing of stone, covered with grass and shrubs;" and, on the authority of persons long resident in New Spain, and who professed to have visited every part of it, he says that "there is not, in all the extent of that vast empire, a single monument or vestige of any building more ancient than the conquest." At that time, distrust was perhaps the safer side for the historian; but since Dr. Robertson wrote a new flood of light has poured upon the world, and the field of American antiquities has been opened.

The ignorance, carelessness, and indifference of the inhabitants of Spanish America on this subject are matter of wonder. In our own country, the opening of forests and the discovery of tumuli or mounds and fortifications, extending in ranges from the lakes through the valleys of the Ohio and Mississippi, mummies in a cave in Kentucky, the inscription on the rock at Dighton, supposed to be in Phoenician characters, and the ruins of walls and a great city in Arkansas and Wisconsin Territory, had suggested wild and wandering ideas in regard to the first peopling of this country, and the strong belief that powerful and populous nations had occupied it and had passed away, whose histories are entirely unknown. The same evidences continue in Texas, and in Mexico they assume a still more definite form.

The first new light thrown upon this subject as regards Mexico was by the great Humboldt, who visited that country at a time when, by the jealous policy of the government, it was almost as much closed against strangers as China is now. No man could have better deserved such fortune. At the time the monuments of the country were not a leading object of research; but Humboldt collected from various sources information and drawings, particularly of Mitla, or the Vale of the Dead; Xoxichalco, a mountain hewed down and terraced, and called the Hill of Flowers; and the great pyramid or Temple of Cholula he visited himself, of all which his own eloquent account is within reach of the reader. Unfortunately, of the great cities beyond the Vale of Mexico, buried in forests, ruined, desolate, and without a name, Humboldt never heard, or, at least, he never visited them. It is but lately that accounts of their existence reached Europe and our own country. These accounts, however vague and unsatisfactory, had roused our curiosity; though I ought perhaps to say that both Mr. C. and I were somewhat skeptical, and when we arrived at Copan, it was with the hope, rather than the expectation, of finding wonders.

Since the discovery of these ruined cities the prevailing theory has been, that they belonged to a race long anterior to that which inhabited the country at the time of the Spanish conquest. With regard to Copan, mention is made by the early Spanish historians of a place of that name, situated in the same region of country in which these ruins are found, which then existed as an inhabited city, and offered a formidable resistance to the Spanish arms, though there are circumstances which seem to indicate that the city referred to was inferior in strength and solidity of construction, and of more modern origin.

It stood in the old province of Chiquimula de Sierras, which was conquered by the officers of Pedro de Alvarado, but not one of the Spanish historians has given any particulars of this conquest. In 1530 the Indians of the province revolted, and attempted to throw off the yoke of Spain. Hernandez de Chaves was sent to subdue them, and, after many sanguinary battles, he encamped before Esquipulas, a place of arms belonging to a powerful cacique, which, on the fourth day, to use the words of the cacique himself, "more out of respect to the public tranquillity than from fear of the Spanish arms, determined to surrender," and, with the capital, the whole province submitted again to the Spanish dominion.

The cacique of Copan, whose name was Copán Calel, had been active in exciting the revolt and assisting the insurgents. Hernandez de Chaves determined to punish him, and marched against Copan, then one of the largest, most opulent, and most populous places of the kingdom. The camp of the cacique, with his auxiliaries, consisted of thirty thousand men, well disciplined, and veterans in war, armed with wooden swords having stone edges, arrows, and slings. On one side, says the historian, it was defended by the ranges of mountains of Chiquimula and Gracios a Dios, and on the opposite side by a deep fosse, and an intrenchment formed of strong beams of timber, having the interstices filled with earth, with embrasures, and loopholes for the discharge of arrows. Chaves, accompanied by some horsemen, well armed, rode to the fosse, and made sign that he wished to hold conference. The cacique answered with an arrow. A shower of arrows, stones, and darts followed, which compelled the Spaniards to retreat. The next day Chaves made an attack upon the intrenchment. The infantry wore loose coats stuffed with cotton; swords and shields; the horsemen wore breastplates and helmets, and their horses were covered. The Copanes had each a shield covered with the skin of the danta on his arm, and his head guarded by bunches of feathers. The attack lasted the whole day. The Indians, with their arrows, javelins, and pikes, the heads of which were hardened by fire, maintained their ground. The Spaniards were obliged to retreat. Chaves, who had fought in the thickest of the battle, was alarmed at the difficulties of the enterprise and the danger to the credit of the Spanish arms, but received information that in one place the depth of the ditch which defended Copan was but trifling, and the next day he

proceeded to the spot to make an attack there. The Copanes had
watched his movements, and manned the intrenchment with their
bravest soldiers. The infantry were unable to make a lodgment.
The cavalry came to their assistance. The Indians brought up
their whole force, and the Spaniards stood like rocks, impassable
to pikes, arrows, and stones. Several times they attempted to scale
the intrenchments, and were driven back into the fosse. Many were
killed on both sides, but the battle continued without advantage to
either until a brave horseman leaped the ditch, and, his horse being
carried violently with his breast against the barrier, the earth and
palisades gave way, and the frightened horse plunged among the
Indians. Other horsemen followed, and spread such terror among
the Copanes, that their lines were broken and they fled. Copán
Calel rallied at a place where he had posted a body of reserve; but,
unable to resist long, retreated, and left Copan to its fate.

This is the account which the Spanish historians have given of
Copan; and, as applied to the city, the wall of which we saw from
the opposite side of the river, it appeared to us most meager and
unsatisfactory; for the massive stone structures before us had little
the air of belonging to a city, the intrenchment of which could be
broken down by the charge of a single horseman. At this place the
river was not fordable; we returned to our mules, mounted, and
rode to another part of the bank, a short distance above. The stream
was wide, and in some places deep, rapid, and with a broken and
stony bottom. Fording it, we rode along the bank by a footpath
encumbered with undergrowth, which Jose opened by cutting away
the branches, until we came to the foot of the wall, where we again
dismounted and tied our mules.

The wall was of cut stone, well laid, and in a good state of preservation. We ascended by large stone steps, in some places perfect,
and in others thrown down by trees which had grown up between
the crevices, and reached a terrace, the form of which it was impossible to make out, from the density of the forest in which it was
enveloped. Our guide cleared a way with his machete, and we
passed, as it lay half buried in the earth, a large fragment of stone
elaborately sculptured, and came to the angle of a structure with
steps on the sides, in form and appearance, so far as the trees
would enable us to make it out, like the sides of a pyramid. Diverging from the base, and working our way through the thick woods,
we came upon a square stone column, about fourteen feet high and
three feet on each side, sculptured in very bold relief, and on all
four of the sides, from the base to the top. The front was the figure
of a man curiously and richly dressed, and the face, evidently a
portrait, solemn, stern, and well fitted to excite terror. The back
was of a different design, unlike anything we had ever seen before,

and the sides were covered with hieroglyphics. This our guide called an "Idol;" and before it, at a distance of three feet, was a large block of stone, also sculptured with figures and emblematical devices, which he called an altar. The sight of this unexpected monument put at rest at once and forever, in our minds, all uncertainty in regard to the character of American antiquities, and gave us the assurance that the objects we were in search of were interesting, not only as the remains of an unknown people, but as works of art, proving, like newly-discovered historical records, that the people who once occupied the Continent of America were not savages. With an interest perhaps stronger than we had ever felt in wandering among the ruins of Egypt, we followed our guide, who, sometimes missing his way, with a constant and vigorous use of his machete conducted us through the thick forest, among half-buried fragments, to fourteen monuments of the same character and appearance, some with more elegant designs, and some in workmanship equal to the finest monuments of the Egyptians; one displaced from its pedestal by enormous roots; another locked in the close embrace of branches of trees, and almost lifted out of the earth; another hurled to the ground, and bound down by huge vines and creepers; and one standing, with its altar before it, in a grove of trees which grew around it, seemingly to shade and shroud it as a sacred thing; in the solemn stillness of the woods, it seemed a divinity mourning over a fallen people. The only sounds that disturbed the quiet of this buried city were the noise of monkeys moving among the tops of the trees, and the cracking of dry branches broken by their weight. They moved over our heads in long and swift processions, forty or fifty at a time, some with little ones wound in their long arms, walking out to the end of boughs, and holding on with their hind feet or a curl of the tail, sprang to a branch of the next tree, and, with a noise like a current of wind, passed on into the depths of the forest. It was the first time we had seen these mockeries of humanity, and, with the strange monuments around us, they seemed like wandering spirits of the departed race guarding the ruins of their former habitations.

We returned to the base of the pyramidal structure, and ascended by regular stone steps, in some places forced apart by bushes and saplings, and in others thrown down by the growth of large trees, while some remained entire. In parts they were ornamented with sculptured figures and rows of death's heads. Climbing over the ruined top, we reached a terrace overgrown with trees, and, crossing it, descended by stone steps into an area so covered with trees that at first we could not make out its form, but which, on clearing the way with the machete, we ascertained to be a square, and with steps on all sides almost as perfect as those of the Roman amphi-

theatre. The steps were ornamented with sculpture, and on the
south side, about half way up, forced out of its place by roots, was
a colossal head, evidently a portrait. We ascended these steps,
and reached a broad terrace a hundred feet high, overlooking the
river, and supported by the wall which we had seen from the
opposite bank. The whole terrace was covered with trees, and even
at this height from the ground were two gigantic Ceibas, or wild
cottontrees of India, above twenty feet in circumference, extending
their half-naked roots fifty or a hundred feet around, binding down
the ruins, and shading them with their wide-spreading branches.
We sat down on the very edge of the wall, and strove in vain to
penetrate the mystery by which we were surrounded. Who were
the people that built this city? In the ruined cities of Egypt, even
in the long-lost Petra, the stranger knows the story of the people
whose vestiges are around him. America, say historians, was
peopled by savages; but savages never reared these structures,
savages never carved these stones. We asked the Indians who made
them, and their dull answer was *"Quien sabe?"* "Who knows?"

There were no associations connected with the place; none of
those stirring recollections which hallow Rome, Athens, and

The world's great mistress on the Egyptian plain;

but architecture, sculpture, and painting, all the arts which embel-
lish life, had flourished in this overgrown forest; orators, warriors,
and statesmen, beauty, ambition, and glory, had lived and passed
away, and none knew that such things had been, or could tell of
their past existence. Books, the records of knowledge, are silent
on this theme. The city was desolate. No remnant of this race
hangs round the ruins, with traditions handed down from father
to son, and from generation to generation. It lay before us like
a shattered bark in the midst of the ocean, her masts gone, her
name effaced, her crew perished, and none to tell whence she came,
to whom she belonged, how long on her voyage, or what caused
her destruction; her lost people to be traced only by some fancied
resemblance in the construction of the vessel, and, perhaps, never
to be known at all. The place where we sat, was it a citadel from
which an unknown people had sounded the trumpet of war? or
a temple for the worship of the God of peace? or did the inhabitants
worship the idols made with their own hands, and offer sacrifices
on the stones before them? All was mystery, dark, impenetrable
mystery, and every circumstance increased it. In Egypt the colossal
skeletons of gigantic temples stand in the unwatered sands in all
the nakedness of desolation; here an immense forest shrouded the
ruins, hiding them from sight, heightening the impression and

moral effect, and giving an intensity and almost wildness to the interest.

Late in the afternoon we worked our way back to the mules, bathed in the clear river at the foot of the wall, and returned to the hacienda. Our grateful muleteer-boy had told of his dreadful illness, and the extraordinary cure effected by Mr. Catherwood; and we found at the hacienda a ghastly-looking man, worn down by fever and ague, who begged us for *"remedios."* An old lady on a visit to the family, who had intended to go home that day, was waiting to be cured of a malady from which she had suffered twenty years. Our medicine-chest was brought out, and this converted the wife of the don into a patient also. Mr. C.'s reputation rose with the medicines he distributed; and in the course of the evening he had under his hands four or five women and as many men. We wanted very much to practice on the don, but he was cautious. The percussion caps of our pistols attracted the attention of the men; and we showed them the compass and other things, which made our friend at San Antonio suppose we were "very rich," and "had many ideas." By degrees we became on social terms with all the house except the master, who found a congenial spirit in the muleteer. He had taken his ground, and was too dignified and obstinate to unbend. Our new friends made more room for our hammocks, and we had a better swing for the night.

In the morning we continued to astonish the people by our strange ways, particularly by brushing our teeth, an operation which, probably, they saw then for the first time. While engaged in this, the door of the house opened, and Don Gregorio appeared, turning his head away to avoid giving us a *buenos dias.* We resolved not to sleep another night under his shed, but to take our hammocks to the ruins, and, if there was no building to shelter us, to hang up under a tree. My contract with the muleteer was to stop three days at Copan; but there was no bargain for the use of the mules during that time, and he hoped that the vexations we met with would make us go on immediately. When he found us bent on remaining, he swore he would not carry the hammocks, and would not remain one day over, but at length consented to hire the mules for that day.

Before we started a new party, who had been conversing some time with Don Gregorio, stepped forward, and said that he was the owner of "the idols;" that no one could go on the land without his permission; and handed me his title papers. This was a new difficulty. I was not disposed to dispute his title, but read his papers as attentively as if I meditated an action in ejectment; and he seemed relieved when I told him his title was good, and that, if not disturbed, I would make him a compliment at parting. Fortunately, he had a favour to ask. Our fame as physicians had reached the village, and he wished *remedios* for a sick wife. It was important to make him our friend; and, after some conversation, it was arranged that Mr. C., with several workmen whom we had hired, should go on to the ruins, as we intended, to make a lodgment there, while I would go to the village and visit his wife.

Our new acquaintance, Don José Maria Asebedo, was about fifty, tall, and well dressed; that is, his cotton shirt and pantaloons were clean; inoffensive, though ignorant; and one of the most respectable inhabitants of Copan. He lived in one of the best huts of the village, made of poles thatched with corn-leaves, with a wooden frame on one side for a bed, and furnished with a few pieces of pottery for cooking. A heavy rain had fallen during the night, and the ground inside the hut was wet. His wife seemed as old as he, and, fortunately, was suffering from a rheumatism of several years' standing. I say fortunately, but I speak only in reference to ourselves as medical men, and the honour of the profession accidentally confided to our hands. I told her that if it had been a recent affection, it would be more within the reach of art; but, as it was a case of old standing, it required time, skill, watching of symptoms, and the effect of medicine from day to day; and, for the present, I advised her to take her feet out of a puddle of water in which she was standing, and promised to consult Mr. Catherwood, who was even a better medico than I, and to send her a liniment with which to bathe her neck.

This over, Don José Maria accompanied me to the ruins, where I found Mr. Catherwood with the Indian workmen. Again we wandered over the whole ground in search of some ruined building in which we could take up our abode, but there was none. To hang up our hammocks under the trees was madness; the branches were still wet, the ground muddy, and again there was a prospect of early rain; but we were determined not to go back to Don Gregorio's. Don Mariano said that there was a hut near by, and conducted me to it. As we approached, we heard the screams of a woman inside, and, entering, saw her rolling and tossing on a bull's-hide bed, wild with fever and pain; and, starting to her knees at the sight of me, with her hands pressed against her temples, and tears bursting from her eyes, she begged me, for the love of God, to give her some *remedios*. Her skin was hot, her pulse very high; she had a violent intermittent fever. While [I was] inquiring into her symptoms, her husband entered the hut, a white man, about forty, dressed in a pair of dirty cotton drawers, with a nether garment hanging outside, a handkerchief tied around his head, and barefooted; and his name was *Don* Miguel. I told him that we wished to pass a few days among the ruins, and asked permission to stop at his hut. The woman, most happy at having a skilful physician near her, answered for him, and I returned to relieve Mr. Catherwood, and add another to his list of patients. The whole party escorted us to the hut, bringing along only the mule that carried the hammocks; and by the addition of Mr. C. to the medical corps, and a mysterious display of drawing materials and measuring rods, the poor woman's fever seemed frightened away. . . .

All day I had been brooding over the title-deeds of Don José Maria, and, drawing my blanket around me, suggested to Mr. Catherwood "an operation." (Hide your heads, ye speculators in up-town lots!) To buy Copan! remove the monuments of a by-gone people from the desolate region in which they were buried, set them up in the "great commercial emporium," and found an institution to be the nucleus of a great national museum of American antiquities! But *quere*, Could the "idols" be removed? They were on the banks of a river that emptied into the same ocean by which the docks of New York are washed, but there were rapids below; and, in answer to my inquiry, Don Miguel said these were impassable. Nevertheless, I should have been unworthy of having passed through the times "that tried men's souls" if I had not had an alternative; and this was to exhibit by sample: to cut one up and remove it in pieces, and make casts of the others. The casts of the Parthenon are regarded as precious memorials in the British Museum, and casts of Copan would be the same in New York. Other ruins might be discovered even more interesting and more accessible. Very soon their existence would become known and their value appreciated, and the friends of science and the arts in Europe would get possession of them. They belonged of right to us, and, though we did not know how soon we might be kicked out ourselves, I resolved that ours they should be; with visions of glory and indistinct fancies of receiving the thanks of the corporation flitting before my eyes, I drew my blanket around me, and fell asleep. . . .

The Ruins Explored. Mr. Catherwood's Difficulties.
Purchase of a City?

At daylight the clouds still hung over the forest; as the sun rose they cleared away; our workmen made their appearance, and at nine o'clock we left the hut. The branches of the trees were dripping wet, and the ground very muddy. Trudging once more over the district which contained the principal monuments, we were startled by the immensity of the work before us, and very soon we concluded that to explore the whole extent would be impossible. Our guides knew only of this district; but having seen columns beyond the village, a league distant, we had reason to believe that others were strewed in different directions, completely buried in the woods, and entirely unknown. The woods were so dense that it was almost hopeless to think of penetrating them. The only way to make a thorough exploration would be to cut down the whole forest and burn the trees. This was incompatible with our immediate purposes, might be considered taking liberties, and could only be done in the dry season. After deliberation, we resolved first to obtain drawings of the sculptured columns [calendar stones, or stelae]. Even in this there was great difficulty. The designs were very complicated, and so different from anything Mr. Catherwood had ever seen before as to be perfectly unintelligible. The cutting was in very high relief, and required a strong body of light to bring up the figures; and the foliage was so thick, and the shade so deep, that drawing was impossible.

After much consultation, we selected one of the "idols," and determined to cut down the trees around it, and thus lay it open to the rays of the sun. Here again was difficulty. There was no axe; and the only instrument which the Indians possessed was the machete, or chopping-knife, which varies in form in different sections of the country; wielded with one hand, it was useful in clearing away shrubs and branches, but almost harmless upon large trees; and the Indians, as in the days when the Spaniards discovered them, applied to work without ardour, carried it on with little activity, and, like children, were easily diverted from it. One hacked into a tree, and when tired, which happened very soon, sat down to rest, and another relieved him. While one worked there were always several looking on. I remembered the ring of the woodman's axe in the forests at home, and wished for a few long-sided Green Mountain boys. But we had been buffeted into patience, and watched the Indians while they hacked with their machetes, and even wondered that they succeeded so well. At length the trees were felled and dragged aside, a space cleared around the base, Mr. C.'s frame set up, and he set to work. I took two Mestizos, Bruno and Francisco, and, offering them a reward for every new discovery, with a compass in my hand set out on a tour of exploration. Neither had seen "the idols" until the morning of our first visit, when they followed in our train to laugh at *los Ingleses;* but very soon they exhibited such an interest that I hired them. Bruno attracted my attention by his admiration, as I supposed, of my person; but I found it was of my coat, which was a long shooting-frock, with many pockets; and he said that he could make one just like it except the skirts. He was a tailor by profession, and in the intervals of a great job upon a roundabout jacket, worked with his machete. But he had an inborn taste for the arts. As we passed through the woods, nothing escaped his eye, and he was professionally curious touching the costumes of the sculptured figures. I was struck with the first development of their antiquarian taste. Francisco found the feet and legs of a statue, and Bruno a part of the body to match, and the effect was electric upon both. They searched and raked up the ground with their machetes till they found the shoulders, and set it up entire except the head; and they were both eager for the possession of instruments with which to dig and find this remaining fragment.

It is impossible to describe the interest with which I explored these ruins. The ground was entirely new; there were no guide-books or guides; the whole was a virgin soil. We could not see ten yards before us, and never knew what we should stumble upon next. At one time we stopped to cut away branches and vines which concealed the face of a monument, and then to dig around and bring to light a fragment, a sculptured corner of which protruded from the earth. I leaned over with breathless anxiety while the Indians worked, and an eye, an ear, a foot, or a hand was disentombed; and when the machete rang against the chiselled stone, I pushed the Indians away, and cleared out the loose earth with my hands. The beauty of the sculpture, the solemn stillness of the woods, disturbed only by the scrambling of monkeys and the chattering of parrots, the desolation of the city, and the mystery that hung over it, all created an interest higher, if possible, than I had ever felt among the ruins of the Old World. After several hours' absence I returned to Mr. Catherwood, and reported upward of fifty objects to be copied.

I found him not so well pleased as I expected with my report. He was standing with his feet in the mud, and was drawing with his gloves on, to protect his hands from mosquitoes. As we feared, the designs were so intricate and complicated, the subjects so entirely new and unintelligible, that he had great difficulty in drawing. He had made several attempts, both with the camera lucida and without, but failed to satisfy himself or even me, who was less severe in criticism. The "idol" seemed to defy his art; two monkeys on a tree on one side appeared to be laughing at him, and I felt discouraged and despondent. In fact, I made up my mind, with a pang of regret, that we must abandon the idea of carrying away any materials for antiquarian speculation, and must be content with having seen them ourselves. Of that satisfaction nothing could deprive us. We returned to the hut with our interest undiminished, but sadly out of heart as to the result of our labours.

Our luggage had not been able to cross the river, but the blue bag which had caused me so many troubles was recovered. I had offered a dollar reward, and Bartolo, the heir-apparent of the lesseeship of our hut, had passed the day in the river, and found it entangled in a bush upon the bank. His naked body seemed glad of its accidental

washing, and the bag, which we supposed to contain some of Mr.
C.'s drawing materials, being shaken, gave out a pair of old boots,
which, however, were at that time worth their weight in gold, being water-proof, and cheered Mr. Catherwood's drooping spirits,
who was ill with a prospective attack of fever and ague of rheumatism, from standing all day in the mud. Our men went home, and
Frederico had orders, before coming to work in the morning, to go
to Don Gregorio's and buy bread, milk, candles, lard, and a few
yards of beef. The door of the hut looked toward the west, and the
sun set over the dark forest in front with a gorgeousness I have
never seen surpassed. Again, during the night, we had rain, with
thunder and lightning, but not so violent as the night before, and in
the morning it was again clear.

That day Mr. Catherwood was much more successful in his drawings; indeed, at the beginning the light fell exactly as he wished, and
he mastered the difficulty. His preparations, too, were much more
comfortable, as he had his water-proofs, and stood on a piece of oiled
canvas, used for covering luggage on the road. I passed the morning
in selecting another monument, clearing away the trees, and preparing it for him to copy. At one o'clock Augustin came to call us
to dinner. Don Miguel had a patch of beans, from which Augustin
gathered as many as he pleased, and, with the fruits of a standing
order for all the eggs in the village, being three or four a day, strings
of beef, and bread and milk from the hacienda, we did very well.
In the afternoon we were again called off by Augustin, with a message that the alcalde had come to pay us a visit. As it was growing
late, we broke up for the day, and went back to the hut. We shook
hands with the alcalde, and gave him and his attendants cigars,
and were disposed to be sociable; but the dignitary was so tipsy
he could hardly speak. His attendants sat crouching on the ground,
swinging themselves on their knee-joints, and, though the positions
were different, reminding us of the Arabs. In a few minutes the
alcalde started up suddenly, made a staggering bow, and left us,
and they all followed, Don Miguel with them. While we were at
supper he returned, and it was easy to see that he, and his wife, and
Bartolo were in trouble, and, as we feared, the matter concerned us.

While we were busy with our own affairs, we had but little idea
what a sensation we were creating in the village. Not satisfied with
getting us out of his house, Don Gregorio wanted to get us out of the
neighbourhood. Unluckily, besides his instinctive dislike, we had
offended him in drawing off some of his workmen by the high prices
which, as strangers, we were obliged to pay, and he began to look
upon us as rivals, and said everywhere that we were suspicious
characters; that we should be the cause of disturbing the peace of
Copan, and introducing soldiers and war into the neighbourhood.

In confirmation of this, two Indians passed through the village, who
reported that we had escaped from imprisonment, had been chased
to the borders of Honduras by a detachment of twenty-five soldiers
under Landaveri, the officer who arrested us, and that, if we had
been taken, we would have been shot. The alcalde, who had been
drunk ever since our arrival, resolved to visit us, to solve the doubts
of the village, and take those measures which the presence of such
dangerous persons and the safety of the country might require. But
this doughty purpose was frustrated by a ludicrous circumstance.
We made it a rule to carry our arms with us to the ruins, and when
we returned to the hut to receive his visit, as usual, each of us had
a brace of pistols in his belt and a gun in hand; and our appearance
was so formidable that the alcalde was frightened at his own
audacity in having thought of catechising us, and fairly sneaked off.
As soon as he reached the woods, his attendants reproached him for
not executing his purpose, and he said, doggedly, that he was not
going to have anything to say to men armed as we were. Roused at
the idea of our terrible appearance, we told Don Miguel to advise
the alcalde and the people of the village that they had better keep
out of our way and let us alone. Don Miguel gave a ghastly smile;
but all was not finished. He said that he had no doubt himself of our
being good men, but we were suspected; the country was in a state
of excitement; and he was warned that he ought not to harbour us,
and would get into difficulty by doing so. The poor woman could not
conceal her distress. Her head was full of assassinations and mur-
ders, and though alarmed for their safety, she was not unmindful of
ours; she said that, if any soldiers came into the village, we would
be murdered, and begged us to go away.

We were exceedingly vexed and disturbed by these communications, but we had too much at stake to consent to be driven away
by apprehensions. We assured Don Miguel that no harm could
happen to him; that it was all false and a mistake, and that we were
above suspicion. At the same time, in order to convince him, I
opened my trunk, and showed him a large bundle of papers, sealed
credentials to the government and private letters of introduction in
Spanish to prominent men in Guatemala, describing me as "Encar-
gado de los Negocios de los Estados Unidos del Norte," and one very
special from Don Antonio Aycinena, now in this city, formerly
colonel in the Central Army, and banished by Morazan, to his
brother the Marquis Aycinena, the leader of the Central Party,
which was dominant in that district in the civil war then raging,
recommending me very highly, and stating my purpose of travelling
through the country. This last letter was more important than anything else; and if it had been directed to one of the opposite party in
politics, it would have been against us, as confirming the suspicion

of our being "enemigos." Never was greatness so much under a shade. Though vexatious, it was almost amusing to be obliged to clear up our character to such a miserable party as Don Miguel, his wife, and Bartolo; but it was indispensable to relieve them from doubts and anxieties, enabling us to remain quietly in their wretched hut; and the relief they experienced, and the joy of the woman in learning that we were tolerably respectable people, not enemies, and not in danger of being put up and shot at, were most grateful to us.

Nevertheless, Don Miguel advised us to go to Guatemala or to General Cascara, procure an order to visit the ruins, and then return. We had made a false step in one particular; we should have gone direct to Guatemala, and returned with a passport and letters from the government; but, as we had no time to spare, and did not know what there was at Copan, probably if we had not taken it on the way we should have missed it altogether. And we did not know that the country was so completely secluded; the people are less accustomed to the sight of strangers than the Arabs about Mount Sinai, and they are much more suspicious. Colonel Galindo was the only stranger who had been there before us, and he could hardly be called a stranger, for he was a colonel in the Central American Service, and visited the ruins under a commission from the government. Our visit has perhaps had some influence upon the feelings of the people; it has, at all events, taught Don Gregorio that strangers are not easily got rid of; but I advise any one who wishes to visit these ruins in peace, to go to Guatemala first, and apply to the government for all the protection it can give. As to us, it was too late to think of this, and all we had to do was to maintain our ground as quietly as we could. We had no apprehension of soldiers coming from any other place merely to molest us. Don Miguel told us what we had before observed, that there was not a musket in the village; the quality and excellence of our arms were well known; the muleteer had reported that we were outrageous fellows, and had threatened to shoot him; and the alcalde was an excessive coward. We formed an alliance, offensive and defensive, with Don Miguel, his wife, and Bartolo, and went to sleep. Don Miguel and his wife, by-the-way, were curious people; they slept with their heads at different ends of the bed, so that, in the unavoidable accompaniment of smoking, they could clear each other.

In the morning we were relieved from our difficulty, and put in a position to hurl defiance at the traducers of our character. While the workmen were gathering outside the hut, an Indian courier came trotting through the cornfield up to the door, who inquired for Señor Ministro; and pulling off his petate, took out of the crown a letter, which he said he was ordered by General Cascara to deliver into the right hands. It was directed to *"Señor Catherwood, à*

Comotan ó donde se halle," conveying the expression of General
Cascara's regret for the arrest at Comotan, ascribing it to the
ignorance or mistake of the alcalde and soldiers, and enclosing,
besides, a separate passport for Mr. Catherwood. I have great
satisfaction in acknowledging the receipt of this letter; and the
promptness with which General Cascara dispatched it to "Comotan,
or wherever he may be found," was no less than I expected from
his character and station. I requested Don Miguel to read it aloud,
told the Indian to deliver our compliments to General Cascara, and
sent him to the village to breakfast, with a donation which I knew
would make him publish the story with right emphasis and dis-
cretion. Don Miguel smiled, his wife laughed, and a few spots of
white flashed along Bartolo's dirty skin. Stocks rose, and I resolved
to ride to the village, strengthen the cords of friendship with Don
José Maria, visit our patients, defy Don Gregorio, and get up a
party in Copan.

Mr. Catherwood went to the ruins to continue his drawings,
and I to the village, taking Augustin with me to fire the Belize
guns, and buy up eatables for a little more than they were worth.
My first visit was to Don José Maria. After clearing up our character,
I broached the subject of a purchase of the ruins; told him that, on
account of my public business, I could not remain as long as I
desired, but wished to return with spades, pickaxes, ladders, crowbars, and men, build a hut to live in, and make a thorough exploration; that I could not incur the expense at the risk of being refused
permission to do so; and, in short, in plain English, asked him,
What will you take for the ruins? I think he was not more surprised
than if I had asked to buy his poor old wife, our rheumatic patient,
to practice medicine upon. He seemed to doubt which of us was
out of his senses. The property was so utterly worthless that my
wanting to buy it seemed very suspicious. On examining the paper,
I found that he did not own the fee, but held under a lease from
Don Bernardo de Aguila, of which three years were unexpired. The
tract consisted of about six thousand acres, for which he paid
eighty dollars a year; he was at a loss what to do, but told me that
he would reflect upon it, consult his wife, and give me an answer
at the hut the next day. I then visited the alcalde, but he was too
tipsy to be susceptible of any impression; prescribed for several
patients; and instead of going to Don Gregorio's, sent him a polite
request by Don José Maria to mind his own business and let us
alone; returned, and passed the rest of the day among the ruins.
It rained during the night, but again cleared off in the morning,
and we were on the ground early. My business was to go around with
workmen to clear away trees and bushes, dig, and excavate, and
prepare monuments for Mr. Catherwood to copy. While so engaged,

I was called off by a visit from Don José Maria, who was still undecided what to do; and not wishing to appear too anxious, told him to take more time, and come again the next morning.

The next morning he came, and his condition was truly pitiable. He was anxious to convert unproductive property into money, but afraid, and said that I was a stranger, and it might bring him into difficulty with the government. I again went into proof of character, and engaged to save him harmless with the government or release him. Don Miguel read my letters of recommendation, and re-read the letter of General Cascara. He was convinced, but these papers did not give him a right to sell me his land; the shade of suspicion still lingered; for a finale, I opened my trunk, and put on a diplomatic coat, with a profusion of large eagle buttons. I had on a Panama hat, soaked with rain and spotted with mud, a check shirt, white pantaloons, yellow up the knees with mud, and was about as *outré* as the negro king who received a company of British officers on the coast of Africa in a cocked hat and military coat, without any inexpressibles; but Don José Maria could not withstand the buttons on my coat; the cloth was the finest he had ever seen; and Don Miguel, and his wife, and Bartolo realized fully that they had in their hut an illustrious incognito. The only question was who should find paper on which to draw the contract. I did not stand upon trifles, and gave Don Miguel some paper, who took our mutual instructions, and appointed the next day for the execution of the deed.

The reader is perhaps curious to know how old cities sell in Central America. Like other articles of trade, they are regulated by the quantity in market, and the demand; but, not being staple articles, like cotton and indigo, they were held at fancy prices, and at that time were dull of sale. I paid fifty dollars for Copan. There was never any difficulty about price. I offered that sum, for which Don José Maria thought me only a fool; if I had offered more, he would probably have considered me something worse.

We had regular communications with the hacienda by means of Francisco, who brought thence every morning a large *guacal* of milk, carrying it a distance of three miles, and fording the river twice. The ladies of the hacienda had sent us word that they intended paying us a visit, and this morning Don Gregorio's wife appeared, leading a procession of all the women of the house, servants, and children, with two of her sons. We received them among the ruins, seated them as well as we could, and, as the first act of civility, gave them cigars all around. It can hardly be believed, but not one of them, not even Don Gregorio's sons, had ever seen the "idols" before, and now they were much more curious to see Mr. C.'s drawings. In fact, I believe it was the fame of these drawings that procured us the honour of their visit. In his heart Mr. C. was not much happier to see them than the old don was to see us, as his work was stopped, and every day was precious. As I considered myself in a manner the proprietor of the city, I was bound to do the honours; and, having cleared paths, led them around, showing off all the lions as the cicerone does in the Vatican or the Pitti Palace; but I could not keep them away, and, to the distress of Mr. C., brought them all back upon him.

Obliged to give up work, we invited them down to the hut to see our accommodations. Some of them were our patients, and reminded us that we had not sent the medicines we promised. The fact is, we avoided giving medicines when we could, among other reasons, from an apprehension that if any one happened to die on our hands we should be held responsible; but our reputation was established; honours were buckled on our backs, and we were obliged to wear them. These ladies, in spite of Don Gregorio's crustiness, had always treated us kindly, and we would fain have shown our sense of it some other mode than by giving them physic; but, to gratify them in their own way, we distributed among them powders and pills, with written directions for use; and when they went away escorted them some distance, and had the satisfaction of hearing that they avenged us on Don Gregorio by praises of our gallantry and attentions.

Mr. Catherwood Goes to Quirigua

QUIRIGUA lies to the north of Copan in a fertile plain by the Motagua valley. It has no high temple pyramid and few stone buildings, but it is noted for exceptionally tall stelae and for altars carved in the form of strange monsters. One of the stelae carries accurate calendrical computations back to four hundred millions years ago.

To recur for a moment to Mr. Catherwood, who, during my absence, had not been idle. On reaching Guatemala the first time from Copan, I made it my business to inquire particularly for ruins. I did not meet a single person who had ever visited those of Copan, and but few who took any interest whatever in the antiquities of the country; but, fortunately, a few days after my arrival, Don Carlos Meany, a Trinidad Englishman, long resident in the country, proprietor of a large hacienda, and extensively engaged in mining operations, made one of his regular business visits to the capital. Besides a thorough acquaintance with all that concerned his own immediate pursuits, this gentleman possessed much general information respecting the country, and a curiosity which circumstances had never permitted him to gratify in regard to antiquities; and he told me of the ruins of Quirigua, on the Motagua River, near Encuentros, the place at which we slept the second night after crossing the Mico Mountain. He had never seen them, and I hardly believed it possible they could exist, for at that place we had made special inquiries for the ruins of Copan, and were not informed of any others. I became satisfied, however, that Don Carlos was a man who did not speak at random. They were on the estate of Señor Payes, a gentleman of Guatemala lately deceased. He had heard of them from Señor Payes, and had taken such interest in the subject as to inquire for and obtain the details of particular monuments. Three sons of Señor Payes had succeeded to his estate, and at my request Don Carlos called with me upon them. Neither of the sons had ever seen the ruins or even visited the estate. It was an immense tract of wild land, which had come into their father's hands many years before for a mere trifle. He had visited it once; and they too had heard him speak of these ruins. Lately the spirit of speculation had reached that country; and from its fertility and position on the bank of a navigable river contiguous to the ocean, the tract had been made the subject of a prospectus, to be sold on shares in England. The prospectus set forth the great natural advantages of the location, and the inducements held out to emigrants, in terms and phrases that might have issued from a laboratory in New York before the crash. The Señores Payes were in the first stage of anticipated wealth, and talked in the familiar strains of city builders at home. They were roused by the prospect of any indirect addition to the value of their real estate; told me that two of them were then making arrangements to visit the tract, and immediately proposed that I should accompany them. Mr. Catherwood, on his road from Copan, had fallen in with a person at Chiquimula who told him of such ruins, with the addition that Colonel Galindo was then at work among them. Being in the neighbourhood, he had some idea of going to visit them; but, being much worn with his labours at Copan, and knowing that the story was untrue as regarded Colonel Galindo, whom he knew to be in a different section of the country, he was incredulous as to the whole. We had some doubt whether they would repay the labour; but as there was no occasion for him to accompany me to San Salvador, it was agreed that during my absence he should, with Señor Payes, go to Quirigua, which he accordingly did.

The reader must go back to Encuentros, the place at which we slept the second night of our arrival in the country. From this place they embarked in a canoe about twenty-five feet long and four broad, dug out of the trunk of a mahogany-tree, and descending two hours, disembarked at Los Amates, near El Poso, on the main road from Izabal to Guatemala, the place at which we breakfasted the second morning of our arrival in the country, and where the Señores Payes were obliged to wait two or three days. The place was a miserable collection of huts, scant of provisions, and the people drank a muddy water at their doors rather than take the trouble of going to the river.

On a fine morning, after a heavy rain, they set off for the ruins. After a ride of about half an hour, over an execrable road, they again reached the Amates. The village was pleasantly situated on the bank of the river, and elevated about thirty feet. The river was here about two hundred feet wide, and fordable in every part except a few deep holes. Generally it did not exceed three feet in depth, and in many places was not so deep; but below it was said to be navigable to the sea for boats not drawing more than three feet water. They embarked in two canoes dug out of cedar-trees, and proceeded down the river for a couple of miles, where they took on board a negro man named Juan Lima, and his two wives. This black scoundrel, as Mr. C. marks him down in his notebook, was to be their guide. They then proceeded two or three miles farther, and stopped at a rancho on the left side of the river, and passing through two cornfields, entered a forest of large cedar and mahogany trees. The path was exceedingly soft and wet, and covered with decayed leaves, and the heat very great. Continuing through the forest toward the northeast, in three quarters of an hour they reached the foot of a pyramidal structure like those at Copan, with the steps in some places perfect. They ascended to the top, about twenty-five feet, and descending by steps on the other side, at a short distance beyond came to a colossal head two yards in diameter, almost buried by an enormous tree, and covered with moss. Near it was a large altar, so covered with moss that it was impossible to make anything out of it. The two are within an enclosure.

Retracing their steps across the pyramidal structure, and proceeding to the north about three or four hundred yards, they reached a collection of monuments of the same general character with those at Copan, but twice or three times as high.

The first is about twenty feet high, five feet six inches on two sides, and two feet eight on the other two. The front represents the figure of a man, well preserved; the back that of a woman, much defaced. The sides are covered with hieroglyphics in good preservation, but in low relief, and of exactly the same style as those at Copan.

Another, represented in the engraving, is twenty-three feet out of the ground, with figures of men on the front and back, and hieroglyphics in low relief on the sides, and surrounded by a base projecting fifteen or sixteen feet from it.

At a short distance, standing in the same position as regards the points of the compass, is an obelisk or carved stone, twenty-six feet out of the ground, and probably six or eight feet under, which is represented in the engraving opposite. It is leaning twelve feet two inches out of the perpendicular, and seems ready to fall, which is probably prevented only by a tree that has grown up against it and the large stones around the base. The side toward the ground represents the figure of a man, very perfect and finely sculptured. The upper side seemed the same, but was so hidden by vegetation as to make it somewhat uncertain. The other two contain hieroglyphics in low relief. In size and sculpture this is the finest of the whole.

A statue ten feet high is lying on the ground, covered with moss and herbage, and another about the same size lies with its face upward.

There are four others erect, about twelve feet high, but not in a very good state of preservation, and several altars so covered with herbage that it was difficult to ascertain their exact form. One of them is round, and situated on a small elevation within a circle formed by a wall of stones. In the centre of the circle, reached by descending very narrow steps, is a large round stone, with the sides sculptured in hieroglyphics, covered with vegetation, and supported on what seemed to be two colossal heads.

These are all at the foot of a pyramidal wall, near each other, and in the vicinity of a creek which empties into the Motagua. Besides these they counted thirteen fragments, and doubtless many others may yet be discovered.

At some distance from them is another monument, nine feet out of ground, and probably two or three under, with the figure of a woman on the front and back, and the two sides richly ornamented, but without hieroglyphics.

The next day the Negro promised to show Mr. C. eleven square columns higher than any he had seen, standing in a row at the foot of a mountain; but after dragging him three hours through the mud, Mr. C. found by the compass that he was constantly changing his direction; and as the man was armed with pistols, notoriously a bad fellow, and indignant at the owners of the land for coming down to look after their squatters, Mr. C. became suspicious of him, and insisted upon returning. The Payes were engaged with their own affairs, and having no one to assist him, Mr. Catherwood was unable to make any thorough exploration or any complete drawings.

The general character of these ruins is the same as at Copan.

The monuments are much larger, but they are sculptured in lower relief, less rich in design, and more faded and worn, probably being of a much older date.

Of one thing there is no doubt: a large city once stood there; its name is lost, its history unkown; and, except for a notice taken from Mr. C.'s notes, and inserted by the Señores Payes in a Guatemala paper after the visit, which found its way to this country and Europe, no account of its existence has ever before been published. For centuries it has lain as completely buried as if covered with the lava of Vesuvius. Every traveller from Izabal to Guatemala has passed within three hours of it; we ourselves had done the same; and yet there it lay, like the rock-city of Edom, unvisited, unsought, and utterly unknown.

The morning after Mr. C. returned I called upon Señor Payes, the only one of the brothers then in Guatemala, and opened a negotiation for the purchase of these ruins. Besides their entire newness and immense interest as an unexplored field of antiquarian research, the monuments were but about a mile from the river, the ground was level to the bank, and the river from that place was navigable; the city might be transported bodily and set up in New York. I expressly stated (and my reason for doing so will be obvious) that I was acting in this matter on my own account, that it was entirely a personal affair; but Señor Payes would consider me as acting for my government, and said, what I am sure he meant, that if his family was as it had been once, they would be proud to present the whole to the United States; in that country they were not appreciated, and he would be happy to contribute to the cause of science in ours; but they were impoverished by the convulsions of the country; and, at all events, he could give me no answer till his brothers returned, who were expected in two or three days. Unfortunately, as I believe for both of us, Señor Payes consulted with the French consul general, who put an exaggerated value upon the ruins, referring him to the expenditure of several hundred thousand dollars by the French government in transporting one of the obelisks of Luxor from Thebes to Paris. Probably, before the speculating scheme refered to, the owners would have been glad to sell the whole tract, consisting of more than fifty thousand acres, with everything on it, known and unknown, for a few thousand dollars. I was anxious to visit them myself, and learn with more certainty the possibility of their removal, but was afraid of increasing the extravagance of his notions. His brothers did not arrive, and one of them unfortunately died on the road. I had not the government for paymaster; it might be necessary to throw up the purchase on account of the cost of removal; and I left an offer with Mr. Savage, the result of which is still uncertain; but I trust that when these pages reach the hands of the reader, two of the largest monuments will be on their way to this city.

Preparations for a Thousand-Mile Journey to Palenque. A Sacred Stone at Tecpan and Ruins of Utatlan. Human Sacrifice.

THE Quiché were a powerful Maya people of the Guatemalan highlands. Their chief city, Utatlan, to the north of Lake Atitlan, was important in the late period of Maya history when it was under Mexican influence.

AND now I would fain let the reader sit down and enjoy himself quietly in Guatemala, but I cannot. The place did not admit of it. I could not conceal from myself that the Federal Government was broken up; there was not the least prospect of its ever being restored, nor, for a long time to come, of any other being organized in its stead. Under these circumstances I did not consider myself justified in remaining any longer in the country. I was perfectly useless for all the purposes of my mission, and made a formal return to the authorities of Washington, in effect, "after diligent search, no government found."

I was once more my own master, at liberty to go where I pleased, at my own expense, and immediately we commenced making arrangements for our journey to Palenque. We had no time to lose; it was a thousand miles distant, and the rainy season was approaching, during which part of the road was impassable. There was no one in the city who had ever made the journey. The archbishop, on his exit from Guatemala eight years before, had fled by that road, and since his time it had not been travelled by any resident of Guatemala; but we learned enough to satisfy us that it would be less difficult to reach Palenque from New York than from where we were. . . .

I was now fortified with the best security we could have for our journey. We passed the evening in writing letters and packing up things to be sent home (among which was my diplomatic coat), and on the seventh of April we rose to set out. The first movement was to take down our beds. Every man in that country has a small cot called a *catre*, made to double with a hinge, which may be taken down and wrapped up, with pillows and bedclothes, in an oxhide, to carry on a journey. Our great object was to travel lightly. Every additional mule and servant gave additional trouble, but we could not do with less than a cargo-mule apiece. Each of us had two *peta-cas*, trunks made of oxhide lined with thin straw matting, having a top like that of a box, secured by a clumsy iron chain with large pad-locks, containing, besides other things, a hammock, blanket, one pair of sheets, and pillow, which, with *alforgas* of provisions, made one load apiece. We carried one *catre*, in case of sickness. We had one spare cargo-mule; the gray mule with which I had ascended the Volcano of Cartago and my *macho* for Mr. Catherwood and my-self, and a horse for relief, in all six animals; and two *mozos*, or men of all work, untried. While in the act of mounting, Don Satur-nino Tinoca, my companion from Zonzonate, rode into the yard, to accompany us two days on our journey. We bade farewell to Mr. Savage, my first, last, and best friend, and in a few minutes, with a mingled feeling of regret and satisfaction, left for the last time the barrier of Guatemala.

Don Saturnino was most welcome to our party. His purpose was to visit two brothers of his wife, *curas*, whom he had never seen, and who lived at Santiago Atitlan, two or three days' journey distant. His father was the last governor of Nicaragua under the royal rule, with a large estate, which was confiscated at the time of the revolu-tion; he still had a large hacienda there, had brought up a stock of mules to sell at San Salvador, and intended to lay out the proceeds in goods in Guatemala. He was about forty, tall, and as thin as a man could be to have activity and vigour, wore a round-about jacket and trousers of dark olive cloth, large pistols in his holsters, and a long sword with a leather scabbard, worn at the point, leaving about an inch of steel naked. He sat his mule as stiff as if he had swal-lowed his own sword, holding the reins in his right hand, with his left arm crooked from the elbow, standing out like a pump-handle, the hand dropping from the wrist, and shaking with the movement of the mule. He rode on a Mexican saddle plated with silver, and carried behind a pair of *alforgas* with bread and cheese, and *atole*, a composition of pounded parched corn, cocoa, and sugar, which, mixed with water, was almost his living. His *mozo* was as fat as he was lean, and wore a bell-crowned straw hat, cotton shirt, and drawers reaching down to his knees. Excepting that instead of Rosinante and the ass the master rode a mule and the servant went afoot, they were a genuine Don Quixote and Sancho Panza, the former of which appellations, very early in our acquaintance, we gave to Don Saturnino.

In the morning the major-domo furnished us with fine horses, and we started early. Almost immediately we commenced ascending the other side of the ravine which we had descended the night before, and on the top entered on a continuation of the same beautiful and extensive table-land. On one side, for some distance, were high hedge fences, in which aloes were growing, and in one place were four in full bloom. In an hour we arrived at Patzum, a large Indian village. Here we turned off to the right from the high road to Mexico by a sort of by-path; but the country was beautiful, and in parts well cultivated. The morning was bracing, and the climate like our own in October. The immense table-land was elevated some five or six thousand feet, but none of these heights have ever been taken. We passed on the right two mounds, such as are seen all over our own country, and on the left an immense barranca. The table was level to the very edge, where the earth seemed to have broken off and sunk, and we looked down into a frightful abyss two or three thousand feet deep. Gigantic trees at the bottom of the immense cavity looked like shrubs. At some distance beyond we passed a second of these immense barrancas, and in an hour and a half reached the Indian village of Tecpan Guatemala. For some distance before reaching it the road was shaded by trees and shrubs, among which were aloes thirty feet high. The long street by which we entered was paved with stones from the ruins of the old city, and filled with drunken Indians; and rushing across it was one with his arms around a woman's neck. At the head of this street was a fine plaza, with a large cabildo, and twenty or thirty Indian alguazils under the corridor, with wands of office in their hands, silent, in full suits of blue cloth, the trousers open at the knees, and cloak with a hood like the Arab burnous. Adjoining this was the large courtyard of the church, paved with stone, and the church itself was one of the most magnificent in the country. It was the second built after the conquest. The façade was two hundred feet, very lofty, with turrets and spires gorgeously ornamented with stuccoed figures, and a high platform, on which were Indians, the first we had seen in picturesque costume; and with the widely-extended view of the country around, it was a scene of wild magnificence in nature and in art. We stopped involuntarily; and while the Indians, in mute astonishment, gazed at us, we were lost in surprise and admiration. As usual, Don Saturnino was the pioneer, and we rode up to the house of the padre, where we were shown into a small room, with the window closed and a ray of light admitted from the door, in which the padre was dozing in a large chair. Before he had fairly opened his eyes, Don Saturnino told him that we had come to visit the ruins of the old city, and wanted a guide, and thrust into his hands Carrera's passport and the letter of the *provesor*. The padre was old, fat, rich, and infirm, had been thirty-five years *cura* of Tecpan Guatemala, and was not used to doing things in a hurry; but our friend, knowing the particular objects of our visit, with great earnestness and haste told the padre that the minister of New York had heard in his country of a remarkable stone,

and the *provesor* and Carrera were anxious for him to see it. The
padre said that it was in the church, and lay on the top of the grand
altar; the cup of the sacrament stood upon it; it was covered up, and
very sacred; he had never seen it, and he was evidently unwilling to
let us see it, but said he would endeavour to do so when we returned
from the ruins. He sent for a guide, and we went out to the courtyard of the church; and while Mr. Catherwood was attempting a
sketch, I walked up the steps. The interior was lofty, spacious, richly
ornamented with stuccoed figures and paintings, dark and solemn,
and in the distance was the grand altar, with long wax candles burning upon it, and Indians kneeling before it. At the door a man
stopped me, and said that I must not enter with sword and spurs,
and even that I must take off my boots. I would have done so, but
saw that the Indians did not like a stranger going into *their* church.
They were evidently entirely unaccustomed to the sight of strangers,
and Mr. Catherwood was so annoyed by their gathering round him
that he gave up his drawing; and fearing it would be worse on our
return, I told Don Saturnino that we must make an effort to see
the stone now. Don Saturnino had a great respect for the priests
and the Church. He was not a fanatic, but he thought a powerful
religious influence good for the Indians. Nevertheless, he said we
ought to see it; and we went back in a body to the padre, and Don
Saturnino told him that we were anxious to see the stone now, to
prevent delay on our return. The good padre's heavy body was
troubled. He asked for the *provesor's* letter again, read it over,
went out on the corridor and consulted with a brother about as old
and round as himself, and at length told us to wait in that room and
he would bring it. As he went out he ordered all the Indians in the
courtyard, about forty or fifty, to go to the cabildo and tell the alcalde to send the guide. In a few minutes he returned, and opening
with some trepidation the folds of his large gown, produced the
stone.

Fuentes, in speaking of the old city, says, "To the westward of the
city there is a little mount that commands it, on which stands a
small round building about six feet in height, in the middle of
which there is a pedestal formed of a shining substance resembling
glass, but the precise quality of which has not been ascertained.
Seated around this building, the judges heard and decided the
causes brought before them, and their sentences were executed
upon the spot. Previous to executing them, however, it was necessary to have them confirmed by the oracle, for which purpose three
of the judges left their seats and proceeded to a deep ravine, where
there was a place of worship containing a black transparent stone,
on the surface of which the Deity was supposed to indicate the fate
of the criminal. If the decision was approved, the sentence was

executed immediately; if nothing appeared on the stone, the accused was set at liberty. This oracle was also consulted in the affairs of war. The Bishop Francisco Marroquin having obtained intelligence of this slab, ordered it to be cut square, and consecrated it for the top of the grand altar in the Church of Tecpan Guatemala. It is a stone of singular beauty, about a yard and a half each way." The "Modern Traveller" refers to it as an "interesting specimen of ancient art;" and in 1825 concludes, "we may hope, before long, to receive some more distinct account of this oracular stone."

The world—meaning thereby the two classes into which an author once divided it, of subscribers and non-subscribers to his work —the world that reads these pages is indebted to Don Saturnino for some additional information. The stone was sewed up in a piece of cotton cloth drawn tight, which looked certainly as old as the thirty-five years it had been under the *cura*'s charge, and probably was the same covering in which it was enveloped when first laid on the top of the altar. One or two stitches were cut in the middle, and this was perhaps all we should have seen; but Don Saturnino, with a hurried jargon of "strange, curious, sacred, incomprehensible, the *provesor's* letter, minister of New York," &c., whipped out his penknife, and the good old padre, heavy with agitation and his own weight, sunk into his chair, still holding on with both hands. Don Saturnino ripped till he almost cut the good old man's fingers, slipped out the sacred tablet, and left the sack in the padre's hands. The padre sat a picture of self-abandonment, helplessness, distress, and self-reproach. We moved toward the light, and Don Saturnino, with a twinkle of his eyes and a ludicrous earnestness, consummated the padre's fear and horror by scratching the sacred stone with his knife. This oracular slab is a piece of common slate, fourteen inches by ten, and about as thick as those used by boys at school, without characters of any kind upon it. With a strong predilection for the marvellous, and scratching it most irreverently, we could make nothing more out of it. Don Saturnino handed it back to the padre, and told him that he had better sew it up and put it back; and probably it is now in its place on the top of the grand altar, with the sacramental cup upon it, an object of veneration to the fanatic Indians.

But the agitation of the padre destroyed whatever there was of comic in the scene. Recovering from the shock, he told us not to go back through the town; that there was a road direct to the old city; and concealing the tablet under his gown, he walked out with a firm step, and in a strong, unbroken voice, rapidly, in their own unintelligible dialect, called to the Indians to bring up our horses, and directed the guide to put us in the road which led direct to the *molina*. He feared that the Indians might discover our sacrilegious act; and as we looked in their stupid faces, we were well satisfied to get away before any such discovery was made, rejoicing more than the padre that we could get back to the *molina* without returning through the town.

We had but to mount and ride. At the distance of a mile and a half we reached the bank of an immense ravine. We descended it, Don Saturnino leading the way; and at the foot, on the other side, he stopped at a narrow passage, barely wide enough for the mule to pass. This was the entrance to the old city. It was a winding passage cut in the side of the ravine, twenty or thirty feet deep, and not wide enough for two horsemen to ride abreast; and this continued to the high table of land on which stood the ancient city of Patinamit.

This city flourished with the once powerful kingdom of the Kachiquel Indians. Its name, in their language, means "*the* city." It was also called Tecpan Guatemala, which, according to Vasques, means "the Royal House of Guatemala," and he infers that it was the capital of the Kachiquel kings; but Fuentes supposes that Tecpan Guatemala was the arsenal of the kingdom, and not the royal residence, which honour belonged to Guatemala, and that the former was so called from its situation on an eminence with respect to the latter, the word Tecpan meaning "above."

According to Fuentes, Patinamit was seated on an eminence, and surrounded by a deep defile or natural fosse, the perpendicular height of which, from the level of the city, was more than one hundred fathoms. The only entrance was by a narrow causeway terminated by two gates, constructed of the chay stone, one on the exterior and the other on the interior wall of the city. The plane of this eminence extends about three miles in length from north to south, and about two in breadth from east to west. The soil is covered with a stiff clay about three quarters of a yard deep. On one side of the area are the remains of a magnificent building, perfectly square, each side measuring one hundred paces, constructed of hewn stones extremely well put together; in front of the building is a large square, on one side of which stand the ruins of a sumptuous palace, and near to it are the foundations of several houses. A trench three yards deep runs from north to south through the city, having a breastwork of masonry rising about a yard high. On the eastern side of this trench stood the houses of the nobles, and on the opposite side the houses of the *maseguales* or commoners. The streets were, as may still be seen, straight and spacious, crossing each other at right angles.

When we rose upon the table, for some distance it bore no marks of ever having been a city. Very soon we came upon an Indian burning down trees and preparing a piece of ground for planting corn. Don Saturnino asked him to go with us and show us the ruins, but he refused. Soon after we reached a hut, outside of which a woman was washing. We asked her to accompany us, but she ran into the hut. Beyond this we reached a wall of stones, but broken and confused. We tied our horses in the shade of trees, and commenced exploring on foot. The ground was covered with mounds of ruins. In one place we saw the foundations of two houses, one of them about a hundred feet long by fifty feet broad. It was one hundred and forty years since Fuentes published the account of his visit; during that time the Indians had carried away on their backs stones to build up the modern village of Tecpan Guatemala, and the hand of ruin had been busily at work. We inquired particularly for sculptured figures; our guide knew of two, and after considerable search brought us to them. They were lying on the ground, about three feet long, so worn that we could not make them out, though on one the eyes and nose of an animal were distinguishable. The position commanded an almost boundless view, and it is surrounded by an immense ravine, which warrants the description given of it by Fuentes. In some places it was frightful to look down into its depths. On every side it was inaccessible, and the only way of reaching it was by the narrow passage through which we entered, its desolation and ruin adding another page to the burdened record of human contentions, and proving that, as in the world whose history we know, so in this of whose history we are ignorant, man's hand has been against his fellow. The solitary Indian hut is all that now occupies the site of the ancient city; but on Good Friday of every year a solemn procession of the whole Indian population is made to it from the village of Tecpan Guatemala, and, as our guide told us, on that day bells are heard sounding under the earth.

Descending by the same narrow passage, we traversed the ravine and ascended on the other side. Our guide put us into the road that avoided the town, and we set off on a gallop.

Don Saturnino possessed the extremes of good temper, simplicity, uprightness, intelligence, and perseverance. Ever since I fell in with him he had been most useful, but this day he surpassed himself; and he was so well satisfied with us as to declare that if it were not for his wife in Costa Rica, he would bear us company to Palenque. He had an engagement in Guatemala on a particular day; every day that he lost with us was so much deducted from his visit to his relatives; and at his earnest request we had consented to pass a day with them, though a little out of our road. We reached the *molina* in time to walk over the mill. On the side of the hill above was a large building to receive grain, and below it an immense reservoir for water in the dry season, but which did not answer the purpose intended. The mill had seven sets of grindstones, and working night and day, ground from seventy to ninety negases of wheat in the twenty-four hours, each negas being six *arobas* of twenty-five pounds. The Indians bring the wheat, and each one takes a stone and does his own grinding, paying a rial, twelve and a half cents, per negas for the use of the mill. Flour is worth about from three dollars and a half to four dollars the barrel.

Don Saturnino was one of the best men that ever lived, but in undress there was a lankness about him that was ludicrous. In the evening, as he sat on the bed with his thin arms wound around his thin legs, and we reproved him for his sacrilegious act in cutting open the cotton cloth, his little eyes twinkled, and Mr. C. and I laughed as we had not before laughed in Central America.

But in that country one extreme followed close upon another. At midnight we were roused from sleep by that movement which, once felt, can never be mistaken. The building rocked, our men in the corridor cried out "temblor," and Mr. C. and I at the same moment exclaimed "an earthquake!" Our *catres* stood transversely. By the undulating movement of the earth he was rolled from side to side, and I from head to foot. The sinking of my head induced an awful faintness of heart. I sprang upon my feet and rushed to the door. In a moment the earth was still. We sat on the sides of the bed, compared movements and sensations, lay down again, and slept till morning. . . .

As we stood on the ruined fortress of Resguardo, [by the site of Utatlan, capital of the Quiché] the great plain, consecrated by the last struggle of a brave people, lay before us grand and beautiful, its bloodstains all washed out, and smiling with fertility, but perfectly desolate. Our guide leaning on his sword in the area beneath was the only person in sight. But very soon Bobon introduced a stranger, who came stumbling along under a red silk umbrella, talking to Bobon and looking up at us. We recognised him as the *cura*, and descended to meet him. He laughed to see us grope our way down; by degrees his laugh became infectious, and when we met we all laughed together. All at once he stopped, looked very solemn, pulled off his neckcloth, and wiped the perspiration from his face, took out a paper of cigars, laughed, thrust them back, pulled out another, as he said, of Habaneras, and asked what was the news from Spain.

Our friend's dress was as unclerical as his manner, viz., a broad-brimmed black glazed hat, an old black coat reaching to his heels, glossy from long use, and pantaloons to match; a striped roundabout, a waistcoat, flannel shirt, and under it a cotton one, perhaps washed when he shaved last, some weeks before. He laughed at our coming to see the ruins, and said that he laughed prodigiously himself when he first saw them. He was from Old Spain; had seen the battle of Trafalgar, looking on from the heights on shore, and laughed whenever he thought of it; the French fleet was blown sky high, and the Spanish went with it; Lord Nelson was killed—all for glory—he could not help laughing. He had left Spain to get rid of wars and revolutions: here we all laughed; sailed with twenty Dominican friars; was fired upon and chased into Jamaica by a French cruiser: here we laughed again; got an English convoy to Omoa, where he arrived at the breaking out of a revolution; had been all his life in the midst of revolutions, and it was now better than ever. Here we all laughed incontinently. His own laugh was so rich and expressive that it was perfectly irresistible. In fact, we were not disposed to resist, and in half an hour we were as intimate as if acquainted for years. The world was our butt, and we laughed at it outrageously. Except the Church, there were a few things which the *cura* did not laugh at; but politics was his favourite subject. He was in favor of Morazan, or Carrera, or el Demonio: *"vamos adelante,"* "go ahead," was his motto; he laughed at them all. If we had parted with him then, we should always have remembered him as the laughing *cura*; but, on farther acquaintance, we found in him such a vein of strong sense and knowledge, and, retired as he lived, he was so intimately acquainted with the country and all the public men, as a mere looker-on his views were so correct and his satire so keen, yet without malice, that we improved his title by calling him the laughing philosopher.

Having finished our observations at this place, stopping to laugh as some new greatness or folly of the world, past, present, or to come, occurred to us, we descended by a narrow path, crossed a ravine, and entered upon the table of land on which stood the palace and principal part of the city. Mr. Catherwood and I began examining and measuring the ruins, and the padre followed us, talking and laughing all the time; and when we were on some high place, out of his reach, he seated Bobon at the foot, discoursing to him of Alvarado, and Montezuma, and the daughter of the King of Tecpan Guatemala, and books and manuscripts in the convent; to all which Bobon listened without comprehending a word or moving a muscle, looking him directly in the face, and answering his long low laugh with a respectful *"Si, señor."*

The heart of the city Utatlan was occupied by the palace and other buildings of the royal house of Quiché. It is surrounded by an immense barranca or ravine, and the only entrance is through that part of the ravine by which we reached it, and which is defended by the fortress before referred to. The *cura* pointed out to us one part of the ravine which, he said, according to old manuscripts formerly existing in the convent, but now carried away, was artificial, and upon which forty thousand men had been employed at one time.

The whole area was once occupied by the palace, seminary, and other buildings of the royal house of Quiché, which now lie for the most part in confused and shapeless masses of ruins. The palace, as the *cura* told us, with its courts and corridors, once covering the whole diameter, is completely destroyed, and the materials have been carried away to build the present village. In part, however, the floor remains entire, with fragments of the partition walls, so that the plan of the apartments can be distinctly made out. This floor is of a hard cement, which, though year after year washed by the floods of the rainy season, is hard and durable as stone. The inner walls were covered with plaster of a finer description, and in corners where there had been less exposure were the remains of colours; no doubt the whole interior had been ornamented with paintings. It gave a strange sensation to walk the floor of that roofless palace, and think of that king who left it at the head of seventy thousand men to repel the invaders of his empire. Corn was now growing among the ruins. The ground was used by an Indian family which claimed to be descended from the royal house. In one place was a desolate hut, occupied by them at the time of planting and gathering the corn. Adjoining the palace was a large plaza or courtyard, also covered with hard cement, in the centre of which were the relics of a fountain.

The most important part remaining of these ruins is that which appears in the engraving, and which is called *El Sacrificatorio*, or the place of sacrifice. It is a quadrangular stone structure, sixty-six feet on each side at the base, and rising in a pyramidal form to the height, in its present condition, of thirty-three feet. On three sides there is a range of steps in the middle, each step seventeen inches high, and but eight inches on the upper surface, which makes the range so steep that in descending some caution is necessary. At the corners are four buttresses of cut stone, diminishing in size from the line of the square, and apparently intended to support the structure. On the side facing the west there are no steps, but the surface is smooth and covered with stucco, gray from long exposure. By breaking a little at the corners we saw that there were different layers of stucco, doubtless put on at different times, and all had been ornamented with painted figures. In one place we made out part of the body of a leopard, well drawn and coloured.

The top of the *Sacrificatorio* is broken and ruined, but there is no doubt that it once supported an altar for those sacrifices of human victims which struck even the Spaniards with horror. It was barely large enough for the altar and officiating priests, and the idol to

whom the sacrifice was offered. The whole was in full view of the
people at the foot.

The barbarous ministers carried up the victim entirely naked,
pointed out the idol to which the sacrifice was made, that the people
might pay their adorations, and then extended him upon the altar.
This had a convex surface, and the body of the victim lay arched,

with the trunk elevated and the head and feet depressed. Four priests
held the legs and arms, and another kept his head firm with a
wooden instrument made in the form of a coiled serpent, so that he
was prevented from making the least movement. The head priest
then approached, and with a knife made of flint cut an aperture in
the breast, and tore out the heart, which, yet palpitating, he offered
to the sun, and then threw it at the feet of the idol. If the idol was
gigantic and hollow, it was usual to introduce the heart of the victim
into its mouth with a golden spoon. If the victim was a prisoner of

war, as soon as he was sacrificed they cut off the head to preserve the skull, and threw the body down the steps, when it was taken up by the officer or soldier to whom the prisoner had belonged, and carried to his house to be dressed and served up as an entertainment for his friends. If he was not a prisoner of war, but a slave purchased for the sacrifice, the proprietor carried off the body for the same purpose. In recurring to the barbarous scenes of which the spot had been the theatre, it seemed a righteous award that the bloody altar was hurled down, and the race of its ministers destroyed.

It was fortunate for us, in the excited state of the country, that it was not necessary to devote much time to an examination of these ruins. In 1834 a thorough exploration had been made under a commission from the government of Guatemala. Don Miguel Rivera y Maestre, a gentleman distinguished for his scientific and antiquarian tastes, was the commissioner, and kindly furnished me with a copy of his manuscript report to the government, written out by himself. This report is full and elaborate, and I have no doubt is the result of a thorough examination, but it does not refer to any objects of interest except those I have mentioned. He procured, however, the image . . . which, without my venturing to express a wish for it, he kindly gave to me. It is made of baked clay, very hard, and the surface as smooth as if coated with enamel. It is twelve inches high, and the interior is hollow, including the arms and legs. In his report to the government, Don Miguel calls it Cabuahuil, or one of the deities of the ancient inhabitants of Quiché. I do not know upon what authority he has given it this name, but to me it does not seem improbable that his supposition is true, and that to this earthen vessel human victims have been offered in sacrifice.

The heads in the engraving were given me by the *cura*. They are of terra cotta; the lower one is hollow and the upper is solid, with a polished surface. They are hard as stone, and in workmanship will compare with images in the same material by artists of the present day.

In our investigation of antiquities we considered this place important from the fact that its history is known and its date fixed. It was in its greatest splendour when Alvarado conquered it. It proves the character of the buildings which the Indians of that day constructed, and in its ruins confirms the glowing accounts given by Cortez and his companions of the splendour displayed in the edifices of Mexico. The point to which we directed our attention was to discover some resemblance to the ruins of Copan and Quirigua; but we did not find statues, or carved figures, or hieroglyphics, nor could we learn that any had ever been found there. If there had been such evidences we should have considered these remains the works of the same race of people, but in the absence of such evidences we believed that Copan and Quirigua were cities of another race and of a much older date.

The padre told us that thirty years before, when he first saw it, the palace was entire to the garden. He was then fresh from the palaces of Spain, and it seemed as if he was again among them. Shortly after his arrival a small gold image was found and sent to Seravia, the president of Guatemala, who ordered a commission from the capital to search for hidden treasure. In this search the palace was destroyed; the Indians, roused by the destruction of their ancient capital, rose, and threatened to kill the workingmen unless they left the country; and but for this, the *cura* said, every stone would have been razed to the ground. The Indians of Quiché have at all times a bad name; at Guatemala it was always spoken of as an unsafe place to visit; and the padre told us that they looked with distrust upon any stranger coming to the ruins. At that moment they were in a state of universal excitement; and coming close to us, he said that in the village they stood at swords' points with the mestizos, ready to cut their throats, and with all his exertions he could barely keep down a general rising and massacre. Even this information he gave us with a laugh. We asked him if he had no fears for himself. He said no; that he was beloved by the Indians; he had passed the greater part of his life among them; and as yet the padres were safe: the Indians considered them almost as saints. Here he laughed. Carrera was on their side; but if he turned against them it would be time to fly. This was communicated and received with peals of laughter; and the more serious the subject, the louder was our cachinnation. And all the time the padre made continual reference to books and manuscripts, showing antiquarian studies and profound knowledge.

Under one of the buildings was an opening which the Indians called a cave, and by which they said one could reach Mexico in an hour. I crawled under, and found a pointed-arch roof formed by stones lapping over each other, but was prevented exploring it by want of light, and the padre's crying to me that it was the season of earthquakes; and he laughed more than usual at the hurry with which I came out; but all at once he stopped, and grasping his pantaloons, hopped about, crying, "a snake, a snake." The guide and Bobon hurried to his relief; and by a simple process, but with great respect, one at work on each side, were in a fair way of securing the intruder; but the padre could not stand still, and with his agitation and restlessness tore loose from their hold, and brought to light a large grasshopper. While Bobon and the guide, without a smile, restored him, and put each button in its place, we finished with a laugh outrageous to the memory of the departed inhabitants, and to all sentiment connected with the ruins of a great city.

As we returned to the village the padre pointed out on the plain the direction of four roads, which led, and which, according to him, are still open, to Mexico, Tecpan Guatemala, Los Altos, and Vera Paz.

[After leaving the ruins of Utatlan Stephens followed the line of the Sierras north-west to Quetzaltenango and then on to Gueguetenango.]

Ruins Near Gueguetenango—an Excavation. Journey to Palenque Continued. Discovery of Stucco Sculptures.

Early in the morning our mules were saddled for the journey. The *gobernador* and another friend of the *cura* came to receive parting instructions, and set off for Guatemala. The Indians engaged for us did not make their appearance; and, desirous to save the day, we loaded the mules, and sent Juan and Bobon forward with the luggage. In a little while two women came and told us that our Indians were in prison. I accompanied them to two or three officials, and with much difficulty and loss of time found the man having charge of them, who said that, finding we had paid them part of their hire in advance, and afraid they would buy *agua ardiente* and be missing, he had shut them up the night before to have them ready, and had left word to that effect with one of the servants of the *cura*. I went with him to the prison, paid a shilling apiece for their lodging, and took them over to the convent. The poor fellows had not eaten since they were shut up, and, as usual, wanted to go home for tortillas for the journey. We refused to let them go, but gave them money to buy some in the plaza and kept the woman and their *chamars* as hostages for their return. But we became tired of waiting. Mr. Catherwood picked up their *chamars* and threw them across his saddle as a guarantee for their following, and we set off.

We had added to our equipments *aguas de arma*, being undressed goatskins embroidered with red leather, which hung down from the saddlebow, to protect the legs against rain, and were now fully accoutred in Central American style. . . .

Our day's journey was but twenty-seven miles, but it was harder for man and beast than any sixty since we left Guatemala. We rode into the town [of Gueguetenango], the chief place of the last district of Central America and of the ancient kingdom of Quiché. It was well built, with a large church or plaza, and again a crowd of mestizos were engaged in the favourite occupation of fighting cocks. As we rode through the plaza the bell sounded for the *oracion* or vesper prayers. The people fell on their knees and we took off our hats. We stopped at the house of Don Joaquim Mon, an old Spaniard of high consideration, by whom we were hospitably received, and who, though a Centralist, on account of some affair of his sons, had had his house at Chiantla plundered by [the rebel leader] Carrera's soldiers. His daughters were compelled to take refuge in the church, and forty or fifty mules were driven from his hacienda. In a short time we had a visit from the *corregidor*, who had seen our proposed journey announced in the government paper, and treated us with the consideration due to persons specially recommended by the government.

We reached Gueguetenango in a shattered condition. Our cargomules had their backs so galled that it was distressing to use them; and the saddle-horse was no better off. Bobon, in walking barefooted over the stony road, had bruised the ball of one of his feet so that he was disabled, and that night Juan's enormous supper gave him an indigestion. He was a tremendous feeder; on the road nothing eatable was safe. We owed him a spite for pilfering our bread and bringing us down to tortillas, and were not sorry to see him on his back; but he rolled over the floor of the corridor crying out uproariously, so as to disturb the whole household, *"Voy morir!" "Voy morir!"* "I am going to die!" "I am going to die!" He was a hard subject to work upon, but we took him in hand strongly, and unloaded him.

Besides our immediate difficulties, we heard of others in prospect. In consequence of the throng of immigrants from Guatemala toward Mexico, no one was admitted into that territory without a passport from Ciudad Real, the capital of Chiapas, four or five days' journey from the frontier. The frontier was a long line of river in the midst of a wilderness, and there were two roads, a lower one but little travelled, on account of the difficulty of crossing the rivers, but at that time passable. As we intended, however, at all events, to stop at this place for the purpose of visiting the ruins, we postponed our decision till the next day.

The next morning Don Joaquin told us of the skeleton of a colossal animal, supposed to be a mastodon, which had been found in the neighborhood. Some of the bones had been collected, and were then in the town, and having seen them, we took a guide and walked to the place where they had been discovered, on the borders of the Rio Chinaca, about half a mile distant. At this time the river was low, but the year before, swelled by the immense floods of the rainy season, it had burst its bounds, carried away its left bank, and laid bare one side of the skeleton. The bank was perpendicular, about thirty feet high, and the animal had been buried in an upright position. Besides the bones in the town, some had been carried away by the flood, others remained imbedded in the earth; but the impression of the whole animal, from twenty-five to thirty feet long, was distinctly visible. We were told that about eight leagues above, on the bank of the same river, the skeleton of a much larger animal had been discovered.

In the afternoon we rode to the ruins, which in the town were called *las cuevas*, the caves. They lie about half a league distant, on a magnificent plain, bounded in the distance by lofty mountains, among which is the great Sierra Madre.

The site of the ancient city, as at Patinamit and Santa Cruz del Quiché, was chosen for its security against enemies. It was surrounded by a ravine, and the general character of the ruins is the same as at Quiché, but the hand of destruction has fallen upon it more heavily. The whole is a confused heap of grass-grown fragments. The principal remains are two pyramidal structures of this form:

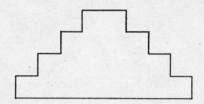

One of them measures at the base one hundred and two feet; the steps are four feet high and seven feet deep, making the whole height twenty-eight feet. They are not of cut stone as at Copan, but of rough pieces cemented with lime, and the whole exterior was formerly coated with stucco and painted. On the top is a small square platform, and at the base lies a long slab of rough stone, apparently hurled down from the top; perhaps the altar on which human victims were extended for sacrifice.

The owner of the ground, a mestizo, whose house was near by, and who accompanied us to the ruins, told us that he had bought the land from Indians, and that, for some time after his purchase, he was annoyed by their periodical visits to celebrate some of their ancient rites on the top of this structure. This annoyance continued until he whipped two or three of the principal men and drove them away.

At the foot of the structure was a vault, faced with cut stone, in which were found a collection of bones and a terra cotta vase, then in his possession. The vault was not long enough for the body of a man extended, and the bones must have been separated before they were placed there.

The owner believed that these structures contained interior apartments with hidden treasures; and there were several mounds, supposed to be sepulchres of the ancient inhabitants, which also, he had no doubt, contained treasure. The situation of the place was magnificent. We had never before enjoyed so good an opportunity of working, and agreed with him to come the next day and make excavacations, promising to give him all the treasure, and taking for my share only the skulls, vases, and other curiosities.

The next morning, before we were up, the door was thrown open, and to our surprise we received a salutation in English. The costume of the stranger was of the country; his beard was long, and he looked as if already he had made a hard morning's ride. To my great surprise and pleasure I recognised Pawling, whom the reader will perhaps remember I had seen as superintendent of a cochineal hacienda at Amatitlan. He had heard of our setting out for Mexico, and, disgusted with his occupation and the country, had mounted his horse, and with all he was worth tied on behind his saddle, pushed on to overtake us. On the way he had bought a fine mule, and by hard riding, and changing from one animal to the other, had reached us in four days. He was in difficulty about a passport, and was anxious to have the benefit of mine in order to get out of the country, offering to attach himself to me in any capacity necessary for that purpose. Fortunately, my passport was broad enough to cover him, and I immediately constituted him the general manager of the expedition, the material of which was now reduced to Juan sick and but one cargo-mule sound.

At nine o'clock, attended by three men and a boy with machetes, being all we could procure at so short a notice, we were again among the ruins. We were not strong enough to pull down a pyramid, and lost the morning in endeavouring to make a breach in one of the sides, but did not accomplish anything.

In the afternoon we opened one of the mounds. The interior was a rough coat of stones and lime, and after an hour's digging we came to fragments of bones and the two lower vases in the plate opposite. The first of the two was entire when we discovered it, but, unfortunately, was broken in getting it out, though we obtained all the pieces. It is graceful in design, the surface is polished, and the workmanship very good. The last was already broken, and though more complicated, the surface is not polished. The tripod at the top of the engraving is a copy of the vase before referred to, found in the tomb, which I procured from the owner of the land. It is twelve inches in diameter, and the surface is polished. We discovered no treasure, but our day's work was most interesting, and we only regretted that we had not time to explore more thoroughly.

In the meantime Don Joaquin had made arrangements for us, and the next morning we resumed our journey. We left behind a mule, a horse, and Bobon, and were re-enforced by Pawling, well mounted, and armed with a pair of pistols, and a short double-barrelled gun slung to his saddle-bow, and Santiago, a Mexican fugitive soldier. Juan was an interesting invalid mounted on a mule, and the whole was under escort of a respectable old muleteer, who was setting out with empty mules to bring back a load of sugar. . . .

In the morning dark clouds still obscured the sky, but they fell back and hid themselves before the beams of the rising sun. The grass and trees, arched by six months' drought, started into a deeper green, and the hills and mountains seemed glad. The alcalde, I believe vexed at our not being willing to make an immediate affair of exploring the ruins, had gone away for the day without sending us any guide, and leaving word that all the men were engaged in repairing the church. We endeavoured to entice one of them away, but unsuccessfully. Returning, we found that our piazza was the schoolhouse of the village. Half a dozen children were sitting on a bench, and the schoolmaster, half tipsy, was educating them, i. e., teaching them to repeat by rote the formal parts of the church service. We asked him to help us, but he advised us to wait a day or two; in that country nothing could be done *violenter*. We were excessively vexed at the prospect of losing the day; and at the moment when we thought we had nothing left but to submit, a little girl came to tell us that a woman, on whose hacienda the ruins were, was then about going to visit it, and offered to escort us. Her horse was already standing before the door, and before our mules were ready she rode over for us. We paid our respects, gave her a good cigar, and, lighting all around, set out. She was a pleasant mestizo, and had a son with her, a fine lad about fifteen. We started at half past nine, and, after a hot and sultry ride, at twenty minutes past eleven reached her rancho. It was a mere hut, made of poles and plastered with mud, but the situation was one of those that warmed us to country life. Our kind guide sent with us her son and an Indian with his machete, and in half an hour we were at the ruins.

Soon after leaving the rancho, and at nearly a mile distant, we saw, on a high elevation, through openings in trees growing around it, one of the buildings of Tonila, the Indian name in this region for stone houses. Approaching it, we passed on the plain in front two stone figures lying on the ground, with the faces upward; they were well carved, but the characters were somewhat faded by long exposure to the elements, although still distinct. Leaving them, we rode on to the foot of a high structure, probably a fortress, rising in a pyramidal form, with five spacious terraces. These terraces had all been faced with stone and stuccoed, but in many places they were broken and overgrown with grass and shrubs. Taking advantage of one of the broken parts, we rode up the first pitch, and, following the platform of the terrace, ascended by another breach to the second, and in the same way to the third. There we tied our horses and climbed up on foot. On the top was a pyramidal structure overgrown with trees, supporting the building which we had seen from the plain below. Among the trees were several wild lemons, loaded with fruit, and of very fine flavour, which, if not brought there by the Spaniards, must be indigenous. The building is fifty feet front and thirty-five feet deep; it is constructed of stone and lime, and the whole front was once covered with stucco, of which part of the cornice and mouldings still remain. The entrance is by a doorway ten feet wide, which leads into a sort of antechamber, on each side of which is a small doorway leading into an apartment ten feet square. The walls of these apartments were once covered with stucco, which had fallen down; part of the roof had given way, and the floor was covered with ruins. In one of them was the same pitchy substance we had noticed in the sepulchre at Copan. The roof was formed of stones, lapping over in the usual style, and forming as near an approach to the arch as was made by the architects of the Old World.

In the back wall of the centre chamber was a doorway of the same size with that in front, which led to an apartment without any partitions, but in the centre was an oblong enclosure eighteen feet by eleven, which was manifestly intended as the most important part of the edifice. The door was choked up with ruins to within a few feet of the top, but over it, and extending along the whole front of the structure, was a large stucco ornament, which at first impressed us most forcibly by its striking resemblance to the winged globe over the doors of Egyptian temples. Part of this ornament had fallen down, and, striking the heap of rubbish underneath, had rolled beyond the door of entrance. We endeavoured to roll it back and restore it to its place, but it proved too heavy for the strength of four men and a boy. The part which remains is represented in the engraving, and differs in detail from the winged globe. The wings are reversed; there is a fragment of a circular ornament which may have been intended for a globe, but there are no remains of serpents entwining it.

There was another surprising feature in this door. The lintel was *a beam of wood*; of what species we did not know, but our guide said it was of the sapote-tree. It was so hard that, on being struck, it rang like metal, and perfectly sound, without a worm-hole or other symptom of decay. The surface was smooth and even, and from a very close examination we were of the opinion that it must have been trimmed with an instrument of metal.

The opening under this doorway was what the alcalde had intended as the mouth of the cave that led to Palenque, and which, by-the-way, he had told us was so completely buried in El Monte that it would require two days digging and clearing to reach it. Our guide laughed at the ignorance prevailing in the village in regard to the difficulty of reaching it, but stoutly maintained the story that it led to Palenque. We could not prevail on him to enter it. A short cut to Palenque was exactly what we wanted. I took off my coat, and, lying down on my breast, began to crawl under. When I had advanced about half the length of my body, I heard a hideous hissing noise, and starting back, saw a pair of small eyes, which in the darkness shone like balls of fire. The precise portion of time that I employed in backing out is not worth mentioning. My companions had heard the noise, and the guide said it was *"un tigre."* I thought it was a wildcat; but, whatever it was, we determined to have a shot at it. We took it for granted that the animal would dash past us, and in a few moments our guns and pistols, swords and machetes, were ready; taking our positions, Pawling, standing close against the wall, thrust under a long pole, and with a horrible noise out fluttered a huge turkey-buzzard, which flapped itself through the building and took refuge in another chamber.

This peril over, I renewed the attempt, and holding a candle before me, quickly discovered the whole extent of the cave that led to Palenque. It was a chamber corresponding with the dimensions given of the outer walls. The floor was encumbered with rubbish two or three feet deep, the walls were covered with stuccoed figures, among which that of a monkey was conspicuous, and against the back wall, among curious and interesting ornaments, were two figures of men in profile, with their faces toward each other, well drawn and as large as life, but the feet concealed by the rubbish on the floor. Mr. Catherwood crawled in to make a drawing of them, but, on account of the smoke from the candles, the closeness, and excessive heat, it was impossible to remain long enough. In general appearance and character they were the same as we afterward saw carved on stone at Palenque.

By means of a tree growing close against the wall of this building I climbed to the top, and saw another edifice very near and on the top of a still higher structure. We climbed up to this, and found it of the same general plan, but more dilapidated. Descending, we passed between two other buildings on pyramidal elevations, and came out upon an open table which had probably once been the site of the city. It was protected on all sides by the same high terraces, overlooking for a great distance the whole country round, and rendering it impossible for an enemy to approach from any quarter without being discovered. Across the table was a high and narrow causeway, which seemed partly natural and partly artificial, and at some distance on which was a mound, with the foundations of a building that had probably been a tower. Beyond this the causeway extended till it joined a range of mountains. From the few Spanish books within my reach I have not been able to learn anything whatever of the history of this place, whether it existed at the time of the conquest or not. I am inclined to think, however, that it did, and that mention is made of it in some Spanish authors. At all events, there was no place we had seen which gave us such an idea of the vastness of the works erected by the aboriginal inhabitants. Pressed as we were, we determined to remain and make a thorough exploration.

It was nearly dark when we returned to the village. Immediately we called upon the alcalde, but found on the very threshold detention and delay. He repeated the schoolmaster's warning that nothing could be done *violenter*. It would take two days to get together men and implements, and these last of the kind necessary could not be had at all. There was not a crowbar in the place; but the alcalde said one could be made, and in the same breath that there was no iron; there was half a blacksmith, but no iron nearer than Tabasco, about eight or ten days' journey. While we were with him another terrible storm came on. We hurried back in the midst of it, and determined forthwith to push on to Palenque. I am strongly of opinion that there is at this place much to reward the future traveller. We were told that there were other ruins about ten leagues distant, along the same range of mountains; and it has additional interest in our eyes, from the circumstance that this would be the best point from which to attempt the discovery of the mysterious city seen from the top of the Cordilleras.

Dangerous Travel—Fireflies and Mosquitoes. Palenque at Last.

PALENQUE is in the north of the Chiapas district of Mexico, and therefore near the western limits of the Classic Maya area. It was a large ceremonial city, and its school of sculpture was perhaps the greatest in Mayan history. The seventh century Temple of the Inscriptions has become famous for the discovery of a richly furnished tomb concealed below it (p. 629, II).

THE country through which we were now travelling was as wild as before the Spanish conquest, and without a habitation until we reached Palenque. The road was through a forest so overgrown with brush and underwood as to be impenetrable, and the branches were trimmed barely high enough to admit a man's travelling under them on foot, so that on the backs of our mules we were constantly obliged to bend our bodies, and even to dismount. In some places, for a great distance around, the woods seemed killed by the heat, the foliage withered, the leaves dry and crisp, as if burned by the sun; and a tornado had swept the country, of which no mention was made in the San Pedro papers.

We met three Indians carrying clubs in their hands, naked except for a small piece of cotton cloth around the loins and passing between the legs, one of them, young, tall, and of admirable symmetry of form, looking the freeborn gentleman of the woods. Shortly afterward we passed a stream, where naked Indians were setting rude nets for fish, wild and primitive as in the first ages of savage life.

At twenty minutes past ten we commenced ascending the mountain. It was very hot, and I can give no idea of the toil of ascending these mountains. Our mules could barely clamber up with their saddles only. We disencumbered ourselves of sword, spurs, and all useless trappings; in fact, came down to shirt and pantaloons, and as near the condition of the Indians as we could. Our procession would have been a spectacle in Broadway. First were four Indians, each with a rough oxhide box, secured by an iron chain and large padlock, on his back; then Juan, with only a hat and pair of thin cotton drawers, driving two spare mules, and carrying a double-barrelled gun over his naked shoulders; then ourselves, each one driving before him or leading his own mule; then an Indian carrying the *silla*, with relief carriers, and several boys bearing small bags of provisions, the Indians of the *silla* being much surprised at our not using them according to contract and the price paid. Though toiling excessively, we felt a sense of degradation at being carried on a man's shoulders. At that time I was in the worst condition of the three, and the night before had gone to bed at San Pedro without supper, which for any of us was sure evidence of being in a bad way.

We had brought the *silla* with us merely as a measure of precaution, without much expectation of being obliged to use it; but at a steep pitch, which made my head almost burst to think of climbing, I resorted to it for the first time. It was a large, clumsy armchair, put together with wooden pins and bark strings. The Indian who was to carry me, like all the others, was small, not more than five feet

Ibid., pp. 273-8, 289-307.

seven, very thin, but symmetrically formed. A bark strap was tied
to the arms of the chair, and, sitting down, he placed his back
against the back of the chair, adjusted the length of the strings,
and smoothed the bark across his forehead with a little cushion
to relieve the pressure. An Indian on each side lifted it up, and the
carrier rose on his feet, stood still a moment, threw me up once
or twice to adjust me on his shoulders, and set off with one man
on each side. It was a great relief, but I could feel every movement,
even to the heaving of his chest. The ascent was one of the steepest
on the whole road. In a few minutes he stopped and sent forth a
sound, usual with Indian carriers, between a whistle and a blow,
always painful to my ears, but which I never felt so disagreeably
before. My face was turned backward; I could not see where he was
going, but observed that the Indian on the left fell back. Not to
increase the labour of carrying me, I sat as still as possible; but in
a few minutes, looking over my shoulder, saw that we were approaching the edge of a precipice more than a thousand feet deep.
Here I became very anxious to dismount; but I could not speak
intelligibly, and the Indians could or would not understand my signs.
My carrier moved along carefully, with his left foot first, feeling that
the stone on which he put it down was steady and secure before he
brought up the other, and by degrees, after a particularly careful
movement, brought both feet up within half a step of the edge
of the precipice, stopped, and gave a fearful whistle and blow. I
rose and fell with every breath, felt his body trembling under me,
and his knees seemed giving way. The precipice was awful, and
the slightest irregular movement on my part might bring us both
down together. I would have given him a release in full for the rest
of the journey to be off his back; but he started again, and with the
same care ascended several steps, so close to the edge that even
on the back of a mule it would have been very uncomfortable.
My fear lest he should break down or stumble was excessive. To
my extreme relief, the path turned away; but I had hardly congratulated myself upon my escape before he descended a few steps.
This was much worse than ascending; if he fell, nothing could keep
me from going over his head; but I remained till he put me down
of his own accord. The poor fellow was wet with perspiration, and
trembled in every limb. Another stood ready to take me up, but I had
had enough. Pawling tried it, but only for a short time. It was bad
enough to see an Indian toiling with a dead weight on his back; but
to feel him trembling under one's own body, hear his hard breathing,
see the sweat rolling down him, and feel the insecurity of the position, made this a mode of travelling which nothing but constitutional
laziness and insensibility could endure. Walking, or rather climbing,
stopping very often to rest, and riding when it was at all practicable,

we reached a thatched shed, where we wished to stop for the night, but there was no water.

We could not understand how far it was to Nopa, our intended stopping-place, which we supposed to be on the top of the mountain. To every question the Indians answered *"una legua."* Thinking it could not be much higher, we continued. For an hour more we had a very steep ascent, and then commenced a terrible descent. At this time the sun had disappeared; dark clouds overhung the woods, and thunder rolled heavily on the top of the mountain. As we descended a heavy wind swept through the forest; the air was filled with dry leaves; branches were snapped and broken, trees bent, and there was every appearance of a violent tornado. To hurry down on foot was out of the question. We were so tired that it was impossible; and, afraid of being caught on the mountain by a hurricane and deluge of rain, we spurred down as fast as we could go. It was a continued descent, without any relief, stony, and very steep. Very often the mules stopped, afraid to go on; and in one place the two empty mules bolted into the thick woods rather than proceed. Fortunately for the reader, this is our last mountain, and I can end honestly with a climax: it was the worst mountain I ever encountered in that or any other country, and, under our apprehension of the storm, I will venture to say that no travellers ever descended in less time. At a quarter before five we reached the plain. The mountain was hidden by clouds, and the storm was now raging above us. We crossed a river, and continuing along it through a thick forest, reached the rancho of Nopa.

It was situated in a circular clearing about one hundred feet in diameter, near the river, with the forest around so thick with brush and underwood that the mules could not penetrate it, and with no opening but for the passage of the road through it. The rancho was merely a pitched roof covered with palm-leaves, and supported by four trunks of trees. All around were heaps of snail-shells, and the ground of the rancho was several inches deep with ashes, the remains of fires for cooking them. We had hardly congratulated ourselves upon our arrival at such a beautiful spot, before we suffered such an onslaught of mosquitoes as we had not before experienced in the country. We made a fire, and, with appetites sharpened by a hard day's work, sat down on the grass to dispose of a San Pedro fowl; but we were obliged to get up, and while one hand was occupied with eatables, use the other to brush off the venomous insects. We soon saw that we had bad prospects for the night, lighted fires all around the rancho, and smoked inordinately. We were in no hurry to lie down, and sat till a late hour, consoling ourselves with the reflection that, but for the mosquitoes, our satisfaction would be beyond all bounds. The dark border of the clearing was lighted up by fireflies of extraordinary size and brilliancy darting among the trees, not flashing and disappearing, but carrying a steady light; and, except that their course was serpentine, seeming like shooting stars. In different places there were two that remained stationary, emitting a pale but beautiful light, and seemed like rival belles holding levees. The fiery orbs darted from one to the other; and when one, more daring than the rest, approached too near, the coquette withdrew her light, and the flutterer went off. One, however, carried all before her, and at one time we counted seven hovering around her. . . .

Early the next morning we prepared for our move to the ruins. We had to make provision for housekeeping on a large scale; our culinary utensils were of rude pottery, and our cups the hard shells of some round vegetables, the whole cost, perhaps, amounting to one dollar. We could not procure a water jar in the place, but the alcalde lent us one free of charge unless it should be broken, and as it was cracked at the time he probably considered it sold. By the way, we forced ourselves upon the alcalde's affections by leaving our money with him for safe-keeping. We did this with great publicity, in order that it might be known in the village that there was no "plata" at the ruins, but the alcalde regarded it as a mark of special confidence. Indeed, we could not have shown him a greater. He was a suspicious old miser, kept his own money in a trunk in an inner room, and never left the house without locking the street door and carrying the key with him. He made us pay beforehand for everything we wanted, and would not have trusted us half a dollar on any account.

It was necessary to take with us from the village all that could contribute to our comfort, and we tried hard to get a woman; but no one would trust herself alone with us. This was a great privation; a woman was desirable, not, as the reader may suppose, for embellishment, but to make tortillas. These, to be tolerable, must be eaten the moment they are baked; but we were obliged to make an arrangement with the alcalde to send them out daily with the product of our cow.

Our turn-out was equal to anything we had had on the road. One Indian set off with a cowhide trunk on his back, supported by a bark string, as the ground work of his load, while on each side hung by a bark string a fowl wrapped in plantain leaves, the head and tail only being visible. Another had on the top of his trunk a live turkey, with its legs tied and wings expanded, like a spread eagle. Another had on each side of his load strings of eggs, each egg being wrapped carefully in a husk of corn, and all fastened like onions on a bark string. Cooking utensils and water-jar were mounted on the backs of other Indians, and contained rice, beans, sugar, chocolate, &c.; strings of pork and bunches of plantains were pendent; and Juan carried in his arms our travelling tin coffee-canister filled with lard, which in that country was always in a liquid state.

At half past seven we left the village. For a short distance the road was open, but very soon we entered a forest, which continued unbroken to the ruins, and probably many miles beyond. The road was a mere Indian footpath, the branches of the trees, beaten down and heavy with the rain, hanging so low that we were obliged to stoop constantly, and very soon our hats and coats were perfectly wet. From the thickness of the foliage the morning sun could not dry up the deluge of the night before. The ground was very muddy, broken by streams swollen by the early rains, with gullies in which the mules floundered and stuck fast, in some places very difficult to cross. Amid all the wreck of empires, nothing ever spoke so forcibly the world's mutations as this immense forest shrouding what was once a great city. Once it had been a great highway, thronged with people who were stimulated by the same passions that give impulse to human action now; and they are all gone, their habitations buried, and no traces of them left.

In two hours we reached the River Micol, and in half an hour more that of Otula, darkened by the shade of the woods, and breaking beautifully over a stony bed. Fording this, very soon we saw masses of stones, and then a round sculptured stone. We spurred up a sharp ascent of fragments, so steep that the mules could barely climb it, to a terrace so covered, like the whole road, with trees, that it was impossible to make out the form. Continuing on this terrace, we stopped at the foot of a second, when our Indians cried out *"el Palacio"* "the palace" and through openings in the trees we saw the front of a large building richly ornamented with stuccoed figures on the pilasters, curious and elegant; trees growing close against it, and their branches entering the doors; in style and effect unique, extraordinary, and mournfully beautiful. We tied our mules to the trees, ascended a flight of stone steps forced apart and thrown down by trees, and entered the palace, ranged for a few moments along the corridor and into the courtyard, and after the first gaze of eager curiosity was over, went back to the entrance, and, standing in the doorway, fired a *feu-de-joie* of four rounds each, being the last charge of our firearms. But for this way of giving vent to our satisfaction we should have made the roof of the old palace ring with a hurrah. It was intended, too, for effect upon the Indians, who had probably never heard such a cannonade before, and almost, like their ancestors in the time of Cortez, regarded our weapons as instruments which spit lightning, and who,

AMERICA   558

we knew, would make such a report in the village as would keep any
of their respectable friends from paying us a visit at night.

We had reached the end of our long and toilsome journey, and
the first glance indemnified us for our toil. For the first time we
were in a building erected by the aboriginal inhabitants, standing
before the Europeans knew of the existence of this continent, and
we prepared to take up our abode under its roof. We selected the
front corridor as our dwelling, turned turkey and fowls loose in
the courtyard, which was so overgrown with trees that we could
barely see across it; and as there was no pasture for the mules
except the leaves of the trees, and we could not turn them loose
into the woods, we brought them up the steps through the palace,
and turned them into the courtyard also. At one end of the corridor
Juan built a kitchen, which operation consisted in laying three
stones anglewise, so as to have room for a fire between them. Our
luggage was stowed away or hung on poles reaching across the
corridor. Pawling mounted a stone about four feet long on some
legs for a table, and with the Indians cut a number of poles, which
they fastened together with bark strings, and laid them on stones
at the head and foot for beds. We cut down the branches that entered the palace, and some of the trees on the terrace, and from
the floor of the palace overlooked the top of an immense forest
stretching off to the Gulf of Mexico.

The Indians had superstitious fears about remaining at night
among the ruins, and left us alone, the sole tenants of the palace of
unknown kings. Little did they who built it think that in a few
years their royal line would perish and their race be extinct, their
city a ruin, and Mr. Catherwood, Pawling, and I and Juan its sole
tenants. Other strangers had been there, wondering like ourselves.
Their names were written on the walls, with comments and figures;
and even here were marks of those low, grovelling spirits which delight in profaning holy places. Among the names, but not of the
latter class, were those of acquaintances: Captain Caddy and Mr.
Walker; and one was that of a countryman, Noah O. Platt, New
York. He had gone out to Tabasco as supercargo of a vessel,
ascended one of the rivers for logwood, and while his vessel was
loading visited the ruins. His account of them had given me a strong
desire to visit them long before the opportunity of doing so presented itself.

High up on one side of the corridor was the name of William
Beanham, and under it was a stanza written in lead-pencil. By
means of a tree with notches cut in it, I climbed up and read the
lines. The rhyme was faulty and the spelling bad, but they breathed
a deep sense of the moral sublimity pervading these unknown ruins.
The author seemed, too, an acquaintance. I had heard his story in

Wine flagons made by early Celtic artists of Gaul. The general shape is based on Etruscan originals, the palmette on the neck is of Greek origin, while the animal handle shows oriental influence. From these borrowings the Celts created their own art. From Basse-Yutz, Moselle, France. Early fourth century B.C.

The face of Tollund man—preserved by a Danish bog for
two thousand years. The man had a leather halter round
his neck, and had probably been hanged either as a
traitor or as a sacrifice to a fertility goddess. C. first century B.C.

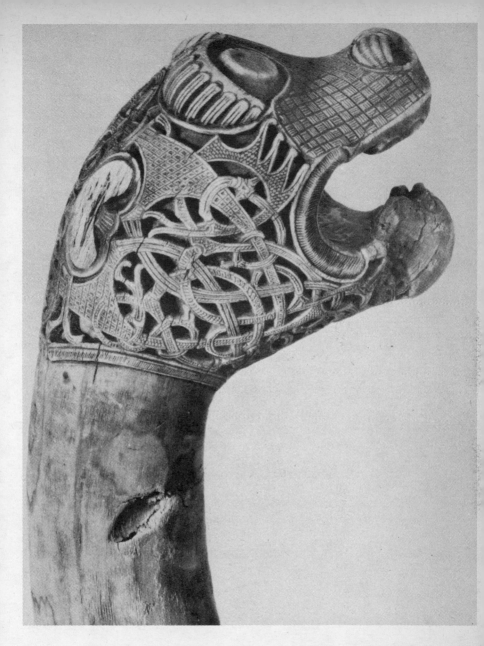

Wooden pole-head, probably of ceremonial use, exemplifying the vigorous and highly stylized art of the Vikings. From the burial ship of Queen Aasa, at Oseberg, Vestfold, Norway. C. A.D. 850

Tikal, a great Mayan ceremonial centre in the jungle of the Peten district of Guatemala. A pyramid, still supporting its crested temple, rises behind the broken stelae of the main court. Classic Maya, fourth to ninth centuries A.D.

RIGHT: An outstandingly fine carved calendar stone (Stela H) from the Mayan ceremonial centre of Copan, Guatemala. This was one of the stelae drawn by Catherwood. A.D. 731

UPPER LEFT: Ceramic figure of a mother and child from Campeche, Mexico: an example of the sensitive and humane aspect of Mayan art. Late Classic Maya, A.D. 600-900.

LOWER LEFT: One of the huge stone heads with infantile features characteristic of the Olmec culture of the Mexican coast. From San Lorenzo, Vera Cruz.

UPPER RIGHT: Ceramic figure of a smiling Totonac youth from Las Remogadas, Vera Cruz, Mexico. The laughing face is thought to express religious ecstasy as the boy was probably a sacrificial victim. Late Classic Maya.

LOWER RIGHT: Ceramic figure of a drummer from Nayarit, Mexico. He is striking a turtle-shell with a deer antler. This sort of percussion instrument is still played in remote Mexican villages. Possibly Classic Maya.

Machu Picchu, a little Inca town on a peak above the
Urubamba Valley near Cuzco, Peru. Late Inca, c. fifteenth
century A.D.

the village. He was a young Irishman, sent by a merchant of Tabasco into the interior for purposes of small traffic; had passed some time at Palenque and in the neighbourhood; and, with his thoughts and feelings turned strongly toward the Indians, after dwelling upon the subject for some time, resolved to penetrate into the country of the Caribs. His friends endeavoured to dissuade him, and the prefect told him, "You have red hair, a florid complexion, and white skin, and they will either make a god of you and keep you among them, or else kill and eat you;" but he set off alone and on foot, crossed the River Chacamal, and after an absence of nearly a year returned safe, but naked and emaciated, with his hair and nails long, having been eight days with a single Carib on the banks of a wild river, searching for a crossing-place, and living upon roots and herbs. He built a hut on the borders of the Chacamal River, and lived there with a Carib servant, preparing for another and more protracted journey among them, until at length some boatmen who came to trade with him found him lying in his hammock dead, with his skull split open. He had escaped the dangers of a journey which no man in that country dared encounter, to die by the hands of an assassin in a moment of fancied security. His arm was hanging outside, and a book lying on the ground; probably he was struck while reading. The murderers, one of whom was his servant, were caught, and were then in prison in Tabasco. Unfortunately, the people of Palenque had taken but little interest in anything except the extraordinary fact of his visit among the Caribs and his return safe. All his papers and collection of curiosities were scattered and destroyed, and with him died all the fruits of his labours; but, were he still living, he would be the man, of all others, to accomplish the discovery of that mysterious city which had so much affected our imaginations.

As the ruins of Palenque are the first which awakened attention to the existence of ancient and unknown cities in America, and as, on that account, they are perhaps more interesting to the public, it may not be amiss to state the circumstances of their first discovery.

The account is that in the year 1750, a party of Spaniards travelling in the interior of Mexico penetrated to the lands north of the district of Carmen, in the province of Chiapas, when all at once they found in the midst of a vast solitude ancient stone buildings, the remains of a city, still embracing from eighteen to twenty-four miles in extent, known to the Indians by the name of Casas de Piedras. From my knowledge of the country I am at a loss to conjecture why a party of Spaniards were travelling in that forest, or how they could have done so. I am inclined to believe rather that the existence of the ruins was discovered by the Indians, who had clearings in different parts of the forest for their corn-fields, or perhaps was known to them from time immemorial, and on their report the inhabitants were induced to visit them.

The existence of such a city was entirely unknown; there is no mention of it in any book, and no tradition that it had ever been. To this day it is not known by what name it was called, and the only appellation given to it is that of Palenque, after the village near which the ruins stand.

The news of the discovery passed from mouth to mouth, was repeated in some cities of the province, and reached the seat of government; but little attention was paid to it, and the members of the government, through ignorance, apathy, or the actual impossibility of occupying themselves with anything except public affairs, took no measures to explore the ruins, and it was not till 1786, thirty years subsequent to the discovery, that the King of Spain ordered an exploration; on the third of May, 1787, Captain Antonio del Rio arrived at the village, under a commission from the government of Guatemala, and on the fifth he proceeded to the site of the ruined city. In his official report he says, on making his first essay, owing to the thickness of the woods, and a fog so dense that it was impossible for the men to distinguish each other at five paces' distance, the principal building was completely concealed from their view.

He returned to the village, and after concerting measures with the deputy of the district, an order was issued to the inhabitants of Tumbala, requiring two hundred Indians with axes and billhooks. On the 17th seventy-nine arrived, furnished with twenty-eight axes, after which twenty more were obtained in the village; and with these he again moved forward, and immediately commenced felling trees, which was followed by a general conflagration.

The report of Captain Del Rio, with the commentary of Doctor Paul Felix Cabrera of New Guatemala, deducing an Egyptian origin for the people, through either the supineness or the jealousy of the Spanish government was locked up in the archives of Guatemala until the time of the Revolution, when, by the operation of liberal principles, the original manuscripts came into the hands of an English gentleman long resident in that country, and an English translation was published at London in 1822. This was the first notice in Europe of the discovery of these ruins; and, instead of electrifying the public mind, either from want of interest in the subject, distrust, or some other cause, so little notice was taken of it, that in 1831 the Literary Gazette, a paper of great circulation in London, announced it as a new discovery made by Colonel Galindo, whose unfortunate fate has been before referred to. If a like discovery had been made in Italy, Greece, Egypt, or Asia, within the reach of European travel, it would have created an interest not inferior to the discovery of Herculaneum, or Pompeii, or the ruins of Paestum.

While the report and drawings of Del Rio slept in the archives of Guatemala, Charles the Fourth of Spain ordered another expedition, at the head of which was placed Captain Dupaix [p. 66, I], with a secretary and draughtsman, and a detachment of dragoons. His expeditions were made in 1805, 1806, and 1807, the last of which was to Palenque.

The manuscripts of Dupaix, and the designs of his draughtsman Castenada, were about to be sent to Madrid, which was then occupied by the French army, when the revolution broke out in Mexico; they then became an object of secondary importance, and remained during the wars of independence under the control of Castenada, who deposited them in the Cabinet of Natural History in Mexico. In 1828 M. Baradere disentombed them from the cartons of the museum, where, but for this accident, they might still have remained, and the knowledge of the existence of this city again been lost. The Mexican Congress had passed a law forbidding any stranger not formally authorized to make researches or to remove objects of art from the country; but, in spite of this interdict, M. Baradere obtained authority to make researches in the interior of the republic, with the agreement that after sending to Mexico all that he collected, half should be delivered to him, with permission to transport them to Europe. Afterward he obtained by exchange the original designs of Castenada, and an authentic copy of the itinerary and descriptions of Captain Dupaix was promised in three months. From divers circumstances, that copy did not reach M. Baradere till long after his return to France, and the work of Dupaix was not published until 1834-5, twenty-eight years after his expedition, when it was brought out in Paris, in four volumes folio, at the price of eight hundred francs, with notes and commentaries by M. Alexandre Lenoir, M. Warden, M. Charles Farcy, M. Baradere, and M. De St. Priest.

Lord Kingsborough's ponderous tomes [p. 66, I], so far as regards Palenque, are a mere reprint of Dupaix, and the cost of his work is four hundred dollars per copy. Colonel Galindo's communications to the Geographical Society of Paris are published in the work of Dupaix, and since him Mr. Waldeck, with funds provided by an association in Mexico, had passed two years among the ruins. His drawings, as he states in a work on another place, were taken away by the Mexican government; but he had retained copies, and before we set out his work on Palenque was announced in Paris. It, however, has never appeared, and in the mean time Dupaix's is the text-book.

I have two objections to make to this work, not affecting Captain

Dupaix, who, as his expedition took place thirty-four years since, is not likely to be affected, if he is even living, but his Paris editors. The first is the very depreciating tone in which mention is made of the work of his predecessor Del Rio, and, secondly, this paragraph in the introduction:

It must be considered that a government only can execute such undertakings. A traveller relying upon his own resources cannot hope, whatever may be his intrepidity, to penetrate, and, above all, to live in those dangerous solitudes; and, supposing that he succeeds, it is beyond the power of the most learned and skilful man to explore alone the ruins of a vast city, of which he must not only measure and draw the edifices still existing, but also determine the circumference and examine the remains, dig the soil and explore the subterraneous constructions. M. Baradere arrived within fifty leagues of Palenque, burning with the desire of going there; but what could a single man do with domestics or other auxiliaries, without moral force or intelligence, against a people still half savage, against serpents and other hurtful animals, which, according to Dupaix, infest these ruins, and also against the vegetative force of a nature fertile and powerful, which in a few years re-covers all the monuments and obstructs all the avenues?

The effect of this is to crush all individual enterprise, and, moreover, it is untrue. All the accounts, founded upon this, represent a visit to these ruins as attended with immense difficulty and danger, to such an extent that we feared to encounter them; but there is no difficulty whatever in going from Europe or the United States to Palenque. Our greatest hardships, even in our long journey through the interior, were from the revolutionary state of the countries and want of time; and as to a residence there, with time to construct a hut or to fit up an apartment in the palace, and to procure stores from the seaboard, "those dangerous solitudes" might be anything rather than unpleasant.

And to show what individuals can accomplish, I state that Mr. Catherwood's drawings include all the objects represented in the work of Dupaix, and others besides which do not appear in that work at all, and have never before been presented to the public; among which are the frontispiece of this volume and the large tablets of hieroglyphics, the most curious and interesting pieces of sculpture at Palenque. I add, with the full knowledge that I will be contradicted by future travellers if I am wrong, that the whole of Mr. C.'s are more correct in proportions, outline, and filling up than his, and furnish more true material for speculation and study. I would not have said thus much but from a wish to give confidence to the reader who may be disposed to investigate and study these interesting remains. As to most of the places visited by us, he will find no materials whatever except those furnished in these pages.

In regard to Palenque he will find a splendid work, the materials of which were procured under the sanction of a commission from government, and brought out with explanations and commentaries by the learned men of Paris, by the side of which my two octavos shrink into insignificance; but I uphold the drawings against these costly folios, and against every other book that has ever been published on the subject of these ruins. My object has been, not to produce an illustrated work, but to present the drawings in such an inexpensive form as to place them within reach of the great mass of our reading community.

But to return to ourselves in the palace. While we were making our observations, Juan was engaged in a business that his soul loved. As with all the *mozos* of that country, it was his pride and ambition to *servir a mano*. He scorned the manly occupation of a muleteer, and aspired to that of a menial servant. He was anxious to be left at the village, and did not like the idea of stopping at the ruins, but was reconciled to it by being allowed to devote himself exclusively to cookery. At four o'clock we sat down to our first dinner. The table-cloth was two broad leaves, each about two feet long, plucked from a tree on the terrace before the door. Our saltcellar stood like a pyramid, being a case made of husks of corn put together lengthwise, and holding four or five pounds, in lumps from the size of a pea to that of a hen's egg. Juan was as happy as if he had prepared the dinner exclusively for his own eating; and all went merry as a marriage-bell, when the sky became overcast, and a sharp thunder-clap heralded the afternoon's storm. From the elevation of the terrace, the floor of the palace commanded a view of the top of the forest, and we could see the trees bent down by the force of the wind; very soon a fierce blast swept through the open doors, which was followed instantaneously by heavy rain. The table was cleared by the wind, and, before we could make our escape, was drenched by the rain. We snatched away our plates, and finished our meal as we could.

The rain continued, with heavy thunder and lightning, all the afternoon. In the absolute necessity of taking up our abode among the ruins, we had hardly thought of our exposure to the elements until it was forced upon us. At night we could not light a candle, but the darkness of the palace was lighted up by fireflies of extraordinary size and brilliancy, shooting through the corridors and stationary on the walls, forming a beautiful and striking spectacle. They were of the description with those we saw at Nopa, known by the name of shining beetles, and are mentioned by the early Spaniards, among the wonders of a world where all was new, "as showing the way to those who travel at night." The historian describes them as somewhat smaller than Sparrows, having two stars close by their Eyes, and two more under their Wings, which gave so great a Light that by it they could spin, weave, write, and paint; and the Spaniards went by night to hunt the utios or little Rabbits of that country; and a-fishing, carrying these Animals tied to their great Toes or Thumbs: and they called them Locuyos, being also of use to save them from the Gnats, which are there very troublesome. They took them in the Night with Firebrands, because they made to the Light, and came when called by their Name; and they are so unwieldy that when they fall they cannot rise again; and the Men stroking their Faces and Hands with a sort of Moisture that is in those Stars, seemed to be afire as long as it lasted.

It always gave us high pleasure to realize the romantic and seem-ingly half-fabulous accounts of the chroniclers of the conquest. Very often we found their quaint descriptions so vivid and faithful as to infuse the spirit that breathed through their pages. We caught several of these beetles, not, however, by calling them by their names, but with a hat, as school boys used to catch fireflies, or, less poetically, lightning-bugs, at home. They are more than half an inch long, and have a sharp movable horn on the head; when laid on the back they cannot turn over except by pressing this horn against a membrane upon the front. Behind the eyes are two round trans-parent substances full of luminous matter, about as large as the head of a pin, and underneath is a larger membrane containing the same luminous substance. Four of them together threw a brilliant light for several yards around, and by the light of a single one we read distinctly the finely-printed pages of an American newspaper. It was one of a packet, full of debates in Congress, which I had as yet barely glanced over, and it seemed stranger than any incident of my journey to be reading by the light of beetles, in the ruined palace of Palenque, the sayings and doings of great men at home. In the midst of it Mr. Catherwood, in emptying the capacious pocket of a shooting-jacket, handed me a Broadway omnibus ticket:

"GOOD TO THE BEARER FOR A RIDE,
"A. BROWER."

These things brought up vivid recollections of home, and among the familiar images present were the good beds into which our friends were about that time turning. Ours were set up in the back corridor, fronting the courtyard. This corridor consisted of open doors and pilasters alternately. The wind and rain were sweeping through, and, unfortunately, our beds were not out of reach of the spray. They had been set up with some labour on four piles of stones each, and we could not then change their position. We had no spare articles to put up as screens; but, happily, two umbrellas, tied up with measuring rods and wrapped in a piece of matting, had sur-

vived the wreck of the mountain roads. These Mr. C. and I secured
at the head of our beds. Pawling swung a hammock across the
corridor so high that the sweep of the rain only touched the foot;
and so passed our first night at Palenque. In the morning, umbrellas, bedclothes, wearing apparel, and hammocks were wet
through, and there was not a dry place to stand on. Already we
considered ourselves booked for a rheumatism. We had looked to
our residence at Palenque as the end of troubles, and for comfort
and pleasure, but all we could do was to change the location of our
beds to places which promised a better shelter for the next night.

A good breakfast would have done much to restore our equa-
nimity; but, unhappily, we found that the tortillas which we had
brought out the day before, probably made of half-mouldy corn, by
the excessive dampness were matted together, sour, and spoiled. We
went through our beans, eggs, and chocolate without any substitute
for bread, and, as often before in time of trouble, composed ourselves with a cigar. Blessed be the man who invented smoking, the
soother and composer of a troubled spirit, allayer of angry passions,
a comfort under the loss of breakfast, and to the roamer in desolate
places, the solitary wayfarer through life, serving for "wife, children,
and friends."

At about ten o'clock the Indians arrived with fresh tortillas and
milk. Our guide, too, having finished cutting up and distributing the
hog, was with them. He was the same who had been employed by
Mr. Waldeck, and also by Mr. Walker and Captain Caddy, and was
recommended by the prefect as the only man acquainted with the
ruins. Under his escort we set out for a preliminary survey. Of ourselves, leaving the palace, in any direction, we should not have
known which way to direct our steps.

In regard to the extent of these ruins. Even in this practical age
the imagination of man delights in wonders. The Indians and the
people of Palenque say that they cover a space of sixty miles; in a
series of well-written articles in our own country they have been set
down as ten times larger than New York; and lately I have seen an
article in some of the newspapers, referring to our expedition,
which represents this city, *discovered* by us, as having been three
times as large as London! It is not in my nature to discredit any
marvellous story. I am slow to disbelieve, and would rather sustain
all such inventions; but it has been my unhappy lot to find marvels
fade away as I approached them: even the Dead Sea lost its mysterious charm; and besides, as a traveller and "writer of a book," I
know that if I go wrong, those who come after me will not fail to
set me right. Under these considerations, not from any wish of my
own, and with many thanks to my friends of the press, I am obliged
to say that the Indians and people of Palenque really know nothing

of the ruins personally, and the other accounts do not rest upon any sufficient foundation. The whole country for miles around is covered by a dense forest of gigantic trees, with a growth of brush and underwood unknown in the wooded deserts of our own country, and impenetrable in any direction except by cutting a way with a machete. What lies buried in that forest it is impossible to say of my own knowledge; without a guide, we might have gone within a hundred feet of all the buildings without discovering one of them.

Captain Del Rio, the first explorer, with men and means at command, states in his report, that in the execution of his commission he cut down and burned all the woods; he does not say how far, but, judging from the breaches and excavations made in the interior of the buildings, probably for miles around. Captain Dupaix, acting under a royal commission, and with all the resources such a commission would give, did not discover any more buildings than those mentioned by Del Rio, and we saw only the same; but, having the benefit of them as guides, at least of Del Rio (for at that time we had not seen Dupaix's work), we of course saw things which escaped their observation, just as those who come after us will see what escaped ours. This place, however, was the principal object of our expedition, and it was our wish and intention to make a thorough exploration. Respect for my official character, the special tenor of my passport, and letters from Mexican authorities, gave me every facility. The prefect assumed that I was sent by my government expressly to explore the ruins; and every person in Palenque except our friend the alcalde, and even he as much as the perversity of his disposition would permit, was disposed to assist us. But there were accidental difficulties which were insuperable. First, it was the rainy season. This, under any circumstances, would have made it difficult; but as the rains did not commence till three or four o'clock, and the weather was clear always in the morning, it alone would not have been sufficient to prevent our attempting it; but there were other difficulties, which embarrassed us from the beginning, and continued during our whole residence among the ruins. There was not an axe or spade in the place, and, as usual, the only instrument was the machete, which here was like a short and wide-bladed sword; and the difficulty of procuring Indians to work was greater than at any other place we had visited. It was the season of planting corn, and the Indians, under the immediate pressure of famine, were all busy with their *milpas*. The price of an Indian's labour was eighteen cents per day; but the alcalde, who had the direction of this branch of the business, would not let me advance to more than twenty-five cents, and the most he would engage to send me was from four to six a day. They would not sleep at the ruins, came late, and went away early; sometimes only two or three appeared, and the same men rarely came twice, so that during our stay we had all the Indians of the village in rotation. This increased very much our labour, as it made it necessary to stand over them constantly to direct their work; and just as one set began to understand precisely what we wanted, we were obliged to teach the same to others; and I may remark that their labour though nominally cheap, was dear in reference to the work done.

At that time I expected to return to Palenque; whether I shall do so now or not is uncertain; but I am anxious that it should be understood that the accounts which have been published of the immense labour and expense of exploring these ruins, which, as I before remarked, made it almost seem presumptuous for me to undertake it with my own resources, are exaggerated and untrue. Being on the ground at the commencement of the dry season, with eight or ten young "pioneers," having a spirit of enterprise equal to their bone and muscle, in less than six months the whole of these ruins could be laid bare. Any man who has ever "cleared" a hundred acres of land is competent to undertake it, and the time and money spent by one of our young men in a "winter in Paris" would determine beyond all peradventure whether the city ever did cover the immense extent which some have supposed.

But to return: Under the escort of our guide we had a fatiguing but most interesting day. What we saw does not need any exaggeration. It awakened admiration and astonishment. In the afternoon came on the regular storm. We had distributed our beds, however, along the corridors, under cover of the outer wall, and were better protected, but suffered terribly from mosquitoes, the noise and stings of which drove away sleep. In the middle of the night I took up my mat to escape from these murderers of rest. The rain had ceased, and the moon, breaking through the heavy clouds, with a misty face lighted up the ruined corridor. I climbed over a mound of stones at one end, where the wall had fallen, and, stumbling along outside the palace entered a lateral building near the foot of the tower, groped in the dark along a low damp passage, and spread my mat before a low doorway at the extreme end. Bats were flying and whizzing through the passage, noisy and sinister; but the ugly creatures drove away mosquitoes. The dampness of the passage was cooling and refreshing; and, with some twinging apprehensions of the snakes and reptiles, lizards and scorpions, which infest the ruins, I fell asleep.

Further Exploration of Palenque. Sculptures and Hieroglyphs.

The interior of the building is divided into two corridors, running lengthwise, with a ceiling rising nearly to a point, as in the palace,

and paved with large square stones. The front corridor is seven feet
wide. The separating wall is very massive, and has three doors, a
large one in the centre, and a smaller one on each side. In this corridor, on each side of the principal door, is a large tablet of hieroglyphics, each thirteen feet long and eight feet high, and each
divided into two hundred and forty squares of characters or symbols.
Both are set in the wall so as to project three or four inches. In one
place a hole had been made in the wall close to the side of one of
them, apparently for the purpose of attempting its removal, by
which we discovered that the stone is about a foot thick. The sculpture is in bas-relief.

The construction of the tablets was a large stone on each side,
and smaller ones in the centre, as indicated by the dark lines in
the engravings.

In the right-hand tablet one line is obliterated by water that has
trickled down for an unknown length of time, and formed a sort of
stalactite or hard substance, which has incorporated itself with the
stone, and which we could not remove, though perhaps it might be
detached by some chemical process. In the other tablet, nearly one
half of the hieroglyphics are obliterated by the action of water and
decomposition of the stone. When we first saw them both tablets
were covered with a thick coat of green moss, and it was necessary
to wash and scrape them, clear the lines with a stick, and scrub
them thoroughly, for which last operation a pair of blacking-
brushes that Juan had picked up in my house at Guatemala, and
disobeyed my order to throw away upon the road, proved exactly
what we wanted and could not have procured. Besides this process,
on account of the darkness of the corridor, from the thick shade of
the trees growing before it, it was necessary to burn candles or
torches, and to throw a strong light upon the stones while Mr.
Catherwood was drawing.

The corridor in the rear is dark and gloomy, and divided into three
apartments. Each of the side apartments has two narrow openings
about three inches wide and a foot high. They have no remains of
sculpture, or painting, or stuccoed ornaments. In the centre apartment, set in the back wall, and fronting the principal door of entrance, is another tablet of hieroglyphics, four feet six inches wide
and three feet six inches high. The roof above it is tight; consequently it has not suffered from exposure, and the hieroglyphics
are perfect, though the stone is cracked lengthwise through the
middle, as indicated in the engraving.

The impression made upon our minds by these speaking but
unintelligible tablets I shall not attempt to describe. From some un-

Ibid., pp. 341-57.

accountable cause they have never before been presented to the public. Captains Del Rio and Dupaix both refer to them, but in very few words, and neither of them has given a single drawing. Acting under a royal commission, and selected, doubtless, as fit men for the duties intrusted to them, they cannot have been ignorant or insensible of their value. It is my belief they did not give them because in both cases the artists attached to their expedition were incapable of the labour, and the steady, determined perseverance required for drawing such complicated, unintelligible, and anomalous characters. As at Copan, Mr. Catherwood divided his paper into squares; the original drawings were reduced, and the engravings corrected by himself, and I believe they are as true copies as the pencil can make: the real written records of a lost people. The Indians call this building an escuela or school, but our friends the padres called it a tribunal of justice, and these stones, they said, contained the tables of the law.

There is one important fact to be noticed. The hieroglyphics are the same as were found at Copan and Quirigua. The intermediate country is now occupied by races of Indians speaking many different languages, and entirely unintelligible to each other; but there is room for the belief that the whole of this country was once occupied by the same race, speaking the same language, or, at least, having the same written characters.

There is no staircase or other visible communication between the lower and upper parts of this building, and the only way of reaching the latter was by climbing a tree which grows close against the wall, and the branches of which spread over the roof. The roof is inclined, and the sides are covered with stucco ornaments, which, from exposure to the elements, and the assaults of trees and bushes, are faded and ruined, so that it was impossible to draw them; but enough remained to give the impression that, when perfect and painted, they must have been rich and imposing. Along the top was a range of pillars eighteen inches high and twelve apart, made of small pieces of stone laid in mortar, and covered with stucco, crowning which is a layer of flat projecting stones, having somewhat the appearance of a low open balustrade.

In front of this building, at the foot of the pyramidal structure, is a small stream, part of which supplies the aqueduct before referred to. Crossing this, we come upon a broken stone terrace about sixty feet on the slope, with a level esplanade at the top, one hundred and ten feet in breadth, from which rises another pyramidal structure, now ruined and overgrown with trees; it is one hunded and thirty-four feet high on the slope, and on its summit is [a] building like the first shrouded among trees, but presented in the engraving opposite as restored. The plate contains, as before, the ground-plan, front elevation, section, and front elevation on a smaller scale, with the pyramidal structure on which it stands.

This building is fifty feet front, thirty-one feet deep, and has three doorways. The whole front was covered with stuccoed ornaments. The two outer piers contain hieroglyphics; one of the inner piers is fallen, and the other is ornamented with a figure in bas-relief, but faded and ruined.

The interior, again, is divided into two corridors running lengthwise, with ceilings as before, and pavements of large square stones, in which forcible breaches have been made, doubtless by Captain Del Rio, and excavations underneath. The back corridor is divided into three apartments, and opposite the principal door of entrance is an oblong enclosure, with a heavy cornice or moulding of stucco, and a doorway richly ornamented over the top, but now much defaced; on each side of the doorway was a tablet of sculptured stone, which, however, has been removed. Within, the chamber is thirteen feet wide and seven feet deep. There was no admission of light except from the door; the sides were without ornament of any kind, and in the back wall, covering the whole width, was the tablet given in the engraving opposite. It was ten feet eight inches wide, six feet four inches in height, and consisted of three separate stones. That on the left, facing the spectator, is still in its place. The middle one has been removed and carried down the side of the structure, and now lies near the bank of the stream. It was removed many years ago by one of the inhabitants of the village, with the intention of carrying it to his house; but, after great labour, with no other instruments than the arms and hands of Indians, and poles cut from trees, it had advanced so far, when its removal was arrested by an order from the government forbidding any farther abstraction from the ruins. We found it lying on its back near the banks of the stream, washed by many floods of the rainy season, and covered with a thick coat of dirt and moss. We had it scrubbed and propped up, and probably the next traveller will find it with the same props under it which we placed there. In the engraving it is given in its original position on the wall. The stone on the right is broken, and, unfortunately, altogether destroyed; most of the fragments have disappeared; but, from the few we found among the ruins in the front of the building, there is no doubt that it contained ranges of hieroglyphics corresponding in general appearance with those of the stone on the left.

The tablet, as given in the engraving, contains only two thirds of the original. In Del Rio's work it is not represented at all. In Dupaix it is given, not, however, as it exists, but as made up by the artist in Paris, so as to present a perfect picture. The subject is reversed, with the cross in the centre, and on each side a single row of hieroglyphics, only eight in number. Probably, when Dupaix saw it (thirty-four years before), it was entire, but the important features of six rows of hieroglyphics on each side of the principal figures, each row containing seventeen in a line, do not appear. This is the more inexcusable in his publishers, as in his report Dupaix expressly refers to these numerous hieroglyphics; but it is probable that his report was not accompanied by any drawings of them.

The principal subject of this tablet is the cross. It is surmounted by a strange bird, and loaded with indescribable ornaments. The two figures are evidently those of important personages. They are well drawn, and in symmetry of proportion are perhaps equal to many that are carved on the walls of the ruined temples in Egypt. Their costume is in a style different from any heretofore given, and the folds would seem to indicate that they were of a soft and pliable texture, like cotton. Both are looking toward the cross, and one seems in the act of making an offering, perhaps of a child; all speculations on the subject are of course entitled to little regard, but perhaps it would not be wrong to ascribe to these personages a sacerdotal character. The hieroglyphics doubtless explain all. Near them are other hieroglyphics, which reminded us of the Egyptian mode for recording the name, history, office, or character of the persons represented. This tablet of the cross has given rise to more learned speculations than perhaps any others found at Palenque. Dupaix and his commentators, assuming for the building a very remote antiquity, or, at least, a period long antecedent to the Christian era, account for the appearance of the cross by the argument that it was known and had a symbolical meaning among ancient nations long before it was established as the emblem of the Christian faith. Our friends the padres, at the sight of it, immediately decided that the old inhabitants of Palenque were Christians, and by conclusions which are sometimes called jumping, they fixed the age of the buildings in the third century.

There is reason to believe that this particular building was intended as a temple, and that the enclosed inner chamber was an *adoratorio*, or oratory, or altar. What the rites and ceremonies of worship may have been, no one can undertake to say.

The upper part of this building differs from the first. As before, there was no staircase or other communication inside or out, nor were there the remains of any. The only mode of access was, in like manner, by climbing a tree, the branches of which spread across the roof. The roof was inclined, and the sides were richly ornamented with stucco figures, plants, and flowers, but mostly ruined. Among them were the fragments of a beautiful head and of two bodies, in justness of proportion and symmetry approaching the Greek models. On the top of this roof is a narrow platform, supporting what, for the sake of description, I shall call two stories. The platform is but two feet ten inches wide, and the superstructure of the first story is seven feet five inches in height; that of the second eight feet five inches, the width of the two being the same. The ascent from one to the other is by square projecting stones, and the covering of the upper story is of flat stones laid across and projecting over. The long sides of this narrow structure are of open stucco work, formed into curious and indescribable devices, human figures with legs and arms spreading and apertures between; and the whole was once loaded with rich and elegant ornaments in stucco relief. Its appearance at a distance must have been that of a high, fanciful lattice. Altogether, like the rest of the architecture and ornaments, it was perfectly unique, different from the works of any other people with which we were familiar, and its uses and purposes entirely incomprehensible. Perhaps it was intended as an observatory. From the upper gallery, through openings in the trees growing around, we looked out over an immense forest, and saw the Lake of Terminos and the Gulf of Mexico.

Near this building was another interesting monument, which had been entirely overlooked by those who preceded us in a visit to Palenque, and I mention this fact in the hope that the next visitor may discover many things omitted by us. It lies in front of the building, about forty or fifty feet down the side of the pyramidal structure. When we first passed it with our guide it lay on its face, with its head downward, and half buried by an accumulation of earth and stones. The outer side was rough and unhewn, and our attention was attracted by its size; our guide said it was not sculptured; but, after he had shown us everything that he had knowledge of, and we had discharged him, in passing it again we stopped and dug around it, and discovered that the under surface was carved. The Indians cut down some saplings for levers, and rolled it over. . . . It is the only statue that has ever been found at Palenque. We were at once struck with its expression of serene repose and its strong resemblance to Egyptian statues, though in size it does not compare with the gigantic remains of Egypt. In height it is ten feet six inches, of which two feet six inches were underground. The headdress is lofty and spreading; there are holes in the place of ears, which were perhaps adorned with earrings of gold and pearls. Round the neck is a necklace, and pressed against the breast by the right hand is an instrument apparently with teeth. The left hand rests on a hieroglyphic, from which descends some symbolical ornament. The lower part of the dress bears an unfortunate resemblance of the modern pantaloons, but the figure stands on what we have always considered a hieroglyphic, analogous again to the custom in Egypt of recording the name and office of the hero or other person represented. The sides are rounded, and the back is of rough stone. Probably it stood imbedded in a wall.

From the foot of the elevation on which the last-mentioned building stands, their bases almost touching, rises another pyramidal structure of about the same height . . . Such is the density of the forest, even on the sides of the pyramidal structure, that, though in a right line but a short distance apart, one of these buildings cannot be seen from the other. . . .

The interior, again, is divided into two corridors, about nine feet wide each, and paved with stone. . . . the front corridor, with the ceiling rising nearly to a point, and covered at the top with a layer of flat stones. In several places on each side are holes, which are found also in all the other corridors; they were probably used to support poles for scaffolding while the building was in process of erection, and had never been filled up. At the extreme end, cut through the wall, is one of the windows . . . which have been the subject of speculation from analogy to the letter Tau.

The back corridor is divided into three apartments. In the centre, facing the principal door of entrance, is an enclosed chamber similar to that which in the last building we have called an oratory or altar. The top of the doorway was gorgeous with stuccoed ornaments, and on the piers at each side were stone tablets in bas-relief. Within, the chamber was four feet seven inches deep and nine feet wide. There were no stuccoed ornaments or paintings, but set in the back wall was a stone tablet covering the whole width of the chamber, nine feet wide and eight feet high.

The tablet is . . . the most perfect and most interesting monument in Palenque. Neither Del Rio nor Dupaix has given any drawing of it. . . . It is composed of three separate stones. . . . The sculpture is perfect, and the characters and figures stand clear and distinct on the stone. On each side are rows of hieroglyphics. The principal personages will be recognised at once as the same who are represented in the tablet of the cross. They wear the same dress, but here both seem to be making offerings. Both personages stand on the backs of human beings, one of whom supports himself by his hands and knees, and the other seems crushed to the ground by the weight. Between them, at the foot of the tablet, are two figures, sitting cross-legged, one bracing himself with his right hand on the ground, and with the left supporting a square table; the attitude and action of the other are the same, except that they are in reverse order. The table also rests upon their bended necks, and their distorted countenances may perhaps be considered expressions of pain and suffering. They are both clothed in leopard-skins. Upon this table rest two batons crossed, their upper extremities richly ornamented, and supporting what seems a hideous mask, the eyes widely expanded, and the tongue

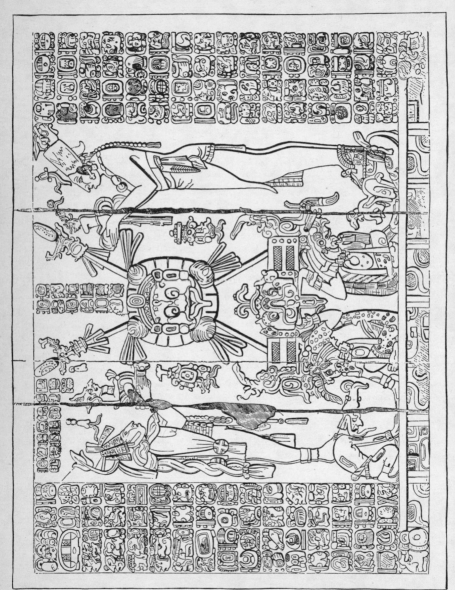

TABLET ON THE BACK WALL OF ALTAR, CASA NO. 3, PALENQUE

hanging out. This seems to be the object to which the principal personages are making offerings.

The pier on each side of the doorway contained a stone tablet, with figures carved in bas-relief. . . . These tablets, however, have been removed from their place to the village, and set up in the wall of a house as ornaments. They were the first objects which we saw, and the last which Mr. Catherwood drew. The house belonged to two sisters, who have an exaggerated idea of the value of these tablets; and, though always pleased with our coming to see them, made objections to having them copied. We obtained permission only by promising a copy for them also, which, however, Mr. Catherwood, worn out with constant labour, was entirely unable to make. I cut out of Del Rio's book the drawings of the same subjects, which I thought, being printed, would please them better; but they had examined Mr. Catherwood's drawing in its progress, and were not at all satisfied with the substitute. The moment I saw these tablets I formed the idea of purchasing them and carrying them home as a sample of Palenque, but it was some time before I ventured to broach the subject. They could not be purchased without the house; but that was no impediment, for I liked the house also. It was afterward included among the subjects of other negotiations which were undetermined when I left Palenque.

The two figures stand facing each other, the first on the right hand, fronting the spectator. The nose and eyes are strongly marked, but altogether the development is not so strange as to indicate a race entirely different from those which are known. The headdress is curious and complicated, consisting principally of leaves of plants, with a large flower hanging down; and among the ornaments are distinguished the beak and eyes of a bird, and a tortoise. The cloak is a leopard's skin, and the figure has ruffles around the wrists and ankles.

The second figure, standing on the left of the spectator, has the same profile which characterizes all the others at Palenque. Its headdress is composed of a plume of feathers, in which is a bird holding a fish in its mouth; and in different parts of the headdress there are three other fishes. The figure wears a richly-embroidered tippet, and a broad girdle, with the head of some animal in front, sandals, and leggings: the right hand is extended in a prayerful or deprecating position, with the palm outward. Over the heads of these mysterious personages are three cabbalistic hieroglyphics.

We considered the oratorio or altar the most interesting portion of the ruins of Palenque. . . . We could not but regard it as a holy place, dedicated to the gods, and consecrated by the religious observances of a lost and unknown people. Comparatively, the hand of ruin has spared it, and the great tablet, surviving the wreck of elements, stands perfect and entire. Lonely, deserted, and without any worshippers at its shrine, the figures and characters are distinct as when the people who reared it went up to pay their adorations before it. To us it was all a mystery; silent, defying the most scrutinizing gaze and reach of intellect. Even our friends the padres could make nothing of it.

Near this, on the top of another pyramidal structure, was another building entirely in ruins, which apparently had been shattered and hurled down by an earthquake. The stones were strewed on the side of the pyramid, and it was impossible even to make out the ground-plan.

Returning to [Casas de Piedras] and proceeding south, at a distance of fifteen hundred feet, and on a pyramidal structure one hundred feet high from the bank of the river, is another building, twenty feet front and eighteen feet deep, but in an unfortunately ruined condition. The whole of the front wall has fallen, leaving the outer corridor entirely exposed. Fronting the door, and against the back wall of the inner corridor, was a large stucco ornament representing a figure sitting on a couch; but a great part has fallen or been taken off and carried away. The body of the couch, with tiger's feet, is all that now remains. The outline of two tigers' heads and of the sitting personage is seen on the wall. The loss or destruction of this ornament is more to be regretted, as from what remains it appears to have been superior in execution to any other stucco relief in Palenque. The body of the couch is entire, and the leg and foot hanging down the side are elegant specimens of art and models for study.

I have now given, without speculation or comment, a full description of the ruins of Palenque. I repeat what I stated in the beginning, there may be more buildings, but, after a close examination of the vague reports current in the village, we are satisfied that no more have ever been discovered; and from repeated inquiries of Indians who had traversed the forest in every direction in the dry season, we are induced to believe that no more exist. The whole extent of ground covered by those as yet known, as appears by the plan, is not larger than our Park or Battery. In stating this fact I am very far from wishing to detract from the importance or interest of the subject. I give our opinion, with the grounds of it, and the reader will judge for himself how far these are entitled to consideration. It is proper to add, however, that, considering the space now occupied by the ruins as the site of palaces, temples, and public buildings, and supposing the houses of the inhabitants to have been, like those of the Egyptians and the present race of Indians, of frail and perishable materials, and, as at Memphis and Thebes, to have disappeared altogether, the city may have covered an immense extent.

The reader is perhaps disappointed, but we were not. There was no necessity for assigning to the ruined city an immense extent, or an antiquity coeval with that of the Egyptians or of any other ancient and known people. What we had before our eyes was grand, curious, and remarkable enough. Here were the remains of a culti-vated, polished, and peculiar people, who had passed through all the stages incident to the rise and fall of nations; reached their golden age, and perished, entirely unknown. The links which con-nected them with the human family were severed and lost, and these were the only memorials of their footsteps upon earth. We lived in the ruined palace of their kings; we went up to their desolate temples and fallen altars; and wherever we moved we saw the evidences of their taste, their skill in arts, their wealth and power. In the midst of desolation and ruin we looked back to the past, cleared away the gloomy forest, and fancied every building perfect, with its terraces and pyramids, its sculptured and painted ornaments, grand, lofty, and imposing, and overlooking an im-mense inhabited plain; we called back into life the strange people who gazed at us in sadness from the walls; pictured them, in fanci-ful costumes and adorned with plumes of feathers, ascending the terraces of the palace and the steps leading to the temples; and often we imagined a scene of unique and gorgeous beauty and magnificence, realizing the creations of Oriental poets, the very spot which fancy would have selected for the "Happy Valley" of Rasselas. In the romance of the world's history nothing ever impressed me more forcibly than the spectacle of this once great and lovely city, overturned, desolate, and lost; discovered by accident, overgrown with trees for miles around, and without even a name to distinguish it. Apart from everything else, it was a mourning witness to the world's mutations.

> Nations melt
> From Power's high pinnacle, when they have felt
> The sunshine for a while, and downward go.

As at Copan, I shall not at present offer any conjecture in regard to the antiquity of these buildings, merely remarking that at ten leagues' distance is a village called *Las Tres Cruces* or the Three Crosses, from three crosses which, according to tradition, Cortez erected at that place when on his conquering march from Mexico to Honduras by the Lake of Peten. Cortez, then, must have passed within twenty or thirty miles of the place now called Palenque. If it had been a living city, its fame must have reached his ears, and

he would probably have turned aside from his road to subdue and
plunder it. It seems, therefore, but reasonable to suppose that it
was at that time desolate and in ruins, and even the memory of it
lost.

Who Built the Ruined Cities?

I have now finished the exploration of ruins. The reader is perhaps
pleased that our labours were brought to an abrupt close (my
publishers certainly are); but I assure him that I could have found
it in my heart to be prolix beyond all bounds, and that in mercy I
have been very brief; in fact, I have let slip the best chance that
author ever had to make his reader remember him. I will make no
mention of other ruins of which we heard at more remote places. I
have no doubt a year may be passed with great interest in Yucatan.
The field of American antiquities is barely opened; but for the
present I have done.

And here I would be willing to part, and leave the reader to
wander alone and at will through the labyrinth of mystery which
hangs over these ruined cities; but it would be craven to do so,
without turning for a moment to the important question, Who were
the people that built these cities?

Since their discovery, a dark cloud has been thrown over them
in two particulars. The first is in regard to the immense difficulty
and danger, labour and expense, of visiting and exploring them. It
has been my object to clear away this cloud. It will appear from
these pages that the accounts have been exaggerated; and, as regards Palenque and Uxmal at least, the only places which have
been brought before the public at all, there is neither difficulty in
reaching nor danger in exploring them.

The second is in regard to the age of the buildings; but here the
cloud is darker, and not so easily dispelled.

I will not recapitulate the many speculations that have already
been presented. The most irrational, perhaps, is that of Captain
Dupaix, who gives to the ruins of Palenque an antediluvian origin;
and, unfortunately for him, he gives his reason, which is the accumulation of earth over the figures in the courtyard of the palace.
His visit was thirty years before ours; and, though he cleared away
the earth, the accumulation was again probably quite as great when
we were there. At all events, by his own showing, the figures were
not entirely buried. I have a distinct recollection of the condition
of those monuments, and have no scruple in saying that, if entirely
buried, one Irishman, with the national weapon that has done such

Ibid., pp. 436-57.

service on our canals, would in three hours remove the whole of this antediluvian deposit. I shall not follow the learned commentaries upon this suggestion of Captain Dupaix, except to remark that much learning and research have been expended upon insufficient or incorrect data, or when a bias has been given by a statement of facts; and, putting ourselves in the same category with those who have furnished these data, for the benefit of explorers and writers who may succeed us I shall narrow down this question to a ground even yet sufficiently broad, viz., a comparison of these remains with those of the architecture and sculpture of other ages and people.

I set out with the proposition that they are not Cyclopean, and do not resemble the works of Greek or Roman; there is nothing in Europe like them. We must look, then, to Asia and Africa.

It has been supposed that at different periods of time vessels from Japan and China have been thrown upon the western coast of America. The civilization, cultivation, and science of those countries are known to date back from a very early antiquity. Of Japan I believe some accounts and drawings have been published, but they are not within my reach; of China, during the whole of her long history, the interior has been so completely shut against strangers that we know nothing of her ancient architecture. Perhaps, however, that time is close at hand. At present we know only that they have been a people not given to change; and if their ancient architecture is the same with their modern, it bears no resemblance whatever to these unknown ruins.

The monuments of India have been made familiar to us. The remains of Hindu architecture exhibit immense excavations in the rock, either entirely artificial or made by enlarging natural caverns, supported in front by large columns cut out of the rock, with a dark and gloomy interior.

Among all these American ruins there is not a single excavation. The surface of country, abounding in mountain sides, seems to invite it; but, instead of being underground, the striking feature of these ruins is, that the buildings stand on lofty artificial elevations; and it can hardly be supposed that a people emigrating to a new country, with that strong natural impulse to perpetuate and retain under their eyes memorials of home, would have gone so directly counter to national and religious associations.

In sculpture, too, the Hindus differ entirely. Their subjects are far more hideous, being in general representations of human beings distorted, deformed, and unnatural, very often many-headed, or with three or four arms or legs thrown out from the same body.

Lastly we come to the Egyptians. The point of resemblance upon which the great stress has been laid is the pyramid. The pyramidal

form is one which suggests itself to human intelligence in every
country as the simplest and surest mode of erecting a high structure upon a solid foundation. It cannot be regarded as a ground for
assigning a common origin to all people among whom structures
of that character are found, unless the similarity is preserved in its
most striking features. The pyramids of Egypt are peculiar and
uniform, and were invariably erected for the same uses and purposes, so far as those uses and purposes are known. They are all
square at the base, with steps rising and diminishing until they
come to a point. The nearest approach to this is at Copan; but
even at that place there is no entire pyramid standing alone and
disconnected, nor one with four sides complete, but only two, or,
at most, three sides, and intended to form part of other structures.
All the rest, without a single exception, were high elevations, with
sides so broken that we could not make out their form, which, perhaps, were merely walled around, and had ranges of steps in front
and rear, as at Uxmal, or terraces or raised platforms of earth, at
most of three or four ranges, not of any precise form, but never
square, and with small ranges of steps in the centre. Besides, the
pyramids of Egypt are known to have interior chambers, and, whatever their other uses, to have been intended and used as sepulchres.
These, on the contrary, are of solid earth and stone. No interior
chambers have ever been discovered, and probably none exist. And
the most radical difference of all is, the pyramids of Egypt are
complete in themselves; the structures of this country were erected
only to serve as the foundations of buildings. There is no pyramid
in Egypt with a palace or temple upon it; there is no pyramidal
structure in this country without; at least none from whose condition any judgment can be formed.

But there is one farther consideration, which must be conclusive.
The pyramids of Egypt, as I have considered them, and as they
stand now, differ most materially from the original structures.
Herodotus says that in his time the great pyramid was coated with
stone, so as to present a smooth surface on all its sides from the
base to the top. The second pyramid of Gizeh, called the Pyramid
of Chephren, in its present condition, presents on the lower part
ranges of steps, with an accumulation of angular stones at the base,
which originally filled up the interstices between the steps, but
have fallen down. In the upper part the intermediate layers are
still in their places, and the sides present a smooth surface to the
top. There is no doubt that originally every pyramid in Egypt was
built with its sides perfectly smooth. The steps formed no part of
the plan. It is in this state only that they ought to be considered,
and in this state any possible resemblance between them and what
are called the pyramids of America, ceases.

Next to the pyramids, the oldest remains of Egyptian architecture, such as the temple of Absamboul [Abu Simbel?] in Nubia, like those of the Hindus, are excavations in the rock, from which it has been supposed that the Egyptians derived their style from that people. In later times they commenced erecting temples above ground, retaining the same features of gloomy grandeur, and remarkable for their vastness and the massiveness of the stone used in their construction. This does not seem to have been aimed at by the American builders. Among all these ruins we did not see a stone worthy of being laid on the walls of an Egyptian temple. The largest single blocks were the "idols" or "obelisks," as they have been called, of Copan and Quirigua; but in Egypt stones large as these are raised to a height of twenty or thirty feet and laid in the walls, while the obelisks which stand as ornaments at the doors, towering, a single stone, to the height of ninety feet, so overpower them by their grandeur, that, if imitations, they are the feeblest ever attempted by aspiring men.

Again: columns are a distinguishing feature of Egyptian architecture, grand and massive, and at this day towering above the sands, startling the wondering traveller in that mysterious country. There is not a temple on the Nile without them; and the reader will bear in mind, that among the whole of these ruins not one column has been found. If this architecture had been derived from the Egyptian, so striking and important a feature would never have been thrown aside. The *dromos, pronaos,* and *adytum,* all equally characteristic of Egyptian temples, are also here entirely wanting.

Next, as to sculpture. The idea of resemblance in this particular has been so often and so confidently expressed, and the drawings in these pages have so often given the same impression, that I almost hesitate to declare the total want of similarity. . . .

There is no resemblance in these remains to those of the Egyptians; and, failing here, we look elsewhere in vain. They are different from the works of any other known people, of a new order, and entirely and absolutely anomalous: they stand alone.

I invite to this subject the special attention of those familiar with the arts of other countries; for, unless I am wrong, we have a conclusion far more interesting and wonderful than that of connecting the builders of these cities with the Egyptians or any other people. It is the spectacle of a people skilled in architecture, sculpture, and drawing, and, beyond doubt, other more perishable arts, and possessing the cultivation and refinement attendant upon these, not derived from the Old World, but originating and growing up here, without models or masters, having a distinct, separate, independent existence; like the plants and fruits of the soil, indigenous.

I shall not attempt to inquire into the origin of this people, from what country they came, or when, or how; I shall confine myself to their works and to the ruins.

I am inclined to think that there are not sufficient grounds for the belief in the great antiquity that has been ascribed to these ruins; that they are not the works of people who have passed away, and whose history has become unknown; but, opposed as is my idea to all previous speculations, that they were constructed by the races who occupied the country at the time of the invasion by the Spaniards, or of some not very distant progenitors.

And this opinion is founded, first, upon the appearance and condition of the remains themselves. The climate and rank luxuriance of soil are most destructive to all perishable materials. For six months every year exposed to the deluge of tropical rains, and with trees growing through the doorways of buildings and on the tops, it seems impossible that, after a lapse of two or three thousand years, a single edifice could now be standing.

The existence of wooden beams, and at Uxmal in a perfect state of preservation, confirms this opinion. The durability of wood will depend upon its quality and exposure. In Egypt, it is true, wood has been discovered sound and perfect, and certainly three thousand years old; but even in that dry climate none has ever been found in a situation at all exposed. It occurs only in coffins in the tombs and mummy-pits of Thebes, and in wooden cramps connecting two stones together, completely shut in and excluded from the air.

Secondly, my opinion is founded upon historical accounts. Herrera, perhaps the most reliable of the Spanish historians, says of Yucatan: "The whole country is divided into eighteen districts, and in all of them were so many and such stately stone buildings that it was amazing, and the greatest wonder is, that having no use of any metal, they were able to raise such structures, which seem to have been temples, for their houses were always of timber and thatched. In those edifices were carved the figures of naked men, with earrings after the Indian manner, idols of all sorts, lions, pots or jars," &c.; and again, "after the parting of these lords, for the space of twenty years there was such plenty through the country, and the people multiplied so much, that old men said the whole province looked like one town, and then they applied themselves to build more temples, which produced so great a number of them."

Of the natives he says, "They *flattened their heads and foreheads, their ears bor'd with rings in them.* Their faces were generally good, and not very brown, *but without beards,* for they scorched them when young, that they might not grow. Their hair was *long like* [that of] *women,* and in tresses, with which they made a garland about the head, and a *little tail hung behind. . . .* The prime men wore a *rowler eight fingers broad round about them* instead of breeches, and *going several times round the waist, so that one end of it hung before and the other behind,* with fine feather-work, and had large *square mantles knotted on their shoulders,* and *sandals* or *buskins* made of deer's skins." The reader almost sees here, in the flatted heads and costumes of the natives, a picture of the sculptured and stuccoed figures at Palenque, which, though a little beyond the present territorial borders of Yucatan, was perhaps once a part of that province.

Besides the glowing and familiar descriptions given by Cortez of the splendour exhibited in the buildings of Mexico, I have within my reach the authority of but one eyewitness. It is that of Bernal Diaz de Castillo, a follower and sharer in all the expeditions attending the conquest of Mexico.

Beginning with the first expedition, he says, "On approaching Yucatan, we perceived a large town at the distance of two leagues from the coast, which, from its size, it exceeding any town in Cuba, we named Grand Cairo." Upon the invitation of a chief, who came off in a canoe, they went ashore, and set out to march to the town, but on their way were surprised by the natives, whom, however, they repulsed, killing fifteen. "Near the place of this ambuscade," he says, "were three buildings *of lime and stone,* wherein were idols of clay with *diabolical countenances,*" &c. "The buildings of *lime and stone,* and the gold, gave us a high idea of the country we had discovered."

In fifteen days' farther sailing, they discovered from the ships a large town, with an inlet, and went ashore for water. While filling their casks they were accosted by fifty Indians, "dressed in cotton mantles," who "by signs invited us to their town." Proceeding thither, they "arrived at some large and very well-constructed buildings of *lime and stone,* with figures of *serpents* and of *idols* painted upon the walls."

In the second expedition, sailing along the coast, they passed a low island, about three leagues from the main, where, on going ashore, they found "two buildings of lime and stone, well constructed, each with steps, and an altar placed before certain hideous figures, the representations of the gods of these Indians."

His third expedition was under Cortez, and in this his regard for truth and the reliance that may be placed upon him are happily shown in the struggle between deep religious feeling and belief in the evidence of his senses, which appears in his comment upon Gomara's account of their first battle. "In his account of this action, Gomara says that, previous to the arrival of the main body under Cortez, Francisco de Morla appeared in the field upon a gray dappled horse, and that it was one of the holy apostles, St. Peter or St. Jago, disguised under his person. I say that all our works and victories are guided by the hand of our Lord Jesus Christ, and that in this battle there were so many enemies to every one of us, that they could have buried us under the dust they could have held in their hands, but that the great mercy of God aided us throughout. What Gomara asserts may be the case, and I, sinner as I am, was not permitted to see it. What I did see was Francisco de Morla riding in company with Cortez and the rest upon a chestnut horse. But although I, unworthy sinner that I am, was unfit to behold either of these apostles, upward of four hundred of us were present. Let their testimony be taken. Let inquiry also be made how it happened that, when the town was founded on that spot, it was not named after one or other of these holy apostles, and called St. Jago de la Vittoria or St. Pedro de la Vittoria, as it was Santa Maria, and a church erected and dedicated to one of these holy saints. Very bad Christians were we, indeed, according to the account of Gomara, who, when God sent us his apostles to fight at our head, did not every day after acknowledge and return thanks for so great a mercy!"

Setting out on their march to Mexico, they arrived at Cempoal, entering which, he says, "We were surprised with the beauty of the buildings." "Our advanced guard having gone to the great square, the buildings of which had been lately whitewashed and *plastered, in which art these people are very expert,* one of our horsemen was so struck with the splendour of their appearance in the sun, that he came back in full speed to Cortez to tell him that the walls of the houses were of silver."

Offended by the abominable custom of human sacrifices, Cortez determined to suppress by force their idolatrous worship, and destroy their false gods. The chiefs ordered the people to arm in defence of their temple; "but when they saw that we were preparing to ascend *the great flight of steps,*" they said "they could not help themselves; and they had hardly said this, when fifty of us, *going up* for the purpose, threw down and broke in pieces the enormous idols which we found within the temple." Cortez then caused a number of "*Indian masons* to be collected, *with lime, which abounded* in that place, and had the walls cleared of blood and *new plastered.*"

As they approached the territory of Mexico, he continues, "Appearances demonstrated that we had entered a new country, for the *temples were very lofty,* and, together with the *terraced dwellings* and the houses of the cacique, being *pastered* and whitewashed, appeared very well, and resembled some of our towns in Spain."

Farther on he says, "We arrived at a kind of fortification, built of *lime and stone,* of so strong a nature that nothing but tools of iron could have any effect upon it. The people informed us that it was built by the Tlascalans, on whose territory it stood, as a defence against the incursions of the Mexicans."

At Tehuacingo, after a sanguinary battle, in which the Indians "drew off and left the field to them, who were too much fatigued to follow," he adds, "As soon as we found ourselves clear of them, we returned thanks to God for his mercy, and, entering a *strong and spacious temple*, we dressed our wounds with the fat of Indians."

Arrived at Cholula, Cortez immediately "sent some soldiers to a *great temple* hard by our quarters, with orders to bring, as quietly as they could, two priests." In this they succeeded. One of them was a person of rank and authority over *all the temples* of the city. Again, "*within the high walls of the courts* where we were quartered." And again: the city of Cholula, he says, "much resembled Valladolid." It "had at that time above a hundred *lofty white towers*, which were the temples of their idols. The principal temple was higher than that of Mexico, and each of these buildings was placed *in a spacious court*."

Approaching the city of Mexico, he gives way to a burst of enthusiasm. "We could compare it to nothing but the enchanted scenes we had read of in Amadis de Gaul, from the *great towers*, and *temples*, and other *edifices of lime and stone* which seemed to rise up out of the water."

"We were received by great lords of that country, relations of Montezuma, who conducted us to our lodgings there in *palaces* magnificently built of *stone*, the timber of which was cedar, with *spacious courts* and apartments furnished with canopies of the *finest cotton*. The whole was ornamented with *works of art painted*, and *admirably plastered* and whitened, and it was rendered more delightful by numbers of beautiful birds."

"The palace in which we were lodged was very light, airy, clean, and pleasant, the entry being through a great court."

Montezuma, in his first interview with Cortez, says, "The Tlascalans have, I know, told you that I am like a god, and that all about me is gold, and silver, and precious stone; but you now see that I am mere flesh and blood, and that my *houses are built like other houses, of lime, and stone, and timber*."

"At the great square we were astonished at the crowds of people and the regularity which prevailed, and the vast quantities of merchandise."

"The entire square was enclosed in piazzas."

"From the square we proceeded to the great temple, but before we entered it we made a circuit through a number of *large courts*, the smallest of which appeared to me to contain more ground than the great square of Salamanca, with double enclosures, *built of lime and stone,* and the *courts* paved with large white *cut* stones, or, where not paved, they were *plastered and polished."*

"The ascent to the great temple was by *a hundred and fourteen steps."*

"From the platform on the summit of the temple, Montezuma, taking Cortez by the hand, pointed out to him the different parts of the city and its vicinity, all of which were commended from that place." "We observed also the temples and adoratories of the adjacent cities, built in the form of *towers* and *fortresses,* and others on the causeway, all whitewashed and wonderfully brilliant."

"The noise and bustle of the market-place could be heard almost a league off, and *those who had been at Rome and Constantinople* said that for convenience, regularity, and population they had never seen the like."

During the siege he speaks of being "quartered in a *lofty temple;"* "marching *up the steps of the temple;"* "*some lofty temples* which we now battered with our artillery;" "the *lofty temples* where Diego Velasquez and Salvatierra were posted;" "the *breaches* which they had made in the *walls;"* "*cut stone* taken from the buildings from the terraces."

Arrived at the great temple, instantly above four thousand Mexicans rushed up into it, who for some time prevented them from ascending. "Although the cavalry several times attempted to charge, the stone pavements of the courts of the temple were so smooth that the horses could not keep their feet, and fell." "Their numbers were such that we could not make any effectual impression or *ascend the steps.* At length we *forced our way up.* Here Cortez showed himself the man that he really was. What a desperate engagement we then had! Every man of us was covered with blood."

"They drove us *down six, and even ten of the steps;* while others who were in the corridors, or within side of the railings and concavities of the great temple, shot such clouds of arrows at us that we could not maintain our ground," "began our retreat, every man of us being wounded, and forty-six of us left dead on the spot. I have often seen this engagement represented in the *paintings* of the natives both of Mexico and Tlascala, and *our ascent into the great temple."*

Again, he speaks of arriving at a village and taking up their "quarters *in a strong temple;"* "assaulting them at their *posts in the temples* and *large walled enclosures."*

At Tezcuco "we took up our quarters in some buildings which consisted of *large halls and enclosed courts."* "Alvarado, De Oli, and some soldiers, whereof I was one, then ascended to the top of *the great temple*, which was *very lofty*, in order to notice what was going on in the neighborhood."

"We proceeded to another town called Terrayuco, but which we named the town of the *serpents,* on account of the *enormous figures of those animals* which we found in their temples, and which they worshipped as gods."

Again: "In this garden our whole force lodged for the night. I certainly never had seen one of such magnificence; and Cortez and the treasurer Alderete, after they had walked through and examined it, declared that it was admirable, and equal to any they had ever seen in Castille."

"I and ten more soldiers were posted as a guard upon a *wall of lime and stone.*"

"When we arrived at our quarters at Jacuba it rained heavily, and we remained under it for two hours in some *large enclosed courts.* The general, with his captains, the treasurer, our reverend father, and many others of us, mounted to the *top of the temple,* which commanded all the lake."

"We crossed the water up to our necks at the pass they had left open, and followed them until we came to a place where were *large temples* and *towers of idols.*"

"As Cortez now lodged at Cuejoacan, in large buildings with white walls, very well adapted for scribbling on, there appeared every morning libels against him in prose and verse. I recollect the words of one only:

'Que trista esta el alma mea
Hasta que la parte vea.'

How anxious I am for a share of the plunder."

"When our party (for I went with Sandoval) arrived at Tustepeque, I took up my lodgings in the summit of a *tower in a very high temple,* partly for the fresh air and to avoid the mosquitoes, which were very troublesome below, and partly to be near Sandoval's quarters." "We pursued our route to the city of Chiapas, in the same province with Palenque, and a city it might be called, from the regularity of its streets and houses. It contained not less than four thousand families, not reckoning the population of the many dependent towns in its neighbourhood." "We found the whole force of Chiapas drawn up to receive us. Their troops were adorned with plumage."

"On our arrival we found it too closely built to be safely occupied by us, and we therefore pitched our camp in the open field. In their *temples* we found idols of a horrid figure."

Now it will be recollected that Bernal Diaz wrote to do justice to himself and others of the "true conquerors," his companions in arms, whose fame had been obscured by other historians not actors and eyewitnesses; all his references to buildings are incidental; he never expected to be cited as authority upon the antiquities of the country. The pettiest skirmish with the natives was nearer his heart than all the edifices of lime and stone which he saw, and it is precisely on that account that his testimony is the more valuable. It was written at a time when there were many living who could contradict him if incorrect or false. His "true history" never was impeached; on the contrary, while its style was considered rude and inelegant, its fidelity and truth have been acknowledged by all contemporaneous and subsequent historians. In my opinion, it is as true and reliable as any work of *travels* on the countries through which he fought his way. It gives the hurried and imperfect observations of an unlettered soldier, whose sword was seldom in its scabbard, surrounded by dangers, attacking, retreating, wounded, and flying, with his mind constantly occupied by matters of more pressing moment.

The reader cannot fail to be struck with the general resemblance between the objects described by him and the scenes referred to in these pages. His account presents to my mind a vivid picture of the ruined cities which we visited, as they once stood, with *buildings of lime and stone, painted* and *sculptured ornaments*, and *plastered; idols, courts, strong walls,* and *lofty temples with high ranges of steps.*

But if this is not sufficient, I have farther and stronger support. After the siege of Mexico, on the re-entry of the Spaniards, a ruthless and indiscriminate destruction fell upon every building and monument in the city. No memorials of the arts of the Mexicans were left; but in the year 1790, two statues and a flat stone, with sculptured characters relative to the Mexican calendar, were discovered and dug up from among the remains of the great Teocalli in the plaza of the city of Mexico. The statues excited great interest among the Mexican Indians, and the priests, afraid of their relapsing into idolatry, and to destroy all memorials of their ancient rites, buried them in the court of the Franciscan Convent. The calendar was fixed in a conspicuous place in the wall of the Cathedral, where it now stands. In the centre, and forming the principal subject of this calendar, is a face, published in Humboldt's work, which in one particular bears so strong a resemblance to that called the mask, as to suggest the idea that they were intended for the same. There are palpable differences, but at all events, in both the peculiar and striking feature is that of the tongue hanging out of the mouth. The calendar is in basrelief, and, as I understand from a gentleman who has seen it, the sculpture is good.

And, lastly, among the hieroglyphical paintings which escaped destruction from monkish fanaticism are certain Mexican manuscripts now in the libraries of Dresden and Vienna. These have been published in Humboldt's work and in that of Lord Kingsborough, and, on a careful examination, we are strongly of the opinion that the characters are the same with those found on the monuments and tablets at Copan and Palenque. For the sake of comparison I have introduced again the engraving of the top of the altar at Copan, and another from a hieroglyphical manuscript published in Humboldt's work. Differences, it is true, are manifest; but it must be borne in mind that in the former the char-

acters are carved on stone, and in the latter written on paper
(made of the Agave Mexicana). Probably, for this reason, they
want the same regularity and finish; but, altogether, the reader
cannot fail to mark the strong similarity, and this similarity
cannot be accidental. The inference is, that the Aztecs or Mexicans, at the time of the conquest, had the same written language
with the people of Copan and Palenque.

I have thus very briefly, and without attempting to controvert
the opinions and speculations of others, presented our own views
upon the subject of these ruins. As yet we perhaps stand alone
in these views, but I repeat my opinion that we are not warranted
in going back to any ancient nation of the Old World for the
builders of these cities; that they are not the work of people who
have passed away and whose history is lost, but that there are
strong reasons to believe them the creations of the same races
who inhabited the country at the time of the time of the Spanish
conquest, or some not very distant progenitors. And I would remark that we began our exploration without any theory to support. Our feelings were in favour of going back to a high and
venerable antiquity. During the greater part of our journey we
were groping in the dark, in doubt and uncertainty, and it was
not until our arrival at the ruins of Uxmal that we formed our
opinion of their comparatively modern date. Some are beyond
doubt older than others; some are known to have been inhabited
at the time of the Spanish conquest, and others, perhaps, were
really in ruins before; and there are points of difference which
as yet cannot very readily be explained; but in regard to Uxmal,
at least, we believe that it was an existing and inhabited city at
the time of the arrival of the Spaniards. Its desolation and ruin
since are easily accounted for. With the arrival of the Spaniards
the sceptre of the Indians departed. In the city of Mexico every
house was razed to the ground, and, beyond doubt, throughout
the country every gathering-place or stronghold was broken up,
the communities scattered, their lofty temples thrown down, and
their idols burned, the palaces of the caciques ruined, the caciques themselves made bondmen, and, by the same ruthless policy which from time immemorial has been pursued in a conquered
country, all the mementoes of their ancestors and lost independence were destroyed or made odious in their eyes. And, without
this, we have authentic accounts of great scourges which swept
over, and for a time depopulated and desolated, the whole of Yucatan.

It perhaps destroys much of the interest that hangs over these
ruins to assign to them a modern date; but we live in an age
whose spirit is to discard phantasms and arrive at truth, and the

interest lost in one particular is supplied in another scarcely inferior; for, the nearer we can bring the builders of these cities to our own times, the greater is our chance of knowing all. Throughout the country the convents are rich in manuscripts and documents written by the early fathers, caciques, and Indians, who very soon acquired the knowledge of Spanish and the art of writing. These have never been examined with the slightest reference to this subject; and I cannot help thinking that some precious memorial is now mouldering in the library of a neighbouring convent, which would determine the history of some one of these ruined cities; moreover, I cannot help believing that the tablets of heiroglyphics will yet be read. No strong curiosity has hitherto been directed to them; vigour and acuteness of intellect, knowledge and learning, have never been expended upon them. For centuries the hieroglyphics of Egypt were inscrutable, and, though not perhaps in our day, I feel persuaded that a key surer than that of the Rosetta stone will be discovered. And if only three centuries have elapsed since any one of these unknown cities was inhabited, the race of the inhabitants is not extinct. Their descendants are still in the land, scattered, perhaps, and retired, like our own Indians, into wildernesses which have never yet been penetrated by a white man, but not lost; living as their fathers did, erecting the same buildings of "lime and stone," "with ornaments of sculpture and plastered," "large courts," and "lofty towers with high ranges of steps," and still carving on tablets of stone the same mysterious hieroglyphics; and if, in consideration that I have not often indulged in speculative conjecture, the reader will allow one flight, I turn to that vast and unknown region, untraversed by a single road, wherein fancy pictures that mysterious city seen from the topmost range of the Cordilleras, of unconquered, unvisited, and unsought aboriginal inhabitants.

In conclusion, I am at a loss to determine which would be the greatest enterprise, an attempt to reach this mysterious city, to decipher the tablets of hieroglyphics, or to wade through the accumulated manuscripts of three centuries in the libraries of the convents.

JOHN L. STEPHENS

Stephens and Catherwood
Return to Yucatan

THE two friends returned to the Yucatan peninsula in 1841, wishing
to make a more thorough examination of Uxmal, Chichen Itza and
other ruins than had been possible on their first journey.

Uxmal

IN working out the plan [of the Governor's palace at Uxmal] on the
spot, it was found that the back wall, throughout its whole length
of two hundred and seventy feet, was nine feet thick, which was
nearly equal to the width of the front apartment. Such thickness
was not necessary for the support of the building, and, supposing it
might contain some hidden passages, we determined to make a
breach through the wall, and to do this in the centre apartment.

I must confess that I felt some repugnance to this work of
demolition, but one stone had already been picked out by an Indian
to serve for mashing maize upon; and as this was likely to be done
at any time when another might be wanted, I got over my scruples.

Over the cavity left in the mortar by the removal of the stone
were two conspicuous marks, which afterward stared us in the
face in all the ruined buildings of the country. They were the prints
of a red hand with the thumb and fingers extended, not drawn or
painted, but stamped by the living hand, the pressure of the palm
upon the stone. He who made it had stood before it alive as we
did, and pressed his hand, moistened with red paint, hard against
the stone. The seams and creases of the palm were clear and
distinct in the impression. There was something lifelike about

From *Incidents of Travel in Yucatan*, Vols. I & II. London: John Murray; 1843, pp.
177-80, 254-7, 287-8.

it that waked exciting thoughts, and almost presented the images of the departed inhabitants hovering about the building. And there was one striking feature about these hands; they were exceedingly small. Either of our own spread over and completely hid them; and this was interesting from the fact that we had ourselves remarked, and heard remarked by others, the smallness of the hands and feet as a striking feature in the physical conformation of the Indians at the present day.

The stones with this red hand upon them were the first that fell as we commenced our breach into the wall. There were two crowbars on the hacienda, and working nearly two days, the Indians made a hole between six and seven feet deep, but throughout the wall was solid, and consisted of large stones imbedded in mortar, almost as hard as rock. The reason of this immense back wall, where everything else had a certain degree of fitness and conformity, we did not discover, and we had this huge hole staring us reproachfully in the face during all the remainder of our residence.

A few words more, and I have done with this building. In the south-end apartment, the façade of which has been presented, we found the sculptured beam of hieroglyphics which had so much interested us on our former visit. In some of the inner apartments the lintels were still in their places over the doorways, and some were lying on the floor sound and solid, which better condition was no doubt owing to their being more sheltered than those over the outer doorway. This was the only sculptured beam in Uxmal, and at that time it was the only piece of carved wood we had seen. We considered it interesting, as indicating a degree of proficiency in an art of which, in all our previous explorations, we had not discovered any evidence, except, perhaps, at Ocosingo, where we had found a beam, not carved, but which had evidently been reduced to shape by sharp instruments of metal. This time I determined not to let the precious beam escape me. It was ten feet long, one foot nine inches broad, and ten inches thick, of Sapote wood, enormously heavy and unwieldy. To keep the sculptured side from being chafed and broken, I had it covered with costal or hemp bagging, and stuffed with dry grass to the thickness of six inches. It left Uxmal on the shoulders of ten Indians, after many vicissitudes reached this city uninjured, and was deposited in Mr. Catherwood's Panorama. I had referred to it as being in the National Museum at Washington, whither I intended to send it as soon as a collection of large sculptured stones, which I was obliged to leave behind, should arrive; but on the burning of that building, in the general conflagration of Jerusalem and Thebes, this part of Uxmal was consumed, and with it other beams afterward discovered, much more curious and interesting; as also the whole collection of vases, figures, idols, and other relics gathered upon this journey. The collecting, packing, and transporting of these things had given me more trouble and annoyance than any other circumstance in our journey, and their loss cannot be replaced; for, being first on the ground, and having all at my choice, I of course selected only those objects which were most curious and valuable; and if I were to go over the whole ground again, I could not find others equal to them. I had the melancholy satisfaction of seeing their ashes exactly as the fire had left them. We seemed doomed to be in the midst of ruins; but in all our explorations there was none so touching as this. . . .

Around the top of the mound was a border of sculptured stone ten or twelve feet high. The principal ornament was the Grecque, and in following it round, and clearing away the trees and bushes, on the west side, opposite the courtyard of the Casa de Palomos, my attention was arrested by an ornament, the lower part of which was buried in rubbish fallen from above. It was about the centre of this side of the mound, and from its position, and the character of the ornament, I was immediately impressed with the idea that it was over a doorway, and that underneath was an entrance to an apartment in the mound. The Indians had cleared beyond it, and passed on, but I called them back, and set them to excavating the earth and rubbish that buried the lower part of the ornament. It was an awkward place to work in: the side of the mound was very steep, and the stones composing the ornament were insecure and tottering. The Indians, as usual, worked as if they had their lifetime for the job. They were at all times tedious and trying, but now, to my impatient eagerness, more painfully so than ever. Urging them, as well as I could, and actually making them comprehend my idea, I got them to work four long hours without any intermission, until they reached the cornice. The ornament proved to be the same hideous face, with the teeth standing out, before presented, varying somewhat in detail, and upon a grander scale. Throwing up the dirt upon the other side of them, the Indians had made a great pile outside, and stood in a deep hole against the face of the ornament. At this depth the stones seemed hanging loosely over their heads, and the Indians intimated that it was dangerous to continue digging, but by this time my impatience was beyond control. I had from time to time assisted in the work, and, urging them to continue, I threw myself into the hole, and commenced digging with all my strength. The stones went rolling and crashing down the side of the mound, striking against roots and tearing off branches. The perspiration rolled from me in a stream, but I was so completely carried away by the idea that had taken possession of me, so sure of entering some chamber that had been closed for ages, that I stopped at nothing; and with all this I considered myself cool and calm, and with great method resolved, as soon as I reached the doorway, to stop and send for Mr. Catherwood and Doctor Cabot, that we might all enter together, and make a formal note of everything exactly as it was found; but I was doomed to a worse disappointment than at El Laberinto de Maxcanú. Before getting below the cornice I thrust the machete through the earth, and found no opening, but a solid stone wall. The ground of my hope was gone, but still I kept the Indians digging, unconsciously, and without any object. In the interest of the moment I was not aware that the clouds had disappeared, and that I had been working in this deep hole, without a breath of air, under the full blaze of a vertical sun. The disappointment and reaction after the high excitement, co-operating with the fatigue and heat, prostrated all my strength. I felt a heaviness and depression, and was actually sick at heart, so that calling off the Indians, I was fain to give over and return to our quarters. In descending the mound my limbs could scarcely support me. My strength and elasticity were gone. With great difficulty I dragged myself to our apartments. My thirst was unquenchable. I threw myself into my hammock, and in a few moments a fiery fever was upon me. Our household was thrown into consternation. Disease had stalked all around us, but it was the first time it had knocked at our door. . . .

The *campo santo* was enclosed by a high stone wall. The interior had some degree of plan and arrangement, and in some places were tombs, built above ground, belonging to families in the village, hung with withered wreaths and votive offerings. The population tributary to it was about five thousand; it had been opened but five years, and already it presented a ghastly spectacle. There were many new-made graves, and on several of the vaults were a skull and small collection of bones in a box or tied up in a napkin, being the remains of one buried within and taken out to make room for another corpse. On one of them were the skulls and bones of a lady of the village, in a basket; an old acquaintance of the *cura*, who had died within two years. Among the bones was a pair of white satin shoes, which she had perhaps worn in the dance, and with which on her feet she had been buried.

At one corner of the cemetery was a walled enclosure, about twenty feet high and thirty square, within which was the charnel-house of the cemetery. A flight of stone steps led to the top of the wall, and on the platform of the steps and along the wall were skulls and bones, some in boxes and baskets, and some tied up in cotton cloths, soon to be thrown upon the common pile, but as yet having labels with the names written on them, to make known yet a little while longer the individuals to whom they had once belonged. Within the enclosure the earth was covered several feet deep with the promiscuous and undistinguishable bones of rich and poor, high and low, men, women, and children, Spaniards, mestizos, and Indians, all mingled together as they happened to fall. Among them were fragments of bright-coloured dresses, and the long hair of women still clinging to the skull. Of all the sad mementoes declaring the end to which all that is bright and beautiful in this world is doomed, none ever touched me so affectingly as this—the ornament and crowning charm of woman, the peculiar subject of her taste and daily care, loose, dishevelled, and twining among dry and mouldering bones.

The Ball Court at Chichen Itza

Passing among these vestiges, we come out upon the *camino real,* and, crossing it, again enter an open field, containing the extraordinary edifice which, on first reaching the field of ruins, we rode in on horseback to examine. It consists of two immense parallel walls, each 274 feet long, 30 feet thick, and 120 feet apart. 100 feet from the northern extremity, facing the open space between the walls, stands on an elevation a building 35 feet long, containing a single chamber, with the front fallen, and, rising among the rubbish, the remains of two columns, elaborately ornamented with sculpture; the whole interior wall being exposed to view, covered from the floor to the peak of the arch with sculptured figures in bas-relief, much worn and faded. The engraving represents the two walls, with this building in the distance. And at the other end, setting back, too, 100 feet, and commanding the space between the walls, is another building 81 feet long, also ruined, but exhibiting the remains of two columns richly ornamented with sculptured figures in bas-relief. The position in which these walls and buildings stand to each other is laid down on the general plan.

In the centre of the great stone walls, exactly opposite each other, and at the height of 20 feet from the ground, are two massive stone rings, 4 feet in diameter, and 1 foot 1 inch thick; the diameter of the hole is 1 foot 7 inches. On the rim and border were two sculptured entwined serpents, one of which is represented in the engraving below.

These walls, at the first glance, we considered identical in their uses and purposes with the parallel structures supporting the rings at Uxmal, of which I have already expressed the opinion that they were intended for the celebration of some public games. I

Ibid., pp. 303-8, 324.

have in all cases adopted the names of buildings which I found assigned to them on the spot, where any existed, and where there were none I have not attempted to give any. At Chichen all the principal buildings have names; this is called an *eglesia,* or church, of the *antiguos,* which was begun, but not finished, and the great open walls present not a bad idea of one of their gigantic churches before the roof is put on; but as we have already one *eglesia,* and there is historical authority which, in my opinion, shows clearly the object and uses of this extraordinary structure, I shall call it as occasion requires, the gymnasium or tennis-court.

In the account of the diversions of Montezuma, given by Herrera, we have the following:

"The King took much delight in seeing sport at ball, which the Spaniards have since prohibited, because of the mischief that often hapned at it; and was by them call'd *tlachtli,* being like our tennis. The ball was made of the gum of a tree that grows in hot countries, which, having holes made in it, distils great white drops, that soon harden, and, being work'd and moulded together, turn as black as pitch. [Undoubtedly caoutchuc or India rubber]. The balls made thereof, tho' hard and heavy to the hand, did bound and fly as well as our foot-balls, there being no need to blow them; nor did they use chaces, but vy'd to drive the adverse party that is to hit the wall, the others were to make good, or strike it over. They struck it with any part of their body, as it hapned, or they could most conveniently; and sometimes he lost that touched it with any other part but his hip, which was look'd upon among them as the greatest dexterity; and to this effect, that the ball might rebound the better, they fastned a piece of stiff leather on their hips. They might strike it every time it rebounded, which it would do several times one after another, in so much that it look'd as if it had been alive. They play'd in parties, so many on a side, for a load of mantles, or what the gamesters could afford, at so many scores. They also play'd for gold, and feather-work, and sometimes play'd themselves away, as has been said before. The place where they play'd was a ground room, long, narrow, and high, but wider above than below, and higher on the sides than at the ends, and they kept it very well plaster'd and smooth, both the walls and the floor. *On the side walls they fix'd certain stones, like those of a mill, with a hole quite through the middle,* just as big as the ball, and he that could strike it through there won the game; and in token of its being an extraordinary success, which rarely hapned, he had a right to the cloaks of all the lookers-on, by antient custom, and law amongst gamesters; and it was very pleasant to see, that as soon as ever the ball was in the hole, the standers-by took to their heels, running away with all their might to save their cloaks, laughing and rejoicing, others scouring after them to secure their cloaks for the winner, who was oblig'd to offer some sacrifice to the idol of the tennis-court, and the stone through whose hole the ball had pass'd. Every tennis-court was a temple, having two idols, the one of gaming, and the other of the ball. On a lucky day, at midnight, they perform'd certain ceremonies and enchantments on the two lower walls and on the midst of the floor, singing certain songs, or ballads; after which a priest of the great temple went with some of their religious men to bless it; he uttered some words, threw the ball about the tennis-court four times, and then it was consecrated, and might be play'd in, but not before. The owner of the tennis-court, who was always a lord, never play'd without making some offering and performing certain ceremonies to the idol of gaming, which shows how superstitious they were, since they had such regard to their idols, even in their diversions. Montezuma carry'd the Spaniards to this sport, and was well pleas'd to see them play at it, as also at cards and dice."

With some slight variation in details, the general features are so identical as to leave no doubt on my mind that this structure was erected for precisely the same object as the tennis-court in the city of Mexico described by Herrera. The temples are at hand in which sacrifices were offered, and we discover in this something more important than the mere determining of the character of a building; for in the similarity of diversions we see a resemblance in manners and institutions, and trace an affinity between the people who erected the ruined cities of Yucatan and those who inhabited Mexico at the time of the conquest. In the account of Herrera, moreover, we see incidentally the drawing of a funeral pall over the institutions of the natives, for we learn that the sport which "Montezuma took much delight in seeing," and which, beyond doubt, was a favourite diversion of the people, "the Spaniards have since prohibited." . . . .

One of these cenotes I have already mentioned; the other I did not visit till the afternoon preceding our departure from Chichen. Setting out from the Castillo, at some distance we ascended a wooded elevation, which seemed an artificial causeway leading to the cenote. The cenote was the largest and wildest we had seen; in the midst of a thick forest, an immense circular hole, with cragged, perpendicular sides, trees growing out of them and overhanding the brink, and still as if the genius of silence reigned within. A hawk was sailing around it, looking down into the water, but without once flapping its wings. The water was of a greenish hue. A mysterious influence seemed to pervade it, in unison with the historical account that the well of Chichen was a place of pilgrimage, and that human victims were thrówn into it in sacrifice. In one place, on the very brink, were the remains of a stone structure, probably connected with ancient superstitious rites; perhaps the place from which the victims were thrown into the dark well beneath.

E. G. SQUIER

An Island of Idols
on Lake Nicaragua

E. G. SQUIER is well known as a pioneer of American archaeology. In the year of the expedition described here he had published his *Aboriginal Monuments of the State of New York,* and in the year before (1848) the *Ancient Monuments of the Mississippi Valley,* which he wrote with Davis.

❦

DEC. 2, 1849.—This afternoon we prevailed upon Pedro—who, with his six stout sailors, had been drunk for a week, but were now sober and anxious to lay in a new supply of *reals* for another debauch—to take us over to the little island of Pensacola, almost within cannon-shot of the old castle of Granada. A young fellow, whilom a sailor, but now in the Doctor's service, on half-pay, as honorary man of all-work, averred that upon this island were *"piedras antiguas"* of great size, but nearly buried in the earth. It seemed strange that in all our inquiries concerning antiquities, of the padres and licenciados, indeed of the "best informed" citizens of Granada, we had not heard of the existence of these monuments. The Doctor was not a little skeptical, but experience had taught

From *Travels in Central America, particularly in Nicaragua,* Vol II. New York: Appleton & Co.; 1853, pp. 33-46.

me that more information, upon these matters, was to be gathered from the bare-footed *mozos* than from the black-robed priests, and I was obstinate in my determination to visit Pensacola.

It was late when we started, but in less than an hour we leaped ashore upon the island. It is one of the "out-liers" of the labyrinth of small islands which internal fires long ago thrust up from the depths of the lake, around the base of the volcano of Momobacho; and its shores are lined with immense rocks, black and blistered by the heat which accompanied the ancient disruptions of which they are the evidences. In some places they are piled up in rough and frowning heaps, half shrouded by the luxuriant vines which nature trails over them, as if to disguise her own deformities. In the island of Pensacola these rocks constitute a semi-circular ridge, nearly enclosing a level space of rich soil,—a kind of amphitheatre, looking towards the west, the prospect extending beyond the beach of Granada to the ragged hills and volcanic peaks around the lake of Managua. Upon a little elevation, within this natural temple, stood an abandoned cane hut, almost hidden by a forest of luxuriant plantains, which covered the entire area with a dense shadow, here and there pierced by a ray of sunlight, falling like molten gold through narrow openings in the leafy roof.

No sooner had we landed, than our men dispersed themselves in search of the monuments, and we followed. We were not long kept in suspense; a shout of *"Aqui, aqui!"* "Here, here," from the Doctor's man, announced that they were found. We hurried to his side. He was right; we could distinctly make out two great blocks of stone, nearly hidden in the soil. The parts exposed, though frayed by storms, and having clearly suffered from violence, nevertheless bore evidences of having been elaborately sculptured. A demand was made for the machetes of the men; and we were not long in removing enough of the earth to discover that the supposed blocks were large and well-proportioned statues, of superior workmanship and of larger size than any which we had yet encountered. The discovery was an exciting one, and the Indian sailors were scarcely less interested than ourselves. They crouched around the figures, and speculated earnestly concerning their origin. They finally seemed to agree that the larger of the two was no other than "Montezuma." It is a singular fact that the name and fame of the last of the Aztec emperors is cherished by all the Indian remnants from the banks of the Gila to the shores of Lake Nicaragua. Like the Pecos of New Mexico, some of the Indians of Nicaragua still indulge the belief that Montezuma will some day return, and re-establish his ancient empire.

I was convinced that there were other monuments here, but the sun was going down, and having resolved to return the next day, I gave up the search,—not, however, without engaging Pedro to be ready, with men and tools, to return at sunrise the next morning.

Pedro, for a miracle, was true to his word (probably because he had no money wherewith to get drunk); and the dew was fresh on the leaves, the parrots chattered vociferously, and the waves toyed cheerfully with the black basaltic rocks, as we leaped ashore a second time on Pensacola. The boat was moored, coffee speedily made and dispatched, and then Pedro's crew stripped themselves naked, and made other formidable preparations for disinterring the idols. But the preparations were more formidable than the execution. They commenced very well, but long before the figures were exposed to view, they were all smitten with a desire to hunt up others,—a plausible pretext for skulking away and stretching themselves on the ground beneath the plantains. I was at one time left wholly alone; even Pedro had disappeared; but the rascals came tumbling together again when I proclaimed that the *"aguardiente"* was circulating. By dint of alternate persuasions and threats, we finally succeeded in getting the smaller of the two figures completely uncovered. It had evidently been purposely buried, for one of the arms had been broken in its fall into the pit which had been previously dug to receive it, and the face had been bruised and mutilated. In this way the early Catholic zealots had endeavored to destroy the superstitious attachment of the aborigines to their monuments. It was, however, satisfactory to reflect that the figures were probably, on the whole, better preserved by their long interment than if they had been suffered to remain above ground. The next difficulty was to raise the prostrate figure; but after much preparation, propping, lifting, and vociferation, we succeeded in standing it up against the side of the hole which we had dug, in such a position that my artist could proceed with his sketch. It represented a human male figure, of massive proportions, seated upon a square pedestal, its head slightly bent forward, and its hands resting on its thighs. Above the face rose a heavy and monstrous representation of the head of an animal, below which could be traced the folds of a serpent, the fierce head of which was sculptured, open-mouthed and with life-like accuracy, by the side of the face of the figure. The whole combination was elaborate and striking.

The stone from which the figure here described was cut, is a hard sandstone, of a reddish color; but the sculpture is bold, and the limbs, unlike those of the monoliths of Copan, are detached so far as could be done with safety, and are cut with a freedom which I have observed in no other statuary works of the American aborigines.

To enable M. to make a drawing of the monument just disclosed, and to relieve him from the annoyance of our men, I deferred proceeding with the exhumation of the remaining one until he had finished, and therefore summoned all hands to search the island for others,—stimulating their activity by the splendid offer of a reward of four reals (equivalent to two days' wages) to any one who should make a discovery. I also joined in the search, but after wandering all over the little island, I came to the conclusion that, if there were others, of which I had little doubt, they had been successfully buried, and were past finding out, or else had been broken up and removed. So I seated myself philosophically upon a rock, and watched an army of black ants, which were defiling past, as if making a tour of the island. They formed a solid column from five to six inches wide, and marched straight on, turning neither to the right hand nor to the left, pertinaciously surmounting every obstacle which interposed. I watched them for more than half an hour, but their number seemed undiminished; thousands upon thousands hurried past, until finally, attracted by curiosity, I rose and followed the line, in order to discover the destination of the procession,—if it were an invasion, a migration, or a simple pleasure excursion. At a short distance, and under the cover of some bushes, the column mounted what appeared to be simply a large, round stone, passed over it, and continued its march.

The stone attracted my attention, and on observing it more closely, I perceived traces of sculpture. I summoned my men, and after a two hours' trial of patience and temper, I succeeded in raising from its bed of centuries another idol of massive proportions, but differing entirely from the others, and possessing an extraordinary and forbidding aspect. The lower half had been broken off, and could not be found; what remained was simply the bust and head. The latter was disproportionately great; the eyes were large, round, and staring; the ears broad and long; and from the widely-distended mouth, the lower jaw of which was forced down by the hands of the figure, projected a tongue which reached to the breast, giving to the whole an unnatural and horrible expression. As it stood in the pit, with its monstrous head rising above the ground, with its fixed stony gaze, it seemed like some gray monster just emerging from the depths of the earth, at the bidding of the wizard-priest of an unholy religion. My men stood back, and more than one crossed himself as he muttered to his neighbor, "Es el diablo!" "It is the devil!" I readily comprehended the awe with which it might be regarded by the devotees of the ancient religion, when the bloody priest daubed the lapping tongue with the yet palpitating hearts of his human victims

It was long past noon before we commenced the task of raising the largest and by far the most interesting idol to an erect position. This was no easy undertaking. The stone, although not more than nine feet high, measured ten feet in circumference, and was of great weight. We were but eleven men all told; Pedro said it was useless to try, we might turn it over, but nothing more. Still I was determined it should be raised, not only for the purpose of observing its effect in that position, but because I was convinced that the under side must exhibit more clearly the finer details of the sculpture than the upper, which had been partially exposed above the ground. I gave each man a prodigious dram of *aguardiente,* which inspired corresponding courage, and after procuring an additional number of stout levers and props, we proceeded to raise the recumbent mass. Our progress was slow and difficult, the sweat rolled in streams down the glossy skins of our sailors, who—thanks to the *ardiente*—worked with more vigor than I thought them capable of exerting. The *aguardiente* was worth more than gold to me that day. The men shouted and cheered, and cried, "*Arriba con la niña!*" "Up with the baby!" But before we got it half raised, a thunder-storm, the approach of which had escaped our notice in the excitement, came upon us, as only a tropical thunder-storm knows how to come. I beat a retreat, dripping with perspiration, into the deserted hut; while the men sat coolly down and took the pelting,— they were used to it! The storm passed in due time, but the ground was saturated, and the feet sank deeply in the soft, sticky mass around the "niña." Still, in order to save another visit in force the next day, I determined not to relinquish the task we had began. But the difficulties were now augmented, and it was only after the most extraordinary exertions, at imminent danger of crushed limbs, that we succeeded in our object. With bleeding hands, and completely bedaubed with mud, I had at last the satisfaction to lead off in a "*Viva por la niña antigua!*"—"Hurrah for the old baby!" I am not quite sure but I took a drop of the *aguardiente* myself, while the shower was passing. Pedro and his crew responded by a "*Vivan los Americanos del Norte!*" which, being interpreted, meant that they "wouldn't object to another drink." This was given of course, whereupon Pedro insinuated that "*Los Americanos son diablos!*"—"The Americans are devils;" which remark, however. Pedro meant as a compliment. The figure, when erect, was truly grand. It represented a man with massive limbs, and broad, prominent chest, in a stooping or rather crouching posture, his hands resting on his thighs, just above the knees. Above his head rose the monstrous head and jaws of some animal; its fore paws were placed one upon each shoulder, and the hind ones upon the hands of the statue, as if binding them to the thighs. It might be intended, it probably was intended, to represent an alligator or some mythological or fabulous animal. Its back was covered with carved plates, like rough mail. The whole rose from a broad, square pedestal. The carving, as in the other figure, was bold and free. I never have seen a statue which conveyed so forcibly the idea of power and strength; it was a study for a Samson under the gates of Gaza, or an Atlas supporting the world. The face was mutilated and disfigured, but it still seemed to wear an expression of sternness, if not severity, which added greatly to the effect of the whole. The finer details of workmanship around the head had suffered much; and from the more decided marks of violence which the entire statue exhibits, it seems probable that it was an especial object of regard to the aborigines, and of corresponding hate to the early Christian zealots.

The sun came out brightly after the rain, and although wet and weary, and not insensible to the comforts of dry clothes and the seductions of a hammock, I could hardly tear myself away from these remarkable monuments—overturned perhaps by the hands of Gil Gonzalez himself, at the time when, in the language of the chronicler, "the great cazique Nicaragua consented to be baptized, together with nine thousand of his subjects, and thus the country became converted." "The great idols in his sumptuous temples," continues the historian, "were thrown down, and the cross set up in their stead." The same authority assures us that "Nicaragua was a chief of great good wit, and though the Spanish captain was a discreet man, it puzzled him much to explain to Nicaragua why it was that so few men as the Spaniards coveted so much gold."

M. returned the next day and completed his drawings, while I busied myself in preparing for a voyage to the great uninhabited island of Zapatero.

The T.'s had volunteered one of their *bongos*, one of the largest and most comfortable on the lake; and as most of this kind of unique craft are only gigantic canoes, hollowed from a single trunk of the cebia, and quite as well fitted, and just as much disposed, to sail upon their sides or bottom up as any other way, it was a gratification to know that "La Carlota" had been built with something of a keel, by a foreign shipwright, and that the prospect of being upset in the first blow was thereby dimished from three chances in four, to one in two. The voyager who has sailed on the restless lake of Nicaragua in gusty weather, with bungling sailors, can well comprehend the satisfaction with which we contemplated "La Carlota," as she rocked gracefully at her moorings, off the old castle on the shore. She was perhaps sixty feet long, and her *chopa* was capable of accommodating four or five persons with lodgings,— something in the pickled mackerel order, it is true, but not uncomfortably, in the moderated views of comfort which the traveller in Central America soon comes to entertain. In front of the *chopa* were ten benches, for as many oarsmen, and places for setting up the masts, in case the winds should permit of their use. "La Carlota," withal, was painted on the outside, and had a figure head; indeed, take her all in all, she looked a frigate among the numerous strange pit-pans, piraguas, and other anomalous and nameless water-craft around her. Thus far all was well. The next thing was to get a crew together; but this devolved upon the junior Mr. T. After two days of exertion, for there was a great conjunction of *fiestas* at the time, they were enlisted and duly paid,—everybody expects pay in advance in Central America! A fixed number of *reals* were counted out for the commissary department, and the *patron*, Juan, solemnly promised to be ready to set sail the next morning at sunrise for the island of *Zapatero*, the "Shoemaker," where Manuel, who was to go along as a guide, assured us there were many *frailes*, friars, some kneeling, others sitting, and still others standing erect, or reclining as if in death, besides many other wonderful and curious things, among which was a deep salt lake.

The Doctor and myself completed our arrangements over night. After breakfast the next morning, which had been fixed for our departure, I proposed to go down to the lake, supposing that as Juan had promised to be ready by sunrise, we might possibly succeed in getting off by nine or ten o'clock at the furthest. The Doctor, however, protested that it was useless to go down so early,—"he was not going to broil in the sun, on the open beach, all the fore-noon, not he;" and he comforted us with the assurance that he had lived in the country ten years, and that if we got off before the middle of the afternoon, we might perform any surgical operation we pleased upon either one of his legs! My time was limited, and these vexatious delays almost worried me into a fever. At eleven o'clock, however, I prevailed upon the Doctor, much against his will, and amidst his earnest protestations that he "knew the people, and that it was no kind of use," to go down to the shore. There swung our bongo, precisely as we had left it the day before, and not a soul on board! The shore was covered with groups of half-naked women, seated just at the edge of the water, engaged in an operation here called *washing*, which consisted in dipping the articles in the water, and placing them on a rough stone, and beating them violently with a club, to the utter demolition of everything in the shape of buttons! Groups of children were paddling in little pools, or playing in the sand; sailors just arrived were landing their cargoes, carrying the bales on their shoulders through the breakers, and depositing them in creaking carts; here and there a horseman pranced along under the shadow of the trees on the shore; and amongst all, imperturbable buzzards in black, and long-legged cranes in white, walked about with prescriptive freedom! Altogether it was a singular mixture of civilized and savage life, and one not likely to be forgotten by the observant traveller.

I was, however, in no mood to enjoy the scene,—and the Doctor's "I told you so!" as he quietly seated himself on a log in the shade, was cruelly provoking. After diligent search, we found two of our crew, with only a cloth wrapped around their loins, lying flat on the sands, their faces covered with their sombreros, and the hot sun beating down upon their naked bodies,—perfect pictures of the intensest laziness. "Where is the *patron?*" They simply lifted their hats, and responded, *"Quien sabe?"* "Who knows?" The eternal *"Quien sabe,"* and uttered without so much as an attempt to rise! This was unendurable; I gave them each an emphatic kick in the ribs with my rough travelling boots, which brought them to their feet in an instant, with a deprecatory exclamation of *"Señor!"* One was dispatched to hunt up the others among the pulperias of the town, with emphatic threats of great bodily harm, if the delinquents were not produced within a given time. The second one, a strapping mestizo, who still rubbed his side with a lugubrious expression of face, was ordered to deposit himself within short range of my form-idable-looking "Colt," with an injunction not to move unless ordered. Directly, another recreant was discovered, doing the agreeable to a plump coffee-colored washing-girl,—nothing chary of her charms, as may be inferred from the fact that excepting a cloth, none of the largest, thrown over her lap, she was *au naturel.* He too was ordered to take up his position beside the other prisoner, which he did with a bad grace, but greatly to the pretended satisfaction of the coffee-colored girl, who said that he was *"malo,"* bad, and deserved all sorts of ill. "A woman is naturally a coquette, whether in a white skin or black," philosophized the Doctor; "that yellow thing don't mean what she says. I'll wager they have just agreed to get married, or what is the same thing in these countries."

It was high noon long before we got our vagrant crew under our batteries; and conscious of their delinquencies, and not a little in awe of our pistol butts, they really exerted themselves in getting the boat ready. Half a dozen naked fellows plunged into the surf, their black bodies alternately appearing and disappearing in the waves, and towed the "Carlota" close in shore, under the lee of the old castle. The sails, our provisions, blankets, etc., were placed on board, and then we mounted on the shoulders of the strongest, and were duly deposited on the quarter-deck. The bells of the city chimed two o'clock, as we swept outside of the fort into the rough water. It was all the men could do to overcome the swell, and the sweeps bent under their vigorous strokes. Once in deep water, the waves were less violent, but they had the long, majestic roll of the ocean. Here every oarsman pulled off his breeches, his only garment, deposited his sombrero in the bottom of the boat, and lighted a cigar; they were now in full uniform, and pulled sturdily at the oars. Juan, the *patron*, drew off his breeches also, but, by way of maintaining the dignity of the quarter-deck, or out of respect to his passengers, he kept on his shirt, a flaming red check, and none of the longest, which, as he bestrode the tiller, fluttered famously in the wind.

One hour's hard pulling, and we were among the islands. Here the water was still and glassy, while the waves dashed and chafed with a sullen roar against the iron shores of the outer rank, as if anxious to invade the quiet of the inner recesses,—those narrow, verdure-arched channels, broad, crystal-floored vistas, and cool, shady nooks in which graceful canoes were here and there moored.

Perhaps a more singular group of islets cannot be found in the wide world. As I have before said, they are all of volcanic origin, generally conical in shape, and seldom exceeding three or four acres in area. All are covered with a cloak of verdure, but nature is not always successful in hiding the black rocks which start out in places, as if in disdain of all concealment, and look frowningly down on the clear water, giving an air of wildness to the otherwise soft and quiet scenery of the islands. Trailing over these rocks, and dropping in festoons from the overhanging trees, their long pliant tendrils floating in the waves, are innumerable vines, with bright and fragrant flowers of red and yellow, mingled with the inverted cone of the "gloria de Nicaragua," with its overpowering odor, with strange and nameless fruits, forming an evergreen roof, so close that even a tropical sun cannot penetrate. Many of these islands have patches of cultivated ground, and on such, generally crowning their summits, relieved by a dense green background of plantains, and surrounded by kingly palms, and the papaya with its golden fruit, are the picturesque cane huts of the inhabitants. Groups of naked, swarthy children in front,—a winding path leading beneath the great trees down to the water's edge,— an arbor-like, miniature harbor, with a canoe lashed to the shore,— a woman naked to the waist, with a purple skirt of true Tyrian dye, for the famous murex is found on the Pacific shores of Nicaragua, her long, black, glossy hair falling over neck and breast, and reaching almost to her knees,—a flock of noisy parrots in a congressional squabble among the trees,—a swarm of parroquets scarcely less noisy,—a pair of vociferating macaws like floating fragments of a rainbow in the air,—inquisitive monkeys hanging among the vines,—active iguanas scrambling up the banks,—long-necked and long-legged cranes in deep soliloquy at the edge of the

water, their white bodies standing out, in strong relief against a
background of rock and verdure,—a canoe glancing rapidly and
noiselessly across a vista of water,—all this, with a golden sky
above, the purple sides of the volcano of Momobacho overshadow-
ing us, and the distant shores of Chontales molten in the slanting
sunlight,—these were some of the elements of the scenery of
the islands,—elements constantly shifting, and forming new and
pleasing combinations. Seated upon the roof of the chopa, I forgot
in contemplating the changing scenery the annoyances of the
morning, and felt almost disposed to ask the pardon of the marine-
ros whom I had treated so unceremoniously.

DESIRÉ CHARNAY

In Camp at Palenque:
Sculptures and Squeezes

DESIRÉ CHARNAY made his explorations in Central America
between 1857 and 1882. He was working on behalf of the French
government (p. 69, I).

HAD Palenque been the capital of an empire, the palace a kingly
mansion, the history of her people, fragments of domestic life,
pageants, recitals of battles and conquests, would be found among
the reliefs which everywhere cover her edifices, as in Mexico, at
Chichen Itza and other cities in Yucatan; whereas the reliefs in
Palenque show nothing of the kind. On them we behold peaceful,

From *The Ancient Cities of the New World*, translated from the French by Gonino
and Conant. London: Chapman Hall; 1887, pp. 246-9, 253-4, 324-5, 346-8.

stately subjects, usually a personage standing with a sceptre, sometimes a calm, majestic figure whose mouth emits a flame, emblem of speech and oratory. They are surrounded by prostrated acolytes, whose bearing is neither that of slaves nor of captives; for the expression of their countenance, if submissive, is open and serene, and their peaceful attitude indicates worshippers and believers; no arms are found among these multitudes, nor spear, nor shield, nor bow, nor arrow, nothing but preachers and devotees.

The interest attaching to these studies is certainly profound and sincere, yet it does not entirely banish the consciousness of our very arduous life among these ruins. The rain is incessant; the damp seems to penetrate the very marrow of our bones; a vegetable mould settles on our hats which we are obliged to brush off daily; we live in mud, we are covered with mud, we breathe in mud, whether amongst the ruins or wandering away from them; the ground is so slippery that we are as often on our backs as on our feet.

No rest for the explorer, is the fiat that has gone forth. At night the walls, which are covered with greenish moss, trickle down on our weary heads and awake us out of our sleep; in the day-time we are a prey to swarms of insects, avadores, mosquitoes, and garrapatas. It is impossible to bear up long against such odds, and first young Lemaire, next Alfonso the cook, are laid up with malaria. Julian and I are the only two of the party whom this scourge has spared. Yet this wretched life is not without some gleams of sunshine. Since our men opened a large space in front of the palace, and cleared the courtyard of the dense vegetation which blocked it up completely, allowing a free passage for the air to circulate, the birds have not been slow to avail themselves of this new retreat, and our mornings and evenings are cheered by their sweet notes. We have our night concerts also, when innumerable creatures, whose names we know not, mingle their voices with the chirping of the cricket, the song of the cicala, the croaking of frogs, followed by the howling of huge monkeys, which sounds like the roaring of lions and tigers; all this is new to us, and not without a certain amount of excitement, yet it sinks into utter insignificance as compared with the great joy of our discoveries, the ever fresh interest of our photographs, the looking forward with immense satisfaction to the time when we shall produce the splendid squeezes of these grand, mysterious inscriptions, not yet found in any museum. Well weighed together, these things are calculated to make us forget the hardships and troubles of the moment.

Quinine has done wonders; our men are themselves again, and

Alfonso, to make us forget the meagre fare he inflicted upon us during his illness, served up a magnificent luncheon to celebrate his recovery. The reader may like to read the menu of a *déjeuner* in the wilds of America:—

Soupe: Purée de haricots noirs au bouillon d'escargots. Olives de Valence, saucisson d'Arles. Poulet de grain, sauté à l'ail et au piment rouge. Morue frite. Chives, pointes de petits palmiers en branches d'asperge. Fritures: haricots noirs rissolés. Crêpes. Fromage américain. Vins: Bordeaux et Aragon. Café habanero et cigares de Tabasco.

I am not sure about the order of succession, but I can vouch for the items being correct, from which it may be seen that even at Palenque, with fine weather and a grateful cook, one need not starve, but he would be greatly mistaken who thought that this was our every day's fare. Let us return to graver concerns.

The Temple of Inscriptions is the largest known at Palenque, standing on a pyramid of some 48 feet high, to the south-west angle of the palace; its façade, 74 feet by nearly 25 feet deep, is composed of a vast gallery occupying the whole front, and of three compartments of different sizes, a large central chamber and two small ones at the sides. The front gallery is pierced with five apertures, supported by six pillars of 6 feet 9 inches by 3 feet 7 inches thick. The two corner pillars were covered with katunes, and the other four with bas-reliefs. No sanctuary is found in the building known as the Temple of Inscriptions, but both the gallery and the central room have flagstones covered with inscriptions. Two panels enclosed in the wall of the gallery measure 13 feet wide by 7 feet 8 inches high, one in the central chamber is over 7 feet by 6 feet. Amidst the katunes of this panel Waldeck has seen fit to place three or four elephants. What end did he propose to himself in giving this fictitious representation? Presumably to give a prehistoric origin to these ruins, since it is an ascertained fact that elephants in a fossil state only have been found on the American continent. It is needless to add that neither Catherwood, who drew these inscriptions most minutely, nor myself who brought impressions of them away, nor living man, ever saw these elephants and their fine trunks.

But such is the mischief engendered by preconceived opinions. With some writers it would seem that to give a recent date to these monuments would deprive them of all interest. It would have been fortunate had explorers been imbued with fewer prejudices and gifted with a little more common sense, for then we should have known the truth with regard to these ruins long since. Of all the buildings the temple was the best preserved, as seen in every detail. The floor, which in the palace is but a layer of plaster, is laid down here with beautiful slabs 9 feet 9 inches on one side by 5 feet by 7 inches thick.

The roof is unfortunately in a very ruinous state, and the dense vegetation which covers it prevents seeing anything of the large figures which presumably occupied its surface; even a photograph is difficult to get, for want of sufficient space. . . .

Notwithstanding the deplorable circumstances in which I had to work, I was able to take more than 325 square feet of impressions; and here I take much pleasure in recording the debt of gratitude I owe Mr. de Laval for his admirable invention, which by means of paper [usually known as "taking a squeeze"] instead of plaster makes the taking of impressions in distant countries comparatively easy, when the difficulty of transport and the expense of plaster would, in our case, have placed the reproduction of reliefs and inscriptions entirely beyond our power. As it was, my impressions, which, had I used plaster, would have weighed at least 30,000 lb., only weighed 500 lb.; but even so, the taking of impressions is not so easily effected as may be imagined, especially in a damp region where the utmost care was required to reproduce faithfully the delicate, faint, and defaced reliefs on these old slabs. It would be impossible to give an idea of the immense and minute brushwork which was required to cover 325 feet square of paper six sheets deep.

Furthermore, the reliefs were only reached by a shaky scaffolding of wet twigs; next came the drying process round huge fires to secure the moulds against the rain getting into them, and the stowing them speedily away before they got spoiled. Well, but we had every reason to be satisfied with our work; the precious squeezes had been satisfactorily stored up in the galleries of the palace, when, on the night of January 26th, a night I shall never forget, a hideous smell of burning startled us out of our sleep to witness the flames which were consuming my mouldings, the result, too, of three weeks' hard labour, now fast vanishing into smoke. To snatch the burning rolls and throw them into the yard, where the Indians were ready to deluge them with water, was the work of a moment, but, alas! to no purpose; the mischief was irretrievable, and we had to begin all over again. Whether done by accident or of malice prepense, it was idle to inquire; we set to work again with renewed ardour, and after ten days of incessant labour we brought out copies finer than the first, and these are now to be found in the Trocadéro.

In Camp at Chichen Itza: the Beautiful Cook

This was not my first visit to Chichen, nevertheless my emotion was profound on beholding again the gigantic outline of El Castillo [the temple pyramid also known as the Temple of Kukul-

TABLET OF THE SLAVES, ABOUT 2.75 x 1.50 METRES,
FROM BUILDING A, PALENQUE, CHIAPAS

can], which we had decided beforehand should be our headquarters, as from its elevated position it offered many strategical advantages, which would secure us against surprise. It was with considerable difficulty that we climbed the steps, which are steep and completely invaded by a vigorous vegetation; as for our great quantity of baggage, none but nimble, sure-footed natives could have succeeded in hauling it up on to the platform of the monument.

Our next thought was how to dispose of ourselves. The interior of El Castillo consists of a rectangular corridor, running along two-thirds of the edifice, pierced east, south, and west by three large apertures, and a gallery giving access to a great hall closed in on every side. We very stupidly gave up the latter to our men, with the idea that we should be cooler and have more air in the open gallery, not taking into consideration that at this altitude, whichever way the wind blew, it would sweep in upon us in fearful blasts, causing perpetual sneezing, coughing, and freezing the very life out of us.

The day was spent unpacking and classifying, and at suppertime we discovered that our cook, who was to have come from Valladolid, had failed us; food we had in tins, but no water, having left our cantaros at Citas, so that we were obliged to go without soup, coffee, or our evening tub.

It may seem unworthy to have been put out by such trivial details with the grand spectacle we had before us: a glorious moon had risen, sailing on her course with her brilliant retinue of scintillating stars, illuminating the vast wooded expanse, like a boundless, heaving ocean on a calm day; fragments of walls, mounds, eminences, shrouded in a sombre vegetation, were distinctly visible, which I pointed out one by one to my companions who, unlike myself, beheld them for the first time. El Castillo occupies nearly the centre of the ruins; below it to the east was the Market-place, and two small palaces which belonged to it; to the north, a stately but ruinous building, the cenote and the temple attached; to the north-west, the famous Tennis-court; to the west and south-west, the Chichan-Chob, the Caracol and the other cenote, the Nuns' Palace, the Akab-Sib; and farther south, the hacienda, which has long been abandoned.

We were conversing in subdued tones of the mysterious past of this dead city, which mayhap our studies and explorations would bring to life again; all was hushed, and the death-like silence was only broken at regular intervals by the cry of our sentinels; and these very cries carried us back to the far-gone days, when the city was perhaps similarly guarded against a sudden inroad from her jealous neighbours.

The morning effects of light and shade were no less beautiful; the broad level wrapped in a transparent mist, pierced here and there by the pyramids and the wooded eminences, looked like a whitening sea interspersed with green islets; while the horizon was gilded with the brightness of the rising sun, who seemed to create, to raise suddenly into life all the objects touched with his golden wand; presently, like a mighty giant he tore asunder and burnt up the white vapour, and lit up the whole sky. . . .

Our excursions in these impenetrable woods, our ascents and descents of the pyramid, the arduous work attending the taking of squeezes, made our life very harassing; it could have been more easily borne had we been able to sleep, but the scorching days were succeeded by icy-cold nights, which kept us awake, so that we rose in the morning more unrefreshed and more tired than when we turned in for the night.

Some compensation we had in our walks round the pyramid, beguiling the time we could not sleep with a cigar, contemplating the fine starry nights and sometimes the lunar rainbows so rarely soon; or we watched the broad shadow of the pyramid cast athwart the white haze shrouding the plain, fringed by an immense brilliant corona, which seemed to float in space. Never had I gazed on anything so curious and fantastic as this terrestrial halo; and if the ancient worshippers of Kukulcan ever witnessed the phenomenon, they must have deemed it little short of miraculous.

We were still without a cook; for Julian was so atrociously bad that I kept him at the squeezes, taking the cooking ourselves in turn, which wasted much valuable time. One evening, after everybody had gone to rest, I was sitting alone writing my impressions, my head full of the ruins and the people who inhabited them. I suddenly looked up, to see standing before me a lovely maiden more like an apparition than a mortal being. Was this the shade of a Maya princess who had returned to the scenes of her former life, conjured up by my imagination? Meanwhile the beauteous figure stood looking and smiling at me. I was amazed, speechless, hardly daring to break the spell, when a third figure stood out from the dark entrance, in whom I recognised the commandant of Pisté.

"You are surprised at our visit," he said.

"Rather, especially at this hour, and in such a night."

"Time is of no account when you wish to serve a friend; I heard that you required a cook, I brought you mine, that's all."

"A cook!" I ejaculated to myself. What a fall! my Indian princess a cook! I looked at her again, and I could not believe that so much youth and beauty were put to such menial occupation. I wondered at the commandant's self-abnegation. I was somewhat embarrassed, nevertheless, as to where I should put her. I called up Julian to prepare a bed for her, but as he was not easily roused, I had time to reflect that with a hundred men about me, El Castillo was no fitting place for a young girl. I was profuse in my acknowledgments to the commandant, observing that as nothing was ready, it would perhaps be better to put off her coming for

a day or two, apologising for the trouble they had taken in coming
through the woods and having to climb the pyramid in such a
pitch-dark night. He knew what I meant. I slipped a coin in the
girl's hand, as she held a bottle towards me. "Drink," said the
officer; "it is Josepha's present to you." I did so, while Josepha
merely put her lips to the bottle. We shook hands, and my two
visitors disappeared in the night. The draught was *Staventum,*
a strong spirit, which made me light-headed, and in a fit of som-
nambulism I wandered about, spouting poetry at the top of my
voice, on the very edge of the pyramid, whence I was fortunately
removed, without any further result than to awake the next
day with a splitting headache. Our long-expected cook arrived at
last, and she was so old, and such a fright, that it relieved me
of all fear on her account.

ANNE MAUDSLAY

In Camp at Copan

SIR ALFRED MAUDSLAY and his wife Anne were working among
Mayan sites of Central America between 1881 and 1894 (p. 69, I).

AFTER crossing the small stream, the laundry of Copan, we rode
on for half a mile, part of the way through a plantation of sugar-
cane, to a stone wall which has lately been built round the ruins.
Passing through a gateway we entered an enchanting grove of
grand old trees which cast their shade over the remains of temples, monoliths, and altars. At last we had arrived and were in
the actual presence of the strange stone monuments whose reproductions in plaster I knew so well. The bridle-path led over

From *A Glimpse at Guatemala.* London: John Murray; 1899, pp. 117-20, 126.

the steep side of a foundation mound into the Western Court, where I found myself face to face with an old friend, who has stood on guard for centuries at the foot of a great stairway. The stately grove of giant tropical trees was of itself strangely impressive, and the glimpses of the grim figures on the monoliths and the strange scrolls and grotesque ornament on the scattered fragments of stone, amongst which we picked our way, added a sense of unreality which was bewildering. Since passing through that little gate in the wall we seemed to have slipped back into a remote past and to be treading the Valhalla of gods and heroes whose patient followers and worshippers had raised monuments which were to outlast the ages, where the spirits of the mighty dead might still haunt the scene of their ancient glory.

It was a distinct effort to return to commonplace things, and to call to mind the fact that the afternoon was far advanced and that I had duties to perform as chief cook and housekeeper. In the middle of the plaza stood the house we were to occupy, an airy structure something like a large bird-cage, which had been built by a party of Americans who for the last two years had been at work in the ruins. The walls were made of rough sticks placed side by side, about an inch apart, and bound together with lianes; the roof was thatched with sugar-cane leaves, one large opening in the wall served as doorway, and windows were certainly not needed, as every breath of air sighed through the gaping walls. One end of the house had been screened off and the walls thatched to the ground so as to form a dark room for photography. Our American friends had left a convenient shed and cooking-place near the house, and I soon had supper ready, and then we settled ourselves for the night.

It only needed one night's experience to convince me that the cross draughts of our airy residence were not suited to our constitutions, and when on rising to make my toilet in the morning, the transparent nature of my dressing-room was borne in on me, my mind was made up, and I ordered the tent to be pitched without delay. Thenceforward we had a thoroughly comfortable bedroom. One end of the tent was left open for ventilation, but we were well sheltered from draughts, and furnished with good thick blankets as a protection against the sharp fall of temperature in the early morning. I only wish one could always secure the same conditions of climate, temperature, and fresh air, for it seemed to me ideal.

We had come to Copan to work, and, as the early morning hours are precious in these tropical climes, dawn always found the camp astir. Fires were soon lighted. As the sun rose Gorgonio would appear at the tent-door with two big bowls of hot

coffee, pan-dulce, and bananas, and by 7 o'clock all were off to
work: my husband provided with note-books, tape-measures, and
drawing-board, followed by the *mozos* with machetes and scrub-
bing brushes, ready for any labour—from clearing bush to scrub-
bing moss and lichens from the sculptures, preparatory to the
moulding-operations, which Gorgonio carried out with such skill
and patience. My duties lay mostly in the camp, and were purely
housewifely in character, for, as no woman could be found in
the neighborhood who had any knowledge of housework or cooking, I had to do the work myself. The cooking was, of course,
the most arduous part of the performance, but the housework
occupied at least an hour in the morning. First, the blankets must
be hung in the sun to keep them dry and free from insects, then
the tent had to be swept out and cleaned of ants and occasional
scorpions. Every few days we sent *mozos* into the hills around
to bring in huge bundles of fresh sweet-smelling pine-needles,
which were spread over the floor of the house as a carpet, and
every morning this carpet had to be attended to. Then came the
preparation of breakfast for three hungry persons, for our party
was increased by the arrival from Copan of Mr. Erwin Dieseldorff, an enthusiastic archaeologist who had come to us on a
visit, and had brought with him Gorgonio's brother Carlos Lopez (an
old assistant of my husband) and three Indian *mozos*.

The tiny kitchen and larder stood beneath the shade of a wide-
spreading Ficus tree, and for convenience of serving the food,
as well as to save me many steps, we placed the table close beside it. It was a charming dining-room in such a climate, for
during the four weeks of our stay not a drop of rain fell to mar
the comfort of our *al fresco* meals. The great Ficus gave us friendly
shade from the noonday sun, and at supper-time the moon played
hide-and-seek between its branches as they were gently swayed
by a soft and balmy breeze.

We shared our dining-room with the birds, who came in flocks
to feed on the Ficus and other fruit-bearing trees, and we were
never weary of watching them at play amongst the branches
overhead. At first the parrots and parroquets vastly outnum-
bered all the others, and appeared to have formed a settlement
in the tree above our tent. These parrots were a boisterous family,
who woke at dawn and began screaming and chattering whilst
they performed round the branches all those gymnastic feats which
I have thought were only devised in captivity to vary the monotony
of cage-life; but the parroquets, who lived in the same tree, appeared to be quiet little creatures who nestled near to one another, whispering and cooing gently, until some sudden impulse
would seize both parties, and they would dash off in the air, flash-

ing circles of gold and red and green as the sun caught the glint of their plumage, and then return as suddenly to the shelter of the trees to chatter loudly over their exploits. An hour or so after sunrise the noise of the parrots ceased, but whether they flew away or hid themselves amongst the thick foliage I could never make out; certain it is that they disappeared until evening, when they again woke the echoes with their cries before settling for the night.

About a week after our arrival, as the fruit ripened upon other trees, the birds greatly increased in numbers, and the air was filled with song and chattering throughout all but the noonday hours. The grey jays perched quite close to us when we were at work, turned their heads knowingly from side to side, and indulged in ribald remarks at our expense; and big toucans, with bright yellow breasts, flew clumsily from tree to tree, as though overweighted by their great green-and-yellow bills. Sometimes an aurora, or yellow-breasted trogon, honoured us with a visit; less gorgeous in plumage than his relation the quetzal, he nevertheless possesses a fair share of beauty, and his dignity of deportment was imposing as for hours together he sat, almost motionless, solemnly contemplating us and our doings. Now and then the gurgling note of an oropendula rang through the grove, and this large cinnamon-coloured oriole, with yellow tail-feathers, would spend half an hour with us, flying from tree to tree and uttering his strange musical cry. The natives told me that there had been numbers of them about the ruins the previous year, as they then had a settlement close by in a tree overhanging the river, where their hanging nests had numbered over two hundred; but some ardent collector had cut off a branch with three or four nests attached to it, to carry home as a specimen, and the whole colony of birds had at once forsaken the tree and formed a new settlement some distance away. Our occasional visitor was doubtless one of the migrants who had ventured to come back to feed on the fruit-trees he had known of old.

I deeply regretted the disappearance of the colony, as it would have been delightful to watch the birds at one's leisure. Only once during our journey did I get the chance of watching them, and that only for a short time. As a precaution against attack, the birds always select for their home a tree with a long clean stem standing out from the surrounding vegetation, and a certain smooth red-barked tree with rather thin foliage seems to be an especial favourite. The long bag-shaped nests, with an entrance at the top, are attached to the spreading branches, and swing freely in the breeze. . . .

It was always a delightful moment for me when my household

duties were over and I could join the workers in the great Plaza, where my husband, with a patience I never ceased to marvel at, was comparing the drawings made for the "Biologia" with the original inscriptions, Mr. Dieseldorff would be clearing the debris from a stairway or tracing the line of a fallen wall, whilst Gorgonio, Carlos, and Caralampio were at work making paper moulds of the sculptured monoliths or heaping up great log-fires to dry the moulds already made.

I wish I could do justice to these imposing plazas, studded with strangely carved monuments and surrounded by lofty mounds and great stone stairways, moss-grown and hoary with age, broken by the twisted roots of giant trees, but very solemn and imposing in their decay. The huge mass of squared and faced building-stones, the profusion of sculptured ornament, boldly-carved human figures, strangely grotesque imps—half human and half animal—elaborate scrolls, graceful and beautiful feather-work, the latter especially crisp and delicate in execution, all combined to make it difficult to believe that no metal tools were used by the ancient Indian workmen. Yet the fact remains that no implements other than stone axes and obsidian flakes have ever been found amongst the ruins, and this adds to the wonder and mystery which enshrouds them, so that one almost fears even to guess at the numbers of centuries or the thousands of busy hands and brains which, under such conditions, must have gone to the accomplishment of the work.

I was always conscious of a longing desire to witness some great ceremony at Copan, such as one's imagination conjures up amid such surroundings, and the thought constantly recurred to me that possibly in the half-Christian, half-heathen rites of the Indian pilgrims and the strange dances they indulge in on certain festal occasions some echo might yet be caught of the ancient ceremonial.

The novelist has already tried his hand both on Ancient Mexico and Yucatan, and that class of theorizer who wants as little data as possible to interfere with his pet schemes has too long occupied the field. Surely here there is scope for the more chastened scientific imagination, and the time has come for the scientific world, the folk-lorists, palaeographers, and archaeologists, who have done so much to recover for us the ancient civilizations of the East, to turn their attention to these wonders of the Western world.

SYLVANUS MORLEY

Chichen Itza:
a Modern Account

THE greatest post-Classic metropolis and sacred city was Chichen
Itza in northeastern Yucatan. The city reached its zenith in the
eleventh and twelfth centuries under Mexican rulers who had
established themselves there in the tenth century. The civic and
religious precincts cover an area nearly two miles long by a mile
wide. While extending over a greater area than Tikal, the groups
at Chichen Itza are less numerous, smaller, and more scattered.

The architecture shows two distinct styles: (1) a Maya period, the
buildings of which date from the eighth to tenth centuries, and
(2) a Toltec period, the buildings of which date from the eleventh
and twelfth centuries and show many architectural features imported from central Mexico.

One of the striking architectural features at Chichen Itza are
the pyramid-temples with feathered-serpent columns. Seven of
these pyramids are known, of which the Castillo, or principal
Temple of Kukulcan, is the largest and possibly the oldest. One,
the Temple of the Chac Mool, is buried in the pyramid supporting the later Temple of the Warriors. These serpent-column temples were dedicated to Kukulcan, the Feathered Serpent, who was
the patron deity of Chichen Itza. The style seems to have been
an importation from central Mexico during the tenth century.

There are seven ball courts known at Chichen Itza: six that were
still in use when the city was last occupied, and an earlier one
buried under a later terrace behind the Monjas. The ball courts
vary in size; the largest, which is in the northern part of the city,
is 545 feet long by 225 feet wide on the outside, while the actual
field of play is 480 feet long by 120 feet wide; the smallest court

Reprinted from *The Ancient Maya*, Third Edition, by Sylvanus Griswold Morley and
George W. Brainerd, with the permission of the publishers, Stanford University
Press. Copyright © 1946, 1947, and 1956 by the Board of Trustees of the Leland
Stanford Junior University. Pp. 279-87, 31-9.

behind the Red House is only 65 feet long and 20 feet wide. A stone ring was usually set into the middle of each long facing wall, and the object of the game was to drive the ball through one of the rings, the openings of which were perpendicular to the ground. The balls were solid rubber, and the description of them given by the early Spanish historians marks the first European notice of rubber. The ball could not be thrown by the hand but had to be struck by the elbow, wrist, or hip, and leather pads were fastened to these parts of the body. The winning stroke was made so rarely that, by an ancient rule of the game, the player

A MAYA COASTAL VILLAGE AS REPRESENTED (12½ x 9 FEET)
IN THE TEMPLE OF THE WARRIORS, CHICHEN ITZA, YUCATAN

making it had forfeited to him all the clothing and jewelry of the spectators. When the ball was thus driven through the ring, all the spectators took to their heels to avoid paying the forfeit, and the friends of the lucky player ran after them to exact it.

Another distinctive feature at Chichen Itza is the use of great colonnades, some of them 400 feet long. Thrones have been found in them, and it has been suggested that they were used as council halls. Colonnades completely surround the Court of the Thousand Columns, a great open plaza of four and a half acres, which may have been the market place of the ancient city. There are so many colonnades in this part of Chichen Itza that it has been called the Group of the Thousand Columns.

One of the most important structures is an astronomical observatory. This round tower, called the Caracol, is 41 feet high and surmounts a rectangular terrace 31 feet high. The tower has a central core of masonry in which a spiral staircase winds up to a small observation chamber near the top of the building. The Spanish name for such a stairway is *caracol,* because of its fancied resemblance to the convolutions of a snail shell. The square openings through the thick walls of the chamber fix certain astronomically important lines of sight. For example, one line of sight through the west wall bisects the setting sun on March 21, the vernal equinox; other lines coincide with the moonset on this same date. The observation room near the top is still partially preserved.

Chichen Itza is probably better known than any other city of the Maya civilization because of the extensive excavations and restorations carried on there by the Ministry of Public Education of the Mexican government and by the Carnegie Institution of Washington since 1924. Quite a large number of buildings have been excavated and repaired, wall paintings and sculptures have been uncovered, and many archaeological specimens brought to light. Among the more spectacular discoveries were a handsome turquoise mosaic plaque and the Red Jaguar throne, a life-sized statue of a jaguar, painted a brilliant red and studded with seventy-three disks of jade in imitation of the markings of the jaguar. The mosaic plaque, found in a covered stone urn, was excavated from beneath the floor of the Temple of the Chac Mool and the Red Jaguar throne was discovered in the temple buried beneath the Castillo.

In the northern part of the city there are two large natural wells or cenotes, which no doubt contributed greatly to the importance of this site in ancient times—the Xtoloc Cenote, which was formerly the water supply of Chichen Itza, and the Well of Sacrifice. During the Mexican Period of the post-Classic, Chichen Itza was the most sacred city in Yucatan. Pilgrims came there from all parts of Meso-America, and sacrifices of every sort were hurled into the depths of this well.

The Modern Maya

The Maya of Yucatan are active, energetic, and hard-working—all on a diet extremely low in proteins. The average Maya's protein intake is only one-sixth of a pound per day. Of everything he eats, 75 to 85 per cent is carbohydrates—maize in one form or another, mostly as tortillas, and to a lesser extent as two beverages called *pozole* and *atole.* The average daily Maya diet contains only 2,565 calories, as compared with our own average caloric intake of 3,500. On this diet the ancient Maya found energy to build the pyramids, temples, and palaces which characterize their great ceremonial centers.

As to cleanliness and neatness, the Maya present a curious contradiction. Their persons and clothing are scrupulously clean, everyone bathing at least once a day and sometimes oftener. When the man of the family returns home. from work in the cornfield, his wife has a hot bath ready for him; under Spanish colonial law, failure to do so gave her husband the right to beat her. None of the houses outside the towns has running water or pumps of any kind, and all water has to be carried from the nearest well or cenote, where it is raised by the old-fashioned bucket-and-rope method, sometimes for as much as a hundred feet. Yet the Maya devotion to personal cleanliness is almost fanatical.

Their thatch-roofed, single-roomed houses are far less clean and orderly, although the Maya housewife cleans house daily and even sweeps the dirt street in front of her home. Chickens, turkeys, dogs, goats, and pigs roam the house at will. In the yard, refuse lies about for years, lending an air of untidiness and disorder.

Some foreigners who have visited Yucatan have thought the Maya cruel, especially toward animals. Perhaps they are not so deliberately cruel as they are insensitive to suffering, not only in others but in themselves; they are stoical under pain, and when they see it in others they are correspondingly indifferent. They will let their dogs slowly starve to death, but they would not think of killing them outright.

The Maya are fundamentally conservative. They have even succeeded in preserving their own language in the face of four centuries of Spanish domination, so that today the affairs of everyday life in the smaller towns and villages throughout Yucatan are conducted in the Maya language and not in Spanish.

Maya dress, especially that of the women, has not changed appreciably in hundreds of years. Their pottery, weaving, and cross-stitch embroidery have remained much the same throughout Maya history. In recent years, under the impact of the machine age, Maya conservatism has at last begun to give ground, at least in the matter of mechanical conveniences. The automobile and the bicycle appear in the larger towns, and hand-operated corn grinders are everywhere replacing the old stone metates. Even in the smaller villages, motor-driven mills are now in general use for grinding corn. Radios are beginning to appear, sewing machines and phonographs are common, and there are even a few electric lights in the homes of the well-to-do of the smaller towns. Most villages now have a weekly or semiweekly movie.

They are a happy, sociable people. They love to laugh, joke, and talk; they are good-natured, trusting, unselfish, and have a strong sense of justice. They are courteous and friendly to strangers, bearing out Bishop Landa's estimate of them nearly four hundred years ago:

The Yucatecans are very generous and hospitable; since no one may enter their houses without being offered food and drink, of what they may have had during the day, or in the evening. And if they have none, they seek it from a neighbor; and if they come together on the roads, all join in sharing, even if little remains for themselves.

The Maya of today show little inclination toward leadership and are generally disinclined to assume administrative responsibility. This seems strange in view of the organized activity of ancient times, as indicated by the great ceremonial centers of both the Classic and post-Classic periods. It is probable, however, that when the Maya civilization was at its peak, leadership and administrative functions were confined to the nobility and the priesthood. The common people were essentially a peasant-artisan laboring class, whose industry and toil built the pyramids, temples, and palaces, but always under the direction of the civil and religious authorities. It was upon these groups that the greatest impact of the Spanish Conquest fell. The Spanish stripped the native authorities of effective political power and the Catholic clergy replaced the native priesthood, so that there were few Maya leaders left. And yet one finds an occasional leader among the modern Maya. Don Eustaquio Ceme of Chan Kom, for example, is an Indian leader of outstanding ability. Chan Kom is a little Indian village of only four or five hundred people, and were it not for the personal qualities of Don Eustaquio it would be like scores of other similar Indian villages. But the energy, administrative ability, and civic pride of this one man have made Chan Kom the most progresssive community of its size in the state of Yucatan. In ancient times he would have been an outstanding figure, playing his role on a much larger stage.

The modern Maya are pronounced individualists and extremely independent. Children early learn to make their own decisions, and their parents respect their individual rights. In making annual series of anthropometric measurements of Maya children in Yucatan the scientists of the Carnegie Institution found it necessary to seek each child's permission anew each year. Each child was paid the equivalent of ten cents in American money for permitting himself to be measured; but in spite of their poverty, their sense of individual independence demanded that they not grant the request too readily.

Competition is not strongly developed among the modern Maya. Even as children their games are noncompetitive, and as adults they seem to be without desire to excel. They are content to be small corn farmers, raising sufficient food for their families and a little more to trade for the few articles they cannot produce themselves. They work in the hemp plantations for little more than subsistence wages. Some of the more able accumulate a few domestic animals and even rise to the higher status of being small storekeepers in their villages, but not many go beyond this.

The Maya have a strong respect for law and a keen sense of justice. Among the semi-independent native groups of Quintana Roo there is an unusually high reliance placed upon community responsibility. The characteristic punishment among these Indians is the *azote* or bastinado. In the case of a heavy sentence, say of a hundred lashes, the culprit receives twenty-five on each of four consecutive mornings. The sentenced man, however, is not kept in prison between successive lashings; he is allowed at large, but the responsibility of presenting himself for punishment each morning rests solely with him. If he is not present at the appointed time, the whole community regards him as an outlaw; any member may kill him at sight without being punished. It is quite conceivable that this sort of group solidarity may have played a part in the remarkable cultural accomplishments of the Classic Maya.

The Maya are not quarrelsome, but if they have been wronged they harbor resentment. Disputes among the Maya of today are chiefly due to domestic troubles and to damage to crops by livestock. In rare cases, a husband may kill his wife's paramour, but often he pardons her or allows her to go off with the other man. Injury to crops by livestock is a more serious matter, and the owner of the animals is obliged to pay for the damage.

As a people the Maya are unusually honest. Petty thieving is almost unknown, and houses are left unlocked most of the time. Rarely does one Indian steal corn from another, in spite of the fact that opportunities to steal are ever present, since the unguarded cornfields are often several miles from the village. One writer says in this connection, "Men who steal from cornfields are killed by the guardian-spirits of the fields and these beliefs are the real locks on the open granaries in the distant bush."

Nor are the Maya given to begging. During the seventeen years the Carnegie Institution carried on archaeological investigations at Chichen Itza, a free medical clinic was maintained for Indians of the surrounding region. Although the Indians came to know that this service was free, after receiving treatment and medicines they invariably offered to pay for them. When payment was refused, the next time they visited Chichen Itza they would bring gifts of food and native embroideries. There was a deep-felt need to repay an obligation.

Foreigners agree that the Maya have a rough sense of humor,

practical jokes being considered the most amusing. A boy will
strike another an unexpected blow behind the knee, causing him to
fall. During the archaeological excavations at Chichen Itza, an
absent-minded wheelbarrow boy would find his barrow quickly over-
loaded by the other Indians. Maya family ties are strong, although
among adults outward demonstrations of affection are rare. Affection
between man and wife is shown by each carrying out his duties in the
home. With their children, however, they are much more demon-
strative. Mothers fondle their babies, talk affectionately to them,
and rarely punish them physically. Children are trained more by
their own desire to conform to established social practices than by
disciplinary measures. When physical punishment has to be administered, however, it is the mother who does it. The older children
take care of their younger brothers and sisters and have authority
over them. Respect for older members of the family is deeply ingrained. The father is the undisputed head of his family and nothing
is done without his approval, though respect for the mother is also
strong. This respect for elders goes back to ancient times, for Bishop
Landa in writing of the sixteenth-century Maya says:

> The young men respected the elders highly, and took their counsels,
> and tried to pass as mature themselves. The elders said to the younger
> ones that since they had seen more, what they said should be believed, so
> that if the youths heeded their counsels, the elders would credit them
> more. So much respect was given to the elders that the youths did not
> mingle with them, except in cases of necessity such as when they were
> married; and with married men they mingled very little.

Bishop Landa remarks upon the extreme modesty of the Maya
women at the time of the Conquest: "The women were accustomed
to turn their shoulders to the men in passing them, and of turning
aside that they might pass; and the same, when they gave them to
drink, until they had finished." Landa also says that in his day
men and women did not eat together: "The men are not accustomed
to eat with the women but by themselves upon the ground, or at
most upon a mat which takes the place of a table." This custom
persists even to the present day. The men eat first, being served
by the women, and later the women of the family eat together by
themselves. Modesty in small children is confined exclusively to
the little girls, who have to wear huipiles (the Maya woman's
dress) from birth. Their little brothers up to the age of six and older
are allowed to play about the house and yard naked.

Sexual promiscuity among married women, and even among unmarried girls, is not uncommon. The former is not regarded with
particular disapproval, except by the jealous husband, while the
unmarried girl with one or more illegitimate children has no more

difficulty in finding a mate than have her more continent sisters. Prostitution, however, is uncommon. Most boys are introduced to sex by older women, while young girls have their first sex experience with their youthful lovers. Incest, though rare, occurs from time to time, usually between father and daughter.

The Maya are not particularly religious. At present Christian worship is carried on almost exclusively by the women, though in ancient times religion was largely an affair of the men. Practically all children are baptized, but few receive additional instruction in the tenets of the Church because of the present scarcity of priests in the smaller villages. Hence the majority know little about the real meaning and significance of Christianity.

If they are not religious, however, all Maya are intensely superstitious. There are countless superstitions, many of them fragmentary survivals of the ancient Maya religion, mixed with Spanish medieval folklore and even perhaps with West African importations. Certain dreams and omens are regarded as sure forerunners of death. If one dreams that he is floating on air, or that he is having a tooth pulled and is suffering intense pain, a member of his immediate family will die; if, in the dream, the suffering is slight, a less close relative will die. To dream of red tomatoes means a baby will die; to dream that a black bull is trying to push its way into one's home or to dream of breaking a water jug indicates that a member of the family will die.

The Maya are fatalistic. What will come, will come. Old people have been known to announce that their time had come and, though not even ill, have lain down in their hammocks and quietly died.

Sickness is caused by dwarfs, for whom gourds of food are placed in the doorway of the house in order to prevent an epidemic. If one gives away embers of burning wood, one's turkeys will die. Eggs set on Fridays will not hatch. This latter belief is suggestive of the bad luck attending Fridays throughout Christian countries.

There are many weather superstitions. Thin cornhusks indicate a mild winter; thick ones, a cold winter. If a swallow flies low, it will rain; if high, it will be clear. Cicadas are honored weather prophets among the Maya, and the time for burning the cornfields is often determined by their chirping. Evil winds take the form of animals, and individuals struck by them will die. If a match drops on the floor and continues to burn, it is a sign of good luck; if it burns to the end, the person who dropped it will have a long life.

The hunter has many difficulties to contend with. If he sells the head, liver, or stomach of a deer he has killed, he will have bad luck in future hunting; should he sell the paunch, he will never be able to kill another deer. To bring bad luck to a hunter, one has only to buy meat from him and throw the bones into a cenote. The

Maya believe there is a king deer in the bush, with a wasp's nest between his horns; if a hunter kills this deer, he will die immediately.

The following signs indicate that visitors are coming: an oriole singing, a dragonfly coming into the house, a butterfly flying high, a cat washing its face, or a fire hissing.

From ancient times, the Maya have lived under the influence of lucky and unlucky days. The modern Maya continue to follow this practice, with one difference: the seven days of the Christian week have now replaced the 260 days of the ancient *tzolkin* or sacred divinatory year. Tuesdays and Fridays are considered unlucky, Mondays and Saturdays lucky. Marriages are usually celebrated on Mondays; Saturdays are considered lucky days on which to buy lottery tickets.

The Maya have always venerated numbers. Nine has always been especially lucky, perhaps because of its association with the nine steps leading to the ancient Maya heaven, or perhaps because of its having been the number of the Nine Gods of the Underworld. If a centipede is found on Tuesday it must be cut into nine pieces in order to bring good luck. If a green snake is seen, it will cause one's death within the year, unless it is caught and cut into nine pieces. Whooping cough may be cured by hanging gourds of fresh *atole* in the doorway for nine successive days, and on the morning of the ninth day it must be shared with one's friends. Nine kernels of ground corn applied to granulated eyelids will cure them; skin troubles may be relieved with a brew of nine pieces of fish skin, nine pieces of corncob, and nine small pebbles.

Thirteen is another lucky Maya number, perhaps because of its important function in the ancient Maya calendar, or perhaps because it was the number of the Thirteen Gods of the Upper World. The use of thirteen as a lucky number seems to be confined chiefly to religious ceremonies, for which offerings of thirteen loaves of bread, thirteen bowls of food, and thirteen cakes made of thirteen layers each are prepared.

Most Maya superstitions have unpleasant connotations. Many more things are thought to bring bad luck rather than good luck. The Maya have a fatalistic strain, perhaps the heritage of their past, where death by sacrifice was common and more of their gods were hostile than friendly.

Opinions differ as to the general intelligence of the Maya. Some American observers have believed them to be very bright; many have classified them as fairly bright; others as average and a few only as rather dull. No one regarded them as downright stupid. They are not inventive, however, but are content to follow the same pattern of living as did their ancestors. Their memory is considered very good and their powers of observation, especially in the bush, are excellent. They are rather imaginative and have a fair sense of beauty, which was probably more highly developed in ancient times than it is today.

ALBERTO RUZ

An Astonishing Discovery: the Noble's Tomb at Palenque

THE discovery of the burial vault of a Mayan prince below the Temple of the Inscriptions at Palenque is probably the most dramatic in all American archaeology. The vault lay slightly below the level of the court outside, and about seventy-five feet below the floor of the temple on the pyramid. It had evidently been made before the pyramid was raised. As Dr. Ruz says, American pyramids were not normally intended as tombs; the nearest parallel at present known is the High Priest's Grave at Chichen Itza, where a vertical shaft led down from the temple floor to a burial place in a natural cave. Dr. Alberto Ruz was Director of Research at Palenque.

WHEN in the spring of 1949 the National Institute of Anthropology and History of Mexico appointed me Director of Research at Palenque, I fully appreciated that this was the most important event in my professional life.

I knew that my predecessors had been explorers, artists, scientists, distinguished men, and that marvellous sculpture had been

From *The Illustrated London News*, August 29, 1953. By permission of Alberto Ruz and The Illustrated London News, holder of World Copyright.

discovered there during the course of 150 years; but I was convinced that many other archaeological treasures still lay hidden in the rubble of the palaces, temples and pyramids, and beneath the dense and mysterious Chiapas jungle which had been their jealous guardian.

A feature of my working plan was one which should always be present in the plans of archaeologists working in Mexico and Central America: to seek for architectural structures of an earlier date and lying beneath the actually visible building. It has, in fact, been proved that the ancient inhabitants of Central America were in the habit of building on top of older constructions, more with the object of increasing their height and bringing them closer to the heavens in which the gods lived than for any practical purpose.

For various reasons I decided to make such a search in the Temple of the Inscriptions. First, because it was the tallest building in Palenque and therefore the most likely to have been built on top of something older; secondly, because of its importance and its containing some fine, large, sculptured panels and one of the largest Mayan hieroglyphic inscriptions; and thirdly, because it had never been explored and its flooring was more or less intact—owing to its being made of great slabs instead of the more usual simple levelled plaster.

This temple is composed of a portico leading to a sanctuary and two lateral cells; and in the central room of the temple one of the slabs of the flooring caught my eye, as it had done with my predecessors on the site. This slab has round its edges two rows of holes provided with stone plugs. After thinking for some hours on its possible purpose, I came to the conclusion that the answer would be found underneath the stone; and accordingly I began to clear the floor beside it, in a place where the slabs had been already removed or broken by treasure-seekers, who had been discouraged from going on by meeting with a heavy filling of large stones.

Quite soon after beginning to remove the rubble I noticed that the temple's walls were prolonged under the floor instead of stopping at its level—a sure sign that there was "something" to be found underneath. Elated by this prospect, I began excavating and on the next day—May 20, 1949—there appeared that stone which, in Mayan buildings is always used to close up a vault. The Mayans did not build a true arch, their vaulting being simply the result of bringing walls closer together by means of inclined facings which converge until there remains only a very small space to be closed with a single flat stone. A few days later I found a step, and then more and more steps. What had been found was an interior staircase descending into the pyramid and which for a reason which we then did not know, had been made impracticable by a filling of large stones and clay.

Four spells of work—each two-and-a-half months long—were needed before we were able to clear the filling from this mysterious staircase. After a flight of 45 steps, we reached a landing with a U-turn. There followed another flight, of 21 steps, leading to a corridor, whose level is more or less the same as that on which the pyramid was built—*i.e.*, some 22 metres under the temple flooring. In the vaulting of the landing two narrow galleries open out and allow air and a little light to enter from a near-by courtyard.

Above one of the first steps we reached we found a box-shaped construction of masonry containing a modest offering: two ear-plugs of jade placed on a river stone painted red. On reaching the end of the flight we found another box of offerings, backing on to a wall which blocked the passage. This time it was a richer offering: three pottery dishes, two shells full of cinnabar, seven jade beads, a pair of circular ear-plugs also of jade, the plugs of which were shaped like a flower, and a beautiful tear-shaped pearl, with its *lustre* pretty well presevered. An offering of this kind, at such a depth, told us without any doubt that we were approaching the object of our search.

And, in fact, on July 13, 1952, after demolishing a solid obstruction some metres thick, made of stone and lime—this was very hard and the wet lime burnt the hands of the workmen—there appeared on one side of the corridor a triangular slab, 2 metres high, set vertically to block an entrance. At the foot of this slab, in a rudimentary stone cist, there lay, mixed together, the largely-destroyed skeletons of six young persons, of whom one at least was a female.

At noon on the 15th of the same month we opened the entrance, displacing the stone enough for a man to pass through sideways. It was a moment of indescribable emotion for me when I slipped behind the stone and found myself in an enormous crypt which seemed to have been cut out of the rock—or rather, out of the ice, thanks to the curtain of stalactites and the chalcite veiling deposited on the walls by the infiltration of rain-water during the centuries. This increased the marvellous quality of the spectacle and gave it a fairy-tale aspect. Great figures of priests modelled in stucco a little larger than life-size formed an impressive procession round the walls. The high vaulting was reinforced by great stone transoms, of dark colour with yellowish veins, giving an impression of polished wood.

Almost the whole crypt was occupied by a colossal monument, which we then supposed to be a ceremonial altar, composed of a stone of more than 8 square metres, resting on an enormous monolith of 6 cubic metres, supported in its turn by six great blocks of chiselled stone. All these elements carried beautiful reliefs.

Finest of all for its unsurpassable execution and perfect state of preservation was the great stone covering the whole and bearing on its four sides some hieroglyphic inscriptions with thirteen abbreviated dates corresponding to the beginning of the seventh century A.D., while its upper face shows a symbolic scene surrounded by astronomical signs.

I believed that I had found a ceremonial crypt, but I did not wish to make any definite assertions before I had finished exploring the chamber and, above all, before I had found out whether the base of the supposed altar was solid or not. On account of the rains and the exhausting of the funds available for this phase of the exploration, we had to wait until November before returning to Palenque. I then had the base bored horizontally at two of the corners; and it was not long before one of the drills reached a hollow space. I introduced a wire through the narrow aperture and, on withdrawing it, I saw that some particles of red paint were adhering to it.

The presence of this colouring matter inside the monolith was of supreme importance. The offerings found at the beginning and the end of the secret staircase had borne red paint; and the sides of the great stone showed traces of having been painted red all over. This colour was associated in the Mayan and Aztec cosmogony with the East, but also it is nearly always found in tombs, on the walls or on objects accompanying the dead person or on his bones. The presence of red in tombs came, therefore, to indicate resurrection and a hope of immortality. The particles of cinnabar adhering to the wire inserted into the centre of the enormous stone block was therefore unquestionable evidence of burial: and our supposed ceremonial altar must therefore be an extraordinary sepulchre.

To prove this it was necessary to lift the sculptured stone, which measured 3·80 metres by 2·20 metres (some 13 by 7 ft.), weighing about 5 tons and constituting one of the most valuable masterpieces of American pre-Hispanic sculpture. The preparations lasted two days in the midst of feverish tension. It was necessary to fell in the forest a hard-wood tree of the kind called in that region "bari," and to cut it into sections of different lengths, lift these along a greasy path to the lorry, convey them by motor to the pyramid, move them by manpower to the temple, lower them by cables through the interior staircase and introduce them through the narrow aperture of the crypt.

The four major sections of the trunk were placed vertically under the corners of the stone and on top of each was placed a railway or motor-car jack. On November 27, at dusk, after a twelve-hour work-

ing day, the soul-shaking manœuvre took place. Every kind of precaution was taken to prevent the stone tipping up or slippping,
and, above all, to prevent its suffering any damage. Handled simultaneously and without any jerking, the jacks lifted the stone millimetre by millimetre, and while this was happening slabs were
placed underneath it to hold it up. When the jacks reached the limit
of their extension, other sections of the tree were inserted and the
operation was repeated. A little before midnight the stone was resting intact 0·60 metres above its original level on six robust logs
of "bari" and a few days later it was lifted to a height of 1·12 metres.

Once the stone left its seating and began to rise it could be seen
that a cavity had been cut out of the enormous block which served
it as a base. This cavity was of an unexpected shape, oblong and
curvilinear, rather like the silhouette in schematised form of a fish
or of the capital letter Omega (Ω), closed in its lower part. The
cavity was sealed by a highly-polished slab fitting exactly and provided with four perforations, each with a stone plug. On raising
the slab which closed it we discovered the mortuary receptacle.

This was not the first time during my career as an archaeologist
that a tomb had been discovered, but no occasion has been so impressive as this. In the vermilion-coloured walls and base of the
cavity which served as a coffin, the sight of the human remains—
complete, although the bones were damaged—covered with jade
jewels for the most part, was most impressive. It was possible to
judge the form of the body which had been laid in this "tailored" sarcophagus; and the jewels added a certain amount of life, both from
the sparkle of the jade and because they were so well "placed" and
because their form suggested the volume and contour of the flesh
which originally covered the skeleton. It was easy also to imagine
the high rank of the personage who could aspire to a mausoleum of
such impressive richness.

We were struck by his stature, greater than that of the average
Mayan of to-day; and by the fact that his teeth were not filed or
provided with incrustations of pyrites or jade, since that practice
(like that of artificially deforming the cranium) was usual in individuals of the higher social ranks. The state of destruction of the
skull did not allow us to establish precisely whether or not it had
been deformed. In the end, we decided that the personage might
have been of non-Mayan origin, though it is clear that he ended in
being one of the kings of Palenque. The reliefs, which we have still
to uncover on the sides of the sarcophagus and which are now
hidden under lateral buttresses, may tell us before long something
of the personality and identity of the glorious dead.

Even if he had not been buried in the most extraordinary tomb
so far discovered in this continent of America, it would still be per-

fectly possible to assess the importance of this personage from the jewels which he wore—many of them already familiar in Mayan bas-reliefs. As shown in some reliefs, he was wearing a diadem made from tiny disks of jade and his hair was divided into separate strands by means of small jade tubes of appropriate shape; and we discovered a small jade plate of extraordinary quality cut in the shape of the head of Zotz, the vampire god of the underworld, and this may have been a final part of the diadem. Around the neck were visible various threads of a collar composed of jade beads in many forms—spheres, cylinders, tri-lobed beads, floral buds, open flowers, pumpkins, melons, and a snake's head. The ear-plugs were composed of various elements, which together made up a curious flower. From a square jade plate with engraved petals, a tube, also of jade, projected and this ended in a flower-shaped bead; while on the back of the square plate (which carries a hieroglyphic inscription) a circular plug was fitted. All these elements would be united by a thread and it would seem that there hung as a counterpoise to them, behind the broad part of the ear, a marvellous artificial pearl, formed by uniting two perfectly-cut pieces of mother-o-pearl, polished and adjusted to give the impression of a pearl of fabulous size (36 mm.). Over the breast lay a pectoral formed of nine concentric rings of twenty-one tubular beads in each. Round each wrist was a bracelet of 200 jade beads, and on each finger of both hands a great ring of jade. We found these still fixed on the phalanges, and one of the rings was carved in the form of a crouching man, with a delicate head of perfect Mayan profile. In the right hand he held a great jade bead of cubical form, and in the left, another, but this one spherical, the two being perhaps symbols of his rank or magical elements for his journey to another world. Near his feet we found another two great jade beads, one of them hollow and provided with two plugs in the shape of flowers. A jade idol of precious workmanship stood near the left foot and is probably a representation of the sun god. Another little figure of the same material must have been sewn above the breech-clout. From the mouth cavity we extracted a beautiful dark jade bead, which, according to the funeral rites of the Mayans, was placed there so that the dead person should have the means to obtain sustenance in the life beyond the tomb. At the moment of burial, the personage wore over his face a magnificent mask made of jade mosaic, the eyes being of shell, with each iris of obsidian, with the pupil marked in black behind. Of the hundreds of fragments, some remained on the face, adhering to the teeth and the forehead, but the greater part were lying on the left side of the head, clearly as the result of the mask's slipping off during the burial. The corpse must have been set in the sarcophagus entirely wrapped in a shroud painted

red, and the same cinnabar colour adhered to the bones, the jewels
and the bottom of the sarcophagus when the cloth and the flesh
decomposed. The mask was fitted directly on the dead man's face,
the fragments being stuck in a thin coating of stucco, the remains
of which fitted to the human face. Nevertheless, the mask had to
be prepared beforehand and may perhaps have been kept on a stucco
head. It is perfectly possible that its main traits, realistic as they
are, represent more or less those of the actual dead man. After
the burial the sarcophagus was closed with its lid and covered with
the enormous sculptured stone. Some jewels were thrown upon
this—a collar with slate pendants and what was probably a ritual
mask made of jade mosaic—and there were placed underneath
the coffin various clay vessels, perhaps containing food and drink,
and two wonderful human heads modelled in stucco, which had
been broken from complete statues. At the closing of the crypt
six young persons, perhaps sons and daughters of important persons
at Court, were sacrificed to act as companions and servants of the
dead man in the other world. In the best-preserved of their skulls
could be noted the cranial deformation and the mutilation of the
teeth which were customary in the nobility alone. A serpent
modelled in lime plaster seems to rise straight out of the sarcophagus and ascend the steps which lead to the threshold of the room.
Here it is transformed into a tube, running as far as the flooring
of the corridor and after this it leads on to the temple, in the form
of an echeloned moulding, hollow and superimposed on the steps.
This amounts to a magical union, a conduit for the spirit of the
dead man to ascend to the temple in order that the priests might
continue to be in contact with his deified being and able to explain
his mandates. Our search for an older building under the Temple
of the Inscriptions could therefore not lead to the expected result,
but in exchange it revealed a tomb whose discovery leads to considerable modification of certain established concepts concerning
the function of the American pyramid. It was formerly thought
that this was solely a solid base for supporting a temple, unlike
the Egyptian pyramids, which are vast mausoleums. Palenque's
"Royal Tomb," as it is now popularly called, with a certain intuitive
propriety, perhaps—brings us a great deal closer to the Egyptian
concept once we grant that the pyramid which hid it, although supporting a temple, was also constructed to serve as a grandiose
funeral monument. The monumental quality of this crypt, built by
thousands of hands to challenge the centuries and enriched with
magnificent reliefs; the sumptuousness of the tomb itself, a colossal
monument weighing 20 tons and covered all over with bas-reliefs
of stupendous quality; the rich jade finery of the buried personage;
all this expensive toil and this magnificence suggest to us the exis-

tence in Palenque of a theocratic system similar to that of Egypt, in which the all-powerful priest-king was considered during life or after death to be a real god. This Palencan Royal tomb also leads us to suppose that the attitude towards death of the Mayan *halach uinic* was very close to that of the pharaohs. The stone which covers the tomb appears to confirm this obsession and synthesises in its reliefs some essentials of the Mayan religion. The presence here, in a sepulchral slab, of motives which are repeated in other representations, gives perhaps the key to interpret the famous panels of the Cross and the foliated Cross (in Palenque) and also some of the paintings in the codices. On the stone in question we see a man surrounded by astronomical signs symbolising heaven—the spatial limit of man's earth, and the home of the gods, in which the unchanging course of the stars marks the implacable rhythm of time. Man rests on the earth, represented by a grotesque head with funereal traits, since the earth is a monster devouring all that lives; and if the reclining man seems to be falling backwards, it is because it is his inherent destiny to fall to the earth, the land of the dead. But above the man rises the well-known cruciform motif, which in some representations is a tree, in others the stylised maize plant, but is always the symbol of life resurgent from the earth, life triumphing over death.

J. ERIC THOMPSON

A Visit to Tikal

TIKAL is in the Peten district of Guatemala. It was already of outstanding importance early in the Classic period; it possesses many stelae dating from the fourth century A.D. The two temples facing the main plaza are 145 and 158 feet high, and their temples are surmounted by huge, ornately sculptured crests.

From *The Rise and Fall of Maya Civilization*. Norman: University of Oklahoma Press; 1956, pp. 14-19, 22-4, 92-7, 119-20. By permission of The University of Oklahoma Press, and Victor Gollancz Ltd., London. © 1959 by University of Oklahoma Press.

As a prologue, I shall give some impressions of my own visit to Tikal, made long before an air-strip was cleared there to facilitate the shipment of chewing gum from the Peten forest.

On that visit to Tikal, over twenty years ago, we arrived on mule-back after losing our way and spending an uncomfortable night in an abandoned, flea-infested camp of chewing-gum gatherers. There was something Chaucerian about the journey of seven days from that modern Tabard Inn, the ramshackle International Hotel in Belize, up the Belize River two days in a launch, and then five days by mule from El Cayo via another Maya city, Uaxactun. We were in a sense pilgrims journeying leisurely to a great shrine, and, as the mules jogged stolidly through the forest at three miles an hour, we had ample time, denied to the air traveller, for speculation on what awaited us.

On earlier journeys in the rain forest of Central America, the exotic surroundings had excited my interest, but with repetition the novelty had worn off, and the impression of the forest on my mind had become one of overwhelming monotony. On this journey, as on a dozen others, we followed endless, narrow, winding tunnels cut in the forest by chewing-gum gatherers. The trees met far overhead, letting through occasional dapples of sunshine or allowing a fleeting glimpse of blue sky or cloud. Below, the serried tree-trunks merged in a dull grey mass, and fallen trees wore the brown of decay. The dense foliage excluded the bright colours one associates with the tropics. Except for a careful eye for an overhanging branch eager to deal one Absalom's fate and a perpetual and largely unconscious struggle between mule and rider, one was free to dwell upon the past, when Maya civilization cut its first teeth on this self-same jungle and which it partly subdued on reaching maturity.

The descent of the trail into the great *bajo* of Tikal fetched me back into the present. That low swamp-land, perhaps a lake when Tikal flourished, is a sea of mud in the rainy season, but it was dry when we crossed it. The few feet of descent brought a complete change, very much for the worse, in the vegetation. Spanish cedars, mahogany, the ubiquitous sapodilla, from the wrinkled trunk of which, when it is slashed with a machete, raw chewing gum drips, and graceful cabbage palms give place to a low, thorny scrub, from the branches of which numberless stinging ants might descend, like paratroopers, upon the rider who incautiously knocked against trunk or limb. The sun beat down on mules and riders as though in punishment for our hours of playing hide-and-seek with him in the

tall forest; the strangely distorted branches of the thorn trees
writhed like souls in Dante's hell.

The trail, which had been meandering southwards, swung to the
west before ascending sharply into rain forest once more. Suddenly
we glimpsed an awe-inspiring sight. Four of the great pyramids
of Tikal, clad in foliage and surmounted by ancient temples of limestone, greyish white against the sky, rose high above the surrounding tree-tops, like green volcanoes with summits wreathed in white
clouds. The pilgrims were at the gates of their New World Canterbury. Just as Chaucer's riders must have lost sight of the cathedral
as they hurried through the narrow streets of the city, so we lost
our view of the Maya temples as we plunged into the forest in that
abrupt climb from the edge of the swamp to the heart of the city.

The trail ascended for about 150 yards to where it crossed an
ancient Maya causeway leading south-eastward to an outlying
group. There we were, so to speak, in the outer downtown district.
Two hundred yards farther west, our eyes were caught by the great
mass, to the right, of one of Tikal's huge pyramids, the blurred outline of its immense bulk rising through the sea-green foliage like
the base of a submarine mountain. To the left were the dispiriting
remains of two parallel mounds, which in better days probably had
been the sides of one of those courts in which the Maya played their
ball game with a solid ball of rubber a millennium before our western civilization had any knowledge of rubber or rubber balls. Impre-
cations of the muleteer, whose mules heeded only the task of
skilfully picking their way across heaps of root-entwined rubble,
echoed in another key the shouts of players and watchers and the
thud of ball on pad or wall—a brighter wall not then in disrepair.

Beyond that narrow passage between pyramid and supposed ball
court the trail enters the great court or plaza of Tikal, great not
because of its size, but because, like the Forum of Rome, it is enclosed by great structures raised by the toil of thousands to a glory
now passed and knit with a faith which was in vain. We unsaddled
and hitched our mules to trees, units in what I would have called
the virgin forest which compassed us about, had I not known that
the forest had been felled in 1881 by the British archaeologist, Alfred
Maudslay, and again in 1904 and 1910 by expeditions of the Pea-
body Museum of Harvard University. Each time the tide of vegetation had engulfed the ruins anew; with the years, saplings had
grown to giants, anchored to the thin soil and the Maya-built floors
beneath by buttressed roots. Lianas—some almost as thick as fire
hose—hung from branches or were looped from tree to tree. A troop
of spider monkeys chattered high in the trees that swept up the
pyramid guarding the west end of the great court, a New World

version of Omar Khayyam's "They say the lion and the lizard keep the courts where Jamshyd gloried and drank deep."

We scrambled up the eastern pyramid, clambering over the slides in the great stairway with the aid of some root working to displace yet another stone of the step or some sapling which now must be a giant. The terraced sides of the pyramid, broken by the actions of roots and rain, were masked by ferns and vines. As we got higher, the cactus-like pitahaya vine with thorny stems triangular in section warned us to climb carefully. The trees thinned out, and we were on the flat crown of the pyramid facing the temple on its summit. We turned to look down the broken stairway we had climbed. The height of the crest of the temple above the level of the court (allowing a few feet for collapse) is almost 160 feet, and each side of the base of the pyramid is a little over a third of a city block in length. So far as we know, there is no natural elevation enclosed in this mass, every cubic foot of which was built without anything that could be termed machinery. The builders were men, and, probably, women and children, who inhabited what is now this forested region 1,200 years ago; and they erected this vast structure not long after Augustine built the Saxon predecessor of the early Norman church, in turn replaced by the Canterbury Cathedral Chaucer's pilgrims journeyed to see. Gangs brought rock and rubble for the core of the pyramid; they faced the building-stone with primitive tools; they cut the wood to heat the lime-kilns; they shaped the sapodilla beams for the temple; and, finally, some of them may have given their lives to the building as sacrificial victims at its dedication. It is likely that their bones or their decapitated heads, each neatly enclosed between pairs of pottery bowls placed lip to lip, are beneath the walls or floors of the temple behind where we stood, or below the bottom steps of the stairway facing us.

From the doorway of the temple we looked out over the tree-tops whose range of hues was not unlike the contrasting green tones of shoal-water. Here and there trees with myriads of scarlet blossoms heightened the effect of a seascape, for they seemed like giant jelly-fish floating on the water's surface. Directly in front, to the west, the grey-white walls of three pyramid-supported temples rose like coral islands above the sea of foliage. A fourth, due south, could be seen by turning to the left. Nearer at hand, a swell in the foliage told of a large building below, not tall enough to break surface. At sunset or dawn deep shadows mapped the contours in better detail.

In ancient times one would have had an uninterrupted view across the city with its clusters of smaller pyramids topped by their temples, its multi-chambered buildings (miscalled "palaces" for convenience), facing courts at different levels, and its endless sur-

faces of cream-white stucco relieved only by shadow and an occasional building or floor finished with red plaster.

In the great ceremonial court and in various smaller courts stood
the stelae, like sentinels, before the approaches to platforms and
pyramids. Those limestone shafts, carved or painted with the static
portraits of gods and with their hieroglyphic texts always recording

STELA II, YAXCHILÁN, CHIAPAS

that overwhelming preoccupation of the Maya with the mystery of
time, are milestones in the history of the city. Every five or ten or
twenty years a new one rose to carry forward the story of conquests,
not of neighbours, but of the secrets of time and the movements of
the celestial bodies. Such impersonal topics would have been unthinkable to the rulers of Egypt or Assyria, eager to commission
the texts which commemorated the triumphs of their reigns.

Just as we forced our way through the tangled vegetation that crowded the courts and surged up mound and across terrace, so, in ancient times, a late arrival at some ceremony must have shouldered his way through the congregation which, packed in the court, intently witnessed a ceremony held on the top of a pyramid before the temple door. I could visualize the priest-astronomer, anxious to check his theories on the length of the solar year or the lunar month, threading his way from stela to stela to see what calculations his predecessors had recorded in the then distant past, or I could conjure up the acrid, sooty smoke of copal incense rising from clay braziers to a sky then fully visible from the great court.

We wandered through the forest, entering temples, climbing pyramids, and once disturbing a herd of peccary feeding on the cherry-like fruit of the breadnut. As darkness fell after that interlude of dusk so brief in those latitudes, we ate, in the ceremonial court, Maya black beans and canned Chicago pork. The mingling of the two foods—one the product of ancient agricultural techniques, the other processed in a modern factory—seemed to symbolize archaeology's task of bringing past and present together.

J. ERIC THOMPSON

The Pool of Sacrifice
at Chichen Itza

EDWARD THOMPSON, who first found Mayan treasures and bones in the cenote, seems to have been a remarkable if rather erratic character. Determined to vindicate the tradition that sacrificial victims had been thrown into the pool, he learnt to dive and employed sponge divers to help him. The pressure may have affected his health, for he is said to have developed paralysis and deafness.

Ibid., pp. 119-20.

Thompson contrived to offend the Mexican government, and was accused of the theft of national property. He chartered a half-finished schooner, and although he was short of food and without navigational instruments, he succeeded in reaching Cuba. Edward Thompson, who was an American, was no relation of J. Eric Thompson.

THE Itza, of course, gave their name to Chichen Itza (it means "at the rim of the well of the Itza"). The name of the city used before their arrival is not surely known, but it may have been Uucyabnal. This could be translated "seven great owners," and reminds one of the seven deserted buildings, from the women of which the Itza were descended. The invaders presumably married native women. Chichen Itza was famed as a centre of pilgrimage for hundreds of years. Indeed, surreptitious pilgrimages thither continued until some time after the Spanish Conquest.

The focal point of these pilgrimages was the sacred cenote, into which sacrifices, both of persons and valuables, were cast to propitiate the rain gods. When this cult began is not surely known. Some carved jades dredged from its muddy bottom are certainly of Classic workmanship. One, carved at Piedras Negras, bears a Maya date equivalent to A.D. 706, and a jade bead, almost surely carved at Palenque, bears a Maya date equivalent to A.D. 690. The problem is whether these jade objects were kept for several centuries as family heirlooms or as temple treasures and then thrown into the cenote, or whether the cenote cult was already active during the Classic Period. Personally, I am inclined to think it was in full swing before the Itza arrived, but received fresh impetus under the Itza. Sacrifice to large sheets of water was a widespread and ancient custom in America, yet it may be significant that the Classic Maya buildings at Chichen Itza are farther away from the cenote than those of the Mexican period.

The sacred cenote (there is another at Chichen Itza which supplied the city with water and, in later centuries, archaeologists with a bathing pool) is about 200 feet in diameter, the level of the water is about sixty-five feet below the surface of the ground, and its depth is about seventy feet. A Maya road connects the great court on which stands the temple of Kukulcan (usually called the *Castillo*) with the cenote. However, I have suspected that this causeway may be older than the great court, and excavation might show that it passed beneath the court to join one of the causeways on the far side. The ruined foundations of a temple stand at the edge of the cenote, and it was almost certainly from here that the sacrifices were thrown in.

Dredging of the cenote by Edward Thompson brought to light large quantities of offerings. These include huge quantities of jade, in most cases deliberately smashed, gold disks, copper bells, copper soles for sandals, wooden spear-throwers, idols and labrets of the same material, balls of copal incense, into some of which jades had been pressed, while others had a core of rubber, idols shaped from copal and rubber, pieces of textiles and basketry, as well as skulls and bones.

Spanish accounts tell of virgins being cast into the well, a detail which has caught the public imagination. Lurid pictures of fair damsels plunging into the pool are common. Actually, of the identifiable remains, thirteen are of men; twenty-one of children ranging in age from eighteen months to twelve years, and of these half were under six years old. Only eight are of women, seven of them over twenty-one, past the normal age of marriage.

The percentage of children was probably far greater than the 50 per cent of the identified remains because children's skulls are more easily broken than those of adults. This high percentage is understandable, as throughout ancient America where human sacrifice was common, children were offered to the rain gods, and the cenote cult was dedicated to the rain gods.

It seems to me most plausible to suppose that the Mexicans chose Chichen Itza as their principal city because the cenote cult had already given the centre renown throughout Yucatan. There must have been some attraction which caused the Mexicans to pick distant Chichen Itza rather than one of the larger Puuc cities, and I think it was the cenote cult.

J. ERIC THOMPSON

The Mayan Philosophy
of Time

WE shall, unfortunately, never know the Maya as we know sixteenth-century Spain or Elizabethan England, but, in time, by integrating all sources of information, we should have material which will satisfy the man interested in this peak of intellectual achievement in pre-Columbian America, and which will at the same time be of value to the student of comparative history.

The purpose of research in every field, as Laurence Houseman said, is to set back the frontier of darkness. With so many frontiers of darkness, even in the study of man, why choose Maya civilization? To that, I think, the answer must be that Maya civilization not only produced geniuses, but produced them in an atmosphere which to us seems incredible. One can never assume the obvious when dealing with the Maya, who excelled in the impractical but failed in the practical. What mental quirks (from our point of view) led the Maya intelligentsia to chart the heavens, yet fail to grasp the principle of the wheel; to visualize eternity, as no other semi-civilized people has ever done, yet ignore the short step from corbelled to true arch; to count in millions, yet never learn to weigh a sack of corn?

In its general aspects Maya philosophy closely parallels the Athenian, for "moderation in all things" was the key to Maya living, as it was to life in Athens. Yet to that philosophy the Maya added concepts which are utterly alien to western thought. The great theme of Maya civilization is the passage of time—the wide concept of the mystery of eternity and the narrower concept of the divisions of time into their equivalents of centuries, years, months and days. The rhythm of time enchanted the Maya; the never-ending flow of days from the eternity of the future into the eternity of the past filled them with wonder. Calculations far into the past or lesser

Ibid., pp. 23-4.

probings of the future occur in many a Maya hieroglyphic text. On one stela at the city of Quirigua accurate computation sweeps back over 90,000,000 years; on another stela at the same site the date reached is some 400,000,000 years ago. These are actual computations stating correctly day and month positions, and are

Maya time-period glyphs: cursive (Dresden Codex), formal, and face signs (from carved stone inscriptions at Copan, Honduras; Palenque, Chiapas; and Yaxchilan, Chiapas (after Bowditch). TOP LINE: *kin (sun or day);* SECOND LINE: *uinal (month of 20 days);* THIRD LINE: *tun (year of 18 uinals, or 360 days);* FOURTH LINE: *katun (20 tuns, or 7,200 days);* FIFTH LINE: *baktun (cycle of 20 katuns, or 144,000 days, approximately 394 of our years). There is a further Great Cycle of 20 baktuns, making nearly 8,000 years.*

comparable to calculations in our calendar giving the month positions on which Easter would have fallen at equivalent distances in the past. The brain reels at such astronomical figures, yet these reckonings were of sufficient frequency and importance to require special hieroglyphs for their transcription, and they were made nearly a thousand years before Archbishop Ussher had placed the creation of the world at 4004 B.C. This was an appraisal of the ages which would have been utterly inconceivable to us even today, had not our minds been conditioned to their vastness by the writings of the astronomers and geologists of the nineteenth century.

Maya interest was not confined to this grandiose aspect of time. Not only the great periods of time, but the very days were divine, for the Maya held, and in some parts still hold, the days to be living gods. They bow down to them and worship them; they order their lives by their appearance. Throughout history man has ascribed favourable or malevolent powers to certain days, but nowhere did those influences attain the importance with which they were invested by the peoples of Middle America. The life of the Maya community and the acts of the individual were rigidly adjusted to the succession of deified days with their varying aspects, for each day was a god who took a lively interest in his duties; happy and sorrowful days succeeded one another. Life passed in this pattern of sunshine and shade was not monotonous. It is not improbable that this strange form of predestination moulded the Maya character or, perhaps, was itself a manifestation of that character which recognized man's small part in an eternity not measured by 400,000,000 years.

There are other aspects of the Maya philosophy of time, such as the strange failure to distinguish between past and future in the prophetic chants. What had gone before and what lay ahead were blended in a way that is baffling to our western minds. Mysticism is not now fashionable, and so writers tend to stress the material side of Maya civilization, but surely it is precisely these (to us) strange aberrations of Maya mentality which pose the most interesting questions.

Why is this Maya mentality so different from ours? Did it produce Maya culture, or did Maya culture produce it? What of its effect on religious conceptions? Can an impractical culture be a successful one by standards other than our own? Did Maya civilization carry within it the seeds of its own destruction? Such, as I see them, are the mysteries that make the Maya a fascinating study.

J. ERIC THOMPSON

The Fall of Classic Mayan Civilization

FOR many years it was believed that for some reason or other the Maya of the Central area abandoned their cities and migrated north to Yucatan and south into the highlands of Guatemala, in both of which regions they established Maya culture, which subsequently blossomed forth into a renaissance. More recent archaeological work has shown that thesis to be untenable; both regions were flourishing centres of Maya culture all through the Classic Period.

For the cessation of activities in the various ceremonial centres a number of theories have been advanced, none of which has much to recommend it. It has been suggested that Maya methods of agriculture (cutting and burning forest for one- or two-year plantings and then allowing the clearings to revert to forest for some ten years) were so wasteful that in time and with an increase of population, lack of food would have forced migration. To refute this theory, one can note that the soil around Quirigua, frequently fertilized by floodings of the Motagua River, is very rich, yet Quirigua was one of the earlier cities to cease functioning.

The explanation has also been offered that repeated clearing of forest was followed by the appearance of grass, which gradually covered the land, producing savannahs which the Maya, having no ploughs or even spades (the shallow soil in many parts would make such implements unusable even if the Maya had possessed them), were unable to break up to plant their crops. This explanation, strongly advocated by my late colleague, Sylvanus G. Morley, was advanced by agronomists of the United States Department of Agriculture. It is quite neat, but I am not certain that it is tenable. It is true that grass will appear in cleared forest land if those patches are kept free of trees and shrubs for several years, but the Maya abandoned their clearings after one or two seasons' use, and

Ibid., pp. 92-7.

in that short time grass cannot establish itself. I have noticed that verges of roads cut in the forests and used for several years to extract mahogany are often of grass, but when those roads are abandoned, they revert rapidly to forest. Some years ago I was in Chicchanha, an important Maya town in southern Quintana Roo until its abandonment in 1852. During its occupation the main plaza and the streets must have been under grass, as in any other Maya town. Yet, when I visited the town, it was entirely covered with deep forest, to a layman indistinguishable from the surrounding virgin forest. In fact, it was not until I saw the walls of houses and gardens and then the ruined church that I realized that I was riding down former streets and across what had once been an extensive plaza. Thus forest will quickly displace grass, even when, as in the plaza of Chicchanha, it had been established for very many years.

The botanist Lundell has modified this theory, supposing that it applies only to regions where the soil is deep, such as the savannahs of Campeche and south of Lake Peten. These are bottom lands and not too extensive. The fact that large Maya sites are not found on or even contiguous to them gives little support for the theory that their growth caused the desertion of the Maya centres. There are no savannah lands around the great concentration of ceremonial centres in the northern Peten, or around Quirigua with its deep soil, or along the Usumacinta. I suspect those savannahs were formed long before the Classic Period reached its peak.

The abandonment of the cities has also been attributed to the incidence of malaria or yellow fever, but both of those diseases are almost certainly of Old World origin, introduced to the New World by the Spaniards. Hookworm is a serious destroyer in this region at the present time, but that, too, is a post-Columbian importation. Moreover, all these explanations call for a gradual death of Maya culture in city after city, but the building already mentioned at Uaxactun with its half-built walls suggest a sudden catastrophe.

I think the fundamental mistake has been to assume that the whole area was abandoned because activities ceased in the great ceremonial centres. As a matter of fact, we know that there was a considerable population around Copan in early colonial days, and Cortés, in his march across the peninsula, came across quite a number of settlements. Friars and military groups in the sixteenth, seventeenth, and eighteenth centuries reported many other groups, although smallpox and other newly introduced diseases had carried off large numbers of inhabitants. Clearly the population of the Central area at the time of the Spanish Conquest was considerably smaller than it had been 800 years earlier, but it is incorrect to suppose that this vast area had been a vacuum for hundreds of years. This later population might have descended from groups subsequently filtering into the region, but it is more reasonable to assume that they are the descendants of the original peasant population of the ninth century.

It is not illogical to suppose that there was a series of peasant revolts against the theocratic minority of priests, "squarsons" (a term for that phenomenon of eighteenth-century English life, the squire who was also the village parson), and nobles. This may have been caused by the ever-growing demands for service in construction work and in the production of food for an increasing number of non-producers. Exotic religious developments, such as the cult of the planet Venus, adopted by the hierarchy, may have driven a wedge between the two groups, making the peasants feel that the hierarchy was no longer performing its main function, that of propitiating the gods of the soil in whom, alone, they heartily believed. I am rather dubious of physical invasion and conquest of the Central area, but there may well have been ideological invasions, as foreign ideas on very late stelae would indicate. Whether degeneracy in art—and it is apparent only in a few cities—reflects a moral weakening in the hierarchy is a question which probably can never be answered. Huxley, I think, showed that Italian art was at its purest when morals were at a very low level. (In our age both seem to have hit bottom together!)

It is suggestive that the collapse of the stela cult seems to have started across the base of the Peninsula of Yucatan, the region most easily invaded by the revolutionary ideas or perhaps even armies of non-Maya peoples or of the nonconformist Maya of the highlands, and its last stronghold was in the very remote region of northern Peten and southern Campeche. This, however, was only a general tendency. Around Comitan, in the Chiapan highlands, which was certainly an outpost of the stela cult on the frontier of the hierarchic empire, monuments continued to be erected until the middle of the ninth century, and there was another hold-out in the middle Usumacinta Valley. However, all sorts of local circumstances may account for these, just as they account for the present distribution of kingdoms in modern Europe.

The gradualness of the collapse over the whole area argues against the view that there was strong central authority and in favour of the city-state theory. In my opinion, and it is one on which I would not stake heavily, in city after city the ruling group was driven out or, more probably, massacred by the dependent peasants, and power then passed to peasant leaders and small-town witch-doctors. The building programme and the erection of stelae ceased abruptly, but the people still repaired to the ceremonial centres for certain religious services and perhaps for markets, but the buildings, no longer kept up, gradually fell into disrepair.

Vegetation began to invade the courts and terraces and to lodge on the roofs of buildings.

There is some evidence for these assertions. Excavation at Uaxactun revealed that after the buildings had been abandoned, burials were still made in the city. One body was placed in the debris of a collapsed room; another lay on an accumulation of dirt in a corner of a court; another (a child) was on a dais or bench, with a few stones and much charcoal placed around it and with a covering of dirt and fall from the roof. In two cases the skulls were deformed, indicating that these were not post-Columbian burials. The child had a piece of jade in the mouth (a common Middle American practice) and two jade beads. As children were commonly sacrificed, the presence of the child with jades and charcoal in this abandoned room would strongly suggest that it had been brought there to be sacrificed. Burials have also been found in collapsed rooms at other sites, notably a burial with pottery of post-Classical types at Copan.

As buildings began to collapse, doorways were slovenly blocked to shut them off, and refuse containing broken pottery and bones is found overlying thin deposits of debris from disintegrating vaults and walls. Shaped spindle-whorls, unknown in the Classic Period of the Peten, occur both at Uaxactun and San José in thin deposits of dirt above the latest floors. A bow was found on the floor of one room at Uaxactun below about eight feet of collapsed masonry.

Such data indicate visits to the sites after their abandonment, half-hearted attempts to keep them in service by blocking off collapsed rooms, and probable use of the buildings for human sacrifices. It is, I think, a fair assumption that these activities can be attributed to the peasant population after the massacre or expulsion of the hierarchy. The jades might have been loot, for peasants would not have owned such valuables; the crude masonry of one of the blocked doorways at Uaxactun suggests that the work was done after the last of the masons working for the hierarchy had joined the great majority.

At Piedras Negras a magnificent dais had been deliberately smashed. This destruction might have been the work of invaders, but, equally well or better, it could have been an act of vengeance or spite by revolting peasants, since the dais was the seat of former rule—a sort of razing of the Bastille. It is also possible that the damage is more recent and is attributable to superstitious fear. Modern Mayas believe that stelae, incense-burners with faces on them, and suchlike relics of the past house evil spirits which, coming to life at night, cause death and sickness, and they frequently destroy them out of fear (the beautiful murals at Santa Rita, in northern British Honduras, were destroyed by Indians probably for that reason, almost as soon as they were uncovered and before they had been completely copied). However, the fact that the figures of gods on the Piedras Negras stelae were not likewise destroyed perhaps indicates that the damage to the throne was inflicted neither by invaders nor by superstitious Indians, but by revolting peasants who attacked the symbol of their civil bondage, but respected the images of their gods.

In Yucatan the epilogue to the fall of the great cities was somewhat different, as we shall see in the next chapter.

In all probability the causes of the collapse will never be surely known, and writers will be speculating on the matter long after this book shall have been forgotten.

Shelley a century and a half ago summed up a like situation in an Old World setting:

> *And on the pedestal these words appear:*
> *"My name is Ozymandias, king of kings:*
> *Look on my works, ye mighty, and despair!"*
> *Nothing beside remains. Round the decay*
> *Of that colossal wreck, boundless and bare,*
> *The lone and level sands stretch far away.*

2. The Aztecs

SIMPLE farming communities long established in the Valley of Mexico developed a high civilization during the early centuries of our era. One of the most extraordinary of their ceremonial cities (which had much in common with those of the Maya) was Teotihuacan on the east side of Lake Texcoco. The pyramids of the Sun and Moon and the temple of Quetzalcoatl are among the most impressive examples of pre-Columbian architecture. Teotihuacan was at its greatest between the sixth and ninth centuries A.D., and seems to have been abandoned a century or two later. Fresh barbarian tribes entered the valley in search of land; they conquered, settled and set up small warring states. Probably with the help of influence from the people of Puebla and Oaxaca, Aztec civilization began to take shape among them. One seemingly small and unimportant group of barbarians had settled to the south-west of Lake Texcoco. Their tribal legends told that they had been led there by their god Huitzilopochtli, who sometimes assumed the form of a humming bird. These Tenochas were an aggressive tribe, believing that Huitzilopochtli intended them to vanquish all other peoples. At first they were worsted, and had to retreat to live on marshy islands off the lake shore. But soon their fortunes changed and the Tenochas became the most powerful of the Aztec peoples of the valley of Mexico. They built their wonderful capital of Tenochtitlan on the islands where they had lived as refugees—and where Mexico City now stands. The Aztec culture owed almost everything to Toltec traditions—including temple pyramids and probably the culture god himself—Quetzalcoatl. The Aztec peoples were also interested in the measurement of time, calendars and religious concepts depending upon them—as is shown by the magnificent Calendar Stone (p. 660, II). Yet they never became obsessed with these matters, nor went as far along the roads of astronomy and mathematics as did the Maya. Instead, when they became all-powerful, the Tenocha Aztecs remained devoted to their destiny as divine warriors. They played an endless war-game to win prisoners for sacrifice to their hungry gods. So it was that when Cortes reached Tenochtitlan, the eagle-vases (p. 661, II) had been brimming with human hearts, and racks in the great square of Tenochtitlan were filled with severed heads.

BERNARDINO DE SAHAGUN

Nobles and Commoners

BERNARDINO DE SAHAGUN was a Spanish Franciscan who arrived in Mexico in 1529, only eight years after the Spanish conquest of Tenochtitlan (Mexico City). He worked among the subject Indians, learnt their languages and collected their myths, legends and traditions. He wrote down all he had observed and learnt in a very large work entitled in Spanish *Historia General de*

AZTEC BOWL, REDDISH BROWN ON WHITE,
16 CENTIMETRES IN DIAMETER

las Cosas de Nueva Espana. This great compilation, a main source
of information about the Aztecs, was not published until the
nineteenth century. The following small fragments are chosen for
their archaeological interest. They give an idea of the living "ruler"
wearing the kind of ornaments that may come to light in excavations; they show the ball court in use and the crowded wares of an
Aztec market. They are also to convey at least something of the
atmosphere surrounding an Aztec sovereign. Elsewhere de Sahagun
described some of the most appalling ceremonies ever devised by
our species.

How the Rulers Were Arrayed When They Danced

THE [head] band with [two] quetzal feather tassels set off with gold,
with which they bound their hair;

A quetzal feather crest device set off with gold, which he bore
upon his back;

A finely wrought headdress of red spoonbill feathers, with flaring
quetzal feathers, and with it a drum [covered] with gold—a device
which he bore upon his back as he danced;

A golden arm band;

Golden ear plugs, which he inserted [in the lobes of his ears];

A wrist band of cured leather, on which was a large, round, green
stone or a fine turquoise which he placed on his wrist; [it was]
treated with Peru balsam, so that it gleamed;

A green stone lip plug set in gold;

A long, white labret of clear crystal, shot through with blue
cotinga feathers, in a gold setting, which he inserted in his [lower]
lips;

A long, yellow labret of amber in a gold setting;

Flowers and tobacco, [which were] exclusively the ruler's; a
mirror in which the ruler looked at himself when he adorned himself. All these were the charge of the artisans when the ruler danced.

Sandals of ocelot skin; cured leather sandals with embroidery—
embroidered sandals.

[There were] two-toned drums and supports for two-toned drums,
ground drums, golden turtle shells, and golden bells;

Singers, a dancer, a player of two-toned drums and one of ground
drums, a drum beater, a singer who intoned the chant.

[There were] chests for the devices, in which were kept all which

From *General History of the Things of New Spain.* Written in mid-16th Century.
The Florentine Codex, Book VIII, pp. 28, 67-9. By permission of the School of
American Research and the University of Utah, who published it in Sante Fé, 1954.

have been described: a large basket-case in which were kept the green stone lip plugs, the gold ear plugs, the golden necklaces, the wigs, the masks, the golden reed serpent.

How the Rulers Took Their Pleasure

When the ruler went forth, in his hand rested his reed stalk which he sent moving in rhythm with his words. His chamberlain and his elders went before him; on both sides, on either hand, they proceeded as they went clearing the way for him. None might cross in front of him; none might come forth before him; none might look up at him; none might come face to face with him.

He sang; songs were learned; chants were intoned. They told him proverbs and pleasantries to pass the time.

They played ball. There were his ball-catchers and his ball-players. They wagered [in this game] all [manner of] costly goods—gold, golden necklaces, green stone, fine turquoise, slaves, precious capes, valuable breech clouts, cultivated fields, houses, leather lcg bands, gold bracelets, arm bands of quetzal feathers, duck feather capes, bales of cacao—[these] were wagered there in the game called *tlachtli*.

On the two sides, on either hand, it was limited by walls, very well made, in that the walls and floor were smoothed. And there, in the very center of the ball court, was a line, drawn upon the ground. And on the walls were two stone, ball court rings. He who played caused [the ball] to enter there; he caused it to go in. Then he won all the costly goods, and he won everything from all who watched there in the ball court. His equipment was the rubber ball, the leather gloves, girdles, and leather hip guards.

The Ordering of the Market Place

The ruler took care of the directing of the market place and all things sold, for the good of the common folk, the vassals, and all dwellers in the city, the poor, the unfortunate, so that [these] might not be abused, nor suffer harm, nor be deceived nor disdained. Thus were things bought, or sold: they arranged them in order so that each thing sold would be placed separately—in its own place or station. They were not spread about in confusion.

Market place directors were appointed to office. They cared for, and attended to, the market place and all and each of the things sold—the merchandise which was there. Each of the directors took care, and was charged, that no one might deceive another, and how [articles] might be priced and sold.

Separate were those who sold gold and silver, and green stone, and turquoise, and emeralds, and quetzal feathers, and [those of] the blue cotinga, and the red spoonbill, and all the various precious feathers of birds, which were needed for devices and shields.

Separate were those who sold chocolate, aromatic herbs, and vanilla. Apart were those who sold great capes, costly capes, embroidered capes, costly breech clouts, embroidered skirts and shifts, large common capes, maguey fiber capes, and thin maguey fiber capes.

DESIGNS FROM AZTEC SPINDLE WHORLS

And all food necessary to them also was sold separately: dried grains of maize, white, black, red, and yellow; yellow beans, white ones, black, red; pinto beans; large beans; gray amaranth seed, red amaranth seed, and fish amaranth; white chía, black chía, and the wrinkled variety; salt; fowl; turkey cocks and hens; quail; rabbits, hares, and deer; ducks and other water birds, gulls, and wild geese; maguey syrup and honey; hot chilis, chili from Atzitziuacan, small chilis, chili powder, yellow chili, chili from the Couixca, sharp-pointed red chilis, long chilis, smoked chilis; small, wild tomatoes, and ordinary tomatoes.

And separately were sold every kind of fruit: the American cherry, avocados, plums, guavas, sweet potatoes, manihot, sapotas, anonas, yellow sapotas, sapotillas, *tejocotes*, tuna cactus, mesquite beans, marchpane, *cacomites*, *cimate* roots, squash cut in pieces, chayote, squash seeds, cassia seeds; and white fish, frogs, and water dogs; water fly eggs, water flies, lake scum, and red shellfish; and white paper made of the bark of trees, and incense, and rubber, and lime, and obsidian; and firewood, and poles, logs, planks, and chips of wood; digging sticks, pointed oaken poles, hatchets, paddles, staves; maguey roots, maguey fiber, and cured leather, and sandals; and copper axes, copper needles, and carpenters' and sculptors' copper chisels; and all manner of edible herbs—onions, water plant leaves, thistles, amaranth greens and heads, purslane, mixed greens, varieties of sorrel; tuna cactus fruit, sweet and acid; squash greens, tender young squash, squash blossoms; bean greens and green beans; green maize, tender maize, tender maize stalks; tamales of maize blossoms, tortillas of green maize, and all edible things—tortillas, tamales, tamales and tortillas with honey, large tortillas, and rolled tortillas.

And also there were proprietors among whom were spread out smoking tubes, pipes, and cigars, [some] quite resinous and aromatic; and tobacco bowls; and large pottery braziers and hearths, and earthen basins, and pots, and jars for storing water, and settling jars, and flat cooking plates, and sauce vessels, and earthen cups, and everything [made of] earthenware.

G. C. VAILLANT

The City of Tenochtitlan

THE history of the Aztecs and their forebears is the most complete record we have of the growth of any Indian civilization. Their conquest was the greatest feat in the European occupation of the American continent. The Aztecs were at their zenith in 1519, when Cortes and his 400 men first landed, and a description of Tenochtitlan, taken from the contemporary records of the conquerors themselves, will show us something of the external character of Indian civilization in America.

Bernal Diaz del Castillo, who left the most personal record of the Spanish Conquest, tells how his comrade-in-arms on first beholding Tenochtitlan, the ancient Mexico City, exclaimed, "It is like the enchantments they tell of in the legend of Amadis! Are not the things we see a dream?"

This is lyric language from hard-bitten men-at-arms, whose chief avocations, while engaged in converting the heathen, lay in acquiring booty and enjoying the charms of dusky Dulcineas. Yet, in contrast to the drab towns and tawny hills of Spain, Tenochtitlan must have appeared a paradise, for its green gardens and white buildings were set in the midst of blue lakes, ringed by lofty mountains. "Gazing on such wonderful sights," wrote Bernal Diaz, "we did not know what to say or whether what appeared before us was real, for on one side in the land there were great cities and in the lake ever so many more, and the lake itself was crowded with canoes, and in the causeway were many bridges at intervals, and in front of us stood the great City of Mexico, and we . . . we did not even number four hundred soldiers."

Although socially and governmentally Tenochtitlan was distinctly an American Indian tribal town, outwardly it appeared the capital city of an empire. A bird's-eye view would have revealed an oval island connected with the mainland by three causeways which converged at the centre of the city. These roads were cut by waterways

From *The Aztecs of Mexico*. New York: Doubleday & Co., 1962, pp. 184-7. (1st ed., 1944). By permission of Mrs. Robert T. Hatt.

over which removable bridges extended. The edges of the island were fringed by the green of the "floating gardens," while at the centre the shiny white of the houses predominated, and the verdure was reduced to tiny green squares in the patio gardens. Thrust above the quadrate masses of the roof-tops loomed the various clan temples, each set on its platform in the form of a truncated pyramid. The city had few streets or open spaces, but was gridded with canals crossed by portable bridges. The two principal plazas were those of the Temple of Tlaltelolco and of the religious centre of Tenochtitlan proper, open spaces which gave a welcome relief from the pyramids and official palaces clustered about them. There must have been a curiously living quality about this grouping, the temples seeming to ride like horsemen among the serrated ranks of the houses.

Were a visitor to have traversed Tenochtitlan from south to north, he would have been struck by the rich variety of sights. Approaching along the causeway, the traveller of that time passed first between expanses of open water. Then gradually tiny islands of green appeared, made of masses of mud dredged up from the bottom of the shallow lake and held in place by wicker-work. White-clad farmers dexterously poled their tiny dugouts through the maze as they went about the cultivation of their gardens. These irregular islets merged gradually into a more orderly grouping where the accumulation of soil had become stabilized as the roots, striking downward, had established anchorage in the lake bottom and created solid ground. This artificially made land reduced the open water of the lake to mere canals.

Save for the broad causeways, roads there were none; and along the canals the traveller saw, in increasing numbers, boat loads of produce headed towards the city. Here and there among the green of the crops and trees he caught glimpses of thatched roofs and wattled walls, the huts of the farmers. Then adobe walls of more substantial dwellings began to encroach on the gardens, and the waters of the lake shrank to a canal following the roadway. The adobe walls gave way to the fronts of more pretentious houses plastered white or washed with powdered pumice, a dull, rich red. Now the visitor could realize how the city expanded through the successive creation of artificial islands which bore first a crop, then a modest hut and finally became integral with the masonry of the city proper.

The causeway had now changed from a simple means of communication into a principal street with all its social complexity. Since canals took the place of roads, space for a saunter was so rare that the causeways were as much recreation grounds as arteries of traffic. Thus people out to see the sights, people on errands, people on their way to the myriad functions of religious import, swallowed up the long lines of trotting carriers who, bowed under their burdens, went to the city with produce and tribute or left with goods for barter. Not a wheel turned or a pack-animal neighed; transport was on the backs of men or in the bottoms of boats.

Outside the city limits the monotony of ant-like columns of laden folk had been but rarely relieved by the passage of a civil functionary, all pomp and feathers, or by a stern merchant with a handful of fighting men, followed by a chain of apprentices, showing the whites of their eyes as they peered from under the press of their tumplines. Now could be seen clan leaders wearing rich mantles and sniffing flowers as they watched the milling crowd, and black-robed priests whose ears were shredded and whose hair was matted with the blood of self-inflicted penance. There was little sound, little hurry, save for the carriers trotting to reach relief from their burdens. There was an intense vitality, none the less, that of a multitude of units participating in complex action, knowing each its allotted part, but never the substance of the whole.

G. C. VAILLANT

Two Monuments: the Calendar Stone and Eagle Vase of Tizoc

THE Calendar Stone is a sculptured disk thirteen feet in diameter and twenty tons in weight. It was quarried on the mainland, and it is recorded that allied rulers sent men to help drag it across the causeways into Tenochtitlan. Eagle-vases (a literal translation of the

wwwwwwwwwwwwww
Ibid., pp. 163-4.

Aztec name) were in fact elaborately carved stone boxes used for the burning and storing of sacrificial human hearts. The ruler Tizoc had an exceptionally large one made to celebrate his conquests. It took the form of a circular cup, eight feet across and thirty inches in thickness.

THE Calendar Stone embodies a finite statement of the infinity of the Aztec universe. In the centre is the face of the Sun God, Tonatiuh, flanked by four cartouches which singly give the dates of the four previous ages of the world and together represent the date of our present era. The twenty names of the days circle this central element, and they, in turn, are ringed with a band of glyphs denoting jade or turquoise, which give the idea of being precious and symbolize the heavens and their colour. This strip is girdled by the signs for stars, through which penetrate designs emblematic of the rays of the sun. Two immense Fire Serpents, symbolic of the Year and Time, circle the exterior to meet face to face at the base. Boring back through these forms to the significance behind them, we have a grandiose conception of the majesty of the universe.

In recent years, under the Presidential Palace in Mexico City, a monolith over a metre high was found, which represented a platform and a stair crowned at the top by a similar solar disk. Reliefs on the sides show Huitzilopochtli, God of War, and Tezcatlipoca, God of the Smoking Mirror, symbolizing the sacred war between night and day. Probably the Calendar Stone was set up in much the same manner, and it is tantalizing to think of the lost reliefs which explained and ornamented the great disk when it was in position.

The historical accounts record that the Calendar Stone was made in 1479 and the great eagle vase of Tizoc during his rule from 1481 to 1486. A trough, extending from the basin to the edge of the vase, has been explained as a drain for blood to run out. However, the design is not keyed to this drain, and the purpose of the basin is to burn hearts, not to receive blood. Therefore, the furrow was probably made by the Spaniards, who sought either to use the vase as a nether millstone or tried unsuccessfully to smash it as an example of idolatry.

The dates of these two monuments indicate that this was the time when Aztec civilization burst into flower. It is a tribute to Aztec artists that, originally fettered by the more lowly tasks of handicraft, they could accept the tremendous economic, social and religious stimulation of their sudden rise to power as a licence to convert craftsmanship into great religious art.

3. The Incas

THE Incas, who were ruling great territories from their Andean capital at Cuzco at the time of the Spanish conquest, resembled the Aztecs in being a people who had recently come to power by expansion and war. But they were quite unlike them in that they had welded their conquests into a united whole. Their empire was kept together by efficient administration and a system of communications, based on roads and runners, that was probably the best in the world before modern times. Also, although they won their ascendancy by fighting or the threat of fighting, the Incas did not glorify war and were not interested in sacrificial victims. As soon as a neighbouring people had submitted they were incorporated in the empire and reasonably well treated. The Inca system has often been likened to that of a welfare state of a particularly despotic kind. It would not be altogether outrageous to compare the Aztecs to the Nazis and the Incas to the Russians—except that the Incas were superlatively good agriculturalists.

Inca history begins with the first chief Inca, Manco Capac, leading his people into the Cuzco valley and establishing his capital there. For two centuries they seem to have done little more than other Andean tribes: they fought and sometimes defeated their neighbours but did not attempt any permanent conquests. These began only after 1438, when an aggressive neighbouring people, the Chanca, had been repulsed and vanquished. Then within the next ninety years the Incas expanded their territories very rapidly. At first they conquered other mountain tribes like their own—including the people who had created the remarkable Tiahuanco culture in the region of Lake Atitlan.

Their most powerful rivals were the Chimu, who ruled a considerable empire of their own from the north coast of Peru. Civilization had a long history in the watered valleys that ran down from the Andes to cut through the arid coastal plains. Agriculture had started there by 2000 B.C., and one has only to look at the Paracas textiles (p. 683, II) to realize what high cultural levels had been achieved by the beginning of our era. Other coastal valley tribes developed some of the finest, most original pottery in all ceramic history. Towns of considerable size were created, and by the fourteenth century the

Chimu had established their kingdom in the Mocha valley. Their capital city, Chan-Chan (near Trujillo), came to cover an area of eleven square miles. By the middle of the fifteenth century, when they themselves were overcome by the invincible Inca army, their dominion extended from Tumbez in the far north almost to Lima. The Inca empire, which was toppled by Pizarro at the head of a few hundred men, included not only the lofty mountain valleys and grilling plains of Peru, but much of Ecuador and Chile as well. It was linked by a mountain highway and a coastal highway, and by cross roads running between and beyond them.

Like many conquering peoples, the Incas were not outstanding in the creative arts. In fact they seem to have been strongly influenced by the more gifted Chimu. They are commemorated today chiefly in their architecture. It did not attain the huge scale or decorative magnificence of Toltec and Aztec building, but was solid and enduring. Inca masonry, either in regular ashlar or with immense blocks fitted together like a cubist jigsaw, has become famous. The three ramparts of the fort of Saccsaihuaman above Cuzco (p. 664, II) could make Tiryns look flimsy. At Machu Picchu the balanced harmony of the architecture is very satisfying.

It has to be remembered that many Inca buildings were painted— and some, like the Temple of the Sun at Cuzco, richly furbished with gold. Gold is certainly the other thing for which the Incas have always been famous. It is sickening to think of the works of fine craftsmanship, brought from all over the empire in the vain hope of ransoming the last Inca, which were melted down by the Spaniards. The quantity was so vast that it is said that it took the Indian goldsmiths a full month to turn these treasures into lifeless ingots.

W. H. PRESCOTT

Cuzco, the Incas
and Their Civilization

WILLIAM PRESCOTT (born in 1796 at Salem, Massachusetts and educated at Harvard) was one of those extraordinary men who— like Gibbon—was determined to be a great author before he knew what he wanted to write about. He cast his net widely before deciding to concentrate on Spanish subjects. He won immediate fame with his history of Ferdinand and Isabella—which was followed after a long interval by the *Conquest of Mexico* (1843) and then, rapidly, by the *Conquest of Peru* (1847). The one-eyed historian (assisted by several two-eyed researchers) worked entirely from written sources and seems to have taken little interest in the material remains of his chosen peoples. The *Conquest* books are, of course, mainly concerned with the history of the Spanish invasions, but his accounts of the native cultures are valuable if not always reliable.

THE ancient city of Cuzco, meanwhile, had been gradually advancing in wealth and population, till it had become the worthy metropolis of a great and flourishing monarchy. It stood in a beautiful valley on an elevated region of the plateau, which, among the Alps, would have been buried in eternal snows, but which within the tropics enjoyed a genial and salubrious temperature. Towards the north it was defended by a lofty eminence, a spur of the great Cordillera; and the city was traversed by a river, or rather a small stream, over which bridges of timber, covered with heavy slabs of stone, furnished an easy means of communication with the opposite

From *The Conquest of Peru*. New York: E. P. Dutton & Co. Inc.; 1908, pp. 8-11, 16-20, 37-41, 57-60. (1st ed., 1847).

banks. The streets were long and narrow; the houses low, and those
of the poorer sort built of clay and reeds. But Cuzco was the royal
residence, and was adorned with the ample dwellings of the great
nobility; and the massy fragments still incorporated in many of the
modern edifices bear testimony to the size and solidity of the ancient.

The health of the city was promoted by spacious openings and
squares, in which a numerous population from the capital and the
distant country assembled to celebrate the high festivals of their religion. For Cuzco was the "Holy City"; and the great Temple of the
Sun, to which pilgrims resorted from the furthest borders of the empire, was the most magnificent structure in the New World, and
unsurpassed, probably, in the costliness of its decorations by any
building in the Old.

Toward the north, on the sierra or rugged eminence already
noticed, rose a strong fortress, the remains of which, at the present
day, by their vast size, excite the admiration of the traveller. It was
defended by a single wall of great thickness, and twelve hundred
feet long on the side facing the city, where the precipitous character
of the ground was of itself almost sufficient for its defence. On the
other quarter, where the approaches were less difficult, it was protected by two other semicircular walls of the same length as the
preceding. They were separated, a considerable distance from one
another and from the fortress; and the intervening ground was
raised so that the walls afforded a breastwork for the troops stationed there in times of assault. The fortress consisted of three
towers detached from one another. One was appropriated to the
Inca, and was garnished with the sumptuous decorations befitting a
royal residence, rather than a military post. The other two were held
by the garrison, drawn from the Peruvian nobles, and commanded
by an officer of the blood royal, for the position was of too great importance to be intrusted to inferior hands. The hill was excavated
below the towers, and several subterranean galleries communicated
with the city and the palaces of the Incas.

The fortress, the walls, and the galleries were all built of stone,
the heavy blocks of which were not laid in regular courses, but so
disposed that the small ones might fill up the interstices between the
great. They formed a sort of rustic work, being rough-hewn except
towards the edges, which were finely wrought; and, though no
cement was used, the several blocks were adjusted with so much ex-
actness and united so closely, that it was impossible to introduce
even the blade of a knife between them. Many of these stones were
of vast size: some of them being full thirty-eight feet long by
eighteen broad, and six feet thick.

We are filled with astonishment when we consider that these
enormous masses were hewn from their native bed and fashioned

into shape by a people ignorant of the use of iron; that they were
brought from quarries from four to fifteen leagues distant, without
the aid of beasts of burden, were transported across rivers and
ravines, raised to their elevated position on the sierra, and finally
adjusted there with the nicest accuracy, without the knowledge of
tools and machinery familiar to the European. Twenty thousand
men are said to have been employed on this great structure, and fifty
years consumed in the building. However this may be, we see in it
the workings of a despotism which had the lives and fortunes of its
vassals at its absolute disposal, and which, however mild in its general character, esteemed these vassals, when employed in its service,
as lightly as the brute animals for which they served as a substitute. . . .

The royal palaces were on a magnificent scale, and, far from
being confined to the capital or a few principal towns, were scattered
over all the provinces of their vast empire. The buildings were low,
but covered a wide extent of ground. Some of the apartments were
spacious, but they were generally small, and had no communication
with one another, except that they opened into a common square or
court. The walls were made of blocks of stone of various sizes, like
those described in the fortress of Cuzco, rough-hewn, but carefully
wrought near the line of junction, which was scarcely visible to the
eye. The roofs were of wood or rushes, which have perished under
the rude touch of time, that has shown more respect for the walls of
the edifices. The whole seems to have been characterised by solidity
and strength, rather than by any attempt at architectural elegance.

But whatever want of elegance there may have been in the exterior of the imperial dwellings, it was amply compensated by the
interior, in which all the opulence of the Peruvian princes was os-
tentatiously displayed. The sides of the apartments were thickly
studded with gold and silver ornaments. Niches, prepared in the
walls, were filled with images of animals and plants curiously
wrought of the same costly materials; and even much of the domestic furniture, including the utensils devoted to the most ordinary
menial services, displayed the like wanton magnificence! With these
gorgeous decorations were mingled richly coloured stuffs of the
delicate manufacture of the Peruvian wool, which were of so beautiful a texture, that the Spanish sovereigns, with all the luxuries of
Europe and Asia at their command, did not disdain to use them.
The royal household consisted of a throng of menials, supplied by
the neighbouring towns and villages, which, as in Mexico, were
bound to furnish the monarch with fuel and other necessaries for
the consumption of the palace.

But the favourite residence of the Incas was at Yucay, about four
leagues distance from the capital. In this delicious valley, locked up

within the friendly arms of the sierra, which sheltered it from the rude breezes of the east, and refreshed by gushing fountains and streams of running water, they built the most beautiful of their palaces. Here, when wearied with the dust and toil of the city, they loved to retreat and solace themselves with the society of their favourite concubines, wandering amidst groves and airy gardens, that shed around their soft intoxicating odours, and lulled the senses to voluptuous repose. Here, too, they loved to indulge in the luxury of their baths, replenished by streams of crystal water which were conducted through subterraneous silver channels into basins of gold. The spacious gardens were stocked with numerous varieties of plants and flowers that grew without effort in this *temperate* region of the tropics, while parterres of a more extraordinary kind were planted by their side, glowing with the various forms of vegetable life skilfully imitated in gold and silver! Among them the Indian corn, the most beautiful of American grains, is particularly commemorated, and the curious workmanship is noticed with which the golden ear was half disclosed amidst the broad leaves of silver and the light tassel of the same material that floated gracefully from its top.

If this dazzling picture staggers the faith of the reader, he may reflect that the Peruvian mountains teemed with gold; that the natives understood the art of working the mines to a considerable extent; that none of the ore, as we shall see hereafter, was converted into coin, and that the whole of it passed into the hands of the sovereign for his own exclusive benefit, whether for purposes of utility or ornament. Certain it is that no fact is better attested by the conquerors themselves, who had ample means of information, and no motive for misstatement.—The Italian poets, in their gorgeous pictures of the gardens of Alcina and Morgana, came nearer the truth than they imagined.

Our surprise, however, may reasonably be excited, when we consider that the wealth displayed by the Peruvian princes was only that which each had amassed individually for himself. He owed nothing to inheritance from his predecessors. On the decease of an Inca his palaces were abandoned; all his treasures, except what were employed in his obsequies, his furniture and apparel, were suffered to remain as he left them, and his mansions (save one) were closed up for ever. The new sovereign was to provide himself with everything new for his royal state. The reason of this was the popular belief that the soul of the departed monarch would return after a time to reanimate his body on earth; and they wished that he should find everything to which he had been used in life prepared for his reception.

When an Inca died, or, to use his own language, "was called home

to the mansions of his father, the Sun," his obsequies were celebrated with great pomp and solemnity. The bowels were taken from
the body and deposited in the Temple of Tampu, about five leagues
from the capital. A quantity of his plate and jewels was buried with
them, and a number of his attendants and favourite concubines,
amounting sometimes, it is said, to a thousand, were immolated on
his tomb. Some of them showed the natural repugnance to the sacrifice occasionally manifested by the victims of a similar superstition in India. But these were probably the menials and more humble
attendants; since the women have been known, in more than one
instance, to lay violent hands on themselves when restrained from
testifying their fidelity by this act of conjugal martyrdom. This
melancholy ceremony was followed by a general mourning throughout the empire. At stated intervals, for a year, the people assembled
to renew the expressions of their sorrow; processions were made,
displaying the banner of the departed monarch; bards and minstrels
were appointed to chronicle his achievements, and their songs continued to be rehearsed at high festivals in the presence of the reigning monarch,—thus stimulating the living by the glorious example
of the dead.

The body of the deceased Inca was skilfully embalmed, and removed to the great Temple of the Sun at Cuzco. There the Peruvian
sovereign, on entering the awful sanctuary, might behold the effigies
of his royal ancestors, ranged in opposite files,—the men on the
right, and their queens on the left, of the great luminary which
blazed in refulgent gold on the walls of the temple. The bodies,
clothed in the princely attire which they had been accustomed to
wear, were placed on chairs of gold, and sat with their heads inclined downwards, their hands placidly crossed over their bosoms,
their countenances exhibiting their natural dusky hue,—less liable
to change than the fresher colouring of a European complexion,—
and their hair of raven black, or silvered over with age, according
to the period at which they died! It seemed like a company of solemn
worshippers fixed in devotion,—so true were the forms and linea-
ments to life. The Peruvians were as successful as the Egyptians in
the miserable attempt to perpetuate the existence of the body beyond
the limits assigned to it by nature. . . .

Those who may distrust the accounts of Peruvian industry, will
find their doubts removed on a visit to the country. The traveller
still meets, especially in the central regions of the table-land, with
memorials of the past, remains of temples, palaces, fortresses,
terraced mountains, great military roads, aqueducts, and other
public works, which, whatever degree of science they may display in
their execution, astonish him by their number, the massive character
of the materials, and the grandeur of the design. Among them,

perhaps, the most remarkable are the great roads, the broken remains of which are still in sufficient preservation to attest their
former magnificence. There were many of these roads traversing
different parts of the kingdom; but the most considerable were the
two which extended from Quito to Cuzco, and, again diverging from
the capital, continued in a southern direction towards Chili.

One of these roads passed over the grand plateau, and the other
along the lowlands on the borders of the ocean. The former was
much the more difficult achievement, from the character of the
country. It was conducted over pathless sierras buried in snow;
galleries were cut for leagues through the living rock; rivers were
crossed by means of bridges that swung suspended in the air; precipices were scaled by stairways hewn out of the native bed; ravines
of hideous depth were filled up with solid masonry; in short, all the
difficulties that beset a wild and mountainous region, and which
might appal the most courageous engineer of modern times, were
encountered and successfully overcome. The length of the road,
of which scattered fragments only remain, is variously estimated
from fiften hundred to two thousand miles; and stone pillars, in the
manner of European mile-stones, were erected at stated intervals
of somewhat more than a league, all along the route. Its breadth
scarcely exceeded twenty feet. It was built of heavy flags of free-
stone, and in some parts, at least, covered with a bituminous cement,
which time has made harder than the stone itself. In some places
where the ravines had been filled up with masonry, the mountain
torrents, wearing on it for ages, have gradually eaten away through
the base, and left the super-incumbent mass—such is the cohesion
of the materials—still spanning the valley like an arch!

Over some of the boldest streams it was necessary to construct
suspension-bridges, as they are termed, made of the tough fibres of
the *maguey*, or of the osier of the country, which has an extraordinary degree of tenacity and strength. These osiers were woven into
cables of the thickness of a man's body. The huge ropes, then
stretched across the water, were conducted through rings or holes
cut in immense buttresses of stone raised on the opposite banks of
the river, and there secured to heavy pieces of timber. Several of
these enormous cables, bound together, formed a bridge, which,
covered with planks, well secured and defended by a railing of the
same osier materials on the sides, afforded a safe passage for the
traveller. The length of this aerial bridge, sometimes exceeding two
hundred feet, caused it, confined as it was only at the extremities,
to dip with an alarming inclination towards the centre, while the
motion given to it by the passenger occasioned an oscillation still
more frightful, as his eye wandered over the dark abyss of waters
that foamed and tumbled many a fathom beneath. Yet these light

and fragile fabrics were crossed without fear by the Peruvians, and are still retained by the Spaniards over those streams which, from the depth or impetuosity of the current, would seem impracticable for the usual modes of conveyance. The wider and more tranquil waters were crossed on *balsas*—a kind of raft still much used by the natives—to which sails were attached, furnishing the only instance of this higher kind of navigation among the American Indians.

The other great road of the Incas lay through the level country between the Andes and the ocean. It was constructed in a different manner, as demanded by the nature of the ground, which was for the most part low, and much of it sandy. The causeway was raised on a high embankment of earth, and defended on either side by a parapet or wall of clay; and trees and odoriferous shrubs were planted along the margin, regaling the sense of the traveller with their perfumes, and refreshing him by their shades, so grateful under the burning sky of the tropics. In the strips of sandy waste which occasionally intervened, where the light and volatile soil was incapable of sustaining a road, huge piles, many of them to be seen at this day, were driven into the ground, to indicate the route to the traveller.

All along these highways, caravanseries, or *tambos*, as they were called, were erected, at the distance of ten or twelve miles from each other, for the accommodation, more particularly, of the Inca and his suite, and those who journeyed on the public business. There were few other travellers in Peru. Some of these buildings were on an extensive scale, consisting of a fortress, barracks, and other military works, surrounded by a parapet of stone, and covering a large tract of ground. These were evidently destined for the accommodation of the imperial armies, when on their march across the country. The care of the great roads was committed to the districts through which they passed, and a large number of hands was constantly employed under the Incas to keep them in repair. This was the more easily done in a country where the mode of travelling was altogether on foot; though the roads are said to have been so nicely constructed, that a carriage might have rolled over them as securely as on any of the great roads of Europe. Still, in a region where the elements of fire and water are both actively at work in the business of destruction, they must, without constant supervision, have gradually gone to decay. Such has been their fate under the Spanish conquerors, who took no care to enforce the admirable system for their preservation adopted by the Incas. Yet the broken portions that still survive, here and there, like the fragments of the great Roman roads scattered over Europe, bear evidence to their primitive grandeur, and have drawn forth the eulogium from a discriminating traveller, usually not too profuse in his panegyric, "that the roads of the Incas were among the most useful and stupendous works ever executed by man."

The system of communication through their dominions was still further improved by the Peruvian sovereigns, by the introduction of posts, in the same manner as was done by the Aztecs. The Peruvian posts, however, established on all the great routes that conducted to the capital, were on a much more extended plan than those in Mexico. All along these routes small buildings were erected, at the distance of less than five miles asunder, in each of which a number of runners, or *chasquis,* as they were called, were stationed, to carry forward the dispatches of government. These dispatches were either verbal or conveyed by means of *quipus,* and sometimes accompanied by a thread of the crimson fringe worn round the temples of the Inca, which was regarded with the same implicit deference as the signet ring of an Oriental despot. . . .

But the worship of the Sun constituted the peculiar care of the Incas, and was the object of their lavish expenditure. The most ancient of the many temples dedicated to this divinity was in the island of Titicaca, whence the royal founders of the Peruvian line were said to have proceeded. From this circumstance, this sanctuary was held in peculiar veneration. Everything which belonged to it, even the broad fields of maize, which surrounded the temple, and formed part of its domain, imbibed a portion of its sanctity. The yearly produce was distributed among the different public magazines, in small quantities to each, as something that would sanctify the remainder of the store. Happy was the man who could secure even an ear of the blessed harvest for his own granary!

But the most renowned of the Peruvian temples, the pride of the capital, and the wonder of the empire, was at Cuzco, where, under the munificence of successive sovereigns, it had become so enriched, that it received the name of *Coricancha,* or "the Place of Gold." It consisted of a principal building and several chapels and inferior edifices, covering a large extent of ground in the heart of the city, and completely encompassed by a wall, which, with the edifices, was all constructed of stone. The work was of the kind already described in the other public buildings of the country, and was so finely exe-cuted that a Spaniard, who saw it in its glory, assures us he could call to mind only two edifices in Spain, which, for their workman-ship, were at all to be compared with it. Yet this substantial, and in some respects magnificent structure, was thatched with straw!

The interior of the temple was the most worthy of admiration. It was literally a mine of gold. On the western wall was emblazoned a representation of the deity, consisting of a human countenance looking forth from amidst innumerable rays of light which eman-

ated from it in every direction, in the same manner as the sun is
often personified with us. The figure was engraved on a massive
plate of gold of enormous dimensions, thickly powdered with emeralds and precious stones. It was so situated in front of the great
eastern portal, that the rays of the morning sun fell directly upon it
at its rising, lighting up the whole apartment with an effulgence
that seemed more than natural, and which was reflected back from
the golden ornaments with which the walls and ceiling were everywhere encrusted. Gold, in the figurative language of the people, was
"the tears wept by the Sun," and every part of the interior of the
temple glowed with burnished plates and studs of the precious
metal. The cornices, which surrounded the walls of the sanctuary,
were of the same costly material; and a broad belt or frieze of gold
let into the stone-work encompassed the whole exterior of the edifice.

Adjoining the principal structure were several chapels of smaller
dimensions. One of them was consecrated to the Moon, the deity
held next in reverence, as the mother of the Incas. Her effigy was
delineated in the same manner as that of the Sun, on a vast plate
that nearly covered one side of the apartment. But this plate, as well
as all the decorations of the building, was of silver, as suited to the
pale, silvery light of the beautiful planet. There were three other
chapels, one of which was dedicated to the host of Stars, who formed
the bright court of the Sister of the Sun; another was consecrated to
his dread ministers of vengeance, the Thunder and the Lightning;
and a third to the Rainbow, whose many-coloured arch spanned the
walls of the edifice with hues almost as radiant as its own. There
were besides several other buildings, or insulated apartments, for the
accommodation of the numerous priests who officiated in the services of the temple.

All the plate, the ornaments, the utensils of every description,
appropriated to the uses of religion, were of gold or silver. Twelve
immense vases of the latter metal stood on the floor of the great
saloon, filled with grain of the Indian corn; the censers for the perfumes, the ewers which held the water for sacrifice, the pipes which
conducted it through subterraneous channels into the buildings,
the reservoir that received it, even the agricultural implements used
in the gardens of the temple, were all of the same rich materials.
The gardens, like those described belonging to the royal palaces,
sparkled with gold and silver, and various imitations of the vegetable kingdom. Animals, also, were to be found there—among
which, the llama, with its golden fleece, was most conspicious—
executed in the same style, and with a degree of skill, which, in this
instance, probably, did not surpass the excellence of the material.

HIRAM BINGHAM

The Discovery
of Machu Picchu

THE small town of Machu Picchu remained intact—and unknown —until 1911 because of its lonely isolation high above the Urubamba valley. Far from being the "principal city of Manco and his sons" as Hiram Bingham briefly suspected, it has been shown by archaeology to have been built quite late in the Inca period.

❧

IT WILL be remembered that it was in July 1911 that I began the search for the last Inca capital. Accompanied by a dear friend, Professor Harry Ward Foote, of Yale University, who was our naturalist, and my classmate Dr. William G. Erving, the surgeon of the Expedition, I had entered the marvellous canyon of the Urubamba below the Inca fortress of Salapunco near Torontoy.

Here the river escapes from the cold plateau by tearing its way through gigantic mountains of granite. The road runs through a land of matchless charm. It has the majestic grandeur of the Canadian Rockies, as well as the startling beauty of the Nuuanu Pali near Honolulu, and the enchanting vistas of the Koolau Ditch Trail on Maui, in my native land. In the variety of its charms and the power of its spell, I know of no place in the world which can compare with it. Not only has it great snow peaks looming above the clouds more than 2 miles overhead and gigantic precipices of many-coloured granite rising sheer for thousands of feet above the foaming, glistening, roaring rapids, it has also, in striking contrast, orchids and tree ferns, the delectable beauty of luxurious vegetation,

From *Lost City of the Incas* by Hiram Bingham. London: Phoenix House Ltd.; 1951, pp. 137-43, (1st ed., 1948). By permission of Phoenix House Ltd. and Appleton-Century, an affiliate of Meredith Press. Copyright 1948 by Hiram Bingham.

and the mysterious witchery of the jungle. One is drawn irresistibly onward by ever-recurring surprises through a deep, winding gorge, turning and twisting past overhanging cliffs of incredible height.

Above all, there is the fascination of finding here and there under swaying vines, or perched on top of a beetling crag, the rugged masonry of a bygone race; and of trying to understand the bewildering romance of the ancient builders who, ages ago, sought refuge in a region which appears to have been expressly designed by nature as a sanctuary for the oppressed, a place where they might fearlessly and patiently give expression to their passion for walls of enduring beauty. Space forbids any attempt to describe in detail the constantly changing panorama, the rank tropical foliage, the countless terraces, the towering cliffs, the glaciers peeping out between the clouds.

You will remember that after passing Maquina where the sugar machinery had been abandoned because it could not be carried across the face of a great granite precipice, we had entered a little open plain called Mandor Pampa. Except where the rapids roared past it, gigantic precipices hemmed it in on all sides.

We passed an ill-kept, grass-thatched hut, turned off the road through a tiny clearing, and made our camp at the edge of the river on a sandy beach. Opposite us, beyond the huge granite boulders which interfered with the progress of the surging stream, the steep mountain was clothed with thick jungle. Since we were near the road yet protected from the curiosity of passers-by, it seemed to be an ideal spot for a camp. Our actions, however, aroused the suspicions of the owner of the hut, Melchor Arteaga, who leased the lands of Mandor Pampa. He was anxious to know why we did not stay at his "tavern" like other respectable travellers. Fortunately the Prefect of Cuzco, our old friend J. J. Nuñez, had given us an armed escort who spoke Quichua. Our gendarme, Sergeant Carrasco, was able to reassure the innkeeper. They had quite a long conversation. When Arteaga learned that we were interested in the architectural remains of the Incas, and were looking for the palace of the last Inca, he said there were some very good ruins in this vicinity—in fact, some excellent ones on top of the opposite mountain, called Huayna Picchu, and also on a ridge called Machu Picchu.

The morning of July 24th dawned in a cold drizzle. Arteaga shivered and seemed inclined to stay in his hut. I offered to pay him well if he would show me the ruins. He demurred and said it was too hard a climb for such a wet day. But when he found that I was willing to pay him a *sol* (a Peruvian silver dollar, 50 cents, gold), three or four times the ordinary daily wage in this vicinity, he finally agreed to go. When asked just where the ruins were, he pointed straight up to the top of the mountain. No one supposed that they would be particularly interesting. And no one cared to go with me. Our naturalist said there were "more butterflies near the river!" and he was reasonably certain he could collect some new varieties. Our surgeon said he had to wash his clothes and mend them. Anyhow it was my job to investigate all reports of ruins and try to find the Inca capital.

So, accompanied only by Sergeant Carrasco, I left camp at ten o'clock. Arteaga took us some distance upstream. On the road we passed a snake which had only just been killed. He said the region was the favourite haunt of "vipers." We later learned that the lance-headed, or yellow, viper, commonly known as the fer-de-lance, a very venomous serpent capable of making considerable springs when in pursuit of its prey, is common hereabouts.

After a walk of three quarters of an hour Arteaga left the main road and plunged down through the jungle to the bank of the river. Here there was a primitive bridge which crossed the roaring rapids at its narrowest part, where the stream was forced to flow between two great boulders. The "bridge" was made of half a dozen very slender logs, some of which were not long enough to span the distance between the boulders, but had been spliced and lashed together with vines!

Arteaga and the sergeant took off their shoes and crept gingerly across, using their somewhat prehensile toes to keep from slipping. It was obvious that no one could live for an instant in the icy cold rapids, but would immediately be dashed to pieces against the rocks. I frankly confess that I got down on my hands and knees and crawled across, 6 inches at a time. Even after we reached the other side I could not help wondering what would happen to the "bridge" if a particularly heavy shower should fall in the valley above. A light rain had fallen during the night and the river had risen so that the bridge was already threatened by the foaming rapids. It would not take much more to wash it away entirely. If this should happen during the day it might be very awkward. As a matter of fact, it did happen a few days later and when the next visitors attempted to cross the river at this point they found only one slender log remaining.

Leaving the stream, we now struggled up the bank through dense jungle, and in a few minutes reached the bottom of a very precipitous slope. For an hour and twenty minutes we had a hard climb. A good part of the distance we went on all fours, sometimes holding on by our fingernails. Here and there, a primitive ladder made from the roughly notched trunk of a small tree was placed in such a way as to help one over what might otherwise have proved to be an impassable cliff. In another place the slope was covered with slippery grass where it was hard to find either handholds or footholds. Arteaga groaned and said that there were lots of snakes here. Sergeant Carrasco said nothing but was glad he had good military shoes. The humidity was great. We were in the belt of maximum precipitation in Eastern Peru. The heat was excessive; and I was not in training. There were no ruins or *andenes* of any kind in sight. I began to think my companions had chosen the better part.

Shortly after noon, just as we were completely exhausted, we reached a little grass-covered hut 2,000 feet above the river where several good-natured Indians, pleasantly surprised at our unexpected arrival, welcomed us with dripping gourds full of cool, delicious water. Then they set before us a few cooked sweet potatoes. It seems that two Indian farmers, Richarte and Alvarez, had recently chosen this eagles' nest for their home. They said they had found plenty of terraces here on which to grow their crops. Laughingly they admitted they enjoyed being free from undesirable visitors, officials looking for army "volunteers" or collecting taxes.

Richarte told us that they had been living here four years. It seems probable that, owing to its inaccessibility, the canyon had been unoccupied for several centuries, but with the completion of the new government road, settlers began once more to occupy this region. In time somebody clambered up the precipices and found on these slopes at an elevation of 9,000 feet above the sea, an abundance of rich soil conveniently situated on artificial terraces, in a fine climate. Here the Indians had finally cleared off and burned over a few terraces, and planted crops of maize, sweet and white potatoes, sugar cane, beans, peppers, tree tomatoes, and gooseberries.

They said there were two paths to the outside world. Of one we had already had a taste; the other was "even more difficult," a perilous path down the face of a rocky precipice on the other side of the ridge. It was their only means of egress in the wet season when the primitive bridge over which we had come could not be maintained. I was not surprised to learn that they went away from home "only about once a month."

Through Sergeant Carrasco I learned that the ruins were "a little further along." In this country one never can tell whether such a report is worthy of credence. "He may have been lying" is a good footnote to affix to all hearsay evidence. Accordingly, I was not unduly excited, nor in a great hurry to move. The heat was still great, the water from the Indians' spring was cool and delicious, and the rustic wooden bench, hospitably covered immediately after my arrival with a soft woollen *poncho*, most comfortable. Furthermore, the view was simply enchanting. Tremendous green precipices fell away to the white rapids of the Urubamba below. Immediately in front, on the north side of the valley, was a great granite cliff rising 2,000 feet sheer. To the left was the solitary peak of Huayna Picchu, surrounded by seemingly inaccessible precipices. On all sides were rocky cliffs. Beyond them cloud-capped, snow-covered mountains rose thousands of feet above us.

We continued to enjoy the wonderful view of the canyon, but all the ruins we could see from our cool shelter were a few terraces.

Without the slightest expectation of finding anything more interesting than the ruins of two or three stone houses such as we had encountered at various places on the road between Ollantaytambo and Torontoy, I finally left the cool shade of the pleasant little hut and climbed further up the ridge and round a slight promontory. Melchor Arteaga had "been there once before," so he decided to rest and gossip with Richarte and Alvarez. They sent a small boy with me as a "guide." The sergeant was in duty bound to follow, but I think he may have been a little curious to see what there was to see.

Hardly had we left the hut and rounded the promontory than we were confronted with an unexpected sight, a great flight of beautifully constructed stone-faced terraces, perhaps a hundred of them, each hundreds of feet long and 10 feet high. They had been recently rescued from the jungle by the Indians. A veritable forest of large trees which had been growing on them for centuries had been chopped down and partly burned to make a clearing for agricultural purposes. The task was too great for the two Indians so the tree trunks had been allowed to lie as they fell and only the smaller branches removed. But the ancient soil, carefully put in place by the Incas, was still capable of producing rich crops of maize and potatoes.

However, there was nothing to be excited about. Similar flights of well-made terraces are to be seen in the upper Urubamba Valley at Pisac and Ollantaytambo, as well as opposite Torontoy. So we patiently followed the little guide along one of the widest terraces, where there had once been a small conduit, and made our way into an untouched forest beyond. Suddenly I found myself confronted with the walls of ruined houses built of the finest quality of Inca stone work. It was hard to see them for they were partly covered with trees and moss, the growth of centuries, but in the dense shadow, hiding in bamboo thickets and tangled vines, appeared here and there walls of white granite ashlars carefully cut and exquisitely fitted together. We scrambled along through the dense undergrowth, climbing over terrace walls and in bamboo thickets, where our guide found it easier going than I did. Suddenly, without any warning, under a huge overhanging ledge the boy showed me a cave beautifully lined with the finest cut stone. It had evidently been a royal mausoleum. On top of this particular ledge was a semi-circular building whose outer wall, gently sloping and slightly curved, bore a striking resemblance to the famous Temple of the Sun in Cuzco. This might also be a temple of the sun. It followed the natural curvature of the rock and was keyed to it by one of the finest examples of masonry I had ever seen. Furthermore it was tied into another beautiful wall, made of very carefully matched ashlars of pure white granite, especially selected for its fine grain. Clearly, it was the work of a master artist. The interior surface of the wall was broken by niches and square stone-pegs. The exterior surface was perfectly simple and unadorned. The lower courses, of particularly large ashlars, gave it a look of solidity. The upper courses, diminishing in size towards the top, lent grace and delicacy to the structure. The flowing lines, the symmetrical arrangement of the ashlars, and the gradual gradation of the courses, combined to produce a wonderful effect, softer and more pleasing than that of the marble temples of the Old World. Owing to the absence of mortar, there were no ugly spaces between the rocks. They might have grown together. On account of the beauty of the white granite this structure surpassed in attractiveness the best Inca walls in Cuzco, which had caused visitors to marvel for four centuries. It seemed like an unbelievable dream. Dimly, I began to realize that this wall and its adjoining semicircular temple over the cave were as fine as the finest stonework in the world.

It fairly took my breath away. What could this place be? Why had no one given us any idea of it? Even Melchor Arteaga was only moderately interested and had no appreciation of the importance of the ruins which Richarte and Alvarez had adopted for their little farm. Perhaps after all this was an isolated small place which had escaped notice because it was inaccessible.

Then the little boy urged us to climb up a steep hill over what seemed to be a flight of stone steps. Surprise followed surprise in bewildering succession. We came to a great stairway of large granite blocks. Then we walked along a path to a clearing where the Indians had planted a small vegetable garden. Suddenly we found ourselves standing in front of the ruins of two of the finest and most interesting structures in ancient America. Made of beautiful white granite, the walls contained blocks of Cyclopean size, higher than a man. The sight held me spellbound.

Each building had only three walls and was entirely open on one side. The principal temple had walls 12 feet high which were lined with exquisitely made niches, five high up at each end, and seven on the back. There were seven courses of ashlars in the end walls. Under the seven rear niches was a rectangular block 14 feet long, possibly a sacrificial altar, but more probably a throne for the mummies of departed Incas, brought out to be worshipped. The building did not look as though it had ever had a roof. The top course of beautifully smooth ashlars was left uncovered so that the sun could be welcomed here by priests and mummies. I could scarcely believe my senses as I examined the larger blocks in the lower course and estimated that they must weigh from ten to fifteen tons each. Would anyone believe what I had found? Fortunately, in this land where accuracy in reporting what one has seen is not a prevailing characteristic of travellers, I had a good camera and the sun was shining.

The principal temple faces the south where there is a small plaza or courtyard. On the east side of the plaza was another amazing structure, the ruins of a temple containing three great windows looking out over the canyon to the rising sun. Like its neighbour, it is unique among Inca ruins. Nothing just like them in design and execution has ever been found. Its three conspicuously large windows, obviously too large to serve any useful purpose, were most beautifully made with the greatest care and solidity. This was clearly a ceremonial edifice of peculiar significance. Nowhere else in Peru, so far as I know, is there a similar structure conspicuous for being "a masonry wall with three windows." It will be remembered that Salcamayhua, the Peruvian who wrote an account of the antiquities of Peru in 1620, said that the first Inca, Manco the Great, ordered "works to be executed at the place of his birth, consisting of a masonry wall with three windows." Was that what I had found? If it was, then this was not the capital of the last Inca but the birthplace of the first. It did not occur to me that it might be both. To be sure the region was one which could fit in with the requirements of Tampu-tocco, the place of refuge of the civilized folk who fled from the southern barbarian tribes after the battle of La Raya and brought with them the body of their king Pachacuti VI who was slain by an arrow. He might have been buried in the stone-lined cave under the semi-circular temple.

Could this be "the principal city" of Manco and his sons, that Vilcapampa where was the "University of Idolatry" which Friar Marcos and Friar Diego had tried to reach? It behoved us to find out as much about it as we could.

HIRAM BINGHAM

Discovery of the House of the Sun

HIRAM BINGHAM went on from his discovery of Machu Picchu to look for this supposed House of the Sun.

❧

TITU CUSI gives no definite clue, but the activities of Friar Marcos and Friar Diego, who came to be his spiritual advisers, are fully described by Calancha. It will be remembered that Calancha remarks that "close to Uiticos in a village called Chuquipalpa, is a House of the Sun and in it a white stone over a spring of water." Our guide had told us there was such a place close to the hill of Rosaspata.

On the day after making the first studies of the "Hill of Roses," I followed the impatient Mogrovejo—whose object was not to study ruins but to earn dollars for finding them—and went over the hill on its northeast side to the Valley of *Los Andenes* ("the Terraces"). Here, sure enough, was a large, white granite boulder, flattened on top, which had a carved seat or platform on its northern side. Its west side covered a cave in which were several niches. This cave had been walled in on one side. When Mogrovejo and the Indian guide said there was a *manantial de agua* ("spring of water") near by, I became greatly interested. On investigation, however, the "spring" turned out to be nothing but part of a small irrigating ditch. (*Manantial* means "spring"; it also means "running water"). But the rock was not "over the water." Although this was undoubtedly one of those *huacas,* or sacred boulders, selected by the Incas as the visible representations of the founders of a tribe and thus was

ꝺꝺꝺꝺꝺꝺꝺꝺꝺꝺꝺꝺꝺ

From *Inca Land*. Boston: Houghton Mifflin Company; 1922, pp. 246-51.

an important accessory to ancestor worship, it was not the Yurak Rumi for which we were looking.

Leaving the boulder and the ruins of what possibly had been the house of its attendant priest, we followed the little water course past a large number of very handsomely built agricultural terraces, the first we had seen since leaving Machu Picchu and the most important ones in the valley. So scarce are *andenes* in this region and so noteworthy were these in particular that this vale has been named after them. They were probably built under the direction of Manco. Near them are a number of carved boulders, *huacas.* One had an *intihuatana,* or sundial nubbin, on it; another was carved in the shape of a saddle. Continuing, we followed a trickling stream through thick woods until we suddenly arrived at an open place called Nusta Isppana. Here before us was a great white rock over a spring. Our guides had not misled us. Beneath the trees were the ruins of an Inca temple, flanking and partly enclosing the gigantic granite boulder, one end of which overhung a small pool of running water. When we learned that the present name of this immediate vicinity is Chuquipalta our happiness was complete.

It was late on the afternoon of August 9, 1911, when I first saw this remarkable shrine. Densely wooded hills rose on every side. There was not a hut to be seen; scarcely a sound to be heard. It was an ideal place for practising the mystic ceremonies of an ancient cult. The remarkable aspect of this great boulder and the dark pool beneath its shadow had caused this to become a place of worship. Here, without doubt, was "the principal *mochadero* of those forested mountains." It is still venerated by the Indians of the vicinity. At last we had found the place where, in the days of Titu Cusi, the Inca priests faced the east, greeted the rising sun, "extended their hands toward it," and "threw kisses to it," "a ceremony of the most profound resignation and reverence." We may imagine the sun priests, clad in their resplendent robes of office, standing on the top of the rock at the edge of its steepest side, their faces lit up with the rosy light of the early morning, awaiting the moment when the Great Divinity should appear above the eastern hills and receive their adoration. As it rose they saluted it and cried: "O Sun! Thou who art in peace and safety, shine upon us, keep us from sickness, and keep us in health and safety. O Sun! Thou who hast said let there be Cuzco and Tampu, grant that these children may conquer all other people. We beseech thee that thy children the Incas may be always conquerors, since it is for this that thou hast created them."

It was during Titu Cusi's reign that Friars Marcos and Diego marched over here with their converts from Puquiura, each carrying a stick of firewood. Calancha says the Indians worshipped the water as a divine thing, that the Devil had at times shown himself in the water. Since the surface of the little pool, as one gazes at it, does not reflect the sky, but only the overhanging, dark, mossy rock, the water looks black and forbidding, even to unsuperstitious Yankees. It is easy to believe that simple-minded Indian worshippers in this secluded spot could readily believe that they actually saw the Devil appearing "as a visible manifestation" in the water. Indians came from the most sequestered villages of the dense forests to worship here and to offer gifts and sacrifices. Nevertheless, the Augustinian monks here raised the standard of the cross, recited their orisons, and piled firewood all about the rock and temple. Exorcising the Devil and calling him by all the vile names they could think of, the friars commanded him never to return. Setting fire to the pile, they burned up the temple, scorched the rock, making a powerful impression on the Indians and causing the poor Devil to flee, "roaring in a fury." "The cruel Devil never more returned to the rock nor to this district." Whether the roaring which they heard was that of the Devil or of the flames we can only conjecture. Whether the conflagration temporarily dried up the swamp or interfered with the arrangements of the water supply so that the pool disappeared for the time being and gave the Devil no chance to appear in the water, where he had formerly been accustomed to show himself, is also a matter for speculation.

The buildings of the House of the Sun are in a very ruinous state, but the rock itself, with its curious carvings, is well preserved notwithstanding the great conflagration of 1570. Its length is fifty-two feet, its width thirty feet, and its height above the present level of the water, twenty-five feet. On the west side of the rock are seats and large steps or platforms. It was customary to kill llamas at these holy *huacas*. On top of the rock is a flattened place which may have been used for such sacrifices. From it runs a little crack in the boulder, which has been artificially enlarged and may have been intended to carry off the blood of the victims killed on top of the rock. It is still used for occult ceremonies of obscure origin which are quietly practised here by the more superstitious Indian women of the valley, possibly in memory of the Nusta or Inca princess for whom the shrine is named.

On the south side of the monolith are several large platforms and four or five small seats which have been cut in the rock. Great care was exercised in cutting out the platforms. The edges are very nearly square, level, and straight. The east side of the rock projects over the spring. Two seats have been carved immediately above the water. On the north side there are no seats. Near the water, steps have been carved. There is one flight of three and another of seven steps. Above them the rock has been flattened artificially and carved into a very bold relief. There are ten projecting square stones, like those usually called *intihuatana* or "places to which the sun is tied." In one line are seven; one is slightly apart from the six others. The other three are arranged in a triangular position above the seven. It is significant that these stones are on the northeast face of the rock, where they are exposed to the rising sun and cause striking shadows at sunrise.

Our excavations yielded no artifacts whatever and only a handful of very rough old potsherds of uncertain origin. The running water under the rock was clear and appeared to be a spring, but when we drained the swamp which adjoins the great rock on its northeastern side, we found that the spring was a little higher up the hill and that the water ran through the dark pool. We also found that what looked like a stone culvert on the borders of the little pool proved to be the top of the back of a row of seven or eight very fine stone seats. The platform on which the seats rested and the seats themselves are parts of three or four large rocks nicely fitted together. Some of the seats are under the black shadows of the overhanging rock. Since the pool was an object of fear and mystery the seats were probably used only by priests or sorcerers. It would have been a splendid place to practice divination. No doubt the devils "roared."

J. ALDEN MASON

Mummies and Textiles
at Paracas

THE dead must have been carried to the Paracas Peninsula from settlements in adjacent valleys. The bodies in the mummy bundles had been placed with their knees up to their chins. The Cavernas

From *The Ancient Civilizations of Peru*. Baltimore: Penguin Books Inc.; 1957, pp. 59-60, 61. By permission of Penguin Books Inc.

type of burial dates from after about 500 B.C.; the Necropolis type from round about the beginning of our era. The embroidered garments from the latter are now to be seen in the National Museum at Lima, where they make one of the most stunning museum displays in the world.

❧

THE known archaeological history of the southern coast begins late, in this experimental period. However, it was doubtless occupied in all four preceding periods, though no sites of these periods have yet been identified. There are known to be great shell-and-refuse heaps on the coast which, when investigated, will almost certainly reveal evidences of an early fishing-and-agricultural population like that of Huaca Prieta on the northern coast. In those days of simple culture the differentiation anywhere on the coast was probably very slight.

The stupendous masonry ruins of the Peruvian highlands and the immense adobe pyramids of the north coast have always been famous, but the ancient civilizations of the south coast, in the valleys of Pisco, Ica, and Nazca, without any impressive structures, were almost unknown until the present century. The cemeteries of the Nazca period with their extraordinary polychrome pottery were discovered by Max Uhle in 1901, those of Paracas with their even more splendid textiles by Julio C. Tello in 1925. In this region it can almost truly be said that it never rains, and the objects buried with the dead in the desert sands are incredibly well preserved. All surface indications of these cemeteries have long since been covered or erased by the drifting sands, and they are found to-day only by the spade of the archaeologist or the probe of the native treasure-hunter.

The Paracas Peninsula, lying about eleven miles (18 km.) south of the port of Pisco, is the seaward extension of a line of low sandy hills known as Cerro Colorado. The red sand is absolutely bare of all vegetation, not a leaf, not a living thing; no stream enters the ocean near by. The nearest human habitation is several miles away where wells tap underground water and a few sedges line the beach. It is the epitome of loneliness and desolation. Yet beneath these sands are found the desiccated bodies of a people unknown to history, together with some of the most magnificent cloths that the world has ever seen. Today their bones lie scattered on the surface, and the winds alternately cover and uncover fragments of the coarser fabrics, discarded by the diggers, still soft and strong after nearly two millennia. For the "mummies" have been removed from

the discovered cemeteries, and either carefully preserved by archaeologists, or rifled and only the saleable goods kept by native
huaqueros.

Two types of burials, known as Paracas Cavernas, and Paracas
Necropolis, were found in this region by Julio C. Tello between
1925 and 1930. They differ greatly in nature and in contents,
Cavernas being characterized by a remarkable type of polychrome
incised pottery and textiles of average quality, Necropolis by magnificent cloths and simple unpainted pottery. . . .

Paracas Cavernas was so named because the bodies are found in
communal bottle-shaped chambers excavated in the rock at the
foot of vertical shafts, at a depth of approximately twenty feet (6
or 7 m.). Many of the tombs also have a stone-lined upper chamber
at the surface. As many as fifty-five bodies were found in one of
these sepulchres, of both sexes and all ages. The heads were artificially deformed, and a large proportion of them had been tre-
phined. The bodies were wrapped in coarse cotton cloths and
accompanied by mortuary offerings. It has been suggested that the
tombs might have been family vaults. The considerable variation in
the quality and quantity of the grave goods placed with the dead
suggests a similar difference in economic conditions during life.

4. *North America*

THE groups of hunters who were the earliest known inhabitants of the American continent (p. 691) are identified principally through the various stone "projectile points" which they made to tip their spears or darts. Some of the oldest of these have been found embedded in the remains of mammoth which at first were their most important game sought by the hunters. Others, generally a little later, have been found similarly lying among the bones of bison.

Although some Carbon-14 analyses have given readings back to over 30,000 years ago for material from human settlements, these are not as yet accepted with confidence. The more cautious archaeologists would say that there is as yet no certain proof that men had entered the continent before about 15,000 years ago, although earlier dates are by no means improbable.

MARIE WORMINGTON

The Peopling of North America

DR. MARIE WORMINGTON, Curator of Archaeology at the Denver Museum of Archaeology, is cautious about the date of man's first arrival in America. In the present extract she only says that it must have been "many thousands of years before" he reached the tip of South America about 8,000 years ago. In the remainder of her book, however, she does not accept outright any date for human settlement before 15,000 years ago, nor does she indicate the existence of any cultures earlier than those represented by the projectile points.

IT IS NOW generally accepted that man did not originate in the New World and that he first came to America by way of Bering Strait, but it should be mentioned that other theories have been advanced, although none is widely held. Among the best known, although the least accepted in scientific circles, are those that take for granted the former existence of now submerged land masses, such as the legendary continents of Mu and Atlantis, which would have provided a link between the hemispheres. Another theory is that at one time North and South America were attached to Europe and Africa but later broke away and moved to their present positions. Most scientists simply classify these as fairy tales, or, at most, admit that land distribution has differed from that of the present but at such remote times in the past that it would not serve to explain the presence of man in the Western Hemisphere.

The possibility of trans-oceanic voyages has also been suggested. Trans-Pacific voyages have been most widely advocated on the basis of certain cultural traits that are common to both Oceania and South America. While it is entirely possible that there was some contact in more recent times, it seems inconceivable to most scientists that people could have reached the New World by this route at any very early date or in sufficient numbers to account for the populating of the New World. The possibility of trans-Atlantic migrations is generally thought to be even more remote.

Still another theory sometimes suggested is that the early migrants crossed from Asia by way of the Aleutian and Komandorski Islands. As there is no geological evidence that ice sheets formed here, even in the glacial period, boats would have had to be used. It is possible that this route was followed by some groups, but it is not generally accepted that the earliest men, or many of the later migrants, arrived by this route. It would have required great skill in navigation, since there are treacherous currents, rocky

From *Ancient Man in North America.* **Denver:** Denver Museum of Natural History; 1957, Popular Series No. 4, fourth ed., pp. 249-52. By permission of the Denver Museum of Natural History and the author.

shore lines, and much fog and wind. Also, some of the islands are so far apart as to be invisible from each other even in the clearest weather.

If, as archaeologists believe, Bering Strait was the only possible route available to people who did not have the watercraft and the navigational skill that would have enabled them to traverse oceans or to go through very difficult waterways, the first people must have come to America from Siberia by way of the Strait. At this point Asia and America are separated by only fifty-six miles of sea broken by three islands. The widest expanse of unbroken sea is only twenty-five miles, and land is in sight on even moderately cloudy days. The gap between the two continents is not thought to have been wider since a time before the last glaciation, and there were times when it did not exist at all.

Although the crossing could have been accomplished by means of very primitive watercraft and with little knowledge of navigation, or by walking across on the winter ice, it is difficult to see what the incentive would have been for such a movement, at least for hunters of grazing animals. It seems more probable that such people would have crossed the Strait at a time when it was possible for the animals on which they depended for food to cross. They would have been able to do so when the two continents were joined by a land bridge. At the height of a glaciation much water was abstracted from the sea to feed the ice sheets, and there was some rise of the ocean floor. A general lowering of sea level resulted, and shallow portions of the ocean became land surfaces.

The floor of Bering Strait would be above water if sea level were reduced by only 120 feet. Due to low precipitation in much of Alaska, glaciers formed largely in the mountains. If the land bridge and adjacent areas were unglaciated they could probably have provided food for grass-eating animals and for men. Palaeontological evidence indicates that in the plains and valleys of Alaska man would have found animal and plant foods to supply his needs.

There is also the problem of how men reached the areas farther south in which evidence of their presence at an early date has been found. During glacial stages there were ice sheets covering large parts of North America. These would have presented a barrier to the movements of men and animals. During interstadials, however, the ice retreated and ice-free corridors were opened. During one or more of the interstadials that preceded the Mankato, as well as in post-glacial times, the Mackenzie Valley was probably free of ice. Those who reached it by moving along the low northern coast line of Alaska could have followed the valley and gained access to the northern Plains. People who moved up the Missouri could have reached the Snake River Plain and the Great Basin. At a later date, movement along the Yukon and down the Liard and Peace River valleys to the Plains, or along the Frazer River to the Great Basin, may have been practicable.

It should be noted, however, that while it is very simple to plot migration routes sitting in an office and looking at a map, the problem assumes new dimensions when one is in the field in this northern country. It takes only a fraction of a second to draw a line half an inch long on a map. However, if that line represents a non-existent path through a hundred miles of muskeg, the situation becomes extraordinarily complicated if one attempts to follow it in person.

As Froelich Rainey has pointed out, "Northwestern America and northeastern Asia, under present climatic conditions, together form one of the most formidable barriers to human communication one can find anywhere in the world." Undoubtedly, there were times when it was possible for people to move through this country, but there must have been times when such movement was not practical. . . . If . . . during stages of widespread continental glaciation the Arctic Ocean was not frozen these might have been the times most favorable for movement by man.

Glib statements pertaining to migrations into the New World often convey an impression of masses of people moving swiftly across the Strait and marching briskly down the continent in search of a pleasanter climate or in pursuit of animals that were rushing south. This is probably far different from the true picture. People dependent on hunting and food gathering cannot move together in large numbers. Furthermore, to the primitive the unknown and the unseen are strange and terrifying, and primitive man does not willingly depart from known familiar things to face the unknown. Only some strong compulsive force, such as the need for food, will cause him to make a drastic change. Also, a warmer climate, even were it known to exist in some distant region, would not necessarily provide an irresistible attraction. In general, people are more likely to make an effort to adapt to conditions in the country that they know.

It seems probable that as J. L. Giddings has suggested, the peopling of the New World was the result, not of migrations, in the sense of predetermined movements, but rather of a spread of population that resulted from the gradual extension of the hunting and gathering ranges of various groups. Population growth would lead to an increase of the range exploited. Variations in climate would, at times, have changed the ecological situation and led to movements into new areas by game animals and the men dependent upon them. Droughts in arid areas could have forced people with some dependence on food gathering into new territory.

Radiocarbon dates from Patagonia indicate that men had reached the tip of South America some 8,000 years go; and, if we eliminate the idea of swift purposeful movement to the south, many thousands of years must have elapsed since the ancestors of these people first reached the Western Hemisphere. The diversity of culture and language among the American Indians also serves to indicate the passage of a very long period of time.

Believing, as we do, that the early American population was derived from northeastern Asia, it is, of course, highly desirable to know something of the archaeological remains found on the Siberian side of Bering Strait. Unfortunately, the writer is unable to read Russian, and it has been impossible to do a proper analysis of the literature pertaining to Siberian sites. All that has been available are the summaries in English published by Lawrence Krader (1952) and Chester S. Chard (1956), and illustrations and partial translations of some of the books of A. P. Okladnikov, which appear to be excellent reports. Scanty as this information is, it serves to indicate that no very early sites have been found; most are attributed to the Neolithic. This is scarcely surprising, however, for Siberia is much like Alaska and northwestern Canada. Those who have worked in the north realize how extraordinarily difficult it is, in such country, to find the scanty traces left long ago by small groups of hunters and gatherers with few possessions and no permanent habitations. The fact that early sites have not been discovered does not mean that they do not exist.

ALEX D. KRIEGER

The Earliest Cultures in the Western United States

IT is still the most widely held opinion that there is no reliable evidence for the presence of man in the Americas more ancient than that provided by the earliest types of projectile point—dated to about 15,000 years ago. Although a few Carbon-14 dates have pointed to the possibility of something like twice this age for the first settlement, every one has been found to be questionable. Dr. Krieger, however, thinks that these Carbon-14 datings, together with the geological and zoological evidence at certain sites, are enough to make a strong case for the arrival of men in the western hemisphere well back in the course of the final ('Wisconsin) glaciation. These earliest hunters would not yet have developed the manufacture of projectile points.

The Wisconsin glacial period, which corresponds to the Würmian of the Old World, was the last of the four great glaciations of the Pleistocene Age. It was broken by a number of warmer interludes, sometimes referred to as interstadials.

It must be added that during 1963 excavations have been undertaken at Tule Springs on the vast scale recommended by Dr. Krieger (p. 693, II). They have failed so far to discover any human traces that can be dated before 13,000 years ago.

❧

ALMOST every archaeologist who writes on the subject of human antiquity in the Western Hemisphere appears to believe sincerely that the oldest cultural remains include some form of projectile point; and that, because the maximum age of such types as the

Reprinted from *American Antiquity*, Volume 28, No. 2, October 1962, by permission of the author and *American Antiquity*.

Clovis and Sandia points is generally supposed to be on the order
of some 12,000 to 15,000 years in the Great Plains and south-
western United States, such a "dateline" must also apply to the age
of man in general in the New World. (This statement does not
apply to certain geographers who have recognized the presence of
pre-projectile point assemblages of crude artifacts, but who have, I
think, greatly exaggerated their age because they recognize only
three indivisible time periods in North America: "pre-Wisconsin"
or "third interglacial"; "Wisconsin," lasting from some 70,000 to
10,000 years ago; and "post-Wisconsin" or "Recent" for the last
10,000 years.) Lately we have been presented with somewhat more
liberal estimates, such as some 20,000 to 25,000 years, but without specific explanation as to whether the earliest projectile points
may be pushed back that much further, or whether this may be a
sort of compromise between, say, 15,000 years for the oldest points,
and a few radiocarbon dates which seem to date human occupation
sites in western North America at various times ranging from
25,000 to nearly 40,000 years.

The general puzzlement and doubt about the validity of these
larger dates in America is only a reflection of the widespread uncertainty that there is a cultural stage in the New World which
may—for want of a better name—be called "pre-projectile point."
It is quite surprising (to me, at least) that to this day there remains
so much doubt about the existence of such a stage. The evidence
for it is fairly abundant in both North and South America, but will
not be very convincing to most archaeologists until it is all brought
together.

As my present topic concerns only the western United States, I
will say no more about evidence for a general "pre-projectile point"
stage in America as a whole beyond the curious fact that, despite
its great importance in the culture history of the New World, so
little attention is paid to it, either pro or con, by archaeologists of
the United States. The "United States" must be specified here because many Latin American scholars feel quite differently about it;
but their occasional use of such terms as "Palaeolithic" for simple
lithic cultures has caused such a reaction in this country that we
have refused even to examine the material so designated, or the
sites from which it comes.

Sellards has recently attempted to interpret seven localities in
the western United States and Baja California as an ecological situation. Although he does not use the term "pre-projectile point" or any
other blanket term for these localities, points have not been found
in any of them and all are probably too old to contain such artifacts.
He divides them into two groups. The first, on which radiocarbon
dates have been obtained, includes Tule Springs, Nevada; Lewis-

ville, Texas; and Santa Rosa Island, Scripps Campus at La Jolla, and Texas Street at San Diego, all on the coast of southern California. The second includes the shores of extinct Lake Manix in the Mohave Desert of southern California and the Chapala Basin in central Baja California; neither has any datings except as might be inferred from association with extinct lakes of late Wisconsin or "pluvial" age. Sellards concludes that:

The use of stone artifacts varies greatly and is not indicative of age but varies primarily with the living conditions, ease of securing food, and availability of rock materials suitable for flaking. Of the seven sites considered in this paper, those in which worked stone implements are rare or absent — Santa Rosa Island, Scripps site, and Texas Street site — are at or near the seashore. Those at which stone artifacts are present in numbers varying from many to a few — Manix Lake, Chapala Basin, Lewisville, and Tule Springs — are inland sites.

Such an ecological interpretation would be interesting if it could be supported by field data. It presumes, in the first place, that all the localities are archaeological and that all have been equally (even if incompletely) explored, which is far from true; and second, it overlooks critical physical factors about the sites themselves. The presence of comparatively many artifacts at the Lake Manix and Chapala Basin sites is easily explained by their open position along the shores of extinct lakes: such sites were never subsequently buried by alluvium or aeolian sand to any extent and therefore are still exposed horizontally for hundreds or even thousands of feet, so that the modern collector may recover artifacts and workshop scrap from what amounts to the full extent of the ancient camps.

A completely different situation obtains at the Lewisville and Tule Springs sites, in which the deposit containing hearths, split and burned bones of Pleistocene animals, and simple but definite artifacts subsequently became buried under two or more later geological deposits, and only an enormous amount of excavation would expose the original extent of the camps, not to mention the full content of cultural material which must lie on them. At Lewisville, partial exposure of the camps was accomplished accidentally by engineers who dug a great borrow pit behind an earth dam; subsequent controlled excavation by archaeologists produced detailed measurements of more than 20 hearths, faunal remains, and a few stone artifacts. At Tule Springs "badlands" erosion revealed scattered exposures of hearths, charcoal, burned and split bones of Pleistocene animals, and both stone and bone artifacts in gully walls; excavations then exposed small amounts of the original camp surface horizontally, but this cannot be more than an infinitely small fraction of the original surface, estimated to be at least one-half mile across. In both cases it is fascinating to speculate on what might be found if it were possible to clear off for horizontal viewing even ten per cent of the original camps! (This will never be possible at Lewisville, now under some 70 feet of impounded water; but with proper facilities it might be done at Tule Springs.)

The three localities in coastal southern California which Sellards discusses present still different physical aspects. That known as the Texas Street site in San Diego is a remnant of river terrace with many lenses of gravel brought down from a short side valley. Sellards' designation of this locality as an archaeological site with "few or no artifacts" is quite inadequate, for Carter has claimed that it contains many artifacts throughout as well as other evidences of culture. Several critics have considered the artifacts to be "eoliths" or naturally fractured rock, while others who have visited the locality not only doubt that there is any reliable evidence of the presence of man here but have also seriously questioned the geological evidence by which Carter places the terrace in a "third interglacial" period.

The Scripps campus site with a radiocarbon date on charcoal of 21,500 ± 700 years, and several sites on the north coast of Santa Rosa Island where Orr has reported burned and split remains of a dwarf mammoth, and radiocarbon dates ranging from about 12,000 years to nearly 30,000 years for the formation containing these discoveries, bear much more promise, in my opinion, of the presence of man than does the Texas Street site. The geological situation at Scripps and on Santa Rosa Island is much the same in that the claimed cultural evidence occurs at different levels within a dense alluvium which can only have been deposited during a glacial stage when the sea was much lower than now. It is difficult to say how far beyond the present coast this alluvium once extended; but it is certain that the alluvium was gradually cut back by a rising sea until the more or less vertical cliffs which now rise some 50 to 75 feet above the narrow beaches were formed.

At the Scripps site there are some thin lenses of charcoal and reddish burned earth at different levels in the cliff face, and at least one of these, the one on which a date of 21,500 ± 700 years was obtained, contained numerous bits of burned shell and bone, and tiny stone flakes which looked like "workshop" material, when I was shown the site by Dr. Carl Hubbs in 1957. Dr. Hubbs also pointed out the location of fossil material collected from lenses of reddish burned earth at lower levels in the same cliff. No artifacts have been reported from here yet, but this could well be due to lack of excavation. While even this evidence for the presence of man may be slim, it is much better than that at Texas Street.

The absence of definite artifacts from the long lines of reddish burned earth, and pockets of charcoal with split and burned bones of the dwarf mammoths on Santa Rosa Island (seen by two groups of specialists in June, 1960, of which I was a member), may also be explained by lack of excavation. It must be realized that these sea cliffs of the coast and islands of southern California present great difficulties in adequate exposure of former land surfaces within the alluvium because of the great amount of overburden. Until such excavation is done, however, it is futile to speculate on whether artifacts are many, few, or absent for some "ecological" reason. In effect, we are at present permitted only an infinitely tiny view of the former camps, if such they were, because we can see only their edges where exposed by seaward erosion and in the banks of arroyos cutting through the cliffs. Furthermore, the original size of the "camps" cannot even be guessed because the present alluvial remnants cannot contain more than a small fraction of the land surfaces which existed from time to time while the sea stood lower and the alluvium was gradually built upward and outward.

Neither can an absence of stone artifacts from such sea-cliff situations be due to a dearth of available stone, as Sellards postulated. While the clay-like alluvium that we see now does not contain sizable stones, in no case would the ancient inhabitants have had to walk as much as a mile to find plenty of gravel and native rock; and in most cases it could have been obtained within a few hundred feet.

In summary, I do not believe that Sellards was justified in drawing any ecological conclusions about the relative number of artifacts found so far in the seven localities he discusses: the differences appear to lie in the nature of the sites and the wide range of sampling afforded by erosion or excavation, or some combination of the two. The coastal localities appear to me to have yielded the fewest artifacts (if any) because sampling of the deeply buried levels has been so minute. It may be that even with extensive horizontal exposure of possible campsites, the artifact yield will still be low in comparison with interior sites, but I know of no way to determine this without excavation.

At least two sites in the western United States with Pleistocene fauna *and* radiocarbon datings seem to be firmly established well back in Wisconsin time: Lewisville, with two published dates of "greater than 37,000 years" which have now been remeasured with the result of "greater than 38,000 years"; and Tule Springs, with its new date of "greater than 28,000 years" and a theoretical possibility that the date may be as much as 33,000 years. These sites have been the subject of considerable scepticism, mainly by persons who have not seen them and merely feel uncomfortable that their cherished notions about the "age of man" in the New World may be upset.

In several recent writings, Lewisville has been summarily rejected because of the discovery of a Clovis fluted point in one of the dated hearths. Unable to accept a date of "greater than 37,000 years" for any New World projectile point, the critics have taken the view that the Lewisville dates are hopelessly wrong and the site has no great significance. I am in agreement that such a date cannot apply to any known type of stone projectile point, and agree with Sellards who postulates that this specimen was either lowered to the hearth level by machinery in the dam borrow pit, or planted in the hearth by a "prankster." The critics have worried about this projectile point to the extent that they have paid no attention to the highly important geological and paleontological data from the site. Not only do the hearths extend to the base of the Upper Shuler formation, which surely represents Upper or "Classic" Wisconsin time, but the numerous faunal remains found in and around the hearths include many occurrences of a giant land tortoise (*Testudo* sp.) as well as some remains of the glyptodon. In the words of palaeontologist Morris Skinner (personal communication), neither of these animals could have lived for twenty-four hours in freezing temperature, and therefore could not have lived in the present winter climate of Dallas. Their presence points to a warmer climate than the present in this area, at least in winter, and the radiocarbon dates agree rather well with a period of climatic amelioration falling midway in the Würm-Warthe glacial stage of Europe (where it is called the Göttweig Interstadial) and in the Wisconsin stage (where its name is still the subject of debate). In Europe this interstadial is believed to have endured for some 15,000 years, from approximately 40,000 to 25,000 years ago, and in America its age and duration may be more or less equivalent. In short, the Clovis point at Lewisville is definitely under suspicion; but the datings and the geological and palaeontological evidence cannot be ignored, and the site may be considered as "pre-projectile point."

What other sites in western North America may be regarded as belonging to a pre-projectile point stage and older than the assumed 15,000 years or so usually assigned to the oldest points? The "elongate-biface assemblage" in the Chapala Basin of Baja California should belong in this category, although I would reject his placement of it in "pre-Wisconsin time" because Arnold, like Carter, considers the Wisconsin to have been a single unit of time beginning some 70,000 or 80,000 years ago. Such an assumption is unwarranted in modern research; yet this assemblage must belong somewhere in Wisconsin time, like the Lake Manix Lithic Industry of the Mohave Desert and the Coyote Gulch material in the same area. In all these cases the lithic material is found on the shores of extinct lakes and consists of large, crudely fashioned, bifacially chipped implements with a notable absence of any artifacts as refined as projectile points or thin bifaced knives. In no case would one be justified in placing the extinct lake farther back than the Upper or Classic Wisconsin stage or last "Pluvial" period unless some specific geological proof were offered.

The Blacks Fork complex in southwestern Wyoming presents a similar problem. Although Renaud and others have collected more than 10,000 artifacts and scrap, all of quartzite, from several sites in this area, and there are no such refined artifacts as projectile points or thin bifaced knives, most archaeologists have persistently ignored this material as having any unusual significance. This is probably due to Renaud's use of European terms for description and the belief that the whole collection is from the surface and therefore useless for chronological placement. The material is, in fact, being exposed by wind deflation (at least on some sites), and therefore must have been buried at one time in a geological deposit; yet no study of this deposit has even been made. The crudity of the artifacts, such as large and thick bifacially chipped tools, very large side scrapers of thick spalls, and choppers, certainly distinguishes this assemblage from any postglacial complex, just as it does the desert material mentioned above from California and Baja California.

Bartlett has described briefly a Tolchaco complex from some 70 sites in the Little Colorado drainage basin of northeastern Arizona. This is featured by crudely made, percussion-chipped, bifaced core implements, "keel-shaped" scrapers, and large flakes, with projectile points absent. Again, the fact that these are surface collections seems to have convinced many archaeologists that they are unworthy of attention.

The Farmington complex in central California provides another situation in which only crude core tools and large flakes have been recovered from no less than 58 sites, with projectile points absent. These collections are not from the surface but have been found in gravels with little or no smoothing from stream transport. The authors cited estimate the age of this complex at perhaps 7000 years, apparently on the assumption that nothing in the western states could be anything but postglacial. Better dating is needed.

Many other localities in the western United States as well as other parts of North and South America could be mentioned, but there is not space enough here. It may be argued that the sites and complexes I have mentioned are not older than those which include stone projectile points because it is quite possible to use wooden spears and dart shafts without stone points. Possibly such an interpretation will hold in some cases, but it ignores such vital factors as the generally low level of stone chipping in the artifacts found; the large size and crudity of the tools, and their narrow range of presumed functions (almost entirely cutting, chopping, and scraping); and the complete absence of pressure flaking or even the refinement of percussion work which is necessary to thin down such objects as projectile points and knives for hafting.

In conclusion, it is my present belief that there is considerable evidence for a "pre-projectile point" stage of culture in the western United States as well as other great regions in North and South America; that in many cases such a stage began long before the appearance of even the oldest projectile points; and that, on present evidence, this stage can be roughly equated in age with a mid-Wisconsin period of warm climate beginning some 40,000 years ago, and the Upper or "Classic" Wisconsin stage beginning some 25,000 years ago. I would not rule out, merely as a matter of principle, the *possibility* of some human migration into America in Lower or "Early" Wisconsin time, nor even in pre-Wisconsin time; but I know of no situation where an age greater than the mid-Wisconsin interstadial can be *demonstrated* to the elimination of other interpretations.

J. L. GIDDINGS

Eskimos and Old Shorelines

J. L. GIDDINGS directs Brown University's Haffenreffer Museum at Bristol, Rhode Island, and teaches anthropology at Brown's Providence campus. An excavator of Arctic archaeological sites since 1939, he has pursued in recent years the Bering Strait problem of American Indian and Eskimo origins.

Reprinted from THE AMERICAN SCHOLAR, Volume 31, Number 4, Autumn, 1962. Copyright © 1962 by J. L. Giddings. By permission of the author and THE AMERICAN SCHOLAR.

ARCHAEOLOGY on the old gravel beaches of western Alaska involves me customarily with the members of an Eskimo family or two. While we work I am inclined to imagine these people as figures of the past and practice with them a little magic to control the motors and the watchful spirits that make or break a camp and a field season.

The Eskimos of Kotzebue and neighboring coasts are Christians all; yet they maintain a pagan respect for things left unhallowed in the ground from the time before missionaries came at the turn of the century. Only a summer ago while waiting at the whaling camp of Shesualek for the ice to move so we could travel up the coast to the digging site, we received a gentle spirit-reminder. A group of adventurous young men of this populous village of white tents at the edge of the sea became impatient in their search for scraps of driftwood at tide level and decided to steal firewood from the old platform burials that still stand on the crest of a beach line marking an earlier ocean front. They advanced on a conical structure of spruce poles guarding the bones and grave offerings of a renowned whale hunter. But as one of the party thrust his hand between the poles to pull at the rusted barrel of a flintlock rifle half-buried in the sand, the gun and the poles began to shake vigorously as though controlled by an underground force, and the project was abandoned. Manifestations such as this we all learn to respect and try to control, although we may continue in our scorn of ordinary superstition.

Weather, if not indeed the spirit Selya who dispatches storms upon the undeserving, has long had a part in determining where on the Arctic coast one should dig. It can determine for me not only where I should dig, but with whom. Bad weather once kept me from a search for forest-edge archaeology, but, permitting work near the sea, led to an important discovery on the beach ridges. That morning the wind blew up when my reconnaissance party was all prepared to travel down the coast with a man who owned a large skin boat and a motor. After some vacillation, the man refused to go, saying that the skies were uncertain and the water overshallow. We looked for a time without success for new means of transportation, and then Almond Savik came along. He said he had a big skiff made of whipsawed river spruce and a motor that, despite its age, we could depend upon. While there were many other things he could be doing, he said, he had always wanted to travel southward along the coast to see that part of the world. He appeared, at first, alarmingly different from the seasoned Eskimos with whom I had worked in previous years. He wore a white

short-billed cap, a black leather jacket with metal studs, dun-
garees, Air Force boots and, just visible under his jacket, a pearl-
handled revolver. Men of this sophisticated dress usually spent
most of their time and a good part of their money in the "jukebox
joints" of Kotzebue. But when I met his young, shy wife and his
two small children, all parka-clad, I felt less hesitation about engaging him as boatman.

Wind and rain increasing as we rounded Choris Peninsula on
our way to the forested rivers, we had to beach the boat. As we
explored Choris on foot, we became aware of a succession of old
gravel ridges, all of about the same height, that had accumulated
through the ages and sealed off an embayment on the ocean side
of the peninsula. The present ocean beach, a mile long, is as broad
on its crest as a highway. Surface evidence, including an early
form of house pit on the lee slope, quickly told us that this beach
ridge, no more than ten feet above sea level, had stood intact for
a few hundred years. As we turned landward on this beach and
walked down into a shallow swale and on to successive crests
to the foot of a steep, tundra-covered hillside, about six hundred
feet from the water, we saw that these older beaches also held
some evidence of human occupation. This was true even of the
beach most remote from the sea. There, unexpectedly, we came
to a cluster of crater-like pits. Excavations soon revealed in them
the remains of a small, but ancient, buried village. The houses
had been immense by Arctic standards—between thirty and forty
feet in length—and our excavations exposed oval floors and no
entrance passages, in contrast to the rectangular houses with passages of nearly all later Arctic dwellers. We now know through
radiocarbon analysis of charcoal from house hearths that this
Choris village dates from about 1000 B. C. Each pole-walled, sod-
covered house, heated by a central fireplace and illuminated by
stone lamps, would have furnished comfortable housing for thirty
or more people. Artifacts and animal bones deposited in the floors
helped to reveal a community of caribou hunters of unknown linguistic stock who spent some of their time at harpooning sea mam-
mals, who kept no dogs, but who practiced the Asian and American Indian trait of divining the future by reading the cracks
formed on a deer's shoulder blades heated over coals.

The lesson of Choris, apart from its purely cultural information, was that if we were going to learn of other early beach dwellers in the region, we could expect to do so only where vagaries
of ocean currents had protected remnants of old shore lines from
the ravages of storms.

Success is contagious. The prehistorians of our party had obtained knowledge at Choris of a new form of culture to report to

our colleagues, and Savik had skillfully steered a river boat along dangerous coasts without ever a serious miscalculation. We absorbed prestige and some little glory from our separate successes, and nothing but lack of funds could have discouraged either Savik or me from another go at this kind of exploration.

Two seasons after the discoveries at Choris, I met Savik again at Kotzebue and we traversed two hundred and fifty miles of the shallow shoreline of Kotzebue Sound in search of other stranded beaches. My party numbered four this time, and Almond's family had grown to five. The boat was the same, yet its cargo had expanded since our last cruise. Loading was a challenge. First we rolled in the drum of gasoline and around it packed the full mixing cans, the case of stove gasoline, the camp stove itself and a wood stove for heating the tent in cold weather; then we loaded a month's supply of food in wooden boxes, the cooking utensils and the washtubs and basins. We arranged the softer duffle bags, bedrolls and individual tents to pad the boxes, and this brought the load well above the gunwales. On top we placed a mattress and Savik's two young daughters. His five-year-old son, equipped with rubber boots, helped as usual with the launching of the craft. By the time Savik's wife had settled with the girls in the center of the mattress and the rest of us had found seats either forward or astern, the skiff seemed to me more than reasonably full—yet Savik assured us that his boat could accommodate a great deal more.

The motor was the same too, the metal worn smooth from many adjustments and repairs. Its case vibrated cheerfully as we pulled away from Kotzebue onto a calm, morning sea. No sooner had we rounded a bend of the beach, however—fortunately out of sight of the well-wishers who gather to see boats off from the shore—than the motor coughed and stopped. Now and then it responded feebly to the starter cord. Savik resorted finally to a long pole, and we to the paddles, to take the boat ashore. Landing on a gravel beach is a happy event for Eskimo women and children whether the voyage has been long or short. The children entered at once into a digging game while their mother made tea and Savik set about carefully dissecting the motor. At length it was decided that we must unload the boat. Through long experience with this kind of travel, I anticipated this standard decision, although I have never known why it is made. Just possibly we unload to convince the motor that we can outwait its stubborn mood. I did not look forward with pleasure, however, to frequent stops that might upset our plans for the summer, and after some meditation I asked Savik if he would consider buying a new motor if I were to advance him the money from his wages. This was a welcome thought. He would—and he just happened to know, he said, that a Kotzebue trader had one suitable motor on hand. This was a 35 h.p. Evinrude with a long shaft, precisely the kind we needed for our journey. Savik quickly reassembled the old motor and I shoved us off while the others of our party remained on the beach. He pulled the cord and we raced back, bow high, to the store in the village, where the strong and beautiful new blue motor lay waiting. I wondered for a moment about this last burst of energy, but remembered that motors here are controlled less by the laws of physics than by the minds of men.

The beaches of Kotzebue Sound were richer and even more promising than I had expected. Traveling long hours with our boat and new motor on good days and exploring the beaches on foot when the wind blew, we learned that wherever beach crests occur in succession, the oldest cultural remains are found by walking inland from the present ocean edge. Regrettably, the older series of beaches at the south side of Kotzebue Sound consist of sand, and crests originally formed by the action of the sea had been altered in successive periods of dune-building and wind-cutting until smothered by a blanket of tough sod. The flints, pottery and remains of campfires in these areas were mainly those exposed in the "blowouts" or wind channels that form from occasional breaks in the surface cover.

The discovery of very old sites large enough to be excavated is not easy under these circumstances, even though surface discoveries at several points confirmed a long succession of cultures from the time when beaches first began to form after stabilized postglacial sea level. We came to prefer hard-packed gravel to shifting sand. In gravel beaches like those at Choris, testing is made easier by both surface stability and the hints of early camp-sites that one learns to see in an arrangement of vegetation and soils. These advantages, Savik lost no opportunity to point out, were to be found at Shesualek, north across the inlet from Kotzebue. I shared only part of Savik's enthusiasm for Shesualek. To our native family it was the festive summer gathering-ground of nearly all the people who spend their winters hunting and trapping in the spruce forests of the lower Noatak River drainage. As far as they know and as far as historic records confirm, they and their ancestors have gone down to the coast and set up their camps at Shesualek at the beginning of each year's whaling season. The small white whales, formerly secured by herding into shoals and harpooning from kayaks, are now shot from motor-driven boats. During the whaling season, racks along the shore become loaded with white-skinned squares of blubber and black strings of drying meat. Modern Shesualek has its post office, temporary, in a tent, and a strip of firm, old beach upon which small planes may land. Savik was right in pointing out that the series of beaches behind Shesualek, composed as they were of packed gravel, would furnish a likely area in which to find early archaeological sites. Toward the end of July we had become established on the beach, surrounded by relatives and friends of the Savik family.

The odds of exploration were against us, however. While many earlier beach crests paralleled the ocean edge at Shesualek, the oldest archaeological site we could find lay a mile and a half distant from the tent village near the edge of a shallow bay on the inner side of Shesualek Peninsula. Here the deep house pits of early Eskimo whale hunters, whose sites had been built at the ocean edge of their time, were those of an aspect of Western Thule culture older than any thus far excavated in Kotzebue Sound. A single square house floor with its long entrance passage and its separate ash-filled kitchen room required more than a week to unearth. As we worked, the neighbors gathered to watch and make an occasional joke or pointed remark. We brought to light the everyday belongings of people long dead—hundreds of things such as wooden buckets, women's slate knives with ivory handles and harpoon heads with their stone blades intact. These were constant reminders of the people who a thousand years earlier had inhabited the houses and left behind the everyday things familiar to modern Eskimos.

I did not know at first, but learned later, that our move from the sea edge to the stagnant shores of the bay had brought about unfavorable comment from the villagers. They did not object to our digging—they themselves (unhappily for science) were not above collecting "relics" to sell to tourists—but they observed that we drank water from a shallow well dug into a swale between old beach ridges. The summer dwellers at Shesualek, it seems, depend for their water upon the saltless old sea ice that floats for more than a month in front of the camp and, when that is gone, upon fresh water transported some miles in barrels and cans from the mouth of the Noatak River. The drinking of water from the ground of the peninsula itself, because of the artifacts and bones buried in it, is thought to result in illness and death—especially the death of small children. The water from our well was sweet and potable, and none who was alien to the locality could have guessed that we were courting disaster. But while we excavated the old house, the weather became miserable. Low clouds moved in, and a steady wind blew unending rain against us and our tents. Only a few visitors walked to the big tent to talk in the evening. The conversation, carried on in Eskimo, frequently held overtones of anxiety. Then one day Savik explained to me about the water. Two infants of Shesualek had recently died, and now within our own group the baby cried continuously with a high fever. While Almond agreed with me that the illness at Shesualek was caused by a virus and said that he did not believe in the superstition about water, we all nonetheless worked and waited apprehensively.

It was during this period of doubt that Savik, possibly as a means of ending our dangerous sojourn at Shesualek, offered a welcome suggestion. He now understood our search for successions of beach ridges and, although still skeptical of my confidence that the older ridges in a series contained the leavings of earlier people, described a place to the north called Sealing Point—Cape Krusenstern, on my map—behind which, he thought, lay a vast expanse of hard-packed gravel ridges covered with sod. We decided to try it, and by the time the wind had finally calmed enough to permit travel up the coast, we observed with satisfaction that the baby was out of danger and the epidemic at Shesualek had apparently passed.

Again Savik was right. The beaches at Cape Krusenstern, barren and forbidding as they may appear to a casual traveler, offered to us the rich vista of crest after crest stretching far into the distance: the beaches upon which tens of generations have walked. Reindeer paths follow the length of the most prominent ridges. We searched these paths and blessed the reindeer for having scuffed occasional flints from under the moss. It is possible to walk as far as eight continuous miles without changing ridges. A still more impressive walk from the historical point of view is taken across the beaches, at right angles to the shoreline. The conviction grows that one is stepping back half a century, more or less, with each of the hundred and more isolable beaches.

The promise of lateral stratigraphy at Cape Krusenstern was fulfilled during three years of digging. Our camp became larger, but never unwieldy. As we summer visitors increased, so did Savik's crew. The best men he could find to help us happened to be his brother, two or three cousins and an unrelated hunting partner, all of whom are winter residents of Noatak village. If at first I had reservations about hiring only so close-knit a group, these doubts soon dissolved as our new workers displayed the same interest and skills as did Savik. We were not clock-watchers on the beach. We worked long hours because of our curiosity

about what lay concealed in the ground. Yet when a fox appeared
on a neighboring beach we diverted ourselves by becoming neighbor foxes, whistling it to distraction. When a seal swam by we
wildly fired expensive ammunition and launched the boat to give
noisy chase.

In the course of three years of excavation, dozens of old tent
sites, burials and lesser camping places were bared, sketched,
photographed and their contents removed. Whole small villages
were excavated, some of them representing phases of culture
previously unknown. Whaling, for example, we found had been
practiced two thousand years earlier than was commonly supposed, by a people who dug multiple-roomed houses deep into
the crest of their oceanfront beach—now three-quarters of a mile
from the sea.

The beach ridges at Cape Krusenstern gave us a nearly complete prehistory for five or six thousand years. Rather than distinct sets of cultures, each waxing and waning, it seemed to
represent a continuity. Some of the beaches still guarded their
contents beneath thick moss, creating thin spots in the record;
yet there seemed good reason to suppose that for as long as
beaches formed in this region, after sea level reached its postglacial heights, people were continuously on the scene. We recognized the main aspects of culture as extending backward through
time in this order: preceding the recent Eskimos were those of
Western Thule times. Thule culture grew out of Birnirk; and
Birnirk, locally, out of Ipiutak, as we have only recently learned.
The Ipiutak culture of two milleniums ago owes its peculiar cast
to art forms of distant parts of Asia grafted onto the Choris and
Norton phases from these and neighboring beaches. Preceding
Choris were the Old Whalers of nearly 2000 B.C. and, before them,
makers of extremely delicate microblades and a variety of in-
set flint edges first found at the Bering Sea site of Cape Denbigh.
The Denbigh people were on hand at Cape Krusenstern when
sea level reached its maximum height, and earlier, for microblades appear on a hillside behind the beach ridge series where
sealing would have been possible only before the sea level had
stabilized and the beach ridges begun to form. And the story
does not end with this ancient shoreline. On a terrace of the
same hill, five hundred feet high, are variously weathered flints
representing hunters of land game, some of whom must have
been there when glaciers still covered large parts of the eastern
continent. These flints of the Palisades closely resemble some
from early mountain passes in the far interior of Alaska and
also some from distant parts of Asia.

The hoard of artifacts and field records now waiting to be transformed into a coherent archaeology are not yet, however, separated completely from either the generations who made them or the Eskimo family who helped to remove them from the ground. Our last season on the beaches it appeared for a while as if the weather and the spirits were at us again. Deep in Savik's new motor a small vital part burned out and rendered the motor useless. We ordered a replacement, but a string of circumstances delayed its arrival. Word came at exasperating intervals that the part was not stocked in Kotzebue; that it was not to be found in Anchorage or Fairbanks; that it was finally on order. Then we learned that it had reached Kotzebue from Seattle—and had been sold by the native storekeeper to the wrong man! With each of these revelations Savik appeared stunned. He assured me, perhaps too often, that the part would soon come and the motor would work for us again.

Airplanes served our camp with some regularity, and on one occasion Savik flew to Kotzebue where without my knowledge he borrowed a boat and motor and started back across the bay. A storm blew up, and for the first time in his career his boat capsized in an attempted landing near a kinsman's tent and he was thrown into the sea. Again he was dismayed at the way his luck had turned. As the season drew to an end, I assured him that we and all our gear could be transferred comfortably by airplane and that he could repair his motor after the season ended, without fear of financial loss. He seemed grateful; yet he insisted upon flying once more to Kotzebue. While he was gone the wind blew and it looked as if we might have one of those fall storms that toss whitecaps to the crest of the beach upon which we camp. During a lull between gusts a motor, incredibly enough, was heard out at sea. Savik, as we shortly learned, had bought a new motor and in a borrowed boat was attempting to come ashore on this beach where there is no harbor or landing place. His plan became clear: he would lie offshore waiting for the seventh wave and then, like a surfboard rider in southern seas, mount its crest and at full motor speed beach himself high on the grassy slope. For a long moment it seemed that his calculations were true—and then the boat outran the crest, turned crazily and lay helpless until engulfed by the wave. Savik fought clear, and members of our crew salvaged the overturned boat.

Despite his strains and bruises, Savik was the victor again, and our camp slowly returned to normal. Neither the sea nor ancestral spirits had overwhelmed a good archaeological season. Nor were outboard motors doomed to replacement by machines in the air. Within hours the missing motor part arrived, and we now had two motors with which to transport ourselves and the cases of artifacts from the beaches at Cape Krusenstern. Days later, as our jet-prop rose into a blue sky from the Kotzebue airfield on the first lap of a long flight east, some of us caught a glimpse of Savik and his family speeding back across a calm bay toward their winter home on the Noatak.

LUCRETIUS

What Lucretius Knew

THIS anthology ends with an extract from Lucretius to show that the stark outlines of the human past were known to him over two thousand years ago. It might be said that as a basis for a philosophical approach to our history, what Lucretius knew was sufficient. But unsubstantiated as it was by any evidence, his rational reconstructions could be overthrown by any myth-maker. And anyway, if archaeology had never been born, if the small army of brave, foolish, gifted, eccentric and fanatical men and women that have created it had turned their energies elsewhere, what a loss it would mean to us all! How much poorer we should be without all the strange, beautiful, grotesque and macabre remains of our ancestors which they have unearthed. How much poorer, too, if our shelves were deprived of all the books they have written about their adventures and discoveries.

And whilst so many lustrums of the sun
Rolled on across the sky, men led a life
After the roving habit of wild beasts.
Not then were sturdy guiders of curved ploughs
And none knew then to work the fields with iron . . . .
As yet they knew not to enkindle fire
Against the cold, nor hairy pelts to use
And clothe their bodies with the skins of beasts;
But huddled in groves, and mountain-caves, and woods,
And 'mongst the thickets hid their squalid backs . . . .

Then from the boiling veins began to ooze

From *Concerning the Nature of Things*, Book V. 2nd century B.C.

O rivulets of silver and of gold,
Of lead and copper too, collecting soon
Into the hollow places of the ground.
And when men saw the cooled lumps anon
To shine with splendour-sheen upon the ground,
Much taken with that lustrous smooth delight
They gan to pry them out, and saw how each
Had got a shape like to its earthy mould.
Then would it enter their heads how these same lumps
If melted by heat, could into any form
Or figure of things be run, and how again
If hammered out they could be nicely drawn
To sharpest point or finest edge.

. . . . Man's ancient arms
Were hands, and nails and teeth, stones too and boughs—
Breakage of forest trees—and flame and fire,
As soon as known. Thereafter force of iron
And copper discovered was; and copper's use
Was known ere iron's, since more tractable
Its nature is and its abundance more.
With copper men to work the soil began,
With copper to rouse the hurly waves of war,
To straw the monstrous wounds, and seize away
Another's flocks and fields . . . .
                              Then by slow degrees
The sword of iron succeeded, and the shape
Of brazen sickle into scorn was turned . . . .

Index

A NOTE ON THE TYPE

THE TEXT of this book was set on the Linotype in a new face called PRIMER, designed by *Rudolph Ruzicka,* earlier responsible for the design of Fairfield and Fairfield Medium, Linotype faces whose virtues have for some time now been accorded wide recognition. The complete range of sizes of Primer was first made available in 1954, although the pilot size of 12 point was ready as early as 1951. The design of the face makes general reference to Linotype Century (long a serviceable type, totally lacking in manner or frills of any kind) but brilliantly corrects the character-less quality of that face.